Behavior
Influence
and Personality
The Social Matrix of Human Action

LEONARD KRASNER

State University of New York at Stony Brook

LEONARD P. ULLMANN

University of Hawaii

Behavior Influence and Personality

The Social Matrix of Human Action

HOLT, RINEHART AND WINSTON, INC.

New York Chicago San Francisco Atlanta
Dallas Montreal Toronto London Sydney

To those who shaped us and maintained our behavior.

ACKNOWLEDGMENTS

The authors wish to thank the following authors, publishers, and agents for permission to quote from copyrighted material:

Excerpted from "The question of Machiavelli" by Sir Isiah Berlin. Reprinted with permission from *The New York Review of Books*, © 1971 NYREV Inc.

Excerpted from "American psychology," by L. W. Brandt, in *American Psychologist*, 1970, pp. 1091–1093. Reprinted by permission of the American Psychological Association.

Excerpted from Chapter 4 of *Two Worlds of Childhood: US and USSR*, by Urie Bronfenbrenner, © 1970 by Russell Sage Foundation, New York.

Excerpted from *Oneida* by Maren Lockwood Carden, published 1969 by The Johns Hopkins University Press.

Excerpted from *What Is History?* Edward Hallet Carr. Copyright © 1961 by Edward Hallet Carr. Reprinted by permission of Alfred A. Knopf, Inc., and Macmillan, London and Basingstroke.

Excerpted from "Galloping technology, a new social disease," by Jerome D. Frank. *Journal of Social Issue*, 22, 1966, 1–14. Reprinted by permission of publisher and author.

Excerpted from *The Hidden Dimension* by Edward T. Hall. Copyright © 1966 by Edward T. Hall. Reprinted by permission of Doubleday & Company, Inc.

Excerpted from *Heavens on Earth: Utopian Communities in America* by Mark Holloway by permission of Dover Publications.

Excerpted from *Please Touch* by Jane Howard. Copyright © 1970 by Jane Howard. Used with permission of McGraw-Hill Book Company.

Excerpted from *Noyes' Modern Clinical Psychiatry*, Seventh Edition, 1968, by L. C. Kolb. Reprinted by permission of W. B. Saunders Company.

Excerpted from *Environmental Psychology* by H. W. Proshansky, W. H. Ittelson, and L. G. Rivlin, 1970. Reprinted by permission of Holt, Rinehart and Winston, Inc.

Reprinted by permission of G. P. Putnam's Sons from *The Psychiatrists* by Arnold A. Rogow. Copyright © 1970 by Arnold A. Rogow. Also reprinted by permission of George Allen & Unwin Ltd, British publishers.

Excerpted from *Experimenter Effects in Behavioral Research*, by Robert Rosenthal. Copyright © 1966. By permission of Appleton-Century-Crofts, Educational Division, Meredith Corporation.

Excerpted from "Anxiety-Reification of a Metaphor" by T. R. Sarbin in *Archives of General Psychiatry*, 1964, Vol. 10. Copyright 1964, American Medical Association.

Excerpted from *Normality Is a Square Circle and a Four-Sided Triangle* by Maggie Scarf. Reprinted by permission of Brandt & Brandt.

Excerpted from *The Making of Blind Men*, by R. A. Scott. © 1969 by The Russell Sage Foundation, New York. Reprinted by permission of Basic Books, Inc., and the author.

Excerpted from *Walden Two* by B. F. Skinner. Copyright 1948 by B. F. Skinner. Reprinted by permission of The Macmillan Company and the author.

Excerpted from *Anton Mesmer* by D. M. Walmsley, 1967. Reprinted by permission of Anthony Sheil Associates Limited, agents.

Excerpted from W. Weiss, "Effect of the Mass Media of Communication" from *The Handbook of Social Psychology, Vol. V*, Second Edition, edited by Lindzey-Aronson, 1969, Addison-Wesley, Reading, Mass.

PREFACE

To write another book on personality may, at first glance, seem to be the height of arrogance. There already exists a wealth of fine books on seemingly every aspect of personality including theory, measurement, and research reviews (Byrne, 1966; Hall and Lindzey, 1970; Bischof, 1970; Mischel, 1968, 1971; Pervin, 1970; Lundin, 1969; Sarason, 1972; Liebert and Spiegler, 1970; Wiggins, Renner, Clore, and Rose, 1971; Millon, 1968; Mehrabian, 1968; and many others). Yet we hope to present an approach to human behavior that adds to the current store of knowledge and justifies the ten years spent between signing the contract for this book and its publication.

We mention this time span because much of the documentation we depend on was produced within the past decade. During this time, a psychology of behavior influence, which at the start was a theoretical hope, became an actuality. Illustrations and support of our assertions would have been far more difficult to find a decade ago. As we will continually emphasize, explanatory models or paradigms shift over time, and we think that the development of behavior influence as a psychological approach represents a basic shift in orientation and a major achievement of the last decade.

We had several goals when writing and living with this book. First, the very concept of personality is presented as a human behavior *in a social context* in contrast to personality as a reified autonomous state. Second, material is presented from other disciplines that are usually touched only lightly, if at all, in typical personality writings but which must be considered as an integral part of a psychology of behavior influence. This material is so extensive that we have had to be. very selective, for both better and worse. There are many relevant observations of human behavior in fields such as sociology, economics, political science, anthropology, and history that most current theories of personality fail to take into account and incorporate.

Third, and perhaps most important, we would like to help create an integrated field of investigation, namely behavior influence. This field already exists in terms of the kinds of investigation now being carried out, but it is not yet in sharp focus. The study of personality as human behavior should take into consideration contextual, economic, sociological, ecological, and organizational variables as well as those traditionally investigated by psychologists. In presenting this material, we are not leaving the domain of clinical and social psychology but rather broadening the conceptualization of personality so that relevant material comes from an increasingly broad spectrum of human observations. In effect, then, our subject is human behavior, and as psychologists we seek to extend the data we use.

There are few, if any, explicit "givens" to human social behavior. Instead, when devising or discussing personality theories, we are dealing with concepts created by humans (that is, concept making is, itself, human behavior). Thus, in order to understand and deal with these ideas, we have to take into consideration the historical context of and the professional influences upon the developers of these concepts. We are all influenced and in turn influence. As psychologists we are quick to detect the influences on others, but it is extremely difficult, and sometimes uncomfortable, to take cognizance of the influences upon ourselves. Just as we should not dichotomize between normal and abnormal behavior or between the impact of heredity and environment, we should not dichotomize between the variables impinging on the personality theorist and the variables he studies. Theories of personality, including our own, are human behaviors and not academic material divorced from social context to be studied in isolation.

Finally, it follows that we are presenting an approach to human behavior which forces explicit discussion of social values. We are arguing that every view of personality reflects implicit beliefs about the nature of "good" human behavior. We cannot dichotomize the behavior of theory making and the social situation in which the theories were developed. Every model of man has social consequences and is a human creation with all of the limitations of time and place that this implies. We view our presentation not as a culmination but as a start.

Our aim is to increase the awareness of our readers, students, professional investigators, and ourselves to the influences upon us, to the potentialities of our influencing others, and to changing our environment. To the extent that we can achieve the goal of increasing the repertoire of environmental-changing behaviors (which we define as freedom)—to that extent, we will feel we have been successful.

Because behavior influence, by definition, must include the influencer as well as the influencee, we have included a sample of pictures of the people who have contributed to this area. As with all other material, our selection has been necessarily arbitrary and space limitations have precluded the inclusion of many others.

We wish to acknowledge the support of Grant #11938 from the National Institute of Mental Health, United States Public Health Service, in many of our research endeavors. Our warm thanks to Peggy Harra for her fine manuscript typing, to Arnold Goldstein and Theodore Sarbin for their cogent and useful review of the manuscript, and to Steve Richards for his comments. We wish to thank our friends and companions, Miriam, Kaloha, Helen, Irma, Stefanie, Charles, Nancy, David, Mike, and Wendy—all of whom, each in his or her own way, enriched our lives.

Finally, a note of dedication and affection for two recently deceased friends who influenced our behavior for the better, Lou Levine and Tom Kennelly.

Stony Brook, New York   L. K.
Honolulu, Hawaii   L. P. U.
January 1973

CONTENTS

ILLUSTRATIONS

Behavior
Influence
and Personality
The Social Matrix of Human Action

PART **1**

Antecedents and Basic Concepts

1

The Psychology of Behavior Influence and Personality

People are interested in other people. In modern life people rather than the forces of nature loom large. We are continually adjusting to and depending on other people. At work or at play our effectiveness involves others for cooperation and for giving satisfaction and meaning to life. The money we earn is exchanged primarily for the goods and services of others. In our society the very manner in which we obtain money depends on a highly complex division of labor. Even the artist—the archetype of the independent man—depends on others, if only for his pigments if he is a painter and for his paper and typewriter if he is an author.

We live in a web of interpersonal structures and respond to intricate cues from other people. On the one hand are the smiles, frowns, and other subtle gestures of the person to whom we are talking; and on the other are the complex social organizations of the family, university, factory, government, law, and custom. The very language we use to communicate with each other is the result of generations of human interactions and of complicated modern manmade communication systems. For example, a monosyllabic word denoting sexual intercourse is usually enough to turn a listener warm or cold. The manner in which this word is pronounced—whether one smiles while saying it or grits one's teeth—and the situation in which the word is said—to one's fiancée's parents or to one's friend on a fishing trip—makes a vital difference in the kind of response the word will evoke. The use of such strong language also illustrates both the impact of social custom and the speed with which it may be changed. Lillian Smith's *Strange Fruit* was banned in Boston twenty years ago because of a single concatenation of the letters *F,U,C,K*, while today the word itself may be found with considerable frequency in novels, plays, movies, graffiti, and even a college psychology textbook.

The reactions to the four-letter word above illustrate that the social effect of a specific act changes with *time*, with *place*, and with *person*. The reference to the use of language indicates that the significance of an act is not inherent in the act itself, but is learned. And among the things learned are the *times* and the *places* when the act will lead to different consequences. We learn not only acts but their consequences, particularly those generated by other people. To a great extent the most meaningful acts in our society involve the manipulation of symbols, primarily in language.

We also deal daily with the predictability of others' responses to our acts. We may feel hurt or angry if someone takes offense when we did not intend it. We may label the people who misunderstand us and our concepts of appropriate human interaction as *stupid, repressive,* or *priggish.* Thus, we categorize people on the basis of relatively small amounts of information. We cannot know (nor would we care to know) *everything* about *everybody,* much less observe them in the entire range of situations to which they might react. Not only is there not enough time in life but the vast majority of others' responses do not relate to our own lives. On the basis of the limited sample we do obtain, however, we place a label on other people; and these labels have an impact on our future behavior.

We become alerted to and expect certain behaviors from others on the basis of the information about them for which the label serves as a convenient summary. In a related fashion, we may use the label we have derived from one set of data as the basis of our predictions about other situations. In short, we may generalize and conclude that if an individual is stupid in one situation he is likely to be stupid in a second situation. Because predictions themselves may alter our behavior, the act of making predictions frequently leads to their being correct. (This procedure has been given the descriptive label of "self-fulfilling prophecy.") We may not only become more alert to evidence of stupidity (and even feel satisfaction for being correct when we observe it), but we may also react to the person as being stupid, giving him cues that we expect stupid behavior to be appropriate from him. Conversely, we may not even give him the opportunity to engage in alternative, intelligent behavior. Thus, our predictions themselves may limit the sample of behavior that we obtain.

Although we are dependent on other people, our response to them is not a passive matter. There is a constant interchange among people of action and effect. How *we* respond will influence the person to whom we respond and *his* response to us in the future. Moreover, we receive both physiological and social feedback as a result of responding. Just as we label others, we can and do label ourselves and our own behavior. This self-labeling may be done in terms of what we see as the immediate consequences of our behavior.

We learn to apply labels to ourselves in the same manner that we learn to apply them to others. Just as labels may influence our predictions about (and responses to) others, so the labels we give ourselves may alter our own behavior. For example, a man who *believes* that he cannot attract a desirable woman may not try to; thus, he would confirm his poor self-image, since he would never do anything that could disconfirm it.

In summary then, we alter and, in large measure, create and control our interpersonal environment by the manner in which we respond. We influence and are influenced by others.

ETYMOLOGY OF PERSONALITY

G. Allport (1937) wrote a book about personality, which by its scholarship and comprehensiveness virtually initiated the modern study of personality as a separate field. Allport pointed out that *personality* is one of the most abstract words in our vocabulary and is "like any abstract word suffering from excess use [p. 25]." There is no single meaning for the term, and many diverse concepts have been attached to it. The term derives from the classical Latin *persona*, which denotes the theatrical mask used by Roman actors. The term soon took on different abstract meanings such as one's outward appearance (but not how one really is); one's part in life; an assemblage of personal qualities; and distinction and dignity. From these four early meanings, Allport traced fifty different definitions of personality.

Included among his derived meanings are the following: external appearance; distinctive personal qualities; prestige and dignity; a freeborn citizen; selfhood; the ideal of perfection; supreme value; a multiformed dynamic unity; the living human being in his or her entirety; superficial attractiveness; one's social stimulus value; the way one really is; a system of habits representing characteristic adjustment to the environment; a style of life. Finally we should quote Allport's definition (1937), which became the standard for many years: "Personality is the dynamic organization within the individual of those psycho-physical systems that determine his unique adjustments to his environment [p. 48]."

Personality—The Metamorphosis of a Word

The human interaction process is ongoing, ubiquitous, and crucial if not for physical survival, then at least for personal satisfaction. Adjustment to the interpersonal environment is similar to adjustment to the physical environment. For a species as free of instinctual determination as humans, both types of adjustment primarily involve learned behaviors. In both instances the goal is *effectiveness*, an increase in what the person has learned implicitly and explicitly as the good life.

To attain mastery of the physical environment, humans have built a view of the world through personal and shared experience. This system has evolved from primitive animism to the physical and biological sciences as we know them today. Certain regularities (models or paradigms) have developed that summarize experience by providing a description of the world that enables the individual, through extrapolation, to understand, predict, and control his physical environment. A paradigm guides the investigations that derive from it, that is, the generation of new data about the world. Any information in conflict with the paradigm may be fought in various ways, such as labeling it heresy or bad science or unfit for publication in reputable journals. However, when enough contradictory or incompatible evidence accumulates, the paradigm is revised or abandoned (Kuhn, 1970).

Models of the physical universe have two advantages over models of human behavior. First, confirmation or disconfirmation of the physical model is likely to be more clean-cut. Second, the subject matter of physical science is far less active and reactive than the data used for models of behavior. While the act of measurement does alter inanimate material, the influence of the investigation process is far greater when living beings, especially humans, are the objects of study (Webb, Campbell, Schwartz, and Sechrest, 1966).

Human interaction, except in the simplest instances, requires special guide-lines (models). These are most likely to be needed in situations of uncertainty. The ability to understand and hence predict the behaviors of others is usually associated with the ability to master or at least to mitigate situations. Two examples are driving an automobile—where knowing what others will do is a matter of survival—and predicting elections—where the correct guess may reflect accurate knowledge, but does not usually affect individual survival.

Let us conceive of a situation in which a person, Beta, may act in a manner that another individual, Alpha, finds unusual or unexpected, or a second situation in which Beta is in a powerful position and Alpha must decide how to react to him. In both Alpha is uncertain; he would like to know the rules Beta is following. In the first instance the rules would help Alpha understand Beta's behavior, and in the second instance they would increase Alpha's chance of doing something that would evoke a favorable reaction from Beta.

If Beta acts in an unexpected manner—that is, in a way that disconfirms the hypotheses Alpha has of how people act in general or of how Beta acts in particular—Alpha will alter his subsequent behavior. As a result of many experiences over time, Alpha will change his behavior in similar situations; in effect, Alpha will *learn* that one course he may take when Beta acts in an unusual manner is to place Beta's behavior in a context different from the one in which he had originally placed it. *The foregoing has been an analysis of Beta's reasons for acting, his "motives," or his identification of the situation.* A shorthand of Alpha's presumptions about Beta is found in the use of labels noted previously.

The solution to Alpha's problem—the description and prediction of others' behavior so that he may be more effective in dealing with them—is one of the objectives of psychology. And *personality* is the academic specialty that most directly studies the theoretical descriptions and explanations offered as the basis of human action.

Personality—The Metamorphosis of a Term

In common usage, personality is applied freely in a number of contradictory ways. It is used as a general description of another person: "He has a pleasing personality." It is used as an explanation: "He has that sort of personality." The first usage involves labeling, similar to calling a person stupid. The second usage is essentially circular; the individual is stupid because he acts stupidly, and he acts stupidly because he is a stupid person.

A third usage of the word is found in professional publications, which in effect *attribute* various interpersonal relations to personality. In this instance there is a progression from a description of people to the offering of an independent cause of people's behavior. The following illustrative quotations are from a widely used psychiatric textbook. This book was selected because it covers an area variously called *abnormal behavior, psychiatry, deviance,* or *psychopathology,* in which professionals describe, explain, and try to alter or control *unusual* behavior. (In many regards, clinical psychology and psychotherapy before 1960 were applied personality theory.)

Personality is perhaps best recognized as each individual's characteristically recurring patterns of behavior [Kolb, 1968, p. 2].

In this quotation, personality deals with *regularities* of behavior and is a *decription*: the regularities permit prediction on the basis of observation of the individual within his social and physical environment. Once such descriptions are obtained, they are usually organized on some reasonable basis.

From the totality of recurring behavior, we move to an organization, or system of behavior:

> Thus, over time, through a prolonged series of social experiencing, more or less enduring and consistent attitudes, beliefs, desires, and patterns of adaptation develop which make each individual unique. The distinctive whole formed by these relatively permanent behavioral patterns and tendencies of a given individual is spoken of as *personality* [Kolb, 1968, p. 34].

From a concept of organization and pattern, of some order within the designated area, it is a small step to think of and to develop concepts of *structures* and *functions*:

> It is convenient to think of personality as having parts or divisions which perform specific functions—in other words, as having structure. Such a concept facilitates the idea of dynamics in the functioning of the personality. However, these parts must not be considered as concrete realities or self-acting entities but as groups of forces and functions [Kolb, 1968, p. 35].

An important matter touched on in this third quotation is that the theorist who studies "personality" faces the same kind of difficulties as any other human observer; he must deal with a complex, changing mass of information. He uses the conceptual tools he has available to organize the information with which he deals. In this regard, the use of the phrase "it is convenient" indicates the human being involved in this process.

The second and third sentences in the quotation introduce a new idea, that of "dynamics." Where personality originally was a description based on recurring behavior, we now find it related to interaction, conflict, and resolution—concepts not unlike forces in physics. At the end of the second of these three sentences we see an interesting and subtle change: instead of "personality," the author talks of "functioning of the personality," an indication that the shorthand designation for regularities of behavior has gained the status of a noun, a thing. Finally, attention should be called to the warning that the entire structure with which Kolb is dealing is a conceptual rather than a concrete reality. This kind of warning is usually well taken, but it is not always honored.

The inclusion of forces and functions in *the* personality leads to the labeling of these entities and to their interaction. The following quotations may illustrate the point:

In the well-adjusted person, behavior simultaneously and successfully meets the demands of the id, the ego, and the superego. [Kolb, 1968, p. 37].

The type of personality pattern the individual works out for himself in his effort to meet the stresses of life will be influenced by many things. Among them will be the nature and number of the defenses which he constructs against aggressive and sexual tendencies and socially unacceptable feeling-attitudes toward persons who have occupied key positions in his life, particularly during childhood. If one develops a multiplicity of such defenses designed to reduce tension and anxiety, a constricted type of personality characterized by rigidity, narrowness, and lack of spontaneity results. If these defenses become pathologically exaggerated or disorganized, they eventuate in the neurotic or psychotic personality. One's basic personality, the kind of person one really is, continues to be the same throughout both prepsychotic and psychotic states [Kolb, 1968, p. 53].

The self-conscious personality with its intense need for a sense of security and self-esteem evokes mechanisms of a protective nature as instinctively as self-preservation prompts the avoidance of approaching physical danger. Just as the body through its physical and biochemical processes strives to maintain a physiological equilibrium or homeostasis, so the personality through automatic and unconscious psychological processes seeks to maintain a psychological stability [Kolb, 1968, p. 55].

In the first of these three quotations, the functions of the personality are in conflict and do not smoothly balance each other. In the first sentence of the second quotation, the person "works out" his own style of personality. This wording confuses levels of communication, because the original definition of behavioral regularities classifies "working out" itself as a behavior, that is, as an aspect of personality. In the second sentence, it appears that defenses are consciously selected, while in the last sentence of the third citation, the defenses are unconscious and automatic. In the second quotation, *the personality* is characterized as narrow, rigid, lacking in spontaneity. There is an implicit presumption of a *healthy* personality, a *normally developed* personality, a *correct* personality, analogous to a condition of physical normality.

This second quotation introduces a concept that is widespread in our culture and that has had a great impact on how people, especially those considered abnormal, are treated. This concept is that of a *basic personality* ("the kind of person one really is"), which exists and functions regardless of the current situation or observed behavior. This idea, taken in association with the last sentence of the third quotation, comprises what has been called the *medical model, disease model,* or the *medical analogue* approach to abnormal behavior (for example, see Ullmann and Krasner, 1965, 1969). The personality deals with stresses and forces to maintain a psychological equilibrium in the same manner that the body maintains physiological equilibrium; and like bodily functions, some basic and important behavioral activities are considered to result from "automatic" and "unconscious" processes. Treatment is therefore aimed at the "underlying cause," and overt behavior is frequently considered symptomatic and not dealt with directly.

In the third and final quotation from Kolb, the personality has been fully reified: it is self-conscious, has needs (for example, security), and evokes protective mechanisms. The reification of personality and its attributes characterizes much research in psychology and psychiatry. The definition of *to reify* makes the point succinctly: "To regard or treat an abstraction or idea as if it had concrete or material existence [Morris, 1969, p. 1097]."

Going beyond the notion of the reification of personality, the following quotation notes how the concepts of personality and structure are "necessary to explain" (that is, to help an observer deal with) behavior.

> Although personality is a product of the social environment of the past, it is not, once it has developed, a mere object of the contemporary environment. What has developed is a structure within the individual, something which is capable of self-initiated action upon the social environment and of selection with respect to varied impinging stimuli, something which though always modifiable is frequently very resistant to fundamental change. This conception is necessary to explain consistency of behavior in widely varying situations, to explain the persistence of ideological trends in the face of contradicting facts and radically altered social conditions, to explain why people in the same sociological situation have different or even conflicting views on social issues, and why it is that people whose behavior has been changed through psychological manipulation lapse into their old ways as soon as the agencies of manipulation are removed. [Adorno, Frenkel-Brunswick, Levinson, and Sanford, 1950, p. 6]

We have used this quotation to illustrate how a theory develops, in order to explain what otherwise would be puzzling or uncertain. This material also illustrates the assumption that behavior is consistent in different situations—an assumption which has disappointingly little empirical substantiation (Mischel, 1968). In fact, we might well wonder about an individual whose behavior did not change when conditions changed. And we might even doubt if he had learned any worthwhile new behavior if it disappeared in the absence of his "agencies of manipulation." These points will be returned to, especially in Chapter 6.

SOME COMMENTS ON THE CONCEPT
OF PERSONALITY

Personality is an intellectual creation of man. An individual has *a* personality no more than he has *a* love, *an* introversion, *a* creativity. Someone may act in a loving manner, an introverted manner, or a creative manner. "Personality" is an abstract way of expressing the individual's characteristics or the regularities of his behavior.

It is more meaningful to ask, *Under what conditions* do we call a person *loving, introverted,* or *creative*? The very behaviors that are so designated differ across times, places, and people. There is love of country, love of parent, love of spouse, and love of work. The label is based on a comparison with other people. A person does *more strongly* or *more quickly* or *more frequently* the sort of things people (including himself and other observers) call loving, creative, or introverted. A person may be loving in one situation and not in another; his love for his work or profession may conflict with his acts of love for his family. A prediction about the person's loving acts based on observations in one situation may not be accurate in other situations. Finally, what is considered loving behavior in a particular situation may be disputed by other equally sincere people. Does the man who volunteers for military service love his country more than the man who protests a war he considers unjust? Does a parent who gives his child everything love the child more than the parent who selectively rewards his offspring?

The examples just given touch on another problem in the use of the abstraction personality. The man who devotes time to his job at the expense of his family may be said to do so because he loves his family. The parent who satisfies his child's every whim may be said to do so to assuage the guilt of "really" hating the child. We are thus faced with a number of pitfalls. One set of problems arises from the distinction between *what* a persons does and *why* he does it. If we cannot be sure that a specific act indicates something or its opposite, then description, prediction, and increased effectiveness become difficult.

Another set of pitfalls is encountered because of the process of abstraction involved in calling acts loving, introverted, or creative. When using the abstraction "love," we are dependent on the evaluative systems of observers. An example is the college male who tells his girl friend, "If you loved me . . ." and means, "Let's make out." His girl friend may begin her reply, "If you loved me . . ." and mean, "Let's not." People can use the same words and be talking about very different things. Conversely, it is possible to use different words to talk about the same things. It is even possible to use different words for the same thing and then to explain one on the basis of the other; for example, anxiety may be called the "cause" of repression, even though a scale of repression-sensitization (Byrne, 1961) correlates very highly with a scale of anxiety (Taylor, 1953; Welsh, 1956)—to the point of operational identity (Wiggins, 1964).

DEFINITIONS OF PERSONALITY

Since human behavior should be approached from a systematic and scientific point of view, we must give operational definitions of the major concepts introduced—behavior, personality, and social influence—and these will be given now and in subsequent sections and chapters.

We will start with the concept of personality. Chapters 2, 3, and 4 detail the changes in this concept from ancient Greece through present times. We are emphasizing the social psychology of the professional labeler; hence it is important to describe the behaviors of and the types of definitions currently used by professional personologists.

Sarason (1972) comes close to defining personality in terms of the behavior of the *investigator* when he says that "We shall consider personality as an area of investigation rather than as an entity, real or hypothetical [p. 15]." In contrast, most definitions clearly consider personality as an entity. For example, Pervin (1970) defines personality as representing "those structural and dynamic properties of an individual as they reflect themselves in characteristic responses to situations [p. 2]"; this definition gives cognizance to the facts that "personality is ultimately defined in terms of behavior [p. 3]" and that people do not operate in a vacuum, but respond to and express themselves in environmental situations. Pervin's definition also indicates the investigator's concern that personality should express consistency and regularity. However, Pervin retains the notion of "enduring properties" of individuals. This aspect of the definition also permeates most other current concepts of personality.

The *Annual Review of Psychology* has institutionalized the concept of "enduring dispositions" by subdividing its chapters on the topic of *personality* between proponents of *dynamics* and *structure*: "A study of structure deals with a description of personality and the organization and measurement of its more stable components. Dynamics, on the other hand, is concerned with the functional interplay of forces within the individual as he copes with the environment [Holtzman, 1965, p. 119]."

Nor is a behaviorist immune to the attractiveness of postulating a personality structure such as we see in Lundin's definition (1969) of personality as "that organization of unique behavior equipment an individual has acquired under the special conditions of his development [p. 7]." This is a more refined way of saying that the individual has enduring properties.

Implicit and explicit models and definitions of personality are further amplified beginning in Chapter 2. At this point it should be clear that in dealing with personality we must involve ourselves with a complex concept, the social psychology of the conceptualizer, and the process of the creation of the concept, as well as with the overt behavior of those to whom the labels are applied.

THE CREATION OF PERSONALITY CONCEPTS

Personality is a human intellectual creation. This means that we should study the development and use of the word and what it signifies in the same way we would analyze any other human behavior. There are difficulties with the concept of personality, but there are also genuine reasons for its use. If we assume that a concept such as personality may have some social utility, then we have two tasks: to describe what the concept should achieve and to determine the specific characteristics of the concept. Can we develop guidelines for what we wish to accomplish when we use the concept? These guidelines will serve in two ways: first, to evaluate what presently exists and, second, to provide a standard for evaluation of suggested revisions, reformulations, and replacements of what currently exists.

The next step after the development of guidelines is a reformulation of personality. We call this reformulation *a psychology of behavior influence*, although it is akin to what others such as Bandura (1969) and Mischel (1971) call *social learning theory* and what we have elsewhere called a *sociopsychological model* (Ullmann and Krasner, 1969).

The structure and method of our approach illustrate our viewpoint. We question rather than accept the use of abstractions. Instead of asking if an abstraction is right or wrong, we ask *what* it purports to do and *what* it actually does. We will outline a method and endeavor to adhere to it. But the method we select and the *values* from which it is derived represent a particular viewpoint. That this formulation is consistent with American general psychology during the midtwentieth century does not alter the fact that our conceptualization is a human behavior resulting from the same conditions as all other human behaviors. We are humans engaged in a human enterprise. The best we can do is a bootstrap procedure; the worst we could do would be to deny our humanity and present our formulation as Truth.

At a more mundane level we will touch on the schools, theories, and topics traditional to the study of personality—but in the context of behavioral influences. We will not fragment the area into *theories of* personality or *issues in* personality as is traditionally done because our orientation is that the *writing* on and the *investigation* of the topic of personality are behaviors as open to study as any behaviors being written about or investigated. And, as we have noted, theories influence *what* will be investigated in terms of *topics* and *how* they will be investigated in terms of *measures* and *methods*.

What Should Be Accomplished by a Definition of Personality

Our definition of personality will attempt to meet several needs. The first goal is an academic or professional one. In some measure *all* knowledge is pertinent to man and his adjustment. Physiological studies tell us about the basic equipment of man and its limitations. Anthropology and sociology tell us of people in groups and social organizations present and past. History, economics, and political science detail further the forms and results of social adjustment. Physiology deals in large measure (but certainly not completely in view of the effects of the physical environment) with the person at a socially isolated level. At the other end of the continuum sociology, economics, anthropology, history, and political science deal with people in the mass. The study of personality highlights the *individual*. He—rather than his bodily endowment or his social context— is the focus of study.

Psychology is a biological *and* a social science. It is hard to conceive of taking a person out of his body. It should be just as inconceivable to take a person out of his social context (although a theory such as Kolb's seems at times to attempt this). One of the fundamental issues we will return to is that the individual cannot be separated from his social and physical environment or the situation in which he finds himself at any given point of time.

The focus is on the individual, but what data about him should be collected? In psychology the specialities of physiology, genetics, and comparative development trace the physical and intellectual growth of individuals from childhood through old age. Classic and fundamental psychological studies deal with the sensory apparatus of individuals—with sensation and perception. While grounded in physiology, these studies seek the consistent relations between physical stimuli, such as magnitude of sound, and human responses, such as reports of noticeable differences. The study of behavioral changes and tendencies resulting from *experience* with the environment is called *learning*.

The study of the differences between people—in endowment or experience —has led to the development of statistical and psychometric methods for dealing with individual differences. Tests sample behavior and compare different responses to stimuli. Finally, the study of man in a social context and the problems arising therefrom are known as social psychology.

The subareas of psychology lead to further groupings in terms of the *activities* of professional psychologists: generalizations to industry or to the clinic have led to applied and clinical psychology; work in schools or the larger community have led to subgroupings of educational psychology, counseling, community psychology, psychologists in public service, and the like. Special theories, such as the functional analysis of behavior (Skinner, 1953), may lead to idiosyncratic groupings as do special topics, such as comparative (animal) psychology, esthetics, or social issues. All of these share some common interest; all are eventually relevant to the individual.

A definition of personality in terms of the activity of the professional is unsatisfying. Such an academic definition would define personality as what its practitioners make it or say it is. This meaning would not offer a clear answer to very real problems and would eventually signify everyone doing his own thing—a definition etched in shifting sands.

We have said that we wish to describe, predict, and respond more effectively. Now we must clarify our aim by asking, What do we mean by *effective*? We have used the word to indicate something good—in the sense that it is worthwhile to be effective. But *effective* might mean to make money, to enslave others, or to increase their happiness (whatever *that* might be).

By effectiveness *we mean to have a consequence, to produce a result, to accomplish or achieve some end, to have an impact.* As will be noted in Chapter 19, we cannot use science alone to designate the goal to which psychology should be applied, but we can use scientific means to measure progress toward designated goals and devise methods to attain them.

We will now introduce an assumption that is quite debatable: *the more accurate we are in observing phenomena, the more effective we will be in the long run.* That is, we should measure or describe only phenomena that actually exist. Further, what we measure should be germane to the goal in which we are interested. A corollary of this rule is that we should introduce as little error as possible from elements such as the observer's preconceptions. The focus of our endeavors to be effective is with people, both ourselves and others. But what about people do we wish to influence through our efforts? The payoff for our efforts is in some sort of action.

In other words, *we are interested in the effects of different conditions on the same person or in differences between homogeneous or randomly assigned groups of people under different conditions. We are interested in differences that are meaningful to our goals.* The thing we can do is to alter a person's psychological environment, that is, his experiences, and determine resulting differences for either himself or for different groups of people in the same or other environments. Three consequences result from this view. The first is that we are dealing with learning, the study of the relationship between prior experience and action. The second is that we cannot separate the situation from either the stimulus or the reaction to it. The third is that the focus of our efforts is differences in behavior. *Both our topic and our data focus on behavior.* Overt activities are the target—whether these activities are at a segmental physiological level, such as blood pressure and galvanic skin response, or at a molar interpersonal level, such as reading, writing, raping, and rioting.

This emphasis on behavior may at first seem to go against common sense. In our day-to-day lives we distinguish between our feelings, thoughts, attitudes, and ideals on the one hand and our activities and behavior on the other. Two features seem to distinguish these categories. The first is volition: overt acts seem much more voluntary and goal-oriented than thoughts and feelings. From everyday experience, however, we can observe that a startle response is overt, but far from voluntary or purposive. At a more epistemological level we can ask what would be implied by thoughts and feelings that neither classify as behavior (as defined by measurable changes in some form of corporeal activity) nor are subject to behavioral formulations. Such a view implies that there is a dualism between mind and body—a notion psychologists do not find acceptable.

The psychologist avoids this implied dualism by asking certain questions. Under what conditions does one have a feeling or a thought? What are the indicants or signs by which the person himself or some other observer knows that someone is having a thought or feeling? And, finally, what are the consequences of such thoughts and feelings?

To the layman behavior implies voluntary muscular control or movement. To the psychologist, however, *behavior* means *measurable differences*, the second feature of the above categories. Beyond this difference in approach, one may "voluntarily" alter one's feelings by placing oneself in different situations or even thinking about different topics. A person may visualize, as clearly as he can, being exposed to an unannounced examination or being surprised in the nude by a member of the opposite sex or winning a contest or engaging in a favorite recreation, such as fishing. The "feelings" may range from fear and rage to shame, pleasure, and quiet contentment. In similar fashion it is possible to ask a person to think of his home phone number or the reasons why marijuana should or should not be legalized.

Thoughts and feelings are behaviors, and as such they can be as fruitfully investigated and dealt with as any other behavior. One key question is the point in time and place at which an observer becomes concerned with the behaviors categorized as thoughts, feelings, or attitudes. A look at attitudes may be illustrative. First, how do we determine whether a person's attitude toward an issue or object is favorable or unfavorable? We obtain a sample of the person's behavior either by asking him directly, for example, "How do you feel about the draft?" or by using an indirect technique, such as the semantic differential wherein the person rates the concept "draft" on a number of conceptual dimensions such as relatively *good* or *bad*, *fast* or *slow*, *weak* or *strong*, *sharp* or *blunt*. Let us presume the person marks the concept "draft" as *strong, bad, sharp,* and *moderately fast*. What next? Does this behavior have an impact different from the rating of the draft as *weak, good, round,* and *moderately slow*? What effects do these checkmarks have in themselves? How will they be used? To what events are these checkmarks related so that they may be meaningfully used?

We are concerned about attitudes *only when they have consequences*. All too many teachers will detail their love of students and speak of how teaching should be more adequately compensated. A cursory observation reveals that such teachers often confuse their speeches with their performance—they blame their classroom mediocrity on the low salary or use the low salary to justify their mediocrity. If but a fraction of the goodwill expressed toward blacks or the poor were manifested in actions, the country would be a better place. These examples show two things. First, when attitudes are measured, behavior (the expression called attitude) is measured. Second, this behavior has impact only when it is related to some further activity.

One of our goals is to collect information about how people act. We are interested in describing their behavior *as it is*, that is, as accurately as possible. We are interested in prediction, or inference from a sample of behavior that we have observed, so that we may react in a way that will increase the likelihood of favorable consequences (for ourselves as predictors) in the future. As professionals we are also interested in prediction because it is a way of testing our formulations.

We observe behavior and we predict behavior—our own and that of others. We are changed because of our experiences, and the likelihood of our actions are increased or decreased as a result.

Are we interested in all behavior? At a theoretical level, yes. But in practice, both personally and professionally, we attend to and study only a very limited portion of the differences and changes in others and in ourselves. In fact, we do not even notice the majority of human behavior. Unless special procedures such as psychophysiological recordings and self-reports are used, many human changes are neither discerned nor discernable. Failure or inability to take these changes into account does not mean they do not exist or are not behavior. The acts we do not measure or notice have an impact on individuals; they may mediate or be parts of the sequences that lead to the responses we do observe. So many behaviors are occurring at any given time that we cannot process and respond to all of our own and others' acts. Rather, we are forced by realistic limitations to select a relatively small sample and may well miss important behavior. This is indeed one way in which interpersonal problems arise. We may not hear or ignore subtle nuances or (if we are married) not-so-subtle ones.

We learn which behaviors are important, that is, have clear consequences for us. The cues that are worth attending to change from situation to situation. A lover is interested in different stimuli than a creditor. Probably a majority of cues do not have meaningful consequences save in special circumstances. Within the limits of fashion, clothing usually makes little difference; yet there are codes of where and when a flower, bow, or necklace is to be worn that are meaningful to those who know the language. The most common example in our culture of this cuing is a wedding ring. Cues must be learned and which cues are worth learning depends on what the individual finds reinforcing.

In short, *our target is the segment of people's behavior that is meaningful to us. Operationally, our target is behavior that influences us or that we wish to influence.* Given this view, we will deal with specifics—whether historical, experimental, or field observations—to draw general rules that may serve in numerous situations.

Guidelines

As noted above, we wish to be accurate, for we think that in most cases accuracy increases effectiveness (there are exceptions to this, such as propaganda). We have written elsewhere (Ullmann and Krasner, 1969, ch. 3) on general considerations of methodology. At this point we wish to stress a number of points relating methodology to accuracy. First and foremost, we must know what we are talking about. Because different acts may be called by the same name, it is necessary to specify what procedures are taken to identify or represent a category of acts. For example, the word *anxiety* is used to describe overt behaviors such as floor pacing, physiological measures such as galvanic skin response, and self-reports such as responses to psychological inventories. While measures from all three of these domains may be called anxiety, the correlations among them, while better than chance, are still discouragingly low. A relationship found between a particular activity and one of these measures of anxiety may not be found with one of the other measures of anxiety. If this occurs, the general concept of anxiety has limited use.

The requisite of having to know how a concept is measured serves as a check on overgeneralization. Creativity has sometimes been measured by the number of original responses a person makes to a word association test. It is reasonable to question whether this is what one means by creativity, or how often such behavior is called for in typical situations. Intelligence is another concept that is to a large extent determined by and limited to the procedures which measure it.

The psychological research worker is frequently faced with a hard decision: he can obtain clear control of relevant variables in the laboratory at the expense of using a minor sample of behavior, or he can obtain data about the specific behavior which he wishes to generalize in a natural setting at the expense of some experimental rigor. The person who makes use of the results of research may well say that the miniature laboratory situation is so far from reality that the results do not reduce his uncertainty about how to proceed in the general environment. In other words, the jump necessary from the manner in which information was collected is so great that the data do not help him become effective. As in so many other areas of research, controversy has arisen between the advocates of the controlled laboratory study and the equally vehement advocates of the naturalistic field study.

Among the variables that may make a research study less useful than hoped for is a population of subjects different from those to whom the work is to be applied. For example, variables of age, race, sex, social class, and amount of prior institutionalization represent different prior experiences that subjects may have undergone. A finding with college students may not be replicated with hospitalized psychiatric patients.

The procedures used to obtain a result may depend on factors that are difficult to duplicate. If *only* a uniquely trained expert can take a particular measure, the utility of the measure is reduced. If another person cannot reproduce the expert's measurements, his findings will not be consistent with the expert's either. Specification of the exact details of experimental procedures helps increase the consistency with which judgments are made. Instances of poor rater reliability with which readers may be familiar are the grading of essay exams and the attractiveness of blind dates. If beauty is in the eye of the beholder, we may find ourselves measuring differences in beholders rather than differences in the beauty of the objects beheld. While studying the behavior of the judges may be interesting, it will not increase our effectiveness in dealing with the material judged.

The individual changes over time and situations. What is appropriate behavior at age two is not at age eighteen; what is fine in the locker room may cause raised eyebrows in church. A man may feel differently after reading a draft notice or after receiving an A on an exam he thought he had failed. In fact, a person would be unusual if he did not. There is no perfect consistency of people over time and situations. Differences in the same person's reaction at different times to the same stimuli may provide us with clues about his intervening experiences and thus be very useful. In a different fashion we may repeat tests to determine whether some intervening experience has had an appreciable effect on the individual. At this point, however, it should be clear that it is neither expected nor desirable that a person *not* change on our measure; and if he *does* change on the measure, this doesn't mean that the measure is no good or that the person is deviant.

A single measure may be made up of parts that have little relationship to each other, so that two people may obtain high scores without overlapping on specific items. An example would be a college exam of several parts. The students' different performances on different parts of the test may well give clues about where the students need extra work—information that is valuable. The point, however, is that we should not treat two people receiving the same overall score in a test as necessarily identical.

These elements of inconsistency may lead us to error and decreased effectiveness. Another general area of methodology deals with what psychologists call *validity*. Our goal is meaningful behavior. For example, an intelligence test may tell us whether an individual is likely to do well in an academic course. For certain academic settings and social classes, an intelligence test may be germane and helpful in reducing uncertainty in making decisions. For other tasks such as assembly-line work or salesmanship, the test may be far less germane. If we make our decisions on the basis of irrelevant data (even though that information is relevant to something else), we will decrease our effectiveness. The foregoing considerations will be elaborated in Chapter 5.

The first two guidelines for accuracy are *discernibility* and *germaneness*. The third is *applicability*. The behavior must be discernible; that is, the operations that bring it to bear must be clear enough for people to agree on the behavioral stimuli and responses. Next, the behavior must be germane; that is, changes in behavior must have an *impact* on the person or his environment.

Manipulating a variable that is not genuinely related to the behavior will not alter the behavior. To illustrate this point, we may hypothesize that a decrease in the number of suicides is socially desirable. On the one hand our hypothesis would be based on the assumption that suicide is "bad," on the other hand on the fact that suicide prevention centers have been established. We might presume that suicides would decrease after a suicide prevention center had been established. Maris (1969), however, presented data that the highest rate of use of suicide prevention centers was by young black females, and the highest rate of suicide was by older white males. The number served by the centers was miniscule compared to the total population, so that the rates of suicide by the two groups could not be explained by use of the centers. In short, suicide prevention centers *may not be effective*; that is, they may not reduce the rate of suicide because they do not serve the high-suicide-risk population. At this point it would appear that suicide prevention centers—while probably valuable social institutions for other reasons—are not germane to the task for which they were intended.

To increase the likelihood of germaneness, or meaningfulness of a procedure or institution, we propose three selection criteria. First, the work should deal as much as possible with populations *in the field*; this means that the data gathered will require fewer assumptions for generalization to other situations than would a laboratory situation. Second, evidence that the variables in the measurement situation are related to the target behaviors as assumed should be available whenever possible. Third, the topics under investigation should involve the concerns of the whole society or at least significant segments of it. This last criterion reflects the author's own value systems and may be called relevancy or common sense. Sometimes, seemingly trivial or esoteric research may have major societal consequences while other, obviously applied, research may lead to a dead end. We cannot know with certainty what will be most meaningful in the future, but we can select areas we think deserve attention.

It is very fortunate for society that not all psychologists are drawn to the same topics, for thus psychology spreads its information net wider. Any single book or person must miss material that will later prove vital. In short, all psychologists make decisions that explicitly reflect what they consider important—whether they write a book, do research, or help an individual with his problem behaviors.

The second aspect of applicability is that the targets of study *be open to change*. On one level this is a matter of experimental method: a different treatment (independent variable) may be found to have a better effect on a target behavior (dependent variable). On another level openness to change is a matter of our judging—with acknowledged fallibility—where we may have the greatest impact, so that we can focus on *what is possible*, given the obvious physical and physiological limitations. The "possible" involves a number of issues. The first is a matter of strategy; we must decide what effort is most likely to yield a return. To invest our time and effort in techniques that are generally ineffective or not germane to a particular problem seems likely to reduce our impact. Second, at a tactical level, we do better to take small but successful steps toward our goal than to demand all or nothing. While we may have a strong conviction about what people *should* do, we will achieve more change and increase our chances of attaining our eventual goals if we accept subgoals and available technologies, rather than if we hold out rigidly for a simple perfect final product.

Social Influence

So far we have discussed differences in the enactment of consequential behaviors between people or by the same person at different times. The problem was to describe general conditions for the prediction, development, maintenance, and alteration of such behavior. One way in which this problem has been approached is the use of the concept of personality. As we have repeatedly indicated, personality is a human, intellectual creation. We will suggest both an approach and a set of generalizations we call *behavior influence* as an alternative, or as a new theory of "personality." By virtue of historical usage, the very word *personality* is focused on an individual, the regularities of his behavior, and the hypothesized "enduring structures" *within him* that mediate between environmental stimuli and subsequent responses. We prefer behavior influence as an alternative concept because it emphasizes that the person acts within a physical and social environment. We wish to emphasize that (1) *the necessary interaction is between the person and his social situation* and (2) *the focus should be on measurable activity rather than hypothesized internal constructions.*

There is a steady interchange between the individual's reactions to his environment and the stimuli to which he will respond in the future. In the physical environment, one of the clearest examples is pollution. Man's style of life has so altered his air, water, and natural resources that he will have to change his future behavior if he is to survive. The same is true for the social environment. The direction of both the physical and sociopsychological environments is now of crucial concern to everyone.

Behavior must always occur in an environment. The individual is located in time and space, and his actions have a physical and temporal geography. In a similar fashion, as empiricists we can conceive only of heredity and environment. An environment is required for the development of hereditary potentialities, from matters as simple as food for growth to matters as complex as the maturation of brain capacity and its full use in intellectual endeavors, language, and other academic and physical pursuits.

The impact of the environment commences with one's conception—which is itself dependent upon a complex set of environmental conditions. The environment is often treated as if it were the person's *history*, but it is also the situation as it *exists* at the *current moment*. The environment includes the person's internal environment (such as his condition of food deprivation) as well as his external environment. The hungry person acts differently if his immediate environment is a lunch counter or a lecture only halfway over. At the lunch counter, the person's behavior differs depending on the amount of money he has and whether it is time for breakfast, lunch, or supper. Finally in this example, the person's behavior is further limited by how busy the counterman is and the content of the menu.

The effects of the person's behavior depend on the environment in which he is at the moment. People learn not only acts but also the times and places for making the acts. This topic will be discussed in detail in Chapter 6. Here we want to emphasize that the act cannot be separated from the situation within which it occurs.

The labeling of acts depends on the situations in which they are made. A person receiving a label such as aggressive is considered to be aggressive sooner, more often, or more strongly than other people *in the same situation*. High frequency, amplitude, and low latency of aggressive acts are expected during a football game and not during a cocktail party. If the player who the coach thinks is "too unaggressive" displayed the aggressiveness he shows on the football field at a party, he would be considered impolite. People learn not only the times and places for their acts but also that they themselves are evaluated as much as their acts in terms of the situations in which they act.

After a person has acted aggressively, it is possible to call him an aggressive person *as if* this label were an explanation of his behavior. The alternative is to ask what conditions led to that particular aggressive act. The latter approach places the major locus of investigation on observable and eventually manipulative aspects of the environment. We believe that this latter approach is more effective both scientifically and interpersonally, and proving this contention is essentially the purpose of this text.

LAST WORD

The concept of personality is an intellectual creation used to guide acts that must be made in the face of uncertainty. As one knows more about the antecedents of the acts to be explained or as one has better control of the future, the concept of personality is likely to be used less frequently. The point of reference then moves from personality to environmental conditions. Behavior has meaning to the individual in terms of its consequences or the reactions it evokes from others. We tend to label our behavior and that of others as an aid in coping with our environment. We tend to react to the label itself and thus make the label come true; that is, the label becomes a self-fulfilling prophecy. Our ideas about people guide us in what we look for and expect in our own and in others' behavior.

Personality theory is a human activity; hence, we can and should study personality *theorists*. A psychology of behavior influence emphasizes the inter-action between the individual and his social situation and focuses on the measurable. We emphasize putting the individual and concepts about him in a historical and social context. *All human concepts have human origins.* Hence, we are interested in the antecedent conditions of behavior, the consequences of behavior, and possible alternative behaviors.

Among human acts are theories of human behavior or personality. These acts have consequences. There are differences in treatment when one follows a psychoanalytic (medical analogue) or sociopsychological (social learning) model. At times, theories are generalized to the level of social policy. Outbreaks of violence may be thought of as manifestations of "human nature" and hence unchangeable. Or outbreaks of violence may be considered as symptoms of frustration or of a "sick" society. In this latter case, the overt acts of violence may be ignored ("they are not the real causes"), and social actions may be aimed at the style of a society rather than at remedies for specific antecedent conditions. The changes made would not be germane to the overt violence, would not reduce such acts, and, therefore, would be abandoned even if they were valuable for other humanitarian reasons. Finally, the overt acts might be given the status of real acts capable of being changed through a program of differential consequences for violence and nonviolence and alteration of the situations to which violence is a response. Once again, we are interested in the conditions that lead to the act, the consequences of that act, and the alternative acts that might have been made.

Theories of personality, the formulations of human behavior, have very real consequences in our attention to, organization of, and response to social stimuli. Our formulations affect the data on which we base our behavior; and our actions alter and thus influence data in the future. The study on which we embark should be a meaningful one for all, since it deals with how we may better understand and deal with human beings, ourselves included.

CHAPTER **2**

Historical Development of Concepts of Human Behavior: From First Models to 1900

The next three chapters will describe the development of the psychology of behavior influence from various perspectives. There are always dilemmas in presenting the background of the field of human behavior. How much of the past must be described in order to give a sufficient picture in which the present and future can be understood and predicted? Another problem in the investigation of human behavior is that there are many established professional domains. Once such a domain is created, a principle of territoriality quickly develops. Dividing the domain of knowledge about man's behavior has fostered a series of arbitrary dichotomies such as those between heredity and environment, normal and abnormal, psychology and economics, sociology and anthropology, religion and philosophy.

Why are we devoting three chapters to a historical perspective? The historical approach introduces a contextual framework and is an integral part of a psychology of behavior influence. While behavior influence may appear to be a new approach to human behavior, it is a theory with many antecedents. And a theory of behavior expresses the social context in which it has developed and in which it is presented.

The personality theories generated at particular times and places are the then-current conceptualizations of how human beings can be influenced by others. A theory at any given time deals with what seems *important* and what seems to *work*. It is a human construction and reveals much about its maker. Investigators continually struggle with the same problems and repeatedly change their paradigms. The very making of theories and use of paradigms are human behaviors that need to be understood. For example, we should deal with the history of psychology, sociology, anthropology, economics, political science, education, jurisprudence, philosophy, and science. The breakdown of man's environmental relationships that attempts to divide them into narrow disciplines is of relatively recent origin and occurred in part to satisfy the organizational needs of academic departments in universities.

This chapter will bring into historical perspective people and ideas which have had and still have influence on theories, research, and applications of the psychology of behavior influence.

On "Great" Theorists

One approach to history is to focus on the theorists and investigators of human behavior. It is not simply a question of an individual "great man" making a crucial contribution, but of a person in a complex social context performing a series of very human behaviors with social consequences. For example, Freud's investigations were a landmark in the intellectual history of Western man, but he has his place in history mainly because of his impact on the behavior of multitudes of other human beings. This influence is not only on people who worked after his time but also affects the evaluation of events that preceded him. A new paradigm fosters a reinterpretation of prior as well as succeeding data. Freud's impact led not only to a reevaluation of his precursors in terms of the concept of unconscious motivation but also to a reinterpretation of literature and history.

Our review will deal with the behavior of key individuals and the consequences of their behavior. For example, Emil Durkheim, one of the founders of modern sociology, published most of his work before 1900. Yet in terms of frequency of citation in current sociology treatises, Durkheim's contributions are very much alive. He is credited with producing "the first clear-cut scientific study of a single social problem in modern sociology [Nisbet, 1970, p. 33]." In his study on suicide in 1897, Durkheim demonstrated empirically and theoretically that this human behavior was related to the organization—or more specifically the disorganization—of the group to which the individual belongs. Both Durkheim's methodology and the theoretical implications of behavior as a function of interaction in a social environment have endured.

Durkheim also illustrated another issue in tracing broad conceptualizations about human behavior, namely, the one-sided viewpoint. A major criticism of Durkheim, particularly by psychologists, is his neglect of "individual dynamics." In fact, Durkheim went so far in the other direction that he seemed to reify the concept of society—ignoring interactions between individuals as though society could exist without individual behavior. The relative importance of individual behavior versus an abstraction called social organization is a theme repeated throughout the development of a psychology of behavior influence. The point here is that the individual who advances a major new paradigm runs the risk of emphasizing his ideas to the exclusion of others.

SOME OBSERVERS OF MAN

Initially, speculations as to the nature of man were also theories of the state and its functioning. For example, the Greek philosopher Plato (427–347 B.C.) argued that the state developed to meet the needs of individuals who could not adequately cope with life by themselves. Plato foreshadowed some later observers in two respects: his belief in an ideal society and his belief that individual behavior should be controlled by the decisions of a ruling elite (in his case, the philosophers, or *lovers of wisdom*) (Jowett, 1892).

After Plato dozens of others observed and commented on man: philosophers, novelists, political scientists, theologians. Their names are legion and include Aquinas, Hobbes, Locke, Shakespeare, Darwin, Tolstoy, Kirkegaard, Bentham, Marx, Nietzsche, Spencer, Machiavelli, Thoreau, Dewey, W. James, Voltaire, Swift, Rabelais, Hegel—and many, many, more. Presenting such a list demonstrates that there have been many acute observers of human behavior throughout history (even before psychologists). Further, theories of behavior have had major influences upon human history. We need but cite the impact of the writings of Hegel, Marx, and Engels, and more recently the influence of Freud's and Skinner's ideas.

The Greeks had several views on human behavior and its causes. There is a clear distinction between Plato's and Aristotle's respective views, which in various forms continues to this day. Plato argued that people behave as they do because they have been *taught* to behave so. According to him, men are born with the capacity to learn and are trained by the society's system of education;

therefore, the way to influence behavior is to change the social system. Aristotle, on the other hand, viewed the individual's behavior as a reflection of the individual's nature. In his view, society is a function of the instinctive and unchanging nature of the human being.

Based on observations of a decaying Greek society, a third theory of individual behavior, credited to Socrates, developed: men *naturally* do the things that *please* them and avoid the things that *displease* them. This was an early form of *hedonism*, which explains human behavior on the basis of pleasure and pain. In some ways hedonism is a variation of the Aristotelian belief that behavior is caused by innate natural forces, and thus is impossible to change.

Another question that divides theorists of human behavior is the desirability of even studying human behavior. McClelland (1951), in assessing the history of man's approach to man, succinctly summarizes the different views on this fundamental question:

> The Hebrews felt that there were dark inscrutable forces within human nature just as there were in the outside world and that even the wish to understand them was in itself bad, in fact a symptom of those evil forces themselves at work. The Greeks, on the other hand, at least in the time of Plato and Socrates, felt that man by reasoning could arrive at understanding and control himself. . . . With such an inheritance from opposing Greek and Hebrew traditions, it can hardly be wondered that beliefs about the feasibility of a scientific approach to personality swung from one extreme to another at different periods in the history of Western civilization [Pp. 6–7].

In effect, then, both the Hebrews and the Greeks agreed that the study of man, in and of itself, has important social consequences. Related to this controversy is the vacillation between the belief in a *fixed* universe—with human behavior predetermined in accordance with a highly moral law, as in the Middle Ages— and a *changing* world—in which man has faith in his ability to control his own destiny, as in the Renaissance.

Locke and his successors in the British associationist school thought that since man was essentially a "blank tablet" at birth, society had the capacity to *influence* him in nearly any manner by the kind of education it gave him. On the other hand, throughout most periods in history, some have argued that man is not a rational animal who can control his behavior, but an *innately* emotional, lustful, and irrational creature. For example, Machiavelli, the Italian political advisor of the Renaissance, argued that man should accept the fact that power was his main concern in life and act accordingly. Karl Marx believed that the profit motive was essentially instinctual and hence could not be understood or controlled. Instead, he felt it had to be accepted and curbed by social arrangements.

The ideas of Freud had a considerable impact on the belief in the feasibility of applying scientific knowledge to the observation of human behavior. Freud combined in his own thinking the two great contradictory beliefs about human nature: those of rationality and of irrationality. He had the Greeks' strong faith in the power of man's ability to understand himself. Yet he was fascinated by the aggressive, antisocial, apparently irrational, and even mystical aspects of man's nature. Freud strongly identified with the faith in science and the power of reason which characterized the educated class of the late nineteenth century. (Freud started out as a biologist and would most likely have developed into an outstanding research worker in this field had not his interest turned to psychology.) Thus Freud represented what at that time appeared to be the synthesis of the Greek and Hebrew streams—that man, despite his irrational and instinct-dominated nature, could be investigated by scientific study.

The Social Philosophers

René Descartes (1596–1650), Thomas Hobbes (1588–1679), John Locke (1632–1704), Jean Jacques Rousseau (1712–1778), and David Hume (1731–1776) are examples of another group of astute observers of the human scene, called social philosophers. Their ideas have had considerable impact not only on their peers but also on subsequent generations. All the conflicting views of human behavior which are part of our current scene (described in Chapters 3 and 4) can be found among their observations.

Descartes argued that the human being and his behavior were subject to the same mechanical laws of the universe as other organisms. The notion of mind-body dualism is usually traced to Descartes, who also emphasized the innate source of man's ideas. Yet Descartes laid the basis for later "scientific" approaches to man.

Hobbes originated a number of concepts that have continued to the present. These include the beliefs that all human behavior is subject to scientific law (going further than Descartes in this regard); that, all other things being equal, man chooses his course of action based on what will give him pleasure (a variant of hedonism); and that the state must control man's natural passion (a view similar to Machiavelli's). Hobbes also developed a view of man which became the basis for the later associationist concepts of Locke. Locke's concept of the individual as coming into the world with a *tabula rasa*, or blank slate, was a counterview to the prevailing doctrine (influenced by Descartes) that the source of man's behavior was inborn. Locke believed that man's ideas and behavior resulted from experience or interaction with the external environment.

Hume was a representative of the Scottish school of moral philosophy, which approached human nature through empirical observation, stressed what was common to and ideal for all mankind, emphasized the importance of emotion as human behavior, occupied itself with ethics and man's "moral sense," and wanted to be in a position to both predict and control human behavior (for man's own good).

The social philosophers shared a general belief in the role of the environment in shaping man's personality—even to the point of viewing man as potentially perfectible. Generally, theorists who emphasize environmental rather than innate influences are optimistic about what can be done to "better" the human condition and tend to focus on human interaction. For example, Burnham (1968) made an astute observation of what was happening to the English language during this period of the Enlightment, when he stated, "At the time when many men were toying with environmentalism, the English language added a large number of a class of words that describe things not in terms of themselves but in terms of the effects that they produce on people: affecting, amusing, boring, charming, diverting, entrancing, fascinating, interesting, pathetic [p. 22]."

These observers of human behavior helped set the stage for one of the more dramatic and influential investigators of personality, Franz Joseph Gall (1758–1828), the originator of phrenology. Gall thought that the explanation of human behavior would be found in the *neurophysiological* makeup of the individual. He believed that fundamental innate attributes (such as pride, vanity, foresight, cunning, sense of property) existed in man and that each attribute was represented by an organ or a part of the brain. Thus a strong development of the particular characteristic (trait or propensity) would be evidenced by the size of that part of the brain. The 37 basic qualities Gall and his coworkers offered were generally accepted by the educated people of his time as representing and explaining human behavior. Phrenology as an approach to behavior and as a social movement stressed its scientific basis and indeed represented the science of the day.

The social philosopher Auguste Comte (1798–1857) was influenced by Gall, particularly in his belief that a physiological substratum was correlated with behavior. Despite this view, Comte also developed the notion of *innate positive social instincts*, which interacted with environmental demands and on which human society was based. Comte tried to cope with the question, How can the individual be at once cause and consequence of society? He was interested in the development of sciences and in many ways foresaw the eventual need for a study of the individual that combined both the biological and social points of view. His work is often taken as a starting place for the fields of social psychology and sociology; and the ideas of some present-day psychological humanists are frequently traced to Comte.

On Blending the Social and the Psychological

Social psychology was that field of an emerging science of psychology which attempted to combine systematically the variables of society with those of the individual. In his historical review of social psychology, Allport (1968) cites

Vico's 1725 observation that "governments must conform to the nature of the men governed" as illustrating that both ancient and modern *political philosophers* were interested in the key problem of man's social nature. Further, from Plato on, virtually all theories of the social nature of man appear to have been tied to theories of the nature of the state or political philosophy.

In 1908, two books, both with "Social Psychology" in the title, were published as introductions to the field; one was by Edward A. Ross, a sociologist, the other by William McDougall, a psychologist. Ross organized his material around the concepts of suggestion, crowd behavior, and other forms of human interaction; McDougall emphasized the concept of instinct. These books crystallized the two traditions of psychological social psychology and sociological social psychology. This division indicated not only a difference in semantics but a different emphasis on where one looks for basic variables—within the person, in the environment, or in the interaction of two sets of independent variables.

Two other key turn-of-the-century sociologists were Charles H. Cooley (1864–1929) and W. I. Thomas (1863–1947). Cooley's contributions were such that a leading modern sociologist (Borgatta, 1969) has argued that Cooley's *Human Nature and the Social Order* (1902) "may be the first modern text in social psychology [p. 1]." Even the title conveys the concept of the individual and society within the same framework. To understand Cooley's break with the prevalent view of society, we must realize that society was conceived of as an entity which involved characteristics *beyond* that of individual actions. Society as a whole was viewed as greater than the sum of its parts (this view later characterized gestalt psychology). Cooley's view is expressed in the following:

> And just as there is no society or group that is not a collective view of persons, so there is no individual who may not be regarded as a particular view of social groups. He has no separate existence; through both the hereditary and the social factors in his life a man is bound into the whole of which he is a member, and to consider him apart from it is quite as artificial as to consider society apart from individuals [Cooley, 1902, p. 3, as quoted in Borgatta, 1969, p. 2].

Cooley's emphasis on the importance of the individual must also be contrasted with the intellectual climate of his time—a time when science was placed on a pedestal; sociology wishfully considered itself to be the synthesizer of theories of man; psychology was doing research on mental functions; and there generally was little empirical data and much theorizing in those fields.

Cooley used the concept of *suggestion* both to observe and explain human behavior:

> The word suggestion is used here to denote an influence that works in a comparatively mechanical or reflex way, without calling out that higher selective activity of the mind implied in choice or will [Cooley, 1902, p. 14, as quoted in Borgatta, 1969, p. 4].

W. I. Thomas was also a major influence on early twentieth-century social psychology and sociology. He developed the ideas of Cooley (as well as those of John Dewey and George Mead) into a comprehensive system of thought and research known as *symbolic interactionism*. For Thomas, the basic unit of study was the *action* of the individual *in a social situation.*

Thomas went beyond his contemporaries in focusing on environmental influences. His entire analysis of human behavior was in terms of human inter-action, and he devoted little attention to intraindividual processes. A current interpreter of Thomas (Petras, 1970) contends that the central thesis of Thomas' work was the view that the individual must always act "as if." The individual evaluates each of the paths of his contemplated behavior on the basis of what will result if he acts in one way rather than another. This planning before any self-determined behavior is the "definition of the situation." Thomas believed that facts do not have a uniform existence apart from the persons who observe and interpret them. Rather, the "real facts are the ways in which different people come into the definition of the situations [Thomas, 1951, p. 30]." Thomas' concept of situationalism became the sociological counterpart of the psychological concept of personality that stresses the effects of internal environment. The situationalists and the personality investigators of that period tended to ignore each other (and still do), but both sides served a useful function by extending their respective concepts to their limits. Recent sociological workers still function in the situational tradition (McHugh, 1968).

CONCEPTS OF HUMAN BEHAVIOR

Human beings have always speculated about the mainsprings of their behavior. Concepts were developed around single key phrases, offered in a manner that apparently would explain all activity. They have included terms such as *suggestion, imitation, hedonism, sex, anxiety, free will*, and currently *reinforcement* and *role*. Here we will briefly examine several of the word-concepts which have had a major influence on how human behavior has been conceptualized by multitudes of investigators in the past (and present).

Instincts

A plausible theory develops, has its brief moment of glory, then fades away but never dies. Such a concept is *instinct*. Darwin's doctrine of natural selection was the foundation for the belief that the basis of all behavior, both human and animal, lay in instincts or basic innate motivational units. McDougall (1908) built a system of psychology upon the concept of instinct, which he defined as "an inherited or innate psycho-physical disposition which determines its possessor to perceive and to pay attention to objects of a certain class, to experience an emotional excitement of a particular quality upon perceiving such an object, and to act in regard to it in a particular manner, or, at least, to experience an impulse to such action [p. 30]." The similarity of McDougall's definition to some later definitions of the function of attitudes is striking in regard to the notion of a predisposition to respond in a particular manner.

Within this rubric of instinct, McDougall explained most social phenomena. All behavior was the result of specific instincts or combinations. This became the generally accepted theory in psychology for many years. By 1932 he had expanded the list of instincts to 18: food seeking; disgust; sex; fear; curiosity; protective or parental propensity; gregariousness; self-assertion; submission; anger; appeal; constructive migratory propensity; a cluster of specific bodily needs—coughing, sneezing, breathing, elimination (McDougall, 1932).

The behaviorists led by John Watson, Knight Dunlap, and eventually B. F. Skinner argued that there was no proof of the existence of instincts and refused to admit the immutability of behavioral patterns implicit in such a formulation. But nobody gave instincts a decent burial, and they are continually resurrected in the garbs of motives, needs, wishes, primary drives, or prepotent reflexes.

Attitudes

G. Allport (1968) considers *attitude* "probably the most distinctive and indispensable concept in contemporary American social psychology. No other term appears more frequently in experimental and theoretical literature [p. 59]." In Chapters 4 and 15, as we discuss current research in personality, we shall see the truth of this statement. Allport adeptly points out that the reason for this popularity is that the concept of attitude is all things to all men. Instinctivists, environmentalists, psychologists, sociologists, individualists, and culturists all can adequately incorporate attitudes within their framework.

If we conceive of attitude as some kind of *state of readiness*, or set, for motor or cognitive activities, then the first experimental research was reported from Germany in the late 1800s. A whole series of attitudes (defined as mental and motor sets that were influencing the thoughts and behavior of subjects during the experiment) were investigated in the laboratory, generally by introspection. Many investigators of the period considered attitudes as *underlying* (causally relating to) other psychological phenomena such as perception, judgment, memory, learning, and thought. In effect then, attitudes became a major determinant and explanatory concept of behavior (in much the same manner as instincts). Many investigators searched for the neurological substrate that would be correlated with attitudes. Freud's explanation of the unconscious gave further impetus to the importance of attitudes, since it appeared to offer an explanation of the dynamic forces behind them. Thomas and Znaniecki (1918) are given credit for the systematic incorporation of attitudes into social psychology and sociology by demonstrating their relevance in a study of the behavior of Polish peasants.[1]

A concept correlated with attitude is *social value*. Attitudes imply direction or movement toward an object; the object itself then represents a value. If love of money is an attitude, then money is the value. If desire for fame is the attitude, then fame is the value.

Hedonism

"Pleasure and pain are our sovereign masters" (Bentham, 1789). "Pleasure stamps in: pain stamps out" (Thorndike, 1898). These quotations represent what is probably man's oldest and strongest belief about the source and control of human behavior. For centuries hedonism (derived from the Greek word for pleasure) has been offered as an explanation, a justification, and a rationale for human behavior. In its simplest terms, hedonism is the belief that the human being does things that are pleasurable for him and tries to avoid events that would be painful. With some variation, diverse theorists such as the Epicureans, Jeremy Bentham, John Stuart Mill, Herbert Spencer, Sigmund Freud, and B. F. Skinner all offer hedonism as an explanatory concept for human behavior. Yet each of these observers has come to very different views about the ways in which human beings actually interact with their environment. These theorists differ in their definition of pleasure and in their interpretation of the manner and degree to which the operation of pleasure-seeking experiences affect the individual's subsequent behavior.

The Epicureans (followers of the Greek philosopher Epicurus, 342–270 B.C.) argued that pleasure was the highest *good* and emphasized that men should seek pleasure of the mind rather than of the body. The nineteenth-century followers of Bentham, the utilitarians, went a step beyond the observation that men maximize pleasure to the moral position that men *should* maximize pleasure.

Important social consequences follow from hedonistic concepts of behavior. If indeed it is human nature to maximize pleasure, then human beings should be left alone (laissez-faire) and few, if any, restraints should be put upon them by the state. Thus, proponents of this view of man in the eighteenth and nineteenth centuries fought against social legislation and used their theory to justify many of the worst excesses of the Industrial Revolution. Herbert Spencer (1899) tied the hedonistic and laissez-faire doctrines to the theory of evolution and used his resultant theory of man in fighting against humanitarian social legisla-

[1] A recent example of the extension of social psychology and particularly the concept of attitude into the area of behavior change is by Suinn, Jorgensen, Stewart, and McGuirk (1971).

tion. He argued that pleasurable activities generally made for human survival and implied that those who had more pleasure than others were "fitter to survive." Spencer took the prevailing sociopolitical view of man's behavior—that of progress and perfectability—and used the science of the day to justify it. Others like Charles Dickens, the novelist, pointed to the human misery that was allowed to continue because corrective social legislation was not enacted because of a possibly erroneous or, at best one-sided, view of human nature.

Sympathy

Other theorists have postulated that, rather than being driven by the selfishness and self-love of hedonism, man may be seen as dominated by more positive feelings of love, altruism, or sympathy. The concepts of *sympathy, imitation,* and *suggestion* comprise the principal triumvirate of explanatory theories in social psychology. This trio can be traced back to Plato's conception of the human mind as made up of three faculties: the abdomen, or seat of emotions; the breast, or seat of striving and action; and the head, or seat of reason. Hence the human mind comprised affection (feeling), conation (striving), and cognition (thought). These faculties developed historically as follows: sympathy came to denote the affective faculty imitation, the conative; and suggestion, the cognitive. Various theorists have stressed one of these concepts at the expense of the others, while some have attempted to combine all three.

Adam Smith (1759), the English economist, hedged his bets by emphasizing human sympathy as a supplement to hedonism and its consequent laissez-faire philosophy. Smith argued for the existence of two forms of sympathy. First was the reflex type of response, in which one experiences the same feeling as the person he is watching. The second type of sympathy, according to Smith, was intellectual, in which one *sympathizes* with a person even though he does not feel as the other does. With these principles, and hedonism, Smith tried to explain social behavior.

In much the same way as Smith, Herbert Spencer also thought that it was necessary to balance hedonism with the more positive instinct of sympathy. Spencer, however, felt that sympathy was applicable only within the narrow limits of the family and not within the broader state. The philosophy of goodness as applicable only in the family led to ultraconservative views, including opposition to free public schools. Rather than "everyone for himself," this theory justified "every family for itself."

A number of writers extended this notion of a sympathetic tendency into an instinct labeled with such terms as *gregariousness, consciousness of kind, human solidarity, social instinct,* and—two current "motives," or not-quite instincts—*affiliation* and *altruism.*

Beyond this, other theorists have considerably expanded the scope of thought about sympathy, but have not necessarily clarified the behavior itself. For example, Scheler (1954) offered a phenomenological analysis of eight forms of sympathy, which was related to the subtleties and flexibilities of the German language. And in recent years there has been a revival of interest in the positive behaviors of man such as altruism and cooperation (for example, see Macaulay and Berkowitz, 1970).

Imitation

Among the key concepts investigators have repeatedly used to explain man's social behavior is *imitation*. But in this case as in so many others, what has been offered as an explanation is actually an acute observation of human behavior. Clearly, a younger generation may learn by seeing what its elders do and then, depending on the consequences, doing the same. Some sociologists have viewed imitation as the key to social organization; Tarde (1843–1904), for example, offered the most succinct observation, "society is imitation."

J. M. Baldwin (1895), an American psychologist, conceived of imitation as a specific mechanism *within* each individual. G. H. Mead (1934) extended the notion by saying that humans imitate by first perceiving what others are doing and then perceiving their own responses to others' acts.

As they have done with so many other concepts, theorists have attributed the simple observations that people learn by imitation to the existence of an instinct (Bernard, 1924; James, 1890). On the other hand, the early behaviorists attempted to explain imitation by either classical or instrumental conditioning. More will be said about imitation and modeling, its modern counterpart, in subsequent chapters.

Free Will

One of the most influential concepts explaining and affecting man's behavior returns to the medieval theory that each human is free to decide whether to follow the ways of God or Satan. This is the theory of *free will*. Many modern individuals probably believe, perhaps vaguely, that as individual entities they possess free will, or the ability to make choices and decisions without outside influence. It must be noted that the medieval theological doctrine did not imply *complete* free choice, but *choice* between two alternative ways of life—the socially acceptable way of God or the socially undesirable way of the Devil. Once a person had selected one or the other, his behavior was determined by his choice. These two modes of conduct were fixed by forces external to man; thus he was not free to will the form of his own society, which had already been shaped.

Although most current investigators of human behavior in psychology and sociology have formally rejected the notion of free will as involving complete freedom of choice, the theory is still found implicitly and explicitly in new forms and terminology, including some of the current personality theories of "growth" and some of the educational notions of "freedom."

Attacks on free will theory have taken many different forms. Among the social philosophers who disputed the theologians was Machiavelli, who viewed human behavior as inherently evil. Machiavelli asserted that if man had free will, he would do harm. The task of the Prince or leader of the state was to manipulate or control his people by any means to prevent manifestations of their innate evil. Thus, success in society would involve obtaining socially desirable behavior by hook or crook and preventing man from destroying himself. By putting his observations on behavior and its contingencies into his guide *The Prince* (written in 1513), Machiavelli's name came to designate underhand, evil manipulative behavior.

It should be noted—as in Chapter 1 on self-fulfilling prophecies and in later remarks on self-control—that current psychological approaches do *not* view man as impotent or unable to change his environment, although they view his acts as the result of multiple antecedent and concurrent influences. The issue of the existence of free will is not only not dead but alive and flourishing (Skinner, 1971). We will return to it in our discussion of values in Chapter 19.

Rationalism

Another important set of concepts which cuts across and influences many others in the investigation of human behavior is that of *rationalism* and *irrationalism*. Allport (1968) has emphasized the relative flow of rationalism and irrationalism in theories of man's behavior and in man's conceptualization of himself. Paradoxically, the hedonism of Bentham, Mills, and the utilitarians was considered to be rationalistic. Hedonism was emotionally (or irrationally) based, but once this starting point was accepted, man's conduct was based on rational choice and his ability to predict the consequences of actions. A more recent statement of this position is by Russell:

> "Reason" has a perfectly clear and precise meaning. It signifies the choice of the right means to an end that you wish to achieve. . . . There is a famous sentence: "Reason is, and ought only to be, the slave of the passions." This sentence does not come from the works of Rousseau or Dostoevsky or Sartre. It comes from David Hume. . . . Desires, emotions, passions (you can choose whichever word you will), are the only possible causes of action. Reason is not a cause of action but only a regulator [Russell, 1962, p. viii].

The rationalist view of man has had many political overtones. An example is in the United States Constitution, in which a system of checks and balances was devised to allow the rational judgments of the voting electorate but to protect against the irrational passions of the mob.

The alternative view of man as an irrational being is that he has no intellectual control over the forces that rule him—be they emotion, instinct, the unconscious, or learned habits. Allport, for example, clearly places most social psychology theory, past and present, within the irrational domain. The major influences were Darwin, McDougall, and Freud, all of whom emphasized the irrational in their uses of instincts. The influence of writers on abnormal psychology with their medical orientation and their postulation of unconscious forces furthered the irrational viewpoint. In contrast, philosopher-educator John Dewey is credited with advocating a more rationalistic, and hence more optimistic, view of man in the twentieth century.

Feeling Rather than Thinking

Many of the themes of this chapter may be illustrated by reference to late eighteenth-century German romanticism, which has reemerged as one of today's popular movements. There are similarities to current existential theories of human behavior in the general social climate of the late eighteenth century.

At the present time, one of the increasingly legitimate and available directions for a growing portion of the college-educated population is the search for direct sensory experiences. One aspect of this will be treated in greater detail in Chapter 17 on social movements, particularly with reference to growth groups. The major feature of this approach is a move away from technology and impersonal relations. Authors such as Goodman (1960) and Maslow (1968, 1971) provide some theoretical rationale (see Chapter 3), while Roszak (1969) provides both a history and label (counterculture). Another statement of this view is Reich's *The Greening of America* (1970), with its emphasis on the value of "Consciousness III," a nonrational, unstudied form of knowing.

The late eighteenth-century intelligentsia in Germany was deprived of political power and opportunity to advance vocationally because of the preference given members of the noble and military castes. One solution was to withdraw from the public arenas (for example, finance and government) and to emphasize inner experience. The educated young man without power or prospects could think of himself as too fine and unique to engage in the current culture. This tactic was adopted also by French youths after the disillusionment of the Restoration of 1815. The coming of the Industrial Revolution in England and the rise of the bourgeoisie and modern capitalism somewhat later in France provided additional impetus for the romantic reaction.

The following quotations have a contemporary flavor:

> The classicist felt himself to be master of reality, he agreed to be ruled by others, because he ruled himself and believed that life can be ruled. The romantic, on the other hand, acknowledged no external ties, was incapable of committing

himself, and felt himself to be defenselessly exposed to an overwhelmingly powerful reality . . . [Hauser, 1958, p. 175].

To all of them the present age seemed to have become stale and empty. The intellectuals isolated themselves more and more from the rest of society, and the intellectually productive elements already lived a life of their own. The concept of the philistine and the *"bourgeois,"* in contrast to the *"citoyen,"* arose, and the curious and almost unprecedented situation came about that artists and writers were filled with hatred and contempt for the very class to which they owed their intellectual and material existence [Hauser, 1958, p. 177].

The inner strife of the romantic soul is reflected nowhere so directly and expressively as in the figure of the "second self" which is always present to the romantic mind and recurs in innumerable forms and variations in romantic literature. The source of this *idée fixe* is unmistakeable: it is the irresistible urge to introspection, the maniacal tendency to self-observation and the compulsion to consider oneself over and over again as one unknown, as an uncannily remote stranger. The idea of the "second self" is, of course, again merely an attempt to escape and expresses the inability of the romantics to resign themselves to their own historical and social situation. The romantic rushes headlong into his "double," just as he rushes headlong into everything dark and ambiguous, chaotic and ecstatic, demonic and dionysian, and seeks therein merely a refuge from the reality he is unable to master by rational means. On this flight from reality, he discovers the unconscious, that which is hidden away in safety from the rational mind, the source of his wish-fulfillment dreams and the irrational solutions of his problems. . . . For him, the irrational has the inestimable advantage of not being subject to conscious control, which is why he praises the unconscious, obscure instincts, dreamlike and ecstatic states of soul, and looks in them for the satisfaction which is not vouchsafed him by the cool, cold, critical intellect. [Hauser, 1958, p. 181].

Their whole hatred, their whole contempt, was now heaped on the middle class. The avaricious, narrow-minded, hypocritical bourgeois became their public enemy No. 1 and, in contrast to him, the poor, honest, open-hearted artist struggling against all the humiliating ties and conventional lies of society appears as the human ideal par excellence. The tendency to remoteness from practical life with firm social roots and political commitments, which had been characteristic of romanticism from the very beginning and had become apparent in Germany even in the Eighteenth Century, now becomes predominant everywhere. . . . The bad manners and impertinences of the bohemians, their often childish ambition to embarrass and provoke the unsuspecting bourgeois, their frantic attempt to differentiate themselves from normal, average men and women, the eccentricity of their clothes, their headdress, their beards . . . their free and easy and paradoxical language, their exaggerated, aggressively formulated ideas, their invectives and indecencies, all that is merely the expression of the desire to isolate themselves from middle-class society, or rather of the desire to represent the already accomplished isolation as intentional and acceptable . . . everything revolves around their hatred for philistinism, around their contempt for the strictly regulated and soulless life of the bourgeoisie, around their fight against everything traditional and conventional, everything capable of being taught and learnt, everything mature and serene. The system of intellectual values is enriched by a new category: the idea of youth as more creative than and intrinsically superior to age. This is a new idea, alien, above all, to classicism, but to a certain extent to all previous cultures. There had naturally been competition between the generations. . . . But youth had not triumphed (previously) simply because it was young . . . [Hauser, 1958, pp. 194–195].

These words were written two decades ago, yet the description of the early nineteenth-century romantics includes nearly every major element of the "new" counterculture. There are marked similiarities in the sociological background both of the general society and the people who became artists, and there are marked similarities in both the need for and form of a new definition of the good life and the good man.

Another observer has presented a similar historical analogy between the hippie movement and behavior during the earlier romantic movement:

Personality configuration and values that have emerged within the contemporary Hippie movement are not new. They have appeared many times in the past, as for example in the Gnostic and similar religious heresies and in the Romantic movement. In each case the personality configuration which I have denoted as the antinominal personality, arose in a time of social crisis and transition when old values and behavior controls were no longer adequate and new ones had not yet emerged to take their place. The antinominal mode with its characteristic emphasis on intuition, immediacy, self-actualization, transcendence, and similar themes familiar in Hippie conduct is an adaptive style manifest in transitional periods [Adler, 1968, p. 332].

FROM THE INDIVIDUAL TO THE CROWD TO THE GROUP

In her excellent reanalysis of social psychology in terms of social role, Heine (1971) points out that the "basic" laws of social psychology—suggestion, contagion, and imitation—were used to explain what appeared to be the mechanical, irrational, and even criminal behavior of "the crowd"; she observes, "moreover, the very language suggested that such behavior spread like a communicable disease and like other diseases required public measures of control [p. 13]." Thus, the crowd was viewed as an entity behaving in a manner different from but analogous to that of the individual.

Le Bon's influential treatise *The Crowd* argued in 1896 for the existence of a "crowd mind" as an emotional manifestation of a vaguely unconscious process. (The belief in the existence of unconscious forces was particularly strong in the late 1800s, as evidenced by the culmination of this belief in the work of

Freud). Along with the other early French social psychologists such as Tarde (1843–1904), Le Bonn emphasized hypnosis and its partner concepts of suggestion and imitation as explanations for *all* behavior, even that of the crowd. It is noteworthy that these concepts were derived in large part from the reports on hysteria and abnormal behavior which were then coming out of clinics and hospitals. This approach to social psychology emphasized the link between investigating man's social behavior and his deviant behavior.

The traditional date given for the establishment of the first psychology laboratory by Wundt at Leipzig is 1879. But research in the early laboratories focused exclusively on performances of individuals *by themselves*. Not until the very end of the nineteenth century did investigators begin to be interested in the influence of others, the impact of the group, on individual performances.

F. Allport (1924) offered a useful distinction between two kinds of small groups, the *coacting* and the *face to face* types. The former includes groups in which several individuals are together when they receive social stimuli and the presence of the others serves as a source of social facilitation. Early twentieth-century social psychology studies focused on coacting groups. Usually the performance studied was found to be enhanced by a social setting. The explanations generally offered were that stress and competition served as social stimulation. Even the *imagined* presence of others was found to have a facilitating effect on behavior. The judgments of experts introduced new sources of influence into these group situations.

The Russians (particularly Bechterev) to a large extent initiated the study of collective as opposed to individual behavior in face-to-face groups, in which the emphasis was on interaction between the participants. These studies were consequences of the Soviet revolution, which introduced a new political emphasis on the importance of *cooperation* in groups. In the United States, investigators led by Kurt Lewin introduced the concept of *social climate*, or group atmosphere. An interesting innovation was the study of *styles of leadership* as they influenced the behavior of group members. These initial studies led to the development of group dynamics, of which more will be said later.

From these early group studies, a series of related investigations developed that traced in increasingly more subtle ways the impact of groups. Among the very first experiments in social psychology were Floyd Allport's studies of *social facilitation*, or the influence of the group upon individual behavior. In a series of experiments at Harvard between 1916 and 1919, Allport found that in rote tasks such as reporting word associations, individuals performed better when in a group of others, in contrast to tasks that involved reasoning, where the individual performed better by himself. Social facilitation at that point referred only to the presence or absence of other people, not to interaction among them.

Another related aspect of Allport's work was the influence of the group (involving actors) upon judgmental decisions. He found that individuals in groups tended to converge in their stated judgments toward a "norm" and to avoid extreme judgments. The social psychological studies of Muzafer Sherif in the 1930s on the *autokinetic* effect also found a tendency for an individual to agree with the group norm. (The autokinetic effect involves making a judgment as to how far a light, really stationary, seen against a dark background, is moving). Sherif's results (1938) indicated that regardless of the norms the person had developed individually, he generally tended to agree with the group norm when tested in a group situation.

Solomon Asch (1946, 1956) investigated the influence of the group on individual behavior in an even more sophisticated manner. Asch also used a judgment task, one involving the length of lines. Again these judgments were made while the subject was alone and when he was in various group situations. But Asch introduced an ingenious condition; the subject was led to believe that he was part of a group of subjects (who were actually confederates), each of whose judgments he could hear in turn. This condition offered the possibility of investigating the individual's judgment as that of the group was systematically varied. Among other things, the technique led to studying "minority" viewpoints, since one or more confederates could be programmed to agree with the individual's judgment or the whole group could make judgments at variance with the individual's.

Richard Crutchfield (1955) extended this work with more complex designs and tasks. He found that in most instances, irrespective of the task, group influences prevailed over the individual. At that point, Crutchfield attempted to bring together social influence and *personality* variables. His findings seemed to demonstrate that in the kind of conformity studies with which he was working, there was a linkage between susceptibility to influence and the scores on a scale of authoritarianism. These findings, linking social influence with personality, will be discussed in more detail in Chapters 4 and 7.

At this point we have briefly traced the development of several lines of investigation, usually labeled as social psychology, of sources of impact upon individual behavior. These investigations of group influences have concentrated upon the effects of more than one person—the group or the crowd—upon the individual. Until recently these investigations showed little concern about the characteristics the individual himself might have brought to the group situation.

The following paragraph, written in 1937, neatly summarizes this concern with the group and much of the earlier history of social influence:

The history of the systematic study of man's social behavior belongs, strangely enough, to the history of economics, ethics, jurisprudence, and other disciplines which have not been primarily concerned with first-hand investigation of human nature. From Aristotle to the early 19th Century, able men were thinking about the laws of social behavior; but whether they called themselves political economists, moralists, jurists, or what not, they all, with one accord, made it plain that they considered the important thing to be the *social interaction* of men; the nature of the *individual man* was left, as a rather irrelevant problem, to a very different person—the psychologist! [Murphy, Murphy, and Newcomb, 1937, p. 3].

ROLE THEORY

As we have seen, we are dealing with manmade concepts which can serve as tools for observing and eventually predicting human behavior. Of these concepts, one of the most useful is *role*. It can be extended to most of the material involved in a psychology of behavior influence. A role is social, ever-changing, external, and probabilistic; a role involves an audience, interaction, and reciprocity in contrast to personality, which is individualistic, internal, difficult to change, and stable.

The term originated in theatrical settings and has been linked with a dramatic metaphor ever since. *Role* derives from the Latin *rotula*, a little or round log. The term originally designated a round roll on which sheets of parchment were fastened. The actors' parts for a particular play were written on these rolls and were read by the prompters to the actors. Thus each part eventually became a "role." Investigators of human behavior who use the concept of role frequently draw analogues from the theatre. Nisbet (1970), in his perceptive survey of society as social bond, introduces and illustrates his chapter on social roles with a quote from "that masterful sociologist William Shakespeare." "All the world's a stage, and all the men and women merely players. They have their exists and their entrances; and one man in his time plays many parts [p. 148]."

We should also note the derivation of the word *person* from the theatrical *persona*, or mask. For role theorists, the concept of person or personality is identical with that of role. Mead (1934) is generally credited with introducing the notion of role as the basic unit of socialization. Personality, or the self, was conceived of by Mead as the *internalization* of social roles. From Mead's position, the concept of role has been elaborated and investigated to the point that it now represents an alternative concept to that of personality (Biddle and Thomas, 1966; Heine, 1971; Sarbin and Allen, 1968).

One advantage and disadvantage of the concept of role, like the concept of personality, is its flexibility. Role has been defined by theorists and investigators in nebulous and vague ways and closely knit and concise ones. Some definitions of role are quite consistent with the social behaviorism of the present volume. Cottrell (1942), for example, defines role as "an internally consistent series of conditioned responses by one member of a social situation which represents the stimulus pattern for a similarly internally consistent series of conditioned responses of the others in that situation. Dealing with human behavior must always be placed in some self-other context [p. 617]." Sarbin (1954) states simply, "A role is a patterned sequence of learned actions or deeds performed by a person in an interaction situation [p. 225]." The concept of role, when carefully specified, is useful in a social learning framework.

Finally, we turn to another kind of concept or belief as to the causes or wellsprings of human behavior. This is the argument that geography influences behavior.

GEOGRAPHIC DETERMINISM

At the end of the nineteenth century, many people believed that one of the major determinants of behavior was climate and geography. Marx and Spencer, with their strong bias toward a materialistic view of the world, argued for the relevance of such variables. Others went even further in making physical influences central to their theories by attributing the *same* personality characteristics to *all* the individuals living in a particular geographic area.

An early investigator who emphasized the influence of geography as a determinant of character was the Greek physician Hippocrates. He postulated as influencing variables the warmth of the climate, the fertility of the soil, and the nature of the food, which depends upon the locale in which it is grown. Geographical influence has been conceived of as being very direct (Hippocrates argued that climate acts on the semen at the time of conception) and very indirect. (Draper, 1867, cited in Burnham, 1968, attributed the outcome of the American Civil War to character differences between the North and South that grew out of geographic and climatic factors. Alternation of seasons in the North made for periods of intense work followed by periods of *reflection* during enforced leisure; whereas, in the South, the weather permitted constant activity and thus fostered *impulsiveness*, since the individual had no time for reflection).

A prevailing scientific concept in the nineteenth century was that individuals could inherit acquired characteritsics. Hence, it seemed sensible to believe that living long enough in a geographic area could result in development of common behavior among the people of that particular area. This formulation became mixed with beliefs about racial and national characteristics (see Chapter 15).

Geographic determination, especially in the form of climate as an influence on behavior, has been briefly alluded to because weather is always present. There has been little systematic research to determine to what extent weather does affect behavior. Geographic variables are not generally included in current paradigms of behavior, although they might very well affect behavior and foreshadow current ecological concerns.

ON PARADIGMS

In 1962 Kuhn, a historian of science, published *The Structure of Scientific Revolutions*, a monograph (revised in 1970), which has had considerable impact on how investigators in various fields have conceptualized the progress of their studies. Kuhn argued that changes in scientific fields come about through basic changes in *paradigms* or models or, put simply, in the way investigators think about the problems in their field. Kuhn argued that progress or change in a scientific field does not involve the linear accumulation of more and more data confirming newer and more comprehensive hypotheses; rather change is a function of major shifts in theoretical models which occur through the competition of new and very different frames of reference. There is bitter competition, real discontinuity, and, frequently, basic crises or showdowns between advocates of different paradigms. More often than not, the issues involve the personal predilections and private interests of the individual investigators as well as the scientific data. Kuhn has illustrated his ideas by drawing from natural science, primarily physics, the field of his own training. In a passage that is observational as well as predictive, he has stated:

> Because it demands large-scale paradigm destruction and major shifts in the problems and techniques of normal science, the emergence of new theories is generally preceded by a period of pronounced professional insecurity. As one might expect, that insecurity is generated by the persistent failure of the puzzles of normal science to come out as they should. Failure of existing rules is the prelude to a search for new ones. [Kuhn, 1962, pp. 67–68].

Kuhn conceptualized this change in paradigms as coming about as the result of "a revolution." By choosing such a dramatic metaphor, Kuhn evoked all the imagery associated with the concept of revolution, albeit in the scientific world:

> Why should progress also be the apparently universal concomitant of scientific revolutions? Once again, there is much to be learned by asking what else the result of a revolution could be. Revolutions close with a total victory for one of the two opposing camps. Will that group ever say that the result of its victory has been something less than progress? That would be rather like admitting that they had been wrong and their opponents right. To them, at least, the outcome of revolution must be progress, and they are in an excellent position to make certain that future members of their community will see past history in the same way. . . . When it repudiates a past paradigm, a scientific community simultaneously renounces, as a fit subject for professional scrutiny, most of the books and articles in which that paradigm had been embodied. Scientific education makes use of no equivalent for the art museum or the library of classics, and the result is a sometimes drastic distortion in the scientist's perception of his discipline's

past. More than the practitioners of other creative fields, he comes to see it as leading in a straight line to the discipline's present vantage. In short, he comes to see it as progress. No alternative is available to him while he remains in the field. Inevitably those remarks will suggest that the member of a mature scientific community is, like the typical character of Orwell's *1984*, the victim of a history rewritten by the powers that be. Furthermore, that suggestion is not altogether inappropriate. [Kuhn, 1962, pp. 165–166].

By such arguments, Kuhn set up an intellectual time bomb not only in the natural sciences but in each of the social sciences. For example, Friedrichs (1970) has attempted to place current sociology in the context of a Kuhnian clashing paradigm by writing a "sociology of sociology." A basic premise of our presentation, influenced by Kuhn, is that we are now in a period in which revolutionary changes in paradigms are taking place in the broad field of man's investigation of his own behavior.

LAST WORD

The historical development of ideas about human behavior offers a necessary framework upon which to base a meaningful psychology of behavior influence. Current conceptualizations of human behavior are not entities by themselves but have meaning only as they articulate with formulations that go back to the origins of man. The process of developing theories of human behavior is itself a human behavior and hence subject to the same influences as all other behavior. The theories of some individuals such as Freud or Durkheim continue to have an impact on current investigations of behavior. However, even the workings of the most brilliant and lucid observers are products of a specific time and place. Further, interpretation and usage of the work of the major theorists is itself a reflection of a specific period. The behavior of the interpreter—be he researcher, critic, or book writer—is determined by social consequences.

One continuing controversy is whether it is possible or even desirable to study the nature of human nature. Certainly, by their attempts to understand man, philosophers, psychologists, historians, and novelists affirm that man can be understood. A small minority argues that man can even be controlled. But if he is to be controlled, it will be by other men subject to the same influence process.

The social philosophers of the sixteenth to eighteenth centuries raised issues, such as that of mind-body dualism which still divide investigators. Can man choose his own course of action? Is man's behavior subject to scientific law? What is the function and duty of the state in controlling man's behavior? And can human behavior be improved or even perfected? Throughout history there has been controversy over the relative contribution of man's genetic heredity versus man's social environment in influencing his behavior.

Only in the late nineteenth and early twentieth centuries have men added a new dimension to their observations of each other. This new element in investigating human behavior was a scientific methodology and experimentation, which was developed by the introduction of an experimental psychology in the nineteenth century and a social psychology in the early twentieth century. Much of what follows in this book is based upon the innovations resulting from this newer approach to people.

Despite the change in the techniques of investigation, the basic explanatory concepts have remained fairly much the same. These basic concepts are of man as being "instinct" driven; as having a state of readiness to respond (attitude); as being hedonistic, or pleasure bound; as being sympathetic to or empathetic with others; as being an imitator (man sees and does); as being a free agent and making his own choices; as being rational and doing that which is most reasonable; as being a feeling, rather than a thinking, individual.

An important concept that has had major impact on the behavior of investigators is that of group influence—the development of a group or a crowd behavior which is something more than an aggregate of individual behaviors. Much of what will be discussed in this book involves people interacting with each other and with larger aggregates of individuals. Much of the behavior of individuals in small and larger groups can be formulated in terms of the concept of *role*, which has been a major concept used by investigators who lean heavily on a social or environmental explanation of behavior.

Finally, in approaching the notion of concepts of behavior, it is necessary to search for the clashes between the paradigms offered by investigators to explain and provide ways to attack the problems. There is a continual stretching and shifting among the accepted paradigms of a given historical period.

It should again be emphasized that the personality theories of the eighteenth century (such as Bentham's) and of the nineteenth century (such as Spencer's) had social and political consequences but, as is true of all personality theories, were also products of the social climate of their day. It would be difficult to determine which came first, since personality theories and the social climates feed upon and justify each other.

Theories of behavior are rarely based completely on scientific evidence. They tie into, relate to, and are products of current political and social atmospheres. For example, the argument for the status quo in any period of time is usually justified on the basis of a fixed, unchangeable concept of human nature. Dewey (1917) has pointed out that "The ultimate refuge of the stand-patter in every field, education, religion, politics, industrial and domestic life, has been the notion of an alleged fixed structure of mind [p. 273]."

Theories of Human Behavior:
The First Half of the Twentieth Century

This chapter describes the major theories of personality and human behavior that have influenced research, clinical practice, social and political application, and other theories in the first half of the twentieth century. We do not intend to offer a standard chapter on theories of personality. Many of these theories are enormously complex and cannot be adequately summarized in a few brief paragraphs. Our primary interest is to describe broad streams of development and some of the key individuals and their impact.

Woodworth (1931) pointed out that by the start of the twentieth century all of the contemporary schools of psychology had been established. The followers of these various approaches can be labeled as psychoanalysts, drive theorists, phenomenologists, existentialists, gestaltists, trait theorists, social theorists, and social behaviorists. It is within these eight general approaches to human behavior that we will present the personality theorists of the twentieth century.

PSYCHOLOGY AT THE TURN OF THE CENTURY

In surveying the schools of psychology in the early 1900s, Woodworth (1931) pointed out that to understand the established psychological order:

> we have to remember that it was itself at one time new and revolutionary. Any school, no matter how radical it seems at first, is likely to become an established order if it has any success, and in time fresh revolts will arise against it. In fact, we are already witnessing revolts against such modern schools as behaviorism and psychoanalysis on the ground that they are "traditional." Similarly, the established order of 1900 was left over from an earlier revolt. A way back at the beginning of modern scientific movement in the seventeenth century, we find such men as Descartes and Hobbes rebelling against the traditional psychology of that day, and so giving us the beginnings of what we call modern psychology in distinction from the ancient and medieval [p. 4].

At the turn of the century, the science of psychology was merging and emerging. The sciences of physiology and physics and the discipline of philosophy were its progenitors. However, a new field also arises out of uneasiness with the current state of affairs and the available sources of reinforcement for serious investigators. Woodworth (1931) notes that

> as psychologists ourselves, we must recognize that the question was not whether the old order was endurable, but whether there was anything in it open to attack. Every young man coming into the game and desiring to make a name for himself looks around for something to attack. If he goes calmly ahead accepting things as they are, nobody will pay attention to him. He looks for flaws, and the bigger they are the better he likes them. Enterprising young psychologists at the turn of the century proceeded to pick flaws, and among them the poor old nineteenth-century psychology was pretty well picked to pieces [pp. 12–13].

The contemporaneousness of this observation is obvious, and it is a safe prediction that will also be descriptive of the situation at the beginning of the next century.

Psychoanalysis

In its day the Freudian paradigm of human behavior was truly revolutionary. We discussed in Chapter 2 man's changing ways of looking at himself from the ancient Greeks through the philosophers, theologians, and political scientists of the eighteenth and nineteenth centuries. Into this scene stepped Sigmund Freud

(1856–1939) with new concepts and a new methodology. Freud's view of man as being driven by strong internal forces of which he was unaware was not new. In fact, the concept of the unconscious can be traced back to the ubiquitous philosophers of ancient Greece (Whyte, 1960). Nor was Freud the first investigator to say that man was ridden by uncontrollable instinctual drives. Such a concept is similar to the ideas of earlier writers including Machiavelli.

Freud's overwhelming contribution was his combining of many disparate strands and notions into a *coherent theory of personality*. Almost all subsequent theories of man's behavior derive from Freud, deviate from Freud, or are in opposition to Freud. Freud became such a powerful influence because he simultaneously offered a *theory* of personality, a treatment *procedure*, and a research *methodology*. Freud's name became synonymous with (and in some quarters infamous for) a view of man—in much the same way that Machiavelli's name became associated with his theory of human nature. In both instances astute observers of human behavior were blamed for the astuteness of their observations. The bearer of bad news was reacted to as the "cause" of the news.

As a movement psychoanalysis influenced several lines of theoretical development. For example, in psychiatry psychoanalysis represented a revolt against the dominant nineteenth-century tendency to concentrate on the somatic aspects of unusual behavior and to ignore the psychic ones (Hale, 1971). Under the impact of psychoanalytic thought, psychiatry began seeking causes of maladjustment in the individual's "mental life," his patterns of thought and styles of action, his suggestibility, and his "lack" of emotional balance—rather than in possible brain lesions. This aspect of Freud's ideas is directly related to the history of hypnotism, which was introduced to scientific and medical attention in 1780 by the Viennese Anton Mesmer (see Chapter 9). It is noteworthy that Freud studied with the leading medical hypnotist of his day, the French neurologist Charcot, and that he used hypnosis in his early therapeutic work.

If we were to select the twentieth-century individual with the greatest impact on thinking in Western society, it would be Freud. Many volumes have been produced to interpret Freud's influence on psychology, psychiatry, literature, sociology, art, and history. In this chapter we very briefly touch upon the highlights of his personality theory, which was of such seminal influence. A distinction must be made between Freud's observations of behavior, based on a time and place in history, and his explanatory concepts, which relied heavily upon metaphors of internal mechanisms.

Freud's three major areas of contributions—the theory of personality, the methodology, and the treatment procedure—are intertwined. The personality theory itself has three major divisions: structure, dynamics, and development. Structurally, the psyche has three parts: id, ego, and superego. The *id* is the part of the psyche influenced by inherited elements—instincts and unconscious forces which demand gratification (tension reduction or satisfaction) such as sex and aggression—and is ruled by the pleasure principle. The *ego* is the part of the psyche in contact with the external world and is determined by the reality principle. The *superego* is the socializing part of the psyche, which represents and internalizes the values and taboos of parental and other social influences.

Since the three parts of the human psyche are in constant tension and conflict, Freud developed a whole complex of dynamic concepts to explain man's behavior. These include the classic defense mechanisms and notions of anxiety and psychic energy such as the libido. In Freudian personality dynamics basic motives or drives are *transformed* to better achieve their objectives, so that the original goal and even its object are disguised. The *libido* is the basic energy available to the individual to carry out various psychic transformations.

An integral part of the Freudian personality theory is the postulation of *stages of development*, which man goes through on the road to maturity. The most important stages of development are psychosexual. According to Freud, the source of man's pleasure or gratification shifts from the *oral* stage (in the first year of life the mouth is a major source of pleasure) to the *anal* stage (in the second year the anus becomes the major erogenous zone and toilet training the source of satisfaction and conflict) to the *phallic* stage (in the third to fifth years the emphasis shifts to the genital area). The phallic stage is the period of the *Oedipus conflict*, in which the child competes with the same-sexed parent for the love and affection of the opposite-sexed parent. The *latency* period (from the sixth year to puberty sexual interest presumably lies dormant) follows and leads to the *genital* period (from puberty to death mature sexuality is characterized primarily by reliance upon heterosexual intercourse and orgasm). When an individual does not progress normally through these stages or becomes *fixated* (arrested growth due to deficit or overgratification) at any one stage, that person is disturbed, unhappy, and "sick."

An amplification of his formulations is crucial to an understanding of Freud and how his personality system was used to develop a treatment procedure and to serve as an explanation of broader areas of human endeavor. Briefly, Freud theorized that man's basic instincts are socially unacceptable if expressed directly; they must be brought under control. But if some form of instinctual satisfaction is not obtained, the impulse will be forced into the individual's unconscious. Since this unconscious is ahistorical, all the thwarted impulses of one's life strive for expression with as great a force as if they were current. Energy (libido) is required to hold these forces in check; and the more energy that is used in the repression of these forces, the less there is available for new challenges and developmental tasks. A solution to this conflict is to partially gratify these impulses by distorting their satisfaction into forms that are more socially acceptable.

For example, the residues of the oral stage may be gratified by talking, smoking, eating, kissing, and the like. The residues of the anal stage may be gratified by unrealistic giving of money or goods; by the smearing of paint such as one finds in abstract expressionist art; or by the withholding, hoarding, or ultraexactitude of the accountant, the miser, or the pedantic editor. Various exhibitionistic behaviors may be related to the phallic stage. Even in the mature genital stage, the best a person can do is to satisfy biological impulses in socially acceptable forms, that is, by sublimation.

In Freud's view the child is indeed the father of the man. On the one hand, this notion provides an explanation of behaviors that seem inexplicable in terms of currently received rewards and punishments. Such behaviors are interpreted as indirect or partial gratifications for past deprivations and difficulties. The person may receive acceptance or tolerance from others for his behavior, but he is not consciously aware of or even able to willfully select his behavior even when it disturbs others. On the contrary, since the buried impulses, especially those of the id, might overwhelm the ego and cause great anxiety, the unappealing pattern of behavior may be maintained as a form of anxiety reduction and thus be resistant to change.

Freud's view of personality provides a drama of forces. It also leads to an increased tolerance of others: if we only understood all, we could forgive all. In its deterministic and overdetermined (unconscious) formulation and its thermodynamic model (forces striving for release dam up and overflow) and its metaphoric language, the theory is a product of the physics and the philosophy of science of its era.

We think the following summary and evaluation—made by Woodworth (1931) before Freud's influence had been fully felt professionally—captures the spirit of many critiques of Freud.

> Freud does not permit us to think of the individual as yielding like putty to "environmental pressures," or as being "conditioned" to any social situation with perfect readiness. The demands of society encounter opposing demands of the individual, whence arise conflict and the need and difficulty of adjustment. Inasmuch as maladjustments of greater or less seriousness occur in all of us, and as what Freud has discovered regarding the more serious neuroses may hold good of the milder maladjustments as well, his contribution to the psychology of personality is obviously very great.
>
> If my personal opinion of Freud's psychology were sought, I should have to say that I cannot believe his system to be true in any absolute sense, or even to rank with the great scientific theories which coordinate existing knowledge and serve as guides to further discovery. With its entities and its dualism, it seems to be retrograde rather than forward-looking. Freud's more limited theories stand on a different footing; they promise to stimulate research, though of course they may be overthrown by the research which they stimulate. Freud's real greatness seems not to lie in the formulas in which he has cast his thinking, so much as in the thinking itself and in the freshness of his approach; it lies rather in his effectiveness as a pioneer than in the conclusions thus far achieved [p. 161].

Subsequent psychodynamic theorists attempt to understand the whole person and to seek out the underlying dynamics of overt behavior. They emphasize data arrived at in clinical situations. They use their own intuitions in dealing with material based upon interviews and with projective techniques which offer opportunity for "deep" material. In contrast to other theorists of behavior, the psychodynamicist argues that seeing is not believing. What a person says or does cannot be accepted at face value. Everything is a disguised or symbolic representation of underlying forces or tensions of which the individual himself is not aware. Their most apt metaphors are an iceberg and a pressure cooker. Man's overt behavior represents only the tip of the iceberg of the human personality. The psychodynamicist also conceives of behavior as a resultant of built-up pressure, which will eventually explode unless a safety valve (symbolic or symptomatic behavior) releases some of the pressure. To the psychodynamicist what is hidden is realer than what is observed.

Carl Jung

Carl Jung (1875–1961) is considered one of the three major psychoanalytic theorists, along with Freud and Adler. He was born in Switzerland and was trained as a physician specializing in psychiatry. Thus part of the raw data from which he derived his theories was based on observation of people in mental hospitals who were more deviant than Freud's outpatients. Jung first became associated with Freud in 1906 and was particularly attracted to Freud's technique of dream analysis. As an indication of the closeness of his relationship with Freud during that early period, Jung became the first president of the International Psychoanalytic Association. However, Jung broke with Freud in 1914 over a number of theoretical issues—particularly the impact of early development on adult behavior. Jung thought of the individual as being able to change his behavior and to achieve self-actualization in later life—a far more optimistic view than Freud's.

Jung developed the *word association* test, which was for many years a useful tool in personality research. But he abandoned interest in empirical work in later life. And despite his early interest in experimental psychology, Jung's overall theory (usually labeled *analytical psychology*) is heavily metaphysical and virtually impossible to test in a laboratory situation.

Two of Jung's concepts, those of the persona and introversion-extroversion, have influenced other theorists. The *persona* is the mask that man presents to society and that hides his true feelings and intentions. Often there is alienation between the mask and the "real" person underneath. This notion implies that the social individual may be continually playing a role, which he thinks others wish him to assume. It also implies that a "real" person exists underneath the mask; and such a belief pervades many personality theories.

Jung's approach to personality is an either/or one, characterized by polarity of issues. For example, his concept of *introversion-extroversion* classifies people as introverts (withdrawn, intellectual, avoiding people) or extroverts (outgoing, sociable, concrete, lose oneself among people). This typology has stimulated considerable research, which on the whole points to a continuum of behavior and the role of situational factors rather than to a polarity among individuals. But the importance of bipolarity for Jung is indicated by his view that any imbalance of forces is by definition neurotic and/or psychotic. On the other hand, a resolution of conflicting forces and tensions results in a state of equilibrium and *self-actualization.*

Jung placed more emphasis than Freud on the hereditary influences on personality. The concept of a collective unconscious as well as a personal one is one of the most controversial and most central of Jung's concepts. The *collective unconscious* includes traces of man's "racial" history. These racial memories are characterized as "predispositions," which enable the individual to react selectively to his world. This characterization led to the possibility that whatever man did, felt, or believed was a manifestation of his *inherent predisposition,* or capacity to do, feel, and believe. Upon this foundation of racial unconscious Jung built a more personal structure of the personality, including the ego and the individual's personal unconscious. The material in the collective unconscious comprises emotionally laden universal ideas and behavior patterns, called *archetypes,* which include death, birth, God, father, heroes, and villains. For example, an Ali-Frazier heavyweight championship fight would illustrate archetypal patterns in which the audience as followers of the sport construct a "good guy" and a "bad guy" out of the situation. This notion of the creation of a hero and a villain illustrates an archetype which man inherited from his primordial past. These archetypes represent powerful forces in the psyche; and thus Jung deemphasized the biosexual focus Freud gave to the libido.

Finally, in comparison with Freud, Jung emphasized the effect of both the past and the future upon man's current behavior. In addition to the past, man is influenced by his "expectations" of the future (*teleology*). Jung emphasized man's creative development and potentiality and the role of destiny and purpose —again a far more optimistic view of man than Freud's.

The reader may be justifiably puzzled by some of these concepts—in part because we have covered considerable material very rapidly and in part because many of the concepts are poorly defined. Yet ideas are popular not because of their comprehensibility or profundity or even their ability to explain behavior. Rather, a major factor in the life of ideas is their compatibility with the zeitgeist, or current way of thinking about life. Jung's ideas have influence on a relatively small but continually growing number of personality theorists, writers, and educated laymen.

Alfred Adler

Alfred Adler (1870–1937), like Freud and Jung, was trained as a physician. Adler is primarily known for the parsimony of his concepts, for his optimism, and for his humanism. In contrast to Freud, Adler believed in the perfectibility of man. The label attached to his system is *individual psychology* (Adler, 1927).

For Adler, the underlying motive source shifted from sex and aggression to the *will to power*, or the drive for superiority. This "drive" applies to the individual's own functions as well as to his functioning in society. It is related to the view that the individual suffers from *organ inferiorities* (real physical weaknesses) and *feelings of inferiority* (which may or may not be realistically based).

The individual must *compensate* for these real or felt inferiorities and to do so he strives to better himself by more perfect living (*functional finalisms*), by developing his *creative self*, or by the manifestation of *social interests*. All of these become characteristic of the individual's unique *style of life*. All people have different environments and different inherited systems, so that no two individuals may be expected to behave in the same way. But a developed style of life has consistency, and the person may consciously follow a *fictional goal*, which he strives to make real. Thus, differences in people develop from the different physical, psychological, and sociological conditions in which they live. Adler recognized the influence of adverse environments such as poverty more clearly than Freud and Jung. Hence Adler was a believer and participant in social causes which would ameliorate unhealthy social environments (Adler, 1939).

Other Psychoanalytic Theorists

A large number of other theorists and investigators have followed, added to, changed, modified, rectified, and deviated from the basic tenets of Freud's classical theories of psychoanalysis. Freud himself wrote twenty-seven volumes of commentary and observations over half a century as his views on many key issues developed and changed. His later writings were not always consistent with his earlier ones. Such prolific and thoughtful writers usually are the source of quotations to fit many sides of subsequent arguments.

A group of theorists influenced by Freud, but deviating from him with their greater emphasis on *social* influence, have been referred to as *neo-Freudian*. Adler was the forerunner of this group, which includes Erich Fromm, Karen Horney, and Harry Stack Sullivan (Sullivan will be described later with the interactionists). The emphasis in this group is upon *man as a social being*. Fromm, for example, talks in terms of a social psychology that views man's behavior as a result of sociocultural and economic conditioning. Man's social character is molded by his experiences in a given society rather than by societal suppression of man's basic instincts. With such a social orientation, Fromm (b. 1900) conceptualizes behavior in terms of positive forces such as man's higher strivings for freedom, justice, and truth. These are considered genuine human attributes and not secondary derivatives of and substitutes for baser human motives. In this respect there is a sharp affinity between Fromm and some of the phenomenologists (such as Maslow and Rogers) who will be described later in this chapter.

Fromm's views (1941, 1947, 1955, 1968) are also relevant to those who stress types or traits. In contrast to Freud's development of types of character based on fixation in psychosexual development (for example, the anal *character*), Fromm postulates traits that develop from experiences with others. For example, an individual develops the *hoarding orientation,* or *type,* from early experiences with a withholding, destructive parent and seeks security in saving what he already has. Fromm's *marketing type* denotes an individual who sees himself merely as a commodity obeying the marketplace laws of supply and demand. Such a person would have *traits* consistent with a view of the world expressed by opportunism, aimlessness, and inconsistency. He would be unprincipled and probably successful in Fromm's conception of a competitive economic system. Fromm's clinical skill permitted him to describe "authoritarian" and "other-directed" people before these terms were popularized by Adorno, et al. (1950) and by Riesman, Glazer, and Denney (1950).

Fromm, as did Adler, conceptualized a desirable and idealized type of person—one with a *productive orientation.* This type results from a close love relationship with others and basically experiences peace and security. The traits associated with the productive person are all good ones such as modesty, pride, loyalty, and flexibility. For Fromm, overt behavior is an outgrowth of early interpersonal experiences and is not foredoomed by the repressive nature of social forces keeping natural instincts under control.

A second group of neo-Freudians are the *ego psychologists* such as David Rapaport, Heinz Hartmann, and Ernst Kris. This group is concerned with the ego process, and in their teaching they deemphasize but do not abjure the importance of instincts, libido, and psychosexual developmental stages. At present Erik Erikson (b. 1902) typifies these neo-Freudians in his concept of stages of *psychosocial* development (in contrast to Freud's psychosexual ones). Each of Erikson's stages represents an encounter with the environment. Each stage designates a conflict between two alternative ways of handling the encounter, one adaptive and one maladaptive. As in Freud, each stage must be resolved before the individual may proceed to the next. These stages and their conflicts and crises are represented by the following: basic trust versus mistrust; autonomy versus shame and doubt; initiative versus guilt; industry versus inferiority; identity versus role diffusion; intimacy versus isolation; generativity versus stagnation; ego identify versus despair. Not unlike Freud, Erikson associates (1963) each stage with specific years in one's life; for example, basic trust versus mistrust occurs in the first year of life, integrity versus despair in the adult. The early stages are also associated with biological functions; for example feeding and elimination are connected with the first two stages.

Erikson also represents an important extension of psychoanalysis in reevaluating historical figures in terms of Freud's dynamic personality theory. Freud himself initiated this approach with his psychosexual interpretations of Leonardo da Vinci (1910), Moses (1939), and Woodrow Wilson (Freud and Bullitt, 1967). Erikson applied his style of historical interpretation to Martin Luther (1958) and Mahatma Gandhi (1969). This has developed into a form of evaluation of the past called *psychohistory* (Hale, 1971; Lifton, 1970).

BEHAVIORISM

We begin this brief look at behaviorism with Woodworth's astute prediction (1931): "I am prepared to believe that the historian fifty years hence, looking back on these first thirty years of the century, will assign much significance to the movement which we now call behaviorism; but I admit that I am puzzled to guess exactly where he will find its significance to lie [p. 89]." Writing about forty years later, we can see that behaviorism is indeed significant, although its full significance may still remain puzzling.

It is important not only to have the germ of an idea but also to apply it, refine it, demonstrate it, and finally be able to formulate and teach it, so that it may spread. As there were many forerunners to Freud, so the germs of behaviorism and its application may be gleaned throughout philosophy and literature. Forms of behavior therapy may be found in Ovid's *Love's Remedy*; and a fair statement of operant conditioning (to be described in Chapter 6) appears in *The Confessions of St. Augustine*:

> It was not that my elders taught me words . . . in any set method; but I, longing by cries and broken accents and various motions of my limbs to express my thoughts, so that I might have my will. . . . When they named any thing, and as they spoke turned towards it, I saw and remembered that they called what they would point out by name they uttered. . . . And thus by constantly hearing words, as they occurred in various sentences, I collected gradually for what they stood; and having broken in my mouth to these signs, I thereby gave utterance to my will [St. Augustine, 1952, p. 8].

Two other examples emphasize the presence of behaviorist ideas in philosophy and literature. In the seventeenth century John Locke described how:

> A grown person surfeiting with honey no sooner hears the name of it, but his fancy immediately carries sickness and qualms to his stomach, and he cannot bear the very *idea* of it; other ideas of dislike and sickness and vomiting presently accompany it, and he is disturbed, but he knows not from whence to date this weakness. . . .

In 1726 Francis Hutcheson, a philosopher, wrote as follows:

> When the prejudice arises from associations of ideas without any natural con-
> nection, we must frequently force ourselves to bear representation of those
> objects, or the use of them when separated from the disagreeable idea; and
> this may at last disjoin the unreasonable association, especially if we can join
> new agreeable ideas to them . . . a few trials without receiving any damage will
> remove the prejudice, as in that against meats . . . [In McReynolds, 1969, p. 93].[1]

In later sentences Hutcheson also touched on the durability of avoidance learning and the use of modeling in social examples.

Behaviorism in America started as an alternative approach to the methodology of introspection rather than as a new discovery. It was soon influenced
by the Russian work on the conditioned reflex done in 1905 in the laboratories
of Pavlov (1927) and Bechterev. Other landmarks in the growth of behaviorism
were the 1898 doctoral dissertation of Edward L. Thorndike (1874–1940) on an
experimental study of animal intelligence; Thorndike's formulation (1911) of
the "law of effect"; John B. Watson's article (1913) urging the application of
the objective methods of animal psychology to human behavior; and E. B. Holt's
formulation (1915) of the notion that words come to be identified with their
meanings through conditioning—so that the words themselves evoke responses
similar to those that would be evoked by what they represent.

John B. Watson (1878–1958) is a figure of particular interest. Watson's
book (1919) on psychology from the viewpoint of a behaviorist was a very
important landmark. Woodworth (1931) captured the scientific rigor and evangel-
ism of this book:

> we find Watson saying that behaviorism is the natural science that takes as its
> field all of human behavior and adjustments, which it studies by experimental
> methods, with the object of controlling man's behavior in accordance with the
> findings of science. He says that the growing success of this natural science ap-
> proach to human problems is causing philosophy to disappear and become the
> history of science, that it envisages the development of an experimental ethics to
> take the place of the old authoritative and speculative ethics, based on religion,
> and that it will gradually do away with psychoanalysis and replace it by scientific
> studies of the child's development and by such control of that development as
> will prevent the psychopathic breakdowns which now have to be treated in adult
> life [p. 91].

In this book Watson asserted that he could take any healthy well-formed
child and make of him anything he chose—provided he had full control of

---

[1] We are pleased to acknowledge the kindness of Professor Paul McReynolds in calling our
attention to this passage. We have modernized the spelling and diction.

that child's environment. Later Watson indicated that this bold statement was meant as a challenge to induce the public to provide support for the extensive research necessary on child development. Yet this bold statement has been repeatedly cited as the quintessence of the faith or folly of behaviorism.

After Watson came a group of investigators who demonstrated a wide diversity within the broad approach to behaviorism. E. R. Guthrie (1935, 1938) returned to the principles of associative learning and emphasized behavior as the result of contiguous pairing of stimuli. Guthrie was among the small group of theorists who attempted to use learning theory in order to change undesirable, or maladaptive, behavior in real life situations. Clark Hull (1884–1952) developed (1943, 1951) a system of quantitative laws based on learning, which had a major impact upon experimental psychology in the late 1940s and the 1950s. Kenneth Spence, Janet Taylor, and Neal Miller are learning theorists who contributed extensive research on the relation between concepts such as anxiety, stress, drive, and learning. J. R. Kantor has been an important link between the early and later behaviorists in terms of his theoretical formulations; he defined personality as "the individual's particular series of reaction systems to specific stimuli [1924, p. 75]." Kantor went beyond Watson in seeking a naturalisitc approach to language and thinking to which later behaviorists turned their attention.

Skinner and Radical Behaviorism

In the history of behaviorism, the contributions of B. F. Skinner (b. 1904) and his followers can be viewed as an extension of the work of earlier experimental and theoretical behaviorists such as Thorndike and Kantor. The Skinnerians can also be placed within the stream of those who have *applied* learning theory to human problems (such as Watson and Guthrie).

The Skinnerians represent a sharp break—possibly a paradigmatic revolution—with the immediate past in their conception of human behavior. When the impact of Skinner's early work began to be felt in American psychology in the 1940s and 1950s, the prevailing conception of human behavior was psychoanalytic and psychodynamic. This was true even of Hull's followers (Dollard and Miller, 1950). Hullians and Freudians alike offered their explanatory concepts in terms of metaphors which explained the inner workings of man. Concepts such as motivation, drive, anxiety, unconscious, libido, and even "habit strength" were all variations of the same theme—the individual being pushed or propelled into action by internal forces the observer had to infer.

Skinner offered an alternative set of concepts and labels, primarily that of operant behavior, which enabled investigators to shift their studies from the individual's hypothesized internal mechanisms to observable environmental characteristics. The notion of operant behavior (which at first appears to be a restatement of Thorndike's law of effect) is deceptively simple: *A behavior which is followed by reinforcing events is likely to reoccur.* We will look at what is implied in this observation of human behavior and what is not. The work started with a rat simply pressing a lever.[2] It has been extended to almost every conceivable action of organisms including such complex activity as motor behavior, language, thinking, and autonomic functioning. *Reinforcing events* have included food, sex, tokens, smiles, the reduction of uncertainty, the achievement of confidence, and the opportunity to "do what you like." The notion of reoccurrence of behavior has been amplified to include the concept of probability and the enormously complex set of relationships involving schedules of reinforcement.

Skinnerian behaviorism has been termed *radical* because it means what it says. The focus is on behavior, its antecedents, and its consequences, and not upon hypothesized internal events. Thus Skinnerian investigators of human behavior have as their prime objective a thoroughgoing analysis of the behavior of an individual. The individual is his own control and provides his own baseline of performance because *his* behavior, not some abstraction, is the target.

The approach of the Skinnerians is a highly individualized one that emphasizes the behavior of the single organism. Since the concept of group norms has little meaning in this approach, it often eschews the more traditional tools of the personality researcher, particularly the use of personality questionnaires. Skinner emphasizes the refinement of experimental variables in own-control designs rather than the use of standard deviations to control for individual variability:

> By discovering, elaborating, and fully exploiting every relevant variable, we may eliminate *in advance of measurement* the individual differences which obscure the difference under analyses. This will achieve the same result as increasing the size of groups, and it will almost certainly yield a bonus in the discovery of new variables which would not have been identified in the statistical treatment [Skinner, 1956, pp. 228–229].

The aim of the Skinnerian is not to obtain a difference that is statistically significant when 20 or 100 people are compared in a brief one-shot exposure, but to achieve a difference that is significant in terms of the organism's own behavior. Moreover, to the extent that everyday life is composed of ongoing influences which may alter in their impact over time, the typical non-Skinnerian design—which does not take into account the organism's history but instead samples his very brief exposure to limited conditions—may very well lead to spurious generalizations. Finally, the object of the Skinnerians is to gain con-

[2] It should be noted how different theories lead to different data collection. The Hullian paradigm traversed a distance with time and errors as dependent variables. Skinnerians counted acts such as lever presses.

trol over the organism's behavior; this means finding the conditions for teaching a behavior or set of behaviors to each subject. A variable is not "significant" or "insignificant"; instead, it has or does not have an impact at a certain time in the sequence. Rather than saying that some variable is not significant, the experimenter must try out his procedures with each subject, tailor a program to each subject, and accept responsibility for each subject. Thus, *there is a change in the approach to data as well as to the subject about whom data are collected.*

Skinner has argued that most human social behaviors involve an organism acting upon its environment, changing its environment, and being changed as a consequence of its actions. Positive consequences such as social reinforcement increase the likelihood of this action reoccurring; unpleasant consequences, lack of attention, and aversive stimulation decrease the likelihood of this action reoccurring, but may serve to increase other, escape or avoidance, behaviors.

Finally, it is ironic to consider Skinner as a theorist of anything, since he is noted for his antitheory position (1950). He views his work as completely empirical and with no need for theoretical antecedents or even theoretical consequences. For him the laboratory with its intensive generation of data is the source of knowledge. He completely eschews the "explanatory fictions" of hypothesized internal variables.

Neobehaviorism

In line with our view of history (and personality) as involving a continual reassessment of the past in terms of current problems, Berlyne's review (1968) of behavior theory as personality theory is pertinent. He categorized the history of behaviorism in the twentieth century in terms of the "early behaviorism" of Watson and the subsequent first and second generations of "neobehaviorism." In contrast to Watson, the first generation of neobehaviorists (Hull, Holt, Skinner, Tolman) were characterized by their willingness to accept verbal reports as useful data, their demand for more rigorous theory construction, and their greater emphasis on the biological setting of behavior. This group of behaviorists split into the "cognitive" and the "S-R" theorists on the major issue of whether to accept the notion of mediating processes. The categorization of this sample of investigators as being within the same group is fairly consistent with the current views of most historians of psychology.

However, in his description of the second generation of neobehaviorists Berlyne offers a more novel group of theorists, most of whom are not usually called behaviorists. These neobehaviorists are typified by new lines of inquiry that have taken shape outside the older neobehaviorist mainstream. Their investigations have developed the "cybernetic notion of gravitation toward a goal by negative feedback and correction of deviation" (p. 636); the concepts of *information theory*; the models supplied by computer simulation; Piaget's ideas on perceptual and intellectual development in the child; and the more recent Russian research on conditioning and complex intellectual processes.

Hebb (1949) is credited with initiating this group with his book *The Organization of Behavior*, which placed major emphasis on neurophysiological correlates of behavior. The human brain became a major area of research—with investigation helped enormously by a developing technology built around the ability to measure characteristics of the brain with the electroencephalograph (EEG).

With his own interest and involvement in *arousal* theories, Berlyne argued effectively that this interest in neurophysiology is what distinguishes the second generation of neobehaviorists from the first. This is illustrated by his own research on exploratory behavior and attention. Berlyne (1968) summarized the spirit of this approach by noting that

> Earlier neo-behaviorists hoped to trace all behavior back to external annoyances or organic needs affecting tissues other than the sense organs and the nervous system. Now, it has become apparent that activities pursued "for their own sake," without any practical consequences of an obvious and immediate nature, take up a large part of the time and energy of higher animals. These activities appear to be self-motivating and self-reinforcing, which must mean that the motivational factors to which they are subject depend on their structure or, in other words, on the relations, harmonious or discordant, between simultaneous internal psycho-physiological processes [p. 638].

Cognition, arousal, physiology, neurology, motivation—all concepts eschewed by one group of behavioral investigators—are central to another group. So who are the behaviorists? Like every other category, the label is defined by its usage and by the goals of the definer.

The Social Behaviorists

There has also emerged in more recent years another group of investigators and theorists who can be called either neobehaviorists or social behaviorists. The various labels the people in this group attach to their approach to behavior include *social learning* (Bandura, Rotter, Patterson), *social behavior* (Mischel), *sociopsychological* (Ullmann and Krasner), and *role theory* (Sarbin). As among the other groups of theorists, there is a wide spectrum of views, although there is a common emphasis on close observation of behavior and its social consequences, social context, and social learning. The research of the group has been primarily in the fields of child, clinical, social, and developmental psychology. We will not go into detail about the views of this group at this point, since much of this book is devoted to the research and theoretical concepts of this approach.

THE SOCIAL THEORISTS

We now turn to theorists who are frequently passed over in personality books—those with the general label of sociologists. Generally these theorists emphasize the impact on behavior of social forces and social institutions. Throughout this text we refer to the sociological work of men such as Charles H. Cooley, Erving Goffman, C. Wright Mills, Howard S. Becker, Robert A. Nisbet, and George C. Homans. The contributions of Emile Durkheim and George Herbert Mead have been a major influence on the work of these current sociologists.

Emile Durkheim

Emile Durkheim (1858–1917), the French sociologist, is preeminent because of his *views* of society, his *impact*, his attempt to make sociology a *scientific* discipline, and his insistence that a social philosophy must have *practical consequences*. Durkheim (1938) saw himself as introducing empirical methodology which focused on the observation, description, classification, and explanation of data. The basic data were social facts, or "things": "All that is given, all that is subject to observation, has thereby the character of a thing. To treat phenomena as things is to treat them as data, and these constitute the departure of science."[3]

Durkheim emphasized the importance and function of *collective representation*, or the influence of a collection of people or society. In fact, Durkheim was criticized (or praised, depending on the source of the critique) for ignoring the psychology of the individual. Durkheim's views of behavior eventually moved in the direction of total cultural determinism. Durkheim went so far as to say that "every time a social phenomenon is directly explained by a psychic phenomenon, we may be sure that the explanation is false [1938, p. 128]."

George Herbert Mead

George Herbert Mead (1863–1931) was an influential theorist who published very little in his lifetime, but had enormous impact through his teaching and the originality of his ideas. Almost unnoticed by his peers during his life, his influence was felt years later and has continued to grow. For example, Mead's

---

[3] More than half a century later, this approach is still considered revolutionary by some people. For example, in a report on behavior therapy in *Time*, August 2, 1971, a psychoanalyst "believes that a human being who submits to behavior manipulation 'is treating himself as object and to some extent, therefore, becomes an object' [p. 41]." In short, Durkheim placed man and his institutions within the realm of scientific study and argued against a "separate creation" or "dualism" or double standard of methodology and evidence.

views on socialization (1934) were picked up by the sociologists of the 1920s and 1930s and used as ammunition against the predominant biological explanations of behavior.

Mead emphasized scientific methodology, gave it a social interpretation, and also rejected individual psychological processes. Mead held to rational views in contrast to the intellectual giants of his day such as Freud, McDougall, and the economist Thorstein Veblen, who stressed the nonrational determinants of behavior. On the other hand, Mead disagreed with the Watsonian behaviorism of his day because it excluded covert aspects of human acts such as thinking as "mental."

Mead called his own approach *social behaviorism*, an apt and useful label which was consistent with his view that the organism is an active rather than a passive recipient of external stimuli. Mead's central thesis was that it is the act or action (behavior) which determines the relation between the individual and his environment. Stimuli are encountered during the act and affect its course. Identical stimuli may function in a different way for different organisms and even for the same organism acting in a different manner. These stimuli may arise in the form of the reaction of others to an individual's behavior. Mead observed that this kind of interaction is a "conversation of gestures." This conversation can be cooperative as among a hive of bees or antagonistic as in a dogfight.

Nor must we attribute self-consciousness to the responding organisms. When a gesture takes on identical meanings to ourselves and to others, it becomes a *significant gesture* or *significant symbol*. Human meaning arises during cooperative group actions and interactions. Every group seems to develop its own system of significant symbols, which are held in common by its members and around which group activities are organized.

Human thought involves designating meanings to one's self and requires one to be a self-conscious actor. The individual delays his action while he attempts to ascertain the consequences of his acts in terms of the *probable* responses of others. This examination involves learning to take the viewpoint of others toward one's self. A child learns to assume many positions toward himself and to organize these views into a system. Childhood games are important in that they help the child to acquire the ability to do this. This learned system of attitudes Mead termed the *generalized other*.

Mead went on to postulate the *me* against the *I* as the two responding sides of the self. The *me* is the controlling, limiting, societal aspect of the person. The *I* is the impulsive side of behavior, upon which the *me* makes a judgment (immediate or delayed) after the person acts. It follows that the *I* is never completely predictable and that the *I* introduces novelty and creativeness into a situation. Unpredictability can both excite and disturb the individual.

Insofar as each individual participates in different groups or participates in identical groups in different ways, no man's *me* is identical with any other's.

This diversity gives ample leeway for an emphasis upon individuality within the broader world of common symbolization. Thus a self-view emerges that is based on previous interaction with others. Mead's ideas were particularly influential in the developments of theories based upon social role (see Heine, 1971; Sarbin, 1964b) and theories of symbolic interactionism which often are similar to those of the social behaviorists.

The views of the current group of sociologists who are basically good reporters of human interaction (for example, Goffman, Homans, Nisbet, and Mills) are utilized throughout this book. We do, however, cite the following passages from Howard Becker (1969) to give one illustration of how the Durkheim-Mead influence is now expressed. In a criticism of approaching human behavior in terms of dynamic personality theories, Becker argues that such approaches

"err by taking for granted that the only way we can arrive at generalized explanations of human behavior is by finding some unchanging components in the self or personality. They err as well in making the prior assumption that changes which affect only such "superficial" phenomena as behavior without affecting deeper components of the person are trivial and unimportant. . . . There are good reasons to deny these assumptions. Brim (1960) for instance, has persuasively argued that there are no "deep" personality characteristics, traits of character which persist across any and all situations and social roles. . . . The process of situational adjustment, in which individuals take on the characteristics required by the situations they participate in, provide an entering wedge into the problem of change. . . . The lesson we should learn from this is that personality changes are often present only in the eye of the beholder. . . . We learn less by studying the students who are alleged to have lost their idealism than we do by studying those who claim they have become cynical. . . . The person, as he moves in and out of a variety of social situations, learns the requirements of continuing in each situation and of success in it. If he has a strong desire to continue, the ability to assess accurately what is required, and can deliver the required performance, the individual turns himself into the kind of person the situation demands. . . . But the notion of situational adjustment is more flexible than that of adult role learning. It allows us to deal with smaller units and make a finer analysis. We construct the process of learning an adult role by analyzing sequences of smaller and more numerous situational adjustments . . . [pp. 257–264].

THE DRIVE THEORISTS

As each group of theorists is presented, we must emphasize its overlap with other groups. Perhaps the most difficult group to justify as being discrete from all the others is the drive theorists. These range from the avid collectors of human needs (Henry A. Murray) to the translators of psychoanalysis into learning theory (Dollard and Miller). What these approaches have in common is the notion of a force within the individual which pushes or propels behavior. Variations on the theme include the concept of a major overall drive (Gardner Murphy's *canalization*) and the notion of a strong single drive pervasively influencing economic aspects of society (McClelland's *need for achievement*).

Henry A. Murray

One of the classic influences in the field of personality was the 1938 publication of *Explorations in Personality* by Henry A. Murray and his colleagues in psychiatry and psychology at Harvard. Among other things, the book offered new techniques for assessment of and a theory of personality with heavy emphasis on motivation. The general theory is similar in many ways to Freud's, with the major new concept the postulation of a hypothetical construct called need.

Need implies an active entity within the organism that organizes perception and cognition of the environment in such a way as to ready the organism to respond in a certain way under given conditions. Murray offers two categories of needs: the 12 primary, or viscerogenic, needs (such as air, water, food, sex, urination, and defecation) and the 27 *secondary*, or *psychogenic*, needs (such as achievement, recognition, exhibition, acquisition, defense, autonomy, aggression, affiliation, and rejection). Any of these needs may be triggered by a real or perceived environmental force called *press*, which arouses the need.

Gardner Murphy

More than any other theorist, Gardner Murphy presents a broad eclectic conception of human behavior, which draws upon personality theory, social psychology, and just about every other phase of human behavior. He has published books on personality, social psychology, general psychology, education, history, parapsychology, and Asian psychology. He is an integrator of many theorists and a bridge between the pioneers of modern psychology (James, McDougall, Thorndike, and Woodworth) and contemporary workers. Much of his influence comes from his impact on the thinking and research of students such as the senior author of this book.

His theories attempt to integrate man's biological and social aspects. There is almost no popular concept from any other theory that he does not incorporate in a logical manner in his own system. These concepts include self, field, psychoanalysis, extroversion-introversion, conditioning, learning, and situationalism. Perhaps the one concept unique to Murphy (1947) is *canalization*, which is defined as "establishing and progressively strengthening a preference for one among several potential ways of satisfying a drive; or the established preference itself: for example, in the United States, the hunger drive is *canalized* into a high preference for ice cream (among other preferences [English and English, 1958, p. 75])."

Dollard and Miller

A sociologist and a psychologist, John Dollard and Neal Miller, authored *Personality and Psychotherapy* (1950), a book of major influence. It represented a triumph for those who ardently wished to integrate the best features of psychoanalysis and learning theory. For Dollard and Miller, the most important elements in the learning process are drive, cue, response, and reinforcement. Any effective stimulus (*cue*) whether from inside or outside the organism can impel action and thus serve as a drive. Motivating cues can be internal (hunger) or external (the sight of a beautiful woman).

In effect, Dollard and Miller translated many of the basic Freudian concepts, particularly those involving repression and conflict, into the learning theory terms of Hull (1943). This translation has resulted in some new research, but surprisingly, very little in the way of new treatment procedures. The primary result of the attempted integration was to make Freud's concepts palatable to experimentally and academically oriented psychologists who had never quite trusted the ideas of Freud, but to whom Hull represented Truth.

THE GESTALTISTS

The gestaltists represented an important turn-of-the-century view of man. Their current impact is represented by their influence on other theorists, in this case the phenomonologists.

Gestalt is a German word for *shape, form, pattern,* or *configuration.* Like the behaviorists, the gestaltists revolted against the notion that the association between elements and events was the complete explanation of behavior. Whereas the behaviorists of that period extended and modified the idea of associationism to include the functional connection between stimulus and response, the gestaltists rejected associationism as explanatory. Rather, the gestaltists argued for the importance of the *relationship* between component parts of a particular situation. This may be illustrated by their view of personality traits. One can list all the traits of an individual obtained by self-ratings or observations. But such a list would tell one very little about the person, since it would ignore the relationship between traits and such crucial factors as which traits are dominant and which are secondary. Most important, the gestaltists conceived of the individual's personality as being *more than* a summary of individual traits. In other words, the human being is an organized whole (a gestalt) and not merely a sum of individual parts.

The founders of gestalt psychology were three young psychologists in the academy at Frankfurt, Germany: Max Wertheimer, Kurt Koffka, and Wolfgang Kohler. Eventually all three came to the United States. Gestaltists were confirmed experimentalists, particularly in the areas of learning and perception. In the field of learning they were primarily responsible for offering the concept of *insight* (a sudden reorganization in the thinking process) as an alternative to the trial-and-error learning of Thorndike and the conditioned reflex of Pavlov.

The gestaltists had their greatest impact in the field of perception. They argued that the way an object in the environment is perceived depends upon the *relationship* of the object to the perceptual *field* rather than upon specific characteristics of the individual object. Their research led to the *field theory* of Kurt Lewin (1936), which was extended to all aspects of psychology and human behavior. Lewin (1890–1947) was particularly interested in spatial relationships and the use of mathematics in specifying such relationships. The *life space* of an individual represented the total facts that determine his behavior at any given moment. Included in the life space was the person (P) and his psychological environment (E), the world as the individual currently perceived it. Thus, the psychological environment represented the individual's subjective evaluation, not an objective array of situational stimuli. The individual's resultant behavior (B) was then expressed in the formula $B = f(P,E)$.

This kind of formulation is an alternative to the notion of personality as involving fixed, unchanging, and immutable traits. Lewin presented behavior as continually changing with changes in the individual's psychological reality— which was itself composed of dynamic forces in the individual and his life space. His final picture was of an individual continually in a tension system in which there was no fixed entities.

Lewin's influence has been felt in social psychology. Behavior was changeable by changing perceptions, hence life space. If the individual's perception of others and of himself as exemplified by attitudes, level of aspiration, and self-concepts could be changed, then behavior would change. A large number of twentieth-century studies in social psychology and personality were carried out in this context (Barker, Dembo, and Lewin, 1941; Lewin, Lippitt, and White, 1939).

THE PHENOMENOLOGISTS

In the development of views in personality, one current of thought can be labeled with the adjectives *self, cognitive, existential,* or more generically, *phenomenological*. Although they are a diverse group, the phenomenological theorists have enough in common to be put into a single category. These investigators emphasize the *experiences* of the individual, his *perception* of the world, his *current relationships*, and his general *being*. They tend to play down (but not eliminate) concepts involving dynamic, motivational, structural, or behavioral explanations. Their key ideas focus on subjectivity, personal experiences, self-actualization, growth, and just plain being human.

If we could trace the lines of the current phenomenologists, some would lead back to such diverse theorists as Jung, Mead, Dewey, Koffka, Kohler, and the existential philosphers. We will refer to a first and second generation of neo-phenomenologists. The second generation is oriented more to groups and applications—as typified by the Esalen Institute, for example, Fritz Perls and William Schutz. The first generation is more oriented to the individual and philosophy; it includes Abraham Maslow, Rollo May, Carl Rogers, and George Kelly. The importance of the second generation is in its impact as a social and therapeutic movement and will be discussed later. The first generation is more relevant to personality theory and research (Snygg and Combs, 1949).

Carl Rogers

Perhaps the most influential theorist in the first-generation phenomenologist group is Carl Rogers (b. 1902). Rogers brought to the field of personality theory a background strongly influenced by philosophy and theology and his experiences as a psychotherapist.[4] His theory of personality coexisted with and grew out of his theory of psychotherapy. Rogers' overview of man's behavior is optimistic. In contrast to Freud's view of man as inherently evil, Rogers viewed humanity as basically constructive and trustworthy.

Rogers' key concept is the *self* as an experiencing mechanism. Rogers (1959) has described the self as an "organized, consistent, conceptual gestalt composed of perceptions of the characteristics of the 'I' or 'me' and the perceptions of the relationships of the 'I' or 'me' to others and to various aspects of life together with the values attached to these perceptions [p. 200]." Ancillary to his concept of self are the concepts of self-actualization, self-maintenance, and self-enhance-ment—all of which lead to the individual operating as a whole. Simply to be alive is to be oriented to fulfilling or actualizing oneself. The organism strives to achieve what it values and to avoid what it does not value or what impedes enhancement.

To understand behavior, Rogers looked at it from the individual's internal frame of reference. The individual adopts ways of behaving that are consistent with his concept of self. Maladjustment occurs when significant sensory expe-

---

[4] This is a good example of the intertwining of ideas. Rogers gained a great deal from the social worker, Jessie Taft, who in turn was indebted to the psychoanalyst Otto Rank, an early apostle and apostate of Freud.

riences are denied to awareness. Adjustment exists when all the sensory and visual experiences of the organism are assimilated symbolically into a consistent relationship with the self-concept. The individual has a strong need for self-esteem as well as social esteem, and from these needs develops an attitude of self-worthiness.

The way to help an individual is to remove the barriers that prevent the growth of the self. Thus, therapy is *client-centered*, and the client is offered unconditional acceptance and warmth by the therapist. This support is intended to enable the client to reexamine his perceptual field so that he can revise his estimation of the worthiness of his self. As the individual experiences warmth and acceptance, he sees himself as an acceptable person and becomes accepting and acceptable.

Although Rogers eschews most of the standard paraphernalia of personality theorists—such as specific biological drives,[5] stages of development, historical motivation, or stable trait characteristics—he does offer two very general types of personality; the fully functioning, or ideal, person and the maladjusted person. The former, having experienced unconditional positive regard in his relationships, is characterized by existential living, spontaneity, freedom, and creativity. The latter person, who may have received only conditional positive regard, is defensive, conforming, distrusting, and inclined to feel that he is continually being manipulated.

Rogers' theory is characterized by the phenomenological emphasis on subjective perception, the importance of experiencing, and the importance of being a person.

Abraham Maslow

The spirtual leader of the humanist branch of the phenomenological theorists was Abraham Maslow (1908–1970). Humanism as a social movement is in its ascendancy in American life and is rapidly developing into a secular religion. We will discuss the implications of humanism as a social movement in Chapter 17.

Maslow's approach (1968, 1971) differs somewhat from Rogers' in that it stresses a hierarchy of needs, which ranges from essentials (food, water) to safety (avoiding pain) to belongingness (intimacy) to esteem (approval) to the ultimate of *self-actualization*. Each need becomes ascendent when the "lower" needs have been satisfied. Human growth naturally develops into self-actualization unless unfortunate environmental circumstances prevent it. Once again, man is seen as innately good, and he must be allowed to be himself. Maslow's overall approach to human behavior includes the three major humanistic concepts: it is organismic, phenomenological, and existential.

---

[5] At times, however, striving for self-actualization and self-consistency seems to be a basic, nearly biological, given for him.

George Kelly

George Kelly (1905–1967) offered a psychology of *personal constructs*, or the ways an individual categorizes his experiences. Kelly (1955) argued that the personality theorist should view man in a way similar to the way man construes his own behavior. Thus Kelly viewed man *as if* he were a scientist. Man looks at the world through transparent patterns, or *templates*, which fit over the realities of the world. These ways of looking at the world are called *constructs*. Every man has his own unique personal constructs. But alternate constructs are always available. In having options to change his views, man has free will.

Kelly argued against the notion of motivation. Rather, man is in motion by virtue of the fact that he is alive. Kelly's fundamental postulate is that "A person's processes are psychologically channelized by the way he anticipates events [1965, p. 46]." This notion of expectancy is central to Kelly's work. His other major concept is *role*, which he defines as "a pattern of behavior that follows from a person's understanding of how the others who are associated with him in his tasks think [Kelly, 1965, pp. 97–98]." Thus training in the taking of roles becomes a major psychotherapeutic technique. The existential nature of Kelly's concepts are underlined by his belief that man is essentially *what he does* and he can only become aware of his true nature *by being*.

THE INTERACTIONISTS

Another group of investigators are the *interactionist*, or *transactional*, theorists. They too overlap with other theoretical views including the psychodynamic, the motivational, gestalt, and social behaviorist.

Robert C. Carson

Carson offers a view of personality based on an analysis of the "smallest possible unit of social interaction, the dyad, or two-person group." Carson's formulation of personality (1969) is similar to that of Kurt Lewin, and, as such, is a good illustration of a compromise position. Carson combines situationalism, perception, cognition, and a notion of traits: "A person's behavior in any situation is jointly determined by the characteristics of that situation as he perceives them, and by the particular behavioral dispositions of which he is possessed at that time [p. 9]."

Carson offers his own conception of interactionism by arguing that a person may be motivated to fashion his interactive behavior in such a way as to prompt a complementary behavior from others:

> If he succeeds in doing so, he is assumed to experience this as a rewarding state of affairs—that is to say, the other person has, in a sense, performed a service for him. On the other hand, a noncomplementary response is nonrewarding and may be experienced as unpleasant, giving rise to anxiety, or a sense of "incongruence." In this case, the person's behavior may be said to have incurred a "cost" for him, in the form of these unpleasant consequences. Moreover, the other person's non-complementary response may be itself a prompt to engage in an altered form of behavior that would incur additional costs to the first person in terms of anxiety, insecurity, self-incongruence, and so on. Our first person is now at an impasse, confronted with two alternatives: (1) He can attempt to terminate the interaction; (2) he can try to salvage it by having another try at getting the other person's behavior into a more rewarding, or less costly, category. And so it goes [Carson, 1969, p. 119].

Harry Stack Sullivan

Carson's approach, like that of most *transactionists*, is based in large measure upon the writings of Harry Stack Sullivan (1892–1949). An American psychiatrist and psychoanalyst, Sullivan's influence has been felt not only among the inter-actionists but also among the socially oriented neo-Freudians previously described. Sullivan specialized in schizophrenic and obsessional patients and was influenced by Freud, Adolph Meyer (a biologically and socially oriented psychiatrist who was one of the influential founders of his profession), and G. H. Mead.

Sullivan conceptualized personality as "the relatively enduring pattern of recurrent interpersonal situations which characterize a human life." Sullivan developed his theories by systematically combining psychoanalytic concepts with the notion of an innate need to grow and to develop; the importance of perceptual events (the personification or mental images of other people); concepts of the self; the belief in stages of development; the role of learning from others; and concepts of reward, punishment, imitation, and anxiety (1953).

Sullivan stressed the necessity for observation of interpersonal relationships. As a clinician Sullivan viewed mental disorders as distortions and complications of the individual's interpersonal relationships. In contrast to many psychiatrists of his day, Sullivan did not view extreme behavior disorders as "mental illness" in which the individual was qualitatively different from normal people. Instead, he viewed deviant behavior within the same framework as all other human behavior (1956, 1962).

A major weakness of Sullivan as a theorist was his lack of contact with the personality and social psychology research of his day, which would have strengthened and altered his views. Those influenced by his thinking have attempted to integrate his ideas into the mainstream of psychology by linking them with subsequent research in learning, perception, and cognition.

John W. Thibaut and Harold H. Kelley

The cognitively oriented interactionists use the theoretical model offered by G. A. Miller, Galanter, and Pribram (1960). The central concept in their approach is that of *plans*, analogous to internal computer programs. This concept provides a link with modern information-processing theory.

As a supplement to the computer analogy, the analysis of J. W. Thibaut (b. 1917) and H. H. Kelley (b. 1924) has been a strong influence on the interactionists. Thibaut and Kelley (1959) have, at least on a theoretical basis, developed a formulation very consistent with that of the social behaviorists. Theirs is a specifically hedonistic application of the law of effect to dyadic relationships: the outcome of a relationship can be determined by the anticipation of the *reward* to be received and the *cost* of that interaction. The terms reward and cost are used in a very general way and are almost synonymous with positive and negative consequences. A reward may be a positive reaction from another person, a chance to do or say what one wants, or the satisfaction of some need. A cost may be a feeling of anxiety, an insult, or any other unpleasant feeling. Reward here is closer to Sullivan's notion of satisfaction than to Skinner's notion of reinforcement. Thibaut and Kelley conceive of interaction in terms of sequences of behavior, or *sets*, designed to obtain some goal or to satisfy some need. This concept is similar to Miller, Galanter, and Pribram's notion of a central plan.

The formulations of Thibaut and Kelley and other interactionists have evolved into a complex theoretical network of dyadic relationships which include traditional sociological concepts such as *power* (to affect a relationship so as to increase or diminish the reward of another person), *norm formulation* (behavioral rules), and *roles* (a class of one or more norms that applies to an individual's behavior toward a specific kind of problem or kind of person). Eric Berne (1964) has taken this kind of transactional analysis and given popular names to typical interpersonal transactions, or the "games people play." Among the jazzy and descriptive titles given to these games are, *Now I've got you, you son of a bitch, Frigid woman, Schlemiel,* and *I'm only trying to help you.*

It is of interest that the interactionists come to the same theoretical conclusion as the social behaviorists about the undesirability of prevailing concepts of mental illness. Instead they offer social psychological interpretations which rely upon the research and writings of Szasz (1961, 1970), Scheff (1966), Schofield (1964), Secord (1959), Sullivan (1964), Braginsky and Braginsky (1967), Haley (1958, 1963, 1969), Goffman (1961, 1963, 1971), and Gergen (1969).

STRUCTURAL (TRAIT) THEORISTS

The human tendency to categorize the behavior of other people into discrete units is found throughout history. Hippocrates placed individuals into four categories: the *choleric*, or easily irritated; the *melancholic*, or easily depressed; the *sanguine*, or optimistic; and the *phlegmatic*, or listless. These temperaments were related to the bodily functions, or humors, of yellow bile, black bile, blood, and phlegm. An excess or imbalance of any one of these humors was thought to result in one of the four types of people. For example, too much black bile made a person depressed, or melancholic. The notion that a relationship exists between overt behavior and specific aspects of physiological functioning or constitutional endowment has continued to the present.

At this point we must distinguish between two terms frequently used in personality observation: *type* and *trait*. A dictionary definition of *type* is as follows: "A group of persons or things sharing common traits or characteristics that distinguish them as an identifiable group or class, a kind, category [Morris, 1969, p. 1388]." Thus, we have the concept of a theoretically discrete category of people such as college graduate, American, or female. In contrast a *trait* is defined as "a distinguishing feature, as of the character [Morris, p. 1361]." Thus, a trait is a characteristic or dimension on which people may differ consistently and which is not itself necessarily discrete but is more likely to vary along a continuum. Characteristics of human behaviors which have been called traits are nearly endless and include intelligence, aggression, shyness, and acquisitiveness.

Gordon Allport

Several theorists approach human behavior with explanatory concepts that are variations of type-trait explanations. The most influential trait theorist is Gordon Allport (1897–1967). His impact derives not so much from his own theory as from his scholarly work (1937). His review of personality theories provided the basis for much subsequent theorizing about traits. Allport's definition of traits as the basic units of personality organization became a classic and has been repeated in various versions for over thirty years. Defined in this manner as generalized dispositions to respond in the same way to similar stimuli, *traits* seemed to explain consistency in behavior. More complex combinations of traits were called *attitudes*. Allport explained behavior in terms of the individual's unique traits and deemphasized the importance of environmental stimuli.

One of Allport's observations became central to many other explanations of behavior. He noted that people start to do things for seemingly obvious reasons, but continue doing them for reasons that appear more obscure—as if performing the particular act has taken on reinforcing properties of its own. The classic example is the middle-aged businessman who first takes up golf to meet customers or to exercise but eventually enjoys it for itself. Allport labeled this effect *functional autonomy*, which is an accurate description but not necessarily an explanation.

Perhaps the major importance of Allport's 1937 book was that in evaluating and reviewing the personality theorists of his day, Allport offered his own personality theory. Throughout this theory, Allport emphasized uniqueness and individuality (the term most descriptive of his approach, centering on the account of individual cases or events, is *idiographic*). Allport became enthusiastic about the development of the statistical techniques of *factor analysis*, which approached traits normatively by clustering together intercorrelated characteristics.

The Factor Analysts

Trait theory has been enormously enhanced by the research of the factor analysts. Psychologists such as Raymond B. Cattell (1950b, 1957) and J. P. Guilford (1959) applied advanced statistical techniques to reduce many descriptive words to the fewest possible commonalities explaining the greatest possible number of differences between people.

Cattell viewed a trait both as a basic construct of behavior and as a mental structure which one may infer from observed behavior. He categorized traits into surface and source traits. The concept of *surface traits* was analogous to the notion of groups of behavior that are observed together. The underlying variables that would account for these overt manifestations are the *source traits*. A surface trait might be labeled as curiosity or altruism, but the source trait would receive a more generic term such as *dominance* or *ego strength*. The approach involves creation of sets of descriptions of behaviors and scales to measure them. Problems with the approach arise because the descriptions are (a) limited to the material in the original factor analysis and (b) may be reified and taken as explanations rather than as the descriptions they actually are.

The Constitutional Typologists

The most obvious and certainly the most popular way of categorizing people is in terms of physical appearance. There is a long and honorable literary tradition linking physical appearance and personality. The title character in Shakespeare's *Julius Caesar* summarized centuries of such belief when he said, "Let me have men about me that are fat; Sleek-headed men and such as sleep o'nights: Yon Cassius has a lean and hungry look; He thinks too much: Such men are dangerous." Such an approach may be labeled *constitutional typology*.

A modern constitutional typologist, W. H. Sheldon (b. 1899), received training both as a psychologist and a physician. He continued his studies and contacts with the major influences of the day both in psychiatry (Jung, Freud, Kretchmer) and experimental psychology.

Thus, Sheldon was in a position to bring together various diverse influences. His research emphasis was on identifying and categorizing the major structural parts of the human body and the major components of personality structure (*temperament*) and investigating the interrelationship between the two. Sheldon argued that the genetically determined *physical structure* of the body is the major determinant of human behavior. The deciding elements of behavior are internal, not in terms of hypothesized constructs, but in real and definable measures of physique. Sheldon (1949) expressed his view of the direction in which psychology as a science should move as follows:

> It has been increasingly plain that the situation calls for a biologically oriented psychology, or one taking for its operational frame of reference a scientifically defensible description of the *structure* (together with the behavior) of the human organism itself. This is perhaps tantamount to saying that psychology requires a physical anthropology for its immediate foundation support. More than that, it requires a physical anthropology couched in terms of components, or variables, which can be measured and quantified at both the structural and behavioral ends—the anthropological and psychological ends—of the structure-behavior continuum which is a human personality [p. xv].

We include Sheldon among the type-trait theorists because of his finding that there are three major physiques—each associated with a particular personality temperament, or *type*. The three basic physiques (the structures or somatotypes) are *endomorphic* (soft and round), *mesomorphic* (muscular), and *ectomorphic* (tall and thin). These are associated, respectively, with the temperaments called *viscerotonic* (friendly, relaxed, and food loving); *somatotonic* (assertive and energetic); and *cerebrotonic* (introvertive, artistic, and apprehensive). Sheldon's observations show considerable agreement with those of Shakespeare's Caesar. But evaluating Sheldon's theory or even asking whether it is a theory rather than an acute observation of behavioral correlates is a difficult task.

Hall and Lindzey (1970) offer the following explanation of Sheldon's data, which is consistent with our own behavior influence orientation:

> One may reason that an individual who is endowed with a particular type of physique is likely to find certain kinds of responses particularly effective while an individual with another type of physique will find it necessary to adopt other modes of response. This conception suggests that *the success or reward that accompanies a particular mode of responding is a function not only of the environment in which it occurs but also of the kind of person (type or physique)*

making the response. The individual with a frail ectomorphic body cannot successfully adopt a bluff, aggressive, domineering manner in relation to most people, whereas it may be perfectly possible for the oversized mesomorph to do so . . . another possibility is that *the relation between physique and temperament is mediated by commonly accepted stereotypes or the social-stimulus value* within the culture in regard to the sort of behavior to be expected of individuals with different kinds of physique. Thus, we may suggest that the individual with a particular physique occupies a social role, which includes a set of behavioral specifications, and in the normal course of events the individual will conform to these specifications. Expectation on the part of the culture will lead the individual with a distinctive physique to show distinctive patterns of behavior and this behavior will tend to be shared by other individuals with the same type of physique who have been exposed to similar expectation [p. 364].

In other words, male or female, black or white, infant or aged, are physiological conditions likely to be associated with differences in behavior; but social role seems a more parsimonious explanation of such differences than does genetic endowment.

Hans J. Eysenck

Hans J. Eysenck (b. 1916), the English psychologist, theorist, and investigator, has been an individual of enormous influence. He is both an originator and a systematizer in whom several diverse streams have converged. These have included experimental psychology, Jungian typology, factor analysis, biological-constitutional emphasis, and, finally, the new therapeutic approach of behavior therapy. Eysenck's wide range of interest is attested to by his numerous papers and books on such diverse topics as psychotherapy, hypnosis, eyelid conditioning, criminal behavior, and genetics (1947, 1952a, 1952b, 1957, 1960b).

Offering a model of man influenced by Pavlov (classical conditioning), Hull (habit strength and laws of learning), Watson (behaviorism), Jung (typology), and Kretchmer (constitutionality), Eysenck uses as his key construct the conditionability of the human organism. He offers the hypothesis that susceptibility to conditioning may well be a constitutional predisposition, and too-susceptible people may develop nonadjustive surplus conditioned reactions, while other people will not develop requisite avoidance behaviors due to low conditionability.

His views are summarized in his definition of personality, which is both *behavioral* and *organismic*: "The sum-total of the actual or potential behavior patterns of the organism, as determined by heredity and environment, it originates and develops through the functional interaction of the four main sectors into which these behavior patterns are organized: the cognitive sector (intelligence), the conative sector (character), the affective sector (temperament), and the somatic sector (constitution) [Eysenck, 1947, p. 25]."

Eysenck's theoretical contribution insofar as a psychology of behavior influence is concerned is that a behavioristic orientation can be comfortably combined with biogenetic influences.

FUNCTIONS AND DIFFERENCES
IN PERSONALITY THEORY

Investigators of personality frequently suggest what personality theories should "do." This is a very reasonable approach, since creations of man such as theories should have a function. Maddi (1968) puts it this way: "There are still some overall principles of theorizing that are generally considered of importance. These frequently mentioned principles are that a theory should be *important, operational, parsimonious, stimulating, usable,* and *empirically valid* [p. 451]."

Hall and Lindzey (1970) argue that a personality theory must lead to "*observation of relevant, empirical relations not yet observed*"; it must permit the "*incorporation of known, empirical findings*" within a simple and logical framework; it must prevent "*the observer from being dazzled by the full-blown complexity of natural or concrete events* [pp. 12–14]."

Rychlak (1968) has offered a different set of functions for personality theory; it is *descriptive* (giving a verbal account of the nature of the phenomena); *delimiting* (fixing boundaries on the scope of the construct); *generative* (providing conceptions, hypotheses, and hunches in the pursuit of knowledge); *integrative* (combining theoretical constructs and propositions into a more consistent and unified whole).

All these functions are reasonable and worthwhile. The point is that a theory of personality should be conceived of as any other intellectual creation and should be interpreted in terms of the goals of its creators and the consequences of its existence.

Categories of Theories

Theories about human behavior can be categorized along many different dimensions; for example, those stressing heredity versus environment, cognition versus behavior, internal versus external control, history versus situations, trait versus type, maturation versus learning, dialectic versus demonstration (Rychlak, 1968).

There have, of course, been many ways of categorizing personality theories. For example, Maddi (1968) categorizes theorists in terms of those who deal with the "core of personality" ("the things that are common to all people . . . the inherent attributes of man") and those who focus on the "periphery of personality" (learned attributes which have a relatively circumscribed influence on behavior and which explain differences among people). Maddi proceeds to classify the core personality theorists into three types; those stressing conflict—for example, Freud, Murray, Sullivan, and the ego psychologists; those stressing fulfillment—for example, Rogers, Maslow, Adler, Allport; and those stressing consistency—for example, Kelly, McClelland, Maddi.

Another perhaps simpler categorization has been presented by Mischel (1971). This author places theorists into the categories of trait and type; psychodynamic; psychodynamic behavior; social behavior; and phenomenological. Our own categorization, while based on Woodworth (1931), is similar to Mischel's.

The Experimental Theorists versus The Clinical Theorists

Two groups of theorists may be distinguished on the basis of their training experiences and sources of data: the clinicians and the experimentalists. In assessing the contribution of clinical theorists (doctors of medicine such as Freud, Sheldon, Jung, and McDougall), we must emphasize that they were not in the mainstream of their profession. Most of the clinical personality theorists were rebels against conventional ideas and practices. They dealt with the psychological rather than physical survival of the individual, since many of them were also psychotherapists involved with neurosis, childhood trauma, and mental health. There is indeed a reciprocal relationship between the theory of personality (or behavior) and the methods used to treat (or modify) that personality (or behavior). On the one hand, clinical personality theorists as therapists did not have to adhere to rigid academic thinking. However, neither did they have the discipline and organized formulations of "scientists."

The experimentalists, on the other hand, might be criticized for the triviality of the behavior that they focused on in their research. This issue emerges as a major one when we consider the research of 1950–1970 in Chapter 4. At that point we shall see how this controversy affected the era, since it involved selection of topics, scientific controls, ethics, social responsibility, and range of applications.

Holistic Theories

Personality theorists, according to Hall and Lindzey (1970), are convinced that "an adequate understanding of human behavior will evolve only from the study of the whole person [p. 6]." This statement can be interpreted as asserting that behavior must be considered in the context of the rest of the individual's life and learning experiences. This statement is in accord with our view that behavior is always emitted by a person and hence holistic, but it does not go far enough to meet one of our cardinal principles—that the context of behavior must also include the behavior of the other people and the environment.

But agreement on the concept of a whole individual and, even more, an individual in a biosocial situation does not mean agreement with a very different assumption made by holistic psychologists and found most clearly in Freudian symptom formation: the psyche is conceived of as an almost human, calculating, intelligence that obtains the most pleasure with the least pain. Thus, any act might be relevant to many different needs. In Freud's terms behavior is not only determined it is overdetermined through having many meanings and satisfying many impulses. The best way to make this clear is with an example. As a consultant the junior author was once presented with the case of a "hysterical whore." His first response was to reject the assumption that the two behaviors were necessarily related; he wanted to talk about a woman who displayed behavior called hysterical who also happened to support herself by a system of free enterprise. The question becomes whether a person learns responses to situations or whether enduring internal systems underlie and even generate responses to situations.

Hall and Lindzey (1970) point out that personality theories are also general theories of behavior—in contrast to "single-domain" theories, such as perception, audition, or rote memory, which deal with a limited array of behavioral events. Conversely, they concede that "in some instances" learning theory may be generalized sufficiently to constitute a theory of behavior and is then no different from a theory of personality. Others describing this field (for example, Bischof, 1970) are willing to accept the growth of behavior theories as *alternatives* to personality theories.

Personality theories appear to be wider, looser, less organized, more complex, and more deeply concerned with the concepts of individuality and motivation than are behavior theories. Motivation is a core concept in many of the older formulations which persist in asking, Why? They are based on a deductive rationale and are frequently rooted in their proponents' experience with deviant populations.

In contrast, behavior theories are expressed in operational terms with testable hypotheses, empirical orientation, and statistical treatment. They seem to ask, How? and What? They are closer to an inductive rationale and are usually rooted in learning theory and the experimental laboratory. Berlyne (1968) brings these differences into focus by documenting the neglect of personality theorists by behavior theorists and vice versa. Behavior theory has been research oriented, whereas personality theory has been practical, clinical, and education oriented. Behavior theorists have stressed environmentalism and the learning process. Personality theorists have stressed heredity, unlearned, instinctive, and ethological data. The behavior theorist first looks for commonality (order out of chaos), the personality theorist for differences between people.

Behavior theorists stress functional situations, reactions, and consequent relationships, which involve control, prediction, and explanation. In contrast, the personality theorists emphasize response-response, or correlational, variables.

The Influence of Texts

Still another dimension one might use to categorize the conceptualizations of behavior is the approaches taken in formal texts. Writers of texts on personality are frequently influential by the very manner in which they order their conceptualizations. For example, a useful kind of dichotomy of themes is described by Maddi (1968) as descriptive of personality books which are written either with benevolent eclecticism or partisan zealotry. *Benevolent eclecticism* is expressed by the author who includes many theories of personality within his book and gives each relatively equal time and space (for example, Hall and Lindzey's *Theories of Personality*, 1957). Books written with *partisan zealotry* express only one theory of personality. Allport's *Pattern and Growth in Personality* (1961) is cited by Maddi as an example of this. Maddi categorizes a third type of book, such as his own, which "borrows the breadth and balance involved in considering many theories of personality, and from partisan zealotry it borrows the conviction that one or a few theories are better than others [p. 2]."

Maddi's analysis is in line with our view that in the personality field we are dealing with *purveyors* of ideas and concepts. Book writing and developing theories are functions of a set of variables which include reinforcement for the writer. The reinforcing stimulus may be what the writer hopes to say, what he wants to convince others about; or it may be royalties for a book that is different and meets a need. But writing is behavior, and what is written is talk about behavior.

As we have repeatedly indicated, authors from many disciplines have theorized about human behavior. But when personality theory was part of a psychology course on "personality," it usually involved psychoanalytic theory with its variations. The publication of Gordon Allport's *Personality* (1937) and Hall and Lindzey's *Theories of Personality* (1957, revised in 1970) helped create a new field, at least a new course, by defining what it constituted. These two texts made it clear that theorizing about human behavior is not limited to the psychoanalysts; it is, in fact, fair game for all. Many excellent books on theories of personality have fed the market created by these pioneers (for example, Bischof, 1970; Gilbert, 1970; Baughman, 1972; Maddi, 1968; Lundin, 1969; Pervin, 1970; Sarason, 1972; Mischel, 1971; Liebert and Spiegler, 1970; Wiggins et al., 1971). Generally speaking, these books have limited their coverage to the psychological or psychiatric theorists and not gone beyond to the sociologist, economist, or political scientist.

A final issue to note is the desirability and feasibility of bringing together the theories into a broader, encompassing *unified field* theory of personality. If such a theory were to emerge, it would be (like all other theories) a product of man. In fact, each of the theoretical orientations which we have discussed— the behavioral, the psychodynamic, and the phenomenological—is in its own way a unifying theory. (Rychlak, 1968, approaches this problem by offering a "philosophy of science for personality theory.") Thus, personality theory begins to take its rightful place within the context of man's seeking of knowledge about man. We think that advancement will come not with more abstraction of theories, but with a spelling out of the differences in the theories as to the nature of man, with the testing of the implications of the theories by systematic observation, and, most important, with the observation of the social consequences of the theory; that is, has it influenced the behavior of the investigators, of other influencers in society, or of anybody else?

LAST WORD

This chapter has given a whirlwind overview of a multitude of theorists and theories of human behavior, beginning with the psychological scene at the start of the twentieh century. The predominant theories of psychology as a science of human behavior include psychoanalysis, behaviorism, social learning theory, drive theory, gestalt, phenomenology, interaction theory, and trait theory.

These theories are far from exhaustive, but in our view they represent the ideas on human behavior that have influenced current theorists and research workers. More broadly, they are ways in which people think about themselves not only as professional personologists but also as observers and influencers of society—be they teachers, novelists, playwrights, political commentators, or lawyers.

We realize that at this point the reader may feel he has been exposed to a mélange of names, with confusion as to who said what, and possible indignation that some favorite author was either omitted or given short shrift.

Rather than treating these theories as the culmination of intensive investigation, we have offered them as examples of the ways in which some professionally trained human beings, products of a time and place, have tried to give some order and meaning to the human scene. When you converse or read about or start to investigate such terms as *ego, unconscious, archetypes, self-actualization, conditioning, role playing, reinforcement,* or *imitation,* you should realize that they do not represent reality. Rather, they are manmade creations which reflect hypotheses about the nature of man and are designed to convey in the only way possible (via a metaphoric language) ideas, beliefs, observations, and hunches about how humans act.

CHAPTER 4

The Development of Research on Behavior: From 1950 to the 1970s

This chapter presents an overview and analysis of the investigations of human behavior in the fields of personality and social psychology during the two decades after 1950. Our intent is to present a *social psychology* of the research and its investigators and not to cover all or even most of the research during this period. First, total coverage would be a physical impossibility because the relevant studies number in the thousands. But more important is our twofold aim: first, to convey the direction of research in this period as the context for our view of personality and, second, to use the material presented to illustrate the *investigation* of human behavior.

Our approach is to compare the state of investigation of behavior influence in 1950 with that in the early 1970s and then to trace the changes that occurred in the intervening period.[1]

The period from 1950 on has been selected for several reasons. It is the most recent; it has been characterized by a plethora of research illustrative of all the major trends traced in this book; it witnessed the development of the principles of behavior influence. Some major points about the study of personality that will emerge are (a) the science of human behavior is actually involved with the social psychology of the scientist; (b) the investigation of human behavior is a behavior subject to the same historical and social contexts and interpretations as the behavior that is being investigated; (c) a continual struggle has gone on between those looking for the locus and impetus of behavior within the individual (for example, in traits) and those seeking the locus of action outside the organism (for example, in situations); (d) a series of investigative techniques were developed, and the resulting study of the tools of research distracted workers from the original purposes of the tools—to provide information about human behavior; (e) the availability of techniques frequently determined the formulation of a problem and the methodology of its investigation. For example, the availability of the Taylor Manifest Anxiety Scale directly contributed to the very large amount of research on the concept of anxiety.

THE MIDTWENTIETH-CENTURY APPROACH

What was thought about human behavior in the midtwentieth century? Many of the traditional terms used by earlier theorists such as *imitation, suggestion, prestige, prejudice,* and *attitude* were being translated into the "basic" psychological concepts or jargon of the day such as *motivation, perception,* and *learning.* The advantage of this translation was that it brought concepts based on either uncontrolled observations of behavior or shrewd philosophical speculations into the laboratory, where they could be systematically investigated.

The problems involved in this kind of transition behavior are summarized by the concern that something may be lost in translation. The basic premise of the scientific approach to human behavior emerging in the 1950s was that the experimenter could transport a segment of real life into the laboratory in order to (a) change behavior and (b) determine of what the change is a function— that is, what features of the human situation are associated with the change. These aims usually allow for an adequate experimental-control procedure, but there is frequently uncertainty about the relationship between the extralaboratory, real life situation and the laboratory experiment. Is the latter a prototype, an

[1] The *Annual Review of Psychology* began publication in 1950 and has appeared every year since. It is a major source of material on the status of particular fields of psychology, and its reviews of personality and social psychology are especially valuable and serve as the basis for the overview presented in this chapter.

analogue, a reproduction of the former, or is it a similar but irrelevant situation which, among other things, has the very different social label of "research" or "experiment"? Thus, investigators in the early post–World War II period initiated several decades of intense laboratory research as well as intense controversy over the value of such research.

Most of the approaches to personality and behavior which have continued to the present time were evident in 1950. For example, one approach, based in large part on Freud's theory of projection, was exemplified by Wolfle's comment (1949) that "an individual reveals his own personality through any change he makes upon any type of material [p. 273]." In contrast, Klineberg (1949) talked of "national characteristics"—differences in personality structure conditioned by cultural products and institutions. The former approach, typified by projective tests (such as the Rorschach ink blots) heralded two decades of intensive research on individual characteristics and dynamics. The latter approach anticipated subsequent investigation into social, cultural, and institutional variables.

During the early 1950s the field of social psychology was the meeting ground for the research of a host of specialists from different disciplines. This meant that either social psychology had *no* field of its own or that *all* the other disciplines were branches of social psychology. Much the same could be said about the field of personality and its relation to other fields of psychology; there was no field of personality or all studies involving humans were really personality studies. In Chapter 3 we described the development of theories and research in personality and social psychology at the beginning of the century. By midcentury, the boundaries between these two fields were becoming obscure.

Personality Types

World War II had left its impact on the investigation of human behavior and influenced the kinds of problems and issues investigated, which were often of social and political interest. This interest can be illustrated by the concern with racial and religious prejudices and the theory that certain types of personality were related to such beliefs. Prejudice was an important American social problem during the post–World War II period. According to investigators who used questionnaires as their primary tool, the "prejudiced" or "authoritarian" personality had many "bad" traits such as being ethnocentric; aggressive; contemptuous of weakness; conformist; moralistic with absolute values; intolerant of ambiguity; uncertain in social roles; rigid in his thinking in attempting solutions to intellectual problems; and valuing power and strength, as exemplified by money, masculinity, and age-status authority. The prejudiced person "saw the world as a dangerous place, full of chaos and unpredictability, with uncontrollable catastrophe ever-impending" (Sears, 1950, p. 117). Based on such early findings, Sears optimistically concluded that "a significant 'character' may be well on the way to isolation [p. 117]." The search for specific personality characteristics seemed at last about to culminate in success.

In fact, one of the most important developments at midcentury was the publication of the large-scale study developed and stimulated by World War II on the *authoritarian personality* (Adorno, Frenkel-Brunswick, Levinson, and Sanford, 1950). The investigators isolated two types of outlook toward the world, namely, the *authoritarian,* or *exploitative,* and the *affectionate, equalitarian,* or *permissive* (note the good versus bad quality of the adjectives). Perhaps to avoid the undesirable label of "type," the investigators referred to the authoritarian *syndrome.* The medical implications of this term had an effect; and before the decade was over the authoritarian was considered a "sick" person by both professionals and the public.

This study on the authoritarian personality was also significant because it attempted to tackle a social problem and to offer a possible solution. The investigators, combining a basic study of human behavior with a zeal to bring about social change, wanted to stamp out the "disease" of prejudice but warned that "symptomatic" treatment was not a cure. In addition to alleviation of social problems, long-term treatment of the dynamic feature of the sick individual's personality organization had to be provided. Here, we have a good illustration of how the theoretical model of man subsumed in a psychodynamic approach to personality resulted in the belief that change can occur only after the extirpation of inner malaise.

Man and Society

As a complement to the controversy over the nature of human nature, theorists also disagreed on the relative influence of society on behavior. The relationship between culture and personality was intensively studied in . the early 1950s. One basic assumption, influenced by Freudian theory, was that early childhood training (which varies in different cultures) determined adult character structure. Orlansky (1949) reviewed the data extant on the relationship between childhood experience—particularly in toilet training and other child-rearing practices—and adult personality and found no evidence that the two were significantly, much less, causally related. Similar negative data were reported by Sewell (1955), although Whiting and Child (1953) found limited positive associations. Orlansky called for the study of "specific psychological effects upon individuals with certain constitutions."

Menninger (1950), a psychiatrist, argued that the two most important factors in psychiatric thinking were that the personality of the child is intimately connected with his society and that the structures of societies differ over the earth. Menninger compared personality development to the process of photosynthesis in that a society supported growth and nourished positive feelings which were synthesized and given back to that society in the form of a useful life. In his view society directly influences man's behavior—even to the tone of feeling expressed in interpersonal relationships.

Linton (1945), an anthropologist, argued that *variations* and *irregularities* within any given culture pattern make for the appearance of changeability in people. He felt that the "status" of the individual was a better predictor of his behavior than his "basic" personality. Status is generated by society, which expects individuals who occupy certain *positions* in its system of organization to exhibit certain traits of personality and individuals in general to meet societal expectations.

Thus, concepts focusing on the influence of society were well represented at this time as were opposing views. For example, MacKinnon (1951) criticized the idea that *status influences behavior* as representing merely the clothes of man and not the real body. People may wear different clothes at different gatherings, but these garments are only superficial indications of the body underneath. This is an appropriate analogy, representing as it does the personality analogue to the disease model of abnormal behavior (see Ullmann and Krasner, 1969). It presumes that a true, fundamental, or basic, personality exists and that overt behavior is superficial if not trivial.

The popular social psychology texts of the early 1950s expressed the contrasting internal and external trends. Krech and Crutchfield (1948) organized social psychology around the concepts of perception and cognitive functions. In contrast, Sargent (1950) and Newcomb (1950) attempted to integrate the social sciences, particularly psychology and sociology, by using concepts such as role, reference group, and group membership.

Social Influences on Behavior

At midcentury lines of inquiry in the study of the *structure* of American society and the impact of that structure on individual behavior were also developing. One line of inquiry was *anthropological* (studies of communities such as Warner's *Yankee City*, 1941). Anthropological investigators attempted an *interpretative* understanding of *social patterns* at a given period. A second approach was *quantitative* and employed systematic procedures and sampling techniques (such as Centers' analysis, 1949, of social class based on interviews). A third approach was *economic* and reviewed the economic basis of social structure and focused on the relationship between man's work and his personality (such as Katona, 1951).

Still another way of looking at the problem of environmental influences on behavior was to evaluate the effects of specific environmental factors such as occupation, social class, and ethnic status (Komarovsky and Sargent, 1949). As far as occupations were concerned, decisive influences on behavior were found to include the type of social interaction on the job and certain technological and economic features of the occupation. The selective attractions of different occupations were also considered. That is, sources of strain in the professional life of an individual might produce anxiety, but certain professions such as medicine might attract an already "anxious" type of person.

Centers (1949) in *The Psychology of Social Class* argued that a person's *economic* status and role impose certain attitudes, values, and interests in both the political and economic spheres. The individual identifies with those who share his values, usually those in his social class (see Byrne's recent research, 1968, on assumed similarity and interpersonal attraction). Hollingshead's *Elmtown's Youth* (1949) described in detail the role of the family and other social institutions in transmitting behavior patterns.

In the same period Newcomb (1950) offered a concept of social *role* that attempted to explain consistent behavior. He theorized that persistency of behavior may be accounted for by the fact that similar role behaviors elicit consistent role responses from others, which maintain the individual's self-perceptions in a given role system. The relationships between status and role-expected behavior may lead to stable culture patterns that continue to be transmitted long after the reasons for the original connections have been lost.

Heredity and Environment

At midcentury the relative influences of heredity and environment on behavior were also intensely debated. Speculations about man's original nature continued. MacKinnon (1951) dichotomized investigators into

> those viewing infants as little savages; or those believing that the natural state is the ideal one and that evils are all imposed from without. Under the influence of the doctrine of original sin and Freud's concept of the id, the former view has in recent years enjoyed wide favor [p. 119].

At that point, however, Maslow (1949) defended the latter view; he argued that man's animal nature had been much maligned. Culture is not necessarily instinct controlling but can also be instinct gratifying. Maslow cited incidents to show that the primitive is not necessarily bad and pointed out that needs for safety, love, and beauty are just as instinctive as drives toward war and crime. He argued that the evidence supported the view that constructive needs were unlearned and that the destructive forces in personality were acquired rather than inherent.

The most important event of this period, according to another psychologist, Eysenck (1952c), who emphasized the impact of the individual's constitution on behavior (see Chapter 3), was the appearance of the twentieth edition of Kretchmer's *Physique and Character* (1951). Kretchmer's system is a typology defined in terms of observed correlations. His methodology is similar to factor analysis. Indeed, Eysenck argued that the word *factor* could be substituted for *type*. Eysenck found Kretchmer's views very "simpatico" and was undaunted by the complete absence of indices of statistical validity in Kretchmer's text. Eysenck himself calculated these indices and found them to be "in nearly all cases" significant at the 1 percent level. As a constitutionalist, Eysenck regarded the literature on the development of personality as being overwhelmingly biased "in favour of environmentalistic hypotheses and a complete disregard of the possibility that the figures given in support of this may find an equally easy interpretation in terms of a nativistic hypothesis [p. 156]."

The context of his arguments makes it clear that Eysenck considered psychotherapy and psychoanalysis as within the environmentalist group. He argued that ignoring the genetic components of behavior is antiscientific. Eysenck noted that the typical personality development study of this period sought to correlate children's and mothers' behavior patterns. When such a correlation was found, it was cited as evidence for the environmentalist position. Eysenck asserted that one could make an equally good, although not necessarily more correct, alternative hypothesis that both the behaviors of the mother and of the child are a function of a third variable, the *genetic*.

Eysenck argued that his own studies (particularly Eysenck and Prell, 1951) on 25 pairs of monozygotic and 25 pairs of dizygotic twins demonstrated that the *neuroticism* factor, which he reported finding, was not a statistical artifact of factor analysis, but had "very definite biological reality." He concluded that

> it does appear clear from this study that heredity plays a very strong part in the determination of personality differences and that psychology cannot go on making the easy and implicit assumption, which is inherent in both psychoanalysis and behaviourism, that environment is the only major variable determining individual differences. This belief, which has acquired a mystical and almost religious fervour in the USSR is also widespread in democratic countries, for reasons which . . . may not be entirely apolitical. It seems a great pity that scientific issue should be clouded in this fashion. [p. 161].

Eysenck's observation gives us not only a good glimpse of the state of the perennial "nature-nurture" controversy at midcentury but also an indication that a relationship may exist between theories of behavior and political forces.

Personality and Perception

The midcentury also witnessed a growing rapprochement between the two types of research on personality then extant, that of the laboratory and that of the field, the more controlled and the uncontrolled. Research in the laboratory was seen as illuminating how personality functions in general life. As an illustration,

Bruner and Postman (1949) were trying to develop a unified theory of behavior in which *perception* was the key to adjustive behavior. Thus, they studied the effect on perception (in the laboratory) of such factors as value and need, emotionality, multiplicity of set, satisfaction and deprivation. The criticisms of the Bruner-Postman studies (and those of earlier perception workers) are typical of criticisms throughout the study of personality. For example, Pastore (1949) argued on the basis of early studies that perception studies were inadequately formulated, contained statistical errors, had methodological flaws, derived from fuzzily stated theory, used undefined terms, and generated contradictory results. Allport's analysis (1959), based on a broader view of these studies, was more balanced but equally unflattering.

Another set of investigators working in the same area, Klein and Schlesinger (1951), offered a *person-centered* approach combining perception and behavior. They described organized perceptual systems as representing and, in fact, directing the person. They offered another variation of the concept of an internal mediating variable—this time called a *perceptual system*—determining behavior.

In a variation of these studies, Witkin and his coworkers (1954) studied perception and personality on the assumption that perceptual tests involving the body directly would be more revealing of basic personality than other measures. The procedures—for example, adjusting a rod to vertical when it was in a tilted frame—measured accuracy and consistency of orientation, which depended upon an effective integration of clues from a number of senses. Size of errors—that is, deviation from true vertical—were associated with personality test scores such as insight, repression, and, particularly, dependence. Important information about significant personal characteristics was expected to emerge from the investigation of perception. Errors on the rod and frame sample of behavior were hypothesized to be typical of behavior in situations in general.[2]

Finally, Katz (1951) interpreted the growth of studies in perception as a healthy reaction to the social behaviorists, who were still refusing to recognize the intervening variables without which the phenomenologists and psychoanalysts have difficulty. But even Katz warned of "a real danger of circularity in a dominantly mentalistic approach [p. 138]." This danger was particularly evident in the clinicians who shifted attention to the personality mechanisms developed as a reaction to the social world. Katz offered this realistic evaluation of the implications of this trend:

> Personality theorists remain one of the influential sources of research and system building in social psychology. Their weakness is their neglect of present social realities and their assumption that society is made up of personalities acting in

[2] Recent investigators of this line (Ihilevich and Gleser, 1971) used ability to perceive embedded figures and scores on a paper-and-pencil test called the Defense Mechanism Inventory. Within this sample of behavior, knowledge of defense permitted a better-than-chance prediction of cognitive style, while knowledge of cognitive style did not help reduce significantly error in prediction of defense.

parallel rather than in interaction. They are too ready to say that discrimination against groups means that there are prejudiced personalities who have been warped in their childhood training, or that group conflict means that there are too many agresive personalities [p. 138].

Other Midcentury Influences

Another area of note was the relation of personality development to psycho-therapy. Rogers (1951, 1959) was the chief spokesman for the view that there was a need for continuous emotional development and that personality should be *developed* through psychotherapy. In effect, this position tied together a theory of personality with a theory of psychotherapy. This was one of the most important theoretical developments and foreshadowed similar positions held by some later psychoanalysts, existentialists, and behaviorists—but justified by each on very different grounds.

One of the more widely held opinions in the 1950s was that all behavior is *motivated*. If one could find the springs which activate the individual, then one could understand (and perhaps control) his behavior. Maslow (1954), among others, did not completely accept this notion. He suggested that there are two kinds of behavior: *coping*, which is motivated, and *expressive*, which is not. Maslow asserted that the individual's uniqueness is most clearly revealed and can best be studied in unlearned, unconscious, uncontrolled, and unmotivated expressive behavior. Maslow cited as examples of expressive behavior the beauty of a lovely woman and the stupidity of a moron. Both beauty and stupidity are determined by the state of the organism and are ends in themselves.

RESEARCH IN THE SEVENTIES

In the perspective of the immediate and more recent past, what is the current scene in research on human behavior? We are writing this chapter at a particular point in history. We might be missing an important series of researches or a new theory which will lead to a major breakthrough in the next decade. However, we do not think such an error is likely, because no major change appears imminent in the direction, issues, experimental critiques, controversies, nit picking, and inconsequentiality of most of the research in the fields labeled as personality or social psychology. Nor is a critical appraisal of such research novel, unique, or daring, since in most instances we are reporting the self-criticism of the investigators themselves. In evaluating the social psychology of behavior influence, we must observe that most investigators engage in a proper amount of humble and critical self-appraisal and self-abnegation—but not enough to change the formulations and tactics of their research.

Adelson (1969), in evaluating the current status of the field, argues that the investigation of personality is characterized by "abundance, diffusiveness, and diversity." He describes the field as a "loose collation of topics [p. 136]," each going its own way without any unity. Large theoretical issues seem to have been abandoned; small squabbles abound. Technology is far ahead of theory in social psychology and personality. To remedy this situation, which he finds undesirable but which others find quite satisfactory, Adelson calls for the revival of inductive and naturalistic approaches. He asserts that the representative study in the field of personality is an experiment in which the experimenter *lies* to an undergraduate. Ninety percent of the papers published in the major journals used undergraduates as subjects and most of these studies ignored the fact that the characteristics of volunteers differ from those of compulsory subjects. (Dohrenwend, Feldstein, and Plosky, 1967.)

Adelson considers this sprawl and diversity in personality research as both a cause of and a consequence of the abandonment of theoretical approaches. Current research has not generated any major new theory, and the general concepts which influence researchers come from authors who wrote thirty to sixty years ago, such as G. Allport, Lewin, Durkheim, Freud, or Thorndike. On the other hand, some critics lament that there is little relationship between theory and actual research. If this is so, it may help explain why most personality research seems unrelated to most other research and why it also seems to a large extent to be irrelevant to the general world of human interaction.

The dominant research approach emphasizes the importance of *hypothesis testing* and *tight designs*, which by their very nature limit stimulus conditions and the range of possible responses. "There is now considerable doubt whether hypothesis-testing via the test of significance is a viable strategy given the quantitatively underdeveloped state of personality theory [Adelson, 1969, p. 218]."

Thus, an assault is under way on the experimental methods currently in vogue. Related to this concern are the serious questions of the *ethics* of contemporary research. The restriction of personality research to the groups available for research raises problems about the validity of generalizations to other populations. There is also widespread concern about other ethical aspects of research, which include disguised observations, confidentiality, research with children, deception, and the data collector himself as a subject of research.

Nor is there sufficient cognizance of the fact that two types of research in the decade of the 1960s should have had devastating effects on most of the remainder of human research—namely, the works on *experimenter bias* (Rosenthal, 1966) and *demand characteristics* (Orne, 1962). These studies demonstrated that major effects in many psychological studies are due to such variables as the experimenter's anticipation of the outcome and the influence of the physical and symbolic characteristics of the situation on the subjects' behavior. These experiments will be described in greater detail in Chapter 8; but here we wish to emphasize that they *should have had* a major impact on research in the area of human behavior. However, few subsequent investigations seem to have attempted to or been able to adequately control experimenter and situational influences. As Adelson (1969) characterized personality research of the late 1960s, "It may be crooked, but it's the only game in town [p. 221]."

Adelson (1969) also goes to the core of the social psychology of research when he points out that a major influence on the frequency and nature of research is the social context of the university and other pressures (for example, to publish) for *quantity* of output with its attendent reinforcers:

> We like to pretend that our choice of methods is dictated by scientific considerations alone. In fact, the exigencies of the academic marketplace play an important and perhaps decisive role. The methodological problems we have noted—the nearly exclusive use of undergraduates, the failure to take account of the experimenter effect, the neglect of naturalistic strategies—all these reflect the pressure for quick publication. There is reason to doubt that there will be rapid reforms in methodology until there is some reform of the university [p. 222].

Perhaps as a compensation for the preoccupation with deception, aggression, and other aversive behaviors, the study of the "moral" domain in both attitudes and behavior has been revived after years of neglect. Relatively little was published in this area before 1964. The early Hartshorne and May (1928) studies had demonstrated that moral conduct was influenced by the situation and no simple relationship existed between moral belief and moral conduct. In contrast to this "external" view, followers of an internal orientation (such as Kohlberg, 1963) pointed to cognitive dimensions such as intelligence and anticipation as key determinants of moral conduct. Currently there is a growing literature on the effects of social influence (external orientation) via observations and modeling on the induction of good, moral, altruistic, charitable, and "delay of gratification" behavior. The recent studies of Bryan and Test (1967) and Rosenhan and White (1967) offer examples of how watching altruistic behavior in others increases the likelihood of similar behavior in the observer.

Thus, after two decades of intensive research into the seemingly most promising variables of personality, there appears to be in the early 1970s controversy over nearly every aspect of the field. For example, in his review of the field of personality at the end of the 1960s, Dahlstrom (1970) is critical of almost all attempts to develop alternatives to the traditional model of intrapsychic causation. Recipients of Dahlstrom's wrath include investigators who describe personality as "an area of investigation" (Sarason, 1972); offer the notion of personality as social stimulus value; look for differences in culture based on differences in role perceptions; view behavior in terms of mutual interaction effects and thus deal with sociopsychological phenomena rather than with pure personality; and define personality in terms of a combination of sociology and psychology.

Mischel's approach (1968) to personality is a particular target of Dahlstrom's criticism because of the negative implications of Mischel's views on current approaches to personality assessment. In a major contribution, Mischel shifted the focus of assessment from the individual himself to the *sources of stimulus configurations and reinforcement patterns* in the individual's specific life situations. Dahlstrom criticizes this formulation as a "mechanical mirror theory" and pointed out somewhat disdainfully, although correctly, that Mischel's views are attractive to sociologists, child psychologists, and behavior therapists.

Dahlstrom (1970) complained that no matter how behavior is conceptualized, such dissenters see no personal stability in it; they ignore "the large body of empirically established correlates of personality scales [p. 5]." Dahlstrom contends that these negativists must substitute for personological constructs identifiable aspects of the sociopsychological culture. He is particularly contemptuous of variables such as sibling rank; racial or ethnic classifications; family structure; socioeconomic status; religious affiliations; geographic, regional, or cultural membership; and even age and sex. He feels all these are merely "descriptors of the situation within which the personality system is found to be interacting [p. 6]." But such descriptors are frequently very good predictors; and a review of the current status of the kinds of personality measures Dahlstrom defends raises many serious questions that have not been adequately considered. We have cited Dahlstrom at length, since he represents a point of view we do not share. In fact, he is most critical of the research we most admire.

Perhaps the best way to summarize this section on the current scene is to cite Adelson's view (1969) of one of this large body of "empirically established personality scales: After all these years and after literally hundreds of studies on anxiety, there is still no general agreement as to what the commonly used scales are in fact measuring, whether it is drive level, maladjustment, affect, degree of defensiveness or several of these in some interaction [p. 233]."

THE FIFTIES AND SIXTIES: BEHAVIOR CHANGE AMONG THE BEHAVIOR CHANGERS

We have briefly looked at the research and theories about human behavior at the beginning and at the end of the two decades of intensive and systematic investigation of the influences on man's social behavior. We have not seen much change in the nature of the major controversies or any great breakthroughs to more fundamental knowledge about man. We now examine some of the issues that arose during the 1950s and 1960s.

Techniques and Procedures

These two decades were characterized by a variety of research on such matters as hypothesized characteristics of the individual's personality state; internal mediating processes; the relationship between internal states and overt behavior; the influences of audiences or other groups of varying number on individual behavior; and the nature of interpersonal relationships. The identifying labels attached to the various kinds of characteristics and processes within these categories included, to name but a few with major impact, authoritarianism, anxiety, anti-Semitism, prejudice, affiliation, achievement, perceptual defense, rigidity, empathy, sense of humor, field dependence, response set, aggression, frustration, response style, opinion leadership, social perception, coercion, introversion, and extroversion.

The concept being investigated, however, cannot be separated from the manner of its investigation. The standard tools of the 1950s and 1960s included interviews, observational ratings, projective techniques, and particularly a series of paper-and-pencil tests such as the Minnesota Multiphasic Personality Inventory (Dahlstrom and Welsh, 1960), Manifest Anxiety Scale (Taylor, 1953), Need-Achievement Scale (McClelland et al., 1953), California F Scale (Adorno et al., 1950), the sixteen-factor personality test (Cattell, 1950a), Personal Preference Scale (Edwards, 1959), Semantic Differential Scale (Osgood, Suci, and Tannenbaum, 1957), and Role Repertory Test (Kelly, 1955).

Anxiety

During the last forty years, the concept of anxiety has played a major explanatory role in formulations of behavior. Behaviors are conceived of as emitted in order to reduce *anxiety*, which is defined as something unpleasant that people act to reduce. Anxiety therefore provides an explanation for many otherwise self-defeating, irrational, and inexplicable behaviors. Problems arise, however, when one examines more closely the nature of or conditions leading to and maintaining anxiety. We will explore the operations and problems involved in the conceptualization and investigation of anxiety in this section and detail the development of anxiety as a metaphoric explanation in Chapter 7.

Several operational definitions of anxiety exist. The first involves overt motor and physiological responses: pacing, sweating, difficulty in performing smoothly. Observers use these cues to infer that a person is *uncomfortable, ill at ease*, or *upset*. A second operational definition deals with physiological measures—most notably galvanic skin response, although muscle tension, blood pressure, heart rate, and other autonomic responses have also been studied. While heavy or spasmodic breathing and other extreme and unusual physiological states may be observed with the naked eye, the measurements in this area are made with very fine and sensitive instruments. The third and final operational definition of anxiety involves self-report, typically in a structured interview such as a paper-and-pencil inventory. The Taylor Manifest Anxiety Scale, also known as the Taylor A or MAS uses Minnesota Multiphasic Personality Inventory (MMPI) items. It is so highly correlated with other self-report measures such as Welsh's anxiety factor, Eysenck's neuroticism, and several ego-strength and facilitation-inhibition measures that it is operationally identical to them. Self-report measures may deal with a general level of behavior or with response to specific situations. This distinction may be called trait versus state. Operationally, a trait measure might ask the individual if he is anxious *in general* or if he is more anxious than most people *most of the time,* while a state measure would ask if he is anxious *on exams* or if he is more anxious than most people *during exams.*

The first important aspect of these operational definitions of anxiety is that while various measures in one domain may correlate highly with each other, the correlations between measures in different domains are of relatively low magnitude and barely attain statistical significance. This is particularly true when the general levels are used; improvement in obtained correlations may occur with specified stimuli. For example, in one questionnaire (Endler, Hunt, and Rosenstein, 1962) subjects rate "You are about to go on a roller coaster" on 5-point scales such as "My heart beats faster" (from not fast at all to very fast) and "I want to avoid the situation" (from not at all to very much). Aside from dealing with a specific situation—*a roller coaster, this interview,* or *asking for a date*— this type of instrument samples physiological (heartbeat, nausea) and avoidance behaviors (effects of "anxiety" such as unease, dislike, or evasion).

In addition to its focus on specific situations rather than on a general (reported) level of anxiety, this approach has a number of other advantages that may lead to the higher correlations obtained across domains of measures of anxiety. First, it samples the physiological and behavioral domains in a specific manner. That is, the person reports on his physiological status and his behavior. A specific definition of the target to be reported on is given the subject: rather than being asked if he is anxious, the person is asked if he wishes to avoid the situation. A second feature is that this instrument is a self-report (one domain) that specifically asks about the other domains (behavior, physiological response).

A very important feature of this type of test is the contrast between *general feelings of anxiety* and such feelings in specific situations. It may well be that one aspect of the important explanatory and predictive material is not in an absolute state of physiological or behavioral "anxiety," but in a contrast between a person's usual level and the level he experiences in response to a given situation. One person may have a lower threshold for reporting anxiety or acting in an anxious manner than another; the important base line may be the individual's usual level and not some general level. Another way of saying this is that the measure is of a *contrast* rather than an absolute threshold.

A second key question—one that has been skirted in the foregoing paragraphs—is, What actually is "anxiety"? What do the measures sample? The general empirical definition (as distinct from psychoanalytic theories) of anxiety involves (a) the physiological and behavioral acts that are (b) correlates of anticipated aversive stimuli. The word *anticipated* is necessary because of the distinction between pain, fear, and anxiety. *Pain* is the impact of a current aversive stimulus; *fear* is a response to an objectively present threat (aversive stimuli, danger); *anxiety* is the anticipation (realistic or not) of some unpleasant threat. The body presumably prepares in an appropriate manner for a current realistic threat, that is, fear or pain. And human beings may use their ability to symbolize to prepare themselves to meet threats in the future. But they may also symbolically present themselves with such stimuli for far more prolonged periods of time than occur with naturally occurring realistic stimuli. Such prolonged mobilizations or responses to stress (that is, anxiety) may lead to physiological changes, some of which may be irreversible.

This empirical definition of anxiety is a good theory and has helped organize a body of observations. But it does have problems. The first is that it presumes the bodily mobilization is so unpleasant that a person will act to reduce the condition or to avoid the stimulation leading to the mobilization. The second is that it views the individual as passive in the process, that the responses to the anxiety-evoking stimulus and their physiological effects are automatic. Though it is related to the second, the third problem is different enough to deserve separate mention: it is the notion of the continued, enduring nature of the anxiety.

The first problem may be illustrated with an example from the previously mentioned questionnaire (Endler et al. 1962): compared to normal experience, going on a roller coaster leads to unusual feelings. We may wish to think of that interesting usage in our language in which a person says "I'm *anxious* for Christmas to come." The Random House unabridged dictionary (Stein, 1967) defines this usage in terms of "eagerness" and "solicitous desire" (p. 68). Physiological arousal is involved in the anticipation of pleasant events, and it is presently very difficult if not impossible to differentiate with purely physical measures the two supposedly separate conditions. *The individual plays an active, crucial role: he labels the situation pleasant or unpleasant*; and then, if he categorizes the situation as unpleasant, changes in arousal may be called "anxiety." Two persons may respond in the same way physiologically to going on a roller coaster, sky diving, or skiing, but one person may refuse such experiences while the other seeks them.

Authors such as Hunt (1961, 1965) recognize this situation by positing a curvilinear relationship between arousal and behavior. Both extremely *low* and extremely *high* arousal lead to debilitating effects. The optimum level for functioning is moderate arousal. If one thinks of anxiety as a drive—a condition whose reduction provides a reason or motivation for behavior—then both indifference and panic over an exam (extremely low and high arousal) are undesirable for studying and subsequent good grades. The student ideally is concerned enough to study, but not so tense that the studying is more aversive than the dullness of textbooks.

The same concept was presented by McReynolds (1956, 1958, 1960) in a beautiful and, unfortunately, overlooked theory that permits integration of many schools of thought. McReynolds viewed psychological life as a series of experiences or percepts. The individual processes or strives to assimilate percepts. Optimum functioning involves novel percepts that can be assimilated. Lack of novel percepts lead to dullness or apathy. On the basis of sensory deprivation studies and similar material, McReynolds hypothesized that a minimum level of novel percepts is almost a biological necessity. The need for assimilable novel precepts is close to an operational definition of Carl Rogers' concept of self-enhancement. Percepts that are unassimilable, however, may lead to overarousal or a situation of "anxiety." In this regard McReynolds both precedes Toffler's *Future Shock* (1970) by a decade and provides a specification of psychological processes into which Toffler's observations may be fitted. Faced with an influx of percepts that he is unable to assimilate, an individual may engage in a variety of actions. He may strive to reduce percepts by withdrawing from sources of stimulation or, as in the societal control of innovations, by striving to eliminate the sources of novelty. Another strategy is to alter the methods of assimilation. For example, a person may create separate and inconsistent categories for different situations or treat percepts in a manner appropriate for similar ones. Finally, a person faced with troubling experiences may engage in new learning. For example, confusion in a foreign country is a good reason to learn the language.

Our remarks on McReynolds provide a bridge to the second problem with the general theory of anxiety: its view of the individual as *passive*. In fact, the individual is not passive; he is an *active participant* in the situation. The reduction of anxiety is viewed as a reason for action or, in behavioral terms, as a source of reinforcement. And we have already noted that the person's labeling of the situation and his consequent arousal is a key aspect in identifying the feeling as anxiety in contrast to pleasant anticipation. We may now add that a person may enter or withdraw from potentially arousing situations, such as roller coasters, dates, or hard courses. Further, a persons' acts provide feedback; that is, a person may view his own behavior with alarm. He may recognize that withdrawing from classes will increase his future difficulties in getting the job he wishes. And he may consider the very acts of becoming upset, tense, nauseated, or the like as indications that he needs to do something differently. *Some of the indicants of anxiety may be the effects of as well as the reasons for actions,* particularly in a cultural setting in which the meaning or evaluation of actions are well defined. Indicators labeled as anxiety may also lead to intercorrelations among different domains of operational definitions of anxiety: the person who experiences physiological upset may call himself anxious with the label preceding further actions that are either called anxious or the outcome of anxiety at a physiological level.

Where the person is actively involved in labeling increased physiological arousal in response to aversive stimuli or other behaviors as anxious, he is also very intimately involved in the larger, more explicit, and presumed molar effects of anxiety on behavior. Very often we have seen people in clinical settings who complained that constant anxiety or depression interfered with their work and who, when asked to take records of their behavior, revealed the following pattern: They would start a difficult and not immediately rewarding task, such as studying, become anxious (that is, recognize increased physiological arousal), cease work, and go out for a cigarette or a cup of coffee. Thus, what *immediately* followed the recognition of the condition called anxiety was escape from an unpleasant activity. This escape operationally reinforced the feeling (or recognition) of the condition called anxiety. We will discuss these learning concepts in detail in Chapter 6.

A person may avoid situations without experiencing any physiological arousal; or, to put it differently, he may avoid situations in order not to be aroused. In college certain professors or courses are reputed to be tough and are accordingly avoided. A student may go to great lengths to avoid these ogres without ever having had any experience with the professors or the subject matter they teach. A person who avoids a situation on the basis of actual (but incorrectly perceived) prior experience is *avoiding* rather than *reducing* the physiological correlates of anticipated aversive stimuli. At this point he may engage in the start of an endless regression: he acts because he is *anxious over becoming anxious*. While we have sometimes seen such cases clinically, the condition is rare and, more germane to the present argument, most human avoidance behavior (the presumed result of anxiety) is not in response to autonomic responses (physiological correlates), but to operants (verbal responses, labels) emitted by the person himself. The person and the acts he emits, including signals to himself, is very crucially involved in the generation of "anxiety," which is anything but automatic and autonomic.

Most theories permit operational definitions of anxiety only with great difficulty. When theories such as McReynolds' offer such a definition, an interesting result arises: the usage of the word *anxiety* becomes extraneous. In general, McReynolds defines the condition of anxiety as one in which there is a surplus of unassimilated percepts. This is a general description, but any given person encounters situations with which he cannot or does not deal effectively. Such situations may be lack of knowledge of a foreign language or material in a course. We have to deal not with the anxiety, but with the conditions giving rise to anxiety—that is, in McReynolds' terms, to the unassimilated percepts.

The concept of anxiety is superfluous in dealing directly with people rather than with theories. In a clinical situation we deal with what is being avoided, with what the person needs to learn or unlearn or relearn. We deal best with the individual by staying with his problem, not by theorizing about his problems. In the words of Singer (1970): "Patients seem remarkably willing to forgive the inanities all too often thrown at them; they seem remarkably willing to understand that at best we know little; but they seem rightfully unwilling to forgive us our intentions of having them prove us right in our theoretical preconceptions [p. 390]."

We may ask a final question: What good does the concept of anxiety do us? What does it add to our effectiveness? In the next chapter we advance the idea that a psychological test is valuable only when it reduces error to a greater extent than if it had not been given. If a test does not reduce error to the extent that makes the time and effort of its administration worthwhile, the justification for its use is open to serious question. The same may be asked for the concept of anxiety. Is it necessary? Is it worthwhile? Does it do something unique or does it impose a level of abstraction that is a barrier to effective treatment of people because it makes us think we know something when we do not and should be looking harder? Many psychologists have devoted considerable effort to the formulation and investigation of the concept of anxiety and have found it useful in their theoretical explanations. But many people's belief in a concept does not make the concept correct or scientifically valid. While anxiety has been a central concept and focus for research during the last quarter of a century, we feel free to ask, Can a psychology of personality exist without the concept of anxiety? We attempt such a formulation starting in Chapter 6.

A strong reciprocal relationship exists between a personality concept and its technique of measurement; the two sometimes become so intertwined that the purpose of the tool is quickly lost and the tool becomes the concept. This is illustrated by the concept of anxiety and the growth and development of the Taylor scale to measure it. Levy (1961) surveyed all the entries in *Psychological Abstracts* from 1945 to 1958 and discovered that the percentage of investigations of the concept of anxiety more than doubled (from 0.5 to 1.2) during this period. No great advances in theorizing about anxiety occurred, but this was the period of the publication of the Taylor A scale. Levy also pointed out in his analysis that the behavioral scientist was controlled more by the availability of techniques than by the intrinsic nature of a problem.

The following evaluation by Blake and Mouton (1959) is typical of the criticism of the Taylor A and the mood generated among investigators about it:

The topic of anxiety holds a prominent place in the minds and hearts of personality psychologists. As much effort is devoted to exploring the ins and outs of the anxiety problem as is extended on any single topic. Results for the present year's work and those from previous years, however, are enough to make the anxiety-oriented psychologist anxious over the topic of anxiety!

The basic reason is that anxiety research doesn't add up very fast, but it certainly does multiply. By this time it is reasonably clear that a valid measure, which permits the anxiety dimension of personality to be employed as an estimate of drive, would provide a most useful research instrument. [Investigators] provide critical studies indicating that the Taylor MAS is not it.

Anxiety measures, as with other indices of personality, do not always correlate with what they are supposed to. They sometimes do with what they ought not. Questions have been raised about the Taylor Manifest Anxiety Scale, and a series of studies of the test have appeared. Unfortunately, the studies themselves do not permit unequivocal acceptance or rejection of the measure [p. 209].

Other aspects of the measurement of anxiety are worth mentioning. One is the fact that the Taylor scale, whatever it measures, measures only one form of "anxiety" at best. Taylor and Spence (1954) found that individuals classified as anxiety neurotics did not score higher on the Taylor A than those not so labeled. This finding questions the usefulness of the scale.

We have indicated that the concept of anxiety serves many functions. As a final example, during this period "anxiety" served as a link between the study of personality and Hullian learning theory. Farber (1954) argued that "manifest anxiety has the functional properties of a drive [p. 3]." In Hullian theory, the reduction of this drive is considered reinforcing. Hence, anxiety was considered to be an *energizer,* or a drive in learning terms. The existence of anxiety as a force or entity was also the basis for research in perceptual defense and for the formulation of the psychoanalytic defense mechanisms. Despite its theoretical importance, one of the major gaps in anxiety research was the paucity of investigations of the reinforcing properties of anxiety reduction at the human level. Most of the theorizing was based on animal studies, such as that of Solomon and Brush (1956).

We have described the research of the last two decades in terms of one organizing concept, anxiety. The questions we asked, however, apply to abstract, organizing concepts in general. We need to ask *what* are we talking about with *what effect* on our behavior.

We next turn to another characteristic of research of this period, the tool of investigation, psychological tests.

Psychological Tests

A review of the testing literature of the 1950s and 1960s seems to point out clearly that "most of the measures used to tap presumably stable personality characteristics have been attacked as not measuring what they are purported to measure [Christie and Lindauer, 1963, p. 201]." Further, it has become increasingly clear that performance on objective personality tests is further confused by the influence of a set of variables considered to be contaminants or spoilers or possibly even "personality characteristics" in their own right. These are the response sets.

The term *response set* refers to a consistency in responding to test items that is unrelated to stimulus differences. *Social desirability* (SD), the tendency to endorse items in a manner to make the respondent look good is the most important response set at the present time.

The SD scales were initiated by Edwards (1957) and by Crowne and Marlowe (1960). "The original interest in social desirability was to eliminate its effects as much as possible as a scaling artifact and many of the arguments centered around the extent to which this was in fact done. Recently the focus seems to be shifting toward interest in personality differences between those scoring high or low in self-ascription of desirable attributes [Christie and Landauer, 1963, p. 203]."

The current role of social desirability as an influence in responding to tests has been summarized by Mischel (1968):

> For example, on psychiatric inventories scores on scales depend on the respondent's willingness to endorse socially undesirable statements such as confessions about bizarre behavior, irregular bowel habits and somatic complaints, or eccentric and socially taboo thoughts. A person's scores therefore may reflect the degree to which he endorses socially desirable items rather than either autobiographical events or underlying traits. Consequently the associations found among different self-report measures may reflect commonalities due to the subject's endorsement of desirable items on diverse scales regardless of specific content. In light of these problems it can be quite misleading to interpret the correlations between inventories as evidence for covariations between the trait labels assigned to the tests.
>
> Correlations between the rated social desirability value of items and the proportion of subjects who endorse them on personality questionnaires tend to be quite high, often exceeding .80 and sometimes even .90. Moreover, high correlations are found between the tendency to endorse socially desirable items (SD) and scores on most personality questionnaires. The correlation between SD and the Manifest Anxiety Scale, for example, was −.84 (Edwards, 1957) [pp. 83–84].

A second major response set is *acquiescence*, or the tendency of people to agree with sentences that involve ambiguous attitude statements irrespective of their specific content. Other response sets include tendency to check extremes, or to check "don't know" answers, or to falsify responses. Many investigators have argued that response sets may account for the major variance on self-report inventories (Couch and Keniston, 1961; Jackson and Messick, 1958; Messick and Jackson, 1961; Wiggins, 1964).

Just as among subjects, so with investigators and critics; there are yea sayers and nay sayers. The yea sayers among the testers such as Block (1965) and Rorer (1965) have presented evidence that response styles do *not* account for systematic variance and scale scores. In contrast, the nay sayers among the critics have interpreted test performance in terms of response sets rather than target "personality traits." The major point is that what is being measured in personality tests is unclear. The second point is that developers of the personality measures have in effect created a circular world in which they test each other's concepts about the nature of their instruments.

The fact that scores of one inventory correlate with another devised in a similar manner leads some experts to talk of personality factors or constructs. This in no way means that the results will lead to greater effectiveness in dealing with people. One of Mischel's most important contributions in his 1968 book was his summarizing how *little evidence there is for the generality of test behavior*. In a recent typical sample, Seitz (1970) found that five tests of depression given to neurotically depressed inpatients generally correlated quite highly with each other but not significantly with psychiatric ratings. One cannot prove the null hypothesis and it is more than possible to quarrel with the criteria of psychiatric ratings. However, *repeated* findings of this nature raise questions about how psychological measurement may be improved.

Holtzman (1965) reviewed the reports on social desirability and acquiescence in paper-and-pencil inventories. His comments and critique are those of a leading proponent of the internal orientation, since Holtzman's own research is well within the traditional personality mode. In reviewing more than fifty publications at the height of the social desirability controversy, Holtzman (1965) commented as follows:

> Indeed, so much attention has been given recently to the internal psychometric characteristics of questionnaires that many investigators seem to have forgotten the importance of demonstrating external correlations with independent, behavioral measures before making strong claims for validity as personality measures [p. 123].
>
> While the last word has hardly been said on the nature of social desirability, acquiescence, and other test-taking attitudes, it is apparent from the work thus far that they vary considerably according to the type of test item and the conditions of administration, as well as the individual taking the test. The behavioral correlates of these stylistic or response set scales are few in number and of questionable significance. As yet they tell us very little about personality structure in spite of the great amount of attention they have received [p. 127].

Similar critical comments about personality research in these two decades are legion. Almost every reviewer of the period had his own pet bête noire. Blake and Mouton (1959) expressed it succinctly:

> "Gad, what a mess!" constitutes one appraisal of personality literature, which emphasizes its brittleness and the fact that results from one study frequently break and disappear under replication. This appraisal also takes into consideration the fact that the area is ridden with results from one experiment which contradict those from another. Another evaluation is that progress will be limited until more valid measures of personality parameters are available. A third is that many improvements are possible in the formulations of problems and in the research designs by which they are approached. All seem to be justified statements, yet they fail to identify the drama of present-day personality research [p. 226].

By "drama" the authors referred to a subtle point about the interest and motivation of the investigators. Based on frequency of empirical reports, the major interest in personality research during the 1960s seems to have been the triumvirate of achievement, anxiety, and authoritarianism. The reasons for the interest and involvement were twofold. First, these areas cover major aspects of contemporary American life. Second, and more importantly, the attractiveness of these topics was due to the availability of psychological tests that supposedly measured them.

The attraction to an investigator of the tool is well expressed by Jensen's astute observation (1958):

> the formula for creating a research craze of proliferation and longevity consists of making available an easy-to-use measuring device with a significant label and fascinating content. Factorially it should be as multidimensional as possible, so that it will yield significant correlations with a host of other psychological measures. Such has been the case with the questionnaires of authoritarian attitudes, particularly the well-known F Scale [p. 306].

Sarason and Smith (1971) added their criticisms to other reviewers' assessments of personality attributes. They summarized the situation by pointing out that "After a test has been published or a new technique announced, it may continue to be used in the absence of any convincing evidence in its favor [pp. 397–398]."

Approaches to Traits

As we have seen in Chapters 2 and 3, the investigation of personality that postulates the existence of certain specific behavioral characteristics such as rigidity or altruism has been enormously popular. A major method of research during this period has been the use of the statistical technique of factor analysis to study traits.

Factor analysis is an attempt to achieve orderliness among disorderly facts. The basic facts are usually discrete yes-or-no responses to questions on objective personality inventories (for example, the MMPI has 550 questions). In seeking the intercorrelations between items, the investigator essentially attempts to determine which items belong together. That is, does a yes to item X mean the person is also highly likely to respond with a yes to item Y? The general procedure is to attempt to discover the *factors* which account for the major portions of variance in response to the personality tests. The development of machines able to do the computations rapidly and inexpensively bolstered this line of inquiry.

It should also be noted that investigators such as Schein (1954) and Seward (1954) argued for a learning theory interpretation of the development of traits. They attributed the development of traits to imitative behavior engaged in under the influence of reward and punishment. Other considerations that might lead to obtained factors may be regularities in the respondents' culture and the structure of the language that is shared by test makers and takers.

Perhaps the major criticism of the factor analytic approach is that its basic data are arrived at from performance on questionnaires and inventories which in no way involve specific situations and interactions with other people. A careful analysis of the array of characteristics that have been found to covary in the various factor analytic studies reveals confusion, overlap, contradictions, and puzzlement. The spirit of this criticism is captured by Allport (1958), one of the theorists most responsible for the development of trait theory: "When units of this sort appear—and I submit that it happens not infrequently—one wonders what to say about them. To me they resemble sausage meat that has failed to pass the pure food and health inspection [p. 251]."

Integrative Theorizing

A major feature of the 1950s and 1960s was a lament by investigators about the lack of integrative theorizing to bring together the mass of experimental data being generated, especially in social psychology. This lack of integrative theory in social psychology contrasted with the data in the personality field, which had no dearth of theoretical possibilities (as we saw in Chapter 3). Whether a lack of theory to guide the gathering of data is undesirable is another question on which there is sharp disagreement. We would contend a theoretical model of man (implicit or explicit) always influences the observations an investigator makes and the kinds of circumstances in which he makes them. This is true even when there is an avowed denial of the existence or even the need for a theory.

Funds and People

Two other aspects in evaluating research for its relevance to a psychology of behavior influence are the source of funding of the projects and the specific population being observed. During the 1950s and 1960s a considerable portion of the research in social psychology was financed by various military and business organizations (Cartwright, 1957). It seems reasonable to assume that at least a portion of these studies were intended to provide information relevant to the goals of the sponsoring organization. This assumption is not intended as a criticism of the research itself, but as an observation of possible sources of influence on the investigator's behavior.

As to the nature of research populations, those reviewing the field have repeatedly criticized the overwhelming reliance upon the college student (usually the sophomore, because that's when introductory psychology is generally taken) as the subject of social psychology and personality research. Since college sophomores are a small part of the total population of the country—being young, bright, verbal, and living in an unusual environment—there should be considerable doubt about the generalizability of conclusions derived from research on this group to the population as a whole or to people in other situations such as a factory or the army.

Dichotomies

The 1950s and 1960s were characterized by dichotomies in theories and ways of looking at human behavior. The most dramatic dichotomy was that between the person and the situation as the focus for investigation. Most personality research has concentrated solely on the person. This is implicit in trait theories, factor analytic approaches, and the use of tests such as the MMPI.

In very broad terms two major theoretical streams, or paradigms, have influenced investigators. One stream is the dynamic, psychoanalytic, cognitive, inner-determined view of man's actions. The other stream views behavior as influenced by situational and social role determinants. Despite the misconception that they are necessarily situationalists, learning theorists may also be dichotomized on this internal-external split. The Hullian learning theory view with its emphasis on drive is internally oriented, whereas the Skinnerian learning theory is far more compatible with situationalism.

A shift has occurred in what are considered to be the generally accepted belief systems of investigators. In the early 1950s the predominant view of investigators of personality was that internal influences were of sole or major importance. Situational determinants were relegated to the amorphous domain of the sociologist. In two decades the situation has changed to the extent that Sarason and Smith (1971) felt called upon to defend personality psychologists who emphasize dispositional variables against the onslaught of situational proponents:

> There can be no quarrel with the position that stimulus factors are powerful determinants of behavior. However, we do question the scientific wisdom of simply relegating, as it were, individual differences to the "error term." Their systematic inclusion in research designs allows not only the study of situational variables, but also assessment of the manner in which individual differences serve to moderate S–R relationships. Every study in which significant interactions emerge between personality and situational variables . . . underlies the fallaciousness of attempts to understand behavior without considering what individuals bring with them to laboratory, clinical, and everyday life situations [p. 393].

It is clear that in this issue each side exaggerates and misrepresents the position of the other. A resolution of the two divergent views would have to involve an interactionist position. People obviously differ in terms of physical and social characteristics and learning history. Any analysis of a current behavior situation must consider the interaction between what the subject brings to the situation because of his prior experiences and genetic constitution, and the many environmental variables discussed throughout this book.

Sarason and Smith (1971) point out that one of the most significant developments in personality research during the past two decades has been an approach that

> incorporated *both* individual differences and experimentally manipulated variables. The aim of researchers who use this approach is to increase the meaningfulness of experimental results by applying treatments not to random samples, but to subjects who differ on theoretically relevant dimensions. The designs employed in this endeavor not only reduce error variance but also provide opportunities to demonstrate construct validity [p. 396].

A related dichotomy that emerged during this period is that between the ideographic and the nomothetic, as typified by the debate between Holt (1962) and G. W. Allport (1962). Holt criticized the romantic movement in science and concluded that there is no need for a special type of science to be applied to individual personalities and suggested throwing out the terms *ideographic* and *nomothetic*. Allport, on the other hand, called for unique repeated questionnaires tailored to the individual to capture peak experiences.

A final dichotomy worth noting is Hebb's designation (1951) of the "right" and "left" wing in psychology. On one side the "narrow mechanists" opposed those with freer but "'vaguer" views. Hebb, like most psychologists, prefers to think of himself as leftwing in this categorization in contrast to "rightwing mechanists." This kind of right-left dichotomy, with its political overtones, has continued to the present day. The investigator with a behavioral viewpoint is imputed to have more conservative social views than his colleague with a nondirective or humanistic approach. The attempt to correlate an investigator's scientific views with his political views is relevant in understanding the aims and impact of certain investigators and is discussed in Chapter 7. We hope, however, that the present volume may give the lie to sweeping statements that behaviorists are mechanistic or even, as Singer (1970, p. xix) implied, "fascists."

Trends in Research

Many trends in research can be discerned in the 1950s and 1960s. Coordinated, programmatic series of researches were developed from a theoretical position through a series of laboratory studies to social applications (for example, McClelland and the need achievement studies). However, most of the research in both personality and social psychology was characterized by one-shot experiments. While these occasionally led to suggestions for new techniques and hypotheses, the results were not usually replicated or followed up and had little relevance for further work.

This lack of followup is in line with the observation of Eriksen (1957) that whereas experimental approaches to personality are becoming increasingly ingenious and sophisticated, scholarship seems to be decreasing. Many investigators have made little effort to relate their findings to those of other investigators. The lack of integration and scattering of effort so characteristic of this period has resulted in the optimistic views of some investigators that everything points our way and the pessimistic views that it's all over for us and our field. The former, optimistic position has been evidenced by diverse writers' views that *cognitive concepts* or *learning theory* (both sides are equally guilty) were now the favored explanatory concepts of the science. In effect, such investigators tended to see the trends in their fields as moving in their own theoretical directions.

The latter, pessimistic position was evidenced in a Blake and Mouton (1959) observation that "As an independent, isolated compartment, personality is on its way to oblivion [p. 203]"; these authors generally contended that "The study of personality is blending with, and, somewhat tortuously, finding its place in a more systematic approach to behavior [p. 204]."

Despite such predictions, the study of personality has not merged into a systematic field of behavior. Research in personality as a *separate entity* has characterized the entire period; and such separate research is not diminishing, despite the repeated predictions of its demise. In Chapter 7, on the role of the influencer, we will look at the kinds of variables that help maintain a line of investigation regardless of its success in solving a scientific problem.

A related trend was the move of personality research to some extent from laboratory to the field; while in contrast, and perhaps ironically, research in social psychology moved in the opposite direction. Personality investigation had been too rigidly bound to the paper-and-pencil inventory filled in by a college sophomore, while social psychology research had frequently been too loose and uncontrolled in its observations of very real social events. The obvious kinds of self-corrections and overcorrections started to occur.

Throughout the decades of the 1950s and 1960s investigators urged that there be greater social relevance in research. The desirability of an area being socially relevant is obviously not a new notion. This is particularly so in personality and social psychology, in part, because of the obvious relationship between these fields of investigation and the general world. Yet most investigators have been frustrated in their desire for relevance and application, primarily because of the weakness of their theories and techniques. While praising the "quality" of research, Heyns (1958) noted that social psychologists are simply unsuccessful in predicting social behavior from the current measures of personality. Festinger (1955) pointed to the "lack of well-defined personality variables which have clear social implications [p. 192]" as the reason for so little research on the relationship between personality and social behavior. In surveying the field at that time, the only exception Festinger spotted was the California F Scale.

Other ramifications of research involve concepts of specialization, communication, criticism, and public consumption of research (particularly that of the psychological test). Wiggins (1968) summarized this aspect of the research situation:

> First, we appear to be in an era of such extreme methodological and conceptual specialization that communication between investigators, never satisfactory to begin with, threatens to break down. Second, the tone of critical writing and convention discussion has taken on an *ad hominem* quality that, at times, exceeds the limits of good taste. Third, despite an unprecedented number of historical reviews and critiques, there appears to be an increased bewilderment as to how the issue arose and where it might be leading us. Finally, let us consider the plight of the much-neglected test consumer who deals with people rather than computers. Battles over alternative explanations of test variance may be viewed from a different perspective when it is realized that the disputed variance is associated with, at best, about 16 percent of the variance of any socially relevant criterion measure [p. 294].

One of the most revealing studies of trends in research was Lambert's content analysis (1963) of the studies appearing in the 1960 volume of the *Journal of Abnormal and Social Psychology*, the major prestige publication in the field of social and deviant behavior at the time. Of the 119 relationships between independent and dependent variables reported, 61 were conceptually explained by one of three general theories: 22 by cognitive theory, 20 by behavior theory, and 19 by Freudian theory. This distribution of theoretical explanation reflects where things were conceptually during the two decades.

Lambert compared the results of this 1963 study to his earlier (1952) investigation. Based on that comparison, during the 1950s, trait theory as an explanatory concept had declined from 17 percent to 7 percent; behavioral explanations had increased from 5 percent to 18 percent; and Freudian and cognitive explanations had also increased slightly; whereas "attitudes" and "mental illness" as explanatory concepts for behavior had sharply dropped. The overall trend indicated a higher percentage of "truly experimental reports," up from 30 percent to 56 percent. Lambert concluded that "most of these studies reflect the fact that different theories identify and deal with different phenomena, although some cross over into what is usually another theory's territory" [Berger and Lambert, 1968, p. 122]." Since different theorists deal with problems in line with their own formulations, studies by different theorists are not really comparable.

Many other events during this twenty-year period are relevant to the study of human behavior. There was no shortage of research and investigation into concepts such as maturation; aggression; social psychophysiology; communication; attitudes; opinions; groups; cognitive dissonance; affiliation; sociometry; congruity; computer simulation; impulse control; awareness; perceptual defense; Guilford's dimensions of aptitude, temperament, motivation, and pathology; and field dependence—to name a few. We are optimistic that enough ideas and data are available to develop an exciting and useful psychology of behavior influence.

LAST WORD

Investigation of human behavior in the fields of personality and social psychology has been reviewed for the period from 1950 to 1970. While a great deal of data was collected during two decades, the net result was an increase in design and technical skill rather than a major breakthrough in either theory or practice. Investigations were influenced by political and social concerns and centered on topics of general interest or relevance such as anxiety, authoritarianism, and achievement. The pay-off behavior in the academic circles from which the majority of investigators were drawn was frequent publication; and the availability of measures, subjects, and financial support strongly biased the direction of research. At times, the very fact that a paper had been published seemed to serve to legitimize a topic as proper for further investigation. Broad issues and controversies continued from earlier periods. These included disputes over the relative influence of.heredity and environment, internal versus external determination of behavior, and the impact of the investigator's theory on his behavior. Current research in this field is characterized by controversy, diversity, laboratory orientation, triviality, tight design, and a growing concern with social and ethical implications.

Measurement of Behavior Influence and Personality

Qualification is a crucial aid in the psychologist's efforts to become more effective. While not all enumeration is scientific, eventually all scientific efforts must quantify. We count in order to keep record, and in so doing have a method for comparing larger groups of instances than we could otherwise handle. There is a limit to the number of objects, people, or experiences that a human can keep in mind with clarity and detail. Thereafter, error is likely to be introduced as some person, instance, or event is overlooked or overemphasized.

Numbering is first and foremost a tool. It is a *means, not an end* in itself. Numbers for the sake of numbers yield the image but not the substance of science; if not used in correct ways numbers may not only *not* help but may actually mislead. Using numbers in erroneous forms is called "lying with statistics," and some classic examples are given in Ullmann and Krasner (1969, ch. 3). Aside from the forms of numbers, the method of assigning numbers may lead to error. The manner of assigning numbers—that is, designating what the numbers stand for—may be trivial, sloppy, or arbitrary in its reflection of variables other than those presumably being measured; in other words, be irrelevant and thus mislead.

Second, numbers are *abstractions*. This quality has both an advantage and disadvantage. We can develop rules for operations on the numbers, and this ability extends our power to reduce massive amounts of experience into usable form. An advanced illustration of this is factor analysis, while a common example is the average used in batting statistics or grade-point standing. The disadvantage of numbers as abstractions is that each categorization and operation removes the material further from the objects, events, and characteristics of the people being measured. *We do not emit average responses, although our responses can be averaged.* Willie Mays may have had a .300 batting average, but he never had a .3 hit.

The concept of average introduces an additional element to the data being analyzed. An "average" is a way of talking *about* an instance but not the instance itself. To be concrete, when a boy says he kissed a girl an average number of times, he actually kissed her once, five, or ten times. Further, he may have kissed her with a forcefulness central on the scale of fervor which is part of the universal osculation index (UOI). But the boy was not making checkmarks to carefully rate his fervor, technique, frequency, pressure, and duration. To say his behavior was average is to talk *about* his behavior, to *compare* his behavior, but is very specifically *not* the behavior itself. We cannot do without enumeration, but we should never confuse the measurement with what is being measured nor give the measurement (an abstraction) as a descriptive, explanatory, or predictive reality that it does not have. Things may happen at the same time or immediately after a rapid increase in the UOI, but *the index is in no way causal or explanatory of these acts.* The point that numbers are abstractions and not the real goods is analogous to our repeated observations that concepts are useful verbal labels, but they are never the same as the events they denote.

THEORY AND BEHAVIOR MEASURED

We are interested in consequential behavior, behavior that is intended to have an impact. The investigator's theory plays a key role in his determination of what behaviors or events to study and hence describe, predict, and alter. If he believes—as did some nineteenth-century psychiatrists (Caplan, 1969)—that the intellect is mediated by the body and that deficits in behavior are associated with bodily defects, then he will measure sensorimotor modalities in a manner

not dissimilar to the early studies of individual differences by the late nineteenth-century psychologists such as Galton and Cattell. If he thinks that man
is actuated by innate needs such as dominance, sex, or aggression, he will measure
these needs. If he thinks that behavior is mediated by physiological changes,
he will focus on measures such as blood pressure, galvanic skin response, and
respiration. If he thinks that the unresolved and unsatisfied yearnings of childhood dominate current life, he will be particularly interested in the individual's
early childhood relationships and their residuals. If he believes that human
capacities are innate, he will measure abilities; if social attainments seem crucial
to him, then achievement tests will be his tool. Thus, an investigator's theory or
model of man's behavior has crucial consequences in determining where and
how he looks and what he finds. We have seen this in the preceding chapters on
the history of man's study of man.

Theories are tested by contact with the world they describe. Data consistent, inconsistent, or irrelevant to a theory can be collected. *But a good theory
leads to hypotheses that can be tested.* Theories that do not permit contact
with reality by having potential for proof or disproof are too vague to be used
to deal with the events which we as individuals must face and eventually alter.

In either freely occurring naturalistic events or controlled experiments,
*enumeration has the goal of altering the behavior of the psychologist or other
consumer of information.* That is, an experiment is designed to influence someone's behavior. The information is developed to be "persuasive," that is, to
offer a minimum number of alternative explanations or theories consistent
with the data.

In similar fashion we collect data (that is, measurements) to be able to
make a decision about or to alter our behavior toward other people. Personality tests or other measures may be used to help decide whether to offer psychotherapy, to hospitalize, to hire, to admit to college or to special training, to
become a pilot, or to play a musical instrument. In contrast to theory testing,
these decisions seem to be different, that is, applied. However, practical, applied
testing is similar in several ways to theory testing. The first similarity is that
the data is collected to help make a choice in the face of uncertainty. Usefulness
does not necessarily depend on perfect certainty, but on reducing the degree
of uncertainty to the point that the person is more effective than he would be
without the data.

A *second similarity is that the data must be germane.* We touched on this
in Chapter 1, but should reiterate that the adequacy of the decision provides a
measure of validity. A comparison of what selected (tested) subjects and
randomly assigned (untested) subjects have gained from training in, say, music
or flying provides a measure of the usefulness of screening in reducing error.
The measures useful in selecting future pilots may very well be irrelevant in
selecting people to study violin.

When a person makes a decision he is implicitly making a prediction about the results of acting on the available alternatives. Both theory testing and applied testing involve such predictions. In the next two sections two other similarities are taken up. The first is that the content of a test is always a *sample* of behavior. The second is that when a test or a sample is used, *theory* plays a vital role in the strategy of interpretation.

Some Testing Considerations

Whenever we refer to dependent variables in experiments, the acts of measurement and experimentation are behaviors emitted by people. *What we collect, analyze, and use for reducing uncertainty are behaviors by people.*[1] The professional selects behaviors that he deems significant; he develops situations that permit him to reduce uncertainty about the consequences of his decision; he generates and uses data that he can evaluate to improve in his later work. *The psychological tester is acting, and his behavior is where testing starts.*

The following example begins to make explicit the similarities and differences between a psychologist working professionally and a typical human being making a decision. Suppose a friend asks you to fix him up with a date.[2] The first thing one usually seeks to establish is the sort of event that is to occur. Things in general will go better if the woman has the abilities the occasion calls for—interest in classical music if the date is for a concert, knowledge of dancing if it is for a prom. Other questions that may be asked are if the friend is interested in a conversationalist, a decorative partner, or a physical or emotional relationship of long or short duration. *The decision starts with what must be decided—with a definition of the task.*

Some of your friend's requirements are relatively easy to measure. First, he wants to date a woman. In similar fashion, he may prefer one who is shorter than he; therefore she should not be more than five feet eight inches. Finally, he has a marked preference for redheads, but he does not exclude the possibility that blondes may also be attractive. The woman's height could be measured with a tape, but in this case an estimate is satisfactory. Given the range provided by art, nature, and the vagaries of lighting, "redhead" designates a sweep of colors and not a definitive identity. While biological femininity is usually clearly established, psychological and social femininity are much more complex and their definitions change both across cultures and during a person's own life. These observations reveal, first, that *seemingly obvious definitions may not be*

[1] Exceptions are (*a*) sociological and demographic variables such as age, birth order, sex, education, social class, biographical data; (*b*) physiological indices such as palmistry, phrenology, and Sheldon body typing; (*c*) astrology. But the *collection* of even these materials is done by human beings and thus comes within the aegis of behavior influence.
[2] Reports from sporadically reliable offspring indicate that the concept of "a date" is becoming archaic. Its usage may illustrate a greater cultural lag than the authors would like to admit.

as simple as they appear and, second, that *some specifications may be within a range and as long as they suffice, they need not and usually will not be explicated further.*

If the date is for a concert, you might think of women whom you had taken to concerts or seen at similar events. And you might think of the opinions they had expressed or interest they had shown. Barring this, you might think of women who select activities likely to be close to concert music; you might think of a student in fine arts rather than in physical education. *Thus, in testing, one moves from what he knows to a probability of response in the future.* Many women studying painting do not like Bach and many future teachers of physical education do. You will make an estimate, and nothing more.

At the next step either you (as a professional behavior influencer) or your friend (if he's not too shy) will call up the woman. She may already have a date for the time of the concert. This point is not trivial: *the decision must be feasible.* Further, *decisions are likely to involve progressions of acts of a go–no go nature.* Telephoning a woman is an action based on a decision. Finding out that she is busy and calling another one is an example of feedback leading to a new progression of behaviors.

Referring back to our example, your friend may want a combination of Wanda Landowska and Raquel Welch. In psychiatric hospitals a frequent recommendation on personality evaluation reports is that the patient receive individual psychotherapy. But, since this resource is very limited, the suggestion is not implemented; the decision is useless and irrelevant, because its consequences are the same as if the evaluation process had not occurred. Either the evaluation process is not necessary—it is so general that it applies to everyone—or it leads to an impossibility, so that no differential action can be taken. The evaluation may be continued, but not for its original purpose of making decisions.

A related consideration is the *cost* of gathering the data on which to base the decision. Some information is easy to obtain without any great effort of time or money; some information is expensive. If the information required to help make the decision is too costly, it will not be collected. For example, you might best be able to ascertain a woman's reaction to concert music if you took her to a concert yourself. You are not likely to do so, however, just for the sake of your friend. You would be making as great an investment of time and money to obtain data as he would. The data would be as costly as the decision. Even if you did collect the data, you would still have to generalize from one concert program to another and one person (yourself) to another (him). A good deal of uncertainty would still remain, even though the cost of the information was as great as the decision.

In applied situations, if the cost of the information is too great, the screening procedure may well be eliminated. If it takes twelve hours to administer, score, and write up a full psychological evaluation in order to decide whether a person should receive brief psychotherapy or not, it seems more reasonable (and time saving) to give a trial program of such treatment.

Finally, the uncertainty reduced by testing is not complete. The cost of the evaluation must not only be lower than the amount risked in the decision but must also be less than the amount lost by a failure to reduce the uncertainty to the extent that the test does. That is, the testing must save time, effort, or reduce uncertainty to an extent that makes it worthwhile.

In research where a theory being tested may be used in many ways, a decision between theories has great value in deciding future behaviors. The collection of data in experiments can legitimately be very costly. In similar fashion, if a result will be used repeatedly, it is permissible for the cost of the first decision to be high. For example, the research involved in evaluating the relative efficacy of two forms of psychotherapy may call for very expensive measures. This cost is acceptable, since one or the other form of therapy will be chosen repeatedly in the future and the cost of the validation procedures can be spread over many future cases. The cost of the first decision will be made up by its repeated later use. Moreover, *no* research would be very expensive in terms of time, money, and effort wasted by an ineffective procedure.

A potential danger, however, is inherent in efforts to test the effectiveness of psychotherapy. Research is expensive and time consuming. Decisions dealing with people frequently have to be made rapidly. The pressure is great to use the best information available, even though the information itself may have been collected in other contexts and for very different purposes. For example, if a form of treatment called systematic desensitization is demonstrably superior to neopsychoanalytic or nondirective therapy in alleviating college students' speech anxiety (for example, see Paul, 1966), is it also necessarily better for businessmen who have speech anxiety—that is, for a different population with the same problem—or college students who have authority problems—the same population but a different problem? Choices need to be made, but the data appropriate for one situation may not exist in another. At this point, data is stretched (psychologists prefer to use the word *generalized*). In addition, students, businessmen, types of· authority problems, and one's conception of anxiety may change over time. When do the data which went into making a choice—even if arrived at in the best scientific manner at the time—become so dated and hence irrelevant that they are stretched too far?

Personality Measurement as Behavior Sampling

As an evaluator of behavior, the psychologist has the same task as a layman fixing a date for his friend. He gathers data relevant to the problem and on the basis of this information makes as good a guess as he can. Some data are presented in terms of what the choice actually is; some data involve ascertaining the range of choices as clearly as possible; and some data are evaluations of the costs of various decisions and data collection. By definition, a professional is one who collects data, although there is an enormous difference in *how* professionals collect data and even in just *what* phenomena they include as data. The sources and the types of data involved may be roughly listed and categorized, although they overlap considerably. The psychologist, for example, may determine (observe, hypothesize, or guess at) the necessary capacities the ideal person should have and measure them in a specific individual. The tools include tests of intelligence for academic work and measures of pitch, tempo, and loudness for musical training.

The psychologist may interview the person about whom he must make a decision. He may formalize his interview to the point of asking set questions through writing (psychological inventories). He may ask the person to observe himself and report on his previous behavior (historical survey, self-report) or he may interview informants (parents, teachers, spouse). He may place the person in an unusual (and controlled) situation and observe his behavior. The situation may be the target activity or one close enough to it to be called a *work sample*.

All these measures deal with the person's behavior. The basic data of tests are *what the person actually did*. The student's heartbeat may increase; he may sweat noticeably and stammer; he may say he is uncomfortable; he may see a volcano on an inkblot; he may rate the concept *interviews like this* as *cold*, *dangerous*, and *unpredictable*; and he may not be able to tell in what way *hot* and *cold* are similar. These are his acts, his behaviors. From these data the psychologist makes decisions.

But if our criterion for tests is efficiency in prediction, we may not even have to go through the rigors of sampling the subject's behaviors. There is considerable evidence that straightforward sociological variables such as age, education, sex, social class, race, or marital status—either singly or in combination—may give us the data necessary to make predictions. The friend who wants a date probably does not have a sixty-year-old married woman in mind.

We have used test and measurement rather interchangeably and will continue to do so, even though tradition holds that a *test* is used to make a decision about an individual, while a *measurement* is used for making general decisions, as in an experiment. Usually we use the word *measurement* for a theoretical purpose, *test* for an applied task; but the distinction is not regularly maintained, especially since devices such as a Rorschach or an intelligence test may be used for both purposes. When the dependent variable—that is, measurement—is a test (for example, the Stanford-Binet) for differences in intelligence quotient after nursery school or no nursery school (independent variable)—the distinction seems trivial. In similar fashion, a measurement may be considered as an assignment of numbers, while a test may be considered as a situation (usually standardized) used to obtain a sample of behavior to which numbers may be assigned. Here the test may be considered the situation and the person's acts the "test responses." This distinction has some value: testing refers to subject behavior, while measurement refers to examiner behavior.

As noted in Chapter 1, the person always acts in an environment. A number of factors are necessary to evaluate a behavior in order to make a decision. The first, as noted above, is a delineation of the decision itself—what is the test to decide? The second requirement is a knowledge of the situation in which the behavior is observed. Because different situations are likely to yield different behaviors from the same person, the psychologist aims to make the test situation as *standard* as possible. He may carefully specify the stimuli, including his own behavior, so that he or another psychologist at another time can duplicate as closely as possible the stimuli which the person being evaluated experiences. Our target is the comparison of people. When differences in the situation cannot be discriminated from differences between the people we wish to investigate, the measure is *confounded* and we cannot rule out alternative explanations. If all women take a psychology course from Krasner and all men take it from Ullmann, and if the women obtain significantly higher test scores, we do not know if this is due to the natural superiority of women over men or of Krasner over Ullmann.

Psychological tests offer a way of keeping *some* of the stimuli in the situation constant. The test materials are not the only stimuli in the situation. The materials—inkblots or true-false questions—should not be confused with the test situation, of which *they are merely a part*. The examiner's ability to establish rapport and the purpose of the test—for a desired job or an unwanted hospitalization—are also aspects of the test situation. Tests may be administered to individuals or groups; tests may be of abilities or personality traits (that is, tests of "power" or tests of "typical behavior"); and tests may use either linguistic or nonverbal responses.

After what is to be tested has been decided and the appropriate test material selected, the third major consideration is the person to whom the test is to be given. We have noted that the testing situation may vary and allow the introduction of different behaviors in response to the same material. But the subject is not born at the time of the test; he brings to it a host of prior learnings. If the examiner does not take these differences into account, he may consider a difference in test behavior as associated with or indicative of something to which it is unrelated. This is particularly likely in intelligence testing. The major variables of the people currently studied are age, sex, race, and social class. Ability, as defined by increasing mental age on intelligence tests, generally increases with chronological age until roughly the midteens, then decreases slowly, and then more rapidly from age fifty onward. A subject's behavior on a test such as the Wechsler-Bellevue must be evaluated in terms of the performance of others of the same age. These comparative data are called *norms*. In similar fashion, if people report that they are interested in cooking, flower arranging, love poems, and home decorations and not in politics, athletics, motors, and adventure novels, we are likely to evaluate the reports differently depending on whether the subjects are men or women. Even such an evaluation may have to be changed because of the rapid social changes occurring in typical sex roles.

Failure to consider differences of sex, age, race, and social class may lead to serious error in testing.[3] When taken into account, these variables may explain much of the variation in people's responses to situations. A skin color or religion does not lead to a difference in response, but may lead to different life experiences, which are in turn associated with differences in responses. For the interim, use of different norms reduces error and offers in itself a basis for prediction of behavior.

A final factor in measurement is *interpretation*, the procedure by which the assigned numbers are used to make predictions. Interpretation in turn leads to further application of theory.

MEASUREMENT CONSIDERATIONS—THEORY

Tests may be used to make applied or social decisions or to increase data supporting or rejecting a theory. The cost of data may be considerably greater when a theory is being tested than when a clinical decision has to be made. A first consideration in theory-based measurement is that *a theory is general in nature*: it applies to a wide range of situations and persons. It can be used with many people and situations, and hence the cost is shared.

Content

If data are being collected to test a theory, the psychologist will select the data that are as germane as possible to the theory—just as material for a work sample should be as germane to the task as possible. Aside from common sense, some empirical data indicate the correctness of such an approach; for example, Goldberg and Slovic (1967) found that items with low "face" (content) validity had low empirical validity, while items with higher face validity (seemingly relevant content) were spread widely in empirical validity. That is, face, or content, validity seems to be a necessary but not a sufficient condition for the appropriateness of what an item purports to measure.

The first order of business in test construction, then, is for the test builder

---

[3] Social class, race, and sex differences may lead to differences in behavior towards an individual that are unrelated to the overt behavior that is purportedly the subject of evaluation. This may occur in the clinical setting (see Gross, Herbert, Knatterub, and Donner, 1969, for a recent example) or in interpretation of a projective test (see Levy and Kahn, 1970, for a recent example). The different values that different professional groups may bring to the evaluation of the same people and behavior is illustrated by the classroom teacher's greater concern with immediate overt behavior such as disruption and the psychologist's greater concern with indicants of longer-term problem behavior or deficits such as social withdrawal (see Ziv, 1970, for a recent example of work in this area).

to determine the task or target. If he is interested in a system of types, he will devise material that he expects will tap the definitive characteristics of the types which interest him. For example, the Allport-Vernon-Lindzey test was constructed of material relevant to economic, social, theoretical, and artistic types. If the investigator is interested in underlying needs or motives, such as followers of Murray, he will design the test to increase the likelihood of eliciting material useful in a motivational interpretation: dominance, nurturance, or need achievement.

The instructions to the subject also will be designed to increase the chances of obtaining relevant and easily scorable material. For example, if one were interested in internal or subjective needs, environmental conditions, the person's actions, and the results of the interaction of these variables, one might show the subject pictures of different interpersonal situations—for example, a young and an older man looking at each other—and ask him to make up a story for each and to tell how each person feels, what he is thinking, what came before, what is happening now, and what will follow. Such a procedure is used in the Thematic Apperception Test (TAT). If the examiner is especially interested in psycho-analytic hypotheses, his test will include pictures dealing with situations crucial to psychoanalytic theory—for example, weaning or toilet training—and he will seek "relevant" subjective reactions and material by the way he structures the task; for example, What is happening? How do the participants feel? How do you, the viewer, feel about the pictures?

If a person believes, as did early psychometricians such as Galton and Cattell, that neurological responsivity is crucial in the collection and processing of environmental stimuli, he will collect data on simple perceptual motor skills such as reaction time. If one hypothesizes that brain capacity is related to be-havior and that such capacity, through exercise or heredity, is associated with greater brain size, one will measure skull bumps (as did Gall and the phrenol-ogists).

If one believes that enduring qualities, or "traits," characterize a person and a wide range of his activities, one might inquire about activities, feelings, and preferences that are actually or theoretically associated with the trait under investigation. Further, the more behaviors, feelings, and preferences that were elicited in the direction of the characteristic, the stronger the trait would be considered to be in the subject. It should be clear at this point that a psycholo-gist's theory affects the content of his test.

Data Processing

The psychologist's theory affects not only the material he collects but how he will use it. A good example is the interpretation of responses to relatively un-structured material labeled as *projective* tests.

The most widely used and discussed projective test is the set of inkblots devised by Hermann Rorschach (1884–1922), a Swiss psychiatrist. The use of inkblots or amorphous forms was not original with Rorschach. Clouds were used as projective stimuli in *Hamlet*. And as a noted art historian has pointed out:

> Alexander Cozens (1717–1786) developed a method of stimulating the inventiveness and originality of landscape composition and painting. Leonardo da Vinci, Cozens noted, had observed that an artist could stimulate his imagination by trying to find recognizable shapes in the stains on old walls; why not produce such chance effects on purpose, to be used in the same way? . . . representational elements may be picked out in the configuration of blots, and then elaborated into a finished picture [Janson, 1962, p. 468]."

The theme of this volume—that the pursuit of the science of psychology is a human behavior—is illustrated nicely by the history of the Rorschach inkblots. "As early as 1857, inkblots had been employed for scientific studies of imagination. Among these earlier, pre-Rorschach investigators were Kerner, Binet and Henri, Dearborn, Sharp, Kirkpatrick, Whipple, Pyle, Rybakof, Bartlett, and Parsons [Reisman, 1966, p. 161]." Rorschach was the son of a public school art teacher and was nicknamed by his schoolmates *Klex*, which means *inkblot* or *painter*. He received his M.D. in 1912 and in 1917 came across the dissertation of a Polish student named Hens, who had devised an inkblot test of 8 cards and administered it to 1,000 children, 100 normal adults, and 100 psychotics. Rorschach was influenced by other writers, most notably Jung. The concept of life style, based on an evaluation of movement and color type responses, was a crucial part of the Rorschach conceptual system. A contemporary psychologist has described Rorschach's difficulties in finding a publisher.

> He sent the fifteen inkblots and the manuscript to seven publishers; all rejected it. Finally, in 1920 it was accepted by a publisher, but only on condition that ten cards rather than fifteen would be published.
> The book appeared in 1921, though with several unsolicited contributions made by the printer. The cards had been reduced in size and their colors had been altered. Furthermore, though Rorschach's original cards had uniformly black areas, the printer in reproducing them introduced a variety of shadings so that forms could be perceived within them. Far from being upset, Rorschach was delighted with the possibilities which the shadings of the blots might afford [Reisman, 1966, p. 163].

Considering the almost mystical veneration some hold for the Rorschach blots, this change from the original research stimuli is illuminating.

The history of the Rorschach test also offers a good illustration of the diffusion of an innovation. Rorschach died in 1922 and it looked as if his work would have few consequences. However, one of the Rorschach's coworkers, Emil Oberholzer, taught the test to the psychiatrist David Levy, who in turn interested the psychologist Samuel Beck in it. Beck wrote one of the major works on the technique and taught it in workshops to a growing number of professionals. With two other psychologists, Hertz and Klopfer, Beck popularized the technique, so that psychologists recalled it later when they were looking for a procedure for depth analysis of personality. What was also necessary was a theory of behavior which could use the inkblot technique, and proponents of Freud's personality theory were then seeking such a method. A fortuitous marriage resulted.

If one follows a Freudian model of personality, what does one do to gain understanding of another person? A major assumption in psychoanalysis is a dynamic unconscious in which repressed material actively seeks expression. Such impulses are defended against, censored, and expressed only when the material is distorted and disguised beyond the recognition of the censor. A number of deductions are made. The first is that everything a person does is expressive of his basic personality structure. The individual *is a* schizophrenic or *a* phobic or *a* homosexual, whose overt behavior reflects a *total* personality structure. The person's overt behavior, including his response to the inkblot, is symptomatic of his personality and revealing of it. The inkblot response is developed in the same intrapsychic manner as a dream, a slip of the tongue, or a socially disruptive psychiatric disorder.

A second deduction is that material gathered in one situation may be generalized to another, or is "prototypical" of the individual's behavior. If a person reacts to a small detail in an inkblot and describes the entire card in terms of this one small part, then he is distorting the whole picture on the basis of a small part. He would accordingly be considered likely to do the same thing in his interpersonal relations and probably to have some real problems in distorting such relationships.

A third deduction is an assertion of the predicate that people who respond similarly in one situation do so in *all* situations. An example of this reasoning follows: paranoids distort and elaborate on the basis of partial information; this subject distorts on the inkblots; therefore, he is likely to be a paranoid. A variation of this assertion is that a particular type of response is emitted only by a certain type of person—let us say people afraid of high places. This subject emits such a response; therefore, he is afraid of high places. This deduction is made even though no behavioral indication of such a fear has been observed. As a final example, a greater percentage of homosexuals than heterosexuals see a squatting or sitting humanlike figure on a certain Rorschach card. If a subject sees such a figure, he may well be designated a latent homosexual, even though not all homosexuals give this response and some heterosexuals (who are more numerous in the general population than homosexuals) do.

A fourth deduction derived from Freudian theory returns to the concept of the reified censor. The more novel, ambiguous, unstructured a situation is, the less defensive the censor will be, since it has had no opportunity to learn socially appropriate responses to that situation. Hence the material obtained will be closer to the unconscious, more dynamic, and, therefore, more interpretable.

The Rorschach test is typically administered in two parts. In the first part the subject gives his responses to the stimuli, and in the second the examiner goes over the responses with the subject and asks questions to determine *where* on the blots the person saw his percepts and *what* about the blots made them appear that way. The first part is called the "free association" and the second the "inquiry."

Theoretically, one might perceive almost any object in the inkblot stimuli. For example, an actual respondent reported perceiving a frog, a bear, boys playing with dirt, a giant, a butterfly, a cat, girls on a teeter-totter, a rocket ship, cowboys, and a horse. Such perceptions are a sample of objects in the subject's culture or life space. If these responses are given by a four-and-a-half-year-old boy—as they actually were—they have different implications for the decision maker than if given by a twenty-five-year-old woman college graduate. A person reporting beaten, dead, and decaying carcasses and explosions has indeed acted in a manner different from a person of the same age, sex, education, race, and so on who reports seeing butterflies, maps, and rainbows.

The content emitted by the subject may be and sometimes is used in the same manner as free associations. Further, some testers follow a tradition in which one Rorschach card is ascribed the status of a mother stimulus and a different card a father stimulus. Other card characteristics involve the presence of color, shading, or separate forms. The total number of responses, the time taken to make a response, and other activities which in some manner may be scorable are included in evaluating the performance of the individual. From the inquiry the psychologist may collect information about the frequency with which the person integrates the entire surface or uses details; the use he makes of shading, color, or form to develop his responses; and the degree to which his perception coincides with the tester's own evaluation of what the blot might look like or what others might see in it.

The test interpreter may base his decisions upon a variety of response characteristics, including the respondent's style (many common responses lead to the notion of a rigid or stereotyped individual), impulsivity (use of undifferentiated color), or anxiety (use of shading, nonhuman tension, or movement as in explosions). He may also note the interpersonal relationship between the subject and the experimenter—whether the subject asked for help, was apologetic, or saw "intellectual" content as "the ceiling of the Sistine chapel." The interpreter may combine clues into a broader picture. A subject may display cues of anxiety in responding to a color stimulus that he perceives as sexual or quasi-sexual or he may interpret as harmful and threatening a card detail that is frequently perceived as sexual.

In short, there is a wealth of material for the user of the test to organize and evaluate. Psychoanalytic assumptions offer him a guide and a rationale for the subject's responses to the Rorschach.

Other aspects of personality investigation may also be used to make decisions based on behavior in response to the Rorschach. If brain-injured subjects are likely to give few responses, to repeat responses, to take a long time per response, and to show poor quality of response, the clinician can develop *signs* of brain injury and state that a subject *acts* on the Rorschach *more like* a brain-injured person than does the average member of his population. (The designation of the population is crucial for baserate data—a problem discussed below—because young children and chronic schizophrenics may as groups emit such responses more than the typical adult.) Thus, criterion validity may be developed for the Rorschach, and scales to which trait names are assigned can be devised.

The Rorschach in particular and projective tests in general provide relatively little normative data and thus permit the psychologist to develop his role in the professional setting. To the extent that the material is complex and difficult to reduce to numbers and from numbers to norms, the psychologist must build norms based on his own personal experience. The projective techniques enable him to be an expert in a unique field of knowledge and to assume a professional role that is his very own and that laymen such as teachers, psychiatrists, and social workers can neither question nor usurp.

The psychologist using projective tests can make dramatic, penetrating statements about personality; the more ambiguous the stimulus, the more dynamic, deep, or unconscious the responses, and hence the more "fundamental" the material dealt with. Aside from providing a service, the psychologist finds the administration and interpretation of projective tests more interesting than use of standardized psychometric procedures such as intelligence tests. Where the well-standardized intelligence test carefully designates the psychologist's behavior during both administration and scoring and circumscribes his interpretive behavior, the projective test provides scope for individual creativity. This is particularly true in terms of the third deduction from Freudian assumptions mentioned earlier in this section: because of the hypothesized unity of the personality system, all material has to be integrated into a single coherent picture. While the quality of a standardized test depends on its reduction of individual differences among psychologists, the projective test permits wide scope and enhances the prestige of the professional tester.

MEASUREMENT CONSIDERATIONS—
SITUATIONAL BEHAVIOR

We have offered two generalizations: (*a*) measurement is decision oriented; (*b*) the differences between people or between the same person at different times should reflect differences relevant to the purpose of the measurement rather than ones that are extraneous (error) to that purpose.

Formal Characteristics

From our knowledge of the effects of "artifacts" in experimental situations (see Rosenthal, 1966) and of the efficacy of placebos (see Ullmann and Krasner, 1965, 1969), genuine changes in behavior may occur that are not associated directly with the ostensible reasons for such changes. Behavior is multiply determined and differences are not fortuitous; but to the extent that differences are interpreted inconsistently with their development, the psychologist is in error. Differences that are not systematically related to the object of measurement are called *random errors.*

Systematic errors—such as measurements by a scale that always overstates weights by five pounds—may be taken into account and corrected. The study of individual differences is generally traced to late eighteenth-century astronomers' development of personal equations of reaction times:

> At Greenwich in 1796, Maskelyne, as every psychologist knows, dismissed Kinnebrook, his assistant, because Kinnebrook observed the times of stellar transits almost a second later than he did. Maskelyne was convinced that all through 1794 there had been no discrepancy between the two of them. Then in August, 1795, Kinnebrook was found to be recording times about a half-second later than Maskelyne. His attention was called to his "error," and it would seem that he must have striven to correct it. Nevertheless, it increased during the succeeding months until, in January, 1796, it had become about eight-tenths of a second. Then Maskelyne dismissed him [Boring, 1950, pp. 134–135].

Our interest in the present section is a discussion of random error and our general view is that recorded differences in behavior are neither erroneous nor correct, but relevant or irrelevant to a specifiable task.

Consistency of Measurement: Reliability

If an event occurs, that is, if a behavior is emitted, we wish to quantify it in such a way that our score reflects as much as possible that event. We may assume that inconsistency of measurement will reduce the accuracy with which the event is observed (reflected in scores) and to that extent will also reduce the achievement of the purposes of measurement.

Consistency is a necessary but not a sufficient condition. Consistency of measurement has many aspects. The first is the consistency of the items composing the situation, that is, *internal* consistency or reliability. In a scale of items that comprise a test such as a trait measure, we wish all the items to pull in the same direction, to be consistent with each other. The degree of internal consistency may be ascertained by devising alternate forms of the test or determining how the items on half of the test correlate with the other half.

A second aspect is time. While people may change over time, trait theories (which deal with enduring characteristics) and psychoanalytic theories (which deal with personality structure) both presume a stability within the person. When dealing with characteristics such as intelligence or musical ability, we wish to *predict* differential responses to training procedures. An assumption underlying this approach is that the person's maximum performance will be relatively stable. Certain intervening events such as a brain trauma or a course of psychotherapy might lead to changes in selected traits. The passage of time—whether associated with physiological decay or increased experience of reality—should also lead to change. The measure of degree of consistency over time is called *test-retest reliability*. For experimental validation of conditions or procedures (such as psychotherapy), a control group—which either receives no treatment or, even better, an irrelevant treatment—is used. Thus, the degree of change (test-retest consistency) may be compared between a group that is expected to change and one that is not.

Once data have been obtained from people, the behavior must be abstracted into numbers, or *scores*. If the scoring procedure calls for a series of complex judgments and good training and written guides are not available, the transformation of behavior to scores may introduce differences associated with the *raters* rather than with the subjects being rated. The more limited the subjects' responses are (for example, writing *yes* or *no* or a specific numeral on a machine-scored sheet), the less chance there is that *rater reliability* will be low. The more complex the behavior to be rated is, the more observers and raters are likely to become inconsistent, that is, unreliable.

The Measurement Situation

The setting in which the measurement is made may affect the obtained behavior to be scored. Moreover, being measured may alter the subject's subsequent behavior.

The most obvious situation is one which has differential consequences for the subject, so that he is likely to try to make a certain impression on the experimenter. For example, there is considerable evidence that people called schizophrenics, who are supposedly socially withdrawn, unresponsive, and out of contact with reality, engage in *impression management* to foster responses by others in a direction that is self-serving (Braginsky, Braginsky, and Ring, 1969).

In a different type of experiment Bernstein (1970, 1973) asked college students who were taking part in psychological experiments, and who were all supposedly afraid of snakes, to report to a setting labeled as a laboratory or a clinic. In both settings the subjects were asked to pick up a snake as part of a study of fear. In the "laboratory" setting far more complied with the instructions and touched the snake than in the "clinic." The labels of each situation signaled a different kind of behavior as appropriate. Frightened behavior may be called for, permitted, and even encouraged in a clinic setting.

The possibility that people may distort their responses has been a particular problem in the use of inventories. The personality inventory was first developed as a rapid structured interview. The earliest inventories were designed by Woodworth for screening draftees during World War I and were composed of yes-no responses to questions a psychiatrist would probably ask in a personal interview with each recruit. In essence, this inventory was a report *by the individual* of whether he manifested or had ever manifested a list of psychiatric signs and symptoms such as social withdrawal, phobic behavior, or bed wetting. Self-reports of such unusual behaviors, which are more frequent in psychiatric populations, remain the primary form of current personality inventories. The obvious problem is that a typical subject is quite capable of realizing what kind of response is socially desirable in his specific situation and culture and what is not. He may then fake in the direction he wishes: to appear unusual to avoid the draft or to appear self-assertive, extroverted, and poised to obtain a job as an insurance salesman.

The result is that the measurement of test-taking attitudes itself becomes an important topic for people interested in developing inventories. One possibility is to gather questions that deal with small failings common in adults—saying nice but untrue things, gossiping, being interested in mildly erotic stimuli. A person who denies many of these common behaviors is presenting himself as an unusually "good" person. There are such people—ministers, boy-scout masters, parents, and congressmen—but in most cases it seems more likely that the unusually good subject is faking "good" than that he is as saintly as he presents himself.

Another technique is to collect items, usually of blatantly bizarre content, that only a small percentage of the population will endorse as self-descriptive. One can then determine if the subject is responding within normal limits, for example, endorsing no more than 5 of 60 items in the unusual direction. Again, people such as severely disorganized patients in a psychiatric hospital, illiterates, and those undergoing a tumultuous psychoanalysis might endorse a number of these items without deliberately engaging in impression management.

A third technique of measuring test-taking attitudes is to locate items checked by subjects asked to fake being insane but not by subjects who reside in psychiatric hospitals. In similar fashion, some patients in psychiatric hospitals who are expected to score in the "bad" direction do not. It is possible to find items that distinguish such subjects from those who admit to the degree of unusual items expected of them.

A variable that has received considerable attention in self-report inventories is *social desirability* (see Chapter 4). Every item may be evaluated for the cultural acceptability of answering it as true or false. Ideally, an even split or no direction of bias would lead to the best measurement; that is, culturally neutral items provide no obvious clues for faking "good" or "bad." A related topic (also discussed in Chapter 4) is yea-saying and nay-saying.

The point here is that the psychologist's interest in making sense of test material leads him to an investigation of the entire test situation and from there to new questions and identification of new dimensions of behavior.

The Tester in the Test Situation

Chapter 8, on the experimental situation, presents a number of examples of the effects of differential expectations by research workers. In a situation in which students rate a speaker, they are acting in a role analogous to the psychologist evaluating a client. Their expectation of the person they observe may have as great an impact on psychologists as on laymen. Goldstein (1962) has documented this point in regard to therapists and Jakubowski (1968) for material reinforced in an experimental situation. Temerlin (1968) indicated that when psychiatrists heard a suggestion that the subject in a taped interview "looked neurotic but actually was schizophrenic," 60 percent indicated he was psychotic and 40 percent that he was neurotic; but when the same tape was played to another group of psychiatrists with the suggestion that the subject was truly well adjusted, 100 percent viewed him as within normal limits. Masling (1960) reported an experiment in which female confederates were *pleasant* or *unpleasant* to graduate student examiners while giving identical responses to a sentence completion test. The pleasantness of the interpersonal relationship affected the evaluation of the responses during interpretation although both sets of responses were identical.

Many psychological test situations are important to the subject but do not offer him a clear indication of what is a proper or good response. This lack of clarity is a situation meeting Frank's conditions (1961) of maximum chance of behavior influence. The examiner usually has a purpose in administering the test, and he may be pleased to obtain information that helps him arrive at a decision. He may therefore direct the interview toward what he considers "significant" material, such as evidence of pathology, by emitting cues as in verbal operant conditioning (see Chapter 8). The significant effects of verbal conditioning on projective tests such as the Rorschach have been demonstrated (See Hersen and Greaves, 1971, for a recent example). And verbal conditioning has been used to increase a variety of behaviors in hospitalized psychiatric patients in the interview (Salzinger and Pisoni, 1958; Ullmann, Forsman, Kenny, McInnis, Unikel, and Zeisset, 1965) and in a TATlike test situation (Ullmann, Krasner, and Collins, 1961; Ullmann, Weiss, and Krasner, 1963) and word association test (Ullmann, Krasner, and Edinger, 1964).

The point here is that the actors in the test situation—*both* the psychologist and the subject—are human beings who reciprocally influence and change each other. Such changes are examples of the social influence process and neither random nor error *in themselves*. But in a measure of enduring characteristics or patterns of behavior, such effects (especially when not taken systematically into account by the tester) may lead to variation that is irrelevant to the purpose of testing and hence may be accurately termed *error of the measurement*.

PROBLEMS OF MEASUREMENT— APPLICATION

Psychological measurement is used to decide between theories and between courses of action to take with specific people. A psychological examination may be viewed as an experiment: material is collected that is relevant to deciding among alternatives. *Interpretation* is the psychologist's bridging of the gap between the specific behaviors he has gathered and processed and the decision he must make on the basis of these data.

As noted already in this chapter, the situation the psychologist sets up for his experiment (the collection of his data and/or the selection of his test) is associated with his theory of personality as much if not more than with the specific decision or purpose of the examination. While imperfect, this consistency among aspects of the professional role of psychologists extends to the use of data during interpretation and is also involved in concepts of validity.

Remarks on Validity

Validity is typically defined as the degree to which a procedure does what it is supposed to do. Validity is the degree to which a test serves a purpose: an intelligence test may be valid in the selection of students for academic training and not valid or helpful in the selection of assembly-line workers. That is, a test is not valid in itself, but only for a particular purpose. Moreover, a measure is valid only if it provides adequate variation: if we are dealing with a sample of people whose intelligence quotients range from 80 to 160, we will find the test more useful in predicting high school grades than if we are dealing with a sample whose scores range from 120 to 130. In the latter case, intelligence has essentially been held constant and other factors such as study habits become more important. Finally, the sample may have lower and upper limits: we might say that unless the person has at least average intelligence, he will find college work both hard and unrewarding. If he has too much intelligence, he may find truck driving boring and his attention wandering from the road, so that his safety record is poor. The basic point, again, is that tests are not inherently valid or invalid, but valid only for a purpose.

A second point is that validity is essentially a reduction of error in making a decision. If we collected no data and randomly assigned people to college, individual psychotherapy, or jobs, we would have some successes and some failures. Validity should be evaluated by the degree to which our *hit*, or success, rate increases over what it would be without any selection or test procedure.

An issue touched on earlier is that the effort saved by the testing procedure (reduction. in error) should be worth the effort or cost of testing. Related to this is the *selection ratio*. A test may have relatively low validity, but if there is a surplus of candidates so that only the very brightest students or the very tallest high school basketball players are taken, a variable that had relatively little usefulness in the past may be increased in effectiveness. Conversely, if there is no selection ratio—that is, everyone is accepted—testing, no matter how valid potentially, is not relevant and hence not used or useful.

A final element of validity is the *mediator variable*: tests may be particularly useful for certain groups. For example, many current tests have an implicitly white middle-class orientation, so that a person from a cultural minority may be mis-scored, misinterpreted, and misplaced. Given this problem of different backgrounds and the fact that certain experiences related or unrelated to the specific task may alter the scores, an attempt is made to keep familiarity with test stimuli constant. One way this may be done is to use material with which everybody in the population is supposedly familiar. But this approach may penalize the person from a different cultural background. Another procedure is to use material presumed to be so unusual that it is novel for all test takers. A point that may be overlooked if one focuses on the test as only a set of materials or questions is that the subjects' experience in taking tests and their trust in the testers may also vary, since subjects bring different backgrounds to the evaluation situation.

Baserates

Our previous remarks about the need for a range of scores and for the cost of testing to reduce error over not testing provide a background for consideration of *baserates*. If there is a shortage of applicants and all who apply will be accepted, the baserate for the decision to accept is 100 percent, and the best prediction of the outcome of testing will be a decision to accept. If in the population screened for admission to a psychiatric hospital, 70 percent of the total are called schizophrenic, then a test would have 70 percent agreement with the concurrent criterion of the psychiatrists' diagnosis if the tester labeled everyone schizophrenic. If the population tested is a random one drawn from the general population or the students in a college classroom, the percentage of people likely to require hospitalization for schizophrenia during the succeeding twelve months is likely to be 1 percent or less. In this case, a predictive validity of 99 percent could be obtained by the psychologist who called everyone normal, regardless of what his test scores seemed to indicate.

Additional complexities arise—particularly when the target for decision making is a behavior of *low frequency*. If the risk of schizophrenia is 1 in 100 per year, and if the psychologist identifies 10 people as schizophrenic—of whom one is later hospitalized—he appears at first glance to be doing ten times better than chance. This improvement is apparent, not real, for the psychologist will have 9 *false positives*—people labeled as schizophrenic when they actually are not (by the criterion of hospitalization for schizophrenia within twelve months). Obvious legal and moral problems are involved in such misdiagnosis and subsequent mistreatment (Burris, 1970).

One of the problems is that the concept of schizophrenia is poorly defined, and the criteria of psychiatric diagnosis and/or psychiatric hospitalization are far from perfectly reliable (see Ullmann and Krasner, 1969). The point of the present discussion is that to be useful a test must not only agree in a percentage of cases but in a percentage of cases significantly *greater* than what would have been obtained if the method had not been used. One must evaluate the costs not only of testing but of test misses and the degree of variation (percentage of subjects falling into each yes-no category). One cannot assume that the distribution is either a fifty-fifty split or is so skewed that the chance of correctly diagnosing or effectively treating a person is so slight that a single outstanding hit or success is given undue weight. In terms of the former assumption, comparing 50 schizophrenics and 50 normals may well be misleading, since the percentages do not reflect the baserates found in either the general or the hospitalized population; and the results cannot be generalized to the target population in which actual decisions are made without some mathematical evaluation and correction. In terms of the latter assumption, only 5 percent of those labeled schizophrenic were released from psychiatric hospitals in the mid-1930s; but in the early 1960s, the discharge rate had risen to 70 percent in a sample admitted to a Veterans Administration hospital (Ullmann, 1967). Even when a control group is available, the baserate must be known and taken into account. This care is, of course, even more necessary when a control group is not available.

The Barnum Effect and Semantic Validity

A problem related to baserates has been called the "Barnum effect" (there's a sucker born every minute) or the "Aunt Fanny effect" (it fits everybody's Aunt Fanny). In a classic and oft-repeated study (Bachrach and Pattischall, 1960; Forer, 1949; Manning, 1968) psychology students complete a psychological test, and each member receives an "individualized personality analysis" during a subsequent session. All the students read their analyses, and most are likely to evaluate the description as true and insightful. One student then reads his analysis aloud to the class, which then learns that everyone has received the same personality evaluation.

Two points can be made from data of this nature. The first is that psychological evaluation is decision making, and decision making requires variation. Variation may be stated in terms of range or baserate or *semantic validity*:

> A *reliably-discriminating* statement is one which is used in the same manner by most clinicians, and which discriminates between data to which it applies and data to which it does not apply. Those statements which are reliably applied to all data or to no data are excluded because they do not discriminate. Those statements which are applied by the same proportion of clinicians to all data, or which might be applied by some clinicians to any data, are also excluded for the same reason. What are left are *nonambiguous* (operationally defined), *nonuniversal* statements [Davenport, 1952, p. 171].

Such statements may be tested for accuracy, that is, whether they apply to certain people and not to others.

Second, a typical basis for the decision to continue using a test in an applied situation is whether it satifies the purchaser of the service. Does the individual who asked for the test—whether a client or professional—think it is worthwhile? In a pure market situation the ultimate test is indeed not whether the procedure is useful or improves decision making, but whether the person for whom the report was written likes it and feels it is helpful. Working clinicians rarely check on the accuracy of their predictions. They are more likely to keep producing that which previously satisfied. Not producing reliably discriminating statements may have an advantage: unreliable statements may be incapable of being proved wrong.

Types of Validity

The problems we have discussed throughout this chapter affect the ability to make useful decisions and should be considered in any measurement. The first type of validity is *content* validity. The content of the test, the behavior sampled, should be judged relevant or representative of the type of behavior to be measured or altered. Content validity is frequently decided on by judges—either the person himself or experts such as psychologists or people skilled in the behavior to be dealt with. A test of content validity might be a work sample, such as a lecture given by an applicant for a teaching position.

Much of what we have discussed in this chapter deals with *criterion* validity, which aims to reduce error in making a decision. The outcome of the decision is the measure of the effectiveness of the test. Criterion and content validity are not mutually exclusive, and tests that lack content validity are likely to have very low criterion validity. Criterion validity may be demonstrated by correlating the test with present behavior, that is, *concurrent* validity, or with future behavior, that is, *predictive* validity. In concurrent validity, the test sample is evaluated in terms of other behaviors, abilities, or characteristics that are known and considered to be more accurate, but which are less available or more expensive for some reason. In predictive validity the association between the test and the outcome of the decision is obtained; and the more that the error is reduced, the more valid the test. As noted, we consider this predictive use of behavior sampling most important for traditional tests, notably because predictive validity is used for classification, placement, and other social decisions. Again, concurrent and predictive validity are not mutually exclusive in test construction (although, almost by definition, they are mutually exclusive in terms of timing). For example. we may wish to determine relative interest in arts and athletics in preferred jobs or in toys selected by groups of males and females. The association between items chosen and the sex of the subjects would be a form of concurrent validity. This scale might later be used to predict the type of work (dealing with people or objects) a person would prefer; and if useful, this test would have predictive validity.

A type of validity particularly interesting to psychologists involved in trait theory is *construct* validity. Where no overt criterion is accepted as definitive and a network of interrelations have been observed, a psychologist may posit a construct as a common element underlying and explaining the empirical findings. Construct validity builds a view of personality by inference from data usually obtained through self-report inventories, although other forms can also be used. Eventually an understanding of the data comprising the correlational matrix draws on content, concurrent, and predictive validities.

MORE ON THE PSYCHOLOGIST
AS DIAGNOSTICIAN

Psychology in general and measurement in particular are human enterprises and as such are fit, feasible, and interesting topics for research. Space permits only a brief, illustrative sampling.

A general question is whether training does any good or even whether psychologists are better judges of people because of their training. This question may be broken down into subquestions that are more easily dealt with and permit a sampling of various operational definitions of *good.* One thing a clinician may be "good for" is improved accuracy in formulating, dealing with, and deducing from human actions. As noted throughout this chapter, how a psychologist does these things depends on his model of man. For example, a frequent assumption is that people are complex and must be approached with a method that takes their complexity into account. A human expert may be thought of as capable of dealing with such complexity and being alert to the exceptional, very infrequent case that would be either impossible to program by computer or not worthwhile to handle in this way. The classic works in this area are by Sarbin (1942) and by Meehl. Meehl (1954, 1965) reviewed 18 and later 50 studies comparing mechanical or statistical procedures with human judgments. He observed that "The current 'box score' shows a significantly superior predictive efficiency in about two-thirds of the investigations (for the actuarial methods) and substantially equal efficiency in the rest . . . [Meehl, 1965, p. 27]." While this finding led to spirited rejoinders, a well-validated personality scale or short biography not only frequently is as helpful as a clinician's effort but is often not substantially increased in effectiveness by the professional psychologist's endeavors.

Hoffman (1960), Goldberg (1968a), and their coworkers approached the matter of training and its effect from the view of the formal data-processing model of clinicians. Using such problems as determination of presence of an ulcer from X rays and selection of people to be admitted to college, these investigators found that while the clinician thought his judgment was complex and weighed many factors, his behavior could be simulated by a simple additive formula—usually of only three factors. The information excluded from the formula was sometimes used by the clinician, but in a way that seemed inconsistent enough to increase error.

Judges' confidence was also investigated, because clinicians had thought they were acting complexly when they were acting in a relatively simple manner and because it might be argued that a clinician's judgments should be evaluated only when he is confident of them or because such confidence might be an illusion. Oskamp (1965) found that judges' confidence levels increased with more information about patients, but the accuracy of their judgments did not. In general, experienced judges are less self-confident than inexperienced ones; but whether confidence is a clue to accuracy has yet to be conclusively demonstrated (for example, see Watley, 1966).

A related problem is whether increasing information increases accuracy. A long line of researchers (Golden, 1964; Kelly and Fiske, 1951; Kostlan, 1954; Sines, 1959) have indicated that at a very early point there is little gain in accuracy from additional information and possibly a decrement (Bartlett and Green, 1966).

So far we have used words such as *expert* and *inexperienced* without defining them. It is possible to take samples of doctoral-level clinical psychologists, clinical psychology graduate students, and nonsocial science undergraduates such as engineers and see how well they do in a judgment task. A representative task is giving the judges a case history or a test protocol and having them select the test response made by that person from among five. It is essentially a multiple choice test. Another task is to ask the judges to distinguish between two diagnostic groups, for example, people entering psychiatric hospitals and general hospitals or persons clinically labeled schizophrenic and neurotic. The typical results (Bendig and Sprague, 1954; Luft, 1950, 1951) were not encouraging. For example, Bendig and Sprague reported that the length of the rating scale (3, 5, 7, or 9 points) accounted for 91 percent of the group variance, while a factor reflecting differences in experience measured 5 percent of the variance. The status of the field has not improved in the period since their study. As Lanyon and Goodstein (1971) have observed:

> There is also substantial though not completely consistent evidence that experienced clinical psychologists may be no more accurate in making judgments based upon interpersonal cues than are clinical psychology graduate students, and that neither group may be as accurate as certain groups of nonpsychologists, such as physical scientists and perhaps personnel workers [p. 175].

Another approach to the problem of judgment is to determine the degree to which training improves accuracy. This topic seems particularly reasonable, because it (*a*) studies rather than presumes an experience variable, (*b*) has implications for future training, and (*c*) provides feedback which may be missing in day-to-day clinical work. In general, inexperienced judges (such as college undergraduates) gain rapidly when they are given actuarial or validated personality scale cues; and in some research undergraduates have improved rapidly and come close to the level of experienced judges (Goldberg, 1968b; Oskamp, 1962; Sechrest, Gallimore, and Hersch, 1967). Feedback and the motivation of knowledge of results have an effect on training, but the upper limit seems to be soon reached. The problem seems to be that actuarial methods do as well as clinical judgments, and both need improvement.

A recent and very interesting topic in the area of training inquires into the development of signs that many clinicians use but which have little empirical validity. This topic, called the study of *illusory correlation*, was introduced and pursued by Chapman and Chapman (1967, 1969) and Starr and Katkin (1969). The careful procedures cannot be given in detail here, but they basically present the subject with clinical material such as a drawing (for example, Draw-a-person test) by a "patient" and two characteristics of the "patient." Characteristics and clinical (Draw-a-person) signs are listed so that every characteristic is paired with every sign an equal number of times. Undergraduates are then exposed to the associations.

Since the signs and characteristics are random and balanced, the purely rational outcome would be no clustering or bias by the subjects when they are later asked to give the characteristic associated with a sign. However, the investigators observed a strong matching of a sign as indicative of a characteristic that was far beyond chance expectations. Essentially, the previously naive subjects associated the signs and characteristics in the same manner found in the clinical psychology literature. For example, a large head is associated with intelligence, atypically drawn eyes with suspicion, broad shoulders with manliness, and elaborated sexual areas with impotence. The obvious question, then, is to determine the basis for such strong associations, which occur despite random pairing during training and lack of empirical validity in the clinic. If one assumes that the concept behind projective drawing is valid, then these repeated pairings make both semantic and common sense in our culture at this time and it is possible to hypothesize that such characteristics would be associated with drawing signs without any professional exposure. This has indeed been the case (Chapman and Chapman, 1967).

Eventually, verbal associative connections may be stronger than either experimentally contrived validity or empirically obtained validity (Chapman and Chapman, 1969). This last finding may serve as a summary of the points in this section: diagnostic work is an all-too-human enterprise and the behavior of professional diagnosticians can and should be the subject of scientific study.

Psychologists' Behavior

We may try to make some rough schematic generalizations about the psychologist's activities, but it should be explicit that even the same person shows enormous variation over time and situations. The psychologist may engage in what Lanyon and Goodstein (1971) call an *empirical approach*. He compares the information obtained through assessment procedures to previous findings in order to make a decision. Consistency of behavior is a necessary assumption here and becomes increasingly necessary as the type of behavior and situation in which the behavior is sampled differ from the original target situation for which the decision was made. The more similar the test is to the criterion, the less difficult consistency of behavior is to assume, but it is still an assumption.

The empirical approach overlaps with what Lanyon and Goodstein call the *personality description approach*. Here, instead of comparing the data obtained from the assessment with empirical data (norms), the psychologist uses the assessment data to develop a description of the individual and matches this description to the decision. That is, rather than a score or direct comparison, the description of the individual or the category in which he is placed is the basis for decision. In short, an additional level of abstraction is introduced, and the psychologist must take care that operationally different abstractions denoted by the same word are not confused.

The third and final general model Lanyon and Goodstein call the *theoretical approach*. Here the data obtained in the assessment leads to a description, and this description is placed within a theory in order to make deductions that lead to a decision. A third level of abstraction is introduced, so that the theory too may be a guide in decision making. The introduction of more levels of abstraction increases the chance for error (that is, variation irrelevant to the decision to be made) and also makes tracking the sources of both accurate and inaccurate test usage more difficult.

A BEHAVIORAL ALTERNATIVE

A constant assumption in the preceding models of psychologists' behavior is that behavior is consistent from one situation to another. Basically, a "personality" composed of enduring predispositions to action is postulated. We have pointed out that as the behavior, situation, or subjects sampled vary, increasing generalization must be made and decreasing accuracy is likely to result. Mischel (1968) has ably marshaled considerable information that empirical findings of consistency from a trait approach are pitifully scant.

This result is expected by one with the view that behavior occurs only in situations: there is no such thing as dominance per se, only dominance over certain other people in certain situations. For example, a teacher may dominate students during a class dealing with his speciality; but he is less likely to dominate them in a class devoted to an area in which he is less expert or in a conversation at a football game. Going further, we postulate that neither a drive to dominate nor an activity of domination exists: there may only be ways of interacting with people that have been learned and sometimes labeled by observers. The label is a shorthand, an abstraction: it has the advantage of speed, but, like many shorthand procedures, it may be difficult to interpret. What one person thinks of as *dominance*, another may think of as *adjustive self-assertion*, and a third as *personal integrity*.

The behavioral alternative starts by focusing on behavior—what the person is doing in the situation. A *situation* is a discriminative stimulus that marks for the individual the time and place for certain acts and not others. The cues on which the discrimination is based may be called demand characteristics, language, perception, and so on.

Once a situation is defined (see Chapter 13, particularly on Barker's research in ecological psychology and behavior settings) we may ask, What acts lead to what consequences? Is the person doing something that gives a maximum or minimum opportunity for reward or punishment? How may the person change, and does he have the prerequisite ability and training to make such changes? If we are to shape the person's behavior, we must know his present situation, because this is always our starting point, and we must also know where it would be useful for him to go, since this is our target.

We count instances of *opportunity* to emit a target behavior and instances of *emissions* of the target behavior over time. The target may be an activity we wish to increase (for example, studying) or decrease (for example, going to the movies when one should be studying). But we always count instances of behavior in situations. We then introduce new aspects to the situation and use our quantifications (baseline measures) to determine the impact of the changes. This procedure may be done with individuals (own-control design) or with groups (classic experimental designs such as Campbell and Stanley, 1966; Underwood, 1957). The impact of changed conditions on behavior leads to further decisions such as whether the procedure is effective, whether a different schedule of reinforcement should be tried, whether a different target behavior (for example, teaching a skill that will make the ultimate target behavior more likely) is needed, or whether training to a discriminative stimulus is necessary.

The next chapter provides a greater background for the behavioral approach, and we return to measurement within this context. At this point we may say measurement is made to determine what needs to be taught (educational) and to ascertain the impact of changes on target behaviors (experimental). Assessment is a sequence of decisions about how to alter or maintain behaviors in situations.

The prime emphasis is on measurable behavior in specific situations. The definition of the situation is crucial. The individual's abilities and learned skills are evaluated as indicants for influence strategies; that is, what needs to be taught and, realistically, what can be taught. The significant others or cost of training must be evaluated as closely as the activity of the person to be influenced.

While behavioral assessment of children, retardates, and hospitalized psychiatric patients is usually made by independent observers, there is no reason why an adult who has minimal social skills and reality orientation cannot be his own observer. That is, a person may collect instances of his own emission of, or failure to emit, target behaviors, situational circumstances (including what he said to himself or how he construed the situation), and consequences of his actions both in terms of others' actions and his evaluation of himself.

There is an interaction between a person's ability and previous learning and the types of training programs that will be most effective. Some decisions must be made after experimentation, but knowledge of the individual's prior social attainments may be very helpful in guiding decisions, while being relatively inexpensive. The subject may be interviewed directly or may fill out a biographical information blank. Material dealing with age, sex, race, marital status, education, and the like may be very helpful in narrowing the range of training programs and reinforcing stimuli from which the teacher, therapist, or behavior influencer may select *a starting point*. Only observation of how the subject reacts, however, will help decide whether the first choice is a good one or requires revision. The behavior of students, clients, and other trainees should guide the influencer's behavior. If a specific program element does not work, it is far more parsimonious theoretically and practically to say the professional did not choose correctly than to say the trainee is stupid, resistant, rigid, or self-defeating.

Because a behaviorist maintains that learning and social influence concepts are true, a failure is not an indication of the theory's falsity, but evidence of a poor application by the professional person. *His theory forces the behaviorist to keep trying with recalcitrant cases.* The theory directly affects its adherent's behavior and puts him on the spot instead of enabling him to blame the client. This approach may at times lead to benefit with people such as retardates and long-term patients on whom others have given up.

This last observation brings us to a major point: the behavior of the professional person, not just the behavior of the client, requires specification and investigation. The influencer's acts and their outcomes become a major object of assessment during any treatment process. The specific targets and the types of people most amenable to different influence tactics is the sort of information each worker should accumulate so that he need not start from scratch every time.

The next chapter deals more fully with the behavioral approach; at this point we wish to emphasize that *rather than dealing with behavior in a vacuum as a characteristic of the person, we wish to deal with behavior in situations.*

LAST WORD

The person doing the measurement, the psychologist, is actively and vitally involved in the selection, administration, scoring, and interpretation of the human interaction called testing. We have particularly emphasized the importance of theory as it affects testing behavior, but we have also made a point of the professional consequences to the examiner. Regardless of the psychologist's theory or immediate professional role, some general considerations may be used to evaluate every test usage. We have discussed these ideas under the topics of cost, reliability, validity, and training. No matter how it is derived or in what context it is used, no test may overlook these considerations without running the risk of defeating its purpose—the reduction of error in making decisions.

The behavioral approach to testing was briefly introduced to indicate how a different conceptual orientation may lead to a different kind of measurement. But the same problems of measurement faced by tests in general are faced in a behavioral orientation. Such pitfalls may be reduced. For example, sampling directly in the area of target behavior reduces problems of generalizability; and making future decisions contingent upon the results of changed conditions on a target behavior reduces problems of obtaining feedback.

Overall, measurement occurs, it follows rules, and it is a human activity. When the theory changes, the type of measures and their use also change.

6

A Social Behavioral View
of Influence

Theories are like guides in a foreign land; they direct attention to and organize a potentially confusing environment. They are not the country itself, and we have discussed previously the pitfalls of confusing a thing with a discussion of that thing. Like guides, theories should offer the widest possible coverage and should be comprehensible and consistent. A guide's work is not final: at best he provides a base from which the traveler can move on his own. The guide presents some rules and procedures, indicates the high points and outstanding features, and does as much as he can in the limited span of a tour. Guiding is a human performance and reflects the guide's experience. Finally, guides are themselves major sources of behavior influence.

Chapter 1 delineated the territory we wish to explore: significant interpersonal behavior. Chapters 2–4 reviewed some of the previous efforts, and Chapter 5 dealt with some problems in investigating and implementing theories. This chapter presents an outline of our view of the development, maintenance, and change of behavior; in short, it presents behavior influence as an alternative approach to "personality."

THE PROBLEM AND THE APPROACH

A typical adult is physically capable of many behaviors in any given situation. In a specific society only a very limited number of these behaviors are appropriate.[1] Adults often may desire to act in ways called *heroic, erotic,* or *nonconforming,* but they rarely do. Their experience may not have prepared them for that kind of behavior and they seldom find themselves in situations allowing it.

We can approach this issue from another direction. In a given situation a person acts a particular way called "conforming." We can ask two quite different questions. *Why* did he act as he did? *What* conditions led him to act in this manner? At first these two questions seem similar but the kinds of investigatory behavior that follow from each have very real differences. It is our belief (or bias) that the latter question, the *what,* is more productive of empirical (hence meaningful) answers than the former.

An analogy is helpful in exlaining what we mean (Lewin, 1936). We observe a ball remaining motionless on a piece of wood. We may think of it as at rest and because *no forces* are acting on it, or we may think of it as at rest because the *forces* on it are *balanced.* To move the ball will require an application of a new external force or a change in the balance of forces already present. In the latter case, no new forces are needed to explain its motion, only a shift in the old balance. Analogously, when we ask why a person acted in a particular manner, we are likely to look for new forces, that is, motives. Just as forces are likely to be sought when the ball starts to move rather than when it is stationary, so we as observers are likely to ask why a human being acts in an unexpected, disturbing, or seemingly self-defeating manner. Just as the ball's lack of movement is taken as a "natural state," so in human behavior conformity is usually taken as a natural state.

---

[1] In Chapter 13, on environmental influences, we discuss some situational constraints on behavior. At this time, the following poetic insight expresses the relativistic nature of evaluations:

> None of us escapes: whenever we judge a person to be a good man or a scoundrel, we do so from the standpoint of the group we have accepted as ours, whether it be as small as our own caste or as large as a religion. If the person we are judging belongs to a group we do not know, we are at sea. We cannot tell if a Masai tribesman is a good fellow or not. If he cuts off the hands of a rival tribe and piles them in a triumphal heap, we can say it is not a thing we would do ourselves, but we are quite open to the suspicion that if we were Masai, we might [Menen, 1970, pp 22–23].

Moreover, when the ball is in motion, one may look for a continuing force being applied to it or may think of the motion as continuing until some counter-force slows it down. An observer who looks at another person's behavior and wonders "why?" is likely to suggest a "motive" (or continuing force) to explain nonconformity.[2] The locus of the force is then placed *within* the individual. Chapters 2–4 provided some examples of the internal and external orientations and the consequences of the locus of forces.

Behavior Influence Is Interactive

This text is about people and what they do. The fact that you are now reading symbols we authors put down in another time and place points to one of the remarkable things about people: certain enormous regularities in life can usually be depended upon. This book discusses the *conditions* that make people's actions seem reasonable, even when they are apparently inexplicable, disadvantageous, or deviant. We use the term *behavior influence* to describe the manipulation of these conditions.

Behavior influence deals with the areas of life in which the individual manipulates the psychological environment to alter and direct the physical and verbal behavior of himself or another person.[3] Through a study of the common elements of the behavior influence process, it is possible to understand and predict many seemingly disparate aspects of human behavior. The behavior influence process is applied systematically and deliberately in *professional* settings to alter socially disapproved behavior. It is utilized in *all* interpersonal situations, usually unsystematically and often not deliberately. The orientation we are presenting can be expressed through an illustration.

Let us examine a situation both mundane and wondrous; it is behavior observed at zoos:

> Begging is a classic case. Visitors actually imagine the begging animals are hungry, even when they are obviously well-fed and even hopelessly overweight. But the food begged for is not important. It is the interaction that counts. Some animals throw the food aside as soon as they have grabbed it, but they soon learn that this cuts down the social interplay, so they munch stoically away and get

[2] Why? is not asked unless conformity is unusually rigid, extreme, and self-defeating. As laymen we usually presume good behavior, and one of the common sources of difficulty in child rearing in our middle-class culture is that desirable behavior (studying, obedience to parents, and so on) is not reinforced. The squeaking wheel gets the oil (attention) both from parents and professionals.

[3] We wish to emphasize that man is not a passive element in the environment. Whether setting an alarm clock, making a note on a calendar, replacing a burnt-out light bulb, signing a contract, working for a graduate degree, or being nice to a member of the opposite sex, each individual alters his environment in ways that will make his own and others' behavior more likely.

fat; sometimes it even kills them. But it keeps people interested and, as any bear knows, people are notoriously easy to train. All the bear has to do is stand on his hind legs, wave a paw, and, hey presto, you do your little trick. Your act is rather repetitive, but you do it willingly. You show your teeth, utter a little "arrr" sound and fling a peanut in his direction. Nothing spectacular, but it helps to pass his day, and if the bear eats the peanut, you'll do it again. All he has to do is wave a paw. If he gets sick too often, of course, the zoo authorities slap a ban on public feeding. He gets healthier, but what does he do all day? Scratch the floor, I suppose [Morris, 1968, p. 81].

The quotation introduces a number of major themes in the formulation of social behavior. The bears are in zoos, that is, in situations with relatively little stimulation. In fact, zoos have been severely criticized for taking animals out of highly stimulating natural environments; we could say the bears have a *deficit* in regard to stimulation, attention, or social interaction. We could infer, therefore, a motive or need for their begging acts. The motive seemingly provides an explanation for a behavior not observed in bears in their natural habitat. The same behavior may alternatively be described from the viewpoint of an external observer, who refers to the situation (lack of stimulation) and the bears' response to it (continued emission of paw behavior and disadvantageous eating).

The behavior of the humans in the zoo situation, however, is what interests us. Consider this contingency: an adult throws food when the bear waves a paw; if the bear does not wave its paw or eat the food, the adult stops. *Usually adults in American cities do not throw food in public.* (Such behavior is rare even in college cafeterias.) The adults are acting in a manner unusual in terms of their other behavior. At the same time they are acting in a manner considered common, reasonable, and even expected *at the zoo.*

The feeding of bears illustrates two major themes of this book: the importance of the situation and the interdependence of the actors. The situation is of crucial importance in the emission of various behaviors. By *situation* is meant the complex of social and physical stimuli responded to by an individual at a given time and place. The word *situation* is used to denote the circumstance or state of affairs reacted to by the individual. The situation is his world, his environment, the totality of stimuli impinging upon him. Factors such as previous learning influence the *choice of stimuli* to which he will eventually respond.

Situations are crucial in the specification of appropriate behavior. Few behaviors are in and of themselves always appropriate or always inappropriate. That is, if one does not know the conditions under which a behavior is emitted, we probably will not be able to say whether the act is socially advantageous, neutral, or disadvantageous. A consideration of the gratification of biological processes in our culture may make this point. Sleeping, eliminating, and reproducing—strongly based biological acts as they are—are appropriate only in limited times and places—even on college campuses.

The second theme in the example of the bears is the *interdependence* of actors: the bear begs, the human throws food. If the bear does not pay attention to the food, the rate at which humans throw food decreases. We may hypothesize the reverse as well: if paw raising did not lead to feeding (for example, if feeding the animals were prohibited), the frequency of paw raising by bears would decrease. One person's response frequently serves as a stimulus for a second person, and the second person's response provides further stimulation for the first person.

We contend that the human being is in large measure directed or guided by other human beings. This does not mean that he is a puppet, since he also directs and guides others. A person's own responses may serve as stimuli for his own later actions. Just as one learns to provide stimuli to which others respond, a person learns to provide and interpret stimuli for himself. In short, a person *influences* and is *influenced*.

Behavior Influence Is Complex

An example in which a person acts in a socially inappropriate or unexpected manner that seems foolish or hard to explain after the fact is being *swindled*. When a person is deliberately defrauded he is led to emit behaviors that are not to his advantage. In current psychology two major approaches investigate the problems typified by the swindling process. The first approach argues that a person is swindled because of a characteristic he possesses. In popular terms, "You can't cheat an honest man." Legally, a person is considered competent except for reasons of insanity, senility, mental deficiency, or youth. A psychoanalyst might argue that the swindled person unconsciously wants to hurt himself, to be punished, to be made a fool.

Such reasoning would naturally lead to research designed to find a group of people who have been swindled and a control group of people exposed to the same inducements and not swindled.[4] The two groups would then be compared on various characteristics such as age, intelligence, suspiciousness, and childhood experiences. The psychoanalyst might, for example, hypothesize that the uncheated were anal personalities (suspicious, stingy, conforming) while the suckers were oral personalities.

If certain traits or characteristics seem to be more frequent (*seem* because of the baserate problem in this sort of research) among persons who had not been swindled, research might be directed toward increasing these "desirable" characteristics. The testable hypothesis would be that people trained to increase the nonswindled characteristic would be less likely to be victimized than those

[4] The after-the-fact criterion presumes that having been swindled does not affect the individual's basic character, an assumption consistent with belief in "enduring systems" within the individual.

without such training, when both groups were later put into an experimental situation.

The outline just presented is the most popular form of investigation in current work dealing with abnormal behavior. One need only replace *swindled* with *schizophrenic* or *suicidal* to see the applications to other categories of human behavior. This line of research makes a presumption: something is different and/or unusual about the person who is swindled (or the person called schizophrenic or suicidal). This different quality, or "defect" (that is, a difference from normal), and its correction are in the realm of enduring characteristics *within* the individual, that is, "personality."

One argument against this approach is methodological: we cannot determine whether a person has been defrauded until we know the situation. The specific acts in the swindle may work out successfully: a swindle is sometimes called making a shrewd investment. In part we need to know the result; and in part we need to estimate how many others in the population behaved in a similar manner. What is considered impulsive, stupid, suspicious, or beautiful is defined by considerations of time, place, and person and varies across different groups and different people in that group. In contrast, personality approaches to behavior, especially trait approaches, assume the *generality* of the characteristic. A person may be called anxious or introverted. This label may lead to the hypothesis that he is more anxious, introverted, or suspicious than his peers in *all* situations. Empirical tests of this presumption have led to disappointing correlations. In everyday terms, a person is not necessarily a social introvert or a social extrovert. He may be extroverted in a situation in which he is competent or expected to lead; and he may be introverted in situations in which he has no special competence or role.

The second, alternative approach to investigating problems such as swindling starts by asking *what conditions will increase the likelihood* that people will become victims of fraud. The presumption is that under designatable conditions everyone is a potential victim. (This is like saying everyone has his price; it does *not* mean that everyone has the *same* price.) This approach also implies that someone is taking the role of swindler, which complements the victim's role.

One condition that may increase a person's likelihood of being swindled is a lack of relevant information, that is, ignorance. Two examples come from colonial America:

> the Dutch swindled the Indians in 1626, buying the island of Manhattan for the equivalent of $24 in rum and trinkets. Actually the Indians swindled the Dutch since the deal was made by members of a roving tribe who didn't even own the island but simply happened to be there when the Dutch landed [Gibson, 1966, p. 8].

> The Indians were accustomed to spitting on strings of blue wampum and rubbing the shell beads vigorously to make sure that they were the hearts of genuine

quahog clamshells and weren't just pieces of cheap white sea shells that had been dyed blue with the juice of wild huckleberries by Indian counterfeiters. . . . The Pilgrims soon found themselves stuck with fathoms of counterfeit wampum. . . . In time, the Pilgrims and other early colonists learned to spit on wampum and rub it, in order to make sure that it was the real quahog [McKelway, 1966, pp. 110–111].

In a similar manner, someone may be swindled when he acts as a helpful, nice person. In one familiar example, the victim of the swindle is a foreigner. The first confidence man makes the foreigner's acquaintance by helping him as a translator. The victim and first swindler become friends and "accidentally" meet the second swindler, who is particularly well dressed and "wealthy." This man presumably has just drawn a large amount of money and carries it in a valise. The three move from one bar to the next, the victim being treated royally. At a certain point the second swindler remembers an appointment and asks the other two to take care of his valise. The first swindler offers his own wallet or watch as surety, and says the victim will show his good faith in a similar manner. For the victim to deny surety would be to act in a manner contrary to the preceding friendly interchanges and in a manner different from the first swindler, who has already "donated" his valuables. The second swindler departs with the surety of both; and shortly thereafter the first swindler excuses himself for a moment but does not return. The victim is left holding the bag (with his valuables gone).

The more the swindler can give the impression that he is an honest man or that his enterprise is legitimate, the more likely he will reap a crop of victims. The swindler may give such evidence by paying dividends at first or by prophesying future persecution by "jealous" elements. It is probably good practice for a swindler to act somewhat hesitant to take the victim's money and to structure the situation so that he appears to be trusting the future victim. In short, the confidence men does things to inspire trust. In this instance, the swindler acts in such a manner that he is labeled as an honest or trustworthy person and is responded to in that way.

We have used the swindling process to illustrate that much behavior is a response to information provided in specific situations, rather than the result of an individual's unique "personality."

Physiological Limits to the Psychological Situation

As noted in Chapter 1, the focus of our interest is behavior. Our measures of topics such as thinking depend on activities, and these are in turn physical. We can measure changes in physical movements, sounds, and similar activities. The individual is a physical being and not to treat him as such is to invite a metaphysical dualism.

Each person also lives in an environment that is physical (see Chapter

13). At one level is his external environment: the air he breathes, the water he drinks, the physical spaces within which he acts out his life. At a physiological level, the person in a New York subway at rush hour in midsummer is in a different environment than the person walking across the vestigial cornfield of a midwestern college campus in the midwinter. The person in a discotheque with a rock band playing at a loudness close to the level of pain, with a light show flickering away, and with packed, spasmodic, writhing peers is in a different physical environment than the individual in a college library ploughing through a text on personality. If anything is remarkable, it is not that people act differently in different environments, but that they manage to stay within cultural limits in different physical environments to the extent they do.

The individual also lives in the environment of his own body, which reduces data from the external environment to physical sensations and encodes them in a manner that permits decoding and processing and, eventually, responses (including go–no go decisions)—which are also encoded, processed, and decoded. Perhaps the best analysis of this situation in information-processing terms is that by Miller, Galanter, and Pribram (1960).

Several immediate considerations arise from a view of humans as information-processing systems. First, the environment as the individual knows it is an abstraction ultimately expressed as electrical stimulation of the brain. Second, the person's environment is limited by his physical apparatus: a blind person lives in an environment different physically as well as socially (see Chapter 13) from that of a sighted person. Third, the individual has minimal, optional, and overwhelming *levels of stimulation*, that is, incoming information.

Fourth, a person's behavior may be altered by changing the physiological structure of his information-processing system. Theoretically, this alteration may be done at the level of input, processing, or feedback. This possibility underlies the use of physical substances (that is, tranquilizers) to treat psychotic patients. In a related manner, the chemical substances may alter stimuli by increasing or decreasing the reactivity of bodily organs. The oldest and most widespread of such chemical agents are alcohol and marijuana: they change the person's environment by altering his information-processing systems.

The investigation of human information processing offers great promise for understanding human beings and for therapeutic efforts. It offers clues to what may comprise optimal environments and methods of pacing educational procedures. In terms of possible therapeutic efforts several alternatives may have important implications. A person may appear behaviorally aberrant if he processes information more slowly than is usual; if he fails to integrate information; if in his process of integration, one set of information interferes with another because of faulty categorization, overlap from other categories, or failure to focus on single categories. Such theories may have a major impact and application in abnormal psychology, where various brain injuries and therapeutic regimens are studied.

There is considerable concern currently about the eventual application of medical discoveries in the control of human behavior. One form of such intervention is selective destruction of portions of the brain as in lobotomy. Another is direct manipulation via electrical stimulation of selected areas of the cerebral cortex (Delgado, 1969). A third involves the enormous possibilities of control through genetic changes and genetic restructuring (Glass, 1965). Still others deal with the impact of widespread dietary changes.

Just as the enrichment of bread, the iodization of salt, and the fluoridation of water are major public health steps that have already been taken, one may speculate about the future possibility of dispersion of tranquilizing or hallucinogenic agents to reduce judgment or of reproductive suppressants to limit population. The technology for such "advances" in the control of people is either already available or will soon be, so that concern that these tools be limited to socially acceptable and ethical usage is appropriate.[5] In fact, many writers who call attention to, defend, or deplore the dangers of the "control of human behavior" refer almost entirely to these biochemical, electrical, genetic, and dietary influences—to the exclusion of the interpersonal, sociocultural, and economic influences we stress (De Ropp, 1961). As intriguing as such speculations may be, we pursue them no further, since we presume we are dealing with an *intact* organism functioning within normal limits.

While denying neither the theoretical nor applied potential of the physiological aspects of information processing, we do see some theoretical and practical limitations. If the information-processing system is physiologically perfect, the adequacy of the program still remains a problem. Investigators following the medical model (Ullmann and Krasner, 1965, 1969) have argued that abnormality is a deviation from and an interference with a normal innate biological progression. The afflicted individual acts in a discordant manner only because there has been a trauma, some damage in either physical or social development. This medical view assumes that a person is normal until a trauma leads him to deviate. In this model it follows that *normality* is the absence of pathology and constitutes an absolute standard.

This concept of normality is acceptable at a physiological level, since we have some standards to delineate the limits of acceptable physiological development and functioning. But this concept is *not* acceptable in terms of social behavior. Different interpersonal situations usually do not alter bodily normality —they alter behavioral normality. In a purely medical view a normal body

[5] In a recent Presidential Address to the American Psychological Association, Dr. Kenneth B. Clark proposed

> a requirement imposed on all power—controlling leaders—and those who aspire to such leadership—would be that they accept and use the earliest perfected form of psycho-technological, bio-chemical intervention which would assure their positive use of power and reduce or block the possibility of their using power destructively [Clark, 1971, p. 1056].

leads to normal behavior; all that is required is undamaged equipment. This view predominated in the last quarter of the nineteenth century and the first half of the twentieth, during which hospitalized psychiatric patients received minimal social stimulation while a physical cure was being devised somewhere. This medical model may still be observed in the physician who prescribes a pill and takes little or no further interest in his patients on the psychiatric hospital ward.

Genetics, Instincts, and Imprinting

We are interested in differences among people. One has only to look at others to note that people come in an interesting variety of sizes, shapes, and colors. In our everyday view of others, we stress the differences, but especially in a survey such as the present one, we should not overlook the far greater similarities of organs and construction that humans share. With the exception of monozygotic twins, all people differ in their genetic endowments; but the similarities among people are overwehlmingly greater than their differences. The question is not whether differences exist, but whether these differences have a significant impact on behavior and, if so, how.

Even in carefully inbred mammals such as rats, differences in maze running and hoarding behavior have been noted. Different breeds of dogs have been noted to respond differently to the same stimuli. For example, different breeds of dogs vary in aggressiveness and responsiveness to training.

The mechanism by which heredity alone would influence behavior may be instinctual or limiting. The latter refers to the physiological potentialities that set limits on the effects of environmental experience. Despite intensive efforts, attempts to train chimpanzees to use language have met with only small success. At a human level the upper limit of size is set by hereditary endowment. The effects of the environment are most manifest when the individual does not reach full potential. The current American college student is likely to be taller than his or her parent, especially if he is the first generation to receive a proper diet. The increase in average height and average shoe size of current college students compared with their parents illustrates (as much as the discarded Chinese practice of wrapping female feet) the effects of the environment on the body. At the same time, the *limits* of size and the similarity of *structure* indicate the extents of the heredity limits.

A second aspect of heredity has been formulated as *instinct* (see Chapter 2)— a word with two meanings. The first, as used by Freud and McDougall, denotes a tendency to action, a motivation. Thus, Freud spoke of "instinctual gratifications" and McDougall used concepts of flight (whose correlated emotion was fear), repulsion (emotion of disgust), curiosity (emotion of wonder), pugnacity (emotion of anger), self-abasement (emotion of subjection), self-assertion (emotion of elation), and parenthood (emotion of tenderness). A somewhat different use of the word *instinct* denotes an unlearned pattern of goal-directed behavior. The organism reacts to a situation in a complex, stereotyped manner that is not learned and that is an aspect of the genetic endowment of a species. If a bird which has been separated from other birds since hatching builds a nest in the same manner as other members of the species, and if, when the sequence of nest building is interfered with, the entire nest is rebuilt, we may conclude with reasonable certainty that the behavior is instinctive. While humans do display reflexive behavior (for example, startle, knee jerk, sneeze, gag, and, at birth, swimming), at present humans do not seem to exhibit the universal, complex, patterned, goal-directed behavior of an instinct.

The notion of *imprinting* involves an interaction between the genetic endowment of a species and the environment. There may well be crucial periods in an organism's life for obtaining certain experiences. The classic illustration of imprinting (Hess, 1959) deals with exposure of ducklings to stimuli during the first twenty-four hours after birth. Usually the stimulus is the mother duck. Throughout the rest of its life the duckling makes succorant and sexual responses to the type of stimulus that was available during this crucial period. In the natural state imprinting to an inappropriate stimulus leads to the organism's death or to its failure to reproduce. A phenomenon similar to imprinting has been reported by Harlow, and his coworkers (1966, 1970), who investigated the disruption of sexual and maternal behavior in primates isolated from parents and/ or peers. For obvious ethical reasons, such experiments cannot be performed with humans.

Specific inherited patterns seem to have a relatively slight effect on human behavior in comparison with the effects of learning. In two areas a person's physiological endowment does have an impact on his behavior. The first is in terms of *general potentialities*; the second is in terms of an endowment given a particular social meaning by others and thus leading to an ascribed *status*.

The sex of an individual is usually established socially at birth on the basis of physical indicants. As noted by Rosenberg and Sutton-Smith (1972, especially pp. 32–36), whether humans are sexually neutral, bisexual, or predisposed to a specific sexual identity biologically may be disputed. Various biological indicants show that when social assignment conflicts with biological assignment, the former has a stronger impact on life style and adjustment at maturity:

1. *Chromosomal sex.* Twenty patients had been assigned to and reared in a sex contrary to their sex chromatin patterns as established by skin biopsy or the buccal smear technique. Without exception, gender role and orientation as a man or woman, boy or girl, were in accordance with the assigned sex of rearing rather than with chromosomal sex.

2. *Gonadal sex.* In thirty patients in whom a contradiction was found between gonadal sex and sex rearing, all but three of them saw themselves in a gender role consistent with their sex of rearing.

3. *Hormonal sex.* Of thirty-one patients whose sex hormones and secondary

sexual body development contradicted their assigned sex and rearing, only five became ambivalent with respect to their gender role. . . .

4. *Internal accessory organs.* This sex variable involves the uterus as the organ of menstruation and the prostate and seminal vesicles as organs concerned with the secretion of seminal fluid. In twenty-two of the twenty-five patients, the gender role was concordant with sex of rearing and was not in accord with these predominant male or female internal accessory structures. . . .

5. *External genital appearance.* In the case of twenty-five individuals who had been raised in an assigned sex that contradicted their external genital appearance, twenty-three of the subjects had come to terms with their anomalous appearance and had established a gender role consistent with their assigned sex and rearing.

6. *Assigned sex and rearing.* Of the more than 100 cases of hermaphroditism involved in the above findings, in only seven of these cases was there any incongruity between sex of rearing and gender role . . . [Rosenberg and Sutton-Smith, 1972, pp. 33–34].

Behavior due to sex status has a great impact, but its specific effects vary widely. In the last hundred years the legal status of women, particularly married women, has changed enormously. In Illinois a century ago a married woman was not a legal entity. The range of activities that women may successfully engage in has increased and continues to increase. Some of the many reasons for this change include the separation of reproduction from sexual intercourse, the move to a technological society in which abstractions rather than muscles play an increasing vocational role, and the pattern of political awareness modeled on the tactics of civil rights movements in the 1960s. The hormonal and muscular differences between men and women may indeed make more likely differences in activity levels, but these physical differences are not sufficient to explain the multitudinous differences in occupation and social role between the sexes. From birth onwards the two sexes are dressed differently, spoken of and to differently, and introduced to different expectations and objects. The methods of gaining social rewards differ so that both opportunities and candidates for earned statuses are associated with sex. One major result of the women's liberation movement of the late 1960s has been to illustrate that many social behaviors expected of women are *culturally*, not genetically, determined.

An even more salient illustration of a genetic difference associated with, but not causally related to, behavior differences is skin pigmentation. A great deal of effort has been expended on demonstrating that a racial difference in intelligence *does* exist or *does not* exist. Such efforts seem futile if not downright wasteful. An empirical science cannot prove that some difference between two groups does not exist—a new measure not known or used may always be discovered. One cannot prove the *null hypothesis* (that no difference exists); one can merely reject it as improbable. On the other side, acceptance of results indicating racial differences in intelligence obtained on contemporary intelligence tests poses two major problems. The first is in the measure itself: How appropriate is the measure to the topic under discussion, namely, functioning intelligently in one's society?

The second problem is that many nongenetic explanations may be offered for any obtained difference between racial groups on an intelligence test. Among these are the groups' different environments, which may or may not (*a*) provide early stimulation, (*b*) encourage the use and manipulation of the kind of abstractions that comprise the tests, and (*c*) reward one for doing well on the type of tasks represented in intelligence tests. Other important variables in performance are the subject's familiarity with the language of the examination and his relationship with the test administrator. Differences in subjects' prenatal and postnatal care and continuing nutrition might also be alternative nongenetic explanations for any obtained differences. In short, if two groups differ on a test and also on some genetic or demographic variable, this does not mean the test difference is *caused* by the variable.

Genetic endowment may indeed lead to differential capacity and performance. The classic work on the influence of heredity on behavior is in the area of intelligence. There are two general lines of evidence. The first compares same sex sibs, same-sex dizygotic (fraternal) twins, and monozygotic (identical) twins. In the following representative data, the correlations between the pairs are given first for intelligence test scores and then for height: same-sex sibs, 0.53, 0.60; same-sex fraternal twins, 0.63, 0.64; identical twins, 0.88, 0.93. The degree of relationship for intelligence is similar to the degree of relationship for height. When identical twins are reared apart, the correlation for IQ decreases to 0.77. For a true test of environment, the children must not only be reared apart but must be reared in markedly contrasting environments. Data on this point is sparse, but while the correlation remains significant, it decreases further. The second line of evidence compares the intelligence test scores of foster children with the academic achievements of their biological and foster parents. The data indicate a low but significant correlation between the children's intelligence test scores and their biological parents' education, while an essentially random one exists between the children's scores and their foster parents' education.

Two remarks are needed at this point. The first is that work on heredity influences is both made possible and limited by the nature of the task used to measure intelligence. It is made possible because an intelligence test score can be assigned with reasonable *reliability* (which cannot be done in research on the genetics of psychiatric deviance). But it is limited by the *validity* of the intelligence test score. The reference to height in terms of degree of association of sibs is germane in this regard. Like the potential for full height, growth of ability to manipulate abstractions probably depends upon adequate input at early crucial ages. Like height, ability to manipulate abstractions has an impact on behavior because both may make positive responses from other people more likely. Women may be more inclined to date men who meet the cultural requirement of being taller than they are. Facility with language and symbols may also make for nonspecific attractiveness to others. In specifiable situations symbol manipulation, like height, is close to a necessary condition. But just as height itself does not make for stardom in basketball (endurance, speed, experience, and coordination have crucial roles), so ability to manipulate symbols does not guarantee success at symbol manipulation tasks. College students know that no matter how bright they may be, at some point they will have to read books and attend lectures.

The foregoing indicates the importance of a man's genetic endowment; it should be clear that genetic givens set firm limits on people's behavior. However, when we think of changing human behavior, we are inclined to work with environmental rather than genetic influences. We can do little to alter an individual's genetic component once he is born. At present we can alter the genetic component of a species only with the utmost difficulty, expense, and time. The changes seen in man's behavior both as an individual and as a species during the last century—or even the last decade—are enormous. Changes due to experience (that is, learning) have replaced evolutionary (genetic) change. Changes in food gathering, transportation, illumination, communication, and social patterns occur with a rapidity that may be destructive to the species; but these changes are environmental and experiential, not genetic or instinctual. If we had to say where the overwhelming variance is in the study and alteration of the behavior of humans, it would be in learning and not in genetics. While we neither can nor wish to deny our genetic substrate, we will leave this topic for ones we think will be more fruitful for our purpose.

The Bodily Environment: Feedback
or Response-Produced Cues

The human body may be considered an information-processing machine, and this assumption implies that the effects of the environment are encoded, abstracted, and ultimately become part of an electrical-chemical interchange. A crucial aspect of any information system is feedback. Input has two major sources: those outside the body that impinge on the sensory equipment and those that arise from the processing and action on inputs. The way the system is programmed affects how the environment is scanned, that is, how new information is gathered (for example, labeling and self-fulfilling prophecies). In addition, the actions taken, or outputs, provide physiological feedback as well as information about consequences.

Reference to labeling reveals that the internal and external loci of information input overlap. A person's responses serve as stimuli for that person and are functionally part of his environment. Schematically, information from the internal domain has two loci, both of which arise from information processing. The first locus is categorizing and labeling information. The second locus—which is the major theme of this section—is feedback, which results from action on previously processed information.

Any time a person acts (including suppression of an overt response) a physical event occurs. These physical events supply information about people themselves as well as about reactions from the external environment. If a person who is not in good physical condition does twenty pushups, he will notice a variety of feedbacks: aching muscles, panting, increased heartbeat, perspiration. These responses may be labeled as "getting old" or "being out of shape"; and either the inputs or their responses may lead to further actions such as a promise to get more exercise or to quit smoking.

This example illustrates a number of generalizations. First, the person's own body is a major part of his environment not only because it mediates stimuli from the external environment but also because its responses to that environment provide feedback, which is a further source of stimulation. Second, the processing, labeling, or valuation of this information may lead to responses that become stimuli for future actions. The third generalization foreshadows the later concept of role: the type of feedback and its evaluation are parts of learned, interrelated patterns of behavior. In the present example the deduction that one should be in good physical condition or that one should quit smoking if one is not conforms to a peculiar midtwentieth-century pattern: the middle-class, middle-aged, intellectual response.

LEARNING AS EXPERIENTIAL INPUT AND BEHAVIOR

We have used the word *learning* to designate the effect of experience on subsequent behavior. In a view of human beings as information-processing systems, learning may be considered as a source of input both in terms of the *data* to be processed and the *programs* by which subsequent data are processed. The following sections conceptualize the learning process in a way which we find congenial and integral to a social behavior view of influence.

Respondent Conditioning

We make the traditional distinction between operant and respondent conditioning, although Miller's brilliant work (1969) indicates this distinction is not perfect.

In respondent conditioning a stimulus *elicits* a response. For example, a stimulus such as light or food (which is originally termed the *unconditioned stimulus*) may elicit a response from an individual such as pupillary contraction or salivation (termed the *unconditioned response*). If this unconditioned stimulus is preceded by or contiguous with a tone or other stimulus that does not normally elicit the unconditioned response of pupillary contraction or salivation, eventually the tone will elicit responses similar to those elicited by the stimuli of light or food. At this point the tone may be called a *conditioned stimulus* and the pupillary contraction or salivation a *conditioned response*.

This situation—labeled as *respondent, Pavlovian,* or *classical conditioning,*—has been of enormous importance to the study of behavior because it designates a measure (for example, the response of salivation) of the differential effects of environmental stimulation, and as such has been and continues to be the subject of numerous careful investigations. Some repeated findings involve concepts parallel to those of operant conditioning discussed in the next section.

One phenomenon is *extinction*: if the conditioned stimulus is presented without the unconditioned stimulus, the conditioned response will diminish and eventually will no longer be elicited by the conditioned stimulus. If, however, a period of time elapses, *spontaneous recovery* will occur: the conditioned stimulus will again elicit the conditioned response. This phenomenon is important in therapeutic applications of respondent conditioning, and it also has the theoretically important implication that conditioning is *not* a purely automatic, passive occurrence.

Two complementary processes in conditioning are generalization and discrimination. If one tone has been established as a conditioned stimulus, a second tone may also elicit a conditioned response. The more similar the two tones, the greater will be the similarity of the magnitudes of the conditioned responses. This observation that the organism will react to a new situation in a manner comparable to that of other similar situations is called *generalization*. If one tone is paired with an unconditioned stimulus (acquisition) and another tone is not (extinction), the first tone will eventually become an effective conditioned stimulus while the second tone will not. This process is called *discrimination*. Like spontaneous recovery, respondent discrimination and generalization are not passive processes. As the difference between the two discriminated tones is reduced, the organism is placed in a conflict over whether or not to respond, and its indications of distress have been called *experimental neurosis*. The situation in which an organism is faced with stimuli calling forth two or more responses that are incompatible with each other is called *conflict*.[6]

Respondent conditioning, especially the establishment of conditioned fears

---

[6] The careful psychologist will designate the conflict and not simply label a situation as "conflictual" or, even more dangerously, infer a conflict as a source of motivation for behavior that is otherwise difficult to explain. The problems in the common and often professional usage of the term "conflict" are similar to those in the use of "anxiety" (see Chapter 4). If the stimuli and conditions making for the conflict or anxiety have to be specified, the terms are likely to be used far less frequently.

and experimental neuroses, led to a model that Watson and early enthusiasts generalized to a greater range of behavior than the data warranted. This overextension is understandable in terms of the pressure to use theory to cover areas of uncertainty; the negative reaction to these theories is also understandable in terms of disillusion.

We wish to illustrate respondent conditioning with several examples. The first is the classic observation of Watson and Rayner (1920). A nine-month-old boy touched and showed interest in a furry animal. Next the animal was paired a number of times with an unpleasant unconditioned stimulus, a sudden loud noise. The child then greeted the sight of the animal with responses similar to those elicited by a sudden loud noise—in effect, a startle response involving crying. A conditioned stimulus (the animal) led to a conditioned response (crying, avoidance) appropriate to the unconditioned stimulus (sudden loud noise). Knowledge of the child's experience made his behavior seem appropriate; without such knowledge an observer might have labeled the child phobic and irrational.

A second area of experimentation is the development of *meaning* or *semantic conditioning*. A series of investigations (Luria, 1961; Razran, 1939; A. W. Staats, 1968) have demonstrated how the meaning of words can be built up by pairing unconditioned stimuli with conditioned stimuli. In much the same way as Watson and Rayner paired old and new stimuli, these investigators demonstrated that man learns the meaning of words. In the development of word meaning, however, this can be done along functional-physical lines or abstract-logical ones. A third series of experiments added a new dimension to the classical conditioning studies and tied them to the behavior influence process. Chapman, Chapman, and Brelje (1969) tested the finding that a person's pupils dilate when viewing a sexually stimulating object. Males looked at pictures of attractive, scantily clothed girls and neutral stimuli. When the experimenter was a young relaxed worker, the finding of greater dilation to sexual than neutral stimuli was replicated. When the experimenter was a square male, the finding was not replicated. These results demonstrated that the *subject's relationship to the examiner* may modify the conditioned responses. Again, it is clear that the conditioning process is neither automatic nor passive.

A pure respondent conditioning model has limitations. First, human social reactions are usually faster than the time required for autonomic encoding and output. Second, second- and third-order respondent conditioning is generally difficult to obtain and maintain; yet such would be required to explain complex human behavior. Third, experimental findings, such as those of Chapman and his coworkers (1969), indicate that the effect of contextual features are difficult to integrate into a simple respondent conditioning model. Fourth, conditioned responses are relatively fragile: irrelevant stimuli must be reduced or eliminated in a sterile laboratory setting that differs markedly from everyday life in order to demonstrate the conditioning effects. Finally, as noted earlier, Miller (1969) has demonstrated operant control of autonomic responses—a finding that indicates a purely respondent approach is an overly simple one.

In short, the phenomenon of respondent conditioning is well established and provides an important historical and theoretical model. But it is not the sole explanation for human behavior.

Operant Conditioning

In operant conditioning the organism emits behavior and the events that *follow* temporally may serve as "reinforcing stimuli," or consequences altering the rate of the behavior's emission.

The paradigm of operant conditioning is an organism such as a rat in a cage with a lever. Pressing the lever has differential consequences. If the rat is hungry and if lever pressing is followed by the delivery of food, the rate of lever pressing increases. If lever pressing is followed by a shock or some other unpleasant stimulus, the rate of lever pressing decreases. If lever pressing terminates an unpleasant stimulus such as shock, lever pressing increases. If lever pressing leads to avoidance of an unpleasant stimulus such as shock, lever pressing increases. If lever pressing is followed by an interruption in a pleasant pursuit such as eating, the rate of lever pressing decreases. Consequences that alter the rate of responding are called *reinforcing stimuli.* Reinforcing stimuli may increase or decrease the rate of responding. Consequences that increase pleasant stimuli or either decrease or avoid unpleasant ones are likely to be associated with an increased rate of that response; consequences that decrease pleasant stimuli or increase unpleasant ones are likely to be associated with a reduced rate of that response.

Extinction in operant conditioning occurs when the rate of response decreases as a function of a reinforcing consequence no longer occurring contingent upon the operant whose rate is being measured. The rate of emission of an operant will also decrease under the condition of *satiation.* The surplus of a reinforcing stimulus decreases the effectiveness of that stimulus. This is one indication of the importance of the internal environment: a well-fed organism will not react to food in the manner it does when it has been deprived of food.

Operant procedures focus on measurable events rather than on inferred motives. It seems a small semantic matter to talk of hunger drive rather than food deprivation for a period of time or the consequences of food contingent on an emitted act. The difference is that the latter two ways of describing the situation carry with them measures while the former is a label and an inference.

As with respondent conditioning, the paradigm is strong because it provides a measure, the *rate of response*, which may be used to evaluate the consequences of the environment. One set of environmental manipulations that have been carefully studied (for example, see Ferster and Skinner, 1957) are *schedules of reinforcement.* Reinforcing stimuli may be presented *regularly* after every single, second, or Nth emission of an act. This is called a *fixed ratio* schedule. The reinforcing stimulus may be presented irregularly on a fraction of the emissions of the behavior. This is called a *variable ratio* scale. The schedule of reinforcement may be fixed in terms of time. It may occur at regular, or fixed, intervals (such as payday on the first of the month) or at irregular time intervals (such as at some time once every five minutes but whether the first, second, third, fourth, or fifth minute of the period is randomly determined). This latter case is called a *variable interval* schedule. Each of these schedules has different effects on timing, rate of emission, and resistance to extinction of the responses being investigated. One of the most important findings in this regard both theoretically and therapeutically has been called "Humphrey's paradox": the rate of response of an emitted act is more resistant to extinction if the response has not been reinforced after every trial. If sheer amount of reinforcement were the sole consideration in establishing and maintaining the emission of a behavior, then a fixed 1-to-1 ratio of reinforcing stimulus to instance of the behavior would seem most effective. The greater resistance variable ratio schedules have to extinction indicates therapeutic applications; and, more importantly, it indicates that operant conditioning is neither automatic nor passive.

As in respondent conditioning, if other things are equal, similar responses will be made to similar situations. This similarity of responses is called *generalization*. As with respondent conditioning, we may also reinforce an operant under one condition—for example, when a green light is on—and extinguish (that is, not reinforce) the same operant when a red light is on. When the organism emits the operant response when the green light is on but not when the red is, *discrimination* has occurred. When an operant is emitted only in the presence of another stimulus, we may say that the operant is under the control of that stimulus, although it is important to note that *stimulus control is not a matter of elicitation as observed in respondent conditioning*. Rather, we may say that the stimulus acts as a *discriminative stimulus*—one that marks the time and place when the emission of an operant will have reinforcing consequences.

Primary and Acquired Reinforcers

At birth the organism may be thought of as responsive to *primary reinforcing* stimuli, that is, stimuli such as food, water, air, and termination of pain that affect biological functions. Other potential primary reinforcing stimuli are a minimum level of novel stimulation and cutaneous contact with another member of the species, in this case, mother. Recent research has located pleasure and displeasure, or pain, centers in the brain that respond to direct electrical stimulation. Such primary reinforcing stimuli as food, liquid, temperature, and reduction of pain are present throughout the organism's life.

Some of the limitations of respondent conditioning have already been noted. Primary reinforcers also have limits. With the exception of direct electrical stimulation of the brain, primary reinforcers may satiate. In addition, as biological maturity and social complexity increase, the response contingency of primary reinforcers to ongoing behavior decreases. Relatively little of a college student's behavior is maintained by primary reinforcing stimuli in the manner that it was when he was two months old.

We have noted that behavior may increase or decrease in association with the presence or absence of a stimulus. The presence of the mother or some other nuturant adult is crucial for crying to have the consequences of hunger or pain reduction. In addition, over time the presence or attention of others serves a widening and *changing* function. *A discriminative stimulus may become an acquired reinforcing stimulus.* People may emit operants to increase the frequency of these stimuli: to turn a red light to green, to have mother present, or to engage a chaperone elsewhere. The functions of acquired reinforcers may also change over time. A classic example is money, which may serve to buy candy at one age, liquor at another, a college education for offspring at a third, and an annuity at a fourth. An interpersonal relationship such as gaining attention of another person may also progress from a discriminative stimulus to an acquired or generalized reinforcer. A college lecturer's efforts to engage his students' attention are different from the acts he made as an infant to obtain his mother's attention, and the consequences that maintain his efforts are also very different.

Acquired reinforcers are less likely to satiate than biologically based primary reinforcers; acquired reinforcers may generalize; the acquired or generalized reinforcer may become relational and symbolic. A college grade, for example, is essentially a symbol, but it is effective in altering behavior because it bears some (albeit imperfect) relationship to remaining in school, obtaining jobs, and the other "good things in life."

EXTENSION OF OPERANT CONCEPTS

Any formulation of human behavior should take a stand on several enduring problems. These questions deal with (a) development of new and complex behaviors; (b) development and maintenance of seemingly self-defeating behaviors; (c) maintenance of behavior over time; and (d) the apparent consistency of behavior over time. The concepts of reinforcement, generalization, discrimination, scheduling, and acquired or generalized reinforcers may be extended to offer possible answers to these questions.[7]

[7] The behavioral approach has been criticized as overly simple because it employs relatively few concepts. Critics have stated that because few concepts are used, the use of these concepts is not complex; a favorite term is that the concepts are *sketchy*.

In reply, we wish to point out that relatively few chemical elements compose that remarkable complexity of organic chemistry that describes man at one level. And our complex

New and Complex Behaviors

Neither the individual nor the environment is stable; both are continually changing. Human social situations are rarely identical. As a person in a complex society matures, different behaviors are expected of him.

A person might indeed learn a new set of responses for each situation. It is more effective and accurate, however, to hypothesize that other things being equal, the person will respond to successive situations on the basis of his previous experiences. The more similar the situations, the more similar will be his immediate responses. Novel responses may sometimes occur because of the generalization of rules learned in one situation to new situations that are different. One may frequently observe such generalizations in the grammar of children. Children appear cute when they extrapolate accurately but inappropriately and say "tooths," not "teeth." One may think of such extrapolations in terms of genetic, or cognitive, levels of development, or one may view them as accurate applications of previously learned rules to situations in which they do not apply.

Skinner (1970) has emphasized the role of accidents or "mutations" in the development of novel art forms. But he also notes that if chance makes a contribution to such effects, the artist learns ways of improving his chances for the effects to occur: "Mutations may be made more probable by making the control of a medium less precise or by encouraging disturbances. . . . [The artist] can violate standards, conventions, and taboos, as a mathematician denies self-evident axioms or a composer uses previously forbidden harmonies [p. 70]." While chance is important so that the artist may create his opportunities, he is not passive. Skinner added, "Mutations, however, must be followed by selection [p. 70]."

A major way in which new behavior may be generated is through a procedure aptly called *shaping*. A notion of what shaping involves may be gained from its alternative name, *successive approximations*. Whether by design of others or through environmental conditions, behaviors that increasingly approximate a final new desired performance may be selectively reinforced. The level of a reinforced performance is *gradually* increased and behaviors which previously were acceptable (that is, reinforced) no longer are. Once an organism is at a new level, its chances of moving further in the direction of the ultimate performance are increased and the procedure is repeated. The level is raised as the organism shows capability of emitting the behavior frequently enough not to be extin-

---

language is written with only twenty-six letters and a few punctuation marks. Similarly, the enormous complexity of RNA and DNA molecules is based upon relatively few ingredients. We simply ask that an approach be chosen for what it does and what descriptions, explanations, manipulations, and experimentation it makes possible. The behavioral approach is presently in a state of gradual development; but to the extent that it is rooted in observation rather than preconception, we think it is the most useful approach available.

guished. An example is the way that successive clarity, complexity, and exactness of children's speech obtains a favorable response from adults. Where an infant's early smiles, babbles, and grunts are a pleasure to his parents, such performances continued too long without progress become a source of concern and at times even displeasure.

Another prime technique is prompting and fading. A stimulus that initially exerted strong control is gradually *faded* (reduced in its clarity, completeness, or saliency) as a new stimulus or performance is developed. For example, handwriting may be taught by tracing over letters that are gradually lightened until the cue is no longer present.

An important way in which many behaviors are added to a person's repertoire is *imitation*. Imitation is probably a procedure that is not innate in humans and must be learned. Baer, Peterson, and Sherman (1967) have presented material on the teaching of imitation to retardates (see Chapter 8). Once imitation has been learned, it may be used as a technique in learning a wide range of other performances.

Once learned, any technique may be used in an instrumental manner to generate new techniques and to guide responses. Man's outstanding accomplishment is language, which is used to provide information, to reinforce, and to warn. Once a person is responsive to language, the easiest way to alter his behavior is to talk to him, to ask him to do something, or to provide him with reasons and methods for acting (compare Skinner, 1968, p. 210). Use of language, however, is an accomplishment that needs to be taught by shaping, chaining, prompting, and fading; and its use is contingent upon continuing consequences.

It is important to note that the skills (such as imitation) instrumental in acquiring other skills can be taught. *These skills eventually are maintained not because of their original reinforcement, but because they continue to make possible complex acts that are reinforced.* It is doubtful that anyone is reading this book solely because of the gold stars he received for reading in second grade.

In *chaining*, a complex series of acts is built backwards. An organism is reinforced for X. When this behavior is firmly established, he does Y so that he can do X in order to be reinforced. After Y is established, Z is taught so that Y can be done for X, and so forth. Each new link in the chain may be taught using shaping, imitation, or any other technique. A child may be taught to read. Then he may be shown how to borrow a library book. Next he may be shown how to use books to do homework. The child may then go to the library, search for a book, withdraw it, and take it home to read in order to do his assignment. Such complex series of acts are developed by shaping, chaining, and changing a previously terminal behavior into an instrumental activity.

Another way of discussing chains and sequences of behavior is to note that the completion of one act may serve as a discriminative stimulus for the next act in the chain. One thing is done so that the next act is meaningful or possible. Finally, not only acts but *strategies* for problem solutions can be and are learned.

At one level experience in dealing with novel situations has an effect. This has been called *learning set* (Harlow, 1949). What is meant here, however, is what Polya (1957) called the "heuristic." Rules can be devised to direct effort to the patterns of acts most likely to lead to problem solving. At an everyday level the person generalizes not only from what he did but how he went about solving previous problems. Put another way, certain patterns of activity—asking advice, listing givens and assumptions, going to the library, thinking of former problems, going to the effects of the solution and working backwards—have been associated with previous problem solution and therefore may be emitted when new problems have to be solved.

Seemingly Self-defeating Behaviors

When we deal with self-defeating behaviors, the word *seemingly* is crucial. We have elaborated elsewhere (Ullmann and Krasner, 1969) the thesis that no behavior is inherently abnormal, but that "abnormality" is an evaluation made by others or by the person himself. While maintaining that so-called abnormal behavior is not different qualitatively or quantitatively in either development or maintenance from so-called normal behavior, it is possible to outline the conditions associated with labeling of a behavior as "abnormal" or "self-defeating." A first condition is that the behavior disturbs someone—the person himself or others—to the point that a change is considered worthwhile. (This aspect of the definition has led some people to the useful step of labeling behaviors "changeworthy" rather than "abnormal.") Second, the behavior falls within the province that society has designated as appropriate for certain change agents. In our own society, for example, alcoholism has only recently been officially designated as a medical rather than a moral problem. The sorts of behaviors our society considers as psychiatric problems are those presumed in the *long run* to be of disservice to the person himself or to those with whom he has contact. Which behaviors are most likely to be so classified rather than considered criminal leads to the third condition: the behavior is *difficult to understand*. For example, the person is unlikely to be taking advantage of opportunities for favorable consequences. If a person's act can be designated the result of lust, covetousness, pride, or other presumably rational reasons for action, he is likely to be treated as a criminal rather than labeled mentally ill. The label provides a quasi-explanation.

Given this background, the task is to investigate conditions for the emission of seemingly self-defeating behavior, in which the person (*a*) does not emit acts that would readily lead to supposedly favorable consequences; (*b*) continues behavior that is seemingly useless or even dangerous for a prolonged period;

or (*c*) emits behavior that differs markedly from that emitted by the majority of people in his culture in similar situations.

A first possibility is that the person has not had the training presumed to be universal. An analogy would be a student taking a college calculus class without any training in algebra. This student would not understand "simple" concepts. He would be labeled stupid—unable to do simple things or grasp simple concepts.

As a result of such an experience, a person might designate other situations for which he does not have the prerequisites as bad ones for himself and engage in various maneuvers to avoid them. Two major concepts are involved: (*a*) secondary deviance and (*b*) maintenance of avoidance behavior.

Sociologists have distinguished between primary and secondary deviance. By *primary deviance* they refer to *rule-breaking acts* such as having sexual intercourse outside marriage or becoming addicted to heroin. The rule-breaking act itself may have little effect on the person, but the consequences arising from it may lead to major changes in behavior called *secondary deviance*. If a woman has sexual intercourse she may label herself several ways—as liberated, cheap, or in love—and recategorize both herself and the realm of behavior appropriate for herself. If her boy friend publicizes her new generosity, her environment may change considerably; and she may interact with others in a far different manner than she had previously, not because of the act of intercourse, but because of the recategorization following it. Once addicted to heroin (primary deviance), a person seeks to keep himself supplied and may engage in theft or prostitution to obtain money (secondary deviance). A final example of the two types of deviance is the person who successfully fakes an illness (primary deviance) to avoid an unpleasant situation and then, after the crisis has passed, must maintain the fiction of the illness (secondary deviance) or face the consequences of having engaged in deceitful practices.

As noted, the frequency of any act that terminates or avoids an unpleasant stimulus is likely to increase in similar situations. We noted in the foregoing section that methods of solving problems may be learned. Not all solutions are necessarily socially desirable, so that the desirability (value) of changing certain behaviors must also be learned.

Avoidance behaviors may lead to secondary deviance and be maintained for long periods without an obvious cause. The person who avoids situations may deprive himself of opportunities to engage in a widening area of activities. While this avoidance may be due partly to generalization, it may also reflect breaks with social requirements. For example, a person who avoids statistics may be avoiding not only a type of mathematics but also a career in psychology.

An act may delay, and hence temporarily avoid, an unpleasant stimulus. If the problem is handing in a paper, the individual can make excuses and promises. These may snowball until the promises all come due at once and the person fails in the same manner as a bankrupt corporation with bad debts. One major problem with avoidance learning is that the person may avoid a situation, even though he or it has changed so that he could adequately deal with it. Since avoidance is followed by no immediate unpleasantness, the avoidance may be maintained far longer than is beneficial; if the person does not discover the change, he may continue to act in a manner that is no longer realistic. The situation avoided may have respondent components. To reduce or avoid these stimuli, the individual withdraws from the situation and avoids anything resembling aspects of the situation.

Implicit in the preceding examples is the observation that short-term benefits may be achieved at the expense of long-term values. Favorable immediate consequences may maintain a behavior that seems self-defeating in the long run. Viewing a movie is certainly pleasanter than studying for an exam that is a week away.

The consequences effective with an individual depend in some measure on his prior history. A person may learn to enjoy stimuli that most people find hard to understand. Such stimuli are called *inconspicuous reinforcers* and may include listening to baroque music or acid rock (although inconspicuous seems the wrong word in the latter instance). Not being heroin addicts, most college students would not work or pay for a shot of heroin and would even avoid a free fix. In psychiatric hospitals, bothersome, repetitive, and self-destructive behavior may be immediately followed by favorable consequences such as attention by the staff. A classic illustration of this concept and a helpful example of what is meant by a discriminative stimulus is presented by Schaefer and Martin (1969):

> In a certain Eastern hospital for the mentally retarded there was an unusually large number of so-called "headbangers." The superintendent, alarmed at this . . . observed conditions on the wards and found something which anybody unfamiliar with behavioral analysis could not help but approve: The nurses were most loving and kind with their patients. As soon as a patient began to hit his head against a wall, the nurse would rush to him and comfort him. In addition, to calm him down or to show her acceptance of him, she would give him a bit of chocolate or other candy. But this superintendent saw that the nurses were using the most powerful behavioral techniques toward a horrible purpose: They were giving tender, loving care to patients smashing themselves bloody against a wall. Not only that, the reinforcers they used had become control stimuli [discriminative stimuli], so that any time a nurse would appear with chocolate or other candy, patients instantly began their headbanging [pp. 47–48].

Seemingly irrelevant or self-defeating behavior may be developed and maintained in a manner called *superstitious*. Here, reinforcement is not related to the act but occurs frequently enough for other reasons that the superstitious act continues to be emitted. A favorite pen or dress has at best only a very indirect effect on a person's examination grade (possibly some effect if it makes the person feel more confident), but if the person does well on enough examinations while using the pen or wearing the dress, the procedure will be continued.

The individual is capable of a great range of behavior. In any subculture or social situation, only a small segment of all the operants a person might emit are considered by himself or others as normal. Viewed in this manner "normal" behavior is a specifically learned pattern of the right act by the right person at the right time and place.

As mentioned, a behavior presumably in the person's repertoire may not have been learned. We must now add that a behavior may have been learned but its emission not maintained. The disuse of the foreign language learned as a Ph.D. requirement is an example. Behavior may be extinguished. If a person finds that favorable consequences do not follow from one pattern of behavior, he is likely to switch to a different set.

A major part of a change in social behavior lies in attention to symbols or discriminative stimuli that are different from those previously attended to. It has been hypothesized (Ullmann and Krasner, 1969, ch. 20) that the behaviors considered symptomatic of patients called chronic schizophrenics in psychiatric hospitals may be deduced from the extinction of normal behavior, and, particularly, what the staff considers the "obvious" salient stimuli in the situation. Two generalizations may then be made: first, both normal and abnormal behavior are learned and need to be maintained; and second, when formulating so-called abnormal behavior, one of the first things done is to ask what the person is doing and what happens (or is avoided) when he emits the abnormal act.

Maintenance of Behavior over Time

Many topics which might well have been included in this section have already been touched on. We would, however, like to add a number of points to the general rubric that behavior is maintained because it *pays off*.

Intermittent or variable reinforcement is more resistant to extinction than schedules in which every instance of an act is reinforced. For purposes of acquisition, a schedule in which reinforcement is frequent is most effective. Over time, however, the schedule of frequency of reinforcement may be "stretched" or "thinned out." This is done gradually. Too rapid or extreme a change would lead to a situation of potential extinction. But, if thinning is done skillfully, an organism may continue a behavior for prolonged periods of time such that his input exceeds the return. A classic example is gambling (Levitz, 1971).

The shifting of the density of reinforcement of a schedule indicates an important point: changes occur over time in the level of a performance (for example, shaping), the schedule of reinforcement, and, the stimuli maintaining any specific act. Reading, for example, usually becomes an act instrumental in attaining a goal, rather than an act reinforced for itself. That is, reading is part of a chain and not a terminal performance for adults. A final generalization is that the original learning situation is not necessarily the cause or crucial condition of current behavior. The continuance of behavior does not require the continuance of the conditions under which it was learned.

Consistency of Behavior over Time

Personality tests have been called tests of typical behavior (Cronbach, 1969). In a different manner, we have noted that the object in testing is to become more effective through accurate description and prediction of behavior. These goals imply a stability in behavior, a consistency greater than chance.

If typical behavior is ascribed to "enduring" qualities of the individual (the "inner" approach) rather than to regularities of interaction between the person and his environment (the external approach), measures of consistency will lead to trait theory—as we have seen in Chapters 2–4. A concept of consistency in traits leads to the hypothesis that an adequate sample of behavior in one situation would be predictive of behavior in another situation. From Hartshorne and May's classic study (1928) through the scholarly summary of the literature by Mischel (1968), which covers four decades of extensive search for trait consistency, the preponderant evidence is *inconsistent* with this hypothesis. As situations become increasingly different, predictions based on traits measured in another situation become increasingly less valid. Two examples may suffice. The reinforcing stimuli available may differ, and hence the particular categories of instrumental acts emitted may differ. In Hartshorne and May's work, children who were below average in athletics were more deceitful (cheated) when athletic prowess was the issue; children from less wealthy backgrounds were less trustworthy in money matters; and students with low grades were more likely to cheat in academic situations. Evidence for a generalized trait of honesty is weak; evidence of reinforcing stimuli appropriate to individuals across different situations is strong.

Our second example involves the traits of social introversion-extroversion and leadership. A variety of studies such as Fiedler (1965) have indicated what most readers have themselves observed: a person varies in degree of social introversion–extroversion and leadership as conditions change. One condition is how competent the person is in the focal activity. Rather than being consistent in terms of a trait or drive, the individual is consistent in emitting behavior in line with his abilities and deficits and with the maximum effectiveness possible in the situation.

There is an additional consistency: if the social situation has been unrewarding or even a time out from reinforcement (in ordinary language, boring) in the past, the person may reduce the frequency with which he enters the situation. In so doing, he is likely to heighten the differences in skill that previously existed. Consistency of behavior may therefore be based on consistency of choice of situations. Consistency may also be based on generalizations of stimuli and responses.

Specific situations impose consistencies on people. In part these may be due to learning what is appropriate in a given situation; that is, generalization from previous experience. Consistency may also arise from what other people are doing, that is, imitation. Consistency may result from attending to stimuli of particular categories. For example, an artist may be alert to paintings in a new room, while a playboy may be alert to members of the opposite sex.

If we had to predict specific acts emitted by an individual, we would probably do better to ask about his age, sex, race, education, and employment than about his traits. If one thinks about specific acts, a college student's whereabouts and behavior can be predicted to a fair extent by looking at his schedule of classes during the day. This can be illustrated by an observation of hallways and their occupancy rate. From ten minutes past the hour until a quarter to the next hour, the halls are essentially deserted. People arriving early for class or dismissed prior to the bell begin to trickle in; a bell rings and from ten to the hour until the bell rings the hour, the halls are packed; a few latecomers straggle along, and then the low occupancy occurs again. On certain autumn Saturday afternoons a stadium essentially deserted at other times draws a dense population. The ebb and flow of population brings to mind a drainage system, as the campus (or offices or factory) empties itself in the late afternoon. The tide of people standing and talking and then apathetically sitting in a room is an indication of behavior under "control" of a discriminative stimulus—in this case, the bell marking the start or end of a class period.

Where Human Behavior Is Complex

Behavior is not solely operant or respondent. In the majority of social situations, the individual is capable of making a variety of responses with varying likelihoods of payoff. Moreover, internal physiological and response-produced symbolic stimuli impinge upon the person and with stimuli external to his body form his immediate environment. Finally, the person both recognizes in himself and in others patterns of behavior to which he assigns labels. Such responses produced by the person himself may serve as plans, strategies, models, or discriminative stimuli for further behavior (Skinner, 1963).

Some of these patterns of behavior we will call *roles*. The person has learned that consistency and accuracy of identifying his own and others' behavior in role-relevant behaviors pays off. A major topic is *self-control*, in which the person manipulates his own environment with himself as the major subject of influence. We will return to self-control in Chapter 12.

Finally, these conclusions lead to the place of *symbols* in human behavior. Symbols permit the bridging of time by application of various acquired reinforcing stimuli. Symbols may be as concrete as a token in a token economy or as a number in a contract or as abstract as a comparison a person makes about himself. Such a comparison may be a concrete score (how many cigarettes smoked, pounds lost, hours studied) or abstract (thinking about whether or not he is a "good" person).

LAST WORD

This chapter has presented behavior influence as an alternative approach to personality. We started the section on operant conditioning by stating that one paradigm involved a rat in a box with a lever to press. But we are *not* presenting observations limited to the situation of a rat in a box. All of the terms used (such as *operant conditioning, shaping, extinction*) are based upon observations of human behavior in both controlled and natural settings as well as upon animals in laboratory settings. We are presenting *manmade concepts* and saying that these concepts are no more "real" than concepts such as personality or ego. Behavioral concepts should not be reified any more than other concepts. For our purposes in developing a psychology of behavior influence and from our point of view, we find these observations of human behavior useful.

An important part of any approach to behavior is the nature of the metaphors (figurative language) into which the theory is put. Every theory utilizes metaphors implicitly or explicitly. Freud made implicit use of a hydraulic metaphor derived from physics; the sociologist Goffman (1963a, 1967) explicitly draws his metaphors from the theater. The investigator is forced to use some kind of metaphor by the need to describe human behavior with language. The terms that are to be used are related to the kinds of words available.

Much of the remainder of this volume applies and extends the concepts outlined in this chapter. Many of the concepts presented in the following chapters supplement and complement the material in this one. Genetics, operant and respondent conditioning, and the concepts attached to them are necessary but not sufficient for a psychology of behavior influence. They are part of the documentable relationships dealing with behavior as a function of environmental events. From observations of these relationships, we may draw some generalizations about the effects of experience and *start* to build an approach to people that will help in our dealings with them. These relationships we describe in the remainder of the book.

PART **2**

Research on Behavior Influence

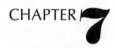

Influences on and of the Influencer

Human behavior can be conceptualized in terms of its influence upon *others* and its *consequences* for the behaving individual. Individuals serve as sources of influence *and* as audiences for or recipients of influence in their relationships with others.[1]

---

[1] We have frequently noted that the influence process is a reciprocal one. The influencer is himself influenced by what he teaches another, as in the effects of role-playing or presenting arguments on both sides of a question. He is affected by assuming the role and label of being an influencer. He learns what behaviors are effective with others and increases such acts, and he learns what tactics are not effective and decreases his use of these. The design of the research reviewed and the simplification required in coverage may obscure this point in the following material, but it should never be overlooked.

THE SOCIAL ROLE OF THE INFLUENCER

The structure of any society incorporates a variety of social roles which affect the behavior of others. For example, current American society sanctions the roles of influencers in spheres that are professional—psychiatrist, psychologist, physician, lawyer, social worker; political—President, congressman, mayor; commercial—salesman, ad writer; moral—priest, minister, rabbi, parent; educational—teacher, professor; and cultural—critic, reviewer, author, movie star, artist.

In this chapter we concentrate on the *professional* influencer to learn about the role itself as well as the general process of influence. To a large extent, the professional influencer attempts to determine the models of human behavior held by other groups of influencers. For example, law generally holds to a model of a rational man, but recognizes that youth and illness mitigate responsibility (such as competence to make contracts). A major issue in the recent past has been the integration of psychoanalytic and other psychiatric concepts into *legal* definitions of insanity. The point is that theories of human behavior are incorporated into the guidelines of other social influencers.

Most of the observations made about the professional influencer apply as well to the other groups. For example, all influencers are affected by and affect their social and political milieu. Investigators of human behavior throughout history have responded to the accepted beliefs of the periods in which they lived. The personality investigator views himself as a scientist, an objective evaluator of behavior. But he too is a captive of his time. This is illustrated by the following analysis of conflict in social science.

> When one studies the "fads" in motivational analysis in social science, one notices how each type of drive has arisen at a time when it was a major component of a public issue. Thus, the *hunger* drive was emphasized during the depression; the *aggressive* drive during the rise of fascism; the *anxiety* drive as America was drawn into World War II; the *dependency* drive with the prolonged separation of families during the war; the *conformity* drive during the McCarthy period; the *achievement* drive during the space race with Russia. In short, all this non-policy and detached, academic research is unwittingly responding to larger public events of immense policy significance. The "unconscious" of social scientists is much more policy-oriented than their theories like to honor [Brodbeck, 1969, cited in DeCecco, 1971, p. 68].[2]

Rather than criticize influencers for being human, we should observe that an investigator *is* a creature of his times in his language and theories. Problems arise when he takes the position that his views represent some final truth.

---

[2] Rather than speaking of their "unconscious," we would note that social scientists work in "important" fields, in which they can readily obtain grants and publish to gain acceptance for "interesting" or relevant generalizations.

The Psychology of the Label

How the influencer *labels* himself and his work provides a starting point for our investigation. The word *influence* appears in the title and hundreds of times throughout this book. We have selected this word to denote the process we are discussing rather than *control* or *manipulation*. The dictionary (Morris, 1969) definition of *influence* as a "power indirectly or intangibly affecting a person or cause of events [or] power to sway or affect based on prestige, wealth, ability or position" comes closest to describing the process we wish to investigate. Influence seems broader and socially preferable to alternatives such as *control*— "to exercise authority or dominating influence over; direct; regulate. To hold in restraint; to check"—or *manipulate*—"to influence or manage shrewdly or deviously."

The development of the usage of the word is also relevant. As detailed in the *Oxford Universal Dictionary* (1955), the verb "to influence" originated in Latin and Middle English usage in an astrological sense and meant to emanate from the stars. The noun also began with an astrological definition: "The supposed flowing from the stars of an ethereal fluid acting upon the character and destiny of man [p. 1002]." By the sixteenth century influence had come to mean "The exertion of action of which the operation is unseen, except in its effects, by one person or thing upon another [p. 1002]." In its emphasis on the consequences of behavior in the interpersonal process, this latter usage comes close to an operational definition of influence. It alludes to a psychological rather than a physical or chemical process.

Our choice of this word should be informative of our views. For example, it indicates our preference to utilize words which have evolved meaning through human usage, rather than to coin a new term. Some may wonder why we have not used Skinner's term, "control." Skinner (1971) has put the problem boldly:

> Good government is as much a matter of the control of human behavior as bad, good incentive conditions as much as exploitation, good teaching as much as punitive drill. Nothing is to be gained by using a softer word. If we are content merely to "influence" people, we shall not get far from the original meaning of that word—"an ethereal fluid thought to flow from the stars and to affect the actions of men" [p. 180–181].

A considerable difference in ideology and model is implied by the use of control or influence. The difference goes beyond the harshness of the former in contrast to the softer, weaker, subtler, and perhaps more ubiquitous latter. *The use of a word itself has consequences.* Describing oneself as an *influencer* has very different consequences from describing oneself as a *controller*. For this reason, we prefer and use influence rather than control. Influence is more descriptive of the process as we see it.

Self-labeling

We have discussed the terms the influencer applies to his model of behavior. But with what label is he willing to designate his professional functioning? Most investigators prefer the label of their own discipline, such as *psychologist, psychiatrist, sociologist*. These terms have such general meanings that they permit the individual influencer a very wide range of behavior and avoid the implication of responsibility for altering other people's lives.

What a professonal does and how he labels it may or may not be related. For example, certain investigators and psychotherapists whose professional functioning are behavioral and social (in our sense of the terms) would be aghast at calling themselves behavior therapists. Conversely, some self-labeled behavior therapists deal with cognitions, anxiety, and other hypothesized internal states in a psychodynamic manner, but would vehemently deny they are anything but behavior therapists.

Individuals, even professional influencers, can call themselves what they like. But such latitude is confusing to clients, students, and the public, who read and try to understand what the professionals are doing.

No self-respecting influencer has ever simply called himself *influencer* much less controller or manipulator (the alternatives mentioned above). The reasons for this are many, the most compelling being that to attach the name of the process to the professional engaged in it would most likely *decrease his effectiveness* in the role. People may well resent being reminded about a fact of life, particularly if it implies they are not complete masters of their own fate.

Most psychologists prefer to use the label of "psychologist" to identify themselves professionally. Lapointe (1970) has reported that the first author to entitle a treatise *Psychology* was the German Rudolf Goeckel (1547–1628), who used the term as a category for the works of various authors: *Psychology, or On the Improvement of Man*. Lapointe has noted that "The moralistic inference in the first title was unavoidable as Zilboorg (1967) remarks, 'Since man's behavior was, and still is, of interest only from the practical standpoint of leading the individual into the path of righteousness, or, as we would put it today, to social adjustment' [p. 640]." Hence from its origin, the term "psychology" implied a process of influencing others to change their behavior.

Characteristics that Affect the Influencer's Role

While encompassing a vast array of data, the field of psychology (including its personality and social branches) has only recently begun to offer material about the "characteristics" of the formal influencer (an experimenter or therapist) that affect the outcome of particular studies. R. Rosenthal (1966) brought most of these studies together in his review of "experimenter effects in behavioral research" as a prelude to and complement of his own studies of experimenter bias. We shall now look at these characteristics. (Chapter 8 discusses the details of some of the actual studies.)

Rosenthal (1966) has summarized the more general relevance of such studies as follows:

> Here we are interested in relating characteristics of the experimenter, not to other of his characteristics, but rather to his subject's responses. The usual study of individual differences is not necessarily social psychological. The relationship between person A's sex and person A's performance on a motor task is not, of itself, social psychological. But, the relationship between person A's sex and person B's performance on a motor task is completely social psychological. That person A happens to be an experimenter rather than a parent, sibling, friend, or child has special methodological importance but no special substantive importance.
>
> It has special methodological importance because so much of what has been learned by behavioral scientists has been learned within the context of the experimenter-subject interaction. If the personal characteristics of the data collector have determined in part the subjects' responses, then we must hold our knowledge the more lightly for it. There is no special substantive importance in the fact that person A is an experimenter rather than some other person because as a model of a human organism behaving and affecting others' behavior, the experimenter is no more a special case than is a parent, sibling, friend, or child. Whether we can generalize from the experimenter to other people is as open a question as whether we can generalize from parent to friend, friend to child, child to parent [p. 39].

The most obvious characteristic of the experimenter-influencer is sex, and numerous investigations have obtained different results depending upon the sex of the examiner-interviewer (for example, see Sarason and Harmatz, 1965). However, although the differences seem to be sex linked, they depend upon a complex interaction with the experimental task and the subjects involved. These sex-related differences may well be attributed to the possibility that males and females *behave differently* toward their subjects and thus elicit or shape different responses. In similar fashion (as illustrated in Chapters 8 and 13), differences in the experimenter's age, race, hair length, accent, and general physical appearance may serve as "demand characteristics": for example, "This hippie (or black, or woman, and so on) probably expects me to . . . ."

In addition to obvious characteristics of appearance, subtler attributes have been inferred from behavior or measured by traditional personality measures. These are the *traits* or characteristics such as anxiety, need for approval, hostility, intelligence, dominance, authoritarianism, and warmth (see Chapters 3 and 4). In fact, any trait or type attributed to humans in general has also been attributed to experimenters (who then may be considered as subjects). Some studies have demonstrated a relationship between performance on the tests measuring these characteristics and differential effects in psychological studies (see Rosenthal, 1966, for a summary). Again, as with physical attributes, there seems to be a highly complex interaction between various kinds of experimenter activities and characteristics, subject characteristics, behavior, and situational components.

A third set of experimenter characteristics includes measurable aspects such as birth order, status, acquaintance with subject, and experience as an experimenter. These are summarized by Rosenthal (1966) as follows:

> From all that has been said and shown, it seems clear that there are a great many variables that affect the subject's response other than those variables which, in a given experiment, are specifically under investigation. The kind of person the experimenter is, how he or she looks and acts, may, by itself, affect the subject's response. Sometimes the effect is a direct and simple one, but sometimes, too, the effect is found to interact with subject characteristics, task characteristics, or situational characteristics.
>
> Not only the kind of person the experimenter "is" but the things that happen to him before and during the experiment affect his behavior in such a way as to evoke different responses from his subjects. The subject's behavior may have feedback effects on his own subsequent behavior, not only directly but also by changing the experimenter's behavior, which then alters the subject's response. . . . In the survey research or test standardization type of research, the data tend to be collected by many different interviewers, examiners, or experimenters. We may be fortunate, and in the given sample of data collectors, the various effects due to their characteristics or experiences may be canceled out. However, they may not be, as when there is a tendency for the data collectors to be selected on strict criteria, implicit or explicit, in such a way that the N different experimenters are more nearly N times the same experimenter [pp. 109–110].

The experimenter himself is an important independent variable. Another way of approaching his impact is via the psychotherapy situation. Goldstein (1962) and Goldstein, Heller, and Sechrest (1966) report research using these concepts directly in the area of therapy. The next section describes one such variable explored within the context of psychotherapy.

The *AB* Variable—Abie's Irish Rose

By subtitling this section *Abie's Irish Rose*, we wish to convey more than a play on words. *Abie's Irish Rose* was one of the longest-running plays in the history of Broadway. It had no great cultural significance but people liked it and it played to large audiences for many years. The *AB* variable in psychotherapy is much the same.

In 1954 Whitehorn and Betz distinguished between two types of therapists who dealt with schizophrenic patients. These investigators retrospectively examined the attributes of psychiatric residents during the previous decade. The seven therapists with the highest rate of improvement for treated schizophrenics and the seven with the lowest improvement rate (averaging 75 percent and 25 percent, respectively) were designated as As and Bs.

Whitehorn and Betz then examined the therapeutic approach used by As and Bs and found differences in (a) the type of relationship between therapist and patient; (b) the formulation of the patient's problems; (c) the strategic goals selected; and (d) the actual tactics used in accomplishing goals. These investigators next sought the personality differences between A and B therapists in a series of studies. A major finding (Betz and Whitehorn, 1956) was a significant difference in performance on the Strong Vocational Interest Blank (SVIB) by the two types of therapists.

After this finding, many other researchers sought to trace the elusive A and B "characters." Howard and Orlinsky (1972) have succinctly summarized the most recent findings and problems in this approach:

> In this period, there were three major reviews of the A-B literature (Kemp, 1970; Chartier, 1971; Razin, 1971) and six research reports. . . . With all this, it is distressing that so much perplexity remains about the meaning of the A-B variable. The fact that it was originally devised as an empirical index to differentiate between more or less successful therapists, rather than as the measure of a theoretical construct, no doubt has contributed to this situation. We are inclined to place the A-B variable in the descriptive category of measures of personal style. However, in view of the fact that so many other person-relevant characteristics among measures of life status, assumptive systems, and adaptive resources (as well as personal style) exist to be studied, we question the wisdom of continuing so nearly an exclusive concentration on this mysterious measure [p. 633].

Roe (1969) reviewed the relatively meager literature on differential personality characteristics of psychotherapists other than the AB variable and noted such findings as the tendency of therapists to score higher (more "masculine") on the masculinity-femininity scale of the Minnesota Multiphasic Personality Inventory (MMPI), to have less interest in mathematics and more interest in persons, and to have higher esthetic and theoretical values than comparable groups in related disciplines.

The point is that *different influencers* have *different effects* on *different people*. If we follow a traditional model of personality, we will continue to seek traits to explain the differences. If we follow a behavior influence paradigm, we will look for differences in influencers' overt behavior in specific situations with specific individuals. At present the former approach is popular; but, like *Abie's Irish Rose*, it may not be very significant.

The Influencer's Political Views

If all kinds of influences affect the behavior of the influencer, then his political views should also have an impact. Belief about what is a desirable social and political way of life may determine what one sees, how one interprets, and to what behavior one reacts. Although this observation seems reasonable, the relationship between the sociopolitical beliefs of the influencer and his behavior has received very little systematic investigation. We are not referring here only to a simple characteristic or trait of an individual (for example, Is he a Democrat or a Republican?) but to the more complex model of the nature of man and society implicit in political labels and individuals' belief systems. These "political beliefs" may be manifested in several ways.

As part of the growing revolt against established institutions in general, a group of therapists is critical of the theoretical and political implications of traditional psychotherapy. The credo and rhetoric of these therapists, who identify themselves as *radical therapists,* are illustrated by the following:

> The therapist touts himself as a magician. But he doesn't follow through. Instead of allying himself to the tradition of soul healing (witch, witch doctor, GP, priest), he allies himself to the status quo—and bolsters it. He sells his skill like a vendor of fried chicken. He uses his prestige to discredit and slur social protest, youth, women's liberation, homosexuality, and any other different kind of behavior. Therapists' rewards come from helping the system creak on. Claiming to be "detached and clinical," therapists never are. They can't be. Their words and acts demonstrate their bias. Current therapy's emphasis on the individual cools people out and/or puts them down. It cools them out by turning their focus from society that fucks them over to their own "hang-up." It puts them down by making them "sick" people who need "treatment," rather than oppressed people who must be liberated [Glenn, 1971, pp. x–xi].

These critics use a political interpretation in recognizing and applying models of human behavior. The radical therapist argues that the traditional therapist uses the "sickness" model to avoid dealing with societal "oppression" of patients. The radicals interpret the traditional therapist's politics as guiding his behavior in therapy to the detriment of his client.

This view of the medical model as having a political position is also seen in professional interpretations of social events such as the student protest movement. Nikelly (1971) reviewed the research on this topic and concluded that the investigator's political views and his model of human behavior influence his observations, his results, and the implications he draws from them:

> The survey of the literature of student protest falls into two major categories. The first views the protesting student as maladjusted, and the second views society and its institutions as culpable. . . .

When the political, educational, economic, or military situation of another country is somewhat opposed to that of our own country, we may easily take for granted that protest in these countries is legitimate and psychologically healthy; however, the rebellion of students in our own country implies to many therapists the operation of an unresolved Oedipal situation, masochism, emotional fixation, the impulse to kill a symbolic father figure, reaction-formation, or dependency. The therapist then searches for these psychological variables and, often enough, finds them; consequently, from the beginning, he treats the student as maladjusted and recommends therapy compromise and rationalization in achieving adjustment to the social and academic milieu. Effects (student rebellion) are treated as the disease, while possible causes (academic suppression) are overlooked. Many psychologists would object to the use of the medical model for explaining anti-social behavior, and also to classifying it in the context of emotional health and illness. They would rather regard it within the context of interpersonal relation-ships, social structure, politics, economics, and ethics [pp. 475–477].

Hughes (1969), a historian, made the same point about the political impli-cations of a sickness model of behavior in a broader context. He pointed out that in the 1930s and 1940s many people, and particularly college students, believed that society's ailments were economic in nature. In contrast, subsequent genera-tions of students have been influenced by the views of many psychologists, psy-chiatrists, and psychoanalysts that society must be approached psychodynamically so that we can "understand" it. This latter approach has led to "a basically un-political aspiration to see through, to unmask, to strip—literally as well as figuratively—down to total nakedness. The goal is psychological or, to use old-fashioned vocabulary, spiritual. And it marks the culmination of a quarter-century of amateur psychologizing among the young [Hughes, 1969, p. 24]."

Hughes connects the labeling of our society as sick to a conservative political position:

There is something profoundly illiberal in the mental set that finds sickness all about us. In the very act of failing to ascribe individual responsibility or to specify the outlines of the society it would prefer, it suggests a despair of reason itself. Reason and liberalism may not be identical, but the attitudes we describe by those terms in fact grew up in historical tandem and were celebrated by an overlapping cast of classical social thinkers. A tendency to write off liberalism, or to give it a premature burial, is a telltale sign of an abdication of judgment that is by no means restricted to the young [p. 27].

If one accepts Hughes' linking of political "illiberalism" with the sickness model, a paradoxical situation results. Most of the influencers who are proponents of such a view—the psychiatrists—are usually political liberals (Rogow, 1970). Conversely, the strong antimedical model position of psychiatrist Thomas Szasz has been endorsed and cited by political conservatives in their attacks upon the "mental health" movement (Scarf, 1971).

The point is that the theories of influencers are used by others to justify a wide spectrum of political views; and the political views of influencers determine to a large extent the kinds of behavior considered desirable not only in society but in the individuals they directly affect.[3]

A Group of Influencers

Systematic observations of the characteristics of influencers as a specific group have been relatively rare, although individual psychologists and psychiatrists have been studied—particularly in a series of studies of scientists by Roe (1953). One investigation of the characteristics of a group of influencers is a report on psychiatrists (based on questionnaires sent to members of the American Psychiatric and Psychoanalytic Association) by a political scientist, Rogow (1970). Rogow used his view of political science (similar to our view of behavior influence) to explain both the goals of his study and to summarize his results:

> To begin with, I conceive of political science as a discipline embracing every institution that shapes values in society, because *ultimately politics in a democracy reflects values much more than it shapes them.* We also have reason to believe, thanks to an increasing volume of research by psychologists, sociologists, and some political scientists, that the political process in a crucial sense begins in the home; that is, the business of becoming involved in politics is affected by the experiences and behavioral patterns that define childhood, adolescence, marriage, adulthood, and aging. The values that emerge from these experiences are central in shaping political views in the end, and it is the aggregation of these views that shapes the nation and, to a large extent, the international community. . . . Since psychiatrists, and especially psychoanalysts, so often deal with people who are themselves influential, psychiatrists and psychoanalysts are strategically placed for shaping values at all levels of society [p. 10].

In his study Rogow accepted the psychiatric model of mental illness and demonstrated how psychiatrists working within this framework may have impact on American society far beyond their numbers.

> Approximately 20,000 psychiatrists, assisted by psychologists, social workers, nurses, and other technicians, are directly or indirectly responsible for the one-half million Americans who are confined to mental hospitals with perhaps another

---

[3] This paradox may be reduced if we consider, as did Bertrand Russell (1962, esp. pp. 19–29), that ethics represents a set of rules developed by people who wish to cooperate. As such, they are manmade compromises, and a final apeeal may be made to a majority opinion. That is, ethics in the public as distinct from the private domain becomes difficult to separate from politics: "What remains the same for every community is that the 'just' system is the one that causes the smallest amount of discontent. It is clear that ethics considered as a matter of give-and-take is scarcely distinguishable from politics [Russell, 1962, p. 29]." We will return to this matter of ethics in Chapter 19 but wish to point out both the role of the influencer's personal beliefs and the ultimate ethical problems raised by changing another person.

half-million in general hospitals and private clinics; one out of every two hospital beds is occupied by a mentally disturbed patient. In their roles as part-time doctors and consultants to corporations, government, the armed forces, universities, labor unions, neighborhood mental health centers, and other agencies, the nation's psychiatrists also deal with a significant portion of the estimated ten per cent of Americans who are suffering from some form of mental illness [pp. 15–16].

Rogow's findings on the characteristics of psychiatrists are interesting but too complex for inclusion here. They may be briefly summarized by Rogow's comment that

it is paradoxical in the extreme that at precisely the time more and more people turn to psychiatrists and analysts for wisdom in all sorts of areas, psychiatrists and analysts are less certain of their goals, methods, and achievements than at any time since the early days of Freud. Hardly less paradoxical is the sad truth that many a psychiatrist and analyst shares in the spiritul malaise, the growing uncertainty, the doubts and the despairs, that characterize our society. . . . In psychiatry and psychoanalysis, as elsewhere, there are many moods, styles, and ways of relating to external as well as internal worlds, and many varieties of feeling about the problems of our time. These professions, too, also have their cynics and nihilists, their reformers and radicals, and those who are not uncomfortable in the world of the Jet Set and Beautiful People. There are even a few psychiatrists and analysts who are self-styled hippies. . . . Younger practitioners seem to be more interested than older colleagues in scientific research and methodological problems, and they may differ in other ways as well. . . . But in truth there is no such person as *the* psychiatrist or *the* analyst, whether young or old [pp. 213–214].

A similar survey of the characteristics of other groups of influencers would probably arrive at similar inconclusive findings. However, each discipline has a fundamental way of looking at and justifying the basis of its professional behavior. These basics cannot be challenged without causing members of the profession serious concern.

We have focused thus far on two interrelated aspects of the influencer variable—the political view and the model of man implicit in the discipline's identification. We now examine a related topic, the influencer's empirical concept of his role.

A Case History in Influence

Christie and Geis (1968, 1970) have offered significant anecdotal and empirical observations of the behavioral scientist as an influencer. Their report indicated how behavioral scientists see themselves and view the art or science of influence. Christie, a social psychologist, describes in detail how he developed the concept of a "Machiavelli scale" while spending a year at the Center for the Advanced Study of Behavioral Sciences in Palo Alto, California. He had observed in years of contact with other professionals and in initial contact with his peers at the Center that "Almost everyone there was a manipulator in the behavioral sciences or the protégé of one. We did a dastardly thing. We conducted unstructured interviews with those of our colleagues who had obtained their doctorates or served in departments with individuals who were generally identified as 'operators' by most knowledgeable behavioral scientists [Christie and Geis, p. 960]."

This attempt at self-examination evolved into a search for an approach to the ways in which people can control others by *psychological* rather than physical means. The next step was an examination of the writing of theorists about the nature of *power*. This investigation included such sources as Kung-sun Yang, a fourth-century B.C. Chinese writer, and Kautilya, an Indian philosopher of 300 B.C. The latter offered useful suggestions on how a king could set up networks of internal and external spies and by bribery protect himself from being stabbed while in his harem. Having convinced himself that the control of human behavior was a subject for study even for the ancients, Christie turned to the writings of Machiavelli: "It was a revelation to reread *The Prince* and *The Discourses*. As an undergraduate these had impressed me as thoroughly detestable. After some years of experience with departmental chairmen, deans, college presidents, government officials, and foundation executives, my reaction was different. Some of them had apparently taken Machiavelli to heart or had independently discovered similar techniques of manipulating others [Christie and Geis, 1968, p. 961]."[4]

Christie then took statements from Machiavelli's essays and rephrased them in modern terms. His goal was to ascertain whether differences of opinion about crucial life problems could differentiate people who had power over others and those who did not. From this point on, Christie followed standard procedure for devising a paper-and-pencil personality scale. The resulting personality test (the Mach Scale) has been used in a wide variety of situations. However, we concentrate only on what the development of this test reveals about the psychology of the influencer.

Christie was reassured to find that the Mach Scale was not significantly correlated with the California F Scale, which is usually taken to be a measure of ethnocentricity or fascism. One may obtain a sense of what these two scales purportedly measure from Christie's observation:

> A hunch is that there is a qualitative difference in agreeing with statements representing the two viewpoints. High scorers on both scales should agree with a simple statement, "Most people are no damn good." Underlying the F Scale, however, is a moralistic and judging predisposition: "Most people are no damn good *but they should be*"; whereas a high Mach might say, "People are no damn good, why not take advantage of them." Those high in authoritarianism tend to evaluate others in moralistic terms, those high in manipulativeness in opportunistic terms [Christie and Geis, 1968, p. 964].

[4] Jay (1968) independently observed the same phenomenon in a business setting.

Christie administered the Mach Scale to a group of students in different medical specialties and to medical school faculty members. Repeatedly, psychiatrists scored highest on the scale and surgeons and obstetricians lowest. One interpretation of these data is that the psychiatrist is involved by his task in interpersonal manipulation. "By definition a psychiatrist is attempting to influence the behavior of his patients, i.e., manipulate them. A surgeon is an 'operator' in the technical but not the popular sense [Christie and Geis, 1968, p. 965]."

Most of the findings of the Mach Scale are still highly tentative and subject to the observations offered in Chapter 4 about personality inventory type scales. Christie's own conclusions have considerable importance for the psychology of the influencer:

> Translations of items relating to interpersonal manipulation appear to be relevant enough to differentiate reliably among respondents who are given an opportunity to agree or disagree with them. . . . Endorsement of such items does not appear to be systematically correlated with known measures of psychopathology, political ideology, or social class. . . . Data to date suggest that the greater the involvement of an individual in a complex of formalized role relationships with others, the greater the endorsement of manipulative tactics. . . . Respondents in agreement with Machiavellian or manipulative statements seem to have greater success in meeting the demands of American society—including getting ahead in college. . . . College students who were selected as subjects for laboratory studies succeeded in out-manipulating their partners roughly in proportion to their agreement with Machiavellian precepts [Christie and Geis, 1968, pp. 971–972].

The validity of the Mach Scale, like other personality measurement devices, may arise from a self-fulfilling prophecy or from the subject's observation of his own behavior. As has been pointed out by investigators such as Bem (1967), self-perception is a special case of interpersonal perception in which the subject learns about himself from his own actions. The influence process is ubiquitous; the advantage of the influencer investigating himself is that *sometimes* he can be objective and systematic in his self-observations. However, the most difficult task of the influencer is to be dispassionate about his own brand of metaphoric explanation.

Reification

Concepts such as personality, anxiety, and mental illness are metaphors that offer hypothesized images about human behavior which are linguistic analogies, or figures of speech. It is a common human behavior to act toward such concepts "as if" they were real events instead of figurative analogies. The professional influencer also is subject to the human characteristic of reifying favorite concepts.

Sarbin has made a major contribution to the psychology of influence by systematically tracing the metaphoric origins of words that have taken on a surplus of meaning and have literally "come alive." Hypnosis, anxiety, imagination, and hallucination have all become reified metaphors (Sarbin, 1950, 1964a; Sarbin and Juhasz, 1967, 1970). The historical development of "anxiety" is most relevant:

> For our purposes we can begin our linguistic analysis of anxiety with the language of the Middle Ages. As an introduction, the natural history of word formation seems to be, first, the creation of words to denote objects and events in the distal environment, such as rain, sun, fire, clouds, rivers, people, and so on. These objects and events are mediated primarily by the distance receptors of vision and audition. Later, terms are invented for denoting proximal events, such as aches, itches, engorgements, tickles, hurts, etc. Symbols already in existence to denote distal events are borrowed through metaphor to denote proximal events. . . . To be sure, the creation of a language to denote distal and proximal events is no mean achievement. Such language arose to serve the purposes of men to communicate about things of importance to their survival. The achievement of a language to denote mental states, however, required a kind of *tour de force*, a special set of circumstances, because empirical events as referents for mental states could not be reliably determined. . . . Let us now trace the etymology of the word *anxiety*. We discover that it came into modern English from the Middle English *anguish*. The term came into the lexicon when the effects of the great religious revivals in Europe were carried to the common man in the towns and villages. Unlike the older ecclesiastical words that denoted the more formal aspects of ritual and ceremony, the new words were intended to represent the inward and personal aspects of faith. Devotion, duty, pity, comfort, conscience, purity, and salvation were other words introduced during the thirteenth century. . . . These ecclesiastical words are unlike terms standing for distal and proximal occurrences. They are intended to denote the activities of a shadow-like spirit in a private world. However, words do not spring from the blue—they spring from metaphor. And, on the theory presented here, the word anguish should have denoted events in the distal or proximal ecology *before* it was borrowed to denote a religious (and later, a mentalistic) experience. As used in medieval times, the antecedent of anxiety, *anguish*, carried the meaning of mental or spiritual suffering. But anguish was the anglicized version of the Old French *anguisse* which denoted a painful, choking sensation in the throat. Thus, we find a bodily, proximal referent for a term which had been borrowed to denote a state of mind. Since one of the commonest forms of metaphor is achieved through composing an analogy, we might reconstruct the origins of anguish as follows: A choking sensation in the throat, produced, let us say, by swallowing a chicken bone, is denoted by the term anguisse or anguish. The death of a loved one, a misfortune, recognition of sin, and similar events often lead to a similar proximal event—a globus in the throat. Here are two proximal events that share one property, namely, the discomfort or pain in the throat. To complete the analogy, their symbols are also shared; the term denoting one is employed to denote the other—ignoring the weighty fact that their antecedents are in different modalities, different idioms. . . .

You will be interested to learn, as I was to discover when I prepared this paper that the word anxiety was hardly used in standard medical and psychological textbooks until the late 1930s. It was a result of Freud's writings about *Angst*, translated as anxiety, that the term now has wide currency. Freud's theories made extensive use of mentalistic metaphors, and his more influential theory of anxiety, published in 1923, was no exception [Sarbin, 1964a, pp. 632–634].

SCIENCE AND THE INFLUENCER

The role of the professional influencer must also be observed within the broader context of science in our society. The following comments from Crichton (1971) capture the self-perpetuating nature of science as a reinforced activity: "One should not forget Dr. Szent-Gyorgi's ironic comment that cancer research has kept more investigators alive than the disease has killed [p. 41]." The pursuit of science is a human behavior subject to the same principles of social influence as any other behavior. Our own bias is to place a high value on this particular pursuit. But to maintain a myth of uniqueness will harm the scientist in the long run.

Each generation has shifting views about the functions and ideals of the scientist. (For an excellent review relating these changes to changes in social and political views, see Daniels, 1971). Important consequences follow from placing scientists—particularly those dealing with human behavior—in the same framework of influences as other human beings are subject to.

The scientist needs to take into account the subtle social and political influences on his investigations. In taking the position that science is a human activity, Brandt (1970) has argued that psychology as commonly pursued in North America is largely a result of the American way of life:

The American way of life is one of doing. The conquering of the new continent, its original inhabitants, and its natural obstacles and resources required doing and not contemplation. People who left Europe and started a new way of life had a sense of urgency and could not sit and wait to see what was going to happen. . . . They had to "predict and control." Saying the same in political terms, they had to enforce "law and order." As scientists they were looking for "law and order" in nature so that they could "predict and control" it. . . . The similarity between the general American ideals as expressed in the American way of life and the principles of American psychology is inescapable. However, American psychologists will object to the conclusion that American psychology is a result of the American way of life. Their objection is based on the contention that their psychology is not the result of the "life style" of American psychologists but the result of "empirical" studies, of observations of observable data, of the experimental testing of hypotheses. In other words, they will, by their objections to the thesis developed here, support that thesis, since their objection must be that there "is" a "consistent," "parsimonious," "deterministic," "knowable" world that can be determined by "prediction and control." These psychologists deny that their picture of the world in general and of man in particular is a result of their general humanness and their particular personalities. . . . American psychology can thus be said to be truly American. It reflects the American emphasis on doing (experimentation) and making (quantification of data and publications), as well as the contradictions inherent in American society, and the feeling of general superiority. By being to such an extent an American product, American psychology fails, however, to meet one of the generally accepted requirements of a science which some psychologists believe to be universal truth [pp. 1091–1093].

The thrust of a growing movement in science to link conceptually the scientist, the social influences on him, and his "discoveries" may be observed in fields other than the social sciences. Kessel (1969) called the attention of psychologists to the implications of a current work on research in the biological and physical sciences. In arguing that it is difficult to divorce the personality of the scientist from his work, Kessel indicated that

Additional and even more striking support comes from a book that recently created quite a stir in scientific circles, J. D. Watson's (1968) *The Double Helix.* The implications of Watson's forthright account of the discovery of the molecular structure of DNA are clear and compelling. So much for impersonal and cold-blooded scientists; so much, too, for the ruthlessly systematic procedures of the scientific method. Watson reveals an infinitely more interesting and complex process, unfolding among personalities of the liveliest variety. . . . But still more important, he shows how differences of personality are not an unfortunate intrusion into scientific research but an essential ingredient in it. . . . Science is thus more intricate, and far more interesting, than the image of cold-blooded eggheads in white coats making breakthroughs. (Davy, 1968) . . . in science, as in any other human activity, personality and competitiveness are ever-present, even determining elements. That they have traditionally been hidden by biographers and historians of science is due to the unusually protracted survival in this field of scholarship of Dickensian stereotypes. Scientists themselves have long been steeped in the illusion that science, by forcing on its practitioners the habit of intellectual integrity, also purifies them of human frailties like aggressiveness and hero worship. (Luria, 1968) . . . the empiricist view of autonomous, objective facts as science's crucial elements is questionable even in the context of justification. Given that paradigms exist, it seems rather fanciful to assert that "the facts speak for themselves." Beyond the level of more trivial scientific observations, it is evident that facts, the reasons for gathering them in a certain way, and the choice of their interpretation cannot be considered apart, that "scientific fact and theory are not categorically separable" (Kuhn, 1962, p. 7). Observer and observed are not separable [p. 1002].

We appear to be seeing a trend of increasing appreciation of perspective, both chronological and interdisciplinary. This trend is evidenced by the scientists cited as well as by social historians and historians of science (Daniels, 1971; Kuhn, 1970; Rothman, 1971) who are placing developments in science, psychology, and other disciplines into the context of the sociocultural developments of a particular historical period.

The pursuit of science is as human an activity as any other described in this book. Thus, the development of a specialized sociology of science (Barber and Hirsch, 1962) is logical. Science as a social phenomenon has a social history, a pattern of organization, a social image, and social responsibility by its practitioners.

Another illustration of the social nature of science is the disputes among scientists over the priority of discoveries. We cite this example because, first, logically it should not exist and, second, it is very typical human behavior. Merton (1957b) reviewed some of the major scientific disputes. Many of the great names of science such as Galileo, Newton, Jenner, Faraday, Darwin, and Wallace were involved at one time or another in violent disputes over the priority of discoveries. At first such a fact seems to go counter to the expected personal disinterest and humility of the scientist. But as Merton notes:

> The value of humility takes diverse expression. One form is the practice of acknowledging the heavy indebtedness to the legacy of knowledge bequeathed by predecessors. This kind of humility is perhaps best expressed in the epigram Newton made his own: "If I have seen farther, it is by standing on the shoulders of giants" (this, incidentally, in a letter to Hooke who was then challenging Newton's priority in the theory of colors). . . . Humility is expected also in the form of the scientist's insisting upon his personal limitations and the limitations of scientific knowledge altogether. Galileo taught himself and his pupils to say, "I do not know." . . . If this contrast between public image ("what I may appear to the world") and self-image ("but to myself I seem") is fitting for the greatest among scientists, it is presumably not entirely out of place for the rest. . . . Like all human values, the value of modesty can be vulgarized and run into the ground by excessive and thoughtless repetition. It can become merely conventional, empty of substance and genuine feeling. There really *can* be too much of a good thing. . . . The quiet, self-appraisal by a celebrated scientist: "I possess every good quality, but the one that distinguishes me above all is modesty" [pp. 464–465].

Merton explains this apparently paradoxical concern with recognition in terms of the reward structure of science, which places heavy value on originality: "Like other institutions also, science has its system of allocating rewards for performance of roles" [p. 484]. The scientist works for his tokens, the strongest of which is peer recognition of originality—be it a new discovery or a praised publication. The economics of exchange are at work on the scientist as on all other humans.

The Influence of Scientific Discipline

Another influence on the scientific investigator is even stronger than his desire for peer recognition. *What* and *how* he observes is influenced by his training in a particular scientific discipline.

Simon and Stedry (1969) offer a useful (albeit sardonic) overview of the arbitrary distinctions between the approaches of different disciplines to human behavior.

> A person who has occasion to wander into various territories in the social sciences is struck not only by the diversity of tribal customs relating to substantive matters—concepts and theories—but by the diversity of methodologies as well. If a social scientist is discovered computing a regression coefficient, he is almost certainly an economist; a factor analysis identifies him as a psychologist, probably working with test data; a *t* or chi-square test, as a social or experimental psychologist, probably working with experimental data, etc. Mathematical statistics has provided a common meeting ground for the statistically sophisticated of all disciplines, but the statistical techniques they have brought back to their own tribes have tended to be somewhat specialized. Scaling techniques and latent structure analysis are hardly known outside of social psychology, the country of origin; the work that has been done on the statistical identification problem is an even more closely held secret of the econometricians. The highly technical nature of some of these developments and the language in which they must be described have hindered their diffusion. . . . The same may be said about empirical methodology. For a traditional economic theorist, an empirical study means going to the reports of the U. S. Census of the Bureau of Foreign and Domestic Commerce. A social psychologist generates new data by experimenting with small groups of college sophomores in a laboratory. The anthropologist-sociologist buys a ticket to New Guinea or Newburyport. The ecologist-sociologist and the demographer-sociologist behave more like the economist, looking largely to official tabulations of aggregative data for their information. The public opinion specialist constructs a stratified random sample and asks questions of a number of respondents. These are some of the principal varieties of social scientists, viewed as data seekers [pp. 306].

Different methodology in approaching the same problems may lead to different results. The diversity is maintained not by questions of which methodology is best, but by the social system within which the investigators are rewarded (by money, promotions, consultantships, prestige) for doing what will protect the "best interests" of the dicipline to which they have devoted years of training. The effect of training is often very specific in the individual. The particular discipline to a large extent determines *where* the budding influencer will observe, *how* he will observe, and *what* answers he will find. Schools of approach do not develop by chance at certain times in certain academic settings. In many instances the mention of a researcher's university and his particular period in time is sufficient for predicting the approach to human behavior used in his research (for example, a University of Iowa psychologist of the late 1940s, a University of Chicago sociologist of the 1930s, a Yale learning theorist in the 1940s and 1950s).

We have pointed out in Chapter 2 how the study of human behavior has been broken down into various disciplines such as psychology, sociology, economics, and political science. Students who read observers in the past such as Freud, Marx, Bentham, and John Stuart Mill are usually astonished by how these writers seem to cut across so many fields. Yet the fault or credit is not these authors'; they covered but *one* field—that of human behavior and influence. Because of a series of historical events such as the university departmental structure (Barzun, 1968), information increase, and a tendency by investigators to perpetuate their own kind, we have now reached a stage of fragmentation and specialization in studying human behavior.

The rewards society offers to the scientific investigator, and any other kind of influencer, are usually greatest when he stays within his particular discipline, school, or model—where his work is more readily "understood" and its relevance recognized. There are exceptions, of course, but the general rule for all types of influencers (as indeed for all citizens) is, "Don't rock the boat."

But, what happens to influencers who do investigate areas that are socially taboo, such as sexual behavior or parapsychology, or at variance with the tenor of their own field because of the questions raised (such as in Rosenthal's "experimenter bias," Sarbin's "metaphors," or Szasz's "problems in living")?

THE INFLUENCER AND UNPOPULAR STUDIES

Certain areas of investigation are not fashionable or reinforceable at given times. Pursuit of such studies may stigmatize the scientists attracted to them. What is acceptable and what is not continually change. For example, in a 1961 symposium at the American Psychological Association investigators reported on their experiences in encountering mostly unpleasant societal and professional reactions to their fields of research—*death, sexual behavior, homosexuality,* and *parapsychology (extrasensory perception)*—which were then among the taboo fields of study. By the end of the 1960s, research in these topics were acceptable, even praiseworthy (especially sexual behavior and homosexuality). Yet taboo areas remain. The New York *Times* (September 7, 1971) reported the accusation of a psychiatrist against a leading psychiatric journal that had refused to accept an advertisement for his book which dealt with "sexual intimacy between patients and therapists." This new field of investigation may be one which creates some discomfort among fellow professionals.

Two current investigators are examples of individuals whose models of behavior are unpopular with some of their colleagues—but for different reasons and with different consequences. One is the psychologist B. F. Skinner and the other is the psychiatrist Thomas S. Szasz. The theories of these two investigators are both relevant to the approach to personality presented in this book. Skinner's research (1938, 1953, 1968) and theories (see Chapter 3) are fundamental to a behavioral approach to personality. His recent book *Beyond Freedom and Dignity* (1971) presents the view that man is not "autonomous"; there is no "inner man." Human behavior is a function of environmental influence (see Chapter 6). The book has evoked considerable controversy and even some criticism from the Vice President who accuses Skinner of attacking "the very precepts on which our society is based (Agnew, 1971)."

Szasz's position (1961, 1965a, 1970) is that basic concepts of deviant behavior such as *mental illness* are metaphors which grew out of a set of social views of a particular period. Moreover, in order to deal with these concepts, it is necessary to study the originators of the metaphors and the social climate in which they lived. The metaphors helped these individuals achieve their goals. Szasz (1970, p. 8) has insisted that the unit of study in "madness" must be the mental patient *and* the psychiatrist (in our terms, the influencer), for it is the latter who has created and maintained the concept of "madness" as "illness."

Thus, each of these investigators points out in his own manner and terminology that the emperor has no clothes. Yet one of them, Skinner, has been honored by his peers to the extent of being rated the most influential living psychologist of his time. The other, Szasz, is considered a heretic by his peers, who are likely in private and occasionally in print to use psychiatric labels to explain his behavior.

The differences in the consequences of the behavior of these two influencers tells us much about the psychology of the influencer. Skinner has many behavior and learning theory antecedents in psychologists such as Thorndike and philosophers such as Locke (see Chapter 2). He literally and figuratively speaks the same language as his peers and predecessors and adheres to the same basic methods of data and proof. His views and particularly their societal implications are labeled as "controversial" in a field where controversy, at least of a mild sort, is accepted as part of the game. If his views began to predominate within his field, this would represent a mild paradigm shift (Kuhn, 1970) which would at least for a period of time strengthen the field. Skinner has established a "school," which means that he has disciples, supporters, journals, TV interviews, and all the trimmings of a successful and powerful influencer in our society. He has even achieved the ultimate recognition of having made it in American society: his face has been on the cover of *Time* (September 20, 1971).

Szasz, on the other hand, is a virtual outcast in his own discipline. Few if any psychiatric investigators support his views, at least in print. He has even been booed by his peers during a presentation at a meeting of his professional group. For a short time he was denied hospital facilities for his teaching. As he and his colleagues realize, the implications of his views question the very existence of his discipline. If his views about "institutional psychiatry"—psychiatrists working in mental hospitals maintain the myth of mental illness and represent the coercive forces of the state impinging upon the rights of individuals to determine the disposition of their own bodies—begin to pervade our society, they would result in the destruction of psychiatry as it now exists. Szasz challenges the rules of data and fundamental assumptions of psychiatry.

Scarf (1971) has offered a popular presentation of Szasz and his impact:

> Szasz has been called everything from a crank and a paranoid to a prophet and passionate humanitarian. In reviewing *Law, Liberty and Psychiatry*, Szasz's third book, the late Manfred Guttmacher, an eminent forensic psychiatrist, complained, "A bird that fouls its nest courts criticism." . . . Szasz has hammered away at virtually every basic assumption of accepted psychiatric thought—and most vehemently at the practice of involuntary therapy . . . . Provocative statements no longer arouse widespread reactions . . . they fall into a well of official silence. No professional colleague has mounted a serious counterattack against Szasz's accusations. Either he is simply ignored or—and this is coming to be far more common—he is conceded privately to be raising some important points. Szasz, nevertheless, is still often regarded as psychiatry's thorn—a fanatic, troublemaker and extremist. Fellow professionals may agree that he has exposed important problem areas in the field, but they cite with distaste his popularity with groups like the John Birch Society and with odd sects such as Scientology. The Birchers, opposing psychiatry as some sort of Communist conspiracy, are delighted with this psychiatrist who attacks fellow psychiatrists. . . . The Scientologists, a quasi-religious society dedicated to salvation through "clearing the mind" have transformed Szasz into one of their spiritual patrons. . . . On the other hand, journals of the far left, such as *The Radical Therapist*, are equally favorable to Szasz; many of the writers for that magazine stand solidly behind his position on involuntary hospitalization, and one recently proposed the establishment of an "Insane Liberation Front." One well-known psychiatrist observes, "Szasz's thought has become the meeting place of radical opinion both from the right and the left."
>
> Says Szasz; "My involvement with these groups is practically nil. I think that most of what they say is nonsense. But in part we are all fighting the same battle, the battle against the legal and moral outrage of involuntary psychiatry. You know there is an old Arab proverb, 'The enemy of my enemy is my friend.' We are all abolitionists" [pp. 40–50].

The consequences of being an influencer with unpopular views are controversy, ad hominem attacks, bitterness, and strange bedfellows. But, despite the reaction within the discipline, views contrary to current paradigms may result in long-term changes by influencing others outside the discipline. In this instance Szasz's views are interacting with those of psychologists and sociologists, and new alternative models of theory and practice may be emerging.

THE INFLUENCER AS A PROJECTIVE DEVICE

A major influencer frequently serves as a device onto which other influencers graft and justify their own theories about human behavior. Freud is perhaps the best example of a theorist whose views have been used to justify a very wide range of interpretation and practice. This process is consistent with the view of the influencer and individual as historian presented in the next section.

Machiavelli provides a useful case history of a writer and observer whose views have served many (and contradictory) purposes of others. Berlin (1971) offers a review of the many interpretations and explanations of Machiavelli's *The Prince,* which we have also discussed within the context of the history of theories of human behavior (Chapter 2). Through the years, the theory of man offered by Machiavelli has been interpreted as

> a satire—for he certainly cannot literally have meant what he said . . . a cautionary tale; for whatever else he was, Machiavelli was a passionate patriot, a democrat, a believer in liberty, and *The Prince* must have been intended . . . to warn men of what tyrants could be and do, the better to resist them . . . a typical piece of its period, a mirror for princes, a genre exercise common enough in the Renaissance and before (and after) it, with very obvious borrowings and "echoes"; more gifted than most of these, and certainly more hard-boiled (and influential), but not so very different in style, content, or intention . . . an anti-Christian piece . . . an attack on the Church and all her principles, a defense of the pagan view of life. . . . Machiavelli is an anguished humanist, and one who, so far from seeking to soften the impression made by the crimes that he describes, laments the vices of men which make such wicked courses politically unavoidable—a moralist who wrings his hands over a world in which political ends can only be achieved by means that are morally evil, and therefore the man who divorced the province of politics from that of ethics. . . . Machiavelli is a cold technician, ethically and politically uncommitted, an objective analyst of politics, a morally neutral scientist . . . he is, above all, a marvelous mirror of his age, a man sensitive to the contours of his time, who faithfully described what others did not admit or recognize, an inexhaustible mine of acute contemporary observation . . . he is a man of deep insight into the real historical (or superhistorical) forces that mold men and transform their morality—in particular, a man who rejected Christian principles for those of reason, political unity, and centralization . . . he is the man of genius who saw the need for uniting a chaotic collection of small and feeble principalities into a coherent whole . . . he is a political pragmatist and patriot . . . [pp. 20–21].

These mutually contradictory estimates of Machiavelli by well-known observers demonstrate that in dealing with conceptions of human behavior, we are dealing with a *reaction* to what the influencer says and to an *interpretation* of his behavior in a specific time and place consistent with the reactor's own values. This behavior is, itself, subject to the influence process.

One of the best current illustrations of this process are the various reactions to Skinner's contributions to utopian and social commentary literature, *Walden Two* and *Beyond Freedom and Dignity*. For example, *Time* magazine (Sept. 20, 1971) revealed that "Rollo May believes that Skinner is a totalitarian without fully knowing it [p. 52]" and quoted Arthur Koestler's reference to Skinner's work as "a monumental triviality that has sent psychology into a modern version of the Dark Ages [p. 52]; as well as historian Peter Gay's mention of "the innate naiveté, intellectual bankruptcy and half-deliberate cruelty of behaviorism [p. 52]."

On the other hand, Sennett (1971) criticized Skinner on a very different basis: "The actual text of Skinner's new book reveals a man desperately in search of some way to preserve the oldfashioned virtues associated with nineteenth century individualism in a world where self-reliance no longer makes sense [p. 12]."

Whereas most reviewers of Skinner's latest work are in agreement with his concerns about the future of society, although not necessarily his proposals for change, one reviewer (in the *Wall Street Journal*) has even questioned the accuracy of what he termed Skinner's "apocalyptic" views of society:

> it does mean that [the individual's] behavior is already operating under a system of external controls that are linked to his need to survive. And this adds crucial weight to the charge that Mr. Skinner talks only of theories and offers no blueprint for social design. For if there is already a kind of invisible hand controlling human behavior, then it is not enough to say that we need to have a designed society; one has to say how a social designer could improve on the system of social design already operating [Anderson, 1971].

The point of these quotations is that as the influencer becomes more visible in his writing, more fundamental in his observation of behavior, or draws wider implications from his theories, he may come to serve as a projective device unto which others place all kinds of interpretations. The wide range of interpretations of Machiavelli's observations will probably soon be matched by the varied analyses of Skinner and his work.

THE INFLUENCER AS HISTORIAN

We present the influencer as historian to offer a point of view about this role and to link it with the notion of daily human behavior as a historical process. The influencer, like the historian, brings together material to fit his theories and his own "needs," or reinforcers. This is not a criticism; it is an observation. Criticism is justified, however, when the influencer is not careful and believes he is dealing with completely objective facts.

The historian Carr (1961) has presented material about the nature of historical "facts" that is analogous to our view of human behavior: the history of man like the behavior of the individual has meaning only in the context of current observations of a student, an influencer, or a historian. Carr puts it this way: "The belief in a hard core of historical facts existing objectively and independently of the interpretation of the historian is a preposterous fallacy, but one which it is very hard to eradicate [p. 10]." We can view the past and understand it only through the eyes of the present. The historian is of his own age and is bound to it by the conditions of human existence. The very words which he uses—words like *democracy, empire, war, revolution*—have current connotations from which he cannot divorce his usage.

As Carr states, "The historian and the facts of history are necessary to one another. The historian without his facts is rootless and futile; the facts without their historian are dead and meaningless. My first answer therefore to the question, 'What is history?' is that it is a continuous process of interaction between the historian and his facts, an unending dialogue between the present and past [p. 35]."

What does the analogue of the influencer as a historian imply? Most personality theorists approach human behavior as if it had a reality of its own (see the preceding section on reification). But *behavior is as real as the facts of history*. In effect, both become meaningful only in terms of a reactor whose interpretation is, itself, a function of (influenced by) the same kinds of variables as all other human behavior. At first glance we are dealing with an infinite regress, since observation of the interpreter of the behavior is also influenced by these same variables. We can break into this cycle by at least (a) pointing out its existence; (b) using as our unit of observation the behavior of the individual, the reaction to the behavior, the behavior of the observer-reporter, and the reaction to it; (c) pointing out that (a) and (b) are merely hypotheses about behavior which may or may not be better than others, but which may help us in terms of what we might do with them.

We emphasize analogizing *behavior* with *facts* in this chapter to point out how his conception of what he is dealing with determines *what* the investigator looks for, *how* he looks for it, and *what* he eventually does with it. Just as the historian seeks facts that fit or test his theory, the personality theorist seeks sources of behavior in terms of his paradigm—be it based on the "motives" or the "conditioning" of the individual. These are inferred explanatory concepts which may be as useful or as deceptive as historical facts.

Dimont (1971) expressed the same view in a slightly different manner:

History can be compared to a vast smörgåsbord, with the facts spread on a prepared table like exotic dishes, each vying for attention. There are two ways the historian can serve himself. He can close his eyes and help himself to a chance sampling of what the table has to offer, in which case he would have that highly praised mode of history known as "objective." Or he can select those facts that suit his concept of history, in which case he would construct that highly criticized mode of history known as "interpretive." We prefer the second school because—to paraphrase an epigram by Oscar Wilde—Objective history gives us the dates of everything and the meaning of nothing. Facts themselves have no intrinsic worth other than that they happened. Meaning can come only after facts have been sifted through the human mind and clothed with value [p. xii].

This point may be summarized by Carr's observation (1961) that "All history is 'contemporary history,' declared Croce, meaning that history consists essentially in seeing the past through the eyes of the present and in the light of its problems, and that the main work of the historian is not to record, but to evaluate; for, if he does not evaluate, how can he know what is worth recording? [p. 22]."

The Historian as Paradigm

One attribute of living beings, including people, is that they are continuously being altered by experience. The psychological problem of what environmental stimuli a human will select, process, and formulate to alter his further behavior is also faced by the professional historian. Carr (1961, esp. ch. 4) has suggested procedures that the average, sane man might follow in evaluating his own life situation in a manner similar to the ways used by historians. The reverse will be done in this section, and we will start with the "average" man as a professional historian.

Carr first addressed himself to the historian's *facts* or, in our context, to what information he will choose to process. Posing the question in this manner reveals something very important about a view of man and his world and leads to the position about theories of personality in this book: namely, that the historian, the personality theorist, and the average sane man all *formulate their experience*, and this formulation is an act which is sometimes worth considering as historically significant.

Carr (1961, pp. 3–4) has contrasted the accepted view of facts at the turn of the century—that with sufficient evidence *the* truth could be established about any phenomenon—with the midtwentieth-century view that knowledge is processed by individuals and therefore is neither impersonal nor objective. "[We] pay the price of prejudice to be involved . . . in activity that has meaning for us but which destroys our objectivity."

The first condition leading to the selection of a fact is its significance in deciding a point. Rather than speaking for themselves, "The facts speak only when the historian calls on them: it is he who decides to which facts to give the floor, and in what order or context [Carr, 1961, p. 9]." The range of facts available to the historian, as to every other person, is limited and many have already been selected. The documents available to a historian are preponderantly ones that someone has saved. Moreover, documentation is usually generated by certain groups and not others and in and of itself already represents a bias. Artifacts are often spared, as in Pompeii, by accidents of nature. A psychologist apparently creates his own significant events through the design of his experiments; but the availability of time, space, equipment, subjects, and ethically permissible manipulations has already limited his operation. The problems that will interest the psychologist and intrigue his colleagues further narrow the range of potential information.

A fact may exist but be so unknown or buried in the professional literature that it has no consequences and is not influential. Finding facts is like fishing: the chances of getting what one wants depends *in part* on where one looks, what methods one uses, and how persistent one is.

There is a constant interchange between the person and the information he receives. He attends to the information most useful in making the decision that has stimulated the information search. The average person will find, however, that if his sampling of relevant information is too biased, the reaction from his peers will be unpleasant.

To summarize, let us quote Carr (1961) once more: "The relation of man to his environment is the relation of the historian to his theme. The historian is neither the humble slave, nor the tyrannical master, of his facts. The relation between the historian and his facts is one of equality, of give-and-take. . . . The historian is engaged in a continuous process of moulding his facts to his interpretation and his interpretation to his facts . . . [p. 34]."

Facets of the Historical Problem

What is the result of the constant interchange between the historian and his facts? First, we must realize that we have no direct knowledge of events; we have instead *knowledge* of history (C. L. Becker, 1935) which, whether personal or professional, is an abstraction: "It is not possible, it is not essential, that this picture should be complete or completely true; it is essential that it should be useful to Mr. Everyman; and that it may be useful to him he will hold in memory, of all the things he might hold in memory, those things only which can be related with some reasonable degree of relevance and harmony to his idea of himself and what he is doing in the world and what he hopes to do [p. 245]."

Carr (1961) has put the matter this way: "The nightmare quality of Kafka's novels lies in the fact that nothing that happens has any apparent cause, or any cause that can be ascertained: this leads to the total disintegration of the human personality, which is based on the assumption that events have causes, and that enough of these causes are ascertainable to build up in the human mind a pattern of past and present sufficiently coherent to serve as a guide to action [p. 122]."

Thus we see that *some explanation and order must be given to experience.* Experience with all its faults is used to guide behavior; it is not perfect, but it is what we call *learning*: "every generation, our own included, will, must inevitably, understand the past and anticipate the future in the light of its own restricted experience, must inevitably play on the dead whatever tricks it finds necessary for its own peace of mind [C. L. Becker, 1935, p. 253]." A person orients himself to his present tasks by referring to what has preceded. Since the present is but the dividing line between the past and the future, anticipation and recollection merge and influence each other. History, both personal and professional, is an instrumental activity.

At a general level the preceding material refers to the view (expressed in Chapter 3) that all theories of personality are makeshifts—the best that can be constructed in any given period of time. "In the history of history, a myth is a once valid but now discarded version of the human story, as our now valid versions will, in due course, be relegated to the category of discarded myths [C. L. Becker, 1935, p. 247]." In Carr's words (1961), "The historian, before he begins to write history, is the product of history [p. 48]."

Humans construct and reconstruct formulations of the world they know in a way that will help them deal with the world they anticipate. The constructions are not eternal; they are constantly being compared to reality. These constructions work satisfactorily or are changed. This is one of Kuhn's major points (1970) in looking at changes in science: when too many discrepancies exist between constructs and reality, a new paradigm is likely to result.

A person lives in a specific historical era. One does well to ask *when* the author was writing in addition to *what* he was writing. Whether they are social, political, or economic, the scientific wellsprings of the activity that the historian uses to order events indicate his own concerns. The very events he selects indicate the author's interests and values. The methods that he describes in which people influence one another are additional sources of information about how he construes social influence. Finally, how he reports the outcomes of action reveals a good deal about the author's view of people and his values, as do the more explicit morals that he draws from his material. In Carr's words (1961), "The beliefs which we hold and the standards of judgment which we set up are part of history, and are as much subject to historical investigation as any other aspect of human behaviour [p. 109]."

The historian and the average person are also similar in their treatment of *unique* events. "The historian is not really interested in the unique, but in what is general in the unique [Carr, 1961, p. 80]." While unexpected idiosyncrasies appear in the midst of dry pages, if they have no impact and are not representative, they remain the cocktail conversation of the historian. The more likely question to ask is whether the unexpected behavior, if not representative of the times or the person, indicates a more pervasive set of conditions that must be taken into account. But if nothing in the future can be predicted from the single instance of behavior, most people will shrug, forgive, and probably forget the whole matter. Again, uniqueness and generalization involve the assigning of significance to behavior.

Another facet of creating history is the development of social science. Carr (1961, p. 179) considers Descartes focal to this development, because of his emphasis on man not only as thinking but as *thinking about his thinking*. In social science man is not only the *actor* but also the *audience*, the *observer*, and the *subject* of observation. Man *uses* history (as noted before, history making is an instrumental activity). "A man's relation to the society of which he is a part must be represented to him in some form; it must be explained and rationalized [Smith, 1964, p. 34]." *It is not that history has a purpose, but that the historian has one or, more accurately, several.*

The historian, like any other professional influencer, has a job. Like other academicians, he must fill space and time, that is, publish and lecture. He gathers material that will help him in these tasks. He will use the methods currently in vogue or justify innovations that solve problems found with prior methods. The questions he asks, the material he prepares, the research techniques he uses, the concepts he calls for in his organization, and, above all, the area he investigates reflect the interests of his era—the material about which he and his audience (department chairman, editor, and even students) wish to gain understanding. While not insensitive to reinforcers such as royalties, authors write the books they wish existed, and professors write books that will help them with the courses they would like to teach. At the time of this writing, books on the urban, the black, the impoverished, and the female experience are on the increase to meet the demands of a new audience. Books on the development, diffusion, and impact of technology; on Asian and African history; and on drugs, American Indians, policemen, consumerism, grade schools, and dissent are also on the increase because these topics have a significance they lacked a decade ago.

In short, similarities exist between the psychologist's and historian's organization of data about the world. As with all people, this organization reflects what the person considers significant and wishes to know more about. What these topics will be and what information is collected reflect the period of time in which the person lives; but once the psychologist or historian has done his work, his efforts affect his time. Marx, Freud, and Einstein are examples of men whose organization of information affected the types of information that followed. There is a constant interchange between the past, present, and future and between the facts that must be explained and the facts collected because of that explanation. The maker of theories is a prime source of influence; his effect is even more pervasive than that of the person who is immediately present, for the theorizer influences the very things to which we attend. While a product of his times, he also creates them.

THE SPREAD OF INFLUENCE

This final section could well be subtitled *From Innovation to Cult*. Many theories about human behavior begin as innovations to impress others and quickly gather adherents and develop into institutions which resemble cults. Such a spread of influence is a major source of satisfaction to the influencer.

An important element in a psychology of behavior influence is how new ideas (which are frequently old ideas reborn) and modes of influence start, grow, spread, become established, and eventually are replaced by newer models. This phenomenon has been illustrated in the field of behavior influence by the growth of psychoanalysis, from Freud's original struggle in Vienna to its world-wide acceptance, and the more recent growth of the behavior modification approach.

We describe the latter development because (*a*) we are sympathetic and involved in it; (*b*) it is still in progress; (*c*) it lays the basis for material to be presented in subsequent chapters; and (*d*) it follows a pattern similar to that of many social movements. Ullmann and Sikora (1970), and Ullmann (1969c, 1972) have placed this growth within more general concepts of social movement. Krasner (1971) has described the development of behavior therapy in a historical context as follows: "There are at least 15 streams of development which have come together within the last part of the 1960s to form a distinctive approach to helping individuals with behavior socially labeled as deviant. These streams, of course, are not independent of each other; the merger of streams to form behavior therapy is far from complete [p. 488]." These streams included investigations in experimental, social, clinical, and developmental psychology as well as the contributions of investigators such as Skinner, Wolpe, Pavlov, and Eysenck. They even included a "stream that can be labeled *utopian* in its emphasis on planning the social environment to elicit and maintain the best of man's behavior. It includes an ethical concern for the social implications of behavior control, as well as offering blueprints for a better life. . . . Thus, behavior therapy is more than a series of techniques of the application of learning theory; it is a broad conceptualization of human behavior. Unless we view behavior therapy in this context, its applications and implications will be irrelevant" [Krasner, 1971, pp. 489–491].

Chapter 9, on behavior modification, details this approach to human behavior. Here we are interested in the ways in which influence is *mediated by the influencer*. As the above streams of development began to merge into a clear, alternative, paradigmatic approach to human behavior, anthologies appeared of the early published material (Eysenck, 1960a; Franks, 1964; Krasner and Ullmann, 1965; Ullmann and Krasner, 1965). At about the same time, journals specializing in publishing articles in this field appeared (for example, *Behaviour*

Research and Therapy was first published in 1963). The availability of a journal signals the arrival of a new approach as well as attracting and stimulating articles. It provides both an outlet for previously rejected publications and an increased audience, since articles germane to the group are no longer widely dispersed.

A concomitant in the spread of innovations is the development of a professional organization; this denotes a growing cohesion and exclusiveness among advocates of the new approach. Thus the Association for the Advancement of Behavior Therapy started in the mid-1960s and served as a focus of professional involvement and enhancement of this approach.

The spread of influence is facilitated and enhanced by workshops, training institutes, programs at professional meetings, graduate and postdoctoral programs specializing in the new approach and by traveling troubadours. The literature in journals and books increases, and specialists develop as bibliographies are compiled.

The general approach is further extended beyond its early clinical origins to the hospital, schoolroom, prison community, and the general society. Finally, personal and professional controversies develop among leading influencers in the movement and splinter groups evolve. Certification and other insignia may be developed to designate who is "truly" qualified.

LAST WORD

The influencer, like the historian, is a product of his times and of the other influencers currently at work. We will resume this theme in several later chapters. In the next chapter we consider the evidence on influence that has emerged from the psychology laboratory. However, we cannot refrain from making one last point about the influence of the influencer: most influencers, at least in American society, deny their influencing role. This is expressed in the following quote from Galbraith (1956):

> The role of power in American life is a curious one. The privilege of controlling the actions or of affecting the income and property of other persons is something that no one of us can profess to seek or admit to possessing. No American ever runs for office because of an avowed desire to govern. He seeks to serve—and then only in response to the insistent pressure of friends or of that anonymous, but oddly vocal, fauna which inhabit the grass roots. We no longer have public officials, only public servants. The same scrupulous avoidance of the terminology of power characterizes American business. The head of the company is no longer the boss—the term survives only as an amiable form of address—but the leader of the team . . . despite this convention, which outlaws ostensible pursuit of power and which leads to a constant search for euphemisms to disguise its possession, there is no indication that, as a people, we are averse to power [p. 25].

In this chapter we have touched on a few of the influences on and impacts of the influencer. The emphasis has been upon the influencer as a human being who is subject in his professional and social roles to the same kinds of influences that affect the behavior of other people.

CHAPTER **8**

The Experimental Laboratory and Behavior Influence

The experimental method and the behavior influence theory of people's actions are intertwined. Overt behavior provides a dependent variable with which to evaluate the impact of different conditions or independent variables. Any tactic that alters an operationally defined dependent measure—that is, demonstrably influences behavior—has import for the view of "personality" being presented in this volume.

Analogue, or circumscribed laboratory, studies permit evaluation of a set of conditions controlled so that alternative explanations can be ruled out. The use of miniature or model situations permits the collection of data rapidly, the random assignment of people, and the manipulation and analysis of several variables at the same time. Ideas are likely therefore to be developed or tested in a model situation. The most obvious disadvantage of the circumscribed study is that the results may not generalize to different, larger, less controlled behaviors and to populations in daily life or clinical practice.

Despite this difficulty, a great number of excellent studies have been produced in the psychological laboratory. This research is now slowly being applied in classroom, clinic, industrial, and community situations (Frank, 1961; Goldstein, Heller, and Sechrest, 1966; Krasner and Ullmann, 1965). This chapter samples some of the many ideas and studies available.

Selection of material is probably more arbitrary in this chapter than in any other because more studies of good quality seemed relevant to behavior influence. In addition to the criteria mentioned in previous chapters, we have tried to sample classic articles that generated additional investigations as well as some more recent works we think likely to have a similar impact.

THE PSYCHOLOGICAL EXPERIMENT
AS A BEHAVIOR SETTING

Two points can be made by starting with the psychology of the psychological experiment. The first is that the participants—both the psychologists and their subjects—are engaging in a social activity that is as describable in terms of behavioral principles as any other activity. To put it a bit differently, while an experiment may study a facet of behavior influence, the people involved in all aspects of the study are themselves subject to behavior influence (see Chapter 7). The second point is related to the first: the experimental situation itself may illustrate behavioral principles beyond those intentionally being tested.

Among the principles most directly illustrated by the participants of experiments are the effects of reinforcing stimuli and self-fulfilling prophecies on the experimenter and the effect of discriminative stimulus control on the subject. We start our discussion with the latter topic.

Discriminative Stimuli and Subject Behavior
in the Experiment

In the next chapter, on hypnosis, we make considerable use of the concept of demand characteristics. A *demand characteristic* may be formulated as a discriminative stimulus. More specifically, demand characteristics are indications (stimuli present) of what sort of behaviors are expected (presumptively) to have reinforcing consequences. The very word *experiment* has a favorable aura in our society in general and on a college campus in particular. The word implies both novelty and discipline within a socially acceptable and protected environment. The person entering a psychological experiment—or, for that matter, situations labeled as psychotherapy, hypnosis, and sensitivity training—suspends normal disbelief. That is, he becomes less critical and more likely to emit behaviors that he would not ordinarily engage in. The discriminative stimuli of daily life and personal responsibility would usually prevail, precluding such behavior.

An example is an experiment in which female college students wore bathing suits, entered a sweatbox, and then chose one of two words presented to them on typed cards; this was not exactly a usual life situation. In another experiment atypical from life (Milgrim, 1963) the subjects administered what they believed to be painful and even harmful electrical shocks to another person (who they did not know was actually the psychologist's confederate and pretending to feel the painful stimuli). It is also not uncommon for subjects in psychological experiments to answer personal questionnaires. In short, the situation overtly labeled as a *psychological experiment* is a special and unique one in which people may emit behaviors that are unusual for them—but unusual only in the sense that the subjects have never been in situations that call for such behavior.

Orne (1962) has related how he was searching for a task which "waking" subjects would not do or would engage in for only a short time so that he could test the effect of hypnosis on compliance in pursuing noxious activities. The task was intended to be annoying, tiring, and boring. College students were presented with a stack of 2000 papers, each of which called for the performance of 224 additions. After instructions were given, the subject was deprived of his watch and the experimenter said, "Continue to work; I will return eventually." After 5½ hours, the experimenter gave up; the subjects were still working! In another phase of the same study, subjects were asked to tear up their work and did so for a number of hours with little hostility. Orne concluded that "It became apparent that it is extremely difficult to design an experiment to test the degree of social control in hypnosis, in view of the already *very high degree of control in the experimental situation itself* [p. 778]." The subjects devised reasonable hypotheses to explain the experimenter's behavior, such as that the task was one of endurance. Orne noted that the students were playing the role of the good subject (that is, giving the experimenter what they thought he wanted) in much the same way as Sarbin (1950) explained the behavior of the "hypnotized" person.

Demand characteristics may be a function of the entire setting or of certain explicit aspects within the situation. The latter possibility is illustrated by a report of Orne and Scheibe (1964). Orne (1962) had defined demand characteristics as the totality of cues which convey an experimental hypothesis to the subject. In sensory deprivation studies, subjects may well be given cues which explain, at least partially, the behavioral decrements and the unusual experiences reported by them.

Orne and Scheibe deliberately manipulated environmental cues to communicate the expectancy of bizarre behavior. Two groups were exposed to the same basic set of physical conditions. In addition, the experimental group was exposed to preexperimental conditions designed to imply that sensory deprivation was expected. The control group was led to expect nothing unusual. Subjects volunteered (at two dollars per hour) to participate in a "psychological experiment in meaning deprivation." For the experimental group the study was conducted in a psychiatric hospital with the examiner wearing a white coat. A medical history was taken; drugs and medical instruments in a labeled "Emergency Tray" were in full view. The instructions stressed the *importance of reporting unusual or hallucinatory experiences*. The subjects were shown a red button marked "Emergency Alarm," which they could press to escape from the situation. They were told that a physician would be immediately available.

The isolation room was well lit, noisy, and large; and the subjects' movements were not restricted. They remained in the room for 3 or 4 hours. The control subjects were treated similarly, except that they were not exposed to the "panic" cues—emergency tray, medical interview, white coat, available physician, and panic button. Instead they were told they were in a control group for a sensory deprivation study. Pre- and posttests of intellectual efficiency were given to both groups. The two groups differed significantly on posttests involving both intellectual tasks and clinical measures of feeling. The experimental group reported a significantly greater number of symptoms of sensory deprivation, including perceptual aberrations ("the walls of the room are starting to waver") and intellectual dullness (inability to concentrate, the occurrence of "blank periods," unpleasant affect, anxiety, spatial disorientation, and restlessness). Orne and Scheibe concluded that the subjects were responding to demand characteristics in the situation. The authors made clear that they do not question that sensory isolation may have drastic effects on behavior, but most studies investigating this phenomenon have not controlled for the implicit demand characteristics.

Placebos

Medicine and other therapeutic procedures are associated with the concept of improvement or change in physiological functioning. However, many medicines have no demonstrable physiological effect. For example, Shapiro (1960) has argued that until limes were given to prevent scurvy all internally ingested substances offered by medical men were placebos. Other substances, such as mild sedatives, have such a pervasive action that, although they do not have relevant specific effects, they may be followed by improvement.

It has been estimated that from 50 to 90 percent of people visiting physicians' offices have problems that can be labeled "psychosomatic" or "nonspecific."

Medicine is administered to these people by the healer and relief follows. This relief is more likely to occur if the healer's ministrations are in a form that is *culturally meaningful* to the patient. The focus of the treatment, usually a pill, should have physical characteristics that have been associated in the past with relief. For example, small pills are that size because their ingredients are so potent; warm-colored pills are likely to pep one up; expensive prescribed medicine is better than aspirin; and, finally, pills should not look like aspirin unless no effects are intended other than the target one (Honigfeld, 1964a, 1964b).

The target for the activity of the placebo may be "real" by all currently known measures. Beecher (1955, 1959, 1960) has shown the impact of placebos on patients who had undergone surgery. Placebo effects are more likely to be effective when the recipient is faced with a situation in which he has *no other way* of alleviating pain. Clinical pain is more likely to respond to placebos than pain brought on in an experimental situation in which the subjects, for obvious ethical reasons, may terminate the procedure when it becomes unbearable. However, even in experimental situations placebo effects have been demonstrated Gelfand, Ullmann, and Krasner, 1963).

The placebo may be viewed as a demand characteristic: it is a cue which indicates to the person how he should act. A placebo, like a demand characteristic, may be viewed as a discriminative stimulus: it indicates a time and place when certain behaviors are likely to be reinforced. Further, if the doner believes in the efficacy of the substance he is giving, he is likely to be pleased and respond favorably to indications of improvement in the person treated. This is a particularly powerful reinforcer for the therapist whose professional worth stems from helping others.

Studies on placebos are important to formulations of behavior influence for a number of reasons. First, behavior does indeed change under the influence of a placebo. There are two possible explanations for this: either the pain or other changed behavior was faked, so that the person influenced by the placebo was not "really" sick. Or behavior, including pain, can be altered by psychological (that is, behavior influence) procedures.

A second reason for the importance of placebos is their connection with the phenomenon of suggestion. Toward the end of the eighteenth century Perkins' tractors and Mesmer's animal magnetism were procedures for changing behavior which were found to utilize *suggestion* rather than physical variables. Neither magnetism nor tractors worked without suggestion; but suggestion worked without the presumed physically potent aspect. While placebos have probably been a crucial aspect of all treatment procedures from the beginning of mankind, the explicit documentation of suggestion—which did not fit any of the scientific models of the day—may be considered the start of "mental healing" (as it was by Zweig, 1932). This historically and empirically important line of investigation is continued in the next chapter.

A third reason for the importance of the placebo literature is that it pro-vides a bridge from the laboratory to clinical situations. An example of a "real life" placebo situation is the following: "South Dakota ordered its communities to start fluoridating their water on July 1. So folks started calling the Sioux Falls City Hall on July 1, griping about the terrible-tasting fluoridated water. They were told gently the city hadn't started flouridation because equipment wasn't delivered yet [Herguth, 1970]."

Fourth, placebo research is important because the giver of the placebo is an influencer of behavior. Studies which inform us about the variables that enhance his influence also offer us hypotheses about influencers in general; and all that has been said about the influencer applies to the individual who utilizes a placebo in whatever context he may do so.

Finally, the investigation of placebo effects has had a major beneficial effect on experimental design. These last two considerations are well illustrated in a research by Paul (1966), whose subjects were students manifesting "performance anxiety." A specific measurable behavior was selected as the criterion of effective-ness for comparing different treatment procedures. The behavior was "anxiety," which was given a clear-cut operational definition. The situation the students responded to with "anxious" behavior was giving a talk to a group of strangers, including psychologists who were evaluating them. The pre- and postmeasures included self-report and physiological measures of anxiety as well as overt be-havior measured by a "timed-behavioral checklist for performance anxiety." This last measure consisted of 20 overt "symptoms" of anxiety such as pacing, swaying, feet shuffling, knee trembling, extraneous arm and hand movements, rigid arms, flushed face, heavy breathing, perspiration, and quivering voice. The presence or absence of each symptom was recorded by four trained observers during the first 4 minutes of a speech presentation.

The subjects were assigned to one of four groups: (*a*) insight-oriented psychotherapy; (*b*) systematic desensitization; (*c*) attention placebo; (*d*) no-treatment control. In addition, there was a fifth no-contact control group. Five experienced therapists, "dynamic and insight oriented" in background, worked individually with 3 subjects in each of the 3 treatment groups for 5 hours over a period of 6 weeks. On completion of treatment, the subjects in the treatment and the no-treatment control groups again presented speeches; and measures of self-report, physiological, and behavioral anxiety were obtained.

The first treatment group received "insight-oriented psychotherapy," which employed the interview approach typically utilized by these therapists. Anxiety reduction was attempted by helping the client to gain "insight" into and under-standing of the historical and current interpersonal aspects of his problem. The second group received systematic desensitization, a behavior therapy technique in which relaxation is paired with increasingly arousing images. This procedure was taught to the therapists, who had had no previous experience with it.

The third, and most important group in the present context, received an "attention placebo." This placebo was given to determine the extent of improvement obtained by *nonspecific social influence* treatments such as the subjects' expectation of relief and the therapist's attention, warmth, suggestion, faith, and interest. This group was given a pill described to them as a "fast-acting tranquilizer," which would work while they were occupied with a "stressful task." The subjects were told that they were being trained to perform under stress without anxiety and that their bodies would develop a tolerance for stress that would carry over to other difficult situations such as speech making. The "fast-acting tranquilizer" was actually chemically inert.

Two control groups were used: the no-treatment controls were administered all the pre- and postmeasures, but received no treatment; and the no-contact controls were never seen by the experimenter, received no treatment, and were unaware they were part of the study. These latter subjects completed a limited self-report measure as part of testing during regular classroom hours.

The results indicated that on almost every measure the desensitization group improved significantly more than the psychotherapy or attention placebo treatment groups. These two groups in turn improved significantly more than the no-treatment group. For example, on the behavior checklist of overt "anxiety" behavior 100 percent of the desensitization group improved as against 60 percent of the insight group, 73 percent of the attention-placebo group, and 24 percent of the no-treatment control group. Comparable figures of "improved" or "much improved" based on change on all three measures used were desensitization, 100 percent; insight, 47 percent; attention placebo, 47 percent; and no-treatment control, 17 percent. Moreover, these effects were maintained on a 6 week and 2 year followup (Paul, 1967). There was no evidence of symptom substitution either immediately after the study or at the 2 year followup.

Of greatest interest in the present context is the gain made by the placebo group. It is possible to hypothesize that placebo manipulations establish a self-fulfilling prophecy that may lead the person to (*a*) more readily emit acts already in his repertoire and (*b*) focus on different aspects of the situation, that is, strengths rather than weaknesses. That is, *placebos direct attention to improvement*.

These hypotheses receive some support from Paul's experiment. The no-treatment control group improved to some degree and in some instances to a greater extent than the no-contact controls. This implies, on the one hand, that "being in a program" and expecting to be helped may in itself have salutory effects. Reviews by Frank (1961) and by Haas, et al., (1963) support this view.

On a theretical level expectation may be a matter of the subject's being "set," or alert to certain stimuli in his environment rather than to others. Thus, he is likely to respond more rapidly to such stimuli and identify them in more instances, so that he responds to them more frequently or intensely. These criteria—latency, frequency, and intensity—have been noted previously as operational definitions of personality variables. Set, attitude, and personality variables may well be operationally overlapping if not identical concepts.

Once there is a measurable behavior—that is, a change by a person in response to the demand characteristic or placebo situation—this change, may be used with a constant stimulus as a *dependent variable*, a measure of the effect of an experimental manipulation. It may also be used by some psychologists as a personality variable. Responsiveness to a demand characteristic such as a placebo might be considered indicative of a trait that would predict behavior in a wider range of situations than the one being immediately measured. As with other traits, no firm evidence on the generality of responsiveness to social influence across situations has been found, despite frequent attempts (for example, Bentler, O'Hara, and Krasner, 1963).

An experimental measurement of expectations of and actual benefit from a placebo medication has been reported by Nash and Zimring (1969). The subjects (whose average age was eighty-two) were residents in a home for the aged and received one of two experimental drugs or a placebo. The target (dependent) measure was short-term memory, which was measured before and after 8 days on each medication. Those given the real drugs did no better than those given the placebo. The subjects' expectations of benefit correlated significantly with their subjective measures of benefit (that is, changed experience) and also with the behavioral criterion of improvement of short-term memory.

An important area for research is the relationship of attitudes and behavior (Kiesler, 1971; Thomas, 1971). In Nash and Zimring's study (1969), expectations of improvement might well be called *attitude* or *set* to improve. If an attitude is defined as "an orientation toward or away from some object, concept, or situation [Hilgard, 1962, p. 614]," it is reasonable to ask whether changed attitudes will lead to changed responses. Krasner, Ullmann, and Fisher (1964) and Krasner, Knowles, and Ullmann (1965) used verbal conditioning—a procedure discussed later in this chapter—to increase the favorability of response toward medical science in an experimental group and compared the result with a randomly reinforced control group. The dependent measure was a dynamometer test. The results indicated that subjects' increasing favorability toward medical science led to their greater effort operationally on the dynamometer test when the task was structured as being done for medical science. In short, an experience dealing with attitudes that could be manipulated led to a change in subjects' overt behavior.

The major point of this section is that subjects in psychological experiments are responsive to behavior influence—most notably to cues on how they are expected to act. The strength of these effects should lead to cautions about research design, a topic relevant to experimental analogues.

EXPERIMENTAL DESIGN

Two topics are pertinent to the design of experiments that stem from considerations raised in the foregoing section. The first is reactive measures and the second experimenter effect.

Reactive Measures

One typical research design has been to administer some device before and after the interposition of an experimental manipulation. For example, in the Nash and Zimring experiment (1969) the residents in the home for the aged received a test of short-term memory. In the Paul study (1966) a battery of self-report, physiological, and overt behavioral measures dealing with speech anxiety were administered before and after treatment. But the test measure itself may influence the results obtained. This problem has been discussed particularly well by Campbell and Stanley (1966) and Webb, Campbell, Schwartz, and Sechrest (1966).

Within the present framework the pretest measure may serve as a demand characteristic. That is, the pretest may *alert* the subject to the research worker's hypotheses. This problem may become particularly acute when (*a*) the experimental condition is administered soon after the pretest and in a manner that leads the subject to connect the two and form hypotheses (which may or may not be accurate) about the purpose of the experiment; (*b*) the dependent measure is a behavior that may be easily changed by the subject such as an attitude scale, in contrast to an ability measure; or (*c*) the subject's insight into the purpose of the research (again whether correct or not) severely alters the independent measures supposedly being evaluated.

While our purpose in this section is to indicate an impact of demand characteristics rather than to present a critique of experimental design, some possible solutions to the problem of design may be suggested. One is to embed the aspects of the design in other ongoing research activities. For example, pre- and postmeasures may be gathered by different research workers in experiments different from the intervening experimental manipulations. Or the subject may be provided with a rationale for the experiment to reduce the likelihood that he will manufacture one of his own. Another technique is the use of measures that are not reactive, but by-products of relevant natural ongoing activities and thus not associated with psychological research in the subject's thinking. A third technique is to *not* administer a pretest to half the subjects in each of the conditions in order to obtain data on the effects of the pretest itself. A fourth technique is to have subjects role play what they *think* others might do under the conditions to be tested. At a general behavioral level one might say that the psychological experimenter enlarges his repertoire to overcome difficulties—in this case, the impact of demand characteristics. Finally, we cannot avoid pointing out that solving this particular experimental design problem leads to broader concerns about the ethical implications of deception (see Chapter 19).

Experimenter Effects

There is a truism that physicians should use new medicine before it loses its potency. This is another way of saying that a professional's belief in his treatment may be a self-fulfilling prophecy communicated to his patient-client. Conversely, the experimenter may cue his subject inadvertently by providing demand characteristics of which both parties are not explicitly cognizant. Subtle cues and unplanned behaviors on the part of the experimenter or the subject may alter the situation and be responded to by the other person.

One such variable is the experimenter's race, a topic reviewed by Sattler (1970). The thrust of the work reviewed by Sattler is that the race of the subject and experimenter can have a measurable effect on the traditional dependent variables of physiological and social psychology. Similar results have been reported for age, sex, and social class, particularly when the setting is an interview aimed at obtaining opinions. Such findings repeatedly point to the influence of the data collector on the results obtained. The literature on experimenter effects is vast and excellent. (Other reviews have been provided by Goldstein, 1962; Kintz, et al., 1965; Masling, 1960; McGuigan, 1963; and R. Rosenthal, 1967.)

From the many studies available, we have selected a number dealing with college students. The first one (Brown, 1953) deals with a relationship between rigidity in thinking as measured by the individual's ability to shift to an easier solution in a waterjar problem (shifting different amounts of water between two jars of specified volume) and his score on an attitude scale of conservative political social attitudes labeled authoritarian. To manipulate the "motivation" of the subjects, the waterjar problem and the attitude scale were presented under different conditions. In the first, in order "to create an ego-involving atmosphere," the experimenter acted in an extremely grave, aloof manner, dressed formally and conservatively, and repeatedly cautioned the subjects against looking at their test materials ahead of time or talking to one another. The general tenor was that the tests were of great importance. Finally, all subjects were required to write their names on all the test materials.

In the contrasting condition, in order to produce a more relaxed atmosphere, the experimenter wore "extremely informal" sports clothes and maintained a very casual, offhand manner. He described himself as a "psych major" carrying out a class project in which he had little personal interest. The subjects were not asked to write their names on the papers until they had completed their tests. There was a significantly higher correlation between the authoritarian and problem-solving rigidity scores under the ego-involving (formal dress and manner) condition than under the noninvolving (casual, informal) condition.

While Brown interpreted his results in terms of a theory of anxiety, achievement motives, and rigidity (the context of the 1950s; see Chapter 4), two points are illustrative in the framework of the present volume and discussion. The first point is that the examiner may influence the results and relationship between scores of a psychological experiment. The second and more general point is that "personality traits" are situation specific and responsive to even slight changes in the environment.

Another illustration of how a seemingly trivial cue may affect judgment (or, more operationally, the evaluations of the experimenter) was shown in a study by McKeachie (1952) entitled "Lipstick as a Determiner of First Impressions." Male college students interviewed women enrolled in a psychology course with whom they were *not* acquainted. For half their interviews, the women wore lipstick; for half, not. The men rated the women on 22 scales; women not wearing lipstick were rated as more conscientious, less interested in the opposite sex, more serious, more placid, and, perhaps unexpectedly, more talkative than women wearing lipstick. Several interpretations of these data fit the behavioral model. First, the work illustrates the effect of small cues on interpersonal impressions. Second, the impression formed led to differential responses by the male interviewers to the females; men felt more at ease with the nonlipstick-wearing women, were therefore better interviewers, and hence the women without lipstick were indeed more talkative. Third, for women in the early 1950s (in contrast to the 1970s), lipstick wearing was part of dating (that is, role expressive), and under this condition the females acted differently when wearing lipstick than when not.

A third experiment, which has been followed up with many variants, was by Asch (1946). Asch read lists of characteristics to two groups of subjects. The lists were identical except that the term "warm" was included in one and the term "cold" in the other. The subjects then wrote personality descriptions of the people having the characteristics. Kelley (1950) repeated this procedure in a classroom in which the description was given prior to the appearance of a guest lecturer. While the results of the Asch experiment were repeated in the sketches by the students, the most interesting finding was that participation in class discussion was greater when the guest lecturer was described as "rather warm" than in classes when he was described as "rather cold." There are two summary points: the first is that judgments are at least partly subjective to the perceiver and do not necessarily describe accurately the behavior of the person being judged. The second is that these inferences or judgments alter the behavior of the perceiver and change the situation of the person perceived and hence may alter the behavior of the perceived person in the direction of the original perceiver.

This concept has been particularly well documented by R. Rosenthal (1966,

1967), who indicated that the experimenter formed hypotheses about his data and might covertly communicate these (or in Orne's terms provide "demand characteristics") to his subjects or research assistants. The soundness of any psychological experiment demands that the possibility of this subjective effect be taken into account, so that results will not be even unintentionally biased. The "Rosenthal effect," however, offers a presumably effective method by which influencers (experimenters) may affect the behavior of influencees (subjects). It would then be possible to take another step and use this effect to attain socially desirable change. Rosenthal proceeded to do so.

The question that R. Rosenthal and Jacobson (1968) posed was, What would the effect be if students were labeled in a positive manner? If favorable evaluation and interaction can be increased by information provided, as in the work of Asch (1946) and Kelley (1950), and if one of society's major training problems is how to influence teachers' behavior, especially toward children of disadvantaged social and ethnic groups, might not a "souce of error" be used as an independent variable?

Rosenthal and Jacobson worked at a school in California with predominantly lower-class children and a strong Mexican-American minority. Their design was a complicated one that permitted evaluation of grade, sex, minority status, and school ability track placement. The procedure used was as follows: in the spring all children who were likely to return next fall were given a test to predict "late blooming" or "intellectual spurting." This device was actually a standardized, relatively nonverbal test of intelligence. In the fall, at the start of the academic year after the first testing, 20 percent of the children in each of 18 classrooms were randomly designated as children about to bloom. The teachers were simply given a list of names and told they might be interested in the findings and were cautioned not to discuss these results with the parents or the children. The children were retested in midwinter and spring of the next academic year. These additional testings were also structured to the teachers as predictions of intellectual growth.

The major finding was that across all children, the control group gained an average of 8.42 points on the intelligence test, while the children designated as "bloomers" (the experimental group) gained an average of 12.22 points, a difference that was statistically significant. Of perhaps even greater import was that the major differences occurred in the first two grades; the first graders (the previous spring's kindergartners) showed gains of 12.0 and 27.4 points for the controls and experimentals, respectively, while the second graders' (the previous spring's first-grade students) average gains were 7.0 and 16.5, respectively. In short, the procedure of providing a label had a generally beneficial effect, and a particularly significant one for the younger children.

It is also interesting to note that when the teachers evaluated the pupils' classroom behavior in the second spring, they rated the experimental group as more interesting, more likely to be successful in the future, happier, and more intellectually curious. Because the teacher's acts toward the child affect how the child acts toward the teacher and, more generally, to the entire school situation, these ratings may have accurately reflected the children's behavior at that time.

R. Rosenthal and Jacobson (1968) have discussed possible media through which the obtained results occurred. Only direct observation, however, can provide information about the specific acts fostered by expectations. A study was addressed to this question by Meichenbaum, Bowers, and Ross (1969). They worked with fourteen female adolescent offenders, six of whom were identified to their four teachers as "potential intellectual bloomers." The study took place at the end of the academic year and three measures were used: (*a*) standardized (objective) tests, (*b*) grading by teachers (subjective tests), and (*c*) appropriate classroom behavior. A particularly great hurdle was that the study was made after the teachers and students had had considerable exposure to each other. It may be hypothesized that the effect of expectancy is greatest when first impressions of the people involved can be influenced and before either the teachers or the students have developed firm patterns of behavior in the situation. A baserate (presuggestion period) was obtained and followed by the same observations after the suggestion had been given to the teachers. The experimental group improved significantly more than the control group (undesignated as "bloomers") on objective exams, but not on the subjective (teacher-scored) exams. This finding is both reassuring and surprising, since it seems to dispute direct teacher bias. The experimental group also behaved significantly more appropriately in class than the control group. The teachers' behavior varied after the giving of the suggestion: some significantly increased their positive interactions, while others decreased their negative interactions with the students designated as bloomers.

Rubovits and Maehr (1971) found that the "Pygmalion procedure" increased the teachers' initiation or request of statements from the "gifted" students; and the teachers' praised these students more frequently than the "nongifted." It is interesting in this regard to note that Kogan and Wimberger (1971) compared mother-child interactions between mothers seeking clinic assistance and nonclinic controls. Kogan and Wimberger reported that the control group mothers tended to direct their children and tell them what to do, while the clinic mothers tended to exercise control by rejecting what their children had already done. The Pygmalion effect may well be mediated through praise, which confirms the expectation of acceptable behavior, rather than by punishment of the child or student's aversive behavior.

The suggestion of being a late bloomer may be made directly to the student, as it was in a study of borderline freshmen engineering students by Meichenbaum and Smart (1971). Compared to two control groups, the manipulation was associated with significant improvement in 2 of 4 courses and with self-ratings of greater self-confidence, expectation of academic success, and—most interesting in the framework of this discussion—perceived relevance of the course material.

Considerable controversy and criticism has been elicited by the R. Rosenthal and Jacobson (1968) study, particularly by certain features of its design and statistical analysis. Despite these critiques, further replications have generally confirmed the study's findings (for example, Anderson and Rosenthal, 1968; Beez, 1968; Burnham and Hartsough, 1968). The effect is certainly not universal or automatic. It is not the "attitude" alone but what the person does as a result of the experimental manipulation that makes the difference.

Studies in "Conforming" Behavior

One of the classic studies of psychology investigated the effects of other people's judgments on an individual's behavior. While imitation and modeling have a long history as explanations of behavior, one of the first empirical studies of this process was carried out by H. T. Moore (1921), who obtained opinions from subjects about grammatical usage, ethical values, and harmoniousness of musical chords. At a later time the same material was presented to the subjects along with the views of "the majority" of "experts." The designation of the choices of the majority led to change in 62 percent of linguistic, 50 percent of ethical, and 43 percent of musical judgments. This procedure was extended and replicated by Asch (1940) and Asch, Block, and Hertzman (1938) and in a number of books and articles by Sherif (1948).

Asch's study (1952, pp. 450–501) of the subject's response to other people's opinions when these judgments were contrary to fact had particular impact on psychology. In this work, a group of seven to nine students met and matched the size of lines. All the subjects making reports save the last one were "shills," that is, students cooperating with the experimenter to purposely and unanimously give erroneous reports on certain trials. On roughly one-third of the trials the naive subject reported an error in the direction of the majority, a rate more than 4 times as frequent as reports by subjects in a control group. Individual subjects differed markedly in the frequency with which they were influenced in the direction of the majority.

Asch himself (1952) reported a number of important variants of the basic design, and numerous research workers repeated and extended his results. One of the most interesting replications was by Crutchfield (1955), who developed a machine which permitted a number of men to be exposed to stimuli and make judgments at the same time. The stimuli were presented on a display board electronically and the supposed judgments of the other subjects (actually fudged data) were also presented in this manner. The position of the subject as first through fifth respondent could be varied, and all subjects were usable (in comparison to Asch's situation which required seven shills to collect data on one genuine subject). Crutchfield reported a number of results using perceptual judgments, logical judgments on a number series completion task, and a decision on a nonsensical answer to an insoluble problem. The rate of conformity to a spurious norm (the supposed answers of the other four subjects) was 46 percent, 30 percent, and 79 percent, respectively.

The type of problem has an impact on the rate of conformity, and a limiting case seems to be decisions that are markedly personal. When questions of preference were asked, such as choice between drawings, the group pressure effect was not observed. Parenthetically, if a question about the quality of the drawings (in which some right or wrong standard was implied) had been asked, the present authors think that a group pressure effect would have been observed.

Another finding reported by Crutchfield (1955) was a group pressure effect on both *political statements* and *self-reports* (of a kind similar to personality tests). The major group of subjects discussed by Crutchfield was composed of men in a profession in which leadership was important. None of the men in a control group, which was not subjected to group pressure, agreed with the statement, "I doubt whether I would make a good leader," whereas 37 percent of those subjected to group pressure toward agreeing with the statement endorsed or agreed with it.

Crutchfield also investigated whether the individual can be *trained* to agree with the majority and if so whether this training will transfer to a different content area. His answer to the first question was affirmative; the subjects were given "correct" answers after they had made their choices. As the sequence continued, subjects in the training condition indicated increasing conformity to the false group standard. In terms of the transfer of training, Crutchfield's results indicated a negative answer. The training was on matters of perception, logic, and vocabulary, in which an indisputably correct answer was ostensibly possible. No transfer of this training was found to expressions of opinions and attitudes; although this lack of transfer does not invalidate the finding of group pressure on such responses. Crutchfield did not report on the direct training of responses on attitude and personal opinion statements, but verbal conditioning has shown that these types of responses are trainable, for example, increasing favorable attitudes toward medical science in the experiment noted earlier (Krasner, Ullmann, and Fisher, 1964).

A final area to which Crutchfield addressed himself was the *type of person* susceptible to group pressure. As noted earlier, the difference between people's performances may be used as a correlate of other performances. Crutchfield found that different groups of people displayed different average rates of conformity to group pressure as measured in his situation and that there were significant correlations between amount of effect of group pressure in his laboratory situation and personality and interview measures; that is, there was some consistency across situations. This finding is of importance in the present volume, since such consistencies lead to presumptions of personality traits such as conformity or submission to group pressure.

Research in this area continues. A noteworthy recent example is by Bruehl and Solar (1970), who combined one of the earliest of the group pressure situations—the autokinetic effect (Sherif, 1935)—with concepts of demand characteristics. Their basic finding was that conformity to the verbal estimates of the confederate was greatest for subjects who believed that the experimenter expected conformity.

MODELING

In the group pressure situations just discussed, the behavior was changed by subjects' observing other people (for example, confederates) or their products (presumed results of actions such as the "information" about other subjects' choices in the Crutchfield experiment). This situation is an operational definition of *modeling: a behavioral change resulting from observing the activities of another person.*

There are many explanations for a person's change of behavior after observing another person. One formulation starts from the empirical observation (Bandura and Rosenthal, 1966; Berger, 1962) that conditioned responses may be developed through observation of another person. For example, if a person sees that a light precedes the model receiving a shock, when the subject is in the same situation and the light goes on, he may himself show a galvanic skin response deflection. Given this finding, it is also reasonable to deduce that observing another person may lead to extinction of a conditioned response. If a person has learned to react with fear or disgust to stimuli such as spiders, snakes, or rodents (animals which probably never have harmed him), seeing another person interact with such animals in an enjoyable way may decrease his unusually severe and seemingly unrealistic avoidance responses. That this sort of beneficial change can occur has been well documented by Bandura, Blanchard, and Ritter (1969) with adults who avoided snakes and by Bandura, Grusec, and Menlove (1967) with preschool children who feared dogs.

Within operant, as distinct from respondent, conditioning paradigms, the observation of another may serve two functions. First, the model may serve as a *prompt*. The way another person deals with a situation—whether it is driving an automobile or interpersonal problems (Ullmann, 1969b)—provides the observer with *information* on how to act. New behaviors may be developed rapidly from observing others, as Bandura and his colleagues have found for aggressive responses in general (which may depend on disinhibition along respondent conditioning lines) and novel aggressive responses in particular (which seem more readily formulated as the results of prompting).

Second, observation of another person may also provide information about discriminative stimuli (the conditions under which specific acts will have meaningful consequences) as distinct from information about the specific acts to be emitted. In this instance, the prestige of the model, his similarity to the observer, and the consequences of his acts are probably particularly important. An everyday example is that one looks to others for which fork to use or when to applaud at a concert.

Modeling has three important areas. The first is documentation of its effects. The second is discussion of how the capacity to be influenced as a result of observing a model is developed. The third is a discussion of the implications of these considerations in a theory of "personality" or behavior influence. Again, there is a wealth of information (Bandura, 1969; Flanders, 1968) and we have selected what we consider to be interesting and important studies.

Effects of a Model

An enduring question about people is how rule breaking and rule following develop (see Ullmann and Krasner, 1969, esp. ch. 12). The behavior of other people may be used to illustrate the range of behaviors that may be emitted (information about acts) and the range of behaviors that may be *safely* emitted. That is, observation of other people may indicate which of the behaviors a person is physically capable of are proper.

An early study that was experimental in design and that took place in the field rather than the laboratory was by Lefkowitz, Blake, and Mouton (1955). At a pedestrian crossing where a "wait" signal was on for 40 of every 55 seconds and a "walk" signal was on the remaining 15 seconds, 2103 adult pedestrians (children and physically handicapped were not tallied) were observed. There were three major conditions: a control condition, in which there was no model; a conforming model, who obeyed the signal; and a nonconforming model, who violated the signal and crossed against the light. A subsidiary condition was the manner in which the pedestrian was dressed. In the "high-status" condition the thirty-one-year-old male model was dressed in a freshly pressed suit, shined shoes, white shirt, tie, and so forth. In the "low-status" condition, he wore scuffed shoes, soiled and patched trousers, and wrinkled denim shirt. The model's dress had no effect on the experimental group when he conformed to the light. Very few of the pedestrians in the conforming model and control groups crossed against the signal (4 of 775 people in the first group, 8 of 750 in the second). A model violating the signal was associated with roughly 9 percent of the people violating the sign (40 of 290 in the high-status model condition and 12 of 288 in the low-status model condition). The presence of a nonconforming model made a very significant statistical difference in the rate of sign violation. Moreover, when the rates of sign violations were compared (a) between the high-status conforming and high-status nonconforming, (b) between the low-status conforming and low-status nonconforming, and (c) between the high-status nonconforming and low-status nonconforming models, all three comparisons yielded statistically significant results.

If sign violation is a mildly "negative" or undesirable behavior, altruism is a socially approved act. In some regards altruism is a "positive abnormality." At first blush it seems rare, unusual, and hard to understand a person helping another for no immediate or ostensible gain. Altruism is also a major topic of interest to psychologists because the development of prosocial behaviors is probably more efficient than the modification of "deviant" ones.[1]

An example of work that used modeling to increase a prosocial behavior in a field setting is by Bryan and Test (1967). In one study the dependent variable was the number of people who would stop to aid a woman who ostensibly had a flat tire. In the model condition, approximately a fourth of a mile from the girl a man was helping a woman fix a tire. Of 4000 passing vehicles, a total of 93 stopped; 35 halted with the model absent, 58 with the model present. The difference in rate of helping behavior was statistically significant. In two other studies reported in the same article, the effect of having a model donating to a Salvation Army kettle was compared with donations during times when no such modeling took place. In both studies, the model increased the rate of people donating.

Schachter and Singer (1962) have demonstrated how modeling affects the meaning attributed to the effects of drugs. The subjects in this study were given a small injection of a drug called Suproxin, actually adrenalin or placebo, depending upon whether they were an experimental or control group. The subjects were placed with another subject (in reality, a confederate) who purportedly had also received Suproxin. With half the subjects, the stooge behaved *euphorically*, while with the other half he behaved *angrily*. The experimenter rated the subjects' subsequent behavior in terms of euphoria or anger. Subjects were more susceptible to the stooge's mood (used him as a model) and were more euphoric or angry when they had no explanation of their own bodily states than when they did. Thus the study demonstrated that individuals are influenced in their enactment of roles by observation of models.

[1] Major reviews of altruism have been written by Bryan and London (1970), Krebs (1970), and Macaulay and Berkowitz (1970). Additional examples of recent experimental reports on the effect of a model increasing sharing or helping behavior are by Aderman and Berkowitz (1970), Bryan and Walbeck (1970), and Grusec and Skubiski (1970), while Doland and Adelberg (1967), Harris (1970), and Mithaug and Burgess (1968) have demonstrated the significant impact of social reinforcement. T. L. Rosenthal and his coworkers (Rosenthal, Moore, Dorfman, and Nelson, 1971; Rosenthal, Zimmerman, and Durning, 1970) have used models to increase effective types of question asking and conceptual behavior of various groups including culturally disadvantaged children. In short, a strong body of research indicates that various prosocial behaviors may be taught and that modeling and response contingent reinforcement are effective ways of increasing such behavior.

THE DEVELOPMENT AND MAINTENANCE
OF A MODELING OR IMITATIVE RESPONSE

There are a number of ways of thinking about the modeling response. One is that it is an *inborn, natural, instinctive* human reaction to situations. As described in Chapter 2, this view has provided a frequent explanation of man's imitative behavior. This position gives a ready explanation for the effect of observing a model or the behavior of crowds: the person is performing a "natural response."

One immediate limitation is that not all people respond to a model all the time. In the study on violation of traffic signals, the model had an impact on roughly 10 percent of the pedestrians; in the work on stopping to help an attractive college woman change a tire, the impact of the model was closer to 2 percent (See also Rhyne and Ullmann, 1972). It is possible to hypothesize individual differences in responsiveness to observing a model. The question then resolves into whether these individual differences comprise a trait manifested across situations or whether the situations affect the emission of imitative responses.

Development of Imitative Responses

If imitation is an operant and its emission is dependent upon both prior experiences and current situations, the first task in investigating its development is to locate a group of people who do not emit this type of behavior and teach it to them. Such groups have been found among retarded and schizophrenic children. Baer, Peterson, and Sherman (1967) worked with severely retarded children who did not imitate others. Imitation was taught by the method of prompting and fading, with food used as a reinforcer. The experimenter would demonstrate a simple response such as tapping the table and then take the child's hand and tap the table (that is, prompt), say "Good," and give the child some food. Fading involved placing the child's hand on the table, and in later trials simply moving it toward the table. Eventually the child performed the behavior immediately after the demonstration. The children were taught to imitate a number of simple behaviors in this way. The children began to demonstrate their having learned to imitate by reproducing new responses after an initial demonstration without prompting.

Of great interest was the finding that as long as other imitative acts were reinforced, children continued to imitate some acts that were never reinforced. That is, imitation is a functional response class that may be maintained by a ratio of reinforcement less than unity; the class is defined by a relation to another person as distinct from the emission or reinforcement of specific acts per se. This result leads to two ideas, both important. The first is that imitation (that is, use of a model) generalizes (Peterson, 1968) and is continued if *some* of the imitational behavior is reinforced. The behavior need not be a specific act but may be a general type of act—in this case, imitating some other person or even some representation of a person. This leads to the second point: imitation demonstrates the learning of an abstract relationship between people rather than a set of particular acts.[2]

Maintenance of Imitative Responses

If imitation is a learned behavior that generalizes, researchable questions arise that are similar to those asked about any behavior. Working with nursery school children, Peterson and Whitehurst (1971) tested out such variables as pre-reinforcement (giving the reward prior to opportunity for the performance), differential reinforcement, and extinction. While these variables had some effects, the general finding was that imitative behavior is relatively durable. A variable that did influence the emission of imitative behavior was a "setting event"[3] or discriminative stimulus—in this case, the presence or absence of the experimenter.

Similar observations on the effect of the experimenter, the person associated with reinforcement, have been made in different contexts by Patterson (1965) and Redd and Birnbrauer (1969). These findings, of the experimenter as discriminative stimulus, illustrate not only that the specific behavior under investigation functions in the same way as other categories of learned behaviors but also illustrate one of the major theses of this chapter and volume. On the one hand, the experimental situation is a denotable, specific environment that may both foster and limit the emission of specific behaviors; and, on the other hand and more generally, behaviors are emitted in and in response to situations.

Numerous studies have indicated that different situational determinants affect the imitation of a model. Two topics have been frequently used to provide dependent variables: aggression and standards for oneself. The degree of similarity of the model to the observer, the observed consequences for the model, and the degree of difficulty (complexity) of the task observed significantly affect the impact of a model. An example of research in this area is a study by Liebert and Fernandez (1969). In this study, naming states in a "game" was the task. The six- and seven-year-old children who served as subjects were exposed to three levels of task complexity. Half in each condition saw a model do the task and be rewarded, while the other half were exposed to a model who was not

[2] Work buttressing that with retardates has been reported for autistic or schizophrenic children by Hartung (1970); Hingtgen, Coulter, and Churchill (1967); Lovaas, Freitas, Nelson, and Whalen (1967); and Metz (1965).

[3] We prefer the term "discriminative stimulus," which is consistent with the terminology used throughout this book. However, the term "setting event," originated by Bijou and Baer (1961) would be more accurate, since no explicit discrimination training had taken place.

rewarded. The more complex the task, the less accurately it was modeled. There is an upper limit to the amount learned from observing a model. The presence or absence of the model being reinforced, however, had its greatest effect on the more complex stimuli condition. A reasonable explanation advanced for this result is that the vicarious reinforcement increased attention. Again, in terms of the limits of modeling, an overly simply task may not yield differences due to the ease with which it is learned.

From the material presented in this section, we may conclude that imitation of a model is a learned behavior responsive to the same effects of prior (Hartup and Coates, 1967) and current reinforcement history as other classes of behavior (Waxler and Yarrow, 1970).

Implications for a Theory of "Personality"

Modeling affects behavior; both in the clinic and in the laboratory, it influences many "personality" traits to such an extent that we may wonder about the meaning of "trait" as applied to the person exhibiting these behaviors. Being influenced by a model is itself a learned skill, as has been demonstrated by Baer, Peterson, and Sherman (1967) with retardates and by Metz (1965) and Lovaas, and his coworkers (1967) with autistic children. Further studies have shown extinction, generalization, intermittent reinforcement, and discrimination effects on imitation. Additional work covered has indicated other situational determinants of modeling behavior. In short, modeling is an instrumental act that is learned and is neither instinctive nor a trait. Modeling as a functional response class indicates that what is involved is the learning of a *relationship* rather than a specific, limited instrumental act. Given the ever-increasing data on the development, maintenance, generalization, and discrimination of modeling behavior, the concept of a "trait" of imitativeness loses its value.

LANGUAGE

One of the most common and important human activities is speech. Speech is a way of influencing the interpersonal environment and being influenced in turn by others and oneself. In the following remarks, we deal with speaking to others and oneself and *not* with linguistics, the study of speech itself. Verbal behavior is one of the most carefully investigated fields of psychology, but we will not deal with the studies of verbal behavior in terms of maturation, rote learning, memory, training effects, and the like. This is not to imply that these works are not important and exciting; there is simply a limitation on space and the authors' abilities. We are interested in speech as *an influence on social behavior.*

Of the many topics that could have been included, we have selected two as examples. The first follows a respondent conditioning paradigm and deals with meaning, or how words may derive their impact. The second, verbal conditioning, is more in the cast of operant conditioning and focuses on the conditions leading to and the subsequent effects of an increase of emission of selected classes of verbal expressions. While we use the operant-respondent distinction for pedagogical reasons, it should be clear that all operants probably have respondent correlates and that there can be operant control of respondents (Miller, 1969). The response elicited by words as acts of the person or someone else may well serve as parts of chains of responses. The response the person makes may become the stimulus or setting event for his next response: in short, it may "mediate" succeeding responses.

Words are tools. Whorf (1965) goes a step further and suggests that one's language shapes one's ideas and concepts of reality. One's linguistic tools direct attention to and limit the types of formulations of events possible. Certainly, language—whether written or spoken—is the predominant vehicle of communication and persuasion (see Chapter 16) and—whether from another person or oneself—it can be a major guide to behavior. One may speak to oneself in terms of labels and self-fulfilling prophecies or in terms of plans, guides, and other forms of self-control (see Chapter 12). An example of the self-generated word as a plan-influencing behavior is the making of shopping lists or topics for coverage in a chapter.

In terms of external sources, language permits the transmittal of experience from one person to another even more rapidly and efficiently than modeling. Recognizing the vast limitations of what follows, we can only refer the reader to volumes dealing with the development of speech ability and linguistics (Mowrer, 1960; Osgood, Suci, and Tannenbaum, 1957; Skinner, 1957; A. W. Staats, 1968).

Meaning and Respondent Conditioning

Let us recall that in the respondent conditioning paradigm a previously neutral stimulus (CS) is followed by an event (US) that elicits a response from the subject. Among early investigators of this paradigm at a linguistic social level was Razran (1938, 1940) who demonstrated that ratings of ethnically labeled pictures of people and sociopolitical slogans could be changed by showing these stimuli under different situational conditions, for example, while the subject was eating a free lunch or was exposed to an unpleasant odor. A recent example of this paradigm is by Griffitt (1970) and Griffitt and Veitch (1971), who found that subjects' interpersonal attraction to a hypothetical stranger was significantly affected by the *climate of the room* in which they made ratings. Specifically, when the subjects had been in a room with a temperature-humidity balance of an effective temperature of 90.6 degrees, they were less favorable than when the effective temperature was 67.5 degrees.

C. K. Staats and Staats (1957) conditioned the evaluative, potency, and activity components of word meaning proposed by Osgood and Suci (1955) to nonsense syllables. The method they used may be illustrated in a second study (A. W. Staats and Staats, 1958) in which national names such as *Dutch* and *German* and personal masculine names such as *Tom* and *Dick* were used. The experiment was structured as one on types of learning. Two types of stimuli were presented: the CS by slide projection, the US orally by the experimenter with the subject requested to repeat the word immediately after the experimenter had pronounced it. The question asked was the effect of this pairing on semantic differential rating scales. The results indicated that the procedure altered the ratings given by the subjects. An elaboration and integration of this and other studies on verbal behavior has been given by A. W. Staats and Staats (1963, esp. pp. 115–258).

If affective responses to words can be established by respondent conditioning in the manner suggested above, the next question is the generalization of this effect. Zanna, Kiesler, and Pilkonis (1970), using an elaborate cover story about testing physiological measures to reduce the chance of demand characteristics, used shock as the unconditioned stimulus (US). Words paired with onset of shock were later evaluated negatively, while words paired with the termination of shock were evaluated more positively on the semantic differential scale. Of additional import was generalization of the effect to words similar in meaning.

A further generalization question would deal with people rather than words as stimuli. Berkowitz and Knurek (1969) illustrated this idea in a study in which male students were first trained to have a negative attitude toward a critical name, either *Ed* or *George* (the other being used as a control). In addition, half the subjects were deliberately angered by the trainer, who told them they had done a poor job. The subjects were then sent to a second experiment in which they talked about juvenile delinquency with fellow students, actually confederates, who happened to be named Ed and George. Unlike the other subjects, the angered men were significantly more unfriendly to the negatively named than to the neutrally named confederate.

Given the previous work on first impressions (for example, Kelley, 1950), we may hypothesize that experiences in prior situations will influence behavior in new ones and the recipients of the behavior will respond in kind.

Verbal Operant Conditioning

Research in verbal conditioning has been one of the major links between the experimental laboratory and clinical applications. The importance of these studies lies in the nature of the behavior involved, namely, human verbalization. The first verbal conditioning study to attract widespread attention was by Greenspoon (1955, but completed in the late 1940s). He used a simple verbal response class of plural nouns. Numerous studies followed (Krasner, 1958, 1962b,

1965a; Salzinger, 1959). Dollard and Miller (1950) seized upon the early reports of Greenspoon's findings to demonstrate their belief that changes in verbalization might be compared to psychotherapy, since they were "automatic and unconscious." Whether this assessment was accurate or not (still a major controversy), Dollard and Miller anticipated the theoretical importance of verbal conditioning for clinical psychology and behavior influence.

In his review of this field, Kanfer (1968) argued that research on verbal conditioning has undergone four stages: (a) demonstration, (b) reevaluation, (c) application, (d) expansion. This classification is useful in summarizing these studies and their relationship to behavior influence research. In the first stage verbal conditioning studies *demonstrated* that verbal behavior can be brought under the control of environmental stimuli and that verbal behavior follows the same principles as other human behaviors. These early verbal conditioning studies were similar to other early operant conditioning studies; they demonstrated that reinforcement under certain conditions can systematically influence verbal behavior. The second stage, that of *reevaluation*, indicated that verbal conditioning is a far more complex phenomenon than was at first thought of by the research workers. Responsivity to verbal conditioning is affected by variables such as social setting, previous experience with the examiner, expectancy, variations in the reinforcing stimuli, and other interpersonal variables. In the third stage, that of *application*, operant conditioning was used to change specific verbal behavior with a therapeutic intent. For example, Williams and Blanton (1968) reported a study in which verbal conditioning was used as a deliberate "therapeutic" technique and found to be as effective as traditional psychotherapeutic procedures.

In another application, various key indicants of the label "schizophrenia" were the target of verbal operant conditioning with hospitalized male psychiatric patients. Ullmann, Krasner, and their coworkers (Ullmann, Krasner, and Collins, 1961; Ullmann, Weiss, and Krasner, 1963) developed a situation in which TAT-like pictures and instructions were administered to the hospitalized men; and after an operant period, the examiner responded to every emotional word with a smile, head nod, and expression of agreement such as "mmh-hmm." These interpersonal cues are considered generalized reinforcers, that is, usually pleasant stimuli in the culture. It was hypothesized that the emission of emotional words would increase, and indeed this was the case. A subsidiary finding was that the pleasantness of the emotional words as well as their frequency increased after the introduction of response contingent reinforcement (Ullmann, Krasner, and Gelfand, 1963).

An independent group using an interview situation (Salzinger and Pisoni, 1958, 1961) also found that the emotional expressiveness of psychiatric patients could be increased rapidly through response-contingent interpersonal reinforcement. These experiments indicated that flatness of affect—regarded by some investigators as one of the prime indicants of schizophrenia—may be altered directly. This finding led to the question of whether stronger reinforcers (explicit tokens for concrete stimuli such as cigarettes, candy, preferred sleeping quarters, passes to town) over longer periods of time (months rather than a single meeting) might not have major beneficial effects. While this query led to another application, that of token economy, it also raised doubts about the nature of the presumed disease of schizophrenia.

Other indicants of schizophrenia such as "bizarre," "sick," or "disorganized" speech (from which disorganized thinking might be inferred) were approached in the same way (Meichenbaum, 1966; Ullmann, Forsman, Kenny, McInnis, Unikel, and Zeisset, 1965; Ullmann, Krasner, and Edinger, 1964) with the same general result. In the limited situation of the experiment, supposedly "sick" and involuntary or unconsciously motivated behavior was directly and significantly altered.

The fourth, or *expansion*, stage of development involves the studies of theoretical issues related to the human capability for self-regulation. These processes include vicarious learning, the role of awareness in learning, self-reinforcement and self-control, and the associative relationships of words (Kanfer and Phillips, 1970).

Examples of Limitations of Analogues

The following material uses verbal conditioning in a major way and is presented in part to illustrate this behavior influence technique. The immediate reason for this presentation, however, is to illustrate a form of psychologist behavior and thought. The researches described are also analogues, and a discussion of their weakness will be germane to many different lines of research.

The first example involves the relationship between a therapist and his client. With the exception of a few situations and limited theories, almost every form of psychological treatment considers a good relationship to be a vital part of successful therapy. But what is meant by a good relationship? Descriptions of good interpersonal relationship in general or descriptions and prescriptions by therapists might provide a starting point. Another approach might be to say that a good relationship exists in successful therapies and therefore the differences between successful and unsuccessful therapies will lead to a description of such rapport. This latter approach fails partly because a good relationship may develop as an *effect* rather than be the cause of therapy movement; that is, success may lead to good feelings rather than the reverse.

People with a behavioral orientation are likely to ask two questions. The first is, How do we know when we have rapport? or What are people doing when we say rapport is good? This question leads to an operational definition of the concept of rapport. One answer might be that both people talk more and that's rapport (the interview research of Matarazzo, 1965, is an investigation of verbal behavior within this context). Or the answer might be given in terms of increased intimacy and self-disclosure of personal material. (Jourard, 1968; Jourard and Friedman, 1970, are examples.) Other definitions might include the criterion of the person returning for therapy over a specified period of time (for example, McNair, Lorr, and Callahan, 1963). Operational definitions may lead not only to different lines of data collection but also to conflicting results. For example, many hours of treatment may be associated with therapeutic *failure* and be randomly or even negatively correlated with amount or content of speech.

The second question likely to be asked by the behaviorally oriented is, What conditions are associated with a difference in rapport, however it is defined? The features of the experiment that permit random assignment of subjects to conditions permit the specification of antecedents and consequents. The conditions selected for investigation are likely to test observations made in the clinic or to be derived from theory.

One study of therapist-client rapport (Ullmann, Bowen, Greenberg, Macpherson, Marcum, Marx, and May, 1968) combined earlier clinical observations (Bandura, et al., 1960; Winder, et al., 1962) with deductions from C. R. Rogers' theory of psychotherapy. It was presumed that *approaching* the person rather than *avoiding* him or being *irrelevant* would increase rapport. It was also presumed that rapport would be better if such approaches were made when the person expressed positive rather than negative things about himself. Out of this set of hypotheses grew four experimental conditions: the interviewer approached half the cases and avoided the other half; for half the subjects in each condition, the approach or avoidance was made in response to subjects' verbalizations of positive or negative things about themselves.

The effects of these conditions, or independent variables, were assessed on dependent variables presumed to be operational definitions of rapport. Rapport was defined in two ways. The first was as an attitude toward the interviewer. For this purpose thirty semantic differential scale ratings of the concept "this psychotherapist" were made by the interviewees after the interview. Second, rapport was operationally defined as an increase or decrease in subject "anxiety," defined by a measure of "state" (Endler, Hunt, and Rosenstein, 1962) or "trait" (general) anxiety (Welsh, 1956).

As noted earlier, a crucial element in any experiment is how it is structured to the subject. Such structure has three goals: the first is to be *ethically* responsible for the subject, to protect and to treat him decently. The second is to make the situation *meaningful* to the subject; for volunteers and members of a pool from an introductory psychology class, this means feedback of some educational value. It also means that in the situation itself the subjects are given some rationale for their participation that will not only not bias them but will also reduce their generation of hypotheses about the nature of the task. Finally, the structuring situation aims to come as close to the target situation as possible within the limits of ethics and meaningfulness.

In this Ullmann et al. study (1968), the subjects were all females taking an introductory psychology course. They volunteered to come in the evening to the psychological clinic. There they were met by a member of the psychology faculty who explained that they would be helping him train people who were learning about psychotherapy, who had or were currently working with children or hospitalized schizophrenics (hence, the night appointment), and who needed their contacts with normal adults sharpened. The experimental conditions were given in a semistructured interview. The ratings of the situation and of the psychotherapist at the end of the study made sense within the training context.

The specific results of this study are not as important as the procedure. However, the results did indicate that approaching or avoiding had an impact on developing favorable feelings. When the "psychotherapist" approached rather than avoided self-references he was rated high on the semantic differential measure as accepting, positive, friendly, reassuring, sincere, encouraging, and sympathetic. When the target was positive rather than negative self-reference, the interviewer was rated as creating a more professional image and described more as consistent, direct, assertive, active, and involved. The measures of anxiety were disappointing, but there was a trend for subjects in the approach-positive and avoid-negative self-reference groups to report the situation as less anxiety provoking than those in the approach-negative and avoid-positive self-reference conditions. We delay the more general discussion to very briefly describe a second analogue experiment.

If indicants of schizophrenia can be directly reduced by behavior influence techniques, it is reasonable to ask if the same sort of procedures may be used to *increase* "schizophrenic" emissions. First, we must determine whether such indicants have a baserate in the behavior of normal people, so that they can be shaped at all. Again, the first question is a matter of selecting an operational definition. In this case (Levitz and Ullmann, 1969) uncommon associations on a word association test and selected types of inkblot responses were chosen. Two parallel experiments were conducted using the same design and experimental conditions. In the first, the word association method was used as a pre- and posttest of generalization, and the inkblots were used for "training" during the experiment itself; in the second, this procedure was reversed so that inkblots were used for before- and after-generalization effects and the word associations for training.

The subjects were college males for whom the situation was structured as the collection of data about inkblots and word associations, topics in which psychologists are interested. The subjects were to give their first responses. After a baseline period, half the students received attention, positive remarks, and other favorable interpersonal stimuli each time they gave a response that was an indicant of disturbed thinking. The other half did not receive any reinforcer. In addition, half of the subjects in each group were told, "I think your responses would be more spontaneous if you let yourself go. . . . This can be done by acting more like the common stereotype of a mentally ill person. That is, act like a person who doesn't care what impression he makes on anyone but says whatever he feels like saying." These instructions might be considered an invitation to role playing; they presume that there is a generally known cultural role of mental illness. Again, without going into detail on results, both reinforcement and instructions affected the rate of emission of indications of disturbed thinking and the results obtained during training showed some generalization to the pre- to posttest measures.

Now the question is, What if any good are these analogue studies? The subjects in the samples were college undergraduates and were neither diagnosed schizophrenics nor currently in psychotherapy. The procedures in the first experiment described were not psychotherapy nor did the procedures in the second make the subjects schizophrenic. In both studies, as in the vast majority of analogues, the duration of the data collection was brief and the contact was terminated, something very different from the ongoing relationships found in psychotherapy or in the majority of behaviors associated with (not only as cause but frequently as effect) the diagnosis of schizophrenia.

Why bother to spend time collecting such data? There are occasions when one might wonder whether there might not be an "emperor's new clothes" effect: not only might the authors of the studies be deluding themselves; but to the extent that their efforts were published and treated seriously, the authors would be reinforced and likely to continue in this type of behavior. Certainly, some of the effort is maintained by professional rewards for a professionally valued behavior, but it is not a complete swindle or delusion.

First, by analogy, one might say that what occurs in a wind tunnel is not what happens 30,000 feet in the sky. The analogy holds or breaks down with the selection of operational definitions. The wind tunnel and the psychological analogue experiment are only effective to the extent that the relationships they propose are found to hold in a larger environment. If the variables studied are not relevant in that larger environment, the analogue research is a waste. However, a background in the laboratory may make the manipulations the clinician tries out in the field more effective.

If a technique based on learning concepts such as a token economy (see Chapter 11) is found to change a person so much that he no longer acts in a manner called schizophrenic, one may *not* logically say that the original behavior that led to the schizophrenic label was due to some unfortunate learning history (either the failure to learn a behavior, the extinction of a socially valued behavior, or the learning of a bizarre behavior). In the same fashion, even if we can influence John Jones by environmental manipulations to appear schizophrenic either on a psychological test or to a team of psychiatrists, we have not logically demonstrated that such manipulations are the basis of Sam Smith's or Bernard Brown's "schizophrenic" behavior. A person on LSD may appear schizophrenic, and a person on amphetamines paranoid. This does not mean that all or even any diagnosed schizophrenic behavior was caused by LSD or that diagnosed paranoia results from "speed."

All the worker in an inductive science can do is to increase the data that are consistent with a formulation. In this context, the analogue study is a test of theory or concepts drawn from practice in a situation that rules out as much distraction as possible. It is aimed at ideas. When refined, these ideas may be more ethically reintroduced into dealings with people. But the gap that generalization must cover between the analogue and the reality cannot be ignored.

LAST WORD

The experimental laboratory offers a major source of data useful for a psychology of behavior influence. The laboratory analogue provides an opportunity to control and to circumscribe the environmental situation in such a way as to better observe the relationship between behavior and certain influencing stimuli (including the experimenter). We have surveyed investigations involving some of the key concepts that have been studied in this way: demand characteristics, placebo response, self-fulfilling prophecy, experimenter bias, conformity, influence of models, imitation, conditioning of language meaning, and verbal operant conditioning. All these studies measure the influence of the behavior of one or more people upon the behavior of other individuals. These studies are also characterized by their demonstration of increasing complexities and subtleties in the mediation of influence. Perhaps the most important distinctions are that the influence process occurs within the experimental situation and this situation offers the best possibility of systematic study. The scientific study of man must investigate the process of investigation itself.

An inductive science builds theories using consistency and probability. No single experiment or series of experiments can construct such an intellectual edifice, although a single piece of information may tear such a structure down. The time and effort of many people go into the development of theories or models, so that there is a genuine force for intellectual conservation and reluctance to change. The bigger theories are the harder they fall, and the greater is the scientific revolution. In an inductive science every model will be altered and eventually overturned. In scientific endeavors we work hard to build an intellectual structure that we know must crumble. Indeed, we insist on rigor of operational definitions so that other people may test our data and find our faults. We are priests to a god who must fail, and our worship hastens his fall. But the scientific method is the best way man has so far devised to increase his knowledge of the world.

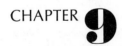

Hypnosis: An Example of the Influencer Influencing

The phenomenon of hypnosis is a prototype of behavior influence because of its history, its public image, and the nature of variables it involves. The study of hypnosis has all of the elements necessary to create interest, excitement, wonder, and bafflement: innocent people "forced" to do things that may be contrary to their moral code; spectacular "cures"; and evidence of social influence variables such as expectancy, social labeling, and demand characteristics. The approaches to personality fashionable in each era have been reflected in the procedures used and the explanations offered by the investigators of hypnosis.

This chapter offers definitions and conceptions of hypnosis, a brief history of hypnosis, a review of the variables involved, the impact of the investigators of hypnosis, the relationship between hypnosis and other modification procedures, and a behavior influence theory of hypnosis. In effect, then, this chapter is a case history of a social concept and its consequences.

ILLUSTRATIONS OF UNUSUAL HUMAN BEHAVIORS

To set the stage for viewing hypnosis as a social influence procedure, it is necessary to offer two descriptions of this phenomenon. The first is a classic description of the typical procedure used by the Viennese physician Franz Anton Mesmer (1733–1815), as described by eyewitnesses:

> Mesmer made use of a peculiar piece of apparatus known as the *baquet* for the purpose of magnetizing several patients at the same time. This was in the form of an oak barrel pierced with a number of holes through which protruded movable rods of iron. Inside the barrel, phials of magnitized water were placed in sockets arranged in concentric circles; all those were immersed in water containing magnetized iron filings, glass filaments, or similar materials. Variation of this type dispensed with the main body of water, using instead only sand or crushed iron ore; and in place of iron rods, there would be cords. Patients sat around holding hands, with knees and feet touching to ensure the circulation of the magnetic fluid. Each of them applied the rod or cord to the affected part of their anatomy. In a corner of the salon, a pianist would play appropriate music, or sometimes Mesmer himself performed on his glass harmonica, soothing passages in a minor key for the most part, more animated when he wished to bring on a crisis. Curtains were drawn to permit only a dim light in the room and the atmosphere was regulated with the aid of a thermometer, a barometer and a hygrometer. Mesmer went around among the patients, fixing on each his penetrating eyes, speaking in a low voice or passing his hand or wand over the body; calming those who were agitated and stimulating the listless. . . . In keeping with the decorum of the proceedings he wore a robe of lilac silk trimmed with lace. . . . Most of the patients were subjected to group treatment. . . . Those who became hysterical and other disturbing patients were removed to different rooms, where they had to await their turn. Having caused the patient to relax, Mesmer sat facing him and began the passes according to the nature of the ailment. In case of a migraine he placed one thumb on the forehead the other on the occiput region at the back of the head, gazing steadily into the eyes. For eye trouble he applied his left hand to the right temple, the right to the left temple and moved his thumb at a slight distance round the affected eye. In some cases he placed his thumbs over the position of the navel, moving his fingers round in a circle or semicircle. Usually his feet and knees were in contact with the patient's. The passes or light massage normally produced a sensation of pain, heat or cold, followed by a crisis or at any rate some relief. When Mesmer wished to magnetize the whole body of the patient, using the maximum power, he placed his hands together forming a kind of cone with his fingers and drew

down the apex from head to foot in front and then behind. Actual contact was not necessary since the magnetic fluid or force could act at a distance; a wand might be used instead of the hands [Walmsley, 1967, 99–101].

The second and briefer description is of a typical performance, usually under laboratory conditions, one would find in many university settings. This would involve the application of a standard scale of measuring *susceptibility to hypnosis*. The most widely used of these is the Stanford Hypnotic Susceptibility Test (Weitzenhoffer and Hilgard, 1959). This is a standardized 15-minute hypnotic induction procedure and involves repeated suggestions of relaxtion, drowsiness, eye heaviness, and sleep. The experimenter administers twelve test suggestions including items such as *hand lowering, arm immobilization, finger lock,* and *arm rigidity.* For example, in the arm rigidity task, it is suggested to the subject that his arm is becoming stiff and he is told to "test how stiff and rigid it is; try to bend it; try." The item is considered passed if there is less than 2 inches of arm bending in 10 seconds. This procedure is carefully prescribed, administered, and scored in an objective manner. It is a far cry from the dynamic flamboyance of mesmerism.

HISTORICAL ANTECEDENTS

The current trends in the study of hypnosis can be traced to the impact of Mesmer in the late eighteenth century. Mesmer had university training in theology, law, and medicine. He was a major patron of Wolfgang Mozart and a virtuoso on the glass harmonica. Throughout his life, Mesmer followed the rules of his science and profession and sought vindication within these guidelines. He believed in the power of the stars, sun, and moon to influence human bodies, just as they affected tides. Newton's concept of gravitation provided a language (metaphor) for explaining human behavior. The study of animal magnetism initiated by Mesmer led to the manufacture of improved magnets and glowing reports of cures obtained by their use. Mesmer himself originally obtained both magnets and information about their use from his friend, Father Maximilian Hell, the Viennese court astronomer and head of the observatory. Mesmer was forty when he started using magnets, and he did not think of magnetism as curative in itself, but as a method of conducting and redirecting the patient's vital fluids.

Another major feature of Mesmer's system, the convulsion, occurred in an early case, a young woman named Franzl, who was a friend of Mozart's. "Mesmer tells us that during his first treatment, the convulsive pains reached an intensity that aroused fears in the bystanders. This is the first indication of the idea of a crisis that became an essential feature of his theory [Walmsley, 1967, p. 54]."

Already, at this time, Mesmer centered on force and fluid rather than magnets. "He kept in touch with Father Hell and in his presence conducted many tests. In order to convince him that magnets had no virtues in themselves, he demonstrated his discovery that almost anything besides steel magnets could act as a conductor of the magnetic force: other metals, paper, wool, silk, stone, glass, water. He found that nine men out of ten had the power in varying degrees, one in ten very distinctly [Walmsley, 1967, p. 54]." Mesmer came to believe that a crisis was necessary before a cure could be obtained; this belief was not unlike some later theorists' beliefs in psychoanalytic catharsis or convulsions from electric shock.

In 1779 Mesmer published a list of twenty-seven propositions as the basis for his procedures. Critics of this period described this work as the product of either a genius or a fraud. Mesmer's conceptions were based on a model of man in which an influence process was central. Although the heavenly bodies were ostensibly the original source of all "responsive influence," this influence could be attached to human beings *under appropriate circumstances*. For our purposes, the most important of the twenty-seven propositions are numbers 10 and 11, which succinctly describe the manner in which influence is mediated.

> 10. This property of the human body that renders it susceptible of the influence of the heavenly bodies and of the reciprocal action of those that surround it manifests its analogy with the magnet, and this has decided me to adopt the term, "animal magnetism."
> 11. The action and virtue of animal magnetism, thus characterized, may be communicated to other animate or inanimate bodies. Both these classes of bodies, however, vary in their susceptibility [Mesmer, 1779, as quoted in Darnton, 1968].

It is of interest to note that Mesmer's magnetic tub—which seated thirty patients at a time as close to one another as possible, so that thighs, knees, and feet touched—has similarities to current encounter groups. Patients would touch hands accompanied by the sound of a piano. Mesmer eventually expanded from one to four tubs; business was good.

Despite his success with patients, Mesmer wanted the approval of the medical establishment. Mesmer's student, D'Eslon, used his political influence in Paris to persuade a royal commission to evaluate Mesmer's work.

The commission's report condemned mesmerism and attributed the results of magnetism to "imagination." It concluded that all treatment by magnetism "must, in the end, be productive of evil results." In addition, there was a caustic note from the King of France, who compared the magnetizer's powers to the emotional attraction that one sex exerts over the other.

The next contribution to the development of hypnosis was made by the Marquis de Puységur, a philosophically oriented philanthropist and pupil of Mesmer. Puységur practiced what he called "magnetic therapy" with farmhands and other members of the lower class. Mesmer had previously observed that some of his subjects would "fall asleep" during his induction procedures. He believed that this sleep was an unfortunate by-product of his technique and sought to avoid it. Puységur noted the same phenomenon when a young shepherd, Victor, with whom he was working began to slumber peacefully. However, Victor remained responsive to Puységur's suggestions and talked and behaved appropriately, even though he seemed to be asleep. Afterwards, Victor did not remember the conversations he had had while entranced.

Puységur expressed his discovery as follows:

> I went to see [Victor] on Tuesday last the 4th of this month at 8 o'clock in the evening. The fever was diminishing, and after making him get up, I magnetized him. What was my surprise to see, at the end of a few minutes this man fall asleep in my arms, quite limp, with no sign of pain or any convulsions. I continued the magnetizing, he trembled and started to talk aloud about his troubles. As he seemed distressed I stopped him and tried to inspire him with more cheerful things. This was very easy to do, and soon he showed every sign of cheerfulness, hopping on his chair and miming a song, which I made him repeat out loud. After an hour in this state during which he sweated freely, I went out of the room. In the evening he ate bread and broth for the first time in five days, and at night he slept well. The next day he could not remember my visit of the previous evening but he said he never felt better [As quoted in Walmsley, 1967, p. 143].

Puységur regarded Victor's case as a very important clue to the nature of mental healing. In his introductory remarks to the case, he used for the first time the term "somnambulism" for the trance—"The most perfect I had ever seen"—into which the patient had fallen after 5 minutes. This word, literally meaning *sleep walking*, continued to be used well into the nineteenth century to describe the Puységur version of mesmerism.

The news of Puységur's success brought several other peasants to be cured. One of the first was a twenty-four-year-old woman who had suffered internal pains for 14 months following a difficult birth. In less than 6 minutes she was relieved, Puységur stated, "merely by the approach of my hand to the affected part." In treatment, she displayed no convulsions, very slight quivering, no crisis, and no aftereffects.

The same phenomenon that had occurred in the cases of Victor and the young woman then began to occur with other patients. Thus, Puységur observed or "created" the trance state which was to become an integral part of the hypnotic procedure. This slumberlike trance contrasted markedly with the crisis Mesmer had felt to be necessary. In addition to somnambulism, Puységur observed (or suggested) many other faculties in his patients such as the ability to diagnose their own ailments and to predict their own cures. Apparently, these behaviors did not catch on as attributes of this phenomenon as had the sleep state.

Through the efforts of its early followers and practitioners, mesmerism spread throughout Europe. We mention a few of the highlights.

The experience of the English physician John Elliotson (1791–1868) illustrated what happens when an influencer deviates too greatly from the accepted procedures of his day. Although Elliotson was a senior physician at his hospital, his practice of the unusual procedures of mesmerism resulted in his dismissal.

During the mid-nineteenth century, mesmerism was used as an anesthetic in surgery. James Esdaile (1808–1859), a British surgeon in India, was the most frequent user of mesmerism. His success was not attributed to his technique, but to the stoicism and gratitude of the Indians for the white man's care.

James Braid (1795–1860), another English surgeon, is a key figure in the history of hypnosis, since he is credited with being the first to use this label. His subjects fell into a trancelike state while looking fixedly at a bright object. He labeled this state of stupor *hypnotism*, from the Greek word *hypnos*, meaning *sleep*. Braid used the procedure to help a number of individuals suffering from paralysis, migraine, and other disorders.

HYPNOSIS AS A SOCIAL MOVEMENT

While modern hypnosis originated from Mesmer's procedures, recent investigators (for example, Darnton, 1968; Walmsley, 1967, esp. ch. 12) have argued that mesmerism in late eighteenth-century France went far beyond a treatment procedure. The church, for example, saw threats to its basic postulates in mesmerism. Scientists saw threats to their basic paradigm of physical causation, despite Mesmer's arguments that he was working with physical rather than psychological (suggestion) forces.

Many of the radical philosophers involved in the French Revolution also identified themselves with mesmerism. The mesmerists organized into political groups and issued pamphlets stating their position. Of particular interest was the attraction of mesmerism for the French and English utopian socialists such as Saint Simon, Fourier, and Robert Owen (see Chapter 18).

What attracted these intellectuals to mesmerism? According to Darnton (1968), "Mesmerism appealed to radicals in two ways: it served as a weapon against the academic establishment that impeded, or seemed to impede, their own advancement, and it provided them with a 'scientific' political theory [p. 164]." It is ironic that mesmerism, which is currently almost synonymous with quackery, represented the best of the science of its day.

Reports of scientific marvels in general filled the popular literature of the 1780s. The emphasis of mesmerism on invisible magnetic fluids was consistent with a physical science just beginning to reveal the power of electricity, the flow of gases, and the force of gravity. The sciences and the pseudosciences of the times nearly merged. Science could do wonders for man. In many ways the attraction was not unlike the excitement and interest generated by the concept of "Consciousness III" (Reich, 1970) among college students of the early 1970s.

Mesmerism was also a revolutionary force within traditional academic medicine. The most common approach to many of the problems which Mesmer and his followers reported curing (by offering documented and often notarized proof) was to use foul-tasting purgatives and bleeding. It is no wonder that mesmerism, which was so much easier to undertake, was said to be the medicine of the common people. One should also remember that at that time most if not all internal medicine was placebo (see Chapter 8).

Other related phenomena such as *perkinism* must be included to place hypnotism in a more complete historical context. (Indeed, Carlson and Simpson, 1970, have recently compared the development of perkinism and mesmerism). "Perkinism" is the technique of alleviating pain by stroking the pained part of the body with pointed metallic instruments such as a knife blade. (Perhaps it can be compared with the current widespread use of copper bracelets to alleviate arthritis pain.)

Perkins was a legitimate and respected English physician who started using this new technique in 1795.

> The first instrument used in his treatment technique was a knife blade which, when stroked across inflamed or painful parts of the body, seemed to bring relief. Japanned (lacquered) metal combs seemed also to alleviate pain, not through stroking, but by being worn constantly in the hair of victims of headaches. Perkins conducted experiments regarding this phenomenon, perhaps trying the efficacy of various metals. He finally settled on a pair of devices fashioned of dissimilar metals, one of a gold, the other of a silver color. They were a little over three inches in length. The tractors were held in the hands of the therapist and repeatedly and gently stroked towards the heart across the affected part of the patient's body [Carlson and Simpson, 1970, p. 17].

A characteristic of new social movements is opposition to, and from, the establishment. In the instances noted in this chapter, the establishment was the medical practitioners and academia. The new approach—be it mesmerism, perkinism, or hypnotism—represented alternative conceptualization of methods of changing human problem behavior (including problems that appeared to be clearly medical). It was a threat to the labelers in authority, since it challenged the concepts and training that legitimized their social and professional positions.

Conversely, different people used mesmerism for different political and social reasons. Mesmerism gave the intellectual with radical leanings a weapon against important elements in the establishment—organized medicine and academia. Mesmerism gave the idealist a means of treating large segments of the population who needed help but who were not getting it from the standard techniques the traditionalists offered. Jacques-Pierre Brissot, one of the leading radical intellectual mesmerites of the period expostulated in a typical pamphlet: "Don't you [academicians] see, for example, that mesmerism is a way to bring social classes closer together, to make the rich more humane, to make them into real fathers of the poor? Wouldn't you be edified at the sight of the most eminent men . . . supervising the health of their servants, spending hours at a time mesmerizing them? [Darnton, 1968, p. 97]." But, Brissot noted pointedly, the academicians had "tried to inflame the government against the partisans of mesmerism," and so he

denounced their medicopolitics: "I'm afraid that the habit of despotism has ossi-
fied your souls [p. 97]."

Thus mesmerism was championed by its followers as a medicine of the
common people. As Darnton (1968) observed:

> Mesmerism would regenerate France by destroying "obstacles" to "universal har-
> mony"; it would remedy the pernicious effects of the arts by restoring a "natural"
> society in which physico-moral laws of nature would drown aristocratic privileges
> and despotic government in a sea of mesmeric fluid. First to go, of course,
> would be the doctors. The program of the mesmerist revolution then became vague,
> but its central proposition remained clear: the elimination of doctors would set
> natural laws at work to root out all social abuses, for the despotism of doctors and
> their academic allies represented the last attempt of the old order to preserve itself
> against the forces of the true science of nature and society [p. 166].

The originators of both mesmerism and perkinism attributed the effects of
their procedures to the then-current concepts of physics such as magnetism and
electricity. They fell into disrepute when they were dismissed as merely dealing
with "imagination" or "suggestion." We may note here that the metaphor one
uses to investigate a phenomenon determines much of others' reaction to the
phenomenon itself (Sarbin and Andersen, 1967). Mesmer introduced the metaphor of *magnetism* to explain his usage of behavior influence. It was rejected as
an appropriate metaphor for psychological influence, because there was no scientific evidence for it. Nor did the alternative metaphor of *imagination* have the
scientific status to justify it as an explanatory metaphor.

The scientific study of mesmerism declined until Braid introduced the
metaphor of sleep through his use of the label hypnosis. This led to a study of
hypnosis based on the physiology of sleep. Hypnosis was used as an anesthetic
for surgery until the advent of ether and chloroform in the mid-nineteenth century. Charcot then introduced a *neuropathological* metaphor, namely, that the
hypnotic state is an *artificial hysteria* and, by the model of the day, a neurological
disorder. Once again, hypnosis became respectable and its proper investigator
became the neurologist with his medical tools such as the reflex hammer. With
Charcot's death, neurological interest in hypnosis quickly declined and some
journals had to be hastily relabeled "neurological reviews" instead of "hypno-
logical reviews." The Charcot era was followed by the modern period, characterized by a considerable amount of laboratory research and controversy about the
theoretical models of hypnosis.

CONCEPTUALIZATION OF HYPNOSIS

A helpful framework in approaching hypnosis is the *skeptical-credulous dichotomy* proposed by Sutcliffe (1960). Although we generally eschew dichotomies
(such as abnormal-normal, presence or absence of traits), here we are describing

a metabehavior—theories about hypnosis—in which there is a clear separation between those who believe that hypnosis is a distinct state and those who do not.

Credulous investigators of hypnosis believe that they are dealing with a unique phenomenon—the *hypnotic trance state*. "They assume that hypnotic suggestions are substitutable for real stimuli as conditions of perception and consequently that hypnotic fantasy is akin in its sensory content to perception produced by parallel real stimuli [Sutcliffe, 1960, p. 189]." The event labeled as hypnosis has characteristics which distinguish it from any other human interaction. If an individual who is being influenced in another situation such as psychotherapy or desensitization exhibits some of the behaviors attributed to the trance state (for example, heightened susceptibility to suggestion or drowsiness), then the existence of a trance state is *inferred* and subsequent changes may be attributed to the effects of hypnosis. The credulous approach to hypnosis may be seen as analogous to viewing human behavior in terms of an entity of personality (Chapter 3) or in terms of uniquely differentiable types of disease in "abnormal" behavior (Ullmann and Krasner, 1969).

The *skeptical* approach does not accept testimony about hypnotic behavior as indicative of the existence of the special trance state. "The 'skeptics' do not accept hypnotic behavior and testimony at face value, as no unequivocal criterion for distinguishing trance behavior and simulation has yet been found [Sutcliffe, 1960, p. 189]." A frequently cited finding is that the behavior obtained in hypnosis (even the most bizarre) is also obtainable by simulation (Barber, 1969) and by role playing (Sarbin and Andersen, 1967). After reviewing all of the extant research literature, Rosenhan (1967) concluded that "without exception, the well-controlled experimental evidence reveals no difference between the performance of hypnotized subjects and either their own or others' waking motivated performances [p. 489]."

The skeptical viewpoint is consistent with and in fact a strong element in our own framework of behavior influence. However, Hilgard (1971), a supporter of the credulous position, has presented this dichotomy in a very different manner. In a discussion of "enemies from within" (the field of hypnosis), he argued that

> Most troublesome are those with scientific credentials, fascinated enough by the problems of hypnosis to experiment and publish in the field, but making a special point of holding a skeptical, debunking attitude. Skepticism in science is a good thing; certainly the demand for proof and replication are of the essence of science. But it is possible to turn this skepticism into a kind of sophistry, a "scientism" that feeds upon itself and gives the impression that all the answers are already known; it thus fails to support the sense of wonder and bafflement out of which scientific discoveries grow.
>
> In sharpening the distinction between a "credulous" and "skeptical" attitude, as proposed initially by Sutcliffe (1961), there has since come about an unfortunate distortion of this polarization. The skeptical attitude is appropriately reflected in some doubts about the nature of hypnotic "induction" and about "trance" as an

explanatory device. But this is then twisted into the position that there is nothing to explain, that all that was mysterious is now clear. By an odd turn of logic, it is the "skeptics" who now have a dogmatic, assured position, and all who think there are unsolved problems are the "credulous" [p. 568].

The fact that there are two mutually exclusive approaches to hypnosis illustrates a point we have been making; namely, that one's theoretical model affects how and what one sees or presents as one's material. Our presentation makes the skeptics the "good guys"; and with the introduction of a loaded word or two (*debunking, sophistry*) in Hilgard's description, the skeptics have evolved into antiscientific "enemies from within."

The Role Metaphor

As social psychology developed, so did a new terminology. Sarbin (1950, 1965) helped to reconceptualize hypnosis within the metaphor of "role": "Drawn from the theater and from everyday life, this metaphor regards the actions of the hypnotist and of the subject as determined in large part by the situation in which both participants are trying to enact reciprocal roles [Sarbin, 1950, p. 256]." The consequence of this metaphor is quite different from viewing hypnosis as a physiological event. Implications drawn from *the theater* help focus observations on reciprocal conduct, acting skill, and the function of the audience.

The concept of role *enactment* is more useful than that of role playing or role taking, since it avoids the notion of simulation. But, in any case, the research by Barber (1969) and Orne (1962) has demonstrated that most if not all hypnotic phenomena can be simulated.

Sarbin and Andersen (1967) offered their own *role* theory analysis of hypnotic behavior within the history of the growth of the skeptical attitude. They argued that the older skeptics have had little impact on their peers because of inappropriate metaphors. Sarbin's (1968) discussion of metaphors in science is one of the keystones in the argument against the reification of trance state metaphors; and Coe and Sarbin (1971) have reexamined factor analytic studies of hypnotic scales in terms of the subjects' ability in role taking.

THE HYPNOTIST AS INFLUENCER

Introducing a recent handbook on hypnosis, Gordon (1967) uses hyperbole and metaphor to refer to hypnosis as "an object of excessive interest." "The terms laid down for hypnosis by an increasing number of investigators are such that it may be purchasing its respectability at the price of much of its identity. Its mystery seems to be fading away, like the Cheshire cat, in an ineffable smog of epiphenomena and artificiality, leaving only the memory of an inscrutable smile. That smile of mystery has been alluring to many investigators [p. 3]."

As in every other type of behavior influence, the focus is not on the technique, but on the user of the technique. Hypnotists, as Gordon (1967) points out, have been a strange lot. "As an obsessive object, hypnosis has attracted the interest of people who are driven to identify themselves with the dark of the moon; it has stimulated the distaste and revulsion of those who are most sensitive to their scientific status in the community of the sciences; and it has been the object of intense ambivalence for those who stand between those poles of the dirty deep and the superficial sterile [p. 4]."

Some investigators have shifted their research emphasis from the characteristics of the subject to the beliefs, values, and behavioral expectancies of the hypnotist. In fact, research in hypnosis such as that of Orne (1959) has set the standards to which other social influence research must conform.

Gordon (1967) makes the further point that "The motives and character of the investigator are made suspect by his interest in hypnosis, a suspiciousness that tends toward self-confirmation as these attitudes restrict the field to the rebels and nonconformists [p. 4]."

CREDULOUS RESEARCH IN HYPNOSIS

Different models lead to different research strategies, which generally tend to confirm the original models that generated them. Hilgard is a credulous investigator, perhaps the leading one at this point. Observing that some people appear to be readily hypnotized and others only with great difficulty, he has focused on individual susceptibility and hence individual differences. His research involves such variables as *depth of hypnosis,* from which quantitative hypnotic susceptibility scales can be developed. These scales then become the tool of the investigator who studies the individual differences associated with differences in depth of trance. Almost every leading investigator of hypnosis sooner or later devises a susceptibility scale (for example, Liebeault, Bernheim, White, Sarbin, Eysenck, Weitzenhoffer, Hilgard, Orne, Shor, Barber, and London).

From his findings, Hilgard (1967) has concluded that hypnotic susceptibility is as stable a trait as intelligence:

> Whenever a human ability is subjected to measurement, the question arises as to how stable that ability is, how enduring it is through time. The historical studies of the constancy of the I.Q. are addressed to this problem, and we face the same kind of problem concerning the stability of the ability to enter hypnosis and to respond to tests of hypnotic susceptibility. The evidence thus far presented, based on retest reliabilities, shows that under standard conditions hypnotic susceptibility is a quite dependable trait, with retest correlations commonly lying in the .80s

and .90s. Like the I.Q., which also shows such retest reliabilities, there is a good deal of room for individual variation, and the assertion of stability is not the whole story [Hilgard, 1967, p. 427].

Hilgard next expresses what could be the core concept for credulous scientists of personality in general and hypnotism in particular.

> To characterize the hypnotically susceptible and the hypnotic non-susceptible has turned out to be a far more difficult problem than might be expected on the basis of the satisfactory criterion measures of susceptibility. One possibility is to reject the whole attempt as essentially illusory, because hypnotic susceptibility is an individual matter depending upon ability, attitude, hypnotist, hypnotic technique, and so forth, thus too whimiscal and emphemeral to be caught by correlation coefficients. Still, as in the study of personality generally, there are some persistent low correlations that encourage the seeker to raise them; if there is a little demonstrated order, there may very well be more underlying order if we are imaginative enough to find it [Hilgard, 1967, p. 432].

Note that a switch is made from hypnosis itself to responses by people who are susceptible to hypnosis. We really are studying a behavior and not a state. It is worth noting further that Hilgard rationalizes the relative paucity of replicable results as indicative of a yet-unmeasured underlying process.

The variables that Hilgard deals with are age, sex, intelligence, personality, and psychiatric diagnosis. He is optimistic about the development of reliable scales for measuring hypnotic susceptibility. He argues that hypnotic ability tends to be quite stable over time and that there is a high common factor to tests of hypnotizability that conforms to the types of behavior commonly included in the social definition of hypnosis—responsiveness to ideomotor suggestions; positive and negative hallucinations; dreams and regression; amnesia; posthypnotic suggestions; and so on. Hilgard (1967) has summarized such research as follows:

> This rather favorable state with respect to the criterion of hypnotizability encourages the attempts to find personality correlates. The results to date seem rather skimpy in view of the efforts expended, but at least we know that some behavior outside hypnosis is rather closely related to behavior within hypnosis (particularly responses to waking suggestion, and role-taking behavior) and some responses on attitude questionnaires and personality inventories show a modest correlation with susceptibility, particularly attitudes giving a favorable evaluation of hypnosis, and "yea-saying" on inventories. Beyond this, it appears from interview studies that global, one-dimensional approaches are likely to yield limited results because there are alternative paths into hypnosis, as illustrated by the roles of adventuresomeness and fantasy. These are illustrative only, and other paths may be available, or these may be partial descriptions of a more fundamental dichotomy [p. 439].

Personality Correlates of Hypnosis

The investigation of personality is closely related to the credulous approach to hypnosis. Hypnosis would seem to be an event in which performance should be related to some special personality characteristic. This search is based on the repeated observation by those involved in hypnosis that not everyone is susceptible to hypnosis. One of the earliest explanations of such susceptibility was the obvious one that the individual was suggestible.

Tests of primary suggestibility (Duke, 1964) correlate fairly highly ($r = 0.60$) with measures of hypnotic behavior. But this is spurious, since the two measures of hypnosis and of suggestibility are nearly identical operationally and should really result in a correlation close to unity. More significantly, Duke found in his review of fifty years' research that the correlation between primary suggestibility tests is directly related to the subject's *experiences with the investigator.* Correlations rise significantly on retesting. This finding indicates the strong interpersonal influence involved in both hypnosis and suggestibility. Duke also found that performance on secondary tests of suggestibility were almost completely independent of performance on primary suggestibility tests, and therefore, whatever they were measuring, primary and secondary performances were not on the same level. Duke (1968) concluded that neither "inner" nor "other" directedness as measured by the Bell questionnaire was predictive of degree of hypnotic ability. Kemp (1969) reported a similar failure. Also related is Klinger's finding (1970) that observation of responsive models results in greater responsiveness on suggestibility tests, at least among female undergraduates. To the extent that external experience, that is, observing a model, increases a behavior, the "internal" personality variables would be less involved.

SKEPTICAL RESEARCH IN HYPNOSIS

T. X. Barber (1969) is representative of "skeptical" investigators of hypnosis. His approach involves a critique of the experimental design of studies on hypnosis as well as the traditional model of hypnosis. Barber (1967), has pointed out that

> most of the data presented in general treatises on hypnotism derive from studies that did not include a control treatment. In the majority of instances, "hypnotized" subjects, but not "waking" subjects, were given suggestions of analgesia, deafness, hallucinations, amnesia, and so on. Although some of the "hypnotized" subjects manifested the suggested effects, it was not demonstrated that the "hypnotic state" was either necessary or helpful in their production. There is evidence to indicate that if "waking" control subjects had been given suggestions of analgesia, deafness, hallucinations, and so on, some of them may also have manifested the effects shown by the "hypnotized" subjects [p. 473].

Barber's approach to hypnosis is typified by the question, "What are the variables associated with the procedures labeled as hypnotic inductions that are instrumental in eliciting behaviors traditionally labeled as hypnotic? [Chaves, 1968]." In answer to it Barber has hypothesized a set of antecedent variables—*instructional, situational, subject, experimenter*—which includes the specific wording of instructions and the characteristics, expectations, and attitudes of both subject and experimenter.

Conversely, Barber has argued that certain variables may *spoil* the usual experimental design in hypnosis studies. (*a*) "Good" hypnotic subjects *try harder* under hypnosis than in the waking state; (*b*) experimental groups based on a preliminary relationship with the experimenter are usually *highly selected* (*hence motivated*); (*c*) the situation is defined as "hypnosis" to the experimental group and as an "experiment" to the control group.

> When the effects of these variables have been systematically assayed, investigators may conclude that it is unnecessary and unparsimonious to postulate a "hypnotic trance state" to explain response to suggestions of analgesia, time distortion, color blindness, deafness, amnesia, hallucinations. . . . Response to suggestions of this type may be found to be a function of the manner in which the situation is defined to the subject; the relationship between subject and experimenter; the subject's interest in the experiment and his attitude toward the immediate test situation; and the subject's motivation to perform well on assigned tasks [Barber, 1967, p. 474].

Almost every form of social influence has a basic set of assumptions which argues its uniqueness. Barber (1969) has pointed out that two fundamental assumptions underlie all discussions of hypnosis. First, it is assumed that the subject enters a "rather" unique state of conciousness. Various terms are used interchangeably to refer to this state of consciousness including *hypnotic state, trance, hypnotic trance*, or simply *hypnosis* [Barber, 1969, p. 5]." As Barber (1969) has pointed out, experts have trouble distinguishing between people in a trance (hypnotized) and people simulating a trance. Second, it is assumed that the depth of the trance is directly related to correlated sets of behaviors such as the specific responses to the hypnotist's suggestion (for example, rigidity, hallucinations), a hypnotic appearance (for example, limpness), reports of unusual experiences (for example, bodily changes), and testimony of having been hypnotized ("I was deeply hypnotized").

One issue which divides investigations is whether or not the features usually attributed to the hypnotic state are universal. On one side is the assertion (Orne, 1959) that the hypnotic state is characterized by changes in the *subjective experiences* of the person hypnotized as evidenced by the subject's testimony that he felt a compulsion to follow suggestions and that he experienced the trance as being *different* from normal.

On the other side, is the counterargument (Barber, Dalal, and Calverley,

1968) that testimony about subjective experiences may be determined largely by the wording of questions in the postexperimental situation. If a subject was asked a negatively worded question such as, "Did you feel you could resist the suggestions?" he was much more likely to state that he could not resist. Thus, experimenter bias may be mediated in hypnosis research by subtle phrasing of questions and instructional sets (for example, see Troffer and Tart, 1964).

Another example of research challenging the function of the trance is by Gandolfo (1971), who gave subjects a suggestion immediately *before* as well as after the induction of a hypnotic trance. Whether or not the subjects received the suggestion during the trance appeared to have little impact, while their expectations and prior experience did.

A frequent topic used to demonstrate hypnosis as a special state is age regression, in which the person in the trance plays the role of a child. Parrish, Lundy, and Leibowitz (1968) cast doubt on the authenticity of this finding when their subjects produced behavior that overshot the mark, in that it was excessively young. Staples and Wilensky (1968) used appropriate controls and found no significant difference in the performance of subjects hypnotically regressed and subjects simulating regression; both groups "regressed," but without a significant difference in the degree to which they enacted the role.

A final challenge to the trance state are studies like that by Miller, Lundy, and Galbraith (1970) on hallucinations. A number in green was projected onto a screen and a bright red light was simultaneously projected, so that the number was not visible to the naked eye. Ten hypnotized subjects were asked to hallucinate a green filter. All the subjects reported doing so and seeing a change in the color of the screen. However, none was able to see the number which should have been visible if the color filters were really working.

Barber's approach has been applied in work explaining the effects observed in stage (entertainment) hypnosis (Meeker and Barber, 1971). In this situation, the subject has a far higher level of responsiveness to "waking" suggestions than is presumed; that is, a "trance" need not be induced to bring about considerable effects. People likely to be responsive to the hypnotist can be selected in part upon their reaction to mild tests such as being requested to relax and to close their eyes. The hypnotist defines the situation as hypnosis and this designation provides demand characteristics (discriminative stimuli) for responsiveness to suggestions beyond normally socially appropriate behavior. Being onstage is a novel and arousing experience for many people. There is an increased pressure to conform or do well; a person who resists or "holds out" spoils the pleasure of the audience and becomes a likely target for the anger of the experienced hypnotist, who may embarrass him.

Under these conditions some people strive to please and actively simulate being hypnotized. And some stage hypnotists whisper private instructions to the subject to help make the demonstration a success. The stage hypnotist may also *not* follow the standard procedures of challenging the subject, that is, testing the person's behavior to see if he is "really" hypnotized. Some stage hypnotists use stooges or pretrained subjects. Others may use "tricks" such as pinching an earlobe before passing a needle through it to deaden what pain may be felt in an area of relatively few nerve endings. By all these procedures, the hypnotist may mislead the audience to believe that subjects are having highly unusual experiences when they are not.

In summary, the skeptical views we have discussed represent a formulation of hypnosis as a behavior that (*a*) requires identification by an observer and (*b*) is increased or decreased by manipulations by another person.

HYPNOSIS AS PARADIGM

In his analysis of Barber's research, Chaves (1968) places the skeptical approach to hypnosis within the context of Kuhn's notion (1970) of changes in scientific paradigms (see Chapter 2). The search for the physiological and behavioral correlates of the hypnotic state and for the factors leading to hypnotic susceptibility represent the traditional paradigm. The underlying assumption is that a hypnotic trance state is instrumental in eliciting hypnotic behaviors. Barber has offered an alternative and "revolutionary" paradigm. Chaves argues that although Barber was preceded by other investigators including Dorcus, Pattie, White, Sarbin, and Sutcliffe, it was he who broke the old paradigm and offered a genuine change in concept and approach.

The major critique of the previous paradigm is its inability to demonstrate the hypnotic state and its circularity of reasoning used to explain the trance. The subjects in a hypnotic state are considered to be highly susceptible to suggestion, and conversely the evidence for being in a hypnotic state is defined as high responsivity to suggestion. There is no independent criterion for being in a trance. The trance is inferred from the behaviors it purports to explain. Sarbin and Coe (1972) present arguments to show that such conceptions as *trance, special state* and *altered state of consciousness* have no utility in accounting for hypnotic behavior. These authors point out that the subject's verbal report is usually taken as the basis for declaring that a trance state exists. But verbal reports, as we have repeatedly indicated, must be analyzed in terms of demand characteristics, subject expectations, and verbal conditioning.

If hypnosis is a separate and unique state, then it should have some physiological correlates that are *unique* to it. For over a century, investigators have unsuccessfully tried to find such an index.

Barber (1969) contends that hypnosis can be approached by a rigorous scientific methodology of antecedent and consequent variables. The behaviors traditionally labeled as hypnotic can then be shown to be a function of a set of denotable antecedent variables "that are very similar to those that play an important role in a wide variety of test situations"; these antecedent variables include subjects' attitudes and expectancies and "motivation to cooperate" and the tone and wording of the instructions.

One argument advanced by Barber is relevant to a historical analogy. The evidence at this time fails to support the notion of a trance state. This concept may well go the way of "ether" in physics or "phlogiston" in chemistry—both concepts depended upon a hypothetical substance to explain how unseen forces of electricity, magnetism, and gravity could be transmitted through the air. Ether began to take on all sorts of characteristics which were necessary to explain physical events. But it soon became clear that the concept was unnecessary to explain observed phenomena. Thus, the notion of a hypnotic trance state may not be disproven, but eventually found to be unnecessary.

We have previously described the origin of the term "hypnosis," with its implications of a special state similar to sleep and the subject's resemblance to a sleepwalker—an individual responding in a dissociated and automatic manner. The credulous investigators do not agree on the meaning of this state, but do agree that it differs fundamentally from the normal waking state. Such a special state, the hypnotic trance, may occur "spontaneously", but it is usually induced by a series of special procedures such as eye fixation and suggestions of relaxation, drowsiness, and sleep. The hypnotic state is expected to last more than a few moments. And the hypnotized subject is expected to be responsive to suggestions that result in special behaviors such as muscular rigidity; age regression; anesthesia; audio-visual and negative hallucinations; deafness; blindness; amnesia; heightened performance on special tasks; and posthypnotic behavior.

Following from this paradigm, most experimental research in hypnosis has accepted the trance as a given and has focused on techniques of inducing *it* and determining the characteristics of individuals who may be most readily susceptible to *it*, and the characteristics of the correlated behaviors associated with *it*.

An alternative paradigm developed by Barber is based primarily on his own research and that of Sarbin (1950, 1965). The assumptions underlying the alternative paradigm are expressed by Barber (1970) as follows:

> It is unnecessary to postulate a fundamental difference in the "state" of the person who is and the one who is not responsive to test-suggestions; both the person who is and the one who is not responsive to test-suggestions have attitudes, motivations, and expectancies toward the communications they are receiving; the person who is very responsive to test-suggestions has "positive" attitudes, motivations, and expectancies toward the communications he is receiving; . . . the person who is very unresponsive to test-suggestions has "negative" attitudes, motivations, and expectancies toward the communications he is receiving; . . . the three factors— attitudes, motivations, and expectancies—vary on a continuum (from negative, to neutral, to positive) and *they converge and interact in complex ways* to determine

to what extent a subject will let himself think along with and imagine those things that are suggested. The extent to which the subject thinks along with and vividly imagines the suggested effects, in turn, determines his overt and subjective responses to test-suggestions; . . . responsiveness to test-suggestions is a normal psychological phenomenon which can be conceptualized in terms of constructs which are an integral part of normal psychology, especially of social psychology . . . the mediating variables which are relevant to explaining responsiveness to test-suggestions include attitudes, motivations, expectancies, and cognitive-imaginative processes. . . . The phenomena associated with test-suggestions are considered to be within the range of normal human capabilities. However, whether or not the suggested phenomena are similar to or different from phenomena occurring in real-life situations that bear the same name is viewed as an open question that needs to be answered empirically [pp. 4–5].

Once one puts hypnosis into this framework, then new questions are asked in new ways. In effect Barber has attempted to demolish the old paradigm, starting with systematic observations of normal behavior. For example, some individuals are highly responsive to suggestions from others even when no attempt has been made to place them in a hypnotic trance. A dramatic example is the fact that when asked to keep their bodies rigid (the human plank feat often seen in stage hypnosis), some persons can remain suspended between two chairs for several minutes, one chair beneath their head and one chair beneath their ankles. Collins (1961) has demonstrated that control subjects could perform this trick just as well as subjects put into a trance; individuals simply told that they were doing a test of imagination have performed similar feats, such as arm levitation, hand lock, thirst hallucination, body immobility, "posthypnotic" response, and selective amnesia.

One of the major foundations of the special state paradigm was the belief that suggestions to highly responsive subjects could cause blisters, cure warts, produce anesthesia sufficient for surgery, and induce other unusual effects like age regression and hallucinations. A review of the literature in hypnosis by Barber (1969) has questioned whether *any* of these occurrences have been demonstrated.

For example, during the special state of hypnosis highly responsive individuals supposedly respond to the suggestion that a blister will form at specified places on the skin. However, the literature reveals that most of these reports occurred before the era of rigorous experimental controls; in most studies no skin changes appeared; no control groups had been used; and, in most instances, positive results were obtained only with people who had or were suffering from skin ailments or who had been labeled as hysterics. Also, it may be relatively easy for an individual to produce a wheal or skin disturbance by self-suggestion.

The literature on hypnosis as anesthesia is even more surprising. "Most 'hypnotic trance' subjects who undergo minor or major surgery without drugs show signs of pain [Barber, 1969, p. 130]." Conversely, a few hypnotic trance subjects show little pain when they undergo survery without drugs. However, it is also true that a few subjects undergo surgery without pain, without drugs, *and* without hypnotic trance. Barber makes a point that certainly warrants verification, namely, that the pain involved in most surgical procedures is "highly overestimated." The skin is sensitive to pain but most of the muscles and organs of the body are relatively insensitive. More evidence against the hypnotic state explanation of pain anesthesia comes from the research on placebo response, particularly in many replicated studies which demonstrate that reported pain can be reduced by inert substances.

Other phenomena characteristic of the hypnotic trance such as hallucinations, deafness, and blindness are difficult to demonstrate objectively and apparently can be reproduced without a trance state. Even spontaneous amnesias attributed to being in a special hypnotic state are usually found to have been suggested implicitly or explicitly by the influencer. In short, the same percentages of individuals with and without "trance" appear to emit the behaviors which are considered indicative of hypnotic trance.

Finally, we must note again that even "experts" have difficulty identifying individuals who are in a "trance" and those who are simulating or role playing. The identification is made in terms of the antecedent events (the label attached to the situation, which serves as a discriminative stimulus for the subject *and observer*).

Instead of a notion of a trance, how can we explain what takes place in hypnosis? Barber has offered an alternative conceptualization, or paradigm, with antecedent variables (input) and consequent effects (output). Barber divides the antecedent variables into procedural, subject, experimenter, and subject-experimenter interaction. The procedural variables include those "subsumed under the term hypnotic induction procedure" (that is, statements which define the situation as "hypnosis, motivational instructions, and suggestions for relaxation, drowsiness, and sleep"). Some examples of procedural variables are the specific wording of the suggestions, the experimenter's tone of voice in presenting suggestions, the method he uses to present suggestions and his specific wording of the questions used to elicit subjective testimony. The subject variables include the personality characteristics, attitudes, and expectations of the subject. The experimenter variables include the experimenter's prestige, characteristics, expectancies, and attitudes. Slight changes, even in words used, in any of these variables influences consequent effects.

Of these antecedent variables, Barber stresses the impact of *intervening variables*—the subject's attitudes, motivations, and expectancies. Despite the cognitive appearance of these variables, the Barber position is quite consistent with a behavioral analysis of hypnosis as a behavior influence situation in that operational definitions of terms are provided for each variable.

LAST WORD

Hypnosis as a procedure and as social movement is a human behavior illustrative of the influencer influencing. It serves as an appropriate historical and theoretical introduction to the detailed discussion of behavior modification to which we now turn. Each of the last four chapters (Chapters 6–9) has presented a view of the variables involved in a psychology of behavior influence from different perspectives: the theoretical framework, the general impact of the influencer, the data from the psychology laboratory, and a procedure which is prototypical of influence. In many ways we now ask the payoff question: To what extent can a psychology of behavior influence affect behavior?

CHAPTER 10

Behavior Therapy: General Considerations

Throughout this book, particularly in Chapter 6, we present a number of generalizations about behavior. Usually these concepts are based upon observations in laboratory situations. The major question for influencer and influencee is how these concepts will work in the nonlaboratory situations in general. It should be clear at this point that the laboratory is also a very real "world," but how the behavioral interactions observed in the laboratory are related to the world in which people usually live remains a key issue for the investigator. As we move from the laboratory we are faced with two problems.

The first is the degree to which the environment can be held constant. The nonlaboratory situation is more complex and much less controlled than the psychological laboratory. In addition, much of the psychological literature is

251

based on the behavior of the bright, young, verbal, and helpful person called the college student. The first task then is to determine how well concepts developed in relatively *brief* and *limited* situations with a *special population* stand up in a more general reality.

The second is that ethical limits on dealing with college students from a subject pool limit the laboratory investigator to the manipulation of relatively trivial behaviors and to the use of relatively circumscribed independent variables. There is a considerable difference between stimuli such as viewing a picture in *Playboy* and dating the girl next door. A college student can be hurt and rewarded far more by examinations and by peers than by contact with a psychologist in a clearly delineated special situation. This does not mean that the psychologist cannot hurt or influence someone (in fact, the psychologist is under a code of ethical conduct designed to make sure that he does not do damage); it simply means that when the psychologist leaves the laboratory, he is dealing with larger, more crucial, and more meaningful aspects of people's lives and that generalizations about behavior may not be valid in these new and different situations.

Several considerations illustrate why such generalizations may be invalid. First, there is the impact of demand characteristics on psychological experiments (see Chapter 8). This impact must have a limit; as the *cost* of compliance with a demand increases, the chance of compliance decreases. In a situation outside the laboratory the costs are likely to be greater, and the exact replication of a demand characteristic effect cannot be assumed. A second consideration is that a curvilinear relationship may exist between the emission of an act and the degree of arousal. For example, if a student is moderately concerned about an examination, he may study more than if he is totally unconcerned. In this instance as concern increases, studying increases. At some point, however, the student may become so concerned or uptight that studying may become aversive, and the material being studied may remind him of the forthcoming dreaded exam. This kind of increased concern may be associated with decreased studying. Work in the laboratory yields information about situations that involve very low to moderate concern, while work outside the laboratory yields information about situations involving moderate to severe concern. This distribution of concern may help explain the fact that a particular laboratory finding may not only not replicate but may even occur in contradictory fashion when made in a nonlaboratory setting. Finally, the laboratory situation serves as a discriminative stimulus, just as do such nonlaboratory situations as classrooms, restaurants, or bedrooms. Behavior may change in each situation; such changes are usually appropriate to the situation.

The goal of behavior therapy research, as of any other investigation of human behavior, is to develop an experiment that can answer a crucial question. The goal is *not* to develop a complex laboratory. The experimental paraphernalia of a laboratory do not make a science anymore than do complex statistical designs.

If the research object is to increase effectiveness in meaningful behavior, a generalization from the trivial social event to the meaningful social event or from the rodent to the human is called for. The general principles may hold, but their explication in specific detail is called for in each instance.

We wish to deal with meaningful behavior and to utilize experimental procedures. The clinical setting provides an opportunity to combine both variables in a manner not possible with undergraduate volunteers. People with clinical problems are acting in ways that someone, including themselves, considers worthy of change. Since therapy is usually sought only after other procedures have failed, it is likely to be persistent and socially meaningful to the person. Further, the changeworthy nature of behavior that calls for professional intervention permits the use of procedures not ethically permissible with laboratory volunteers. Individuals entering a treatment procedure implicitly contract for a change of behavior in return for their time, energy, and possibly money. In the present volume we are not primarily interested in the fields of abnormal behavior or treatment. We have written on these matters elsewhere in some detail (Ullmann and Krasner, 1965, 1969). Our interest here is in illustrating behavioral formulations in the realm of peoples' overt social behavior.

The clinical situation not only permits the application of stronger procedures to larger units of human behavior but has historically been a realm in which personality theories were applied and tested. The theories of Freud and Carl Rogers led directly to therapy procedures. It must be repeatedly emphasized that if a form of treatment is effective, it does not follow logically or empirically that its theory is necessarily true. Logically, an effective method of change does not have a necessary relation to etiology, nor does the specific treatment have to be the only one that might have been deduced from the theory. A treatment may be empirically effective, but its active ingredient may be very different from that presumed by the therapist as work on placebos has illustrated. These limitations should be remembered; however, it is possible to present how some investigators are using behavioral principles and the results of their efforts. Here again we emphasize that our goal is to illustrate the process of behavior change in human beings.

WHAT IS TO BE MODIFIED?

The basic notion of the behavioral approach is that no act is in and of itself abnormal. Rather, people are capable of a wide range of responses to the environment. Given age, sex, social class, and social situation, a limited number of the acts a person could emit are considered correct or appropriate. Acts that are unexpected, disturbing, or disadvantageous to someone, including the individual himself, are likely to be *called* deviant, and the form of deviance that sanctions the intervention of shamans such as clinical psychologists is called abnormality or mental illness. Calling a person abnormal or mentally ill solves a social problem to the extent that it explains behavior and legitimizes action such as hospitalization. Because we think that the very definition of abnormal behavior requires a *social context* and a *social evaluation*, we have called what follows a *sociopsychological model* (Ullmann and Krasner, 1969).

Psychiatric Diagnosis and After

Once a person has been designated mentally ill, either by himself or others, he is treated differently. While relatively few regularities are observed among diagnostic groups (Zigler and Phillips, 1961), those that do occur may be a *result* of the differential treatment of people so labeled rather than the *cause* of the differential treatment. This possibility may be particularly true of hospitalized patients (Ullmann, 1967) and illustrates secondary rather than primary deviance (Lemert, 1967; Scheff, 1966; see Chapter 6 of this text).

Primary deviance is a specific act such as speeding on the highways or injecting heroin. *Secondary deviance* is *the effects of that act*, including being caught and publicly labeled. If the person is not caught for speeding, he may speed again in the future and his pattern of behavior will not be greatly altered. If he is caught and loses his driver's license, however, he may have to alter his vocational or recreational habits. Drug use provides an even clearer example of primary and secondary deviance. Drug use in itself may not lead to a major change in life style, as evidenced by data from England, where drugs are provided by the National Health Service, or from American physicians who are drug users. If the person becomes addicted and has neither money nor a ready supply, he may engage in criminal acts such as theft or prostitution in order to obtain funds to buy drugs. He may limit his social circle to fellow users. In short, his life style changes. Being caught and jailed for a specific act may lead to loss of job, change of peer identification, and a stigma that makes it difficult to obtain employment at the level of one's capabilities. In addition, many parolees are faced with limitations on their mobility and choice of friends that are not imposed on people who have not been jailed. Thus, the effects of being caught and labeled may be far greater and far more damaging than the effects of the deviant act itself. It must also be made explicit that the person may apply a label to himself; he need not be officially caught and publicly labeled. A person may assign to himself a label, which may become a self-fulfilling prophecy. An example that counselors see on college campuses is the undergraduate who says he or she is not attractive to members of the opposite sex, makes no efforts to be pleasing to others, and thus is ignored and lonely.

In the vast majority of cases, people are brought to professionals by nonprofessionals. The person may come himself (self-referral) or at the behest of a teacher, parent, policeman, minister, spouse, or employer. For both diagnostic and treatment purposes, the professional fits the person's behavior into a system because there must be legitimization of the professional's subsequent actions. Especially when working with an adult who is not self-referred, the professional categorizes the person within the diagnostic system of the International Classification of Disease or of the American Psychiatric Association (DSM II 1969). There is a great social as well as a professional pressure to categorize the person, because by analogy to physical health, if a person does not manifest a mental disease, he is normal. (See Ullmann and Krasner, 1969, chs. 12–13, for a discussion of these social pressures and the frequently poor reliability of psychiatric diagnoses.)

The professional may well categorize the person in terms of a disease concept and then treat the disease rather than the behavior that caused the referral. There are a number of reasons for this procedure. The first is that the behavioral problem may be formulated as an indication of the disease which thus must be "cured" before behavioral change can be expected. The second reason is that the notion of a disease legitimizes the treatment procedure. The third reason is that the treatment facilities may offer little opportunity to treat the behavioral problem; if, for example, the problem is sexual, isolation of the person away from members of the opposite sex seems one of the poorest procedures for the development of socially typical sexual behavior.

The sociopsychological variables previously discussed also function in the diagnostic situation as well as in the laboratory situation. Social class and ethnological differences influence decisions. The material emitted by the person to be treated may be influenced by verbal conditioning and demand characteristics. Of prime interest, however, is the fact that the labeler, the professional, is also subject to the influence process. A classic in this regard is the work of Temerlin (1968) on the role of suggestion effects on diagnostic decisions.

Temerlin first developed a tape of a "supernormal" man who got along well with his family and coworkers. This recording was then played before various groups of people who evaluated the subject's mental health. Table 1

Table 1: The Effects of Suggestion on Evaluation of Mental Health of a Tape-Recorded Subject by Mental Health Professionals (after Temerlin, 1968, p. 351).

CONDITION: SAMPLE AND SUGGESTION		PERCENTAGE IN EACH CATEGORY		
		Psychotic	Neurotic	Mentally Healthy
Mentally healthy	$N = 20$	0	0	100
Employment interview	$N = 24$	0	29	71
No suggestion	$N = 21$	0	43	57
Psychiatrists, psychotic	$N = 25$	60	40	0
Psychologists, psychotic	$N = 25$	28	60	12
Psychology graduate students, psychotic	$N = 45$	11	78	11

summarizes the data. The tape was played to various groups of mental health professionals, and just before each group heard it, an outstanding professional remarked loudly to the person next to him that this tape was unusual. If the condition was "mental health," he noted that the subject was that great rarity, a truly normal person. In the last three conditions reported in Table 1, the influencer said that the case was very interesting because the subject appeared neurotic, but was psychotic.

As may be seen from Table 1, when mental health was the suggestion, all the professionals rated the subject as mentally healthy. The second and third conditions described in Table 1 may be considered a measure of baserate of evaluation of mental illness or health by such a group of professionals, since there was no suggestion or a neutral suggestion (that is, employment interview). Under such conditions, none of the workers rated the subject in the range of psychosis, but roughly one-third rated him consistent with neurosis. The last three conditions, where psychosis was the suggestion, speak for themselves. The suggestion greatly increased the evaluated presence of indicants of psychosis.

In summary, just as bringing a person to a professional is a learned behavior, so the succeeding acts by the professional are also learned and altered by social influence (Kadushin, 1969).

Development of Changeworthy Behavior

In every system of behavior change, a number of issues must be touched. These are (a) How does disturbing or changeworthy behavior develop? (b) What maintains such behavior which on the surface appears disadvantageous to the person as well as aversive to others? (c) On what basis does the therapist make his decision to treat? (d) What material does the therapist think important for his therapeutic maneuvers? (e) How is this relevant material obtained during therapy? (f) How does the therapist deal with the material, so that the person being treated is aided to alter his behavior? (g) Once there is a change in behavior, how is this change maintained?

Some enduring therapy topics center on question (f) above. These deal with (a) the establishment of rapport, (b) the use of interpretation, (c) the therapist's responsibility to and for the patient, (d) the limits of ethical therapist behavior, (e) confidentiality, and (f) the therapist's evaluative behavior beyond or in addition to diagnosis.

The Effect of the Label: Treatment

In examining the effects of labeling, we now discuss three partially overlapping treatment situations: institutionalization in a psychiatric hospital; outpatient treatment for adults with problems not severe enough to disrupt the majority of their social activities; and imposed outpatient treatment such as that given to children at a clinic or within a day school. In all three situations, becoming the object of treatment alters the person's environment.

We have discussed at length elsewhere (Ullmann, 1967; Ullmann and Krasner, 1969) the effect of being placed in a psychiatric hospital. Such placement results in the person being trained to adjust to the hospital far more than he is prepared for life in the extrahospital situation. The typical hospital treats a disease—for example, schizophrenia—rather than social behavior and is likely to offer somatic therapy (shock, tranquilizers) or custodial treatment (protected routines) rather than training in adjusting to work, spouses, recreation, and unsupervised daily life. Behaviors typical of the person living outside the hospital may well appear maladjusted within the framework of the large psychiatric hospital. Normal patterns of responsibility and self-assertion in the person may literally be extinguished; and because he is labeled as sick and irresponsible, his attending or responding to important social stimuli may also be extinguished. If the person is labeled as *out of contact with reality* or *disorganized thinking* or *regressed*, what he says and does no longer has the same impact as when these acts are emitted by so-called normal people. Socially positive and socially aversive acts are treated the same. The end result is likely to be a pattern of withdrawal and avoidance of punishment, decision making, and responsibility. Ways of counteracting this pattern, which leads to the severe apathy that is the greatest therapeutic problem of patients hospitalized for two years or more, are discussed later in this chapter when we take up token economies.

Goldstein (1962, 1971) has provided major reviews of the interaction of the therapist and client's expectations in outpatient psychological treatment. The expectations of both alter their behaviors and may increase or decrease the success of the therapy. In addition, being in treatment has both obligations and benefits. In some select populations having a "shrink" is a status symbol. More generally, in a parallel to the medical situation, having an illness may excuse one from the society's typical level of responsibility. Many people experience a period of struggle prior to seeking or accepting professional help and literally undergo a process of socialization to therapy (Kadushin, 1969). Entering therapy may then be a major step for the person, with consequences not only in how others label him but how he looks at himself.

In adult outpatient treatment, as in the case of hospitalization, the client is trained in how to be a patient. In all psychological treatments there is an assumption that the person receiving treatment will be more open with the therapist than he is with other people. The psychoanalytically influenced therapist has a fundamental rule of *free association* in which the client says whatever comes into his mind. A second assumption is that the therapist is an *expert* capable of helping the client. From these first two follow two related assumptions: that the therapist, as a professional person, will not take advantage of his client for personal satisfactions and that the therapist will indeed help the person change his behavior.

Whether psychoanalytic, existential, client-centered, or behavioral, the therapist will *instruct* the client in what he is to do in order to benefit from the treatment. Adult outpatients are usually assumed to wish to change and hence to give the procedures a fair trial. The expectation of change as well as the realistic investment of time, money, and effort may lead to improvement that is not necessarily related to any specific therapy maneuver. This improvement may be termed a placebo effect and also illustrates social influence.

A third treatment situation involves children, who are likely to be brought to the therapist by someone who wants their behavior changed. Whether in individual or environmental therapy, the professional bears a particularly great ethical responsibility. He must evaluate whether change is called for or whether a change would be more reasonable in the person disturbed by the child's behavior. Underlying this decision is the implication that the professional has a standard to which he can compare the child and his situation in order to decide if and in what regard change is justified.

An example of this problem is the use of tests and other behavioral samples to designate children *likely* to have behavioral difficulties at a later date. What a middle-class school teacher may consider a behavioral difficulty may be appropriate behavior for the child in a particular subgroup. A second and immediately pertinent problem is the effect of designating a child as one who is *likely to have future behavioral difficulties*. Even if we assume that the standard psychological tests and school-oriented criteria are correct, we may still ask whether such "preventive" procedures are justified.

Such criteria typically designate a third of the population as in need of help. While more children who will have problems are identified *than would be expected by chance*, such statistical significance leads to many "false positives," that is, children labeled as in need of help who will *not* have serious problems. If one-tenth of the unselected population will have later severe problems and if the selection devices are twice as accurate as chance, but place one-third of the children in need, the following situation will occur: of every 100 children, 6 of the 10 true positives will be identified. However, another 24 children will be false positives; that is, four times as many children not in need of help will be referred. And 4 of the 10 true positives will still be missed.

The second problem is that a great many children will be flagged. If, as in the Pygmalion effect discussed in Chapter 8, giving a child a good name may result in a self-fulfilling prophecy, we may hypothesize that giving a child a bad name—potential deviant, troublemaker, or the like—will have an adverse effect. This negative result of classification is one of the problems of school track systems, which may with the best of intentions have many aversive social effects. Another problem of flagging procedures that needs to be faced is that diagnoses are not stable, especially if formal labeling does not occur. When conditions change, people change, and the same behavioral manifestations may be evaluated differently at different ages. The data on stability of deviant behavior over time, especially that of children, strongly argues for caution (Clarizio, 1968; Scheff and Sundstrom, 1970).

In summary, the very fact of being treated—regardless of the specifics of treatment—may have effects on the person. Treatment may have favorable effects, as in the placebo response of outpatient treatment; or it may be self-defeating, as in labeling that leads to negative self-fulfilling prophecies in schools or to training in dysfunctional behaviors in psychiatric hospitals. But the point remains that receiving special treatment has an impact in and of itself irrespective of the nature of the treatment.

Treatment Targets

What treatment aims to change is the behavior of a person. This may involve an increase or a decrease of an act or a change in the locale or the timing of an act. The act itself may be disturbing to others or it may be a disturbance the person feels at someone else's behavior. The decision whether or not to alter a specific person's behavior and, if so, what new behaviors to encourage depends on concepts of what is good, right, useful, proper, and so on. That is, an ethical question always exists in behavior change in regard to the legitimacy of the change and the direction of the change. These ethical questions are returned to in Chapter 19.

METHODS OF THERAPY

In general, science is a matter of collecting data to provide generalizations. The typical scientist collects data to test or establish abstract statements about relationships. The scientist moves from his specific data to the general universe; the applied scientist does the reverse. He takes general statements or principles and applies them to specific situations, problems, and individuals. Behavior therapy is the application of general principles from fields such as learning and social psychology to the alteration of the behavior of particular people in specific situations.

The key difference between behavior therapy and more traditional, psychotherapies that have been called "evocative" (Frank, 1961) lies in a deduction from the formulation of the nature of the target problem. If, as in psychoanalysis, the behavior is viewed as an indirect partial gratification and symptom of an unacceptable need, then the appropriate procedure is to deal with the underlying conflict first. A deduction from this position is that if the symptomatic behavior is changed without treating the underlying problem, a new behavioral difficulty will arise. This is called the hypothesis of *symptom substitution*. A correlate of this hypothesis is that since the present symptom is the most economical one that could occur, the new maladaptive behavior should be even more disruptive or disturbing than the present one it supplants. A second feature of this position is that since the difficulty is intrapsychic, the person may be cured without primary reference to the extratherapy situation.

Two more concepts are correlated with this psychoanalytic view. The first is that the therapist's making suggestions about daily life or otherwise entering into the nontherapy situation will dilute the transference which is considered to be basic to the psychotherapeutic situation. The second is that the nature of the disturbing behavior is an indication of a deviation from the normal progression of psychosexual development. The analogy is made here to physical difficulties in which disease is always an indication of an abnormal condition. Again, if the intrapsychic difficulty is *cured*, changed behavior will automatically follow. The therapist, therefore, should not need to deal with the extratherapy situation. The restoration of health becomes its own justification, both in terms of ethical considerations and therapeutic goals.

A second type of evocative therapy is the client-centered approach originated by Carl Rogers. The formal assumptions implicit in this approach are that man has an innate drive towards self-actualization and that he strives for self-consistency (see Chapter 3). External stimuli may be integrated, ignored, or repressed. In the course of life, events may be inconsistent with each other or with the way the person would like them to be. Difficulties arise when stimuli are not integrated or ignored, but are avoided or repressed—that is, not permitted symbolization in the person's awareness. The person avoids further exposure to such stimuli and thus restricts his life span. This behavior may instigate a vicious cycle in which increasing areas of the person's life are restricted, that is, not self-actualized.

The therapist offers a nonthreatening, nonevaluative situation in which the person may investigate his own life without fear. As he does so, he comes face to face with inconsistencies; but because of the nonthreatening situation and because, "When such discrepancies are clearly perceived, the client is unable to leave them alone [Rogers, 1951, p. 148]," the client obtains new and more mature views. By the atmosphere he creates, the therapist helps the person to evoke the repressed material and deal with it, so that it becomes adequately symbolized in the person's awareness. This leads to more mature view of the life situation, an increasing rather than decreasing life space, and a greater congruence between how the person would like to be and how he thinks of himself as actually being. The necessary and sufficient condition for the client's gain is the therapist's *unconditional positive regard*. Treatment is a procedure that can be fostered by the therapist, but it results from the nature of the person. The therapist is responsible for creating the conditions, but not for the outcome. Suggestions, training, or other forms of direction or instigation by the therapist within treatment or in the extratherapy situation are ruled out because the mechanics of the change process are concerned only with therapeutic interaction.

A THEORETICAL OUTLINE
OF BEHAVIOR THERAPY

We have noted that Freudian and client-centered procedures do not deal *directly* with the disturbing behavior. This is the crucial difference between these techniques and behavior therapy. Using the questions on the development of change-worthy behavior, we present a brief outline of behavior therapy and then go on to present some techniques as examples of the application of behavioral principles and of the behavior influence process.

The first question is, *How does disturbing or changeworthy behavior develop?* The essential issue here is how any behavior develops, for the behaviorist makes no judgment of normality on the basis of the behavior itself. He considers the observed behavior as the reasonable outcome of the person's heredity, history, and current situation. If the behavior is satisfactory to the person himself and/or to those who observe and are affected by it, it is "normal" in the sense that no one is upset by it to the extent of calling for professional assistance.

A person may develop his behavioral repertoire in a manner reasonable and "normal" for him, but may act in a way disturbing to others. A first possibility may be he has a *genuine physical deficit*. A classic example is tertiary syphilis, which affects the brain and changes "personality," so that he acts in a different and unexpected manner. Frequently an early indication of change is grandiosity, indifference to the niceties of social usage, and poor economic judgment. With lessened capability, the person is not able to deal with situations in his previously successful ways. He may try to bluff or he may substitute what he wishes for what he can do. Another example of physical deficit is a lack of capability based on *genetic endowment*. A person's ability to deal with abstract concepts may be such that even though he studies diligently he has difficulty with college subjects such as calculus. The first effect on such a person may be failure and frustration. A second effect may be avoidance of classes calling for calculus or similar abstractions and attendant behaviors that excuse or neutralize his failures. For example, the poor calculus student may come to believe that the calculus teacher hates him. A person who is tone-deaf is well advised not to set his heart on becoming a violinist; a physically uncoordinated person should not try to be a professional gymnast; a woman who looks like a typical college coed should not set her heart on becoming Miss USA.

The basic point is that failure to emit the "normal," expected behavior may be due to lack or impairment of a necessary physical prerequisite. In some instances, medical treatment may provide crucial help, as in the use of antibiotics with syphilis. In other cases, at least at the present stage of knowledge, after the source of difficulty has been specified, selection of another vocational or avocational interest may be called for.

Another possible reason for failure to emit an expected or "normal" behavior is failure to have learned *expected prerequisites*. A knowledge of algebra and some trigonometry is usually presumed in college calculus courses. A person who has not mastered these earlier subjects may well fail. In a similar fashion, addition, subtraction, and multiplication all play a role in long division. A child who transfers schools and has not learned these tools as well as his classmates have may appear "stupid" to the teacher.

In adult social situations quite complex performances are taken for granted. Typically, adults provide each other with subtle cues as to how the other's behavior is being received. In some regards this is a matter of custom, and in other ways it is a method for permitting investigation of another person's feelings without running the risk of either being insulting or rejected. A prime example is a college couple; usually the male makes some very slight gestures to determine if further advances will be acceptable. He may hold a hand or put his arm around the female. The manner in which the female disengages herself or leans closer may provide cues for the male's next step. In similar fashion, by geographical proximity, posture, and smiles, a woman may signal her interest in a man. The great social advantage of such gradual, subtle behaviors is that the person may terminate a sequence without overtly hurting the feelings of the other party. Another method of accomplishing the same goal is to present the truth in jest so that if it is rejected, one can always claim, "It was only a joke, so why are you so uptight?"

The behavior of others serves as discriminative stimuli. That is, they mark the times and places when certain behaviors will have reinforcing consequences. People within a given culture expect others to recognize and react appropriately to such cues. Failure to respond to an invitation is considered a lack of interest. One who thinks that an invitation has been given when the opposite is the case is likely to be called anything from a clod to a rapist. A person may act in an unexpected, stupid, or disturbing manner because he has not learned what the other person thinks he has. Once the difficulty has been determined, the focus of treatment is on the *training* that is required.

A person may act in an unusual and disturbing manner if he fails to practice behaviors considered appropriate. A person may have the required intelligence for academic courses and may have mastered the prerequisites adequately. But if he does not study the right way, he may still have trouble. He may not have enough study time. Another may be studying in an ineffective manner—either the so-called studying time is really time in the company of the book, or the time is used to drill on irrelevant material. Every college lecturer has had the experience of being asked by the class if some topic is relevant, that is, Will it be covered on the exam? Students learn how to find out what the professor wants. In athletics, hobbies, work, and social situations, a smooth performance requires practice. The therapeutic procedure, once the difficulty has been determined, involves encouraging the person to practice and not to give up after a single trial.

The previous paragraphs dealt essentially with the development of a normal repertoire. The following material deals in some ways with the development of an appropriate response to unusual learning situations. A person may have his emission of so-called normal behavior extinguished. One theory (Ullmann and Krasner, 1969), for example, has argued that the person called schizophrenic has had his attention to the stimuli presumed to be salient in his environment extinguished.

Extinction of a response that has previously been well learned and practiced may be observed in everyday situations such as sexual relationships. At the start, sexual favors may have been granted only when both partners were in the mood. After a while such a mood may cease to be a discriminative stimulus: the sexual act may take place whether or not both partners feel romantic. The man may decrease his romantic behaviors, since they may be less necessary to attain his goal. The woman may similarly be less seductive. The marital counseling strategy is to endeavor to have the partners provide strong go-no-go reinforcers, so that the discriminative stimulus of the romantic mood is once again worth working for.

In a more general fashion, a major change in life style is frequently preceded by a period in which a former life style is no longer effective and hence extinguished (see Ullmann, 1969c). The life style being extinguished may be a socially valued one, such as studying hard, or it may be evaluated by others as unfavorable, such as being dependent or annoying the nurse in a psychiatric ward. In terms of the latter, Ayllon and Michel (1959) have shown how various behaviors considered schizophrenic were reduced in emission when they no longer were responded to with attention and interest. Examples of the former, the extinction of socially favored responses, may be the disillusionment of people in therapy who find it ineffective (Toch, 1965) or the defection of members from a political party (for example, Crossman, 1950, *The God That Failed*).

If a person delays gratification and studies hard for a long time and then finds no increase in his skills, he is likely to engage in alternative behaviors. This may be the case of a black who finds that his skills do not lead to employment; a graduate who finds no market for his Ph.D. in foreign languages; or a student who finds that being an upright person in the manner defined by his mother, minister, and former scout leader does not turn on his college peers.

Different times, places, and economic conditions lead to the maintenance of different behaviors. In growing older a person may be placed into different situations in which his previous behaviors are at best insufficient and at worst inappropriate and aversive to others. Moving from kindergarten to grade school, high school, college, employment, and retirement calls for a steady *change* in behavior (and not for a consistent "personality"). At an extreme, the Peter Principle—that every man rises to his level of incompetence—is an example of this concept. A person may be promoted in an organization on the basis of a good performance in a lower-level job. When he no longer performs well, he remains at the new level, the one in which he is incompetent. The basic point is that performances required of the individual may change, and continuing a once-favorable pattern may prove decreasingly effective.

A person may label situations inaccurately, that is, in a way that does not jibe with either the physical or social realities. A person may learn to avoid situations through observing the responses of others. This is an instance of vicarious learning of an avoidance or inappropriate arousal ("anxiety") response. Many negative labels that lead to responses of avoidance or repugnance, and hence distortion of the actualities of the world, are developed in this manner. Relatively few people in our culture actually have had unpleasant experiences with snakes, mice, or spiders, yet fear of these animals is quite common among college students to the point that one in a hundred has difficulty viewing pictures or reading about these animals. In similar fashion, responses to certain minority groups, sexual practices, and statistics courses are developed without actual experience. These responses may lead to *avoidance*, so that the *information contrary to the stereotype or mislabeling is not obtained.* If a person does not take statistics, he will not fail the course, but he will also not expose himself to the fascination of the subject and will reduce his range of behavior by cutting himself off from pursuits for which statistics is a prerequisite. The technique of treatment is gradual exposure to the situation, symbolically, vicariously, or in actuality, with care that the experience be as pleasant as possible.

Mislabeling may also result from overgeneralization or a failure to obtain or benefit from discrimination training. The person emits the behavior appropriate in one situation in another situation that is similar but different in some crucial manner from the first. The difference may be small in terms of physical or functional dimensions, but very meaningful socially and presumed obvious to members of a society. Many of these mistakes may be seen in young children who apply grammatical rules in irregular or colloquial situations.

Related to overgeneralization or failure of discrimination is the condition in which the person has a very severe deficit or lack of a particular stimulus. In our society such a deficit most frequently exists in sexual satisfaction. Because sexual activity is especially satisfying to such a person, he may more often identify situations as potentially sexual more than the typical person. He may make partial or anticipatory sexual acts more readily, more strongly, and in a wider range of situations than the typical person, and thus he might become disturbing or aversive to others. The reader should note in this example the increase in frequency and amplitude and the decrease in latency of response— the criteria for what has been called a trait. The person may be said to be overly sensitive to sexual opportunities: he mislabels situations and sees sexual meaning where none is intended. Similarly, a person may be alert to cues, so that he sees threat, disdain, or prejudice in situations where they may well be absent. In similar fashion, a person who is satiated or complaisant may not respond to cues that are present and emitted with the intent to evoke behavior.

Another instance of mislabeling seen in complex social situations is the *maintenance* of *overly high standards*. Our society in the past was one that fostered delay of gratification, modesty, and continued striving—elements of the so-called Protestant ethic. The *inner-directed person* (Riesman, Glazer, and Denney, 1950) strives in terms of his own standards rather than more external, objective accomplishments. Such an orientation may at times lead to socially valuable work, but it may also lead to a situation in which the person may functionally deprive himself of self-reinforcement or put himself on such a low ratio of reward to effort that he risks extinction of his efforts. We sometimes see college students for whom a less than perfect grade in all courses is a tragedy. An approach that may have been functional in grade school no longer is.

A person's overly high standards may be maintained by reference to a very select social group. To an outsider, the dedication of some people to abstruse interests, such as represented by publications of university presses or special avocations, are difficult to understand. The person with a special reference group may develop a jargon and value performances that only another expert can recognize. A figure skater (double-axle) or a chess player (Nimzo-Indian defense) may spend hours every day refining a skill that removes him from other, more common social pleasures. His social circle becomes restricted to those who "understand" him. These examples are of socially acceptable behaviors, but the concept may be observed in the narrowing of social circles by those who join the drug culture or restrict their socializing to their peers in the American Psychological Association.

While the gradual thinning of reinforcement and increasing levels of shaping have impact prior to the delivery of self- or external reinforcement, a different schedule of reinforcement is found in *superstitious behavior*, which is reinforced fortuitously. If reinforcement is frequent enough, the behavior will be maintained on an aperiodic schedule and be quite resistant to extinction. If, in addition, the behavior is not particularly costly in terms of effort, time out from other reinforcement, or aversiveness to others, it may be continued for long periods. With a long history of reinforcement, change of circumstance, and a low but adequate rate of reinforcement, some superstitious behaviors that are apparently disadvantageous to the individual may continue to be emitted.

Superstitious behavior has a negative connotation and is frequently used (and possibly overused) as a paradigm for the development of so-called abnormal behavior. It is therefore worth pointing out that some of the elements of stimulus control used in self-control (as described in Chapter 12) may also be considered superstitious in terms of their fortuitous relationship to reinforcement. For example, the authors know a psychologist who must have a cup of coffee at hand, a cigarette in mouth, and a Mozart quartet on the record player before he starts to write. This environment has been followed often enough by satisfactory work for him to maintain the arrangement. The psychologist probably could work in other situations, but the behavior will continue because it is not particularly disturbing. It would become a matter of concern to him and others if circumstances required him to write in a public library.

Most complex adult human behavior is under control of discriminative stimuli. Acts are made at the socially appropriate time and place, that is, "under control of" discriminative stimuli, which indicate that certain behaviors will have reinforcing consequences (whether favorable or unfavorable). Behavior and language appropriate in the locker room is likely to be aversive to one's fiancee's mother. The distinction between superstitious behavior and inappropriate discriminative stimuli is not always absolutely clear, although the trend is to use superstitious behavior to designate the emission of specific operants rather than external stimuli such as the physical and social characteristics of other people.

In our society, for example, the ideal situation for sexual gratification is in privacy with one's spouse, who is a member of the opposite sex and roughly one's own age. If a person is aroused *only by* certain characteristics of his partner that are not typically considered crucial or even relevant for sexual gratification, the result may be called *fetishism*. For example, to be sexually arousing his partner may have to be dressed in a certain manner or have to engage in clearly dominant behavior. To the extent that behavior emitted under such limited circumstance is followed by pleasure and to the extent that increasing one form of outlet decreases time and energy for others, such fetishes are likely to be maintained. If one considers that the overwhelming majority of people are capable of a wide range of physical gratifications, being aroused only by one's spouse reflects the same principles of behavior influence as being aroused only by members of the same sex or women in black stockings. The development of such a pattern of behavior may start through fortuitous reinforcement such as first orgasm occurring while one is dressed in or handling clothing of the opposite sex (Bandura, 1968, 1969; Buckner, 1970). The behavioral difficulty is in identifying situations as sexual on the basis of stimuli that are not crucial to sexual gratification nor considered relevant by most other people.

A group of behaviors considered changeworthy are those in which a single uncrucial aspect of the situation leads the individual to respond to the total situation as if it were a prior one in which that cue had been central. In classical conditioning a previously neutral stimulus is paired with a stimulus that elicits a response. Eventually the previously neutral stimulus elicits the response without the associated original eliciting (unconditioned) stimulus. The classic example (Watson and Rayner, 1920) is the child who responded to a furry animal as if a subsequent loud noise was an aspect of the stimulus. While the response to the furry animal was reasonable and understandable in terms of the child's history, the response of fear and crying at the sight of a furry animal or other similar objects was unusual and changeworthy. In such situations, adults may label and avoid situations, so that avoidance decreases the chance of extinction or learning that reality is different than it may once have been.

A person's methods of avoiding situations or neutralizing (rationalizing) his own behavior may become disturbing in themselves and hence become the focus for treatment. For example, if a person is inept in social situations and likely to be hurt or to feel inferior in them, he may avoid them by becoming an overly serious student. Aside from the inherent gratification of studies and rewards for good grades, the person who is studying has a socially acceptable reason for not entering the situations he wishes to avoid. We have purposely chosen such "compulsive studying" rather than some classic compulsive behavior such as hand washing because of the challenge in deciding at what point a socially acceptable behavior is changeworthy. We cannot offer any definitive statement, but we can offer some of the guidelines we have used in our clinical practice. One is that the person who overstudies reduces the ratio of gain to effort. Related to this decrease in the rate of reward is the potential for satiation, which decreases the person's effectiveness in studying. In more general terms, the person does not sample the social, intellectual, and physical environments as widely or as thoroughly as he might. The important point, however, is that the conditions that support many changeworthy behaviors are not direct gains so much as avoidance of presumed aversive consequences. In these situations, treatment would start with an attempt to ascertain the situations being avoided and then to focus on increasing the behaviors that lead to a pleasurable or at least competent response to these situations.

Aside from the response of fear or avoidance itself being disturbing, a person may be upset over his upset. Not only may a person not deal well with a situation, he may also be angry, anxious, or disturbed with himself for the way he has acted. His own poor performance may lead to further labels of "inadequacy" by himself or others.

The fact that a person may respond to a part of a situation as if it represented the total situation is similar to Piaget's concept (1929) of "centering." The person pays disproportionate attention to *one element* rather than to the total situation or the context of the stimulus. Another way of saying this is that the person may *overgeneralize*. For example, a person who has been in an auto accident while driving with a long-haired student in a red car during a sleet storm may thereafter feel acutely uncomfortable when entering cars—particularly if they are red, the road conditions are poor, or the driver has long hair. The person responds as if the former situation will recur. Only the road conditions are necessarily meaningful; the color of the car and the driver's hair length are fortuitous circumstances. The procedure of systematic desensitization described below has been used with good effect in such difficulties. The point is that a person may respond to (mislabel) a situation *on the basis of stimulus elements that are fortuitous and out of context*. To act as if red cars are followed by accidents is similar to acting as if furry animals are followed by sudden loud noises.

A final and perhaps major source for the development of changeworthy behavior is learning through the application of the procedures presented in Chapter 6 such as selective reinforcement, chaining, and prompting and fading (including modeling). A person learns to adjust to the complex, changing, and at times seemingly inconsistent demands involved in maturing in a social environment. He learns certain patterns of behavior and not others. Even in formal school curricula, where lessons are planned and measures (examinations) are taken of what has been learned, the effects on students are uneven. Just as behavior that is evaluated as *good, normal,* or *expected* may be taught, so by the same means behavior that is evaluated as *bad, abnormal,* or *unexpected* may be taught.

Some of this training may be consciously engaged in by power figures such as parents, teachers, police, and peers. The stimuli with which a person is presented and the types of responses that are reinforced are influenced by the person's sex, race, socioeconomic status, nationality, and the like. The person raised as a red-blooded, patriotic, respectful, trusting, trustworthy, God-fearing, moral American a generation ago may find his assumptions and behaviors severely challenged by contemporary American college students such as his children.

Some of the training that leads to disturbance at a later time may not be planned, although it clearly follows the general concepts of behavior influence. Many American parents and teachers seem to believe that children are innately good and will naturally behave themselves. Thus, when the children are quiet and constructive, they are likely to be ignored. Attention is frequently paid to disruptive behavior rather than to socially desirable behavior. The same paradigm may be observed in the larger context of campus and minority disturbance: in a number of cases social amelioration has followed a riot or civil disturbance after orderly procedures for change have failed. The success of extreme measures has led some activists to state that change can be obtained only through confrontation. *When* reinforcing stimuli are applied has a great deal to do with what is functionally reinforced.

A Summary Comment

This section has been a lengthy response to the first question every behavior change and personality theory must face: How does changeworthy behavior develop? We have spent considerable space on this effort because it illustrates and extends the material of Chapter 6 as well as providing a basis for understanding the assessment procedures in behavior modification. The behavioral approach to personality can provide a formulation of supposedly deviant as well as supposedly normal behaviors without recourse to special events, structures, or concepts.

Each practical situation is complex and requires careful analysis of what needs to be learned and what needs to be altered. There is no reason to believe that people should have single problems or unitary deficits. For example, a person may have failed to learn adequate ways to deal with authority figures and may have been in an auto accident. His friction with a boss and fear of automobiles do not have to be related; and having one problem certainly does not protect an individual from having another.

Complexity may also be increased if a particular difficulty leads to others. This possibility has been touched on in our mention of primary and secondary deviance. A person who does not know how to deal with a situation may avoid it or alienate people when in it. These acts may increase the aversiveness of the environment in which he lives. Fortunately, the converse is also true: behavioral change toward socially effective behavior is usually welcomed and supported by significant others, so that a change in the individual may well lead to a change in his social environment.

A third feature that may increase complexity is that verbal and nonverbal reinforcers emitted by the same person at the same time may convey different messages. Bateson, Jackson, Haley, and Weakland (1956) have theorized about this possibility and called it "double binding"; Mehrabian (1970, 1971) has reported valuable research on it. Social behaviors and social situations are both complex. Such complexity makes analysis difficult, but does not alter the principles involved.

A reason for complexity is that the reinforcing stimuli maintaining a behavior may *change over time*. For example, the person reading this book is not likely to be doing so for the reasons that he or she first learned to read. Reading has become part of a chain. It is an act instrumental in obtaining reinforcing stimuli such as good grades. In similar fashion, a changeworthy behavior such as fear of driving in automobiles may develop as the result of an accident; but a wife, for example, may avoid driving for many years, in part at least, because it provides a control over her husband or leads to his doing the shopping.

In short, just as the number of genes or chemical elements are relatively few, so the number of behavior principles are relatively few. But as with genes or chemical elements, application may lead to challenging complexity.

WHAT MAINTAINS CHANGEWORTHY BEHAVIOR?

What maintains changeworthy behavior has been touched on in both Chapter 6 and in the preceding section of this chapter. The first answer is that the behavioral model makes no distinction between normal and abnormal behaviors in themselves; hence, one answer is that changeworthy behavior is maintained in the same way as any behavior: behavior is maintained or altered as a result of experience, notably consequences.

Two points should be reiterated. The first is that the *stimuli maintaining a behavior may change over time*. That such changes occur does not mean that the behavior is *functionally autonomous* and perpetuated for its own sake. We previously used the example of reading to show (*a*) how the reinforcing stimuli that obtained when one was learning to read do not explain current reading behavior by college students and (*b*) how an activity that was a terminal behavior may become an instrumental act. The second point is that if there is no major cost to a behavior or if no new experiences are provided, the behavior will continue when relevant situations arise. This continuation is particularly true for avoidance or escape behaviors and is why a full functional analysis of a situation includes as crucial questions, *What should the person be doing? What is he not doing at present that would be expected, typical, or have favorable consequences?* These questions not only provide a target behavior to increase but frequently yield clues to situations being avoided and hence to the stimuli maintaining seemingly compulsive behavior.

UNDER WHAT CONDITIONS DOES
THE THERAPIST DECIDE TO TREAT

The basic problem the behaviorist, whether therapist or theorist, faces in deciding when to give treatment is that there is no implicit distinction between normal and changeworthy behavior. *Changeworthy behavior* has been selected as a designation because it indicates that someone has considered a change in his own or someone else's behavior to be worthwhile. This decision leads to an ethical as well as a diagnostic problem. This ethical problem is not as explicit in psychoanalytic work. In Freudian formulations certain behaviors are in themselves indicants of a failure to achieve or of a regression from full psychosexual maturity. In the realm of sexual activity, in psychoanalysis, anything other than heterosexual genital union between appropriate partners is considered deviant and a fit target for treatment. The term "appropriate partner" is advisedly included not only to rule out incestuous relations but also to point out that some (but not all) psychoanalysts are prepared to consider almost any deviation from the cultural ideal as indicative of the desirability of behavior change, that is, therapy. An example is extramarital sexual relations. As one author (Hunt, 1969) has noted:

> A few quotations will illustrate the prevailing outlook among Freudian-oriented professionals:
>
> "Infidelity, like alcoholism or drug addiction, is an expression of a deep basic disorder of character." Frank Caprio, M.D., *Marital Infidelity*.
>
> "Infidelity is often ˜a neurotic and sometimes psychotic pursuit of exactly the man or woman one imagines or needs. . . . It is primarily a return to behavior characteristic of adolescence or earlier." Leon Saul, M.D., *Fidelity and Infidelity*.
>
> "Infidelity may be *statistically normal* but it is also psychologically unhealthy. . . . It is a sign of emotional health to be faithful to your husband or wife." Hyman Spotnitz, M.D., and Lucy Freeman, *The Wandering Husband*.

We have repeatedly noted that one's theory of personality has implications for one's behavior. The difference between the psychoanalytic and behavioral approaches provides a good illustration. The psychoanalyst (*a*) may designate a behavior as "sick" or a deviation from normality and suitable for treatment and (*b*) because the trouble is *intrapsychic* may "cure" it without reference to the people with whom the patient interacts. The decision to treat can be made with theoretical and ethical ease by a therapist with a Freudian orientation.

The behavior therapist is faced with the decision to change behavior that he formulates as normal and appropriate, given the person's background and current situation. While the behavior may be disturbing or disadvantageous, it is not *in itself* sick or changeworthy. The therapist must evaluate a total social context. In addition, he tries to bring about a change, not a cure. The locus is not intrapsychic, but in the extraperson, extratherapy situation. For these reasons, the behavior therapist faces a major ethical as well as tactical problem when he makes a treatment decision. This problem has been discussed before (Ullmann, 1969c) and is returned to in Chapter 19.

A person's request for a change in himself does not necessarily justify helping him achieve the change he desires. The behaviorist must also consider the people with whom the client interacts and the effect of a change on them. This does not mean that the inconvenience of others should stop a program of behavior change. An example of what is being discussed is a student in a class graded on the curve. The student tenses up during examinations so that he does less well than his capabilities and studying justify. If the student does better on his tests, some of the other students in the class will receive lower course grades. Most therapists would not hesitate to treat the examination difficulties; they would generalize that the student was being helped to emit the socially acceptable performances of which he was capable. On the other hand, if the person reports becoming so tense when he is about to steal, cheat, or lie that he does not engage in such behavior, most therapists would not "help him."

Two situations that may test the therapist's generalizations about legitimate behavioral change can be presented briefly. The first is a change in a person who does not request and may not even recognize that he is being treated. Notable in this regard are children who have been brought to the therapist's attention by teachers or parents. In such cases the therapist may be ready to impose response-contingent aversive stimuli in order to reduce the child's emission of self-injurious behavior such as severe headbanging or scratching of eyes. The general principle is whether a behavior is to the long-range benefit of a child growing up in the society. In other instances the therapist may consider counseling the parents to change their views as more appropriate than altering the child's behavior.

The second situation is one in which the psychologist's various roles put him in conflict. For example, a psychologist may assume an *advocate role for a minority group*. Are there times when he, as advocate, should foster the minority's violent confrontation of his employers in order to obtain changes which may have long-term benefits for the minority group?

Another set of considerations involved in the decision to treat or not centers on tactics. Essentially the therapist asks, "Can I be of assistance?" A negative answer would be likely to end the treatment or at least treatment by that particular therapist. Therapies relying heavily on speech and concepts such as insight are likely to be restricted to relatively bright, young, verbal, educated, middle-class, and unpsychotic individuals. Behavior therapy techniques such as token economies require a fair degree of control of the environment and the cooperation of many people. If this cooperation is not carefully developed beforehand, the therapy is likely to fail.

Where the psychoanalytic or Rogerian forms of treatment see the locus of change as intrapsychic, the behavioral orientation sees acts and their consequences as central. The behavior therapist therefore attends to what occurs outside the therapy situation both during treatment and thereafter. For example, if a juvenile deliquent trained in a pattern of effective studying behavior and work for pay is released to an environment in which these behaviors have no favorable or even aversive consequences (such as alienating his friends), we would expect the new behaviors to diminish (to be extinguished) and alternative (probably previously reinforced) behaviors to be emitted.

WHAT MATERIAL IS IMPORTANT
TO THE THERAPIST?

The question of material that is important to the therapist returns us to the *what* questions of a functional analysis of a behavior. The behaviorist is interested in what the individual is doing, what behaviors he should increase or decrease, what he might be doing (his options), in what situations he emits target behavior, what features of the environment the client himself or significant others may alter, and what the long- and short-term consequences of various behaviors are. The behavioral focus is on current behavior and consequences. Historical material is collected in order to gain clues about target behaviors. Under what conditions was a target behavior observed? What acts in the person's repertoire are currently being emitted rarely and might be increased? And what things have helped or hindered the person in the past?

Aside from emphasizing the present, the behavior therapist is likely to consider material with a relatively positive flavor important. He conceives of his job not as decreasing a disturbing behavior, but as helping a person to deal differently and more effectively with situations that now lead to difficulty for himself or others. For example, it is not enough to extinguish a behavior by withdrawal of reinforcing stimuli or to suppress an act by response contingent aversive stimuli (that is, punishment). The behavior therapist must concern himself with how the person will deal with the situation. The therapist prefers not to leave this to chance. There is no theoretical reason why the new behavior, if not carefully programmed, should necessarily be more effective than the old. In actuality, behavior usually becomes more socially acceptable because the person has observed others (modeling or prompting) and his trying out of similar responses is likely to be reinforced. But the most effective way of obtaining new behavior rapidly and durably is to systematically develop a socially useful response to situations.

A related aspect of behavioral therapy that stems from the what orientation is that the material be as concrete and specific as possible. The client is asked to give examples in terms of actual behavior. When he uses abstract concepts or labels, such as *inferiority feelings, anxiety, alienation, shyness,* or *uptightness,* he is asked to tell under what circumstances he has such feelings and what the feelings actually mean as defined by his behavior. One immediate effect of this procedure and of the behavior therapist's general formulation of changeworthy behavior is that the client's difficulty is viewed as something he does in a particular time and place rather than as the result of a generalized "deviant personality." The person is not a schizophrenic or a phobic or a homosexual, but rather a person who *acts in certain limited and specifiable situations in a manner that is changeworthy.* There is a great increase in the person's optimism and favorable feelings toward himself when this distinction is made and he begins to realize the full consequences of this view.

The behavioral focus on concrete acts is also associated with counting behavior. Records of how often and under what conditions the person emits both desired and changeworthy behavior are kept. These records may provide clues for further therapy procedures. But they also provide a measure of progress or its absence. If there is progress, this fact is encouaging to both the therapist and client. Frequently discussion may center on what the client did differently and how behaviors that worked out well may be increased in the future. If there is lack of progress, this can be quickly identified and the tactics reevaluated. The keeping of records not only acts as a monitor and reinforcing stimulus but also indicates that the client is an active partner rather than a passive recipient of treatment.

The foregoing material may be contrasted with a view that the difficulty is the result of a deviation from normal psychosexual adjustment usually related to some early childhood experience. If the intrapsychic problem involves socially unacceptable impulses, the therapist may be especially interested in behavior or desires embarrassing to the client. If the "real" problem is repressed and by definition (that is, in the formulation of symptom) not directly accessible, then free associations, fantasies, dreams, and slips of the tongue become particularly important.

HOW DOES THE THERAPIST OBTAIN
TARGET MATERIAL?

The Freudian psychoanalyst believes that target material will express itself because the unacceptable impulse continually strives for expression. Because it is unacceptable, the impulse will be *distorted*, so that dreams and the other indirect methods mentioned above must be used to reveal it. The Rogerian practitioner also believes that if the situation is properly managed (that is, the therapist is properly permissive, favorable, and accurately empathetic) the process of growth will occur. For both Freudians and Rogerians therapy is a process.

The behaviorist makes no assumption about either the therapy process or the evocation of useful material. Rather, a relationship more closely paralleling that of student and teacher is developed. The behavior therapist questions, makes assignments, and observes or receives reports on the person in extratherapy target situations. Rather than depending on a special therapy process, the therapist conceives of and strives to make the therapy situation as germane as possible to the extratherapy one.

HOW DOES THE THERAPIST HELP
THE PERSON ALTER HIS BEHAVIOR?

All therapies with adults aid the person to gain a rationale for his behavior and to relabel his acts. This may be done in terms of childhood experiences, deficits, and psychosexual development, or it may be done in terms of prior and current learning. The Rogerian, client-centered therapist creates an appropriate atmosphere and through his presence and empathetic responses helps the client remain on the topic; and quite possibly through what he selects to reflect, the therapist directs the client's attention to certain topics and behaviors. The client-centered therapist both encourages new perceptions and, through *reformulation* and *reexperience*, encourages the client "to adequately symbolize in awareness" experiences that had been inconsistent and not attended to.

The Freudian therapist helps principally through *interpretation*. It is hypothesized that the patient has an observing portion of the ego, a mature portion of the personality. Becoming conscious of the reasons for his actions—his impulses and needs that strive for expression—may lead to his more mature and realistic evaluation of these impulses and more socially acceptable outlets to provide satisfaction. The highest adjustment in a Freudian system is *sublimation*, the abreaction of the impulse in a socially acceptable fashion. The therapist helps the person achieve such conscious formulation or insight by interpreting. That is, the analyst points out relationships or concepts that are not yet conscious. A good interpretation is one that helps the client and that he can accept and use to generate additional material and insights—and is not so dynamic, sweeping, or revealing of repressed material that the patient rejects it.

The manner in which a behavior therapist helps his client follows the teacher-student model. The therapist seeks to provide experiences that will encourage alternative behaviors and that are as close and relevant to the extra-therapy target situation and behaviors as possible. Specifics of procedures may be found throughout this volume (especially in Chapter 11).

HOW IS BEHAVIOR CHANGE MAINTAINED?

The target of evocative therapists such as Freudians and Rogerians is *personality reorganization*. Difficulties are presumed to be the result of intrapsychic problems and to be curable. The cured and now normal person presumably deals with situations in such a realistic or mature manner that further problems do not arise. Difficulties after therapy are viewed as indications of incomplete treatment.

As so often noted in this chapter, the behaviorist does not distinguish between normal and changeworthy behavior. *The new behavior is maintained as long as the consequences for its emission are favorable.* If the maintaining stimuli and conditions are changed or withdrawn, the person may emit the formerly reinforced behavior. For example, a former transvestite remains physically capable of donning the opposite sex's attire. Behavior does not disappear; it simply is not emitted at certain times and places.

While the behavior therapist does his utmost to take into account all the specific stimuli in a social situation and to provide verbalized generalization of principles (Ullmann, 1969b), there is no guarantee that circumstances will not change or that behavior someone considers changeworthy will not develop. The behavior therapist, however, it not completely at the mercy of the fates.

We have already mentioned that a behavior is maintained by its consequences. We have also noted that when a person changes in a favorable manner, significant others in his environment become more favorable toward him. This possibility may be fostered by enlisting the aid of spouses (in sexual difficulties), teachers (in classroom problems), and parents (in children's home behavior). A second manner in which the therapist can increase the chances of maintenance of an act is through applying the behavioral principles touched on in Chapter 6. He may gradually increase the length of chains; stretch out, thin out, or make more variable a reinforcement schedule; remove prompts until the person is prompting himself; and raise the level of complexity of a reinforced act through shaping.

But the fundamental behavioral concept is that *there is no discontinuity between treatment and reality, between normal and changeworthy behavior.* The treatment is direct because the focus is on the behavior as real rather than symbolic.

LAST WORD

In this book on behavior influence and personality, we have described treatment concepts in some detail for several reasons. Psychotherapy is a formal socially sanctioned manner of bringing about behavior change. In addition and perhaps even more important for our purposes, there is a direct connection between theories of psychotherapy, theories of "personality," and more generally theories of behavior change.

We have offered a brief outline of the key questions with which every therapy approach has to deal. We have also discussed in some detail the behavioral approach—both as an extension of Chapter 6 and as a prelude to Chapter 11, on behavior modification. We have emphasized that *different formulations* lead to different behaviors being considered changeworthy, to different types of behaviors being attended to and encouraged within and outside therapy, and to different notions about the types of people who may be helped. In this regard, as throughout this book, personality theories are social behaviors with consequences.

CHAPTER 11

Behavior Therapy: The Changing of Behavior

The term "behavior therapy" was first used in 1953 in the psychological literature on the application of operant conditioning to hospitalized psychotic patients (Lindsley, Skinner, and Solomon, 1953; see Chapter 7 of this text and Krasner, 1971, for historical and intellectual contexts). This term was used independently by Lazarus (1958) to refer to the work of Joseph Wolpe (1954, 1958), who developed procedures for dealing with interfering autonomic responses (anxiety) following a Hullian or Pavlovian conditioning model.

In a third independent development of the concept, Eysenck (1959) used behavior therapy to refer to the application of what he termed "modern learning theory" to change the behavior of neurotic patients. This later usage was based in large part on the procedures of a group of investigators then working at the Maudsley Hospital in London, who approached each patient contact as if it were an experiment (Yates, 1970).

The term "behavior modification"[1] has also been used in a variety of ways: interchangeably with behavior therapy; as a generic term which includes behavior therapy and other procedures; as a reference solely to the clinical application of operant conditioning (to distinguish it from the behavior therapy derived from Wolpe and Eysenck). Homme, et al. (1968) have offered still another related term, "behavioral engineering," to refer to a combination of the technologies of "contingency management" and "stimulus control."

As in every approach to changing human behavior, there is a spectrum of opinion as to what aspects of theory are subsumed within the behavioral approach. One influential group of investigators has consistently defined behavior therapy in terms of *learning theory*. For example, Wolpe (1969) has offered the following definition: "behavior therapy, or conditioning therapy, is the use of experimentally established principles of learning for the purpose of changing unadaptive behavior. Unadaptive habits are weakened and eliminated; adaptive habits are initiated and strengthened [p. vii]." This definition implies a greater agreement on the "established principles of learning" than may be warranted, but it does represent a learning theory framework characteristic of much behavior therapy.

An alternative and perhaps more encompassing framework has been provided by those who view behavior therapy in the broader context of *social learning* or *behavior influence*. Ullmann and Krasner (1969), for example, have described behavior therapy as "treatment deducible from the sociopsychological model that aims to alter a person's behavior directly through application of general psychological principles [p. 244]." This is contrasted with "evocative psychotherapy," which is "treatment deducible from a medical or psychoanalytic model that aims to alter a person's behavior indirectly by first altering intrapsychic organizations. [Ullmann and Krasner, 1969, p. 244]."[2]

Another way of approaching behavior therapy is to categorize it into four general groupings (Kanfer and Phillips, 1969): *interactive therapy*—requiring an

---

[1] Graziano (1970) has noted the use of the term by J. S. Gray in the title of an article published in 1932.

[2] A similar conceptualization has been given by Patterson (1969).

It seems to me that future trends will of necessity involve a greater reliance upon principles available from social learning. The term *social learning* as used here refers to the loosely organized body of literature dealing with the changes in learning, or performance which occur as a function of contingencies which characterize social interaction. . . . Many of the mechanisms which have been described for bringing about these changes have been based upon principles from social psychology rather than learning theory; they would include such processes as persuasion, conformity, and modeling [p. 342].

extended series of personal interviews using the therapist's verbal behavior to catalyze changes in the patient; *instigation therapy*—using suggestions and tasks to teach the patient to become his own therapist; *replication therapy*—changing behavior by replicating a critical segment of the patient's life within the therapy setting; *intervention therapy*—disruption of narrow response classes as they appear in the patient's interactions with his natural environment. "A consistent behavioristic view requires an understanding of the entire range of psychological principles which can be brought to bear on the problem of an individual patient, from his presentation to his discharge [p. 448]."

Bandura's "social learning" conceptualization (1969) of behavior therapy places major emphasis on controlled laboratory studies of efficacy; as he states, "By requiring clear specification of treatment conditions and objective assessment of outcomes, the social learning approach contains a self-corrective feature that distinguishes it from change enterprises in which interventions remain ill-defined and their psychological effects are seldom objectively evaluated [p. v.]."

The conceptualization of behavior therapy offered in this book views it as a way of formulating cases and using a series of specific techniques derived from the experimental laboratory, usually but not exclusively based on learning theory, and applied in a social influence situation. Behavior therapy thus involves a technology built upon a base of behavior influence.

The technology of behavior therapy is most effective only within a context that maximizes social influence. It is important to emphasize that behavior therapy involves *both* the technology and its social influence base (Ullmann, 1970a, 1971). Some behavior therapy investigators clearly recognize this fact, but many others ignore it. The behavior therapist is both a social reinforcing and discriminative stimulus. The metaphor of the therapist as a "social reinforcement machine" (Krasner, 1962b) indicates a therapist who is deliberately applying current behavioral principles within a relationship (defined in social reinforcement terms) to bring about change in another person's life situation.

Social psychology is still in the early stages of merging with learning in the behavior therapy field. This merger is occurring in two ways. First is the approach of investigators (such as McGinnies, 1969; McLaughlin, 1971) who have reconceptualized most traditional social psychological studies such as small group research into behavior principles. As indicated in Chapter 4, this approach was a development of the late 1960s.

The second point of contact between social psychology and behavior therapy is typified by the application of specific social psychological theories or research to specific types of behavior therapy. For example, "attribution theory" (Thibaut and Kelley, 1959) has generated considerable interest in the hypothesis that changes in behavior which the individual attributes to his own efforts will be more longlasting than changes he attributes to external sources. The behavior therapist follows the model of teacher or coach; he may give ideas or schedule practice, but the client actually plays the game.

Goldstein (1971) has offered a rationale for studying *interpersonal attraction* as the major variable in the therapist-patient relationship. Although such investigations derive from social psychological research, they also belong within the behavior therapy framework we are describing. Thibaut and Kelley (1959) view a person's attraction to another as a function of the extent to which the person achieves a reward-cost ratio above a minimum level in his interactions with others. These views and those of others (for example, Homans, 1961) have led to the development of a social psychology of interpersonal attraction which seeks to discover the behaviors and events people find rewarding.

Unfortunately, the investigation of new ideas may lead to a haphazard after-the-fact description (as in Dollard and Miller, 1950) rather than serve as a basis for a priori selection of procedures based on a theoretical rationale. The notion of behavior therapy offered in this chapter does not include *anything* that seems to work, because it would then include fortuitous, superstitious therapist behavior. Further, behavior therapy, as noted in Chapter 10, is *a way of formulating human behavior* and *not a mere set of techniques*.

Following are some elements of the belief system common to most behavior therapists: (*a*) the statement of basic concepts that can be tested experimentally; (*b*) the notion of "laboratory" as ranging from the animal mazes or shuttle boxes through basic human learning studies to hospitals, schoolrooms, homes, and the community; (*c*) the concept of research as treatment and treatment as research; (*d*) an explicit strategy of therapy; (*e*) the demonstration that a particular environmental manipulation was indeed responsible for producing a specified behavior change; (*f*) the goals of the modification procedure are usually determined by an initial functional analysis or assessment of the problem behaviors; (*g*) the direct treatment of overt behavior considered changeworthy. In effect, behavior therapy involves an integrated set of questions to be pondered carefully in every instance: What are the environmental determinants, maintainers, and consequences of current behavior, and what possible alternatives can be developed?

We have previously traced the history and development of behavior therapy in the context of the social influencer (Chapter 7) and in the history of paradigm clashes in the study of human behavior (Chapter 2). Now we turn to specific techniques.

The major techniques used in behavior therapy can be classified in five general categories: (*a*) positive reinforcement, (*b*) desensitization, (*c*) aversive procedures, (*d*) modeling, and (*e*) other procedures. It should be clear that this listing is a convenience, since in actual practice these procedures overlap considerably. In most clinical work more than one procedure may be used at any given time and different procedures may be used sequentially as what the subject needs to learn and what he can use changes.

POSITIVE REINFORCEMENT

Fuller (1949) was probably the first investigator to report on the deliberate application of operant conditioning in a clinical setting by shaping arm movements using a warm sugar milk solution as a reinforcer for an eighteen-year-old "vegatative idiot." Some of the most useful applications of positive reinforcement have been in work with children in the classroom (see Chapter 14). Here we use the token economy as an illustration of systematic contingent positive reinforcement.

Token Economy

One of the most widely used techniques which have emerged from the early operant studies has been the use of tokens in place of primary reinforcers. Staats, Staats, Schutz, and Wolf (1962) were the first to utilize a backup reinforcement system in a reading discrimination program. They used tokens exchangeable for a variety of edibles and toys. This meant that the therapist, or experimenter, was no longer dependent upon the moment-to-moment value of the item to the subject (for example, the M & M candy frequently used as reinforcers in early studies). Tokens opened an almost limitless world of reinforcers. Unlike food (but like money in the general society), tokens are not as likely to result in satiation.

Tokens have several characteristics which enhance their value in a program of remedial assistance. They offer concrete and worthwhile indications of another human being's approval. To strengthen this approval, they must be backed up (as is money) by being exchangeable for valued goods. Tokens also provide a time bridge between the emission of an act and a later explicit reinforcement. Moreover, tokens may be given with greater flexibility and frequency than food and may be less disruptive of ongoing behavior than food that is eaten on the spot. (When M & Ms or other candy are saved until a complex task is completed, they function as tokens). The giving of tokens also focuses the influencer's attention and may facilitate his recording procedures.

Although material indicants are required, every effort is made to eventually replace the concrete reinforcing stimulus with a social one by pairing social reinforcing stimuli (for example, verbal praise, smiling) with the tokens. This pairing is a step toward the usual performance of people in our society. Self-control is the topic of the next chapter, but we should note here that in our culture the person seemingly reinforces himself.

Tokens may be used to shape and to develop chains of behavior. Reinforcement schedules may move from every instance of a behavior to ratios of diminishing frequency for each act or to greater delay between the act and the reinforcement. The reinforced behavior may be required to become more complex as it progresses, so that an original terminal behavior becomes instrumental and part of a series of acts.

A *token economy* may be defined in terms of the operations involved in planning it, setting it up, and carrying it out. First is systematic *observation* of the behavior of the people for whom the program is intended and the *consequences* of their behavior in the specific situation in which it occurs—whether in the classroom, a hospital ward, the home, or the community. The unit of observation goes beyond an individual's specific act to include the responses from the environment to the behavior. Thus it would be insufficient to observe in a classroom situation that a child left his seat. A full observational unit might note that "When the task was dull, the child left his seat, the teacher said, 'Go back to your seat,' three children laughed, and the observer put a check on his pad to indicate that a disruptive behavior had occurred."

Second is the *designation* of certain specific behaviors as *desirable*, hence reinforceable. This may include such behaviors on a hospital ward as dressing oneself or making a bed or such behaviors in a classroom as staying in one's seat or raising a hand to be recognized. These behaviors are usually those which someone (the teacher, ward nurse, or the individual himself) has determined are socially useful and *of relative initial low frequency*. Deciding whether a certain behavior (for example, sitting in seat) is changeworthy (see Chapters 14 and 19) clearly is a value decision.

Third is the determination of what environmental events may serve as *reinforcers* for the individual. What are the good things in life for this individual? What is he willing to work for? Reinforcers for the hospitalized adult may include a bed, a pass, or a chance to sit in a favorite chair. Reinforcers for the child in the classroom may include candy, toys, or a chance to go on an interesting trip. As treatment progresses, different events and objects may become reinforcers.

Fourth is the *medium of exchange*, the token, which links desirable behaviors with reinforcers. The token *stands for* the backup reinforcer and can act as a discriminative or reinforcing stimulus or both. The token may be a tangible object such as a plastic card or a green stamp, or it may be a mark on a piece of paper or a point scored which the individual knows about, but to which he has no direct access. Despite the label of token economy, the tokens in themselves are merely a gimmick—a training device to help the teacher, nurse, parent, or individual himself learn how to *observe behavior and its consequences*, how to *use his own behavior in a reinforcing manner*, how to *respond contingently*, and how to *arrange the environment* in order to maximize the possibility of receiving reinforcing stimuli at an appropriate time.

Fifth are the *exchange rules*. The planning of a token economy must specify the *economic relationship* between the amount of tokens an individual may earn and the cost of the good things in life. If a person can earn only 10 tokens a day and the cheapest item he can purchase costs 100 tokens, the system will not work. Conversely, if he can earn 100 tokens and only 10 tokens will take care of all his desires, the system will not work. We must consider the economic constraints which determine the values and effects of specific reinforcers.

Examples of Token Economy

Ayllon and Azrin (1965) reported the results of the first use of a token economy program in a psychiatric hospital ward. As a model for most later programs, this study has had considerable impact on subsequent investigators. The behaviors selected for reinforcement included serving meals, cleaning floors, sorting laundry, washing dishes, and self-grooming.

Although it was widely believed that few stimuli are effective reinforcers for schizophrenic patients, Ayllon and Azrin made no a priori decisions about what might be an effective reinforcer, but *observed the patients' behavior* to discover what the patients actually did. They applied the general principle expressed by Premack (1959) that any behavior occurring frequently when freely allowed can be used as a reinforcer. Thus, the reinforcers they utilized included such items as rooms available for rent; selection of people to dine with; passes; a chance to speak to the ward physician, chaplain, or psychologist; opportunities for television viewing; candy; cigarettes; and other amenities. Ayllon and Azrin placed particular emphasis on the objective definition and quantification of responses and reinforcers and upon programming and recording procedures.

Ayllon and Azrin (1965) reported a series of six experiments within the context of their token economy; and in each they demonstrated that target behavior changed systematically as a function of the token reinforcement. One experiment is typical of the procedures they developed. The response they were interested in was work assignments off the ward. A patient selected the job he preferred most from a list of available ones for which he could receive tokens. After ten days he was told that he could continue working on this job but would receive no tokens for his efforts. Of the 8 patients observed, 7 selected another job immediately and the eighth patient switched a few days later. In the third phase of the experiment, the contingencies were reversed and the jobs that the patients had originally preferred were again paying tokens. All 8 patients immediately switched back to their original jobs.

The results of Ayllon and Azrin's six experiments demonstrated that the token reinforcement procedure was effective in maintaining the desired performances. In each experiment the subjects' performances fell to near zero when the established response-reinforcement relationship was discontinued. On the other hand, reintroduction of the reinforcement procedure restored performance almost immediately and maintained it at a high level.

The Ayllon and Azrin token economy was used on a ward for long-stay female patients in a midwestern state hospital. Another token economy program (Atthowe and Krasner, 1968; Krasner and Atthowe, 1971) was set up in a Veterans Administration hospital in California with male patients (average age, fifty-eight years) hospitalized for a median time of twenty-four years. Most of these patients had been labeled as chronic schizophrenics and the rest as having organic brain syndrome. As a group their behavior was apathetic and indifferent; the patients were inactive, dependent, and socially isolated. The procedures used were similar to those developed by Ayllon and Azrin, except that the experimenters had less control, since this program took place on an *open ward* where patients could come and go if they had sufficient tokens. The token economy had to compete with the economy (which used dollars and cents) outside the ward. Many economic problems were encountered, and special procedures were developed to deal with them; for example, a banking system to foster savings, a monthly devaluation to cut down hoarding, and special color tokens to prevent stealing.

Before the introduction of tokens, most patients refused to participate in any of the available activities and showed little interest in their environment. They sat or slept in the ward during the day; this inactivity resulted from years in which compliant and apathetic institutional behavior had been encouraged. The investigators made the value decision that these patients could spend their time better than sitting in the ward. Among the behaviors selected as valuable for enacting the role of responsible people were being adept at self-grooming, keeping living quarters clean, dressing neatly, keeping a job, and interacting with other people. Responsibility in this sense also included responsiveness to normal social reinforcement. Thus, whenever tokens were offered, they were accompanied by social reinforcement such as *Good, I'm pleased, Fine job,* and an explicit statement about the contingencies involved; for example, "You received 3 tokens because you got a good rating from your job supervisor."

This token economy program was a significant success, as measured by changes in specified behavior, observers' ratings, and reactions of hospital staff. Changes in behaviors, such as attendance at group activities, were found to be a function of the number of tokens (value) given for the activity. Group attendance increased as more tokens were given and decreased when the payoff returned to its lower value.

The greatest change was in the appearance and atmosphere of the ward and in the *staff expectations of the patients' capabilities.* The morale increased enormously when staff members found that their participation in the token economy had a therapeutic effect on the patients' behavior; it became a matter of prestige throughout the hospital to work in the token ward. Other wards in the hospital adopted similar token economies because of the apparent therapeutic effect of the program.

Schaefer and Martin (1966) have described the effects of a token economy program in a California state hospital on a *specific type of patient behavior—apathy*. They noted that the overt behaviorial pattern of apathy is a manifestation of a *limited* response to the environment. As the environment changes, the patient does not. Schaefer and Martin first recorded patients' behavior at half-hourly intervals on three scales: (*a*) mutually exclusive behaviors—walking, running, standing, sitting, lying down; (*b*) concomitant behaviors—talking, singing, playing music, painting, reading, listening to others or to the radio, watching television, group activities; and (*c*) idiosyncratic behaviors—rocking, pacing, chattering. They reviewed clinical records to designate patients as withdrawn, apathetic, or uninterested and found that *the absence of concomitant behaviors* was an excellent measure of what is generally called apathy. Once a behavioral target had been selected, the next step was to determine whether this behavior could be influenced within the framework of a token economy.

The sample in Schaefer and Martin's study consisted of 40 long-stay schizophrenic patients whose medical records indicated apathy. Half the patients were randomly allocated to the experimental group, which participated in the token program, and half to a control group, which received routine ward treatment procedures. The patients were first checked on the three scales on five consecutive working days every half-hour. The reinforcement procedure was then started in the experimental group and the patients were again observed every half-hour during a five-day work week after one and after two months. Patients in the control group improved slightly but not significantly, whereas improvement in the experimental group was statistically significant. That is, the number of observations in which concomitant behaviors were not emitted decreased significantly in the experimental group. Thus, the token program was successful in improving the specific target behavior of apathy.

Winkler (1970) has reported a series of studies on token economy programs which extends their usefulness into an important new area—testing predictions from economic theory. He investigated the complex relationships between the variables of prices, wages, and savings, and how they influence individual behavior. Token economies were found to operate according to principles similar to those economists have found in national, money-based economies. Token economies not only look like "real" economies but also function like them; and research in this field has linked behavior therapy with social and utopian planning.

Token economy principles have also been applied to antisocial delinquents (persons sometimes referred to as having "character and behavior disorders"). The basic assumption in all such token programs is that antisocial behavior is "acquired, maintained and modified by the same principles as other learned behavior." Cohen's analysis (1968) of alternatives to delinquency behavior resulted in the selection of *academic work* in the form of programmed instruction as the target behavior to be shaped. Cohen and his group (1966) then developed a special environment, which included classrooms, study booths, control rooms, library, store, and lounge. Clements and McKee (1968) used a variation of token reinforcement procedures by combining contingency management with "performance contracts" in their work with 16 prison inmates. Such contracts are an important element in the development of self-management or self-control, since the individual really sets his own behavioral goals.[3]

Token Economy in the Classroom

The use of rewards in the classroom is not new; but the *systematic* use of contingent reinforcement by a teacher trained in the procedure does represent a basic change. The principle behind the use of tokens in the classroom—contingency reinforcement of desirable alternative behaviors—is the same as in mental hospitals, but there are challenges unique to the classroom. These are discussed in Chapter 14, on education.

Token Economy in the Community

One of the most important recent developments has been the extension of token programs from the hospital and the schoolroom directly into the community (Tharp and Wetzel, 1969). Henderson and his group at Spruce House (1969) have reported on a token program that bridges the gap between a residential institution and the community for adults who had seriously disturbed behaviors.

Miller (1969) has described a program which extends the principles of token economy to a community organization of low-income mothers. The focus of the program is to train the mothers in self-help. The participants' self-help activities are reinforced by means of "freedom credits," a form of token system. In this program a group of community mothers were trained to run their affairs and *to begin to control their own environment*. Tokens were earned for attending meetings and performing various jobs that benefited themselves and others. The self-help projects involved job training, mutual aid, and education.

An illustration is a food project which provided a major portion of the reinforcers for the freedom credit system. Such food items as meat, canned

---

[3] Other successful token economy programs with adult psychiatric patients have been reported by Gericke (1965); Lloyd and Garlington (1968); Marks, Sonoda, and Schalock (1968); Sletten, et al. (1968); and Steffy et al. (1969). Token economy programs have been extended to other groups including mental defectives (Birnbrauer, Wolf, Kidder, and Tague, 1965), delinquents (Fineman, 1968), adolescents (Girardeau and Spradlin, 1964), and children with classroom behavior problems (O'Leary and Becker, 1967). See review by Kazdin and Bootzin (1972).

goods, and produce were exchanged for freedom credits. Club members staffed the food project and were paid freedom wages for duties such as transporting foodstuffs, sorting, marking, and clerking. The club members were also paid with freedom credits to attend adult and consumer education projects. The program has been an everexpanding one. As the tokens are used to influence and shape new and increased self-help activities, the mothers are able to obtain more and more power in getting their rights.

The Training of Reinforcement Dispensers

Tokens serve several purposes, one of which is as a vehicle (or excuse) for training key environmental figures such as nurses, aides, parents, and teachers on *how to observe the behavior* of others and *how to use their own behavior* to reinforce the desirable behavior of others. Kuypers, Becker, and O'Leary (1969) have discussed the failure of a classroom token program which neither trained the teacher in behavior therapy nor coupled *social reinforcement* with the tokens.

Patterson (1969) has also viewed behavior therapy intervention as an attempt to *modify the dispensers* who provide reinforcement contingencies in the social environment. The target behaviors included how to observe and how to reinforce behavior. Training is given individually and in groups with the aid of devices such as programmed books, films, closed circuit TV, and "bug in the ear" (a small, wireless, radio receiving set placed in the ear) that can be used in the laboratory, the home, and the schoolroom. The training itself is done by psychologists, technicians, parents, and teachers. Patterson's conclusions (1969) about family intervention procedures within the overall research utilizing positive reinforcement is that "this body of research represents one of the few developments within psychology in which the data have the dual characteristics of being replicable and meaningful."

Patterson, Shaw, and Ebner (1969) have described the use of peer reinforcers and a work box for training *attending behavior*. They illustrated how the operant training strategy worked even though the child whose behavior was being modified was aware of what was going on and protested that it wouldn't work.

Wahler (1969) successfully modified extreme oppositional behavior in children by altering their parents' reinforcement practices. In the initial part of the program, parents ignored their children's resistance to requests and rewarded cooperative behavior with approval. This procedure proved to be relatively ineffective. The next procedure involved a reinforcement system which combined parental approval with tokens exchangeable for toys. This more sophisticated approach dramatically increased cooperativeness. Then the tokens were gradually withdrawn and cooperative behavior was maintained by social approval alone.

SYSTEMATIC DESENSITIZATION

Systematic desensitization is a *technique* which involves the gradual substitution of a favorable (relaxed) response which is incompatible with an unfavorable (tense) response to a stimulus. However, Wolpe's *concept* (1958) of reciprocal inhibition has stimulated the research and clinical application characteristic of the subsequent decade. In a recent description of reciprocal inhibition, Wolpe (1968) summarized his theory as follows:

> A competing response is made to interfere with the response that one wishes to abolish. The competing (incompatible) response must therefore be elicited in the presence of the stimuli that would evoke the undesired response and must be "stronger" than the latter. The undesired response is then inhibited, and the strength of its habit consequently diminished. Since the source of the inhibition is the competition of a second response, and since under other circumstances the situation could be reversed and the second response could be inhibited by the first, it is appropriate to describe the process of change as conditioned inhibition based upon reciprocal inhibition [p. 234].

The term "systematic desensitization" has been widely used to designate one technique used to achieve the goal of response substitution. Wolpe (1969) has conceived of systematic desensitization as "the breaking down of neurotic anxiety-response habits in piecemeal fashion. A physiological state inhibitory of anxiety is induced in the patient who is then exposed to a weak anxiety arousing stimulus. The exposure is repeated until the stimulus loses completely its ability to evoke anxiety [p. 91]." Using the conditioned inhibition notions of Hull, Wolpe devised a series of animal experiments which resulted in the development of a technique of replacing an anxiety response by a relaxation response.

Jacobson's technique (1938) of progressive relaxation offered the possibility of a response that could be influenced by the therapist and that when developed would be incompatible with anxiety. Wolpe paired muscular relaxation with visualized scenes and objects to which inappropriate anxiety responses had been made. The potentially threatening situations with which relaxation was paired ranged in a series of small steps, or a "hierarchy," from the least to the most threatening situation.

Evaluation of Desensitization Studies

Paul (1969c) has offered a comprehensive and critical review of all available controlled studies of individual and group desensitization. Covered in detail are 75 papers (most published beween 1959 and 1968) on the application of systematic desensitization therapy to almost 1,000 different clients by over 90 different therapists. Paul's conclusions are important because of his thoroughness and critical approach.

> While 55 of these papers were uncontrolled case reports or group studies without sufficient methodological controls to establish independent cause-effect relationships, 20 of the reports were controlled experiments, and 10 of the controlled experiments included designs which could potentially rule out intraclass confounding of therapist characteristics and treatment techniques. The findings were overwhelmingly positive, and for the first time in the history of psychological treatments, a specific therapeutic package reliably produced measurable benefits for clients across a broad range of distressing problems in which anxiety was of fundamental importance. "Relapse" and "symptom substitution" were notably lacking, although the majority of authors were attuned to these problems. Investigations of equal quality and scope have not been carried out with other treatment techniques deemed appropriate for similar problems, and cross-study comparisons where control is absent have little meaning [pp. 158–159].

When writing in 1968, Paul found only 8 studies sufficiently controlled to rule out confounding variables. All of these found evidence for the effectiveness of systematic desensitization. Of these, only Paul's own study (1966, described in Chapter 8) adequately compared desensitization with traditional therapeutic procedures. Since that time modeling and reinforced active contact have been found to be even more effective than systematic desensitization alone in reducing avoidance of specific stimuli (Bandura, Blanchard, and Ritter, 1969).

Desensitization in Action—Frigidity

A target behavior to which systematic desensitization has been successfully applied is frigidity[4] (Brady, 1966; Lazarus, 1963; Madsen and Ullmann, 1967). The process of changing this behavior is *prototypical of the change process in behavior therapy*. Systematic desensitization is not a simple technique but a highly complex set of diverse operations.

A first and major step in the decision to change a behavior is the action taken by the individual in contacting a therapist. There are various paths. The first is when a husband urges his wife, whether for her own pleasure or to enhance his feelings of competence, to seek help; another is when the woman seeks help after having been successfully helped with a different problem; and a third is when she asks for assistance under pressure of, for example, women's magazine articles which deal with sexual response.

[4] We use the traditional term for purposes of communication although we agree with the superiority of the term *orgasmic dysfunction* used by Masters and Johnson (1970).

A number of typical beliefs about sex held by these clients must be dealt with early in the modification program. The first is the idea that sexual activity is not pleasurable. Many of the women who come for help in this area have had parental and religious training that has led them to think of sexual activity as dirty, immoral, degrading, and a duty. In order to obtain the cooperation required for useful behavior therapy, the therapist discusses the ideas the woman has *about* sex with her. It would be easy to label the behavior being worked with as "attitudes," but this designation would tell us little. Attention must be devoted to the sensory experiences *themselves* (Masters and Johnson, 1970, use the term "sensate focus"). The shift is from abstract attitudes *about* the sexual experience to experiencing the actual sexual sensations. The level of discourse or meta-communication is different or changed. The aim is to enhance an open, unbiased, even mildly pleasant labeling of these experiences. An individual makes anticipatory and covert responses, both physiological and verbal; and these responses in turn serve as stimuli. How these stimuli are *labeled* (another response by the person) is crucial (see Chapter 8). These verbalizations are dealt with in the early sessions, so that later physiological experiences can be evaluated accurately.

A number of problems frequently dealt with in the interview should be noted. The first is that the woman may feel that she has been forced into treatment in a manner not dissimilar to being forced to have intercourse. These feelings should be dealt with openly, and treatment should be presented as something to the woman's advantage and not merely another favor to keep her husband happy. Another problem is the woman's fear of loss of control if she should enjoy sexual intercourse. All a therapist can do is point out that the effect is usually the opposite: pleasurable sexual contacts are likely to cement marital relationships and decrease promiscuity. Still another frequent problem is contraception.

An important early task in the procedure is to obtain a sexual history, with particular reference to how the client learned about sex and the outcome of her early sexual encounters. At times we may find specific instances in which fear or pain was associated with earlier sexual or quasi-sexual activities. At a later time, sexual contacts may be made in terms of stimuli that are no longer actually present. A single traumatic incident is not a permanent deterrent, but worry about it may reduce sexual arousal, so that sexual intercourse is repeatedly uncomfortable or painful. Another effect of early unfortunate experiences is the avoidance of sexual contacts altogether.

The therapist's aim is to help the client formulate herself as a normal person, who as a result of certain experiences has learned a number of responses being maintained by current consequences (including responses she herself makes). There is an important difference between having learned something and being a person defined by that learning, that is, between being *a normal person who has failed to learn to enjoy a human potential* and being a *frigid woman.*

Throughout these interviews the therapist models an optimistic yet matter-of-fact approach to the area of sex. The woman may have a chance to discuss sexual material for the first time in her life *as a natural topic* without guilt, anxiety, embarrassment, or other emotional correlates. While some extinction may occur, a much more active form of teaching takes place. In part this is due to modeling, in part to the therapist's encouragement of new and different verbalizations and labels. Often the therapist will not accept a label or idea as final but will challenge and help the client to investigate it fully for the first time.

Much of the procedure thus far may be called *rapport building* and overlaps traditional evocative therapy procedures. Indeed, rapport is built so that the client can progress smoothly in the situation and so that the treatment situation itself does not become aversive. While there are apparent similarities to evocative therapy, the reasons for the use of such procedures follow from a very different model of both human behavior and treatment procedures. Basic to the behavioral approach is the concept of dealing with *a normal person* who may be taught new behaviors directly. The past is used to understand the present, but present behavior is what is to be altered.

Systematic densitization involves three components: the first is relaxation, usually taught by Paul's modification (1966) of Jacobson's procedure; the second is a hierarchy of scenes of increasing difficulty; and the third is a pairing of the first two.

In a typical clinical case one of the greatest problems is selecting the hierarchies. Frequently a person is asked to use a notebook to list situations throughout his day that are particularly distressing and particularly pleasant. The various aspects of these situations are discussed to find the tasks or stimuli *that are avoided* or with which the person has difficulty. Usually once the situations or variables have been agreed upon, the making of hierarchies (in terms of time, distance, or intensity) is less difficult.

In working with frigidity, deciding on the hierarchy is relatively straightforward. The hierarchy is constructed by both the wife and the husband (who has now become part of the process). While the ostensible purpose is the development of the steps of increasing intensity for purposes of systematic desensitization, the making of the hierarchy provides an opportunity for the couple's discussion of what the wife likes and dislikes. The task-oriented nature of the situation permits a freer interchange between the spouses because the purpose is to devise a helpful procedure and not to criticize the husband or his technique. It is a rare husband who does not learn something of worth from such discussions about how to proceed; and the wife learns that the husband is eager for feedback from her on how to improve his behavior. The idea is to change and not to blame; to find out what to do in the future and not why something was or was not done in the past.

Once the hierarchy has been devised and relaxation learned, the husband (rather than the therapist, as in other uses of systematic desensitization) reads the scenes to be visualized, keeps time, and cues when, after 10 seconds, the image is to be "erased" by the wife by thinking of something else or checking that she is completely relaxed. At the first sign of any increase of tension, the image is erased. The therapist stands by to clue the husband (usually by written message) on the presentation of images. In this situation, as in behavior therapy in general, the *therapist is a teacher and a coach*. He can and does give suggestions, but the client, like the student and athlete, plays the actual game.

During this period of therapy, the husband and wife are asked to engage only in sexual activities that the wife finds pleasant and actively seeks. The discussions during the development of the hierarchy and the signaling of tension during desensitization (pairing) proper provides some practice for the wife in expressing her response to her husband's activities and in slowing down or redirecting his behavior.

The object is a desensitization in practice: a gradual approach in which each successive intimacy is engaged in only when a prior one is completely pleasant. In many ways the situation is not unlike that of courtship or the period in our culture of the middle and late teens in which necking and petting is engaged in for prolonged periods.

A major difference from the teen-age behavior is that the wife's obligation is to give explicit feedback: asking the husband to slow down is not a rejection of him as a person, but is specific to the time, place, and act. A request to slow down redirects the sexual contact; it does not stop it.

The avoidance of complete sexual intercourse at this time removes a source of concern for the wife, so that she can enter more freely into the situation and focus on the pleasant sensations that are present rather than pain and disappointment she has previously felt and tried to avoid. Both a fear and a burden have been removed from her. The greatest problem from the delay of intercourse is usually that the wife worries about the deficit for her husband. Husbands usually are delighted to make a short-term investment of roughly two months for the return of decades of improved marital relationships.

Improvement is aimed at increasing the joy of the sexual contact. It should be noted that as sexual relationships progress and improve, interpersonal relationships are also likely to improve. Masters and Johnson's procedure of having the couple on vaction for a number of weeks in a large city is ideal; but it is possible, less expensive, and easier for generalization to work with a couple who remain in the ongoing home situation.

The person being treated makes a response (relaxation) to an aspect of the target situation. The object is to reduce the disruptive tension responses which were previously made and competed with the client's pleasurable sensations.

If we think of direct generalization of learned responses, it may be argued that sexual arousal and active operants are called for in the actual sexual situation. Sexual arousal rather than relaxation seems appropriate, and in fact Davison

(1969) and Marquis (1969) have devised ways to use such arousal. With the exception of vaginismus—in which the woman so tenses her muscles that penetration is painful if not impossible—systematic desensitization seems more a matter of reducing irrelevant stimuli than teaching specific responses.

Systematic desensitization also has operant aspects. The images that the person visualizes are *responses* to the situation. The person's activity is not unlike role rehearsal or role playing; at the first point of tension, the image is erased and then after further relaxation again emitted. The systematic desensitization procedure may include informational aspects in addition to pairing approach or increased intensity responses with the absence of irrelevant tension responses. This is perhaps clearest in examination problems, in which studying for examination is a major part of most therapeutic hierarchies; but some of these elements may be found in work with frigidity. We have noted how the building of a hierarchy by husband and wife may provide information to the husband. The steps and gradual procedures involved may highlight a more appropriate technique for the husband, but the role playing involved during visualization may also be the wife's first investigation and attention to sexual stimuli *as they really are*.

Aside from the aspects so far discussed, the entire range of social influence variables may be observed in the systematic desensitization procedure. While research workers such as Paul (1966) make every effort to reduce the effect of suggestion and demand characteristics as they strive to evaluate and isolate different therapy procedures, this is not the case in clinical practice where the goal is service to the client and not the demonstration or evaluation of a technique. If nothing else, the therapist reinstitutes conversation and activity. At later stages of treatment, the clients are expected to engage in sexual activity so that both progress and difficulties may be discussed and evaluated.

The major point of this section has been to illustrate how many different techniques may be used at the same time and how the same technique may serve many different purposes at the same time. Behavior therapy is the application not of a single technique, but of a multitude of techniques integrated with the social influence base.

AVERSION PROCEDURES

Aversion techniques are the most controversial major area of behavior therapy in terms of theory and ethical implications. Men have always used noxious stimuli to influence the behavior of others—sometimes to coerce them, sometimes to treat them, and sometimes to do one under the guise of the other. Within the context of behavior therapy there are two broad types of aversion methods: those derived from operant and those derived from respondent conditioning. Bandura (1969), for example, has categorized aversive control into the use of *negative reinforcers, contingency systems,* and the *removal of positive reinforcers.* Kanfer and Phillips (1970) have distinguished between *punishment*—an aversive stimulus contingent on a response expected to *decrease* its frequency—and *escape and avoidance*—in which an organism under noxious stimulation *increases* the frequency of acts which *terminate* the stimulus. Rachman and Teasdale (1969) in their analysis of the application of aversive therapy to behavior disorders have emphasized the controversy over the use of *chemical* or *electric* aversion techniques and leaned toward the latter approach.[5]

A case report by Lang and Melamed (1969) has important theoretical and practical implications. These authors used aversive conditioning with a nine-month-old infant suffering persistent ruminative vomiting for which no organic basis had been found and for which all therapies had failed. Observation and physiological recordings indicated that vomiting occurred within ten minutes of intake and the onset of vomiting seemed to be signaled by distinctive throat movements. The treatment procedure was to give one-second electric shocks, sufficient to be painful, to the leg at the start of vomiting and at one-second intervals during vomiting. The vomiting stopped completely before the sixth session. Cessation of vomiting was accompanied by weight gains, increased activity level, and general responsiveness to people. A six-month followup indicated no recurrence of vomiting and a healthy, normal child. These procedures can be fitted into either classical avoidance conditioning or operant conditioning paradigms. Other examples of the use of aversive stimuli to stop serious self-injurious behavior have been reported by Tate and Baroff (1966).

McLaughlin (1971) has summarized much of the literature on aversive stimuli as follows:

> In short, research indicates that punishment can be an effective means of controlling behavior when carefully applied. A number of investigators have suggested that the effects of punishment are more closely related to the attendant withdrawal of attention or affectional responses than they are to physical pain as such. Support for this contention comes from the finding that the more nuturant the agent of punishment, the more effective punishment is. Additional support is obtained from studies in which, under certain conditions, low-intensity punishments are found to be more effective than high-intensity punishments. In such cases punishment seems to focus the child's attention on disapproved activity and to signal disapproval on the part of the agent of socialization. Since weaker, less intense forms of punishment—particularly verbal reproaches—are more common than stronger, pain-inducing punishments in normal socialization, the most important effects of punishment may be discriminative and cognitive, rather than affective and emotional [p. 259].

---

[5] For more theoretical discussions of aversive procedures, see Azrin and Holz (1966), Solomon (1964), and the studies on "learned helplessness" (Seligman, Maier, and Geer, 1968).

Aversive Stimuli Used Clinically

Unpleasant consequences may be used in many ways by the behavior therapist, but he must always keep one overriding rule in mind: *the object is for the person to deal effectively with situations. Suppressing a response that is disturbing is only half the task. The person must be taught to emit an appropriate. and satisfactory response to the situation.* Sometimes, as in the Lang and Melamed (1969) case, such a response occurs spontaneously; frequently through observation of others or emission of acts already in the person's repertoire, socially appropriate responses seem to occur spontaneously and with little or no formal effort by the therapist. But unless some alternative behavior is encouraged and maintained, the client will either resume his prior activity, become apathetic, or otherwise indicate that the therapeutic task has not been completed. On the other hand, a mildly aversive consequence is sufficient when an acceptable alternative is made available (that is, taught). What maintians the new behavior is not the aversive stimuli, but the ongoing positive consequences.

An aversive stimulus may be presented contiguously or soon after the person has made an act or perceived a stimulus to which he has been responding inappropriately. Because such aversive conditioning is relatively rapid, it may be used with behaviors that are self-injurious but followed by pleasurable effects or decreased unpleasant ones. People who drink to excess (alcoholics) or who engage in sexual activities that are disturbing to themselves or others give prime examples of such behavior. As the drinker lifts his glass or is about to swallow, he may receive an electrical shock. Various principles previously discussed may be used: shock may be aperiodic; shock may be avoided by lowering the glass or otherwise interrupting the drinking sequence. Nausea-inducing drugs may also be used so that after swallowing the person experiences vomiting. After a course of such experiences, a genuine conditioned response may be established so that nausea is associated with the stimulus (alcohol) or the stimulus created by the person's behavior (lifting a glass containing alcohol). Because the cessation of drinking to excess is encouraged by significant others, we presume that the person receives considerable reinforcement for his changed behavior through naturally occurring environmental events. Roughly half the cases treated by aversive stimuli in this manner remain abstinent for six months.

The fact that only half the people receiving such treatment do remain abstinent is important. In a similar vein, Freund (1960) reported up to two-thirds success in the aversive conditioning of homosexuals who wished treatment and less than one-tenth success with men who received aversive treatment under court order. Just as avoidances that are socially disturbing may be learned and extinguished, so avoidances that are socially useful may be and are extinguished.

In the case of homosexual behavior, even more than in excessive use of alcohol, other people are required for a satisfactory alternative behavior. The teaching of dating skills and reduction of avoidance of women due to irrelevant, distracting tension may be taught in a manner parallel to the treatment of orgasmic dysfunction described earlier in this chapter.

Among the most classic work on the use of aversive stimuli in an operant context (that is, as a consequence of an undesirable behavior) is the work on self-injurious behavior. A classic study of aversive stimuli used to generate the reinforcing effects of escape or avoidance of unpleasant stimuli is by Lovaas (1968) in which *approach and attention to other people led to termination* and later avoidance of an electrical shock.

As we move to adult outpatients, the active cooperation of the person whose behavior is to be modified can be used. The next chapter deals with self-control, but at this point we should note that the person may provide himself with images of the ultimate unpleasant consequences of his behavior (getting fat, being dismissed from school, losing his friends or job, being jailed). A use of these procedures in a more Pavlovian-Hullian model is called *covert sensitization* and is associated with the work of Cautela (1966, 1967). Such personal rehearsal of ultimate aversive consequences—from eternal damnation to being unprepared for the next day's class—is probably one of the major ways most adults control their own behavior and put aside immediate gratification for long-term benefits. It should be clear that *an ethic must be taught*, and such teaching hypothesizes a stable world in which delayed gratification will be rewarded.

Pocket shock equipment has been devised so that the person may provide himself with an aversive stimulus and control his own behavior. This procedure is done at the very *start* of a chain of events and not at its consummation, in part to give the shock when the strength of the potential reinforcing stimuli is relatively low, in part to avoid making the normal consummatory responses (eating, orgasm) the target. In effect, the operant of attending to or placing certain stimuli in an unwanted context (that some person might be a sexual object, that a martini or cigarette would be awfully good) is followed by an unpleasant consequence. Because self-produced aversive stimuli can be applied in many field settings, generalization is facilitated.

Finally, the relationship between the punisher and the punished in aversive procedures must be considered. Social influence variables are as basic to aversive conditioning as to any other behavior therapy procedure. Studies reported by Patterson and Reid (1970) with children in the family setting have emphasized the mutually coercive relationships among family members.

Risley (1968) noted that only after elaborate training did mothers shift from frequent use of aversive control to a specific positive control, demonstrating one of the paradoxes of our time. Society generally uses aversive procedures to control deviant behaviors at the same time that it deplores aversive control. The unfortunate fact which seems to emerge from much of the work in training parents is that most people simply do not use positive reinforcement as frequently as they should. They seem to think that good behavior is natural and virtue is its own reward.

Three other techniques derived mainly from the operant approach may be noted: satiation—the excessive use of positive stimuli; time out—access to positive reinforcement is blocked contingent on occurence of an undesirable behavior; and response cost—reinforcement penalties are imposed per response (Weiner, 1962).

The notion of *response cost* has been used in several ingenious ways. For example, Harmatz and Lapuc (1968) worked with obese male patients who were put on an 1800-caloric diet and were weighed weekly. Patients who failed to lose weight during the week forfeited a portion of their financial allotment. This response-cost group did not differ initially in weight loss from other patients in group therapy or in a diet-only control group. The important result was that those exposed to the response cost procedure continued to lose weight during a one-month followup period, whereas the controls regained the weight they had lost. The notion of response cost and its application in the classroom and in the mental hospital represents another important link between the laboratory and the clinic.

MODELING

Modeling and the use of vicarious processes in the acquisition and modification of patterns of behavior have become major techniques of behavior therapy. Bandura (1969) has observed that

> research conducted within the framework of social-learning theory . . . demonstrates that virtually all learning phenomena resulting from direct experiences can occur on a vicarious basis through observation of other persons' behavior and its consequences for them. Thus, for example, one can acquire intricate response patterns merely by observing the performances of appropriate models; emotional responses can be conditioned observationally by witnessing the affective reactions of others undergoing painful or pleasurable experiences; fearful and avoidant behavior can be extinguished vicariously through observation of modeled approach behavior toward feared objects without any adverse consequences accruing to the performer; inhibitions can be induced by witnessing the behavior of others punished; and, finally, the expression of well-learned responses can be enhanced and socially regulated through the actions of influential models. Modeling procedures are, therefore, ideally suited for effecting diverse outcomes including elimination of behavioral deficits, reduction of excessive fears and inhibitions, transmission of self-regulating systems, and social facilitation of behavioral patterns on a group-wide scale [p. 118].

The above quotation summarizes a large range of research which has only recently (through the efforts of investigators such as Bandura, Kanfer, Lovaas,

Baer, and their collaborators) become an integral part of behavior therapy. Investigators in this area have used a variety of labels under which to classify their work such as *modeling, imitation, vicarious learning, vicarious reinforcement, identification, prompting* and *fading* and social psychological terms including *role playing, social facilitation,* and *contagion.* The application of modeling procedures to the modification of specific kinds of behavior has occurred within two different but not mutually exclusive frameworks. Those working within operant concepts have tended to view the introduction of modeling procedures as an additional training technique to overcome incomplete behavior repertoires. Baer, Peterson, and Sherman (1967) have summarized the approach to the use of imitation particularly in obtaining verbal behavior in children. These investigators described the initiation of their research as "not from a basis of clinical ambition to improve behavior, but rather out of a curiosity about the fundamental nature of imitation. Is imitation a type of learning qualitatively different from operant conditioning, or only a more complex organization of the results of operant conditioning than is the simple discriminated operant? [p. 12]." Baer and his colleagues opt for the latter answer.

On the other hand, a study by Bandura, Blanchard, and Ritter (1969) derived in part from the avoidance learning research, particularly of Solomon and his collaborators. Bandura and his colleagues have placed their study within the "dual process theory of avoidance behavior [according to which] threatening stimuli evoke emotional arousal which has both autonomic and central components. It is further assumed that these arousal processes, operated primarily at the central level, exercise some degree of control over instrumental avoidance responding [p. 173]." Bandura (1965b) had previously demonstrated that avoidance responses can be extinguished if the individual is exposed to a graduated sequence of modeling activities beginning with those that have low-arousal value (in effect, vicariously eliminating fear arousal). Based on these earlier results, Bandura, Blanchard and Ritter administered either symbolic desensitization, symbolic modeling, live modeling combined with guided participation, or no treatment control to 48 snake-phobic individuals. In contrast to most snake phobics used in research work, the subjects in this study were individuals whose lives *were restricted in some way* because of their fear of snakes. Although all three approaches produced reductions in fear arousal, the modeling with guided participation proved most powerful and achieved virtually complete cessation of phobic behavior in every subject. The favorable changes produced toward the phobic object were accompanied by fear reduction in other threatening situations.

The deliberate use of the therapist's behavior (or an individual trained by him) as an example, illustration, or model to influence the behavior of another person has occurred in the one-to-one interview (Ullmann, 1969b); has been combined with reinforcement in training a retarded child (Baer and Sherman, 1964); has been used as an "observational learning opportunity" with juvenile delinquents (Sarason, 1968); has been used in films depicting social interaction between children to enhance social behavior in preschool isolates (O'Connor, 1969) and to decrease fear of dogs in preschool children (Bandura and Menlove, 1968).

OTHER PROCEDURES

An important extension of the behavior therapy paradigm which has both theoretical and practical implications involved the *control* of *autonomic functions*. The basis of this work is the demonstration that autonomic responses can be strengthened by reinforcement after their emission. Techniques have been developed for the direct training of autonomic systems through feedback and operant shaping.

Shearn (1962), for example, demonstrated the *operant conditioning of heart rate acceleration*. A series of studies followed which showed that heart rate may be stabilized within narrow limits when feedback is provided (Lang, 1970); spontaneous increase in heart rate can be brought under control of operant verbal conditioning (Ascough and Sipprelle, 1968); blood pressure may be brought under control by feedback and reinforcement; and states of psychophysiological relaxation can be produced by the use of electromyograph feedback from striate muscles. An important demonstration has been that people can be taught to control some of their own brain wave patterns by hearing a buzzer whenever the desired pattern is occurring (Kamiya, 1968). They learn to associate their subjective mental state with the buzzing so that by reproducing that mental state, they can reproduce the brain wave patterns without the buzzer.

Paul (1969d) demonstrated with undergraduate females that relaxation training (and hypnotic suggestion) significantly decreased *arousal* effects in physiological measures (heart rate, respiratory rate, tonic muscle tension, and skin conductance). Craig and Lowery (1969) have reported the vicarious classical conditioning of both galvanic skin response and heart rate by the use of electric shock to a model.

The experiments of Miller and his associates (1969) on curarized rats have provided the most sophisticated and convincing demonstrations of operant control of autonomic functions. Miller suggests that psychosomatic conditions may develop through attention and other reinforcing consequences. It should then be possible to modify some of the visceral responses that occur in psychosomatic disorders by extinction and differential reinforcement.

Implosive Therapy

The extensive research on fear reduction has evolved in two directions. First has been systematic desensitization designed to *gradually* reexpose the individual to the feared situation. *Implosive therapy* has evolved from the opposite direction by utilizing the principle of exposure to the fear situation *at maximum intensity*. Stampfl and Levis (1967) have developed a treatment paradigm based on a simple extinction theory. Rather than the graded hierarchy presentation used with relaxation, Stampfl has presented only the items at the top of the hierarchy, the most frightening, maximal anxiety scenes. It is assumed that the anxiety response will be extinguished with the repetition of these scenes and that this extinction will transfer from imagery to life in general.

Cognitions as Behavior

In contrast to the initial focus of traditional forms of psychotherapy (dependent on verbalization and insight) on the young, attractive, verbal, intelligent, and successful (YAVIS; Schofield, 1964), behavior therapy started with the aged, the unattractive, the mute, the retarded—those whom everyone else had given up. Individuals with severe learning deficits and unable to be controlled by language provided problems of therapy implementation that were akin to problems in dealing with organisms that do not have the use of language.

The success of treatment by behavior therapy throughout the 1960s had numerous effects. The first was an increased confidence on the part of the practicing behavior therapist. The second effect was the spread of news about their expertise by word of mouth, students, and to some extent mass media. A third effect was that attention to the process that made the treatment package effective increased. The early behavior therapists used the most generally accepted learning principles with little sophistication. As their work progressed, increasingly complex theoretical questions needed to be answered. A fourth, and related, effect was the observation that social influence techniques not previously considered as learning procedures were effective. Language and imitation are prime examples of areas that were reinterpreted within learning frameworks and also tested the limits of current learning theories. A fifth effect was that the behavior therapist was challenged by his more traditional colleagues to deal with problems that were considered inherently "cognitive" and "complex."

New clients have provided new challenges such as the so-called existential problems of college students (see Ullmann, 1972). The behaviorist does not categorize people, but performs a functional analysis of each person's behavior. After such a procedure the supposed existential problems may be found to be matters of genuine career choice, overly high standard setting, satiation with reinforcers, lack of interpersonal skills, or assumption of counter-culture roles not currently valued by the larger culture.

The major thrust of the new populations served and problems presented is that behavior therapists are dealing with people who are highly skilled in the use of language and who can and often will help themselves. While the behaviorists have maintained their adherence to "what" questions and operational definitions, they have found that new *techniques* can be based on older principles.

A major concept is that a person's *own behavior serves as a source of stimuli.* Because it is hard to observe another's covert behavior such as thought, there has been a lag in work effectively labeling internal states (Ullmann, 1970a). Thoughts seem to occur to people in a manner beyond their control and seem to be involuntary or spontaneous acts, different from overt acts requiring major muscular expenditure. Despite Skinner's insights (1953) and increasing evidence (Bem, 1967; Festinger, 1964) that *activity may precede rather than follow change in attitudes and emotions*, work using these behavioral insights in the clinic has been slow.

A major clinical force has been Albert Ellis (1962), who stresses that a distorted evaluation by the individual probably occurs between the situation and a self-defeating response to it. While this concept was not unlike that of theorists such as Rotter (1954) and Staats (1970), whose attitude-reinforcer-discriminative (ARD) system has broad implications for both theoretical and applied psychology, Ellis presented and proselytized a clinical procedure called "rational emotive therapy." To more dedicated behaviorists, Ellis' work is based on modeling effective verbal responses to situations, prompting and fading, reinforcement by the therapist for progress in accurate thinking, and the assignment outside the therapy hour of tasks which seem close to shaping behavior or following hierarchies of desensitization through practice. An example from the junior author's clinical work is offered to indicate how cognitions or complex conditions may be dealt with within a behavioral framework.

> I have twice worked with students who report difficulty in studying due to "unwanted" disruptive thoughts. Because I viewed these "thoughts" as behaviors, I made use of the Premack principle. In the situation, the "thoughts" had a greater likelihood of emission than studying behaviors. The students were instructed to write down the "thoughts" and after completing a study segment (that was gradually increased in length) were told to actively give themselves to thinking about these topics rather than "fighting against them." To the extent that the thoughts were higher probability behaviors, they acted as reinforcing stimuli for the completion of the study assignment. A "disruption" was changed into a reinforcing stimulus for the task that was previously disrupted [Ullmann, 1970b, p. 203].

LAST WORD

Behavior therapy is the application to behavior change problems of a theoretical formulation of human behavior, the value and belief system of the therapist, a series of specific techniques, and the deliberate utilization of the principles of behavior influence. Many of the critiques of behavior therapy are based on a very limited, narrow view of what this concept involves. We have presented an extended discussion of the approach to one difficulty, "frigidity," to indicate the many different factors involved in behavior therapy. Our view is that all of the material we are presenting in this book on behavior influence is relevant and necessary for the practicing therapist. For convenience of exposition, we have tried to emphasize that these topics are *integrally related* to all aspects of the behavior influence process.

In terms of research, one benefit of the behavioral approach in general and the research in systematic desensitization in particular has been the focus on *behavior as a dependent variable*. The problem to be dealt with has become reconceived in terms that are overt, measurable, and culturally relevant (that is, changeworthy by the very nature of the sample selected). The specification of independent variables (therapeutic maneuvers), the use of explicit and testable assumptions, and the general interest in the method have fostered considerable research on behavioral approaches.

CHAPTER 12
Self-Control

We can no more escape from the impact of *differential social situations and contingencies* than we can escape from the real world; in effect, the two are identical. As noted in Chapter 6, the individual's behavior is a very important part of his environment. Behavior implies *organism change* or action. The person responds to situations, and his own responses may serve as effective stimuli affecting further behavior. This self-stimulation may occur at a relatively molecular physiological level as the result of changes during respondent conditioning, fatigue, or ingestion of drugs. Or it may result directly from prior experiences (learning) involving the labeling of physiological effects or the manipulating of symbols so that situations are avoided or their impact changed (neutralized). The person's own responses—"That's a bargain," "That's a violation of academic freedom"—are part of his environment. The act of emitting these behaviors changes his environment. Another way of saying this is that the individual *listens to himself and responds.* In Kanfer and Karoly's formulation (1972), self-direction and self-control imply a behavioral input-output loop.

CONTROL

Self-control calls for two concepts: self and control. We say an act is under control of a stimulus to the degree that it is emitted in the presence of that particular stimulus complex, and is less likely to be emitted when that stimulus complex is not presented. The term "stimulus complex" is used rather than "stimulus" for a number of reasons. An example may make the matter clearer. Getting undressed and going to bed is an act in the repertoire of most people. It is more likely to be emitted, however, if the person is tired, if his work is done, if the time is his usual bedtime, if he is at home and/or in a bedroom, and so forth. The stimulus complex may also involve the *absence* of stimuli incompatible with the act. All the above conditions may be met, but the person may not get undressed if there is an unwanted person in the bedroom, if there is a tornado warning, or if there is a really good movie on the late, late show.

Stimulus control is not a compulsion, it is a *probability.* An example of stimulus control is *fetishism.* The fetishist is frequently aroused by stimuli most members of his society consider nonsexual; and, conversely, he is not aroused as frequently as other people are by supposedly sexual stimuli. A high-heel, black-stocking fetishist will respond with sexual arousal more frequently, more rapidly, and more strongly to these stimuli than the majority of people of the same age, sex, and status groups. If, however, the shoes and stockings are worn by a man instead of a woman or if a policeman, husband, or the dean of students is present, the fetishist may not respond. In the same vein, a fetishist may not respond to a woman who is not wearing the crucial attire as often, as quickly, or as strongly as the majority of men in his culture. Notice that the presence of the fetish is measured in terms of relative probability, frequency, latency, and amplitude similar to the basic operations of the measurement of "traits" (see Chapter 3).

Control is both positive *and* negative; that is, it involves probabilities of both *increased* and *decreased* emission. Many so-called compulsive, ritualistic, habitual, or impulsive behaviors vary dramatically with situations. It has been noticed, for example, that nail biting decreases sharply when the person is under obvious scrutiny. We may again call attention to other stimuli that increase or decrease "traitlike" behavior. As in the Hartshorne and May (1928) studies of deceit, one aspect is the presence of reinforcement. Another may well be an "internal" or "covert" response: becoming aroused and labeling oneself anxious may be responses that serve as stimuli.

A third and final point is that the vast majority of stimulus control is learned. With the exception of reflexive or unconditioned respondent stimuli, the emission of responses in the presence of certain stimuli and not in the presence of others is learned.

Who Controls?

The word *control* implies a controller, just as the word *education* implies an educator and a student. We cannot avoid influencing others and in turn being influenced by their reactions to our methods of influence. Further, the regularities of social life within a society lead to regularities of activity and response. For example, we college lecturers deliver material in speeches to large groups of students. From one time to the next, our lectures are altered by what was effective. "Effective" in this context may be our own evaluation that the class got the idea or stayed awake, and not necessarily that what we said altered the course of science, psychology, and Western civilization, or even led our students to treat other humans differently.

Teachers are taught by their students; but the controls that students have over their teachers—for example, favorable responses during lectures, good performance on semester exams, ratings, and enrollment—are also learned and not innate to students. Teachers also are differentially treated in meaningful ways by administrators, deans, and professional organizations. The principles of influence on a person who manipulates controlling and reinforcing stimuli are the same principles he himself applies. Second, the sources of influence are numerous, complex, and sometimes contradictory. But above all the person engaged in influencing is being influenced whether by fortuitous, cultural, or physical regularities or by factors explicitly planned by other people. *Influence is never a one-way street, and the influencer is never uncontrolled.*

For purposes of exposition we may think of teachers and students, but we must not forget that teachers are taught and also play a student role. And, as we emphasize in this chapter, a person learns from his experience and *may come to teach himself.*

By teaching oneself, we mean that the person learns to act so that he provides himself with stimuli that are both controlling *and* reinforcing. There are at least two ways for him to do this. A person may provide himself with controlling stimuli for awakening by setting an alarm clock and may provide himself with reinforcing contingencies for performance such as not reading a book on art or sex until a lecture is outlined. In both instances the person eventually arranges his own environment (Stuart, 1972).

SELF

The conception of the self which we use here represents a combination of the theories of G. H. Mead (1934) and James Taylor (1962). One of the givens of common experience is a concept and feeling of selfhood, or personal identity. There is an "I" that does things and a "Me" that experiences things done by external agencies. There is a concept or feeling of identity, uniqueness, and continuity. There is a locus of personal activity, memory, and consciousness that is bounded by a body, experiences sensations, and even strives toward some fuller expression of potentiality. At times (English and English, 1958, p. 485, definition no. 4; Hilgard, 1962, p. 632) the self and its structures are viewed as nearly equivalent to the "personality." Moreover, "an adequate concept of self" is considered by many as a prerequisite for mature behavior. An early task of childhood is the differentiation of the boundaries of self (Erikson, 1963). The failure to develop or the loss of such boundaries provides some theorists with a definition of severe psychological difficulty such as depersonalization or schizophrenia. The concept of self is subject to the same reification as the concept of personality.

As with other concepts and situations, the first approach of a behaviorist is to determine *what* is the topic. An attempt must be made to specify what the label covers rather than take the label as a real object. What is designated by the term "self"?

First, there are several different levels of discourse. There is the realm of *self-psychology*, an academic area. The classic author in this area is Wilhelm Stern (1938) and recently Snygg and Combs (1949) and client-centered workers such as Rogers (1959). The argument is proposed that a person may be understood and hence predicted, measured, and helped only in terms of his own frame of reference. To be effective in altering behavior, new experiences must be related to the recipient's method of evaluating or processing information. At first glance, this is not a major deviation from concepts which note that (*a*) whether a stimulus is reinforcing depends upon the organism's state of deprivation and (*b*) whether a stimulus is attended to (that is, is an effective discriminative stimulus) depends upon the recipient's attentive responses which in turn depend upon his prior history of reinforcement.

What is different between self-psychology and the behavioral approach is the limitation of methodology implicit in self-psychology: only the recipient can supposedly divulge his idiosyncratic frame of reference. Self-report takes the place of observation of overt responses to different stimuli. Taken to its extreme, this assumption leads to *solipsism*, or the belief that the self is the only object of real knowledge. This in turn leads to impotence on the part of the external observer and finally to a denial of the teacher's obligation to plan, act, or assume responsibility for the outcome of interactions (see existentialists such as May, 1961).

At a second level, self refers to the individual's designation of himself as *initiator* and *recipient* of environmental stimuli and activity. The individual makes statements, overt and covert, about the environment, including his own body and the feedback of his own acts. The self is the result of these acts. Following Taylor's concept (1962), *consciousness is the result of activity*. The stream of words, images, percepts, sensations, and the like are the result of acts by the person; the "contents of consciousness" are a portion of the acts the person makes. Thus, this theory states that we become conscious through activity; if there is no activity, there is nothing to be conscious of and hence no consciousness.

The development of the contents of consciousness, the increase of certain acts and the decrease of others, follow the general principles of operant and respondent conditioning. The importance of the acts of others at an early age has been emphasized by G. H. Mead, who observed that the response of others to our acts is a prime source for (*a*) our differentiation of ourselves from the rest of the world, and (*b*) the evaluations that we apply first to separate acts and later generalize to larger classes of our potential as well as emitted behavior.

The data of consciousness, the seeming givens of sensory experience, are the result of complex acts by the person, who processes stimuli prior to any formal recognition of the stimulus. In particular, differences in the environment must be discriminated before any formulation that permits labeling of environmental contingencies can be made.[1] Discrimination precedes *awareness*, which is defined here as the emission of a verbal operant—whether to oneself or others, whether correct or incorrect—about the relationship between different aspects of the environment. Further, the awareness, like other concepts which summarize the environment, is expressed in a language that is learned; this expression is an indication of the learned operant nature of awareness and consciousness.

Hefferline (1962) has reported a series of studies that attempted to link discrimination, self-awareness, and self-control. He reported the conditioning of escape and avoidance responses in human subjects without their "observation" of the behavior. He pointed out that when the response to be conditioned is a voluntary one, the results are usually neither easily predictable nor reproducible compared to those obtained from animals. This unpredictability is due to the uncontrolled variables labeled as "self-instruction." To circumvent this problem, Hefferline worked with a thumb twitch, a "response so small as to preclude a history of strengthening through discriminable effect upon the environment—in fact, so small as to occur unnoticed by the subject [p. 127]."

An ingenious study (Hefferline, et al., 1959) demonstrated that a small thumb

---

[1] Staats (1970) has carried this attitude-reinforcement-discrimination process further than we are presently inclined to.

twitch could be conditioned to terminate or postpone noise stimulation. For our exposition, the significant result of this study was that the experimental groups could be trained (via verbal instructions on what to look for and a meter giving specific feedback on their performance) to discriminate this previously unnoticed behavior and to control it. Hefferline pointed out that it would be possible to make the occurrence of a small response such as the thumb twitch (with a secondary reinforcement of an increase in score) an effective discriminative stimulus for a reporting response such as "I did it."

It is worth noting that the individual may *observe his own behavior and its effects* in the same manner as he observes the behavior of another and its effects. We may say that a person learns from himself in the same manner that he learns from a model; he can and does observe himself (Bem; 1967). He adds and modifies not only acts in his repertoire but also acts that are metastatements about himself and his total environment.

The person's effective, conscious environment is an abstraction. It is first abstracted in terms of the changes that occur with the processing of sensations. Further abstraction is involved in the particular language a person uses and his covert operation on such data. Finally, actions are contrasted with prior experience, and these data are also abstracted as the process continues. At this point we may summarize our definition of self by reference to Skinner's comment (1953) that the self is "simply a device for representing a functionally unified system of responses [p. 285]."

Language and Self

A. W. Staats and Staats (1963) consider the self or self-concept as a series of labeling utterances that the individual acquires for his own physical and behavioral stimulus qualities and for the responses that other people make toward him. The principles involved in the formation of such verbal behavior are summarized by these authors as follows:

Various environmental stimuli come to control certain specific speech responses; internal drive stimuli come to control certain speech responses; the stimuli produced by one's own responses come to control speech responses; printed and written verbal stimuli come to control the appropriate speech responses; verbal stimuli (or speech responses) come to elicit implicit responses through classical conditioning. These implicit responses may be called meaning responses; these meaning responses produce stimulus characteristics that come to elicit speech responses having a similar component of meaning; word stimuli (or speech responses, through the stimuli they produce) come to elicit other word responses. Sequences of speech responses may be formed in this manner; verbal stimuli (written, auditory, and those produced by one's own speech responses), as well as the stimuli produced by meaning responses, come to control certain motor behaviors; the child acquires vocal responses that produce sound stimuli that "echo" or "match" those produced by an authority source, as well as other types of verbal "matching" responses. The matching stimuli that result become conditioned reinforcers [A. W. Staats and Staats, 1963, p. 183].

Thus the development of language may be viewed as the development of a self-control procedure. To this, Kanfer and Karoly (1972) have added that statements of behavioral intentions are verbal operants subject to conditioning.

WHAT IS CONTROLLED IN SELF-CONTROL?

We may now incorporate our material on self and on control: *Self-control is the learned behavior in which a person brings his own acts under stimulus control.* This may be stated in other ways; for example, the person learns to be his own teacher, therapist, or behavior influencer. What is crucial is not that behavior is under stimulus control, but that the person plays a major role in arranging the stimulus conditions and contingencies under which he will emit a behavior. In this light, self-control is learned behavior about behavior and indicates the multiple conceptual levels at which people act.

This definition of self-control is different from the typical usage. In common parlance, self-control is used to designate restraint in expression of feeling or action. In English and English's words (1958); self-control is "the ability to inhibit either impulsive or goal-seeking behavior for the sake of a more inclusive goal [p. 486]." The behavioral definition offered in the preceding paragraph includes the operation by which such behavior is attained. It should also be noted that the more typical definition of English and English implies that the person has impulses that might be immediately gratifying but which must be suppressed or inhibited to achieve a "higher" goal.

THEORIES AND EXAMPLES
OF SELF-CONTROL—OVEREATING

While material dealing with smoking, dating, and other social behaviors will also be used, the major substantive material illustrating self-control in this section deals with *eating*. The reasons for selecting eating are practical as well as theoretical. First, a number of studies have demonstrated the effectiveness of behavioral self-control procedures in eating. These studies are by Harris (1969), Wollersheim (1970), and Hagen (1970) and are all well-designed experiments. Second, a psychoanalytic and psychological literature on eating exists and provides considerable data. Third, at a theoretical level, eating is an activity necessary for survival. If need be, a person may give up alcohol completely and still live. However, a person must learn to regulate (control) his calorie intake, a matter that is harder, at least conceptually, than complete avoidance.

The following material deals with *overeating* by persons who are physiologically within normal limits but ingest more calories than they use. Mayer (1968) has suggested that there is probably a strong hereditary factor in obesity, whether of a regulatory or metabolic nature; but this knowledge should lead to greater care in formulating eating habits rather than to fatalistic beliefs that nothing can be done. In addition, endocrine, neurological, and other medical disorders may increase the difficulty of weight control. By speaking of overeating rather than overweight or obesity, we wish to call attention to the overingestion aspects of the problem—the area in which behavior control has a role to play—and to make clear that the discussion here is relevant to obesity and overweight only after medical problems have been ruled out or stabilized. *Overeating* is a direct reference to a problem behavior in contrast to *obesity* or *overweight*, which are undesirable consequences of the problem behavior.

The Problem: Social Aspects

Estimates of overweight in the United States population range from 10 to 40 percent. Mayer (1968, p. 82) has pointed out that an increasingly mechanized society leads to less muscular activity and an increased chance to consume more calories than one uses. Overweight has two major areas of impact. The first is medical: the presence of obesity worsens the prognosis in essentially all illnesses. The increased risk in respiratory difficulties, cardiovascular dysfunctions, diabetes, and kidney diseases is such that overweight is highly correlated with decreased life expectancy.

A second and even more interesting area to psychologists is the denigration and discrimination against the overweight in a manner similar to other minorities. Mayer (1968, pp. 84–91) has provided examples from the Bible, fiction, and English letters to indicate a stereotype equating obesity with stupidity and slothfulness. At best a fat man is considered a good-humored slob. It seems permissible to call attention to and poke fun at a person's shape, although not at his other personal characteristics. Clothing styles and other visible models are geared to the slim. Numerous positions in the army, police, and airlines have mandatory weight limits. While a woman who wants to be a stewardess may no longer be refused because of marital status or skin color, she is rejected if overweight and may later be fired for overweight (although this latter action is being challenged in the courts). Mayer (1968, p. 91) has found a strong bias in college admissions against the obese, especially in the case of women. An equally qualified obese female has only one-third the chance of entering the "prestige" college of her choice that a nonobese girl has.

More generally, overweight women are considered unattractive in our culture. This may decrease their range of dating and marital partners. Because overweight is considered the person's fault, the person, again especially female, is faced not only with the psychological as well as social consequences of not being as valued as her slimmer peers, but with having to blame this situation on herself rather than the establishment or the system. "In both Manhattan and in Sweden, as social class and income decreased, obesity in women increased. The prevalence of obesity was seven times higher among women reared in the lowest social-class category as compared with those raised in the highest category [Mayer, 1968, p. 90]." Whether this was due to social pressure, money for better diets, or even a drift caused by the obese woman having trouble being admitted to prestige colleges and marrying quality young men is moot. What may be said is that the approved cultural model is slimness.

In short, overeating has adverse physical, social, and psychological consequences. We may seem to be reciting the obvious in detailing these negative consequences, but we are really demonstrating the first step in a program of modifying the behavior of overeating. In developing such a program Ferster, Nurnberger, and Levitt (1962) started with such information about the "ultimate aversive consequences" of overeating and found that, surprisingly, most "fat" people were at best only vaguely "aware" of these consequences. At a more general level, we are offering biological and social considerations that make overeating changeworthy behavior in our present society.

Theories of Overeating

The most satisfactory general theory of overeating is Mayer's statement (1968) that there are less demands for energy expenditure and hence an increased likelihood of obesity in a mechanized society; as he states, "I am convinced that inactivity is the most important factor explaining the frequency of 'creeping' overweight in modern societies [p. 82]." Mayer has called for programs of increased activity. The alternative is a lifetime of weight control.

While genetic and other physical factors are likely to influence the difficulty of weight control, the basic problem remains one of eating too much. How may one account for an individual's engaging in an activity with long-term aversive consequences for himself?

The psychoanalytic answer is the concept of unconscious motivation which views the overeating as an indirect, partial gratification and hence a symptom of a more basic intrapsychic problem. If a person fully understands the consequences of overeating and consciously and honestly wishes not to engage in the activity, and yet continues to do so, the reason is presumed to be a matter of which he is not conscious. He is not conscious because the truth would be overly threatening, unless it was revealed during a psychoanalysis. Eating can easily be related at a verbal-conceptual level to the oral stage of development.

Psychoanalytic theories of inappropriate eating have included food as a sub-stitute for love, overeating as a sign of immaturity, and excessive weight as a defense against being attractive to members of the opposite sex. A flavor of this literature may be gathered from the following quotation:

> Wulff has described a psychoneurosis, not infrequent in women, which is related to hysteria, cyclothymia and addiction. This neurosis is characterized by the person's fight against her sexuality, which, through previous repression, has become especially greedy and insatiable. This sexuality is pregenitally oriented, and sexual satisfaction is perceived of as a "dirty meal." Periods of depression in which the patients stuff themselves (or drink) and feel themselves "fat," "bloated," "dirty," "untidy," or "pregnant" and leave their surroundings untidy, too, alternate with "good" periods in which they behave ascetically, feel slim, and conduct themselves either normally or with some elation. The body feeling in the "fat" periods turns out to be a repetition of the way the girl felt at puberty before her first menstruation, and the spells often actually coincide with the premenstrual period. The menstrual flow then usually brings a feeling of relief: "The fat-making dirt is pouring out; now I am slim again, and will be a good girl and not eat too much." The alternating feelings of ugliness and beauty connected with these periods show that exhibitionistic conflicts also are of basic importance in this syndrome. Psychoanalysis discloses that the unconscious content of this syndrome is a preoedipal mother conflict, which may be covered by an oral-sadistic Oedipus complex. The patients have an intense unconscious hatred against their mothers and against femininity. To them being fat means getting breasts, being uncontrolled, incontinent or even pregnant. The urge to eat has the unconscious aim of incorporating something that may relax the disagreeable inner "feminine" tension, eating meaning reincorporation of an object, whose loss has caused the patient to feel hungry, constipated, castrated, feminine, fat; that is, the food means milk, penis, child, and narcissistic supplies which soothe anxieties [Fenichel, 1945, p. 241].

Kolb (1968) may be cited to illustrate that the above is not unique:

> The development of obesity often occurs in a family setting in which the parents compensate for their own life frustrations and disappointments through their attachment to the child. In most instances the mother is the dominant family member and holds the obese child or children by anxious overprotection, including a pushing of food. The mother frequently has high expectations for achievement for the child, achievement to compensate for the failures of the parents and those of their children. The child is not cared for as an individual with particular problems that require emotional support, and, as the aims of the parents are pre-dominant, the child fails to develop personal independence or self-esteem. Often the mother's attitudes reflect her own early sufferings and hardships coupled with resentments toward her family's and her own childhood experiences. Toward her-self she appears self-pitying, yet intent on saving her children from similar experi-ences. In many instances the obese child is not a wanted child. He is often one who has passively accepted the indulged role without rebellion because of his

own demanding attitude, which cannot be met outside the home. On the surface, the obese individual, as a child and as an adult, is most frequently seen as submissive and unaggressive. Yet this is not really the case. His demands are met in the family setting by the balance provided through the food expression of love and satisfaction. . . . When exposed to social frustrations with their consequent arousal of hostility, the overweight person seeks his satisfaction in over-eating and by this means symbolically obtains an expression of his aggression, as if the food represents to the patient evidence that he is the best loved. . . . Obesity at a later stage then becomes, in itself, the rationalization for failure. In some, the overweight is used as a means of escaping the anxieties requisite for the pursuit of a creative social existence. . . . The psychology of the obese person, as discussed, explains the usual failure of medical therapies to effect continuing change in the overweight state. Since simple loss of weight in those with developmental obesity threatens their psychological defenses, symbolized by the satisfactions of eating and the personal concept of strength in size, the failure to obtain gratifications either through fantasy or through becoming slender results in relapse. . . . Successful treatment of the obese person requires a knowledge of his total personality, also that the goal of treatment be directed beyond the mere reduction of weight. With young people these aims are not likely to be obtained unless the parent in the parent-child symbiosis that led to the over-eating is also willing to participate in the treatment, even in some instances to the point of undertaking simultaneous psychotherapy [pp. 428–430].

These lengthy quotations serve a number of purposes. They illustrate the material on psychoanalysis presented in Chapter 3. Finally, they point out, as in the end of the last quotation, that a formulation leads to a course of treatment, that is, work with the entire "personality."

Comment

One may deduce from the foregoing material that the overweight person should be adversely affected in terms of adjustment. This should be true whether the maladjustment is a cause of overeating or an effect of being overweight. Wollersheim (1968) has reported that

in spite of many personality studies, it has not been possible to define psychological characteristics of obese persons which will consistently distinguish them from nonobese persons. [These] investigators undertook an assessment study in which responses of overweight and normal weight college women were compared on major personality variables, including general anxiety, extraversion-introversion, situation-specific anxiety, as well as eating in response to anxiety, and reported level of physical activity. In addition, a detailed assessment of reported eating patterns was included. Results indicated that, in general, overweight women were no more maladjusted than normal weight women nor did the reported level of physical activity differ between the two groups. The obese consistently differed from the nonobese only in the reported incidence of eating more in response to both nonemotional and emotionally toned situations. A factor analysis of the detailed report of eating practices showed that overweight women scored significantly higher on five of six factors indicating more inappropriate eating. Additionally overweight women indicated that eating was one of the main pleasures in their lives. On the basis of their literature review as well as the evidence from their own study, Wollersheim et al. concluded that while, from a physiological point of view, obesity may result from multiple etiologies, overeating has been the only behavioral or personality characteristic consistently distinguishing the obese from the nonobese . . . overweight individuals simply eat *too much* for their activity level [pp. 3–4].

While one can never prove the statistical null hypothesis—that a difference does *not* exist—and can never be sure that all potential measures have been taken, the inconsistencies between the theoretical explanations in the psychoanalytic literature and Wollersheim's report of data strongly suggest that the psychoanalytic theory of overeating may be needlessly complicated.

A second point can be made from the writings of Hilde Bruch, who has contributed considerably to the psychoanalytic literature. Bruch (1969) has noted that hunger refers not only to a physiological state of severe food deprivation but also to a psychological experience or a desire for food; she has put forth the hypothesis that *"hunger awareness is not innate biological wisdom, and that learning is necessary for this biological need to become organized into recognizable patterns* [p. 130, italics added]." From a variety of sources, but particularly her clinical work, Bruch (1969) has noted that (*a*) insight therapy is not as effective as it should be; (*b*) rather than lacking willpower obese people have a deficit in their functioning in regard to recognition of bodily sensations; and (*c*) "The direction of my questions changed from trying to understand the *why*, the unconscious motivation of the disturbed eating patterns, to *how* it had been possible for a body function as essential and basic as food intake to be transformed in such a way that it could be misused . . . [pp. 131–132]."

These statements by Bruch provide a bridge to the immediately following section. First, her movement from why questions to how questions parallels the behavioral move from why questions to what questions (for example, Ullmann and Krasner, 1969, pp. 240–241). Second, her emphasis on what needs to be learned or learned differently also parallels the behavioral approach. Finally, the problem of learning to recognize hunger leads to social psychological experiments.

Social Psychological Research on Overeating

There is general agreement that the obese are less accurate than those with normal eating patterns at evaluating when they are hungry. Given a difficulty of *functioning* of this sort (whether learned or inherited), it is reasonable to ask what the behavioral result is. One obvious deduction is that since the obese person uses "internal" physiological stimuli less (regardless of the reason or combination of reasons), he should be more dependent than the nonobese on external or environmental stimuli.

A person may use an "inner," or "biological," clock; if his inner clock is not as accurate as it needs to be, he will use a mechanical clock (external control) or else be too early or too late for his appointments. The person who overeats may be thought of as a person who does not use his inner clock because it is defective or because he has neglected it.

A series of studies have indicated that this is indeed the case. These studies are of both the experimental, laboratory manipulation type and the field, observational type. Schachter and Gross (1968) used clocks that gave a false time, so that subjects thought it was earlier or later than their usual dinner times. While filling out a questionnaire as part of the ostensible experiment, the subject was left alone for a standard period of time and allowed to eat as many crackers as he wished while working. Obese subjects ate more when they thought it was after their usual dinner hour, while no such effect was observed for the nonobese subjects.

Nisbett (1968a) asked subjects not to eat after 9 A.M. and saw them after at least four hours of food deprivation. After a monitoring task and bogus physiological measures, the subjects went to a second room in which they filled out a questionnaire. In this room a refrigerator filled with food was available to them. Because they had not eaten prior to the experiment, they were offered lunch. The experimental variable was whether *one or three* sandwiches were placed on the table at which the subjects were filling out a questionnaire. Obese subjects who were offered three sandwiches ate more than the nonobese; when only one sandwich was placed on the table, obese subjects ate less than the nonobese.

In an experiment on "the relationship between hunger and the ability to concentrate," (Nisbett, 1968b) subjects were asked to skip a meal prior to the experiment and then were given ice cream just before the experiment. Half the subjects received excellent ice cream, while the other half received an inferior type spiked with quinine. The obese were more responsive to the external cue, taste, while the nonobese were more responsive to the internal cue, deprivation. Schachter, Goldman, and Gordon (1968) also manipulated deprivation as well as fear and found that nonobese subjects ate more when calm and deprived, while obese subjects ate roughly the same amounts in all experimental conditions.

Goldman, Jaffa, and Schachter (1968) presented three field studies. In the first, they hypothesized that if an external criterion such as taste affects their eating, obese students should more frequently terminate college eating contracts than the nonobese. This indeed was the case. In the second, they hypothesized that not being as dependent on inner (deprivation) stimuli, obese

Jewish students would more frequently fast on the Day of Atonement (Yom Kippur) than the nonobese. This was the case—with 83.3 percent of obese religious Jews fasting in contrast to 68.8 percent of the nonobese. Finally, Goldman and his colleagues hypothesized that relatively obese flight personnel—being more influenced by external stimuli than inner, biological clocks—would have less trouble with time zone changes than the nonobese. This hypothesis also was upheld. Nisbett and Kanouse (1969) observed people shopping for food at supermarkets. Nonobese subjects bought more food and took more time when they had not recently eaten, while the reverse was true for the obese.

Schachter (1968) has reported work by Hashim and Van Itallie (1965) in which the subject was allowed as much food as he wished, but in which the food was unappealing and the eating situation devoid of all social and domestic trappings. The situation did not affect the caloric intake of nonobese subjects, but this regimen led to a significant decrease (an average of up to 80 percent) in obese people's caloric intake. In Schacter's words (1968), "Only when the food was dull and the act of eating was self-initiated and devoid of any ritual trappings did the obese subject, motivated or not, severely limit his consumption [p. 753]."

The reader should remember this quotation when we discuss control of the environment in eating. For the present, we may summarize the social psychological data by noting that it adds strength to the concepts that the overweight are more affected by external stimuli and less affected by internal stimuli than the nonoverweight. The degree to which differential stimuli affect eating behavior in humans is a major contribution not only to the specific topic of eating but to general considerations of the modification of biological behavior.

The Behavioral Approach to Overeating

Whether the task is treatment or theory construction, a behavioral approach starts with a decision about *what* is to be accomplished. At this point, three generally agreed-on concepts about overeating must be taken into account. Some people overeat and suffer physically and socially, so that they or their friends consider a change worthwhile; such people are likely to be less capable than others in identifying or utilizing internal stimuli that signal the appropriate occasions or amounts to ingest; and such people are more under the control of external stimuli than those without overeating problems.

Until a medical prevention is developed, and probably even after, rehabilitation measures will be needed (to retrain people's behavior even after the cause is cured). We may also ask if the obese individual's relative lack of regard for internal stimuli is not the result of a primary physiological defect. Can overeating occur on functional grounds? Here formulations about the disturbed communication between mother and child may well be correct for specific cases.

Bruch (1969) has written that "Many mothers would report with pride how they always 'anticipated' their child's needs, never permitting him to 'feel hungry.' A generation ago such mothers would report with as much self-satisfaction that they waited for exactly the minute for which the feeding was scheduled, and made sure that the child took every drop of the prescribed amount [p. 137]."

This quotation makes two points. The more general one is how strong in terms of behavior a theory of good childrearing may be. The more specific and immediate point is that both types of mothers essentially extinguished their children's response to the internal stimuli of hunger by making these stimuli irrelevant in terms of food delivery.

A second and somewhat different manner in which the functional basis of overeating and reliance on external cues may develop is the emphasis on eating everything on one's plate. Under a dogmatic regimen of this nature, the food made available ("on the plate") rather than the internal stimulus ("hunger") is crucial. At a severe enough extreme, the child may be reinforced to eat more than he wishes in order to avoid the punishment that follows food being left on the plate. Again, he is being extinguished for internal stimuli and learning to be controlled by external ones.

Nisbett (1968a, p. 1255, table 2), has offered information consistent with this possibility by presenting information on the association between weight and reports of cleaning one's plate. Of 82 underweight subjects, 26.8 percent reported that they nearly always cleaned their plates, while 23.2 percent reported that they nearly always left something. For 83 subjects of normal weight, the respective percentages were 38.8 and 14.5 percent, while for 95 overweight subjects, the respective percentages were 53.7 and 9.5 percent. These data do not explicitly tell what the subjects' situations were during early childhood; they are merely consistent with one way in which overeating may develop.

A third formulation of how overeating may develop historically relies strongly on the hypothesis that food is a strong reinforcing stimulus and to some extent a suppressant of anxiety. Food is given to the individual in place of or as symbolic of interpersonal interest and comfort. "Anxiety" or "need for emotional supplies" then serves as the discriminative stimulus that is learned for eating; at later times, when anxiety stimuli are present, the person eats whether he is physiologically in need of food or not. To the extent that food is pleasant and incompatible with anxiety (Wolpe, 1958), the association is maintained.

A fourth behavioral formulation stems from observation of current behavior. The overweight person eats in many nonmeal situations—while studying, while watching television, while talking to other people, and so on. The discriminative stimuli for eating are very widespread. Put differently, eating is paired with many experiences, some of which serve not only as discriminative but also as reinforcing stimuli. This may even be true of eating while studying or writing term papers or writing a chapter on overeating. A close look at these situations may reveal that smoking, drinking coffee, or eating a sandwich is done at a rough or boring spot and momentarily removes the person from an unpleasant situation. This is reinforcement based on escape. A different form of reinforcement may occur at a cocktail party, where one snacks while talking to attractive members of the opposite sex. A careful analysis of the contingency of eating and other activities is required for each person. In each case, however, eating is likely to be associated with many other activities.

While additional formulations using learning theories may be offered, the foregoing material should suffice to indicate that (*a*) in addition to a possible physiological predisposition that decreases the saliency of internal cues, attendance to and use of such cues may either be underdeveloped or extinguished; (*b*) numerous formulations may be developed to explain that different people have different histories, but all have been influenced by their learning experiences; and (*c*) specific historical antecedents may be different from and less important than current activities and reinforcements.

The Behavioral Treatment of Overeating

The behavioral approach first asks for a definition of the problem. Appropriate eating involves *what* the person eats, *how much* he eats, and *when, where,* and *how often* he eats. While we will not go into detail, extreme undereating (anorexia nervosa) requires the same considerations in assessing the problem as does overeating (for example, see Bachrach, Erwin, and Mohr, 1965).

For balanced nutrition and for most effective weight reduction, a person requires some knowledge of nutritional requirements and caloric value. Just as a person learns the rules of the road and obeys them without having to test the potential ill effects of routinely running red lights and driving in the opposite lane, so a person may be taught that potatoes, pie, and alcohol should be avoided. The procedure may derive some of its effect from conditioned meaning (as A. W. Staats and Staats, 1963, suggest), but its major feature is probably operant discriminant control, where the label is the discriminative stimulus and the selection of food is the operant.

Experience indicates that such academic or "cognitive" instruction is relatively easy to attain. In a different context Bruch (1969) has noted that the obese easily acquired insight but used it as "just one more thing they had passively accepted from their therapists [p. 131]." Knowledge facilitates but is not sufficient for weight reduction; the information must be translated into decisions and used.

How much the person eats in calories depends, in part, on what he eats and how often he eats. It also depends on the size of the portion. Because the ultimate goal with people who overeat is the establishment and *continuance* of appropriate eating as well as weight reduction, crash dieting is not encouraged. If proper eating patterns are not established, weight reduction is not likely to be maintained. Crash diets focus on teaching a diet that is to be discarded rather than a behavior the person is to continue. Moreover, the deprivation of a crash diet may well heighten the reinforcing value of food.

When and how often a person eats involves cultural considerations; eating situations differ with different societies. If extreme deprivation and a resulting increase in the reinforcing stimulus of food are to be avoided, the dieter must be educated not only about types of foods but also about having more frequent but smaller meals. Snacks, however, are a crucial target of most weight reduction programs. A frequent observation is that the overweight eat in many situations in addition to typical mealtimes. While eating at mealtimes may be relatively appropriate, between-meal snacks are likely to be frequent, high in calories (peanuts, pretzels, beer), and indulgent in amount. In addition, the problem arises of numerous behavioral settings as discriminative stimuli for eating and the eating, in turn, is reinforced in those settings.

At least four studies have indicated the value of the behavioral approach to self-control in the area of overeating. All of these studies used appropriate comparison and control groups. The studies are by Hagen (1970), Harmatz and Lapuc (1968), Harris (1969), and Wollersheim (1970). What follows is drawn from these sources, from our own experience, and from articles such as those by Ferster, Nurnberger, and Levitt (1962), Goldiamond (1965), Homme (1965), and Stuart (1967).

Different workers emphasize and use different procedures. A composite such as the one that follows may start at different points. In practice the order may differ, but the ideas are usually introduced in some sequence to keep from overloading the client with so many new procedures that he does not carry out some or uses them so poorly that their effectiveness is obviated.

Motivation

Clinical workers very often stipulate that a person must be properly "motivated" in order to be successful in undertaking new behavior. In this usage motivation seems to be something the individual brings to treatment. The therapist may do his best to increase "motivation" and also protect the client against situations likely to lead to disappointment and dropping out.

One way in which this may be done is by giving the client a rationale for his own behavior and for the difficulties he has met before. For example, food is a relatively immediate pleasure, while the unfavorable effects of overeating— whether physical illness or social unattractiveness—are delayed. No single piece of cake, bar of candy, or milkshake by itself has led to clothes not fitting. An accumulation of such instances leads to the trouble. The person wishing to lose weight "knows" this as well as the therapist. The therapist makes the point in order to (a) show understanding (b) prepare the person for later steps, and (c) prepare the person for difficulties so that failures may be somewhat discounted. But the crucial thing is that the therapist offers the client something concrete to meet the contingency.

The effects of overeating provide *ultimate aversive consequences* to the individual. The therapist may therefore train the client on these. The form of treatment may be role playing or repeatedly visualizing circumstances of overeating and their consequences. For example, a college woman may be asked to visualize herself as being overweight and having to wear unattractive clothes to a party attended by men with whom she would like to interact, but who are ignoring her for slimmer, undeserving sorority sisters who are having a ball.

Implied in this example is the eventual reinforcing consequence: the attention of members of the opposite sex or the avoidance of the ultimate aversive consequence. Paying attention to ultimate aversive consequences also lengthens the chain between desire for food and eating.

Given the immediate gratification of eating versus the delayed aversive consequences of overeating, the person who wishes to alter his eating pattern may devise various ways to provide himself with immediate positive experiences for not eating. This may be done in terms of avoidance of an unpleasant experience: he may think of the ultimate aversive consequences that he has escaped; he may penalize himself by having to contribute a sum of money, for example, an amount equivalent to the cost of the snack, to a cause that he dislikes; or, as in some work with cigarette smoking (Ober, 1967), he may give himself an electric shock.

On the other hand, he may allow himself pleasant experiences if he maintains his eating plan. For example, he may budget himself for 1500 calories the day, and if at the end he has used only 1350, he may grant himself a cocktail. Inappropriate eating during the day will diminish his chance of the reward, and appropriate eating will bring him closer to it. A person may make other pleasant experiences such as movie-going, novel reading, or smoking contingent on his daily success. For example, overeating could lead to loss of smoking privileges at the rate of one cigarette per 100 calories. The payoff should be daily and not delayed for a week or a month.

It is important that the dieter's goals be attainable, as was touched on in our remarks on shaping. Because a lifelong pattern of eating is the goal and because unrealistically high levels of aspiration lead to lack of reinforcement, the tasks set must be attainable. A person cannot realistically say that he will never again indulge in the riotous delights of a vanilla milkshake; he can say that he will not have his usual milkshake during the next twenty-four hours.

Records

In self-control work the individual acts as his own therapist. A great part of behavior therapy is keeping records of the response. Record keeping provides information both about what the person is doing and about his progress (how he is doing).

A person is requested to record *for all food intake* the food eaten, the amount, the number of calories, and the occasion—including the events and emotions before, during, and after eating. The recording of all intake diminishes the possibility of double-entry bookkeeping in which some of the day's calories are charged to a future time. Records point out the danger times and places, which *are not to be avoided*, but to be worked on as particularly vital. That is, records help pinpoint where all the client's calories come from. Records may also indicate whether other work is required. For example, a person may over-indulge (usually alcohol rather than food) in social situations. In that case, he may be introduced to techniques for dealing with the situation such as systematic desensitization to reduce tension.

Record keeping serves as a potential source of reinforcement. One may think of all reinforcing stimuli as feedback, and records serve this function. Records may help by specifying situations and acts and permitting the individual to grade himself. The clearest use of records in this way—for acts to be done and self-evaluation—was by Rehm and Marston (1968) in a study of dating. Here, situations entered in terms of closeness to members of the opposite sex could be specified as a hierarchy and thus made clearer for the subject, who could then evaluate his progress in terms of frequency, type of situation, and how well he acted in the situation. For overeating, records should also be kept of times when food was desired but not taken. In addition to the information on the ingestion of food, the client should note what helped him resist temptation.

A different sort of record involves the result of reduced eating. While the goal is not weight reduction but appropriate eating, loss of weight and smaller clothing sizes are correlated and rewarding feedback. To avoid errors of measurement (fluctuations in water retention, for example) and discouragement at slow progress, a third of a pound a day is an excellent and possibly maximum healthy loss (but well within the error of measurement of most scales). The client is asked also to make a weekly weighing record.

Making one's effort and one's progress public may provide an additional source of commitment. There may be social pressure of success or failure. The person may select an observer and may also deposit a reinforcement with that person to be returned contingent on reasonable weekly progress. The very act of going public may be an incentive.

The Act of Eating

The object of dieting is not to stop eating, but to eat appropriately. If anything, the object is to enjoy eating rather than to stuff oneself. The person is encouraged to eat slowly. At an early stage, the person may put down the eating utensil after putting food in his mouth and not pick it up again until he has slowly and thoughly chewed and genuinely savored and swallowed his food. The ideal is for a person to be a gourmet rather than a gourmand.

This procedure has additional advantages. At a psychological level the person does not use placing food in his mouth as a stimulus for starting to place more food in his mouth. A new chain is being created. In addition, if the overweight person is relying too much on external stimuli, this procedure begins drawing more of his attention to internal stimuli and away from the external stimulus of available food. Thus, the person is encouraged in another new pattern: he is requested *to deliberately leave some food on his plate*. The food-on-plate discriminative stimulus is no longer to control his behavior. A third feature is that attention is called to the actualities of eating, to the stimuli currently present. We return to this last point in the next section.

At a physiological level, there is approximately a fifteen-minute lag between food ingestion and the resulting physiological changes. A person may eat great amounts not because he needs them, but because he has not yet felt the effects of the amount he has already swallowed. The same changes may be obtained in the same time with less food, and this is the aim of the enforced slowdown (through putting down fork, chewing, and checking each bite).

The Eating Situation

As noted, the obese person seems to be more influenced by external than internal stimuli than is the nonobese. As a step in altering eating behavior *and not as a terminal behavior*, the person may eat only in the presence of certain stimuli he has selected for himself. The eating situation should be clearly demarcated— candles, silverware, startling purple tablecloth, linen napkin, and the like may be used. Eating is made a unique occasion—an aim consistent with the gourmet approach of slower eating.

This special situation approach may be carried further when feasible. Much inappropriate eating is done on an eat-and-run basis. If a person cooks his own meals, he should not taste them until he is properly seated. The discriminative stimuli of the table and its setting are incompatible with much bed, couch, television, and street snacking. If circumstances permit, as they may in a private home, the eating situation should be located geographically in an area that the person enters rarely and hence only for eating. Separation of the dining and cooking areas adds a link to the chain. The specification of the eating locale may also aid in separating eating from other activities that provide reinforcing consequences.

A matter on which there is professional dispute is whether the person should avoid eating situations. What is clear is that a person may increase the chances of an act by being in the locale where the act is likely to take place. For example, dating behavior may be decreased by staying in one's room, drinking by avoiding bars, and religious services by going to bowling alleys on Sunday morning. If one has regularly had a cup of coffee and two donuts at 3 P.M. in a favorite shop, one may reduce the chances of this snack by choosing a different route from class to dormitory. If the object is to break the pattern of the 3 o'clock snack, the avoidance of the smell, sight, and sounds of the bakery may make the task easier. But the ultimate goal is not control by avoidance, but by *new appropriate eating habits*. To eventually establish new behaviors, one must practice and be reinforced for them in target situations.

A final cue that the overeater should learn is hunger. Time is an important discriminative stimulus for eating in our society and should be used. The person who is learning new eating patterns may be counseled to welcome hunger pangs as stimuli to be experienced, as inner stimuli he may not have adequately used. In this regard the person should eat unfavored foods when he is most hungry. Favored foods such as desserts, should be eaten when the hunger has decreased, so that these foods' reinforcing quality is weakened. This is especially true if the individual's favored foods are of the rich, high-calorie kind.

Broader Situational Control: Supplies

Our society being what it is, one method of avoiding food is to have little or no money. Thus, the reducing person might leave his home in the morning with only enough money for foreseeable necessities. (In the same manner, smoking can be drastically reduced by not carrying cigarettes so that one is reduced to social begging, known as mooching.) The general point of this chapter is illustrated by such a strategy: the person can act in such a way that he places, that is, controls himself environmentally with desirable results. In weight reduction such environmental self-control may lead to a short-run gain; but in terms of altered eating habits this strategy seems most effective in breaking rather than replacing behavior patterns.

A person may organize his environment in a way that will help establish eating patterns of long-term value. The general rubric may be called *lengthening* the chain of events between impulse to eat and actual ingestion. Lengthening may be accomplished by removing all high-calorie prepared food from the premises. If no peanuts, candy, and potato chips are available, the person cannot immediately follow his impulse to eat with consummation. Further, to satisfy the impulse the person must make an extra effort to obtain the food—something that may be a time out from reinforcement (that is, that may have a cost).

This idea can be extended. Only food that is low calorie and/or requires time and effort to prepare might be purchased. Some authors suggest that purchases be made *after* eating, when the drive is low, but evidence on the relative lack of internal stimulus control in those who overeat seems to argue against this timing. Instead, a list of purchases should be made prior to shopping. If the person realizes at the store that something vital is not on the list, for example, salt, he may not purchase it until after he has returned home and written the item down on the list. The idea is not to punish forgetfulness, but to reduce impulse buying and to place the accumulation of supplies under stimuli other than those externally present at the store.

Self and Social Reinforcement

Both the new patterns of eating and the more general strategy of self-control must pay off for the person or suffer the fate of any nonreinforced operant, namely, extinction. The person may look for high-probability behaviors in his life and schedule such reinforcing events on the basis of his good eating behavior or weight loss. The person *makes a contract with himself*. Among such contracts, as time progresses, are limits on eating at occasions where food will be served. The person decides on the acceptable caloric limits beforehand and may later reinforce himself for keeping the bargain. Another maneuver is to set aside a sum of money (even giving it to another person as an agent) and to earn it back by maintaining weight loss or making further progress.

Two eventual outcomes are hoped for. The first is that eating will come under the control of naturally occurring stimuli as the previous overeating pattern had.

The second is that the dieter's feelings of improved health and social stimulus value will be sources of reinforcement for his new eating pattern. An increase in social reinforcement such as favorable attention by the opposite sex is neither automatic nor always welcome. Changes in body build may be disconcerting to a woman who has not previously been an object of male attention. This upset is not a rejection of womanhood, as some might hypothesize, but is due to lack of practice in dealing smoothly with members of the opposite sex. A change in a person's behavior or body—that is, his stimulus value for others—may lead to a change in his environment. At a treatment level he may have to learn roles and social skills not involved in eating. The point at a theoretical level is that a person may control his own environment and alter his behavior within it; and having accomplished this, he may find even more changes in his environment. Finally, the person may learn that he can change and control his environment and his behavior. A person may be discouraged and label himself negatively not only because he overeats but also because he "cannot" (that is, does not) change. Success at self-control not only aids the target behavior but also encourages changes in more general feelings and self-perceptions.

Recapitulation

In the foregoing material we have indicated that a person *may act as his own therapist*. A knowledge of the target behavior, a functional analysis of the situation, and the application of deductions from behavior influence concepts may lead to the person's alteration of his own behavior and social environment. A person's behavior is a function of his heredity, his past experiences, and his current situation. The person's past experiences provide him with tools for actively dealing with his life situation. Of the successful behavioral treatments of overeating cited above, the most germane is that of Hagen (1970), who presented his material as "bibliotherapy." He wrote out in far greater detail the types of ideas briefly presented here. The women in Hagen's bibliotherapy group made use of written information. That is, their learned ability to read made change possible on the basis of written communication. Reading—a performance that was a terminal behavior in grade school—became an instrumental skill.

THEORETICAL AND LABORATORY COMMENTS

If a person can control another's behavior, he should be able to control his own. The relatively clinical material just presented on overeating has indicated a number of ways a person may arrange his environment to learn to eat appropriately. The person who has effectively arranged his own environment and reinforcement contingencies no longer overeats. Is this person manifesting "self-control"? He is controlling himself and, therefore, we think he is.

In the preceding sections, a number of interesting and challenging psychological questions have been brushed over. Theoreticians and research workers such as Bandura (1969), Kanfer (1971), and Mischel (1971) have worked on various aspects of this area.

Kanfer (1971) has noted that three processes may be involved in self-regulation, and that each leads to testable research questions. These three processes are *self-monitoring, self-evaluation,* and *self-reinforcement.* The question may be asked differently: How does a person learn to control himself? And if a person does control himself, what does he need to do?

The typical laboratory procedure has been to work briefly with subjects, usually children, under different conditions, and to indicate how the presence of models, differential reinforcement, instructions, and the like may lead to group differences in behaviors that are aspects of the broader concept of self-control. Among these topics are standard setting (for self-reinforcement), delay of gratification (resistance to temptation), and reduction of impulsivity.

Standard setting is a crucial aspect of self-control because it touches on self-critical behavior. A person may evaluate his behavior before changing it or accepting it as not changeworthy. Observation of one's own behavior may also lead to satisfaction. Thus, standard setting may be considered as a precursor of self-reinforcement, and self-reinforcement usually is the dependent variable in standard setting experiments.

An interesting variable that has received less attention is *sufficient satisfaction* (or dissatisfaction) to lead a person to continue or stop a task (Weiner, 1970). Experiments have shown how the standards set by a model may affect the self-reinforcement behavior of observers (Bandura and Kupers, 1964; Bandura and Whalen, 1966; Kanfer and Duerfeldt, 1967; Kanfer and Marston, 1963a, 1963b; McMains and Liebert, 1968). Modeling in this case may well have an effect in terms of providing *information as to appropriate behavior*, especially when situations are novel and the subject may not be sure what is appropriate.

Akin to self-reinforcement is *delay of attaining a reward* (Mischel, 1966; Mischel and Grusec, 1967; Mischel and Masters, 1966; Mischel and Staub, 1965). These general findings may be simplified by saying that the value of the reward and the probability of attaining it seemed to be key elements in delay or nondelay of self-reinforcement.

It is likely that children use overt and covert acts such as speech to provide stimuli for themselves in rule following and matters requiring delays of gratification (Meichenbaum and Goodman, 1969a, 1971; O'Leary, 1968). Some classic measures of stylistic behavior such as reflection-impulsivity (Meichenbaum and Goodman, 1969b) have been significantly affected by experimenter instructions that led to interposition of self-prompting behaviors and reward (Baird and Lee, 1969). Of great interest is the finding that such behaviors may have the impact, that is, be useful in the teaching of "moral" behavior (Bandura and McDonald, 1963; Burchard, 1970).

These researches, which are all within the last decade, indicate both increased theoretical interest and careful empirical analysis of those behaviors that later may be labeled "self-control." In broader measure, they lead to an analysis and eventual increase of society-maintaining and society-building behaviors such as cooperation (Mithaug and Burgess, 1968), sharing (Elliott and Vasta, 1970; Harris, 1970), and altruism (Bryan and London, 1970; Krebs, 1970).

LAST WORD

Rather than asserting that humans have certain capacities or traits, the behavioral research discussed has centered on carefully defining and increasing certain behaviors as functions of operationally defined and replicable manipulations. The investigation of biological, social, and personally generated feedback—the "self," if one wishes to use such a label—is one of the most interesting areas of investigation at this time. From our more general view as experimenters influencing and being influenced, we think this investigation is not only an outgrowth of the development of the science and profession of psychology but also a response to the needs of our age to find better ways of living with each other and with ourselves.

PART 3

Influences of Broader Contexts
on Human Behavior

CHAPTER **13**

The Interaction of Behavior and Physical, Organizational, and Social Environments

Behavior occurs in social and physical settings. A constant theme of this volume is the impact of the social environment on resultant action. The environment is a major factor in *setting limits to the range of potential behavior*. This is at times overlooked, just as until recently the availability of pure air and water was taken for granted. One focus of this chapter, then, is the effect on behavior of *physical* aspects of the environment—including *natural* influences such as weather, *inadvertent* by-products of man such as pollution, and *deliberate* products of man such as architectural spatial arrangements. These influences are complemented by the manner in which men are trained (or learn) to deal with their physical environment.

Only rarely does a physical aspect of the environment lack a social meaning. All environmental stimuli including the physical must be considered as being *social*, since the individual has learned their meaning and how to react to them.

The physical, political, economic, and organizational aspects of the social environment have received relatively little attention in texts on personality which often seem to present the individual alone in a sterile world. Rarely is the environment considered a setting event or antecedent for action in contrast to such usual concepts as "anxious man" or "authoritarian personality."

Much of what a person does is learned in terms of previous responses to his behavior (see the discussion of G. H. Mead, Chapter 3). Concepts such as "role" and "status" are a verbal shorthand for this learning about relations to other people. Assumptions about what is right and proper may be so ubiquitous that challenging and changing them involve major social changes. At a physical level, one might cite the challenges to self-evident truths posed by the heliocentric theory and the development of Boolean algebra. The same holds for the impact of a social movement: a revolution in the Kuhnian sense (involving basic paradigms; see Chapter 3) is literally required to alter the person's responses to himself. Without such a drastic change, he places constraints on his own behavior (controls himself; see Chapter 12) that are anything but self-evident or innate. Lists of instincts or motives made in the nineteenth and early twentieth centuries (see Chapter 2) seem almost quaint, so great have been the changes in what is "self-evident."

(*a*) Major limitations on the behavior of which a person is capable are learned by the responses others make to the person, that is, the social environment; (*b*) this social environment is so ubiquitous *within* a given time, place, and subculture that there is a danger it will be overlooked as an influence on behavior; and (*c*) when the social environmental effect limits rather than evokes specific acts, it may be overlooked. The impact of the cultural relativists (see Chapter 2) during the last part of the nineteenth and first half of the twentieth century provided the kinds of data that support this environmental view.[1]

THE ENVIRONMENT AS VOCATION

While belief in the influence of the moon and stars on behavior has a long history and while chemistry and physics have been prime topics in Western civilization, the systematic investigation of man's *reciprocal interaction* with his environment has been a recent development. The word *environment* has become a slogan for what needs "fixing" for a better life—be it air, water, or other people's behavior.

The dictionary defines *environment* so broadly that it can mean almost any-

[1] Among the more systematic and recent volumes illustrating the impact of the social environment are those by Kluckholm and Murray, 1948; Sargent and Smith, 1949; Shibutani, 1961; Smelser and Smelser, 1963; and Spitzer, 1969.

thing: "The total of circumstances surrounding an organism or group of organisms, specifically: (a) the combination of external or extrinsic physical conditions that affect and influence the growth and development of organisms; (b) the complex of social and cultural conditions affecting the nature of an individual or community [Morris, 1969, p. 438]."

With the recent interest in the environment, many traditional disciplines have begun to incorporate the term and the concept into newer modes of investigation. For example, a group of economists including Kenneth Boulding has criticized the economist's traditional concern with consumption. Instead, these economists focus on the *nature of environmental quality* such as air and water. Their approach is typified by the title of the 1971 book, *Environmental Economics* (Crocker and Rogers).

Changes in the conception of sociology have also led to an environmental sociology. The flavor of this new development is captured in the following quote from Mann and Hagevik (1971).

> Sociology has been both conceptually and empirically isolated from concerns of the physical environment from the decline of the Chicago school of urban ecology until the very recent past. In the era of Parsonian dominance, empirical space was abstracted to a point where theoretical constructs seemed more real than did the urban environments which were mere "anchoring points" of the social system (Parsons, 1959). For a variety of reasons, this has now changed, and environmental sociology is hardly lagging behind environmental psychology. It is now respectable for the builders of sociological curricula to search for a sociologist with "space vibes." While there is not yet (to our knowledge at least) a reader in environmental sociology, there almost inevitably will be soon. For one thing, as we have noted, many of the people so easily coopted by environmental psychologists are really environmental sociologists. And the sociologists are in a much stronger position since they already have a viable theoretical framework for environmental sociology in Kolaja's *Social System and Time and Space* (1969) plus a cogent summing up of the relevant literature in Michelson's *Man and His Urban Environment* (1970) [p. 345].

Michelson has summarized what he considers to be the relevant sociological environmental variables influencing behavior in the urban environment, namely, physical access to relatives, to other people, to activities, and to services; land use patterns; neighborhood density; noise levels; changes of residence and the position and outlook of doors determining spatial proximity.

Environmental Psychology

It is reasonable to predict that the emerging field of environmental psychology will have a major impact upon and eventually merge with the psychology of behavior influence.

The first step in an emerging discipline is its gaining a label, and the publication of *Environmental Psychology: Man and His Physical Setting* (Proshansky, Ittelson, and Rivlin, 1970) has already marked this step. The credo of this approach is manifested in the following quotation from Proshansky et al.:

> All living organisms engage in a complex interchange with their environments in the course of which they modify, and are modified by, what they encounter. Some such interchange is essential for the maintenance of life and usually is involved in definitions of the concept of life itself. Living necessarily involves changes wrought on the environment by the organism, changes that may subsequently alter the organism itself, chemically, biologically, or behaviorally. . . . The archaic view of a fixed environment that organisms must adapt to or perish is being replaced by a view that emphasizes the organism's creative role in shaping his own environment. . . . From the viewpoint of the social sciences, man's social and psychological environment is largely a product of his own creation, and he, in turn, is fundamentally influenced by this product. Indeed, the social effect on man of the environment he himself has created may prove to be the most important aspect of this relationship. . . . The magnitude and complexity of man's effect on his environment would be little more than an interesting biological curiosity were it not for man's capacity to predict the consequences of his behavior. This characteristic makes it possible for him to do more than blindly operate on the environment; it permits planned manipulation of the environment. . . . Man the builder is also man the planner. But for the most part man's planning, with respect to the environment, has been limited to the physical effects of his alterations. Understanding and predicting the effects of these manipulations upon himself, while operationally inseparable from the fact of manipulation, have tended to be separated conceptually and, until quite recently, largely ignored. . . . it is evident that the scope of man's manipulations of his environment makes essential an understanding of the consequences of these manipulations for human life itself. . . . In summary, the environmental sciences, as we understand them, have four identifying and defining characteristics. They deal with the man-ordered and defined environment; they grow out of pressing social problems; they are multidisciplinary in nature; and they include the study of man as an integral part of every problem. In short, the environmental sciences are concerned with human problems in relation to an environment of which man is both victim and conquerer. . . . Ultimately all environmental sciences are concerned to a greater or lesser extent with questions of human behavior. They must then turn to environmental psychology, which can be characterized, in keeping with our general discussion, as the study of human behavior in relation to the man-ordered and defined environment [pp. 1–5].

Environmental Psychology is a collection of 65 articles reporting research on such topics as the anthropology of space, behavior-contingent physical systems, function and meaning of the physical environment, the ecology of isolated groups, the ecology of privacy, privacy and the bathroom, the uses of sidewalks, office design, factors which determine hospital design, human movement, and architecture and behavioral maps.

Similar evidence for the existence and growth of an enviromental psychology is given by Craik (1970), who systematically approaches the impact of the physical environment and the "built" environment on behavior. He points out that

> The adoption of the designation "environmental psychology" seeks to profit from the rich connotations that the term "environmental" has acquired through many recent efforts to analyze systematically the character of the total contemporary physical environment, including its natural and man-influenced, professionally designed and haphazardly formed manifestations. In keeping with this new and liberating perspective, the disciplines of architecture, landscape architecture, design, and city and regional planning signify the interrelated nature of their pursuits by organizing themselves under the common calling of "environmental design". . . . Furthermore, environmental science, the study of strictly physical aspects of the environment, has been joined by an environmental physiology . . . and, perhaps, by an environmental sociology. . . . Thus, the term "environmental psychology" conveys both the domain of the new field and its interdisciplinary potential. It must also be noted that "architectural psychology" . . . while more limited in implication, and "ecological psychology" . . . which places less clear-cut emphasis upon the physical environment, are also serving as effective designations for significant portions of the research reviewed [p. 5].

Other evidences of the merging and emerging of new fields come from the existence of new training programs such as that in environmental psychology at the City University of New York, ecological psychology at Michigan State University (Tornatsky, Fairweather, and O'Kelly, 1970), and social ecology at the University of California at Irvine. New journals have appeared such as *Environment and Behavior*, which is described by its editors as an "interdisciplinary journal concerned with the study, design, and the control of the physical environment and its interaction with human behavioral systems." (See also Wohlwill, 1970, and Wohlwill and Carson, 1972.)

All these signs indicate that the environment has become a focus for the influencers of the seventies and eighties. Scientists are reacting to the relevancies of their own environment.

VARIATIONS IN ENVIRONMENTAL STIMULI

Because the major interest of this chapter is physical aspects of the environment, the following variables will be noted briefly at this time insofar as they relate to the physical environment.

Prenatal and Physical Disease Factors

The physical environment operates on the individual from the moment of conception, and *foreign substances* or *nutritional deficits* may have a severe impact. A major example is the birth defects caused by the drug Thalidomide.

An interaction always occurs between the child and the social world he enters. Roger Barker (1968), for example, has reported on the changes in behavior effected by the settings which crippled children entered, and their level of participation once in the setting.

While the ultimate limitation on behavior associated with physical disease is death, nonterminal conditions may also have a severe impact. The loss of hearing, sight, sensation, limbs, and so forth frequently caused by a traumatic event such as an auto accident casts the person into a world that is markedly different from that of the majority of people not so afflicted. This impact is manifested in various ways. The blind person must find sources of information as best he can. He may use audio aids, take notes with tape recorders, read with braille, and attend to sensations that most people have but do not need to utilize or develop. The social environment of the blinded is thus very drastically changed.

The blind person experiences the effect of his limitations in dealing with the environment—basically a difficulty in obtaining information about stimuli that are at a distance and that usually provide data via visual input—in a social matrix which *adds* greatly to his difficulties and which leads to similarities among the blind that are not necessarily, logically, or directly related to their physical handicap. The blind person must learn to deal with the physical environment in a manner that illuminates *the process of learning the social meaning of physical events.*

In an excellent book, *The Making of Blind Men*, Scott (1969) has contended that being blind is a *learned social role.* In what follows, the reader may wish to replace the words *blinded person* with *aged, black, female, young, imprisoned, psychiatric patient, hippie,* or many others.

Scott (1969) has advanced two basic theses:

> The first is that many of the attitudes, behavior patterns, and qualities of character that have long been assumed to be given to blind people by their condition are, in fact, the result of ordinary processes of socialization. The second is that organized intervention programs for the blind play a major role in determining the nature of this socialization. Blindness, then, is a social role that people who have serious difficulty seeing or who cannot see at all must learn how to play [p. 3]."

Scott points out that there are "commonsense" explanations and stereotyped expectations of the blind. Because their world is "less gross," the blind are expected to be more spiritual than other people. But, by the same sort of deductions, the blind are expected to be depressed, frustrated, helpless, and docile. Sighted people learn these stereotypes and interact with the blind on the basis of them.

The first context in which a blinded person learns these stereotypes is in childhood. Here it is important to note the distinction between the *congenitally blind*—those blind from birth or shortly thereafter—and the *blinded*—those who lose their sight later, usually late in life. (A temporal distinction has differential behavioral consequences in other areas also. If a child is brain injured from birth or shortly thereafter, he is called retarded; if an adult suffers severe damage through disease, auto accident, war incident, or the like, he has a *chronic brain syndrome*.) The vast majority of blind people are in the blinded category; the point is that during their sighted years, they learn the social role which is first directed toward the blind, and then later toward themselves as blind. A similar effect may be observed in the area of psychiatric difficulties: the patient has a concept (whether accurate or not) of the role of the "mentally ill" prior to hospitalization (Levitz and Ullmann, 1969) and of "therapy patient" prior to treatment (Kadushin, 1969).

A second context of socialization is in interaction with people who treat the blind person as helpless, docile, and dependent. The assumption that the person is helpless may be a self-validating hypothesis, since he may be denied the opportunity to practice the skills he has and to demonstrate his competence to others and himself.

A third context is interaction with the social agencies created to help the blind. Agencies for the blind are so numerous that they may even compete for this limited population in order to justify their own existence (a phenomenon not limited to agencies for the blind, but true frequently for agencies created to assist with particular social problems). There is a blindness *network, system,* or even *industry*.

> The legitimacy of this profession is in large part based upon its practitioners' claims to specialized knowledge and expertise concerning problems of blindness. Through the years, this knowledge and expertise have become increasingly formalized, so that in blindness organizations today, there are a number of more or less distinct approaches to blindness. These approaches are based on beliefs and assumptions concerning the fundamental problems experienced by people who are blind, the necessary and appropriate solutions to these problems, and the reactions of people when they first become blind and during each successive stage of their rehabilitation. These beliefs and assumptions serve to guide practitioners in dealing with clients in the clinical setting of the blindness agency. The approaches are expressed as the blindness workers' expectations of the attitudes and behavior of those they are trying to help. For blindness workers, one key indicator of the success of a rehabilitation endeavor is the degree to which the client has come

to understand himself and his problems from the workers' perspective" [Scott, 1969, pp. 18–19].[2]

People react differently to a person considered blind than they do to one considered sighted. But this differentiation is not made unless people perceive the person as blind. While this statement seems obvious, it is not; the most frequent definition of *blind* is central visual acuity of 20/200 or less in the better eye with correcting lenses. Many readers of this book who wear glasses, as does the junior author, can gain some indication of what this means by taking off their glasses. For example, the eye examination starts and the physician says, "Read the first line of the chart," and the junior author, without glasses, honestly responds, "What chart?" Without glasses, most of the world assumes the broken, hazy aspect of an impressionist painting, and newsprint is a strain to read even from a distance of three and a half inches. While definitely handicapped in comparison to others when not wearing glasses, persons such as the junior author probably consider themselves very far from blind.

The matter of self-labeling is made more salient when, we note that "because of the way most Snellen charts are graduated, persons are classified as blind if their corrected vision is poorer than 20/100, rather than 20/200 or worse, as prescribed by the currently accepted administrative definition. On most Snellen charts there are no gradations between 20/200 and 20/100. If a person is unable to read the letter corresponding to 20/100 but able to read the letter corresponding to 20/200, he is classified 20/200 [Scott, 1969, p. 41]." Many people, therefore, may not be blind by the administrative definition, which is not sensitive to how well the person functions in his world.

Scott (1969) has noted that close to half the people considered blind have corrected acuity of 20/200 (p. 47); moreover, two-thirds of the blind are aged fifty-five and over (p. 50); and while the rate of blindness is roughly 2.5 per 1000 between ages eighteen to forty-four, it is roughly 30 per 1000 after age sixty-five (p. 51). Two final facts are of great importance: first, only 36 percent of the blind between eighteen and twenty-four, and 26 percent between twenty-five and thirty-four have visual acuities poorer than 20/200 (p. 51); second, clients of blindness agencies comprise only a small, select portion of the total blind population and rehabilitation is geared to those who are young and have the highest probability of success (p. 70). This second point will be particularly important when we return to socialization by agency.

---

[2] This situation, both of an industry and socialization by a "service" agency, is also seen in work with psychiatric patients. Loeb (1957) has pointed this out in terms of the use of jargon and "dynamic" formulations by patients interacting with therapists. Dunham and Weinberg (1960, esp. pp. 48, 122–128) have made this point on the ward vis-à-vis nursing assistants. Bloom (1963) has written that the new admission "is taught, first of all, *how to behave* in his new role as a hospital patient [p. 191]." See also Kim (1971), Scott (1967), and Wellford (1967).

To return to our earlier considerations, the individual must first be identified as being blind. He is then assigned a new role. Of import and typical of personality theory, blindness is not considered an attribute limited to relevant situations—such as contact with distant physical objects—but is viewed as a constant set of characteristics across most, if not all, social situations. In line with our earlier discussion in Chapter 2, we may even say that we are dealing with the concepts of a *trait* of blindness. As Scott (1969) has noted:

> It is impossible for blind men to ignore these beliefs; they have no choice but to respond to them. These responses vary, but in a highly patterned way. Some blind people come to concur in the verdict that has been reached by those who see. They adopt as a part of their self-concept the qualities of character, the feelings, and the behavior patterns that others insist they must have. . . . Such blind men might be termed "true-believers"; they have become what others with whom they interact assume they must become because they are blind.
>
> Not all blind people are true believers; there are many who explicitly, indeed insistently, reject the imputations made of them by others. They thereby manage to insulate a part of the self-concept from the assaults made on it by normals. The personal identity of such a person is not that of a blind man, but of a basically normal person who cannot see. For the blind man who responds in this way, there remains the problem that most people who see do not share the view he has reached about himself. Some blind men respond simply by complying with the expectations of the sighted, in a conscious and deliberate way. They adopt an external facade that is consistent with the normals' assumptions about them, but they are aware that it is a facade, and they are ready to drop it whenever occasions permit them to do so. Ordinarily, the reason for acquiescence is expedience; in fact, every blind man, whether he accepts or rejects the social identity imputed to him, will be found to acquiesce at least some of the time. For example, several blind people have told me that when they use public transportation, fellow passengers will occasionally put money into their hands. When this occurs, a blind man cannot very well give a public lecture on the truth about blindness; in fact, to do anything but acquiesce and accept the gift will leave him open to charges of ingratitude and bitterness. There are other blind people who use the acquiescent facade not for expedience but as a weapon. Those who beg, for example, deliberately cultivate it in order to encourage people to give them money. The beggar strikes up an unstated pact with the world: he agrees to behave exactly as others insist that he must, and in exchange he makes the normal person pay with money. How dear this price is, of course, depends upon the beggar's ability to exploit their notions that lead his victims to expect him to acquiesce in the first place [pp. 22–23].

But the world of the blinded is not dictated merely by stereotypes or attitudes. Blindness has an effect on overt behavior, and this effect is sharpened by actual interchanges. The cues used by sighted people such as head nods of agreement are not effective. Because his hearing is the more important channel in conversation, the blind person may turn his head away from the sighted person—

emitting a cue that would be one of disinterest in a sighted person. Unless experienced, the sighted person does not know how to act, especially when to help and when not to. He wants to do the right thing and yet not call attention to the blind person's handicap: Should he help him to his chair, guide his hand to the cup of coffee or cigarette, use phrases such as "I see what you mean"? The sighted person may hesitate to respond to the blind with the same directness that he would to a sighted person. He may suppress some of his normal responses lest he hurt the blind person. In short, the blind person makes the sighted person constrained, uncomfortable, and even frustrated.

The blind person not only faces this difficulty in communication but may also be placed in a dependent and compliant position because he cannot return favors as easily as the sighted. The relationship may be more like that between parent and child or teacher and student because it is less one between equals. As a result of these situations, people who were originally different may come to act in similar ways.

To these factors, we may now add the impact of service organizations. First, it should be noted again that blindness is not defined as total lack of sight and that many people who would meet the official definition remain in the general population and, while having difficulties in seeing, are not thought of by themselves or others as blind. A person with severe vision problems may be referred to an agency serving the blind, be *labeled blind*, and then be treated *as if he were totally blind*. Thus, there is a redefinition of the problem both by the person and those serving him. This is similar to what occurs when a person enters a psychiatric hospital because of a particular behavior, is diagnosed as schizophrenic, and then is treated for schizophrenia rather than for his overt behavior. The situation is made more difficult because many of the techniques of the service agency are devised for people who are totally blind, but are applied to people who have partial vision. For example, a person who would be able to function with enlarged print may be taught braille. Further, the presenting difficulty may have been marital, psychiatric, financial—that is, specific to one area of life. But because the person happens to have visual difficulties, he may be referred to an agency serving the blind.

A person may wish better optical aids or other specific services. The blind person believes his trouble lies in specific areas. "The personal conceptions that blinded persons have about the nature of their problems are in sharp contrast with beliefs that workers for the blind share about the problems of blindness. [The service worker views blindness as a total process affecting all aspects of life.] Beneath the surface of awareness lies a tremendously complicated mass of problems that must be dealt with before the surface problems can ever be successfully solved [Scott, 1969, p. 77]." This attitude of the service worker parallels closely the approach of the traditional therapist, who believes that the underlying problems ("personality") must be changed before behavior can change. The service worker must therefore discredit the client's ideas about his own problems. *The client must learn to accept the agency's formulation*: "in face-to-face situations, the blind person is rewarded for showing insight and subtly reprimanded for continuing to adhere to earlier notions about his problems. He is led to think that he 'really' understands past and present experiences when he couches them in terms acceptable to his therapist. If he persists in viewing his 'presenting problems' as the real ones, he is labeled 'unacceptable' or 'uninsightful.' The client is said to be 'blocking' or resisting the truth [Scott, 1969, p. 79]."

To be fully rehabilitated and to earn the related rewards such as progress in the program, the individual must accept the agency's formulation. There are two general concepts of work with the blind. The first may be called restorative, the second accommodative. The goal of *restoration* is return to community functioning. While the most ambitious program for the blind—and in the hands of some agencies such as the Veterans Administration, the most successful— restoration is often commingled with a process of "mourning and rebirth" that may well be unnecesary, unrealistic, and poetic.

The majority of work is *accommodative*, that is, aimed at helping the person accept and adjust to reduced abilities. "Clients are rewarded for trivial things and praised for performing tasks in a mediocre fashion. This superficial and over-generous reward system makes is impossible for most clients to assess their accomplishments accurately. . . . The unstated assumption of accommodative agencies is that most of their clients will end up organizing their lives around the agency [Scott, 1969, p. 85]." The parallel to the custodial hospital for the psychiatric patient is striking; the person is taught to adjust to the agency, and "A blind person who has been fully socialized in an accommodative agency will be maladjusted to the larger community [Scott, 1969, p. 86]."

We may now ask, What conditions lead to the adoption of the theories and practices of an accommodative agency? One factor (which also works in the development of large psychiatric hospitals) is that the accommodative agency removes blind persons from the awareness of the remainder of the population. A second is that by considering the blind person's difficulty as severe, the agency worker enhances his own dedication and expertise. Blindness agencies may have a real vested interest in maintaining the general public's stereotypes. Public education may be more frequently directed to the availability of the agency rather than to the actualities of blindness.

Because "results" are desirable in terms of increased accommodation, the person who is old or multiply handicapped is less likely to be served than the younger, less disabled person. This may also be due a carry-over of the goals of earlier blindness workers, who charted the field when fewer sick children and old people survived and blindness frequently occurred in industrial settings.

Agencies are constrained by their source of funding and, particularly when supported by private philanthropy, must meet the desires and stereotypes of their sources. The number of clients who meet the standards of an agency are limited, and "When an agency has the opportunity to provide services to a suitable blind person, it is reluctant to let him go completely [Scott, 1969, p. 99]." The agency strives to keep its workload of people served high.[3]

The worker in the blindness agency is locked into the system almost as much as the blind client. Especially if his expertise has been gained on the job in an agency, not in a professional school, he is dependent on the existing system for his status and salary. Procedures may be continued because they fit the presumed needs of the blind, and needs may even be invented to justify procedures.

In summary, "there is nothing inherent in the condition of blindness that requires a person to be docile, dependent, melancholy, or helpless; nor is there anything about it that should lead him to become independent or assertive [Scott, 1969, p. 14]." The similarities observed among the blind stem from what people are taught. In the context of this book, similarities in the teaching of the social behaviors of being black, female, old, a psychiatric patient, or student follow the general outlines given here for the blind, with much the same consequences.

SOCIAL STATUSES

The preceding section on blindness dealt with the impact of physical indicants on people's behavior. Individuals also learn how to respond to a number of personal physical attributes, which serve as major environmental stimuli for behavior. Although there are many such stimuli, we shall concentrate on age, sex, and race, the ones we believe are most readily associated with differential overt behavior.[4] In this matter, we agree with Linton (1945) that "the division of society's members into age-sex categories is, perhaps, the feature of greatest importance for establishing the participation of the individual in the culture. In practically all societies, the great majority of activities and occupations are ascribed to the members of one or a very small number of age-sex categories and prohibited to members of others [pp. 63–64]."

Age

At the time of this writing, every age group seems to feel that it is the object of discrimination. The clearest instances are requirements of age which bar a person from behavior of which he is capable and in which he could engage pleasantly and productively. At one end of the continuum is a policy of enforced

[3] The situation may also be observed in psychiatric hospitals in which new applications per bed (assuring an adequate average daily patient load) were significantly associated with rapid release and measures of patient turnover (Ullmann, 1967).

[4] Other variables could have been selected such as hair color or length (T. L. Rosenthal and White, 1972).

retirement at some specified age such as sixty-five. Aside from the financial impact of such rules, in our culture a person's employment is an indication of worth. Working is one aspect of being mature; loss of work may lead to feelings of debility. At the other end of the continuum are restrictions on drinking, making contracts, holding office, and the like until one reaches twenty-one. Even white, middle-class, and middle-aged men may feel that they are the objects of outrageous fortune: heavily taxed and endlessly working to make ends meet in the face of rising costs, they find themselves called anything from "racist pigs" to "establishment." Giving much and getting little thanks or recognition, many a middle-aged Archie Bunker feels exploited in the midst of a youth culture.

Beyond physiological limitations, distinct opportunities, expectations, and obligations severely define what behavior will be positively reinforced and what behavior is likely to be extinguished if not punished.

While the dependence of the infant on adults is related to age regardless of the society, probably the major source of difference in values widely called "the generation gap" results from the fact that Americans of twenty, forty-five, and seventy have been born into remarkably different worlds. The work of Kinsey, Pomeroy, Martin, and Gebhard (1953) was consistent with its forerunners in indicating that one of the major predictors of a woman's sexual behavior was whether she had been born before or after 1900. A poignant glimpse of what having grown up in a different era means may be gained from Bertrand Russell's word picture (1968) of his grandmother, who incidentally was the wife of one of Britain's great prime ministers:

> It was obvious from her conversation that she never came anywhere near to knowing what it feels like to be in love. She told me once how relieved she was on her honeymoon when her mother joined her. On another occasion she lamented that so much poetry should be concerned with so trivial a subject as love. . . . I do not think that she ever understood the claims of animal spirits and exuberant vitality. She demanded that everything should be viewed through a mist of Victorian sentiment. . . . Her morality was that of a Victorian Puritan, and nothing could have persuaded her that a man who swore on occasion might nevertheless have some good qualities. . . . Marriage was a puzzling institution. It was clearly the duty of husbands and wives to love one another, but it was a duty they ought not to perform too easily, for if sex attraction drew them together, there must be something not quite nice about them. Not, of course, that she would have phrased the matter in these terms. What she would have said, and in fact did say, was "You know, I never think that the affection of husbands and wives is quite such a good thing as the affection of parents for their children, because there is sometimes something a little selfish about it" [p. 14–16].

A product of her time and social class, the range of operants that Lady Russell emitted clearly differed from those of a contemporary, liberal, college-educated woman.

Gender

Anthropologists (M. Mead, 1935) and those working with physiological anomalies (Money, 1968) have indicated the wide range of social roles that may be labeled appropriate for men or women. But within any particular time and place, only a small segment of these roles are deemed correct or optimal; and only slowly and recently in our own culture has the range of choices open to women increased. As work shifts from muscular to intellectual and interpersonal, the rational basis for work discrimination based on sex decreases. But from time of their birth males and females have notably different social worlds in terms of dress, toys, and—of greatest import—behaviors that are modeled and encouraged. To call a woman masculine or a man effeminate is a serious insult. Socialization into sex role moves from toys to athletics, hobbies, assertiveness, dating behaviors, and vocational expectations. The documentation of the discriminatory impact of such socialization and the variety of forms used is increasing daily. (The growing volume of publications on women's liberation includes Friedan, 1963; Millet, 1970; Steinem, 1970; and *Ms.*, a magazine whose name symbolizes many women's desires for changed social roles.)

A relatively small item involves clothing, but perhaps only a man who has to keep his bad back straight can realize the constraint on operants involved in wearing a miniskirt. A report from a school for delinquent girls provides an illustration of grooming as a potential form of stimulus control:

> Our worst days are when we have a snowstorm because, realistically, the girls say that they have to wear slacks. . . . This is the day we know there are going to be at least 10 fights. When they dress in a way that gives them greater freedom . . . in a somewhat masculine way, they are going to act up. But no girl particularly wants to act up when her hair is well done, when she has had a manicure, when she's made up . . . she doesn't want to bother; she doesn't want to disturb it [as quoted by Anspach, 1967, p. 329].

Fashion also provides examples of the interaction of the social environment and body structure that is far more rapid than the genetic drifts of "natural selection": "The result of this emphasis on youth and slimness is that the retailer now sells ten times as many size 16's as size 40's, something not true 20 years ago. If any woman allows her figure to go beyond a size 16, she is banished to unexciting styles and conventional colors [Anspach, 1967, p. 277]." Women are likely to exercise and diet to be able to wear desirable clothes. The effect is a decrease in the market for youthful designs in larger sizes, so that fewer are available and the cycle is repeated.

Even a professionally held theory of personality (see Chapters 2 and 7) can be a means of discrimination against women. Gilman (1971) has reviewed the justifiable complaints of many women against Freud and psychoanalytic theory, which through its belief that "anatomy is destiny," has contributed to a subtle discrimination toward women by both sexes. The social setting of Freud's Vienna influenced his theories about the Oedipus complex and penis envy, which in turn have had enormous influence on how men and women interpret their own lives and behavior.

Race

Genetic differences in skin color are difficult to associate causally with the well-documented plight of many American blacks and Indians. Rather, the discriminative practices of the social environment over four centuries have given an unfortunately clear demonstration that citizens residing in the same country in the same era may live in worlds that are crucially different. In our day we are faced with changes in both how the white should view the black and how the black should view himself.

Strongly associated with race and geographical origins, such as Puerto Rican in New York City and Spanish-American in the Southwest, is the environment called the *culture of poverty*. Differences in diet, housing conditions, and family constellation are accentuated by differences in the meaningfulness of study for self-improvement, delay of gratification, and indulgence in abstract intellectual rather than immediate sensory experiences. Variations in potential employment are both an association and a consequence of these added differences. While this material is also considered in succeeding chapters on economic, social, and political considerations, the point here is that there is a vast difference in the environment and hence in the range of potential operants that are associated with a particular subgroup such as "the poor."

Organizational and Professional Influences

Adjustment to the work situation (Presthus, 1962; Thompson, 1961; Whyte, 1956) may lead to the development of "types" of behavior patterns as well as specific task behaviors. This is especially true for professional training (W. E. Moore, 1970; Slocum, 1966; Vollmer and Mills, 1966). The occupations of teacher, housewife, policeman, and physician predict types of behavior and settings in much the same way that the label *middle-aged white married college-educated male* aids in specifying limits of expected behavior.

PHYSICAL VARIABLES OF THE ENVIRONMENT

We now focus on the effects of physical environment on behavior; on stimuli other than other human beings; on the arrangement of human beings as physical stimuli; and on the arrangement of physical objects by human beings. Various observers of American society have pointed out the behavioral effects of aversive environmental stimuli such as air and water pollution, noise, DDT, detergents, artificial food additives, and defective industrial products.

Another important reason for environmental interest is the recent exposure of man to a variety of a new, special, and unique environments, including the weightlessness and isolation of space travel, undersea exploration, radiation, and communes and planned cities.

The Physical Environment

A distinction between the psychological and the physical environment is purely a matter of organization of the sequence of material and emphasis. We are constantly interacting with the physical environment and altering it. The alterations made by man on purpose such as roads, dams, and plowed lands and those made without plan such as pollution as by-products of the industrial process have received increasing attention in the last few years. While the allocation of resources and the concern of the public will hopefully alter our future behavior drastically, we concentrate here on currently available data. While the range is modest compared to the broader problems of behavior influence, the relatively small environmental variables currently being studied may indicate how great the potential effects are.

If we had to justify our inclusion of the physical environment in a book on behavior influence, we would cite and agree with the following quotation from Craik (1970): "Using environmental design to achieve socially valued outcomes places it among the standard behavior modification techniques, next to hypnosis, psychotherapy, education, persuasion, and brainwashing, and raises the question, what leverage does the environmental designer possess to influence behavior? [p. 37]."

Cultural Differences

Differences in conceptualization and use of space are far more than a matter of geographical or technological availability. The very vehicle of abstraction and thought, language, poses a cultural barrier when physical reality is processed by a person. Further, the person's formal and informal training leads to a selection of objects which he will attend to or "ignore" or adapt to. For example, in *chess* the player may advance bishops, rooks, and queens until they are blocked by another piece. The player is trained to consider control of space such as the center of the board abstractly and to value it for the increased maneuverability it allows his pieces. In *go* the player learns to place stones at intersections, with the object being to encircle and control space.

A person who has played both chess and go will have some feel for the following statements by Hall (1966):

> The European systems [of city plans] stress the lines, which they name; the Japanese treat the intersecting points technically and forget about the lines. In Japan, the intersections but not the streets are named. . . . When Westerners think and talk about space, they mean the distance between objects. In the West, we are taught to perceive and to react to the arrangements of objects and to think of space as "empty." The meaning of this becomes clear only when it is contrasted with the Japanese, who are trained to give *meaning* to spaces—to perceive the shape and arrangement of shapes; for this they have a word, *ma* [pp. 99, 142–143].

This difference in spatial conception may be reflected in the Western trend to place furniture and objects along fixed walls, while the Japanese place furniture in the center of the room space, use the same location for different purposes, and move walls and furniture rather than themselves when the function changes.

Privacy

Privacy is something that contemporary Americans assume is good and even necessary. But Hall (1966, pp. 142, 148) has noted that the Japanese and the Arabs do not have a word for this concept. In addition, imaginary geographical lines such as boundaries are not used by Arabs. Hall (p. 152) has also reported that he was unable to discover an Arabian concept resembling the Western one of trespass and that in the Arabian context *who* a person is, rather than *where* he is, is the crucial variable.

People from different cultures may dislike each other and, perhaps even worse for interpersonal and international relationships, think that members of other cultures dislike them because of different concepts of space. Hall (1966) has related how he was seated in an empty hotel lobby waiting for a friend in a spot from which he could scan the elevators and entrance when a man came and stood so closely to him that Hall could hear his breathing; Hall moved his body away, an indication of annoyance in American culture.

> Strangely enough, instead of moving away, my actions seemed only to encourage him, because he moved even closer. [Hall identified the man as an Arab.] In describing the scene later to an Arab colleague, two contrasting patterns emerged. My concept and my feelings about my own circle of privacy in a "public" place immediately struck my Arab friend as strange and puzzling. He said, "After all, it's a public place, isn't it?" Pursuing this line of inquiry, I found that in Arab thought I had no rights whatsoever by virtue of occupying a given spot; neither my place nor my body was inviolate! For the Arab, there is no such thing as an intrusion in public. Public means public . . . I learned, for example, that if A

is standing on a street corner and B wants his spot, B is within his rights if he does what he can to make A uncomfortable enough to move. In Beirut only the hardy sit in the last row in a movie theater, because there are usually standees who want seats and who push and shove and make such a nuisance that most people give up and leave. Seen in this light, the Arab who "intruded" on my space in the hotel lobby had apparently selected it for the very reason I had: it was a good place to watch two doors and the elevator. My show of annoyance, instead of driving him away, had only encouraged him. He thought he was about to get me to move [pp. 145–146].

This anecdote raises a crucial question about personality traits such as "aggressiveness" or "obnoxiousness." The Arab certainly annoyed Hall, but given cultural perspectives on privacy and public space, is it useful to say that Hall was responding to a "personal trait" or to a "national characteristic"?

Space around the Body

Hall (1966, pp. 110–122) has listed four kinds of distance in personal relationships: intimate, personal, social, and public. He further subdivides each into a *close* and *far* phase and gives approximate footage for each. This is a conceptual scheme, and the distances vary across different cultures. Not only are there cultural differences but within a culture the distance at which a person feels comfortable with another person may be indicative of his feelings about the other.

At an *intimate distance* the person can feel the body heat, smell, breath, and even muscle changes of the other as well as see and hear him, although vocalization may be involuntary and slightly blurred. At the far intimate distance, roughly 6 to 18 inches, heat, odor, and breath can still be felt, talk is likely to be about internal feelings, and the stance has aggressive or sexual overtures for middle-class Americans and Northern Europeans. When forced to this degree of closeness in crowded conditions such as subway rush hours, the Westerner becomes immobile and acts as if the other person did not exist, as if he were a "nonperson."

Personal distance is the typical distance separating members of a group not accustomed to huddling together. Close personal distance for most Americans is from 18 to 30 inches; it may best be described as the distance that a wife may enter with impunity or no comment, but which she will resent when another woman approaches her husband. Far distance is arm's length, or 30 to 48 inches. The voice level is moderate, the face can be seen without distortion, but body heat and most odors are not sensed.

Social distance, from 4 to 7 feet, is the typical distance for business; far social distance, 7 to 12 feet, permits a view of the whole person. Close *public distance*, 12 to 25 feet, calls for a raised voice and a more formal style of speech. At far public distance, over 25 feet, speech is further slowed due to potential echo, and an ostensible barrier is placed between the people. Details become indistinct and a person such as an actor may deliberately exaggerate facial expressions in order to transmit nonverbal cues.

Different groups of people learn different concepts of personal space early in life (Aiello and Jones, 1971; Meisels and Guardo, 1969). Southern Europeans are more likely than Northern Europeans to move closer to other people with whom they are talking. What is social distance for one group is personal distance for another. The person may retreat to maintain what he finds is a comfortable social distance and nonverbally communicate rejection of the other person. This rejection may be conscious, as in the case of a young lady who deliberately did not wear gloves when going to meet a young man during the height of winter cold. That way she had to keep her hands in her pockets rather than give the young man, who was being sent a message, a chance to hold her hand.

Of greater import are unintended messages, particularly when they are communicated among representatives of groups of people. To quote Hall (1966, p. 149): "Olfaction occupies a prominent place in Arab life. . . . Arabs consistently breathe on people when they talk. . . . To the Arab, good smells are pleasing and a way of being involved with each other. To smell one's friend is not only nice but desirable, for to deny him your breath is to act ashamed. Americans, on the other hand, trained as they are not to breathe in people's faces, automatically communicate shame in trying to be polite [to Arabs]."

Eye Contact

Different postures, distances, and gestures alert people in the same groups to the feelings or likely responses of others. Small gestures may communicate without the use of explicit invitations, rejections, or other interpersonal stances that would put a person into an extreme position. Psychotherapists and poker players may consciously train themselves to be alert to changes in positions of the limbs, tones of voice, or pace of speech, while most people respond to such cues without trying to specify them. Many a young man has learned about the boundaries of space when he has wanted to move from an armchair (social space) to the sofa beside the young lady with whom he was talking (personal space) and realized that his change would clearly signal his desires.

Of the many possible gestures that might have been used, we have selected *eye contact*. Again, different groups of people have different patterns of eye contact, and major errors may be made when the meaning assigned by a gesture in one culture is assumed to hold in a different one. *Gestural languages are as learned as semantic ones.*

To start with, Hall (1966) has pointed out that

Englishmen in this country have trouble . . . when they want to interact. They never know for sure whether an American is listening. We, on the other hand, are equally unsure as to whether the English have understood us. . . . The English-man is taught to pay strict attention, to listen carefully, which he must do if he is polite and there are not protective walls to screen out sound. He doesn't bob his head or grunt or let you know he understands. He blinks his eyes to let you know that he has heard you. Americans, on the other hand, are taught not to stare. We look the other person straight in the eye without wavering only when we want to be particularly certain that we are getting through to him.

The gaze of the American directed toward his conversational partner often wanders from one eye to the other and even leaves the face for long periods. Proper English listening behavior includes immobilization of the eyes at social distance, so that whichever eye one looks at gives the appearance of looking straight at you. In order to accomplish this feat, the Englishman must be eight or more feet away [p. 134].

As the Englishman moves away to obtain the distance he needs, he may seem standoffish to an American.

In contrast to the Englishman is the Arab, who not only moves close but looks at others with an intensity that is challenging: "One Arab informant said that he was in constant hot water with Americans because of the way he looked at them without the slightest intention of offending. In fact, he had on several occasions barely avoided fights with American men who apparently thought their masculinity was being challenged because of the way he was looking at them [Hall, 1966, p. 151]." In America looking at and establishing eye contact is a way of expressing interest; two male strangers at a bar whose eyes meet typically look away rapidly. To hold another's gaze, whether male or female, is often a sign of sexual interest.

Rubin (1970) in validating a paper-and-pencil test of *romantic love* predicted that college dating couples who had high scores would spend more time gazing into one another's eyes than would couples who received a lower score. The prediction was substantiated. Efran (1968) found that visual interaction in an experimental setting was influenced both by the subjects' expectation of approval and the relative importance they attached to the people from whom they would receive approval.[5]

In terms of influence, then, eye contact is a major measure of interpersonal relationship and is affected by many situational factors. This important operant may have different modes of expression and communicate different messages

[5] Other studies of eye contact are by Argyle and Dean (1965); Exline, Gray, and Schuette (1965); Lefcourt, Rotenberg, Buckspan, and Steffy (1967); and Modigliani (1971).

depending on context and culture. A mouse may look at a king, but he should do it in the right way.

This last point has been made within a single culture in an experiment by Ellsworth and Carlsmith (1968). In the setting of a discussion of research on birth order effects, the interviewer, who did not know the birth order of the subjects, either looked at the subjects very frequently or not at all. This was the look or no-look variable. The experimenter made remarks about "firstborn" and "laterborn" children. These remarks were very one-sided, for example, that firstborns were dependent, unloved, generally incompetent, and so forth (the negative condition). In the positive condition, he made the reverse of these statements—firstborns were independent, lovable, competent, and so on. It was presumed a subject who was firstborn would have a negative experience with negative statements and a positive experience with favorable statements. Thus the amount of eye contact and the nature of the situation were evaluated together. The subjects later made confidential ratings of both the interview and interviewer. The findings on both variables (ratings of interview and interviewer) were the same: when the content was favorable, the interviewer's looking at the subject increased the favorability of his rating by subject; when the content was unpleasant, *not* looking at the subject led to increased favorability of the rating by the subject. In short, the effect of eye contact depended on the topic and was not in itself an intimate or pleasure-giving behavior. At times, it is courteous not to look.

Enclosed Space

In all man's interactions with meaningful spaces—but especially those in which he has a role as creator—it is hard if not downright foolish to separate cause and effect in the *structure*. A middle-class American thinks of home as a dining room, bedroom, living room, family room, study, kitchen, and so on; and while there are variations among families, in general there is a clear idea of where and when each member of the family or visitor may go. Separate rooms for various family functions are a relatively recent invention dependent upon heating systems and other architectural and technological innovations. Hall (1966, p. 97) has stated that rooms having fixed functions were introduced at the start of the eighteenth century. Prior to that time rooms opened into each other rather than onto a hallway, and as they moved from one space to another, people went through each other's rooms. Whether differentiation of family roles—such as children not being treated as young adults—can be related to such a change in the room structure is disputed. More easily accepted are indications that Americans express a desire for privacy in terms of their rooms, that is, physical cues, and need not use the personal, nonverbal expressions of privacy necessary for people in other cultures. Whether at home or work, a middle-class American may close his door to indicate that he does not wish to be disturbed.

The layout of an office building or home may foster or hinder interaction among people. "Increasingly, the designer's immediate clients are not the future inhabitants or users of his structures, but private developers, public administrators, corporation committees, and other intermediary agents. The actual user-clients are often unidentified until the designs are developed and, when they are known, cannot specify their own requirements." [Craik, 1970, p. 18]." The environment of a large high-rise, low-cost urban redevelopment may be at severe variance with the patterns of the people who will live there. The builders have a model of the behavioral pattern or "personality" of those who will inhabit their structures; the further this model is from reality, the greater will be the adjustments necessary for the inhabitants and the greater their discontent—as evidenced by behavior in many urban "housing developments."

The second point is that the inhabitants will try to adjust the structures to their living patterns. There is, however, a limit to which brick and board can be modified. A city neighborhood may be functionally like a small village. Kin and friends are close by; one's language is spoken in shops that stock the foods one knows how to cook. A person living in a particular neighborhood in Boston or New York may rarely move more than ten blocks away from his home. When urban renewal occurs, the effect on women may be particularly great: patterns of socialization on stairwell, stoop, and street are broken, along with mutually supportive relationships. (Fried, 1963; Fried and Gleicher, 1970; Gans, 1960).

In enclosed spaces such as offices and housing, people who like each other are likely to move closer. Conversely, people who move closer are likely to come to like each other—especially when they are similar and choice is restricted. People who are geographically close increase in interaction and liking in situations as varied as offices, military barracks, student housing, and dormitories (Festinger, 1951; Festinger, Schachter, and Back, 1950; Gutman, 1970; Priest and Sawyer, 1967; Wells, 1965).

Furniture Arrangement

While considerable anecdotal material is available on the effects of urban renewal and massive changes in the environment dealing with transportation or other industries, little experimentation is available in manipulation of variables for which there is a major capital investment. At this point in the development of the field, experiments are likely to deal with far more modest aspects of the environment—notably the arrangement of furniture in hospital wards and classrooms. To what extent the fact that students and psychiatric patients are also relatively passive, unorganized, dependent, captive, available populations influences the choice of research settings is not known. The theory advanced in this volume would argue that the environmentalist's choice has not been made by chance.

Among outstanding observations of the use of space are those of Esser, Chamberlain, Chapple, and Kline (1965) and Mehrabian and Diamond (1971). Sommer (1969) has brought together his own classic work in this area. After a hospital had spent considerable money on renovation, the patients (older women) interacted little with each other. Sommer noted that the chairs in the day room were set against the walls, a design that is traditional in institutions and makes life easier for the janitors when cleaning and the nurses when looking for patients. In addition, this arrangement permitted traffic to move rapidly through the ward hallway. Such a side-by-side arrangement, however, is likely to reduce conversation. People can stare straight ahead and avoid eye contact, while conversation requires their turning their bodies toward the other person.

Sommer's eventual solution involved the irregular spacing of tables in the center of the room to encourage people to sit close to and view each other. Not too many tables were used, so that sitting with another person was encouraged. The tables had magazines and flowers placed on them. Both brief and sustained interactions increased dramatically (see Sommer, 1969, p. 85, table 4).

Another situation in which participation and conversation is considered desirable is the classroom. The typical school layout has students facing the teacher; the students may be packed together, but the teacher has space to move. This design is similar to that of a theater and is likely to hinder student-initiated interaction, especially when class size moves over forty. This arrangement puts a barrier of space between teacher and students and casts the teacher as the active agent who must lead, entertain, and take responsibility for the passive students. The imposition of such public distance leads to slow and ponderous speech. Sommer (1969, pp. 111–119) has reported work that indicated a strong trend for students at the front of the room to participate more than students in the back and for students in the center to participate more than those on the sides. Students may exercise some self-selection in terms of where they sit. And seating probably has some effect on the teacher in terms of his prior experience and his focus for recognizing students, as well as probably having a major positional effect on eye contact. The entire question of classroom layout has been reopened by the proponents of "open" education. The impact of the spatial layout on behavior in the classroom is discussed in Chapter 14.

Sommer (1969, pp. 20–25) has also discussed leadership. Leaders in group situations such as a jury or college committees, generally sit at the head of the table. This provides optimal eye contact. In jury situations, upper-status people are more likely to select the head of the table, and a person who sits in this position is more likely to be elected foreman, to participate in the discussion, and to be evaluated later as having made the most significant contributions to the task of the group. Further support for these ideas has come from Hastorf (1965) and Pellegrini (1971). The former found similar effects in terms of amount of conversation and evaluated degree of contribution in a situation in which he manipulated, through selective reinforcement, the amounts different people spoke. While the person's prior history (for example, social class and confidence in the situation) interacts with the position he takes, his position in the room affects his behavior and others' responses to him.

Closeness and Likability

If *self-disclosure* is a behavior valued for itself or as part of psychotherapy, then conditions which will enhance it are worth specifying in the same manner as increased participation in classrooms. Jourard and Friedman (1970) found a combination of "experimenter modeling" and "light touch" as they guided the subject to the chair as most effective in obtaining the target behavior of self-disclosure. Hasse and Di Mattia (1970) showed pictures of four seating arrangements in counseling to administrators, counselors, and patients. The major finding was that administrators preferred an arrangement of two chairs facing each other with a desk intervening far more than did counselors, who liked it considerably less than the three other arrangements, each of which reduced physical barriers between interviewer and interviewee.

The task influences the preferred seating pattern. Sommer (1969, p. 62, fig. 3) had students rate six types of seating arrangements at six-person, rectangular tables. People conversing with each other led to selection of people sitting together at the corners or facing each other across the table; people cooperating to sitting next to each other; and people working separately (coacting) to sitting diagonally across from each other. These locations make sense to us as members of the same culture, because we associate distance and eye contact with the task at hand.

The attitude change induced by a friendly or hostile speaker is affected by his distance (1 to 2, 4 to 5, or 14 to 15 feet) from the recipient of the message. In an experiment by Albert and Dabbs (1970) the further away from the subject the speaker was, the more effective he was; the most interesting finding was that when the "hostile" speaker was close, his effect was negative in terms of attitude change in the direction he asserted.

The most extensive and rigorous series of experimental studies on the communicative aspects of nonverbal cues has probably been carried out by Mehrabian (1968a, 1968b, 1969, 1971). The person's degree of relaxation in arms and legs, forward or backward lean of body, standing or sitting, head raised or lowered, and the like may indicate liking for the other person and the assessment of status relative to him.

Mehrabian (1970, esp. pp. 64–77) has noted that verbal and nonverbal messages may disagree with each other; for example, a woman's hesitant "No" combined with certain nonverbal gestures may mean, Oh! Yes! The presence of more than one channel of communication may lead to confusion. This confusion may occur in cross-cultural situations (such as those discussed by Hall in the preceding section), in which information is misinterpreted because the same cues have different meanings or in one's own culture because the person contradicts himself in the messages he sends. Because nonverbal communication is informal and rarely explicitly taught except to some actors, salesmen, and therapists (Little, 1965), it is sometimes given great weight in the evaluation of what a person is "really" communicating.

Mehrabian and Ferris (1967) found that attitudes communicated facially were a stronger influence on "liking" than attitudes expressed vocally (tone of voice), which in turn were stronger than the words themselves. There are two possible therapeutic uses of these types of data. The first use, in a diagnosis of a person's social troubles, may lead to the discovery that the person is sending messages that are confusing and annoying or that reward behavior in an unintended manner. The second use is as an aid in influencing their clients. When not used systematically or intentionally, the different channels may lead to experimenter effects as noted by R. Rosenthal (see Chapter 8); when used intentionally, they may be added to the manipulations reviewed by Goldstein, Heller, and Sechrest (1966) in their suggestions for applying the material of social psychology to psychotherapy.

Given such potential purposes, questions that may be answered experimentally arise about the ability to encode or send messages by tone of voice and facial expression and ability to decode or interpret accurately such messages. Once messages are established and the most important cues identified, training programs may be established to improve the skill (operationally defined as encoding and decoding more effectively). An example of work required in this program is an article by Zeidel and Mehrabian (1969), who had subjects tape record the words *maybe* and *really* while expressing five degrees of like and dislike of an imagined addressee. At the same time photographs were taken. Later, other subjects judged this material as communicating positive, negative, or neutral attitudes. Among the results was the finding that the facial channel was generally more effective than the vocal channel; that negative attitudes were usually more effectively communicated than positive attitudes; and that females were better at communicating negative attitudes, while males were somewhat better at communicating positive attitudes.

Closeness and Intrusion

Physical proximity, like eye contact, may communicate negative as well as positive responses. At an anecdotal level, this has been illustrated by Hall's story of the Arab in the hotel lobby. Violation of spatial boundaries is a violation of social expectations. Sommer (1969, p. 30) noted this duality in the work of one of his students, who found that students given praise sat closest to his chair, ones interviewed neutrally next, and ones given stress instructions farthest away. Frankel and Barrett (1971) have investigated this effect in terms of whites reacting to black males. Kinzel (1970) has reported the fascinating and useful finding that violent prisoners showed far larger *body-buffer zones* than nonviolent prisoners.

Another of Sommer's students (1969, p. 35) investigated social expectations about space in a college library setting. When the reading room was empty, the social expectation was that a person would sit at an empty table rather than at one which another person was seated. Using the next person entering the library as a control, the investigator found that sitting next to or across from the experimental subject led to the experimental group's departure sooner than the departure of control subjects. Yet only one of 80 students asked the experimenter to move over. Discomfort—which Sommer also observed with psychiatric patients and to some extent with invasion of visual space (staring)—seemed to be a distinct influence, but sitting at the same table with someone else was not against formal rules, so that there was no justification for overt complaint.

In other studies Sommer (1969, pp. 52–56) investigated the defense of chairs by the leaving of articles. When the reading room was filled to "high density," an object that was personal and had dollar value had a strong effect on keeping a chair vacant when left as a marker, compared to the use of no marker or impersonal, littertype markers. Magazines piled neatly in front held a vacant chair for 77 minutes, while the same magazines randomly scattered held the chair for only 32 minutes.

"Keeping one's distance," is a colloquial expression of respect or of dislike. This may refer to the barrier of public space; the better and larger space that usually coincides with improved status; the respect a guest has for his host's space; or a measure of aversion, as in isolation for disease or segregation of minorities. Just as a stressful interview led to increased distance from the questioner, so designation of a person as "stigmatized," such as being an epileptic, may lead to an increased physical distance being maintained (Kleck, et al., 1968).

Population Density

Observation of different species in the field and under experimental conditions (Calhoun, 1962; Dubos, 1965, esp. pp. 100–109) has led to a finding inconsistent with Malthus' theory of population limitation. The upper limit of population does not seem to be set so much by food (as Malthus postulated) as by the effect of *crowding* or the disruption of patterns of behavior that may be largely instinctive as in rodent or learned as in primates. The disruptions of patterned behavior are stressful as measured by enlargement of the adrenals.

A direct extrapolation from nonhumans to humans is never safe, but it seems reasonable that undermanned and overmanned situations lead to different pressures and opportunities for individuals. Barker (1968, esp. pp. 178–205) has presented theory and data on this point, particularly as it refers to a school situation. Human crowding is likely to disrupt the traditional patterns of attaining goals and to lead to new, nonspatial ways of attaining privacy and status. For example, in the New York rush hour, other people are treated as if they do not exist—as if they are nonpersons—even when they are in the zone of intimate space. One of the worst things a person can do in a packed subway train is to apologize to another because this act recognizes the other's existence.

In one of the rare studies attempting to test these ideas in a laboratory setting, Skolnick, et al. (1971) placed undergraduate volunteers in an analogue of an "urban condition," a dense crowd with 8 square feet per person, or in a "non-urban condition," with 16 square feet per person. The results suggested that the behavior of subjects in the urban environment was "fragmented and that they resisted organization," whereas in the nonurban environment the students remained cohesive and well organized:

> In the crowded group, subjects made claims to territory, engaged in aggressive games and activities, and failed to maintain clean surroundings. Another detrimental aspect was the habituation of subjects to their adverse environmental conditions. Despite the hot, crowded, and stale atmosphere, most subjects remained for the entire experiment, and on a post-experimental questionnaire indicated their reluctance to leave and their willingness to participate longer. By comparison, subjects in the uncrowded group made no territorial claims, engaged in creative, non-aggressive inter-personal activities, and adequately maintained clean living conditions [Skolnick et al., 1971, p. 15].

The authors concluded that their data were consistent with the hypothesis that high population density and crowding have detrimental effects on human behavior. Griffitt and Veitch (1971) also found that hot and crowded conditions negatively affected interpersonal liking.

Another approach to the relationship between density and behavior has come from a field study of room density and user satisfaction (Sommer and Becker, 1971). The investigators used a single classroom and determined the effects of the considerable variation in the number of people using it and the satisfaction the users felt. The method of investigation involved the collection of ratings from 32 separate classes ranging in size from 5 to 22, meeting in a room with 22 chairs over a period of four years. The rating scales concerned all aspects of room environment such as ventilation, lighting, and storage areas. The results indicated a significant relationship between the population density and dissatisfaction with the physical aspects of the room. The lower the number of students in the classroom, the greater the overall satisfaction with the room. Sommer and Becker concluded that an "ecological perspective will require concepts of people-in-situations rather than of people on the one hand and situations on the other [p. 417]."

Finally, based on a survey of existing animal and human research and their own survey of various community areas in Chicago, Galle, Gove, and McPherson (1972) have concluded that "overcrowding may have a serious impact on human behavior and that social scientists should consider overcrowding when attempting to explain a wide range of pathological behaviors [p. 29]."

Ecological Psychology

We live in physical and cultural environments as much as we do in environments of earth, air, fire, and water. We are likely to become cognizant of environmental variables only when a change in them affects our behavior. At the present time increased industrialization and improved communications have led to a public awareness and to a general and deep-felt call for a change in national priorities.[6] What is meant by goals and priorities is what we want, what we will work for, and what is reinforcing. In largest measure, the physical and social environments are the contexts of reinforcement. Knowledge of these environments tell us "who, what, when, where, and why."

Barker (1968, pp. 2–4) has made two relevant points about man in his environment. The first is that while chemists and entomologists know much about the distribution and action of chemicals and insects, respectively, *in the general environment*, psychologists who have sought the control provided by the laboratory know little about the distribution and rate of occurrence of punishment, hostility, friendliness, frustration, reward, and the like *in the natural social setting*. Barker's second point is that in many psychological experiments and theories the environment is treated in a passive manner, and man acts in accordance with a program he carries around within himself (or what has traditionally been called "personality"). "But research at the Midwest Field Station and elsewhere indicates that when we look at the environment of behavior as a phenomenon worthy of investigation for itself, and not as an instrument for unraveling the behavior-relevant programming within persons, the situation is quite different. From this viewpoint the environment is seen to consist of highly structured, improbable [non-chance–ed] arrangements of objects and events which coerce behavior in accordance with their own dynamic patterning [Barker, 1968, p. 4]."

As Barker (1968) has stated: "The ecological environment of a person's molar behavior, the molar environment, consists of bounded, physical-temporal

---

[6] One effect already observable is the dramatic change and controversy in the last three to five years in attitudes and laws about abortion and dissemination of birth control information and supplies. The greater openness about sex and the greater emphasis on personal sensory experiences may also be associated in some measure with increased population density.

locales and variegated but stable patterns in the behavior of people en masse [p. 11]." Examples are a road as a track (physical attribute) for travel by people (behavioral attribute), a store as a place where goods (physical attributes) are kept and sold (behavioral attributes), and a park as a piece of ground (physical attribtute) kept for recreation (behavorial attribute). Abstractions such as a mile, a minority group, and a bureaucratic system are not ecological units.

Patterns of behavior are characteristic of people in a behavior setting and persist even though participants change. For example, a store, a church service, or a ball game leads to similar behaviors regardless of specific individuals. Conversely, the behavior of individuals changes markedly as they move from one behavior setting to another. An example would be the behaviors exhibited by a child as he went from reading class to recess to music class. In typical psychological parlance, the specific behavior that will be emitted can probably be *predicted more from the situation* than from individual differences among people in that situation.

Barker (1968) has provided careful rules for detailing the behavior settings of a locale and for determining a variety of characteristics. From his survey methods, it is possible to answer questions as to how many settings a person may and does enter, his degree of activity or participation in the setting, and the activities possible in the setting. This type of data provides a systematic description of the behavior (at least in public settings) of an entire social entity (for example, a town). It is possible to compare one entity (town) with another, on the number of settings (complexity), the percentage of settings devoted to religion, business, or artistic pursuits, and the number of settings that have the same programs (cultural similarity). It is also possible to describe systematically rather than impressionistically the range and degree of participation (penetration) in different settings associated with a person's age, physical handicap, sex, or race. Many of the tragedies of urban renewal and environmental planning could be avoided if the designer's model of man was checked against the realities of people's behavior.

Through a knowledge of physical and social environments and methods of teaching the patterns of appropriate behavior in that environment, a great amount of human activity can be dealt with effectively. This approach should provide the theories, data, and decisions for a psychology of activity satisfying to both psychologists and citizens.

LAST WORD

We conclude this chapter on environmental influences with a quotation from Jerome D. Frank, an observer of the American environment. We cite this passage because it is an able review of the impact of some of the physical aspects of our environment on behavior. Frank made these observations in 1966, before it was fashionable to focus on the environmental dangers in our society. And Frank linked his concerns with the role of the influencer by observing his own society as a physician and psychologist and attempting to sound the alarm for dangers of which many individuals were not yet aware. As Frank (1966) put it:

Our galloping technology has created or aggravated problems of unemployment, urbanization, racial and international tensions, war, overpopulation, and many others. . . . But "social disease" in my title refers to the other, old-fashioned medical meaning of the term—namely, illness caused by the conditions of social living. My particular training has made me sensitive to the direct effects on life and health of man's reckless conquest of the environment, a topic that has been largely neglected by social scientists. The most obvious reason for this neglect is that the problems present themselves as medical or technological. My thesis is that, although the new menaces to life and health may be caused by new machines and poisons, the remedies lie mainly in the realm of human behavior. . . . In its medical meaning, the term "social disease" referred to illnesses contracted, directly or indirectly, by misbehavior, and therefore blameworthy. Most commonly, of course, it was a euphemism for veneral disease, but it was also used for illnesses like tuberculosis, presumably contracted by living under unhygienic conditions. These diseases were reprehensible because our forefathers blamed the slum dwellers for the circumstances under which they were forced to live. . . . Of the social diseases caused by galloping technology, those caused by air pollution might be thought of as analogous to tuberculosis, whereas injuries and deaths caused by reckless driving—a voluntary, pleasurable, but disapproved activity—would be analogues of veneral disease. . . . Like their medical counterparts, technological social diseases can be acute or chronic. The most virulent and acute form, which fortunately has not yet broken out, would be modern war. The threat to survival posed by modern weapons is receiving so much agonized attention from most of us that there is no need to dwell on it. . . . I shall assume, without any really valid grounds, that humans will shackle the self-created monster of modern weapons before it is too late. Otherwise there would be no point in continuing with this address, which deals with the causes and cure of chronic forms of technological social disease. These are the subtle, insidious dangers that are the unwanted and incidental by-products of fabulous achievements in raising the level of human welfare. These dangers are at present more apparent in the United States because our society is the most technologically advanced, but in due course they are certain to plague all nations. . . . The dangers can be grouped into three categories: pollution of the living environment, the biosphere; accidents; and drugs. Let me start with the only brand new danger, of small consequence at present but potentially one of the greatest—the pollution of the biosphere by radioactive products of nuclear power plants . . . some living creatures accumulate certain isotopes which become increasingly concentrated as they move up the food chain. For example, algae concentrate radioactive zinc to about 6,000 times that of the surrounding water. The algae are eaten by bluegill fish, in whose bones the concentration is about 8,700 times that of the water. Fortunately, humans do not eat bluegill bones, but who knows what edible tissues will be found to store other radioactive substances in the same way? . . . Dangers of the same type are created by pesticides. In terms of the amount of chemical per unit of body weight, most pesticides are equally toxic to all living creatures, though immunity for some can be built up in time. They kill insects and not men simply because the former receive enormously greater doses in proportion to their weight. . . . Furthermore, some pesticides, like radioactive isotopes, cause cancer in animals on repeated exposure, and some are suspected of damaging the germ plasm, so that their deleterious effects, though long delayed, may eventually be very serious. . . . A more serious, immediate menace to health is atmospheric pollution from factories and automobiles. It is estimated that 133,000,000 tons of aerial garbage are dumped into the atmosphere of the United States each year—more than the weight of our annual steel production. . . . A particularly subtle form of air pollution, which may have the most inexorable effects, is the slow increase in carbon dioxide in the atmosphere produced by industrial use of fossil fuels. This blocks the radiation of heat energy back to outer space, so that the temperature of the earth is gradually rising. The average temperature today is 8% higher than it was in 1890. This, of course, could be due to other causes. In any case, if it keeps up, among other unpleasant consequences, it will melt the polar ice caps, flooding the world's seaboards. . . . Accidents have become the leading cause of death from ages 1 to 37 and the fourth cause of death at all ages, being exceeded only by heart disease, cancer and stroke. Their prominence obviously results, in part, from the sharp reduction in natural causes of death, especially in the younger age group, but in absolute figures they claim an impressive toll . . . floods of new medications are being put on the market. Despite increasingly stringent laws, some that cause serious damage to health or even death get past the guards. Examples were the contaminated strain of polio vaccine, and, more recently, the malformed babies caused by an apparently harmless sleeping medicine, thalidomide. . . . Finally, there is the growing menace of drugs that alter states of consciousness, including sedatives, stimulants, mood-lifters and so-called psychotropic drugs such as LSD. Most of these drugs were thought to be harmless when first introduced. . . . A further difficulty in identifying the damage to health caused by noxious environmental agents is that illnesses have multiple causes, so in any given case it is hard to single out what really is to blame. If an elderly man with chronic lung disease dies during a heavy smog, who can say for certain that the smog was the cause of death? In other terms, statistical variations in various environmental and internal factors are so great that the true noxious agent may be hidden by them. . . . Finally, although the damage done by environmental poisons is constantly increasing, the increments are very small compared to the base level. So, in accord with a well-known psychophysiological law, they do not rise above the threshold of awareness. Humans may be in the same plight as a frog placed in a pan of cold water, which is very slowly heated. If the rise in temperature is gradual enough, he will be boiled without ever knowing what happened to him [pp. 1–7].

14

The Influence of Formal Education
on Behavior

Society is so organized that the formal educational process—involving living in classrooms for up to six hours a day from roughly age four to twenty—is the major systematic vehicle by which people are prepared to enact social roles. The educational process has two aspects; *what* shall be taught and *how* it shall be taught. The former deals with values and goals, the latter with methods of attaining these goals. Both aspects are demonstrably subject to many forms of social influence.

SELECTING GOALS

Silberman (1970) has defined education as "the deliberate or purposeful creation, evocation, or transmission of knowledge, abilities, skills, and values. To emphasize the deliberate and the purposeful is not to deny that non-deliberate influences may be more powerful; it is to assert that man cannot depend upon a casual process of learning. Unless men are to be forced to rediscover all knowledge for themselves, they must be educated, which is to say that education, to be education, must be purposeful [p. 6]." In other words, the first step in the educational process, as in all social influence, is the value decision, implicit or explicit, as to the goals, objectives, or target behavior of the process.

There is a relationship between broad social objectives and what takes place in the educational institution. There is considerable debate in our society about this relationship at all school levels but particularly in college. What is the purpose of college? Is it to prepare one for a job, to develop a well-rounded person, to alter the college and the town in which it is located, to prepare social revolutionaries, to dispense a "liberal education" (whatever that may be defined as), to provide a preparation for graduate studies, to help one become all one is capable of or simply to do one's thing?

There is less obvious dispute at the elementary school level. The goals seem to be more clearly expressed in terms of behavioral objectives such as ability to read specific material or to perform specific arithmetic procedures. Although educators insist that much more is learned in the classroom than the specific content of reading, writing, and arithmetic, there is no clear behavioral objective or measure for these other goals, which are often expressed as attitudes, morality, human concern, awareness, good citizenship, and patriotism. Skinner (1968, p. 18) has suggested that appeal to such indistinct goals may indicate classroom failure: a vague, unmeasurable goal is appealed to in the absence of a measure of attainment. Frequently, broad social objectives and specific content merge. For example, the early achievements of the Soviet Union in the space race led the United States and President John F. Kennedy to set a national goal of a man on the moon in a decade and a change in curriculum that emphasized achievement in science and mathematics. The recognition of the pervasive deleterious treatment of blacks has led to a rewriting of history books to include their contribution and viewpoints. In the history of education in the United States (for example, Rudolph, 1962), what seems most striking is that there never has been a period when education was not in ferment and changing. Kuhn's paradigm (1970) of scientific revolutions may be translated into the educational setting: new goals (revolutions), procedures, and paradigms are formulated rapidly as "normal" education (the status quo) is found wanting and no longer doing its job. What the educational objectives were and who selected them provides a clear glimpse of the larger social currents of each era.

361

The view of *what is a good education* and *who shall receive it* has moved from a reading knowledge adequate for the Bible to liberal, technical, and professional education, so that each person may not only contribute more effectively to society but also enrich his personal life. The curriculum of universities has moved from the preparation of ministers and educated gentlemen capable of understanding the nuances of philosophy and literary allusion to the preparation of persons trained in scientific theory and application. The curriculum has moved from a unified education in classics to diversity and specialization and to a return to some general shared body of knowledge obtained in survey courses. The organization of the university has moved from a few teachers to a complex of departments, institutes, and schools specializing in specific areas or domains (Barzun, 1968).

Concepts about the *specific nature of goals* directly affect the behavior of the teacher. As long as there was satisfaction with the current store of information, *transmitting* accumulated information was the duty of the teacher. The teacher helped the student learn (at times memorize) the wisdom of the ancients. Education was a means of conserving the past and passing it on to the next generation. Such a view is usually associated with a relatively stable stratified society in which one's accent and one's associations are strong prerequisites for social position. The teacher as a channel of transmission could be—and, in Hellenic civilization was—a slave; as happens all too often in current elementary and secondary education, he may be a servant of the system, whose intellectual and personal innovation is discouraged.

If the proper goal of an educational institution such as a university is the generation of *new information*, the teacher assumes a more professional role. In his teaching he emphasizes methods of data collection rather than data already collected. He is a creator rather than a transmitter. His status is enhanced. (The change is analogous to that in plastic art in which the role of the artist changed from that of an artisan reproducing forms of reality to one of creating new forms and expressing his needs rather than satisfying a function whether that of the church or of Madison Avenue.) The teacher now demands to be evaluated in terms of his profession, that is, by peers and specialists, rather than superiors at his institution. Because he is visible outside his place of work, he is more capable of moving from it and less dependent on it.[1] In many ways, he is an entrepreneur, working for himself and dependent on his own efforts. His teaching *load* (an indication of a view of information transmission) is reduced and he may restrict himself to "better" students (those who need less instruction). Criteria of advancement come to depend not upon how hard he works in terms of hours, but upon what he accomplishes in a nonclassroom setting.

This model is breaking down at the present time. Rather than being a con-

[1] The influence of economics on behavior is illustrated by the degree to which this statement does not hold during an academic recession such as that of the late 1960s and early 1970s.

servation of the past or preparation for future accomplishment, education is being valued as a meaningful *experience* in itself; and this outlook has been associated with an increasing emphasis on personal satisfaction and student voice in policy. Other correlates are an emphasis on the teacher as a person rather than as a servant of society or scholar.

To whom is the teacher responsible—the parents and legislature who pay him, his scholarly profession, or his students? May he teach material that his employers consider subversive? May he require his students to read material they consider irrelevant?

The goal of education is to offer experiences that will change people in a "good" direction. Good may be defined theologically, and from this definition deductions may be logically made about course content and student decorum. Or good may be defined as success in a particular society at a given time; and again curriculum and approved social behavior will follow. Whether education is *preparation for* the good life or *is* the good life itself makes a great difference and is an example of how the nature of theories affect behavior.

Concepts of Man and Educational Procedures

In Chapters 10–12, we have noted how theories of personality have a direct effect on the alteration of behavior considered undesirable and hence change-worthy. All therapy is teaching, even though all teaching may not be therapeutic. We might say that psychotherapy is aimed at reducing disruptive behavior and formal education at increasing prosocial behavior, although the distinctions overlap. The point, however, is that both education and psychotherapy apply theories of personality in general and theories of learning in particular.

If ideas are real, continuing, ultimate entities, then they may be considered to reside in all people and only the correct conditions are required for their retrieval. This concept is illustrated by Plato in his presentation of the Socratic method. The teacher is a midwife who helps draw out but is not responsible for the product. This concept is almost diametrically opposed to the associationist position, which considers the person at birth to be a tabula rasa—a clean slate. The material is presented by experience and by contiguity and other arrangements. In his novel *Emile*, Rousseau advanced a theory in which much of the teacher's arrangement of material was done in an effort to preserve the pupil's accuracy of impression from the corruption (prejudice, in its meaning of pre-judgment) of societal formulations. Stimulation, preparation, and enjoyment were major elements in the pedagogical concepts of Maria Montessori that are having a renewed usage today.

An interesting combination of both a belief in the *rational aspects of thinking* and an emphasis on contexts and *learning to learn* rather than the specific subject matter may be found as a result of the impact of John Dewey. His successors (for example, progressive schools from Betrand Russell's venture to Summerhill) emphasize the attitude or relationships of the student to his teachers, to his peers, and to his material. They believe that the individual has a *natural drive* to know, experiment, manipulate, and—if no unfortunate emotion has intervened—to master and conceptualize. The child develops by experiencing; he will organize, select, and abstract on his own—not unlike the infant who while going on binges of certain foods eventually self-selects a favorite diet. Therefore, the teacher must be a caterer, not a dietitian. Any obstacle to the student's natural inclination will lead to emotional "blocks," while a free spirit will eventually learn whatever is required in a reasonabe and enthusiastic manner. Another corollary of progressive theories is that feelings about school, teachers, peers, and learning are more important than specific curricula.

Another investigator who has had considerable influence on education is the educational sociologist. These specialists have observed the behavior of people in typical American cities such as Middletown (Lynd and Lynd, 1929) and Yankee City (Warner and Lunt, 1941). To the extent that the goal of education is to shape children's behavior to *that which already exists* in a given community, these sociological observations are of importance.

Finally, a new interdisciplinary group of observers is having considerable impact on the current American scene. These are the sociological-educational-journalist-essayist group of critic-practitioners such as Goodman (1960), Holt (1969), Illitch (1971), Kozol (1967), and Silberman (1970). The focus of their *social criticism* is the classroom in the context of a dissatisfied society.

PSYCHOLOGY AND EDUCATION

One may view the role of the psychologist as influencer in the educational system in terms of measurement and in terms of manipulation. The classic aspect of psychological measurement is the work by Binet and Simon (1913) in France and Terman (1916) in the United States on intelligence testing. One problem was how to distinguish between the student who was bright but lazy and the one who was hard-working but stupid. It was felt that different types of student should be treated differently. The role of the psychologist was that of selector; he helped decide *who* would be taught, not *how*. Placement by testing has only recently been challenged; the testing movement, *when uncritically and incorrectly applied*, may have done major injustice to minority students and those not fluent in English.

Of the many recent textbooks on personality, only one (Sarason's 1966 edition) contained a chapter referring to the "school experience." Sarason points out that if we consider a variable such as test anxiety, it is insufficient to "consider only what the student brings with him to the classroom [p. 474]." It is necessary to inquire into the characteristics of the *classroom as a stimulus*. Recent efforts have focused on the role of the teacher in the classroom and his relationship with individual students. Sarason suggests that the teacher-student relationship be viewed as an analogue of the parent-child relationship. But the model the teacher provides must also include some of the characteristics of the psychiatrist and scholar. "The roles of teachers are to a large extent determined by the society in which they work and by their own upbringing. As the values and goals of society change, so do the tasks assigned to the teachers [Sarason, 1966, p. 475]."

Thus, in approaching behavior influence in the classroom, one must first look at the teacher and the social influences on the teacher. The view that the educational institution *shapes behavior* is usually not acceptable to the educator. Only with rare exceptions such as Montessori (1964) is there an acknowledgement of this kind of educational goal. For a considerable period of time the key educational concept was *readiness* (Cronbach, 1950), a trait concept.

The educator's guiding belief was that the child must grow and develop at his own pace, as if this pace were predetermined by some programmed maturational pattern which would unfold sometime. The task of the educator closely approximated the theory of laissez faire: Don't get in the way, just let the child develop. This view did represent progress over the previous emphasis on a rigid, structured, authoritarian technique. The laissez-faire view was "child-centered" and hence more "humanitarian"; its underlying concept was that the child would do the right thing "naturally," as in Rousseau's *Emile* or Carl Rogers' self-actualization.

In many ways the concept of readiness in education is analogous to the concept of sickness in deviant behavior. Both place emphasis on an internal process—in the first instance a normal one, in the second a pathological one—which serves as an explanatory concept for current student behavior and teacher inactivity. For example, visualize a first-grade child who does not sit still and fidgets during reading instruction period and hence is labeled a *nonreader*. During the reading period another first grader gets out of his seat and physically bothers the others in the class, even hitting his neighbor. In the first instance, the teacher labels the child as "immature" and thus not ready for reading instruction; the teacher recommends that he be held back from promotion with the view that he will become more mature and "ready" for reading with time. In the second case, the teacher recommends that the disruptive child be placed in a class for emotionally disturbed children and be seen with his parents by a psychiatrist. The teacher has labeled this child's behavior as *sick* and hence in need of attention from society's appropriate healers. In neither case does the teacher assume responsibility.

In both instances the teacher's explanatory concepts have aversive consequences for the child and his family. These cases illustrate how *a theory of learning or personality implicitly guides the teacher's behavior.* Instead of observing the classroom situation for the stimulus conditions which are the major determinants of behavior and which the teacher should be able to manipulate, the teacher blames the child's behavior on maturation, adjustment, or intelligence—that is, on traits of the child. In addition, the teacher gives the child information about his stimulus value to other people: thus, the child is taught a role and label of self.

Our task is to focus on the *teacher as behavior influencer, how his behavior is influenced, and how he, in turn, influences*. First, the teacher influences role models. It may be argued that the middle-class teacher is a poor role model for the child of a deprived background, but one could respond that the goal of society is to mold all its members into a homogeneous middle-class value system. This goal implies that a standard set of behaviors is optimum for all children. This belief has been typical of most parts of American society, but is no longer acceptable to an increasing proportion of the population, particularly in urban areas.[2]

Second, the teacher is a planner of social environments. How he organizes the classroom and distributes various materials the children will work with will alter the behavior of the children. This role of the teacher is illustrated in our discussion of the open classroom later in this chapter.

What are the influences upon the behaviors of the teacher and student in the classroom? We have seen how certain general theoretical concepts on the nature of man influence the teacher's approach to his task. In our examination of the influences of theory on the teacher, it should be clear that we are dealing with three separate but overlapping sets of theories—those of *learning*, of *teaching*, and of *what* is to be learned or taught. The first theory is about a *process*, the second a *technology*, and the third a *value* system.

Educational Philosophies

An educational philosophy that is influencing current techniques is called *learning by discovery*. Forerunners of learning by discovery include Jean-Jacques Rousseau, Maria Montessori, and John Dewey. A clear-cut definition is virtually impossible. The term "discovery" is often used to denote a presumed or guessed-at unobservable intervening cognitive event. Wittrock (1966) has pointed out that despite the strong claims for learning by discovery, "almost none of these claims has been empirically substantiated or even clearly tested in an experiment [p. 33]." As he has stated:

> Herein lies the crux of the dilemma among educational psychologists about discovery learning. When learning and discovery are measured by one event, discovery cannot be given as a cause for learning. It does no good to say tautologically that those who discover learn. For example, the desired result is an event named

---

[2] A scholarly documentation of this point in the area of child welfare is by Billingsley and Giovannoni (1972).

learning by discovery. The treatment designed to produce the result is also an event named learning by discovery. A tautological conclusion easily follows. The discovery learners learned by discovery, therefore their treatment was the better one, regardless of the data [p. 35].

In short, the conditions for the learning and the learning itself are lumped together.

A more useful approach is to deal with "conditions of learning" (Gagné, 1970). Gagné used this term as the title of a book in which he attempted to present knowledge about the *process* of learning that could be used in designing better education. Gagné defines learning as "a change in human disposition or capability which can be retained, and which is not simply ascribable to the process of growth [p. 3]" and focuses on dealing with *sets* of circumstances that exist when learning occurs. From his point of view, learning must be linked to a *design of instruction* after consideration of the different kinds of capabilities being learned.

Several investigators differentiate *theories of instruction* or teaching from theories of learning. As an example, DeCecco (1968) has argued that a theory of learning is broader than and basic to a theory of teaching. He has offered such a theory of teaching based upon Glaser's model (1965), which divides the teaching process into four components: instructional objectives, entering behavior, instructional procedures, and performance assessment. This model offers four steps which are analogous to the assessment procedures used in behavior modification.

Gage (1963) also has argued that to the extent that the instructional process is unique, integrated theories pertaining to teaching cannot be assembled merely by collating a series of subtheories on selected aspects of the process. Thus, he conceives of *instructional theories* as developing *alongide of* rather than by inference from theories in other behavioral sciences. Gage has asked for a theory of teaching that can answer three questions: How do teachers behave? Why do they behave as they do? and What are the effects of their behavior?

Gage and Unruh (1969) have made important points on the dichotomy between research on teaching and research on the relationship between learning theory and teaching. First, they have commented on the revolution in teaching *technology.*

A revolution in teaching is being fomented. If successful, it will overthrow the hegemony of the centuries-old pattern whereby one teacher and 20 to 40 pupils engage for most kinds of instruction in a teacher-dominated discourse. The revolutionary force is programmed instruction, broadly defined (Corey, 1967) as instruction in which objectives are described with special care and explicitness, behaviors are analyzed with much psychological sophistication, sequencing is based on an experimental approach, revisions are made after empirical evidence, instructional stimuli are carefully developed and controlled, frequent and explicit responding by the learner is procured, and relatively quick knowledge of results is provided the learner. If the revolution succeeds, the teacher will spend much less time each day with groups of students in time-honored ways, discussing, lecturing, tutoring, demonstrating, and so on. And such traditional activities will need to be justified rather than taken for granted [p. 3].

Another cleavage in approaches to teaching research is between describing the way teaching *is* (Jackson, 1966), and concern with improving and determining what teaching *ought to be* (Stolurow, 1965). The descriptive approach regards teaching as a realm worth studying simply because it exists and is sociologically fascinating. The second deals with teaching as something that needs to be improved because it is not as good as it ought to be. The first approach resembles that of the anthropologist neutrally studying cultures; the second, that of the inventor working on a better way to meet a practical need.

The protagonists of these approaches have difficulty understanding each other. The describers believe that the improvers tamper with humanistic values and do not understand the human condition. The improvers feel that the describers are indifferent to the inadequacies of the conventional classroom or are bent merely on improving knowledge of obsolescent forms. Describers have produced detailed analyses of what goes on in present-day classrooms. Improvers such as Glaser, Skinner, and Stolurow regard the present-day classroom as inconsistent with "known" facts about (individual) differences among learning situations, with the difficulties of appropriately structuring and sequencing subject matter in the heat of teacher-learner interaction, and with the needs of learners for a multitude of reinforcement contingencies.

Skinner (1968) has offered a view of learning and teaching that—for practical purposes—equates a theory of learning with a theory of teaching. According to Skinner, all of the traditional learning and teaching theories can be categorized by three expressions, each of which is incomplete in itself: learning by *doing*; learning from *experience*; and learning by *trial and error*. Skinner's own view of learning is expressed in his critique of these theories as each representing an essential part of the learning situation: learning by doing emphasizes the response; learning from experience emphasizes the occasion upon which the response occurs; and learning by trial and error emphasizes consequences. Skinner has argued that no one part can be studied *entirely* by itself and that all three parts must be recognized in formulating any instance of learning or effective teaching.

Acquiring knowledge is viewed as a process in which every new capability is built on a foundation established by previously learned capabilities. By this reasoning, one cannot argue that a child is not mature enough to learn any particular content: "A student is ready to learn something new when he has mastered the prerequisites; that is, when he has acquired the necessary capabilities through preceding learning. Planning for learning is a matter of specifying and ordering the prerequisite capabilities within a topic to be learned, and later perhaps among the topics that make up a 'subject' [Gagné, 1970, p. 27]."

Instructing involves analyzing the content of the material to be learned, so that it can be presented in sequence of difficulty, and then arranging the conditions of learning external to the learner. It is necessary to construct the conditions step by step, taking into account the requirements for retaining previous learning and the specific stimulus situation needed for the next stage of learning. Thus, instruction is quite intricate; it may be predesigned, as in a well-constructed textbook, workbook, or in a programmed teaching machine, or extemporaneously designed in the classroom by the teacher. Instruction may also be designed in terms of *planning the classroom environment so that certain kinds of learning experiences are likely to occur.* Implied in the process of specifying the conditions of learning are the choice of specific media of instruction and classroom materials, which are considered the resources for learning.

Atkinson (1968) has offered another approach in presenting a *mathematical model* for "optimizing" the learning process. Atkinson, a pioneer in setting up programs based upon computer-assisted instruction (CAI), has argued that a viable theory of instruction and a corresponding theory of learning will be an interactive enterprise with advances in each area influencing the concepts and data base of the other. He anticipates that CAI will be both a tool for research and a mode of instruction, from which will evolve newer concepts of learning theory as well as a corresponding theory of instruction. Silverman (1962) found that 48 out of 80 studies dealing with experimental manipulations of instructional programs *failed to obtain significant differences* among the treatments compared. Groen and Atkinson (1968) have argued that such equivocal results in the field of programmed instruction are due to the absence of a clearly formulated learning theory as well as to misapplication of statistics.

Another way of approaching the impact of learning theories and research on educational policies and planning is historical. The articles in the *Annual Review of Psychology* on various aspects of psychology offer a useful yearly review of research in this field (see Chapter 4). In the first volume, two articles were relevant to learning and its application in the educational system: Melton's chapter (1950) on learning and Cronbach's chapter (1950) on educational psychology. Melton cited much of the research in that period as influenced by the experimental psychologists Tolman, Hull, and Thorndike; and he identified the major theoretical differences of the time as "environmentalism" and "nativism." Cronbach pointed out that educational psychology had "broken the bonds which confined it to Thorndikean studies of drill and individual differences [p. 235]" and had moved from the *goal of efficiency* in formal education to the *goal of total socialization* of the individual. It is interesting to note again that in 1950 the central concept in educational theory was "readiness," which embraced "aptitude, maturation, motivation, and experiential background [Cronbach, 1950, p. 236]."

In recent years (1966 to 1973) there has been no *one* article on the topic of human learning and only one on educational psychology in the *Annual Review*. Instead a variety of chapters have discussed memory and verbal learning; instructional psychology; verbal learning and memory; the learning of psychomotor skills; perceptual learning; cognitive functions; operant conditioning and verbal learning; and the comparative psychology of learning.[3] This plethora of material reflects not only the increase in sheer volume of research but also growing diversity, disagreement, and controversy about the relationship between theories of learning and their application in the classroom.

ORGANIZATIONAL AND COMMUNITY INFLUENCES

We have started with the impact of theory on teacher behavior in the classroom. Before returning to the specifics in planning the classroom environment, we must briefly describe other important influences on the teacher as an influencer.

The situation in New York City is an example of how diverse community and organizational elements may affect education. Perhaps the unique feature of New York is the availability of documentation, the great complexity, and carrying of strife to its logical and illogical extremes.

The sociologist D. Rogers (1968) has investigated the impact of the policies and maneuvers of a centralized board of education on the behavior of the individual teacher and student. His study originally concerned desegration in the schools, but his observations illustrate the impact of an institution. An earlier study (Alison, 1951) had documented "the system's many weaknesses in the 1930s and forties. Political patronage in board-member selection, corruption among board members overly responsive to real estate and construction interests, anti-Semitism and racism among school officials, the Red-baiting of school officials (many of them highly competent and committed to improving ghetto schools), and the pedestrian nature of curriculum and instructional methods were among the system's main features [p. 4]."

Rogers (1968) was interested in the process of change in the organization: "Plans for changes in the public school system, and the implementation of such plans, are affected by the actions and attitudes of many 'constituencies,' ranging from professional groups inside the school system to community groups, real estate interests, and politicians. The Board of Education and the superintendent

---

[3] The personal function of most research in the area of learning is to meet a professional or career requirement, such as the doctoral dissertation, rather than to solve a problem. The worker does the sort of research that will be instrumental in attaining his goal; he does research that is safe and that parents and administrators permit. Therefore, the starting point of study is likely to be problems that arise from theoretical formulations and not from the classroom or a "natural setting."

act within what students of administration call 'zones of acceptance' or 'conceptions of legitimacy.' If the board is to implement new plans, it must mobilize support within the school system and in the community [p. 5]."

Rogers summarized the role of the centralized board as a source of influence as follows: "The system is a 'total institution' for its officials and they are preoccupied with its internal politics and status order. They are at the same time withdrawn from and often suspicious of or arrogant toward outsiders. Such comments as, 'We're tired of studies by people who have never taught in the system,' and 'Nobody could be effective as a superintendent unless he had been in the system for many years,' reflect this attitude . . . [p. 11]."

One of the many pressures on the teacher's performance in the classroom is the local community. An illustration of community pressure occurred in the New York City school system in 1968. The issues involved controversy over concepts of centralization and decentralization; a predominantly white teachers' union versus a predominantly black community; and community participation in curriculum decision making. Each side had its own version of the issues, and the controversy culminated in two teachers' strikes. These strikes illustrated how important an influence on the teacher as an influencer is the *social and political climate of the community*. In his review of the situation, Mayer (1969) began by stating that "the teacher strikes of 1968 seem to me the worst disaster my native city has experienced in my lifetime [p. 18]."

Prior to the late 1960s control of the New York City school system was held by a centralized board of education. In the early 1960s, the political climate resulted in a push for decentralization of the system to make the schools accountable to the community. By the mid-1960s, the proportion of black and Puerto Rican schoolchildren had passed 50 percent. The vast majority of the schoolteachers were recruited from the New York City colleges, which meant that they were primarily white, middle-class, and Jewish—with less than 10 percent black or Puerto Rican.

Ocean Hill, a school district in Brooklyn, was about 70 percent black and 25 percent Puerto Rican. The Ford Foundation selected this district to have a model decentralized, community controlled school program. At the same time activist elements in the community set up their own unofficial "People's Board of Education" in reaction to the citywide Board of Education. The teachers of the district were at first strongly behind decentralization but soon became disenchanted. A citywide strike of the teachers' union at the beginning of the 1967 school year over issues not directly related to the Ocean Hill controversy accentuated the rift between teachers and local community. When school resumed, so did an open conflict with the teachers, the Board of Education administrators, and the union on one side and the local school board and the students and parents of the community on the other. Eventually a second teachers' strike occurred, which was to last five weeks, with the major demand that the Ocean

Hill project be ended. By this time the issues of the controversy seemed to go far beyond local problems. The issues involved most of the social, political, religious, and racial controversies of the United States in the 1960s. The specific issues included whether the local board could fire or transfer tenured teachers (who were also union members) considered professionally capable but unsympathetic to community control. The local conflict was resolved by a series of compromises which did not really satisfy any of the parties involved.[4]

In short, the context of the teacher is the community, parents, the union, the bureaucracy, his own education, religion, and politics, as well as his classroom, students, and subject matter.

CULTURAL INFLUENCES ON EDUCATION

Education reflects the values of the society in which it takes place. An example is a report by Bronfenbrenner (1970), in which he has offered a cross-cultural comparison of American and Russian education. The major national difference which emerged from his study was the Russian focus on peer relationships at every stage of child development and education in contrast to the American focus on parent-child relations. In the classroom different kinds of behaviors are reinforced. The Russians focus on training for altruism, for group activities, and peer social criticism. In contrast, the American classroom emphasis is usually on competitive individual behavior and accomplishment.

We may examine further the influence of peers. Bowerman and Kinch (1959), working with several hundred students from the fourth to the tenth grades in the Seattle school system, studied age trends in the tendency of children to turn to parents or to peers for opinion, advice, or company in various activities. In general there was a turning point to peers at about the seventh grade. Before that the majority of children looked mainly to their parents as models and guides of behavior. Thereafter, the children's peers had equal or greater influence. In a study about a decade later, Condry and Siman (1960) reported on children's reliance on parents versus peers as sources of information and opinion. The results showed a much greater percentage of dependence upon peers at every age and grade level than did the earlier study. Thus, the shift from parents to peers as the child's major source of information appears now to occur at an earlier age and to be more pervasive and influential on the child's behavior.

Bronfenbrenner (1970) has summarized many studies on peer influence as follows:

---

[4] A similar problem involving roles and finances may well arise over the awarding of performance contracts to private industrial corporations which receive pay for specific student achievements through application of their program. The role of the teacher (and of his union) are considered to be put in jeopardy and the ability of these organizations to achieve any greater success than the traditional schools has been seriously challenged.

In summary, the effect of a peer group on the child depends on the attitudes and activities which prevail in that peer group. Where group norms emphasize academic achievement, the members perform accordingly; where the prevailing expectations call for violation of adult norms, these are readily translated into action. In short, *social contagion is a two-way street.* . . . How early in life do children become susceptible to the effects of such contagion? Professor Albert Bandura and his colleagues at Stanford University have conducted some experiments which suggest that the process is already well developed at the preschool level [p. 109].

Bronfenbrenner's observations (1970) on the cross-cultural differences in peer influences are most relevant to the complex and subtle ways in which socio-cultural norms influence behaviors.

The peer group need not necessarily act as an impetus to antisocial behavior. Among Soviet youngsters, it had just the opposite effect. Why? The answer is obvious enough. The Soviet peer group is given explicit training for exerting desired influence on its members, whereas the American peer group is not. Putting it another way, the Soviet peer group is heavily—perhaps too heavily—influenced by the adult society. In contrast, the American peer group is relatively autonomous, cut off from the adult world—a particularly salient example of segregation by age. . . . It is noteworthy that of all the countries in which my colleagues and I are working, now numbering half a dozen both in West and East, the only one which exceeds the United States in the willingness of children to engage in antisocial behavior is the nation closest to us in our Anglo-Saxon traditions of individualism. That country is England, the home of the Mods and the Rockers, the Beatles, the Rolling Stones, and our principal competitor in tabloid sensationalism, juvenile delinquency, and violence. The difference between England and America in our results is not great, but it is statistically reliable. England is also the only country in our sample which shows a level of parental involvement lower than our own, with both parents—and especially fathers—showing less affection, offering less companionship, and intervening less frequently in the lives of their children . . . [pp. 115–116].

Sex Role Learning in the Classroom

The learning of sex role behaviors is an illustration of how the classroom influences behavior. An analysis of sex role stereotyping in elementary school readers (Doubrovsky, 1971) has given some details about the stimuli to which students are exposed. The investigator studied 144 reading primers for their portrayal of male and female sex roles. First, there was a preponderance of stories built around boys or males as against girls or females (for example, 72 percent boy-oriented stories for the 49 percent boy population in elementary schools). Within the stories the behaviors expected of males and females were sharply differentiated:

"Girls are associated with helping their mothers or brothers, playing with kittens, getting into minor forms of trouble and being helped out by their brothers. Patterns of dependence, passivity, and domesticity are apparent . . . boy story lines begin to offer specific achievement for boys as well as contacts with adults outside the home . . . girls in the same book have no outside contacts or achievements other than shopping expeditions. They begin to show tendencies to minor stupidities and mishaps [Doubrovsky, 1971, p. 14]." Derogatory comments about girls in general were found to be quite common; for example, "Girls are always late." "She is just like a girl, she gives up."

The stories in the primers also contain the sex role stereotypes of adult males and females, such as male bravery and female domesticity. It may be argued that these stories reflect the attitudes, beliefs, and expectancies of the adult society. But, it is to these sex role behaviors which are taught early in life that women's liberation groups strongly object. The issue here is the influence of an important stimulus in the classroom, the "reader," in offering verbal descriptions of sex role models. These supplement and guide the child's observation of adult behavior in the classroom, the home, the community, the movies, and on TV.

THE TEACHER AS A BEHAVIOR CHANGE AGENT

As in the general process of behavior modification (see Chapters 10–12), the teacher is a user of behavior influence concepts in the classroom. As a behavior change technician, the teacher must first determine the objectives of his course— What is to be accomplished by the learner? *What behaviors are to be changed?* Here we are talking about careful observation in a functional analysis of behavior. Second, once the teacher has determined the behavior to be changed, he can initiate the specific conditions in the classroom necessary to bring about change. Third, the teacher must be in a position to evaluate the effectiveness of his techniques.

In a study illustrating these steps (Winett, Richards, Krasner, and Krasner, 1971), a second-grade teacher set up an individualized reading program. The objective was to develop the behavior of *independent reading* in each child. The teacher's observation of the children during the individualized reading period indicated that some were not reading. In order to change this behavior the teacher instituted a token program which involved specific reinforcement of independent reading behavior. Measures of time spent reading both before and after the instructional procedure were taken. The amount of time spent by children in independent reading significantly increased after the introduction of a token system. The implication of this study is that the teacher saw her role as that of a behavior change agent and acted appropriately.

We may recapitulate material previously presented in different contexts in terms of concepts about education. First, a person must not only learn *what* to do, but also under what conditions he should act in a particular way.[5] It is not enough merely to repeat a behavior under the instruction of a teacher, follow a proof passively, or make a mark on a multiple choice exam. Teaching should enable the student to gain mastery in contexts that are novel, to generalize, and to be able to deal with new situations. This goal may be stated in three different ways. The first way is by saying that the terminal behaviors of education are not tests or other current formal educational measures of "learning," but *activities after school* and *outside the classroom.* The second way is that the teacher may act as a prompt or discriminative stimulus for the behavior, but eventually *the behavior should be brought under the control of the student* and the *subject matter* and the *relevant situation itself.* As Skinner (1968) has noted: "Priming repertoires are misused when the teacher accepts the simple execution of behavior as a goal regardless of whether the student is likely to behave in the same way after the primes have been withdrawn [p. 211]." The third way is that the targets of teaching include not only specific acts but *strategies* for making acts. This last statement moves teaching into the realm of self-control, thinking, decision making and originality.

In the typical classroom situation, the student is presented with a task to master (read and remember) or some pages in a text or a problem to solve; and the resulting behavior is evaluated (after varying periods of delay) by the teacher. No measures or training of what the student does when he studies, thinks, or solves problems are undertaken. These activities may be formulated as gifts or traits that can be improved only through reward of the final behavior. That is, these skills or acts are not taught. The student is left to find his way alone. If we wish to increase problem solving and creativity, we would do better to study what the person does when he is being "creative" and the conditions under which he is most likely to perform and then to teach students to increase these behaviors.

Among the elements of critical thinking that may be explicitly taught are gathering and selecting relevant material, concentration on specific features of the problem, rejection of irrelevant material and details, self-criticism in the rejection of wrong solutions, and tolerance of indecision. Polya (1957) has given some general rules for problem solving such as reflection on a similar problem, evaluation of the meaning of the final solution, and manipulation of givens. The thrust is to make explicit the parts of the activity that were once overt but that are now so well practiced by the effective problem solver that he pays no more attention to them than the skilled automobile driver does to the moves required in driving his car.

---

[5] Skinner (1968, p. 33) has offered the stimulating idea that the conditions under which a behavior is emitted, especially if it is appropriate, are the basis for the traditional inference of "motivation."

"Instructional contingencies are usually contrived and should always be temporary [Skinner, 1968, p. 144]." This does not mean that such techniques should not be used, but that they should be used only until learning becomes complete; then they will no longer be necessary. The most general sequence for the elementary school may be (*a*) instigation by the teacher such as telling or showing the student what to do; (*b*) gradual fading of the teacher's instigatory, setting, and reinforcing stimuli, as he gives fewer hints and moves the student from physical to social to self-reinforcement, from schedules of immediate and inclusive reinforcement to more variable and delayed schedules, and increases the frequency and complexity of a reinforceable act to the point where a formerly reinforced act is now instrumental or a smaller part of the product considered adequate. The idea is for the person to eventually become his own therapist (Ullmann, 1969b) or his own teacher. We can teach self-mastery only after we have first analyzed it so that we can be explicit in our instruction.

To the extent that an act or strategy is taught, the student seems less creditable and more dependent on the teacher. A frequent criticism of the view of education being expressed here is that it does not allow for creativity or originality. If we can identify what we mean by *originality* (for example, not merely novelty or difference, but *valued behavior*), we may obtain some cues to problem solving and identify and later maximize the conditions for such valued behavior. We have discussed originality in terms of problem-solving strategy; we now approach creativity by a series of suggestions. First, it is good for the student to have as much mastery of the prerequisites as possible: *creativity is more likely* when the person has *facility* and *knowledge*. An alchemist might make a discovery by random mixing; a contemporary chemist probably would not. But creativity means a novel combination or arrangement. Behaviors as such must not be too tightly bound to stimuli.

One strategy is to try new ways of solving old and already solved problems. The new solution to the old problem, even if more costly than the old solution, may generalize to new related problems. New theories may be generated as bridges over unknowns that a person does not have time to solve; new stimuli (mixed media in art, new givens or their removal in mathematics) may lead to new ideas and arrangements. Sometimes difficulties may be deliberately introduced to produce accidents or to obtain a new slant. Again, the plastic artist may be stimulated by the work of people in other cultures, children, or naive painters. It is said that the artist Kandinsky's final breakthrough to totally nonobjective art came from seeing one of his paintings on its side in the dusk.

Another technique is to work backwards, to ask what would be a novel solution (for example, utopias of Chapter 18) and what conditions and intervening acts would be involved. If an intervening condition or act would be aversive, how might it be changed? The investigator plays with materials, symbols, and systems, while he holds severe criticism (necessary at a later stage) in check. Such intellectual play can be taught and welcomed. The point is that if the behavior influencer labels an area of activity as beyond modification, he will not analyze or investigate it. Once he approaches it as a human activity, he will at least increase the likelihood of more desirable behaviors being emitted, although he may never gain complete control. The earlier in the sequence of creativity that this effort is made, the more likely the prerequisites and conditions that can be manipulated will be identified.

The general principles of behavior influence apply to the classroom. The challenge is to specify, analyze, manipulate, and measure; the student may learn approaches to problem solving as well as solutions to specific problems, and the eventual goal is *effectiveness in new contexts with the actual material and problems*, not recitation to a teacher about past materials or problems.

THE CLASSROOM AS A PLANNED ENVIRONMENT

As a planned environment the classroom belongs within the context of behavior influence, that is, the same set of social influence variables that we have been dealing with throughout this book. Two complementary approaches to the classroom have developed in recent years; and both are integral parts of behavior influence in the classroom. These are the concepts of *token economy* and the *open classroom*.

In Chapter 11, we introduced token economy within the context of behavior modification. We begin our review of token economy in the classroom with several illustrations.

Token Economy in the Classroom

O'Leary and Becker (1967) introduced the use of a token reinforcement program in a public school class ($N = 17$) of children with behavior problems. Observations focused on the eight most disruptive children. Two observers recorded undesirable behaviors (for example, pushing, talking, making a noise, and chewing gum) every 30 seconds for an hour and a half on three days in a week. *All token programs begin with careful observation of specified responses.* Behaviors manifested during the observation periods were classified as either disruptive or nondisruptive.

On the first day of training, the experimenter wrote the following on the blackboard: *In Seat, Face Front, Raise Hand, Working, Pay Attention, Desk Clear.* The experimenter then explained that tokens would be given for these behaviors and that the tokens could be exchanged for *backup reinforcers* of candy, comics, perfume, and so on. During several brief class interludes, the teacher rated the extent to which each child had met the criteria.

For the first three days tokens were exchanged at the end of each period.

Tokens were then accumulated before being cashed in, first for two days, then for three and, finally, four days. The process was designed gradually to fade out the backup reinforcer so that the more traditional acquired reinforcers of teacher's praise and eventually self-reinforcement would take over. In addition, group points (exchanged for ice cream) were awarded for quietness during the rating period. Further techniques of verbal praise, ignoring (extinction), and time out from reinforcement were used when appropriate. During the baseline observation period, the disruptive-deviant behavior characterized 66 to 91 percent of the observations. The daily mean of observed deviant-disruptive behavior dropped to a range of 4 to 32 percent during the period of token training. The authors concluded that "With the introduction of the token reinforcement system, a dramatic, abrupt reduction in deviant behavior occurred. . . . The program was equally successful for all children observed, and repeated anecdotal evidence suggested that the children's appropriate behavior generalized to other situations [O'Leary and Becker, 1967, p. 637]."

This program already contained most of the elements that were to characterize future token programs in the classroom and which had appeared in the earlier mental hospital and retardation applications; namely, systematic observation, explicit selection of the desired behaviors with the assistance of the teacher as alternatives to undesirable behavior, the exchange system, the training of the teacher in his new role, the use of additional behavior influence techniques such as social reinforcement, and the careful charting of behavior by trained observers.

O'Leary, Becker, Evans, and Saudargas (1969) replicated the earlier study in a more systematic manner to determine the separate effects of the variables utilized in the previous study. They worked with 7 children in a second-grade class of 21 children. After a period of baseline observations, they successively introduced *Classroom Rules* (for example, on the blackboard, "We sit in our seats"), *Educational Structure* (for example, the teacher structured her program into four sessions of 30 minutes each), and *Praising Appropriate Behavior* while *Ignoring Disruptive Behavior*. None of these procedures consistently reduced disruptive behavior in 6 of the 7 target children; the three procedures were successful with one child. When a token reinforcement program was introduced, the frequency of disruptive behavior declined in 5 of the remaining 6 children.

Withdrawal of the token program then resulted in increased disruptive behavior in these 5 children. The reinstatement of the token program reduced disruptive behavior in 4 of the 5 children. Followup data indicated that the teacher was able to transfer control from the token and backup reinforcers to the reinforcers existing within the educational setting such as stars and occasional pieces of candy. Improvements in academic achievement during the year may have been related to the token program; and attendance records appeared to be enhanced during the token phases. The token program was utilized only in the afternoon and the data did not indicate any generalization of appropriate behavior from the afternoon to the morning.

To quote the authors' comparison of the results of the two studies:

> Although a Token Reinforcement Program was a significant variable in reducing disruptive behavior in the present study, the results are less dramatic than those obtained by O'Leary and Becker (1967). A number of factors probably contributed to the difference in effectiveness of the programs. The average of disruptive behavior during the base period in the 1967 study was 76%; in the present study it was 53%. The gradual introduction of the various phases of the program was probably less effective than a simultaneous introduction of all the procedures, as in the previous study. In the earlier study, the children received more frequent ratings. Five ratings were made each day at the introduction of the 1.5 hr. token program, and they were gradually reduced to three ratings per day. In the present study, the children received four ratings per day during a two-hour period. In the 1967 study, the class could earn points for popsicles by being quiet while the teacher placed ratings in the children's booklets; in the present study, group points were not incorporated into the general reinforcement program. In the 1967 study, the teacher attended a weekly psychology seminar where teachers discussed various applications of learning principles to classroom management. An *esprit de corps* was generated from that seminar that probably increased the teacher's commitment to change the children's behavior. Although Mrs. A received graduate credits for her extensive participation in the project, she did not attend a seminar in classroom management. A number of children in the present study had an abundance of toys at home and it was difficult to obtain inexpensive prizes which would serve as reinforcers; in the earlier study, selection of reinforcers was not a difficult problem since the children were from disadvantaged homes [O'Leary et al., 1969, pp. 11–12].

Thus, any evaluation of token programs must also consider baseline levels of the target behaviors; the phasing of the program; the frequency of certain teacher behaviors; the use of group reinforcers; the consequences of a teacher-training program (and available reinforcers for the teacher); and the availability of meaningful reinforcers for the children in their total environment. Other complexities also exist, as we shall determine after descriptions of other programs.

Another example is an elaborate study by Hewett, Taylor, and Artuso (1969), in which 54 children with learning and behavior problems (most of whom had been labeled "emotionally disturbed") were assigned to six different classrooms with 9 students each. The children ranged in age from eight to eleven. Hewett and his group described their program as an "engineered classroom" rather than a token economy. However, the principles overlap. The experimental condition of the project involved rigid adherence to the engineered classroom design and systematic reliance on the giving of checkmarks. The control condition of the project used any approach the teacher chose to follow (including aspects of the engineered design) except for tangible or token rewards. Conventional grading, verbal praise, complimentary written comments on completed assignments, and privileges for good work were all acceptable. The independent variable was adherence to the engineered design. The dependent variable was the student's "task attention" and academic functioning level in reading and arithmetic. Specific criteria for a student's task attention as measured by observers were established.

Because of the complexity of the design, the results cannot be presented simply. Students' task attention was significantly facilitated when the experimental condition was introduced to emotionally disturbed children after their placement in either a regular or control class. Task attention was facilitated by removal of the experimental condition from classes which had become accustomed to it over one semester. Reading achievement was not significantly affected by either the experimental or control condition, but gains in arithmetic fundamentals were significantly correlated with the presence of the experimental condition.

The authors concluded that "certainly evidence was provided that the use of tangible rewards on a temporary basis does not doom children to dependence on them. On the contrary, it appears such rewards may be extremely useful in launching children with behavior and learning problems into successful learning in school [Hewett et al., 1969, p. 529]."

The Hewett et al. study has been a model for studies applying token programs to "disturbed" children. This program was more complex than usual in its involvement of numerous teachers, use of comparative control groups rather than own-control baselines, focus on academic target behaviors, and testing of the removal and reinstatement of the token programs.

Wolf, Giles, and Hall (1968) have reported on a token economy designed to develop and maintain the academic behavior of children with low scholastic achievement in a community setting. This report described the results of the first year of afterschool remedial education for such children from the fifth and sixth grades in a deprived urban area. The remedial program incorporated standard instructional material, the mastery of which was supported by token reinforcements.

The reinforcement procedure resembled a trading stamp plan. Each child was given a folder containing groups of four differently colored pages divided into squares. The different colors signified different rewards. After a child had completed an assignment correctly, he was given points by the teacher who marked the appropriately colored squares. At first, points were given after each problem that was worked correctly. As the student improved his output, the amount and/or difficulty of work needed to obtain points were gradually increased.

The number of points given to a child for particular work was decided by the teacher. This decision was sometimes determined through negotiation with the child—a unique feature of this program. Filled pages of points were redeemable, according to their color, for a variety of goods and events including weekly trips to outdoor events or the cinema; food; money; articles available in the school store; and long-range items such as clothes, inexpensive watches, and secondhand bicycles. The children could earn tokens in three areas: regular classroom work, work completed in the remedial classroom, and six-week report card grades.

With this basic paradigm, Wolf, Giles, and Hall (1968) performed several experimental analyses of the token procedures. In the overall program they compared the academic achievement of their experimental students during the year with that of a matched control group. The results indicated that the remedial group gained 1.5 years on the Stanford Achievement Test as compared to 0.8 of a year for the control group; these differences were significant at the 0.01 level. There was a similar significant difference in report card grades. The authors concluded:

> The remedial program's effectiveness in maintaining the children's participation was indicated by the high attendance record, and the fact that whenever the opportunity was given them the children chose to attend class on regular school holidays. . . . The cost of the program, which was substantial, must be contrasted with the long-term cost to society in terms of human as well as economic resources lost by not educating these children adequately. The cost could be reduced significantly by utilizing the potential reinforcers which already exist in almost every educational setting. Properly used, such events as recess, movies, and athletic and social activities could be arranged as consequences for strengthening academic behavior [Wolf, Giles, and Hall, 1968, pp. 63–64].

This study was the first to apply tokens to "the disadvantaged," to use changes in price structure to shape the quality and quantity of classroom work; to let the child enter the decision-making process; to introduce long-range goals; to suggest utilizing reinforcing events outside the classroom as well as making greater use of the "natural" reinforcers of the classroom.[6]

[6] Other token programs have used money receipts with institutionalized female adolescent offenders (Meichenbaum, Bowers, and Ross, 1968); given tokens for good performance on a "news" test (Tyler and Brown, 1968); used plastic-washer tokens as tickets for special events (Bushell, Wrobel, and Michaelis, 1968); given tokens to school dropouts in a Neighborhood Youth Corps who were "hired" to complete remedial workbook assignments (Clark, Lachowicz, and Wolf, 1968); used contingent tokens in a remedial reading program (Haring and Hauck, 1969); given points as tokens along with time out and parental involvement to disruptive fourth to sixth graders (Walker, Mattson, and Buckley, 1969); used poker chips to increase "instruction following behavior" in retardates (Zimmerman, Zimmerman, and Russel, 1969); given tokens to extinguish tantrum behavior (Martin, et al., 1968). See O'Leary and O'Leary (1972) for a comprehensive over-view of these studies.

Target Behaviors

A major step in the education process is the specification of the behavior to be influenced. Implicit in such a specification is a value judgment as to the desirability of the behaviors being affected. The behaviors that are to be shaped tell us much about what the teacher (and/or investigator) values as "good" behavior.

Bushell et al. (1968, p. 55) used as dependent variables the desirable behaviors of *attending quietly* to instructions, *working independently or in cooperation with others* as appropriate, *remaining with* and *attending to assigned tasks*, and *reciting* after assignments had been completed. Conversely, the undesirable behaviors were "disrupting others who are at work, changing an activity before its completion, and engaging in 'escape' behaviors such as trips to bathroom or drinking fountain, or gazing out the window [p. 55]." Both sets of behaviors indicate value judgments.

In a critique of the goals of behavior modification in the classroom, Winett and Winkler (1972) reviewed publications in the *Journal of Applied Behavior Analysis* from 1968 to 1970 in which behavior modification was applied to relatively normal classrooms; they stated, "Our purpose was not to evaluate specific techniques or results but rather to investigate the kinds of target behaviors that were either reinforced or in various ways proscribed." The authors cited as illustative a study by Thomas, Becker, and Armstrong (1968) which rigorously classified "appropriate" and "inappropriate" behavior. Labeled as *inappropriate* were such behaviors as getting out of one's seat, standing up, walking around, running, hopping, skipping, jumping, moving chairs, racking chairs, tapping feet, rattling papers, conversing with other children, crying, singing, whistling, laughing, turning one's head or body toward another child, showing objects to another child, and looking at another child. *Appropriate* behavior included attending to the teacher, raising one's hand and waiting for the teacher to respond, working in one's seat on a workbook, and following the lesson in a reading text.

The desirable behaviors quite clearly tend to be in the direction of *quietness* and *nonmovement*, whereas the undesirable behaviors tend to be in the direction of *movement* and *interactive* stimulation. Thus, the behavior modification approach in the classroom, as typified by token economy, has usually been used to support the implicit behaviors held desirable as part of the traditional school approach. Winett and Winkler (1972) have drawn this bleak picture of current goals: "Just what do those present goals seem to be? Taken as a fairly accurate indication of what public schools deemed as the 'model' child, these studies described this pupil as one who stays glued to his seat and desk all day, continually looks at his teacher, or his text/workbook, does not talk to, or in fact look at other children, does not talk unless asked to by the teacher, hopefully does not laugh or sing (at the wrong time), and assuredly passes silently in halls."

The issue of target behavior is not peripheral but central to the application of behavior modification in the classroom. Many of these early applications in the classroom were attempts to demonstrate that the application of learning principles could indeed change behavior. The particular behavior was selected on the basis of its being readily *observable, countable,* and *important* to the teacher. Little attention was given to evaluating the desirability of the behaviors themselves. The social and ethical implications of target behavior have increasingly become more focal.

Reinforcers

In our discussion of the use of reinforcers in token economy and planned environments, two aspects must be considered. As indicated in an earlier section, tokens are only symbolic of some other object or event. Theoretically, tokens should take on reinforcing properties because of the desirability of the *backup reinforcers* which they represent. Yet it is clear from observation that tokens take on reinforcing properties of their own. The clearest analogue of this is the individual who works for money far beyond his needs. The token, money, becomes highly desirable for itself. Moreover, *tokens call attention to behaviors and provide information to the student.* The teacher also alters his behavior because he is on a schedule to reinforce the child's behavior. The teacher is encouraged to observe, to respond, and to record. Thus, the program both guides the teacher's behavior and provides him with information via the feedback provided by the records of his reinforcing behavior.

The tokens used include checkmarks, stars, rings, chips, and tags. O'Leary and Drabman (1971, p. 389) have offered a list of the desirable properties of tokens: their value should be readily understood; they should be easy to dispense; they should be easily transportable from the place of dispensing to the area of exchange; they should be identifiable as the property of a particular child; they should require minimal bookkeeping by the teacher; they should be dispensable in a manner that diverts as little attention as possible from academic matters; they should have some relevance to real currency if the aim is to teach mathematical or economic skills which will be functional outside the classroom; and they should be dispensable frequently enough to ensure proper shaping of desired behavior. As for the backup reinforcers, every conceivable object or event that can be considered desirable has been used. These have included such diverse objects as candy, food, clothing, watches, and access to events such as movies, sports events, and circuses.

Natural reinforcers—those present in the environment prior to the onset of the systematic program—are shapers of behavior; they help evoke behavior. For example, the teacher may place an Indian headdress in a corner of the classroom. It is a reinforcer (that is, an object of curiosity and manipulation). The presence of the headdress increases the likelihood of the child going to this corner. Further, the child is likely to perform certain behaviors with the headdress because of previously learned associations. He may pick up the headdress, put it on his head, and then jump up and down as he makes sounds like an Indian whooping. He may open books with pictures of Indians on them. He is more likely to display behavior indicating an interest in matters Indian.

Another material object that may combine the qualities of a reinforcer and an evoker of behavior is an ordinary bathroom scale. Putting a scale in a corner of a second-grade classroom not only serves as a fun reinforcer for the child going into that corner but increases the likelihood of various mathematical activities such as comparing weights with one's peers; making size comparisons; making weight estimations and testing their accuracy; and representing in pictures the data collected. Any and all these behaviors may reflect desirable goals of the teacher.

These two illustrations indicate the close connection between the concept of natural reinforcers and the evocation of desirable behavior in a planned classroom environment.

Generalization

Behavior change takes place in a specific context. The question is, Does behavior generalize from one situation to another? Although both laboratory and individual case studies with operant procedures have attempted to approach problems of generalization across time (Do changes in the morning carry over to the afternoon?) and across situations (Does change in the classroom extend to the home?), most token economy programs have not attempted such measures.

The key observation on the problem of generalization has been made by Baer, Wolf, and Risley (1968): "Generalization should be programmed, rather than expected or lamented [p. 97]." With a few exceptions, the token programs do not result in generalized behavioral change in other situations. But most of the token studies were not intended or designed to bring about change in other situations.

O'Leary and Drabman (1971) have offered a list of ten procedures which may be useful in enhancing generalization:

> Provide a good academic program, since in many cases you may be dealing with deficient academic repertoires—not "behavior disorders." . . . Give the child the expectation that he is capable of doing well by exaggerating excitement when the child succeeds and pointing out that if he works hard he can succeed. . . . Have the children aid in the selection of the behaviors to be reinforced and as the program progresses, have the children involved in the specification of contingencies. . . . Teach the children to evaluate their own behavior. . . . Teach the children that academic achievement will "pay off." . . . Involve the parents. . . . Withdraw the token and backup reinforcers gradually and utilize other "natural" reinforcers existing within the classroom setting, such as privileges. . . . Rein-

force the children in a variety of situations and reduce the discrimination between reinforced and non-reinforced situations. . . . Prepare teachers in the regular class to praise and shape the children's behavior as they are phased back into the regular classes. . . . Look at the school system as a large-scale token system with the distribution of token and backup reinforcers and extending from the school board to the superintendent, to the principal, to the teacher, and finally to the children [pp. 395–396].

The problem of generalization is really one of carefully explicating the circumstances (*when*, *what*, and *how*) under which the specific response can be reproduced. To the above list it is necessary to add such concepts as the effect of different reinforcement schedules (such as periodic and thinned out); the verbalization of rules; behaviors likely to be reinforced outside the classroom; the teaching of strategies as well as specific acts (such as using concepts of self-control through environmental arrangements and self-reinforcement, as described in Chapter 12).

The Token Economy as a Real Economy

A modified form of a token economy program has extended the use of these techniques in the classroom (Krasner, 1973). Whereas previous token programs had emphasized *remedial goals*, in this classroom the development of the token economy served as a *learning experience* itself. Thus, token economy and open classroom were brought together. A fifth-grade teacher read about token economies in educational journals and decided to initiate such a program in the form of a simulated society.[7] He brought into class a dozen bottle caps as the first tokens (initial capital) and proceeded to start a classroom society with himself as a king with divine rights.

From this beginning the token economy developed and soon took on a life of its own. The behavior of the children was determined by the shifting directions of the economy as it progressed from a system of slavery to capitalism and then to socialism. The following excerpts are from interviews with the teacher and several of the students in the class, including the eventually elected president of the society, on the development of the program and their reactions to it.

INTERVIEWER (LK): What was the next step?
TEACHER (GM): . . . When kids couldn't pay taxes, I made them indentured servents and sold them. If a kid didn't work, he wasn't worth anything and he remained as an indentured servant 'til he paid off his debt. At this point, the humor disappeared and it became a serious matter. I was taxing the kids with money. A middle class formed consisting of the kids that produced a lot of

[7] Our thanks to the teacher of this class, Mr. Gerald Martin of the Three Village Central School District, Setauket, New York, for his cooperation and innovative ideas.

products. There was no tax schedule; I fired kids and gave jobs (three or four of them) to kids that I had told were my favorites, whether they could do the job well or not. There developed a lot of antagonism. But the economy was healthy because the kids still circulated money, except that there were larger lower classes and the middle class was supporting me and my friends.

LK: Could you tell us about the revolution?

GM: . . . I told them if they want a revolution, then they have to study it economically and see how they could get rid of the king by taking away his power economically. I would respect it if they could get 80 percent of the class to sign a petition. They studied recession and depression that happened after the Russian and American revolutions and a turnover in government. . . . They did quite a bit of work and wrote up a constitution.

LK: How were you finally overcome?

GM: What they did (I was not aware of it at the time) was to take up a collection in class. They got the support of the indentured servants and collected 60 bottle caps and put them in Mr. H's [principal] office and called it their "Swiss Bank Account." One kid said he had to leave the classroom to go to a music lesson and he went to get the money from the "Swiss Bank Account." But Mr. H. would not see him or give him the money without a receipt (which they had not gotten). This kid was going through some sweat because he needed to get government jobs going. The economy was collapsing and they were nervous about it. They had to stimulate the economy quickly, but Mr. H. was holding the bottle caps. But I couldn't help them.

LK: They had left the money in the "bank" without a receipt?

GM: The kids threatened to change the tokens, that is, to change the nature of the economy. They said to Mr. H. that if he didn't hand over 56 bottle caps, [they conceded the interest] they would change the monetary value and he would be holding garbage. That's how they got their money back! Then they were running a democratic form of government-free enterprise and I stepped out completely. The economy, itself, has stayed the same, but they now have the individual freedoms that they looked for. They also have a lot of controls, same as in a democratic system. They also have problems; they have a welfare system, a congress, and a president with a six-week term of office. . . .

LK: Mr. President, tell me a little about your job and what you do.

PRESIDENT (P): Well, my job is to give the country leadership and to hold it together and to provide it with its defense, its protection, and its people with mostly what they need to live with, which would be in this case money, which is what I'm trying to do right now.

LK: Last time I was here, I saw you collect the taxes. Could you tell me about that? How did that work out?

P: My taxes work. There is a certain amount of money taxed. People have between 10 and 20 bottle caps. They get taxed differently from people with 70 or 80, and it works out pretty well. I've tried to lower the budget, just today, so that welfare could be put in.

LK: Tell me about the welfare.

P: Welfare programs will be given to people with under 2 bottle caps, until their wealth exceeds 5, which would give them some money to live with. They work for the government to earn this money so that they wouldn't just sit back on their behinds and get it. You can only apply for welfare three times in an interval so many weeks apart.

LK: What kind of comment can you make about how things have been going . . . about the way the country's run?

P: I think that I don't have enough time to meet with the Senate. I would like to have more, but generally I don't think we've run into much of a crisis except that I don't think I've been able to do what I really want to do.

LK: What would you like to do if you could?

P: I'd like to meet with the Senate and Congress more to try to get more passed. Right now I can only meet twice a week and during recess most of the time.

LK: How much are you paid?

P: I'm paid 4 bottle caps per week but according to the new budget, I get paid 3 bottle caps so we can pay for welfare.

LK: Oh, so you're taking a cut to pay for welfare.

P: Yes, I'm also trying to cut the low jobs . . . the low-paying jobs.

LK: What made you decide to run for president?

P: I was not going to run for president at first. I thought I'd like to be a representative more and then I asked people how many would like me as their president and how many would vote for me and I got about 18 so I decided to run for president. After I became president, I decided I did the best thing because I think in this economy I can do more as a president than as a representative.

What was most striking in visiting this program and observing it in action was the life and vitality of the economy. The children had become quite sophisticated in economic and reinforcement principles. Everyone in the classroom was involved in the program and enjoying it.

The token economy programs we have described have implications for the training of teachers in methods of planning the classroom environment and even for the community. The concepts of the open classroom and behavior modification clearly move the role of the schoolteacher in the direction of becoming a planner of social environments and an agent of social change (Krasner and Krasner, 1973).

Open Classrooms

Most of the published literature on the open classroom is enthusiastic (for example, Featherstone, 1971; Holt, 1967; Plowden, 1967; Silberman, 1970; Weber, 1971), but hard data are rare. The major elements of the open classroom approach, as it developed from its origins in the post-World War II

British Infant Schools, are the integrated day, individualized instruction, and family groupings. The concept of the *integrated day* encompasses a total environment in which there is a blurring of distinctions between work and play, between subject matters, and between inside and outside the classroom. Weber (1971) has described it this way:

> In planning for the free day there is no separation of activities or skills and no separate scheduling of any one activity other than the fixed points (Morning Service, P.E., Music and Movement, and lunch) designed for all children in the school. As a result, one might see all aspects of the environment—reading, writing, number, painting, acting, music—in use at all times. A group getting the teacher's special help or stimulus could be found at any time. . . .
>
> It should be emphasized that the undifferentiated day was not conceived simply in terms of simultaneity, of all different aspects of the environment, nor in terms of a child's use of any one aspect as a separate use at a single moment in time. The English viewed a child's use of the environment as cutting across subject areas in pursuit of his interests. This kind of scheduling not only supported a child's integration of experience but also sustained his involvement [p. 91].

In effect, the integrated day denotes the concept of having available in the environment a wide variety of stimuli and conditions which should make learning more interesting, exciting, and meaningful to the child.

A second characteristic of open classrooms is that of *family* or *vertical grouping*. This type of nongraded grouping spans three years, combining five-, six-, and seven-year-old children together. The word *family* is used to describe the arrangement because the class is deliberately set up to resemble a family. Older children help with the teaching of younger children,[8] and the classroom is designed as an extension of the home. The rationale behind this arrangement is that children learn from each other. A third basic aspect of the open classroom is the emphasis on an availability of *environmental materials*. Wide use is made of inexpensive materials readily found in most environments such as water, sand, and common household utensils.

The open classroom approach has frequently been confused with the "free" school. This has resulted in an image of children entering a class and doing what they like or not doing anything if they so desire. In fact, however, the open classroom is a carefully structured and planned environment.

One of the arguments presented for the use of the open classroom approach is that it discards much of the "conventional wisdom about teaching." Yet this is not necessarily so. For example, the notions that there are some common general goals for all children, and that the teacher should plan and schedule the work

---

[8] Among the most impressive work on the use of fellow trainees, both in terms of methodolgy and content, is work on pyramid therapy with retardates (Whalen and Henker, 1969, 1971).

program for his students are still present, but in a way which should increase the likelihood of accomplishing these goals. As a planner of the environment, the teacher must make decisions about what learning experiences to expose the child to and the best way to maximize the likelihood that the child's behavior will be changed in a personally and socially desirable manner.

The question arises whether the open classroom approach merely repeats the earlier idea of progressive education—learning by doing—which was deemed a failure. A major difference between the two seems to lie in goals. The earlier movement stressed goals of self-growth, personality development, and self-expression. Based on Piaget's research (1954) on how learning takes place, the newer movement stresses learning and more closely links the concepts of competence with self-control and self-direction as goals. These new goals of learning can probably be measured—a difference from the older ones which often precluded evaluation.

LAST WORD

One of the largest budget items for state and local government is education. One of the largest investments of a person's youth is in education. Through education society perpetuates itself; through education the individual is prepared to cope effectively as an adult. In terms of time, effort, and money, education is probably the most important single behavior influence institution in our society.

There are two immediate questions: What shall be taught? And how shall it be taught? The goals of education involve major value decisions and reflect the group's current concerns and aspirations. Given a pluralistic society in which differences should be respected, the increasing trend to input from parents becomes an ethical imperative.

This chapter, however, has been devoted to the *how* of education. Educational technology is an application of social science. Regardless of the goals selected, the manner of achieving them may be improved. The effects of different theories of personality and education have been touched on and major attention given to the classroom as a planned environment. Another major theme of the chapter has been that the teacher is not a baby-sitter, but a professional who strives to alter the behavior of students in what he and the community consider a socially desirable direction.

Both what is taught and how it is taught affect how the future adult citizen will deal with economic and interpersonal problems; in short, what sort of a person he will be. The behavior influence approach leads to suggestions for the technology of teaching. Theories of personality involving concepts of "readiness" or "giftedness" may help the teacher reinforce the child for appropriate acts, but leave almost to chance the procedures that will help the child to achieve. By increasing the chances for achievement, we think we may help children become competent adults, so that at a later date a traditional observer will remark on how "integrated" their personalities are. The classroom has no inherently correct structure. Setting up a classroom with straight rows of desks is a value decision with implicit expectancies of certain kinds of behavior. Whether these behaviors are good or bad is not the issue. The aim is to communicate to the teacher that he or she as an agent of social change should be able to state goals and to utilize the role of environmental organizer and learning facilitator to achieve them.

CHAPTER 15

Economic, Social, and Political Influences on Behavior

Certain influences on human behavior are usually ignored, misinterpreted, or at best underestimated in treatises on personality. Generically, these influences may be labeled as *social, economic,* and *political.* As in Chapter 13, on environmental influences, and Chapter 16, on social movements, we are dealing with a contextual influence on individual behaviors. We are not introducing concepts such as society, culture, or economy as explanations of behavior, nor are we attempting to explain economies and sociology in terms of individual psychology. Rather, we wish to show that man's behavior and his social organizations *reciprocally* affect people and are affected by them.

Thus, in this chapter, we look at the situations involved with *work*—man earning the means of supporting himself; *governance*—the way man organizes to rule himself; *nationality*—the behaviors expected of an individual because he is a citizen of a particular nation; *subculture*—the influences on man's behavior because of his birth into a particular socioeconomic or ethnic group. While most investigators of human behavior readily acknowledge the theoretical importance of these kinds of influences, these are factors frequently ignored by psychologists.

Words often designate overlapping categories. This is particularly so of terms such as *nation, society, state, culture*, and *country*. Culture, for example, may comprise both a conglomerate of learned and shared behaviors, patterns, attitudes, *and* all available objects in a particular setting. Society may indicate organizations of people in some specific administrative grouping. The two concepts overlap with each other and may overlap with the concepts of nations, professions, and the like. We may talk of American culture or Western civilization as though they include all people, but we must realize that we are designating only a fraction of the population.

INFLUENCES OF NATIONALITY

Whether political or economic, a *nation's immediate goals* have an *enormous impact* on the *life of its citizens*. The most extreme example is the influence on behavior of living in the zone of a hot war. Children growing up in Vietnam and Switzerland or Sweden learn about different worlds. While many other differences are also present in a war zone, one's personal security and ability to predict long-range relationships are decreased. Poverty, disease, presence of foreign troops, and a host of other conditions make actions consistent with values such as honesty, trust, and kindness to others hard if not impossible.

At the time of this writing, a set of policy changes in the goals of the administration of the United States have led to emphasis on reducing inflation, certain military spending, and funding of some aerospace endeavors. The point here is not whether these decisions are correct or sufficient, but that they create economic conditions that gravely influence segments of the population such as engineers and craftsmen in the aerospace industry. Some of these people have sought employment in other areas, creating, for example, a buyer's market in science teachers. For some middle-class families the result has been a change in living habits, family structure, and personal security that is drastic, pervasive, and contrary to many of their assumptions about themselves and their world.

National Character

Do people behave in a specific, predictable manner because they are from a specific nation? Is one more likely to behave, for example, in an aggressive manner if he is a citizen of the United States rather than of Sweden? This might be a meaningful question if we were dealing with a unified society, but the population of the United States is fractionated, segmented, and divided along many lines. Membership in an age, sex, social class, or racial group is likely to lead to greater predictability of behavior than national character.

In this section we focus on the manner in which the concept of "national character" is approached by various professionals, since most investigators *seek* and *find* the national character that supports their theory.

Inkeles and Levinson (1969) have offered an overview of the relation between national character, concepts of personality, and sociocultural systems. They put the question in this manner: "To what extent do the patterned traditions of life in a particular society give rise to certain distinctive patterns in the personalities of its members? To what extent, that is, does the sociocultural system produce its distinctive forms of 'social character,' 'basic personality structure,' or 'modal personality'? Further, what are the consequences, if any, of this patterning in personality for stability or change in the societal order? [p. 418]."

The concept of national character itself can be defined in terms of the *history* of the investigation of "national characteristics." Anthropologists were the first to approach the problem of the relationship between individual personality and the norms of a society. The late nineteenth-century approach was to ascertain what behaviors were socially expected in diverse societies and then to assume that individuals behaved in conformity with these prescribed norms. However, a later group of investigators (for example, Boas, 1940, and Sapir, 1948) recognized the possibility of deviance from expected behavior based upon how the individual had learned appropriate behavior.

A major landmark in this field was the publication in 1934 of Ruth Benedict's *Patterns of Culture*. Benedict went beyond the description of individual behavior as the product of a particular culture. She attempted to characterize the patterns of behavior or the "psychological coherence" of the society. Perhaps the fact that she did not start with a formal integrated theory of personality to guide, bias, or obscure her observations worked in her favor.

Benedict (1934) borrowed from the philosopher Nietzche the terms "Apollonian" and "Dionysian" to apply to broad patterns of behavior and to express "two diametrically opposed ways of arriving at the values of existence [p. 72]." The *Apollonian* way of life was based on the qualities attributed to the Greek god Apollo—*poise, restraint, serenity, esthetic appreciation*. The Pueblo Indians of the Southwest were an example of this kind of culture. They were considered to be gracious and easy in their manner and steady workers. From these general patterns of culture, specific inferences about behavior can be made, such as that this Apollian society would be one in which individuals made beautiful pottery.

In contrast, the *Dionysian* way of life is *impulsive, violent, primitive, orgiastic, savage,* and *exotic*—qualities attributed to the Greek god Dionysus. The Dionysian values *excess*, be it in behavior, emotion, drunkenness, or frenzy. As the poet William Blake wrote, "The path of excess leads to the palace of wisdom [as quoted by Benedict, 1934, p. 72]." The Indians of the Great Plains such as the Sioux and the Blackfoot were classified as Dionysian. In order to prove his manhood in these societies, a boy had to fast and go without water in order to have a *vision*. Men danced to the point of exhaustion or passed wooden skewers through the muscles of their chests so that they could hang suspended in the sun. These deeds provided proof of their manliness. Benedict also described several other patterns of behavior in societies such as the Dobu people of New Guinea and the Kwaikiutl Indians of Vancouver Island. What she dramatically demonstrated was that a specific behavior or a pattern of behavior accepted as the *norm* in one society was considered *deviant* in another. For example, the Dobuans' day-to-day behavior—involving as it did the use of complicated rituals, suspiciousness of neighbors, treachery, secretiveness, aggressiveness, and belief in black magic—might be labeled paranoid in our society.

A feeling both of Dobu's society and Benedict's approach to it is indicated in the following passage:

> Life in Dobu fosters extreme forms of animosity and malignancy which most societies have minimized by their institutions. Dobuan institutions on the other hand exalt them to the highest degree. The Dobuan lives out without repression man's worst nightmares of the ill-will of the universe, and according to his view of life virtue consists in selecting a victim upon whom he can vent the malignancy he attributes alike to human society and to the powers of nature. All existence appears to him as a cutthroat struggle in which deadly anatagonists are pitted against one another in a contest for each one of the goods of life. Suspicion and cruelty are his trusted weapons in the strife and he gives no mercy, as he asks none [Benedict, 1934, p. 159].

An event which had major impact on the concept of national characteristics was World War II. Teams of American investigators, particularly anthropologists and psychoanalysts, used their talents to observe and interpret the behavior of the German and Japanese enemies (Bateson, 1942; Benedict, 1946; Gorer, 1943; LaBarre, 1945; Mead, 1942). This period culminated in Kardiner's classic psychoanalytic formulation of society (1943), *The Psychological Frontiers of Society*. But the involvement of anthropologists in the study of national character ended; it was as if these specialists had come to a dead end in psychoanalytic applications to society and could go no further.

In the postwar period psychologists focused on the individual's learning or perceptual processes independent of social setting or context. However, the research of a number of investigators involved cross-national comparisons on specific kinds of behavior. For example, McClelland (1961) reported on national differences in *achievement motivations*.

He hypothesized differences in the strength of the need for achievement between Protestant and Catholic countries based upon Max Weber's *The Protestant Ethic and The Spirit of Capitalism* (1930). According to Weber, a

Protestant ideology should cause parents to stress the importance of achievement, self-reliance, and self-denial in their children's training. If this thesis is correct, Protestant families should produce sons with high achievement motivation which would be expressed in various economic and entrepreneurial endeavors leading to a more rapid national economic growth. To test this hypothesis McClelland compared the economic development of Protestant countries (England, United States, Sweden) with that of Catholic countries (France, Spain, Italy) in 1950. For example, one index of such development was the kilowatt hours of electricity consumed per capita. The differences in this particular measure tended to confirm McClelland's hypothesis as to greater growth in the Protestant countries. In another related study McClelland compared assessments of the achievement motive level in children's readers in these same countries with various estimates of national economic development between 1925 and 1950. He found the same kind of national relationship and concluded that the level of achievement motivation in a particular country could be used to predict subsequent increases in its rate of economic growth.

Sociologists have also approached the concept of national characteristics. Those influenced by G. H. Mead (see Chapter 2) found their ideas to be quite compatible with the notion of national social norms (or roles) learned by the individual and then manifested in specific behavior. However, an alternative approach influenced by Durkheim (see Chapter 2) argued for purely sociological and social structure explanations and implicitly delegated the study of individual behavior to psychology.

One sociological report had a major impact on the direction and behavior of subsequent investigators. *The Lonely Crowd* (Riesman, Glazer, and Denney, 1950) presented the notion that certain personality types characterized American society. The authors differentiated three character types, depending upon the predominant sources of social control of behavior. The first is a "traditional-directed" individual, whose behavior is guided by the formal and *traditional* standards and norms of the society. The second is an "inner-directed" individual, whose behavior is primarily affected by individualized *personal* standards. The third type is the "other-directed" person, whose behavior is guided by conformity to the particular standards of the *social group* in which he finds himself. They argued that in the midtwentieth century, the American modal personality was shifting from the inner-directedness characteristic of the pioneers to other directedness, which placed great reliance on feedback and approval of others, particularly peers. As broad observations of behavior, these designations seem most perceptive. As delineation of "types" of people, they suffer from the same limitations as all other typologies.[1]

It is difficult to see how a psychology of behavior influence based on social learning can ignore the impact on the individual of living in a particular

---

[1] Fromm's conception (1947) of receptive, exploitative, hoarding, marketing, and productive orientations is closely related, but stems from a psychoanalytic rather than a sociological theory.

nation or culture. Every major nation has developed an image or a set of norms for expected behavior that acts as a self-fulfilling prophecy. However, national character is also a very dangerous concept because erroneous and misleading conclusions may have dangerous political consequences.

> The importance attached to studies of national character has fluctuated with intellectual fashions and also in terms of the requirements of applied work. It is a field inevitably "contaminated" by lay stereotypes about groups and nations and by the scientific effort to get away from these, if not to deny their relevance completely. Easy assumptions of the fixity of national character contradict the evidence of human plasticity provided by studies of acculturation, and the history of societies such as the English or Swedish reminds us that peoples now well-known for stability and law-abidingness were, in the eighteenth century, a valiantly disorderly people [D. Riesman, 1967, p. 37].

The basic criticism of the concept of national character is twofold. First, any nation-state at this point in civilization is so complex in terms of social, economic, and political classes, races, ages, and geographic regions that to expect behavioral similarities between its diverse elements seems highly unrealistic. Second, the term "character" has the same implications of internal organization that personality does and hence omits any reference to situational impact. On the other hand, in a modern technological society such as the United States, many environmental forces are at work to enhance communality of expected behavior in specific kinds of situations. These include a common language, television, movies, architecture, supermarkets, and suburbia.

While no investigation has yet demonstrated an American "national character," there have been many observations of American behavior which at best are suggestive. An example is the following observation by Riesman (1967) about Americans in the Peace Corps,

> More striking still has been the overseas experience of young college-educated Americans in the Peace Corps and like ventures who have regarded themselves as almost "un-American" in their rejection of material greed, of vulgar ethnocentricism, and, in general, of many of the tastes, pursuits, and styles of the middle-brow, middle-aged, Americans. In the training programs where I have encountered them, for example, many volunteers have assumed that they could readily adapt to work with host-country nationals if the latter were sufficiently underprivileged since what was "really" human would unite them underneath the sham societal forms. Their real culture shock came at their discovery of how "American" they were in spite of themselves, being imbued with egalitarianism, activism (or at least nonfatalism), candor, and impatience [p. 40].

Riesman has further noted the ways in which the mass media influence American behavior.

It is the longer-run impact of the media that seems to me of far greater import for character and conduct. The media help to tutor us in how to be American: to be cheerful rather than sullen and forlorn; slender rather than fat; peppy rather than inert; aspiring rather than resigned; hedonistic and gregarious rather than pinched, postponing, or withdrawn. In the term "media" I include not only the images of movie and television screen and of advertising, but also the manner in which the more mobile Americans carry themselves, the way they publicly greet each other, and the way they design houses, cars, and public places [p. 43].

One other way to look at national characteristics is in terms of the models and metaphors used to observe and to communicate to others (see Chapter 7). Metzger (1963) has discussed one approach which is consistent with our view of the social influence process, namely, the "dramaturgical" model:

[This includes the] social behaviorism of George Herbert Mead, the developmental studies of Jean Piaget, the theatrical metaphors of Erving Goffman and other sociologists [as well as the psychologists Newcomb, Sargent, and Sarbin; see Chapter 3 of this text].

The central idea that emerges from these varied sources is that every society, in order to achieve its goals, requires its members to play set roles that are usually assigned on the basis of age, sex, class, and occupation. Becoming a socialized person means acquiring thespian skills—knowing what the part of male or adolescent or doctor calls for, making the performance of that role seem authentic to the audience, and guarding against discrepant gestures (acts) that would give the play away. These skills are acquired slowly by instructive social interactions; the novice becomes a polished actor not so much by direct tuition as by continuous practice in required roles. . . . Let character trait denote the style with which an individual plays a specific social role, and character the style that infuses the individual's playing of his many roles. Then, national character may denote the style which the troupes constituting the nation bring to the roles within their repertory [p. 92].

In short, Metzger's analysis links national character and the social influence process. The person is taught his roles, and both sociologists and anthropologists provide evidence of the difference in roles that are available and valued.

Cultural Concepts of Time

As much as we live in a physical environment, we spend our social lives within the confines of learned formal, informal, and technological ideas. On the basis of ways of organizing and communicating experience, such as language, we are able to predict what others will do and how they are likely to react. As long as we remain within our own culture, we are likely to be accurate, effective, and comfortable. Because our constructs usually work, we may be oblivious to them and unaware of their influence on our own behavior. This is particularly true of our concepts of time and space.[2]

Time is a concept that seems obvious and unquestionable, but which differs widely among cultures. The members of the dominant culture of the United States think of time as a continuous path toward the future that is divided into recognizable and identifiable segments. Time is treated very much like a physical substance: it is earned, saved, spent, wasted, and carefully measured. This is expressed by the slogan of the efficiency experts, Time is money. Time spent adds up: sixty minutes to the hour, 365 days to the year, so that every part of a period of time can and must be accounted for. We plan our time and we base many of our economic practices, such as payment for our services and interest on money, on concepts of time periods. Promises to do something within a given time or at a certain time are considered binding by both participants. At a formal level we think of being up to five minutes late for an appointment as within the acceptable range, fifteen minutes late as reason for apology; and forty-five minutes or more as a serious breach of expectation and even an insult.

There are variations of all sorts. Mormons are a group reputed to be particularly punctual, while people in the Northeast and Southeast are less so. The typical mode in the United States is to do one thing at a time and then move to another. If one activity is allowed to interfere with another, by implication the first is more important than the second. If a meeting is delayed, the person kept waiting may feel that his importance has been demonstrably reduced. What is punctual or permissible and what requires an apology may vary with situations. Work, classes, and other occupational situations start relatively on time. Athletic events that are televised start more punctually than those that are not; but once games start in which the time factor is important, as in football compared to baseball, time is kept to the second.

Time is also informal and taught by example and social context rather than by explicit precept. Here the same words, *soon, in a little while,* and *not too long* may have different meanings depending on the situation. *Soon* may mean five minutes before supper; for example, "Wash your hands, we're eating soon." Or it may mean half an hour when an impatient child asks when the ride to grandma's will be over. Time that is equal by the clock may also be long or short depending on with whom or how it is spent. A daughter may say, "I practiced my flute a half hour"—implying a long time—or she may say, "I listened to television half an hour"—meaning a short time. We think of time passing faster if we are actively engaged in a task and if there is a variety of input. Time passes slowly when there are urgent demands or if we have to wait

---

[2] The following material draws heavily on Edward T. Hall's *The Silent Language,* first published in 1959, but now available in paperback (1969).

for an event we greatly desire. A person may use the word *eternity* to signify the two days until the dance.

The situation in which the time is being measured makes a major difference. If one has an invitation for dinner and the hostess has a dish in the oven and the other guests are presumably hungry, he normally tries to be punctual and arrive within five or ten minutes of the given time. If the invitation is for a cocktail party and no major preparation or activity depends on one's presence, he is less likely to be punctual. In the same vein, a date for coffee may be made for half an hour later, but a woman may turn down an offer for a Saturday night date if it is made too short a time before the event—possibly because of the implication that she has nothing else planned. An exception occurs when the couple increases its commitment to each other: when each has established the worth of the other, the act of asking about specific engagements assumes less importance.

While people in the United States plan in terms of time, the span in which they plan or expect to see results is relatively short. To the extent that major elections occur every two to four years, there may be a political basis to the desire for rapid visible results. A relatively youthful population may also increase pressure for rapid effects: an academic year may seem a more sizable piece of time for an undergraduate than a professor who has seen thirty such years. Additionally, an undergraduate's life on campus may well end before he has seen changes he deems necessary, while the faculty has a longer time span.

Finally, time may be dealt with at a technical, scientific level. Here the range may be from minute portions of a second to millennia. Time is set by scientific standards and is as free of cultural and other influences as possible. The person using technical time does so under professional rules that are explicit, teachable, and usually abstract. Further, the time span involved in scientific concepts is so great (or small) that most people simply do not attach emotional meaning to such statements as, Life has existed on earth for a billion years.

We may contrast the American concept of time with that of some other people. In the Arabic world to plan for the future is close to heresy, since only Allah knows the future. For the Navajo "only the immediate gift has reality; a promise of future benefit is not even worth thinking about [Hall, 1969, p. 23]." The span of time in many Asian countries is such that a century is a short period of time and plans for future goals are considerably longer. One might say that there is less urgency than in the United States and hence time passes more rapidly or, perhaps more accurately, *less slowly*. The difference in American and Asian concepts of time has been repeatedly evidenced by different expectations about the length of the Vietnam war.

The past is a very brief period for Americans. Many events such as the Great Depression of the 1930s, World War II, the Truman presidential victory of 1948, and the impact of Senator Joseph McCarthy that are very real to people over forty years of age are as ancient history to their children as Washington crossing the Delaware. If we think of variety of stimulus input, time moves rapidly in our present society. There is such a great amount of change in our culture—in fact, change and novelty are positive values in science, art, and the marketplace—that the wisdom of elders which derives its power from stability is decreased. A contemporary high school student is likely to know more advanced physics and mathematics than his father's teacher did twenty-five years ago. The current situation may be contrasted with a culture which has had less technological change, less varied input, and less social and geographical movement of the population. In the Pacific island of Truk, for example, events in the past are treated as if they had just happened and grudges are held indefinitely.

Other differences among cultures may be noted. Many Southern European and South American officials and businessmen do not work on the assumption of one thing at a time. Rather, a number of jobs are moved along at the same time and the waiting room—in which people spend what would be for United States citizens intolerable periods of time—is a place for socialization.

Time need not add up or even be specific in the manner that we think of it. To the Hopi, time is a *characteristic sequence* rather than a measurable duration. Time is what happens when the corn matures or an animal grows up. In a similar vein, the American orientation is to isolate time from sequences of events and treat it as if it had a reality of its own. (In this sense, time joins "personality" and other reified metaphors.)

An extended quotation from Hall (1969) may serve to illustrate and bring together many of the issues in this section.

> Not so long ago, a man who was introduced as the superintendent of the Sioux came to my office. I learned that he had been born on the reservation and was a product of both Indian and white cultures, having earned his A.B. at one of the Ivy League colleges.
>
> During a long and fascinating account of the many problems which his tribe was having in adjusting to our way of life, he suddenly remarked: "What would you think of a people who had no word for 'time'? My people have no word for 'late' or for 'waiting,' for that matter. They don't know what it is to wait or to be late." He then continued, "I decided that until they could tell time and knew what time was they could never adjust themselves to white culture. So I set about to teach them time. There wasn't a clock that was running in any of the reservation classrooms. So I first bought some decent clocks. Then I made the school buses start on time, and if an Indian was two minutes late, that was just too bad. The bus started at eight forty-two and he had to be there."
>
> He was right, of course. The Sioux could not adjust to European ways until they had learned the meaning of time. The superintendent's methods may have sounded a bit extreme, but they were about the only ones that would work. The idea of starting the buses off and making the drivers hold to a rigid schedule

was a stroke of genius; much kinder to the Indian, who could better afford to miss a bus on the reservation than lose a job in town because he was late.

There is, in fact, no other way to teach time to people who handle it as differently from us as the Sioux. The quickest way is to get very technical about it and to make it mean something. Later on these people can learn the informal variations, but until they have experienced and then mastered our type of time, they will never adjust to our culture [pp. 25–26].

A Discussion and Recapitulation

The first point illustrated by the preceding quotation is that concepts of time differ widely among cultures. The presumption that all humans share the same concepts about such apparent universals as time and space is manifestly wrong, even though in our own thinking concepts of space and time are so funda-mental that it is hard to conceive of other time and space systems or even—without the help of people such as anthropologists—to raise the issue. Once it is pointed out that people live in different worlds in which the social environ-ment is differently construed, different concepts of time seem obvious and one wonders why one did not realize their existence before.

Three points about behavior influence follow. The first is that one person trying to influence the behavior of another will be far less effective in his efforts if he does not take into account the other person's world. The person being in-fluenced may view the influencer as thoughtless, rigid, mad, childish, or just plain uneducated and not worth cooperating with. The influencer will find him-self less effective than he would be with "normal" people, that is, ones who shared his cultural orientation.

This leads to the second point—one that is central to this volume. When an influencer finds that he is not succeeding—that is, the person does not change in the manner the influencer expects—he may apply the labels *lazy, stupid, un-grateful, irresponsible,* and *dingbat* to the "offender." That is, the unsuccessful in-fluencer applies the personality trait designations that would be attributed *if a person of his own culture acted in such a way.* The concept of personality be-comes an explanation of ineffectiveness that saves the self-respect of the ineffectual influencer. Unfortunately, it also maintains the ineffective behavior of the person who wants to be an influencer and does not change the behavior of the person who was to be influenced.

If one wants (that is, will find it positively reinforcing) to change another's behavior, frequently the most efficient method is to change the relevant and specific instrumental acts, in this case, the concepts of time. The third point is that the prime method for bringing about change is to make the cues that are important to the influencer important to the influencee. The designated time of an appointment is a discriminative stimulus that certain acts will have reinforcing consequences; occurring too far before or after that time, the acts will not have the same consequences. It is quite possible that favorite TV and, in an earlier era, radio programs have reinforced this form of meaningful time for children in the dominant American culture. The role of technology in concepts of time is also alluded to in Hall's example about the Sioux's provision of accurate timepieces. If such instruments of measurement are not available and used, agreement on time is necessarily less exact. While not causal, the equipment facilitates the cultural concept. We return to technology in the next section.

The teaching of a concept such as time leads back to how *any* concept is taught. We note that meaningful distinctions are taught, and this process is an integral part of learning the meaning of words. The persons has to learn *what goes with what, what cues indicate special cases,* and *how groups fit together.* A final and key point, that of values, is involved in Hall's quotation. From cues in the quotation, it seems that the author, Hall, approves of the superintendent's procedure. Hall is both sensitive and sensible; yet while he is far freer of his cultural prison than most of us will ever be, he presumes that the teaching of the white man's concept of time is a good thing. Less than two decades after he wrote the illustration, the appropriateness of such a change would be questioned by more than a few people in the academic community (and for all we know by Hall himself). Sioux time has little survival value in a white man's world, but the reverse is also true. The question then becomes, Under what conditions is it permissible to enforce the learning of a new scheme of time?

Other Cultural Influences

DeVos and Hippler (1969) have pointed out that "no student of human behavior today seriously considers the theory that motor behavior in its differing forms among different cultures is hereditarily determined [p. 325]." Just as we have previously noted national differences in concepts of time and space, there are vast differences in ways of *gesturing* despite the fact that most individuals would consider such gestures to be natural. If an American were asked to point to himself, he would most likely point to his chest. In response to the same question, a Japanese would point to his nose.

Efron (1941) reported on the differences in hand and shoulder gestures accompanying the language of New Yorkers who were Italian immigrants or Jewish immigrants from Eastern Europe. There were systematic patterns in the *spatial directions* of the gestures. For example, the Jews' gestures were frontally oriented and turned inward in contrast to the more lateral and open gestures of the southern Italians. Further evidence of the influence of the environmental situation on the learning of gestures came from Efron's observation that acculturated Jews living in New York did not use hand gestures when speaking English, but accompanied their Yiddish speech with the familiar gestures.

Thus when an individual is under the discriminative stimulus of his own behavior, Yiddish or English, he makes the gesture appropriate to the situaation (speaking to someone who understands Yiddish or English).

ECONOMIC IMPACT ON BEHAVIOR

Each section in this chapter can be qualified by a variation of the phrase, "There is much more evidence we could cite to indicate the influence of (national, social, political, cultural, organizational, and so on) factors on the behavior of the individual." In the "economic" area we will truly skim the surface. Although rarely acknowledged in texts on human behavior, it should be obvious that the relationship between what an individual receives for his labor and what he has to pay for the items enabling him to subsist has a major impact on his behavior. It may even be argued that this economic relationship is *the* major influence on behavior.

Simon and Stedrey (1969) reviewed the relationship between the disciplines of psychology and economics.[3] They have pointed out that the field of *macroeconomics* is concerned with the economy as a whole (or the big economic picture) and is not too concerned with individual behavior, since it assumes that human beings are creatures of objectivity and *rationality*. Thus, predictions can be made without the need to observe actual individual behavior. It also assumes *rational competition*, in which the better competitor is considered more likely to survive. Macroeconomics assumes that what is rational is right and permanent. Thus, the irrational must logically be wrong and transient, so that it can be safely ignored.

The other aspect of economics is called *microeconomics* and focuses on the behavior of the individual economic man. A major concept in this field is the *utility function* of the consumer. This view hypothesizes that for any pair of alternative actions available to him, the individual as a consumer can tell which he *prefers* and will react in line with his preferences. Thus, we have a picture of a rational man making a rational decision based on his own self-interest. This was obviously too simple an observation, and more sophisticated views have been developed. For example, the theory of von Neumann and Morgenstern (1944) relates "games and economic behavior," thus bringing the notion of "uncertainty" into the theory of consumer choice.

Man as an economic being behaves no differently than man in any other situation. Economic behavior (buying, selling, saving, hoarding) is still behavior and subject to the same general principles and analyses described throughout this book.

---

[3] Riegel (1972) offers an interesting linkage of psychological theories of child development with political and economic ideologies. He focuses on the behavior of influencers rather than that of the influenced (children).

The few attempts at linking economics and psychology have involved the application of the current psychological and sociological concepts and labels—attitudes, choice, level of aspiration, expectancy, decision making, social norms—to the traditional concerns of the economists. Psychology and economics should be *one field* based on the kind of observations of human behavior we have been describing. Simon and Stedrey (1969) have emphasized that the major difference between economics and psychology is methodological:

> Recent years have seen an increasing amount of borrowing of empirical methodologies among disciplines, though the average experience of social scientists trained in one discipline, but using the data-gathering techniques of the others, is very slight. A few economists are now using questionnaires and the interview as a means of learning about economic behavior. An even smaller group is exploring the possibilities of actually observing behavior within the business firm. A few studies, easily counted on the fingers, have attempted to elucidate economic phenomena by laboratory experimentation. . . . As we survey the various aspects of methodology, then, we observe a slow but significant diffusion of empirical techniques from the behavioral sciences to economics and a return traffic in statistics and mathematics (pp. 306–307).

The technique of token economy (see Chapters 11 and 14) represents a link between behavior influence and economics.

Krasner (1968) has pointed out that "Token economy procedures need a combination of social and economic planning. When an economist (for example, Galbraith, 1967) relates a 'general theory of motivation' to the economic structure of society, he is presenting hypotheses that can be tested in small social units, such as hospital wards, by means of a token economy [p. 172]." If token economies are to be regarded as true economies, then it should be possible to demonstrate the operation of at least simple principles that have been reliably observed in larger, national economies. Demonstrations of this type would strengthen the argument that token economies do in fact function as economies.

In a token economy for chronic psychiatric patients, Winkler (1970) has shown that the relationship between patients' total income and patients' total expenditure is successfully predicted from consumption schedules such as found in national economies. In both national and token economies, expenditure rises with income and stays within ± 10 percent of income over most of the income range, except at the low extreme where expenditure exceeds income and at the high extreme, where expenditure falls well below income.

While the field of economics augments the theoretical base for understanding token economies, it can also provide ideas for the design of new and perhaps more effective token economies. Many different types of economic systems have been developed throughout the world, each with its own particular aspects and each the topic of considerable study. Present token economies are most often what are labeled *command economies*, which means that they have no free market or private ownership and there is little relationship between the cost of producing goods and their prices.

The economic system has an effect on behavior, and different forms have different effects. (Fromm, 1947, stressed this point for psychological aspects of the behavior of people in these systems.) Therefore, viable token economies must search for economic systems which require, strengthen, or reinforce "healthy" and therapeutically desirable behavior. For example, in a program described by Winkler and Krasner (1971), patients were trained in the behavioral skills required for survival outside the hospital. An economy based on aspects of a semisocialist economic system such as that in Yugoslavia was devised for the ward. In such countries, many enterprises are run by workers elected from their peers, and worker income is a function of the *businesses' income*. A program preparing female patients to return to the community was entirely funded by the profits of a canteen owned and operated by the patients in the program. Each patient-worker received pay in proportion to the profits of the day's sales to the patients in other programs. Each patient therefore was receiving money *according to the success of her group's work* (profit sharing) and was, in effect, paying for her own treatment program while learning the many skills required to run a successful canteen.

Typically, economists are forced to gather data through nonexperimental techniques such as analysis of census reports, government records, business operations, and so on. The variables economists discuss are usually not theirs to control directly, and as a result the empirical evaluation of much economic theory is very poorly developed as various economists (Juster, 1970; Leontief, 1971) have pointed out. In token economies not only can detailed measures of important variables be obtained directly but these variables can also be directly controlled for research purposes (Kagel and Winkler, 1972).

Economic concepts that may be tested are those of inflation and depression. For example, if a therapeutic goal is to reinforce the hospitalized patient's prosocial behavior, then it is desirable that he should spend his tokens. If the rate of pay is overly high, the person may easily earn more tokens than he uses, and at a certain point be either hoarding or not using the backups, extrinsic reinforcers for which tokens are exchanged. One way to alleviate this situation is to raise prices; another is to devalue tokens so that at the start of each month, the previous month's tokens are worth only, for example, one-third of their original value.

Other analogies might be made to social classes: if an increasingly long period is introduced between work, receipt of tokens, and exchange of tokens for backup reinforcers, then we approach the more general situation of a set weekly or monthly payday. A step-level process may develop in which a person at an advanced level earns a *status*, in which he pays to obtain a credit card entitling him to backup reinforcers without having to spend tokens each time.

In similar fashion, a person at a higher level may have the open ward or geographical mobility that permits him a wider range of more interesting or better paying jobs. A person may even buy jobs that may eventually lead to greater remuneration. This is like earning a college degree as a key to a job. How to keep the consumer spending most of his earnings while still saving a portion of his income for future greater gains is the problem of the ward psychologist as well as the economist.

A final problem is that a high level of prosocial activity is desired. Thus, the token economy member may be placed in a situation of sufficient scarcity that encourages activity with enough of a payoff to make work meaningful but continually necessary. Ideally, he lives like a college professor or a donkey: working hard but never getting too far ahead.

The same results of scarcity, reward, and continual work occurred during the late ninth to the mideleventh centuries of European civilization, or what might be called the early Middle Ages. Central government had broken down and there were not sufficient funds for the upkeep of the army, especially for the introduction of new heavy armored cavalry. The only method of payment for military service was a gift of land, at first for a limited period, but eventually hereditarily. This led to the end of the absolute monarchy, since the great landowners had territory and power while the king had only his personal estates.

The economy became organized around the manor rather than towns, and trade decreased, for as Hauser (1958) has noted, "As money and means of communication, cities, and markets are mostly lacking, people are forced to make themselves independent of the outside world, and to forego both the acquisition of others' products and the sale of their own. Thus a situation develops in which there is almost no incentive to produce goods in excess of one's own needs [vol. 1, p. 179]." Not only are extra goods not produced, the competition involved in making these goods more attractive to prospective buyers is not present. The emphasis is not on discovery or improvement—values that are today taken almost for granted in both art and science—but on confirmation, reproduction, and corroboration of already revealed truth. These features are prevalent in a totalitarian society, in which the individual's intellectual and personal mobility and freedom to change are markedly reduced. In short, political, economic, and social behaviors are clearly interrelated.

THE INFLUENCE OF TECHNOLOGY

Technology refers to tools, "the organization of knowledge for the achievement of practical purposes [Mesthene, 1970, p. 25]." Man extends his ability to change his physical and social environment through tools, which create new opportunities. But tools themselves are developed within a social environment. It is hard to say which comes first—whether the society develops technology or whether technology creates new social patterns. Further, technological innovation may have unforseen consequences such as public health measures leading to a rapidly expanding population, the use of fertilizers and pesticides to increase food production and pollution. Modern technology frequently is of such complexity that specialization is fostered, as in medicine, and job segmentation, as in mass production. Modern technology is both a source of pressure and a solution which makes possible increasingly large concentrations of specialized people in factories, universities, and governments. Increasing dependence on others leads to an increase in both formal and informal rules. Because any one of numerous groups can bring a complex, interdependent society to a halt, controls over the range of choices available to the individual are increased. Legislative and contractual obligations by experts representing groups takes the place of face-to-face bargaining.

The technological innovation perhaps most interesting to the person interested in behavior influence deals with the *interchange of information*. There has been an explosion of both material to communicate and methods by which to store, transmit, and receive information. Such technological developments may enable an informed electorate to aid in the selection of decision makers and even to help make a few crucial decisions, but technology is also available for societal control of the individual and invasion of his privacy. Information is disseminated more rapidly, more widely, and—if one seeks it—in increasing depth; but the speed and variety of information has decreased the opportunity for calm reflection and studied action. Movies, television, and magazine advertisements present hard-to-attain ways of life as not only desirable but necessary.

In summary, the availability of new tools for travel, communication, and an easier life has shaped the places in which we live, broadened and changed our horizons, and led to a different environment not only physically but also socially. This technology in and of itself has become a major determinant of our behavior (see Muller, 1970).

We may bring economic and technological considerations together by asking the reader to think of the consequences of increasing the cost of some common object which is part of his daily life, such as an automobile or television set. If a government tax raised gasoline to ten times its current price, we suspect that the number of private automobiles would decrease. The usage of public transportation might well increase, while the number of gas stations, auto dealers, auto repair shops, tire stores, and associated auto industries would decrease. Shopping plazas in the suburbs would probably become smaller, while the number of neighborhood stores and restaurants would increase. To the extent that more select clienteles would be served and turnover of inventory would be less, the special tastes of specific groups might be more frequently represented. The trend in American culture towards homogeneity might be slowed.

The Organizational Context

Schools, clubs, teams, leagues, churches, factories, governmental agencies, hospitals, companies, cooperatives, charity drives, political parties, grocery chains, and the like—we spend our lives working for and using groups of people banded together in certain patterns to attain selected goals.

This bonding together is not new to the United States and was commented upon by Alexis de Tocqueville over a hundred years ago:

> Americans of all ages, all conditions, and all dispositions constantly form associations. They have not only commercial and manufacturing companies, in which all take part, but associations of a thousand other kinds, religious, moral, serious, futile, general or restricted, enormous or diminutive. The Americans make associations to give entertainments, to found seminaries, to build inns, to construct churches, to diffuse books, to send missionaries to the antipodes; in this manner they found hospitals, prisons, and schools. If it is proposed to inculcate some truth—they form a society. Wherever at the head of some new undertaking you see the government in France, or a man of rank in England, in the United States you will be sure to find an association [as quoted by Kaufmann, 1967, p. 6].

The organization is a setting for behavior that deeply influences the range of people's behavior. Of the many aspects of organizations, we have chosen to deal primarily with size and secondarily with complexity. Technological innovation interacts significantly with large manufacturing corporations: technology makes the large corporation both possible and necessary and in turn is furthered by such organizations. In many ways, organization—the arrangement of effort as it develops—is itself a technology. Civilization depends on groupings of people: administrative organization to ensure irrigation, storage, and protection of crops were as necessary as implements to turn the soil in the development of the Egyptian and Mesopotamian civilization.

"Perhaps the minimum definition of formal organization is that collective effort is explicitly organized for specific ends [Blau and Scott, 1962, p. 223]." Large size makes increased and specialized effort possible and is conducive to specialization, hierarchy of authority, rules, and impersonality. These four characteristics—specialization, hierarchy, rules, and impersonality—are basic to the definition of bureaucracy (Blau, 1956, p. 19). Increased size and specialization lead to an increased need for coordination among units, which leads to supervisors of supervisors and coordination of interdependent units. In short, *a new group of workers dealing with the relations among people* rather than production of objects themselves comes into being. This leads to a new field of study—not the conduct *of* the corporation, but conduct *in* the corporation.

W. E. Moore (1962, p. 34) has spoken of a "social landscape" in the manner that Barker (1968) talked of a behavior setting. The jobs within the organization are described in terms of task and then evaluated in terms of personal requirements such as knowledge and experience required to do them. A person is hired to fill a position; while the person may resign, retire, or die, the task and position are likely to continue. The person is fitted in and the position description outlines certain work behaviors and lines of authority. Jobs are not fitted to people; *people are fitted to job descriptions.*

Because the organization is most efficient when previous solutions are made routine, there is a corporate emphasis on categorizing situations so that rules and precedents may be applied. The brusqueness of a representative of an organization, whether a secretary or a dean, may well be due to the probability that an exception to the rule will require increased effort by the employee or the organization. The more an organizational employee knows about an exceptional case, the less likely he will be to find a comfortable category for that situation that would permit a solution by the book. The *book*, that is, the written rules representing prior solutions, permits each person to be treated "properly." Characteristics of the "case" lead to categorizations that indicate what action can be taken. This situation is the basis of the concept of impersonality: all people who are equal in a manner relevant to the rules are treated in the same way.

The employee is not authorized to deal with exceptions and must refer the individual up the line to his supervisor until some person or office is found that is authorized to make the decision. Both the specific decision and any new general rules are then put into writing. The written word provides the memory of the action to take in a given situation because the person who made the decision may forget or leave the organization. The forms and rules of the organization increase, and it is not too inaccurate to say that a body of law similar to more formal legislation is developed. One problem is that the client (student, customer) is not privy to this law; another problem is that the majority of employees do not know the full extent of the rules either and may apply only those they know of or choose to. Thus the more rules promulgated in the organization for justice and equality, the less likely it may be that these ends will result.

Rules dominate an organization. The rules are of two major sorts: the arrangement of *who is responsible to whom for what* and *the specification of what should be done in each position.* To quote W. E. Moore (1962):

> The greatest single advantage of the model administrative organization over other forms of human interaction is the capacity for inducing strangers and even potential enemies to cooperate in accomplishing the collective mission. This is accomplished not by brainwashing or conversions in character but by the single process of employment. Cooperation consists of persons performing tasks that are related to other tasks. . . .
>
> . . . In large organizations persons who are unseen by and unknown to one another are caught up in webs of reciprocal or sequential dependence. . . .

This mechanical cooperation permits the use of radically divergent personality types and trained skills, allows the organization to go on while its human components are being shuffled and replaced, and achieves collective goals out of the efforts of individuals who perhaps couldn't care less. It is really remarkable what money, in the form of wages and salaries, can do in dissolving human apathy and antipathy [pp. 36–37].

First, then, the concept of corporation is one of *order* (Drucker, 1964, p. 173). Second, this order is manifest in assignment of *supervised* tasks. Messages officially should move through superiors (the channels) until a person who has the authority to make a decision is reached. At times, to communicate in an official manner with each other, two people occupying relatively low positions on the hierarchy must go through many steps until they arrive at the lowest common administrator, that is, a person who has authority over both their positions and thus can make a decision.

This procedure is cumbersome, but has the advantage of making behavior predictable and permitting the assignment of authority and responsibility. It has the disadvantage of delaying action. The safest thing to do is opt for the status quo; and as each person in the upward movement of a message may be able to veto it, change may go through many levels and interdependent offices before it is approved if ever.[4] Similarly, change may lead to reorganization to accomplish a task; and reorganization is costly, since new boundaries and assignment of authority may be needed. It is imperative not only that each order be checked but that it be checked by only one clearly specified person, lest confusion of authority arise. That is, not only are tasks and responsibility clear, the limits of responsibility must also be clear.

A person has only a limited span of time and attention, or *range of control*. As the location or nature of tasks becomes more complex, the shorter is this span of control and the greater is the need for another level of supervision. The further the person in authority is from the site of actual work, the more he must deal with problems as abstractions and make his decisions general. This leads him to the behavior of simplifying and categorizing the complex, which eventually becomes a source of maladaptive behavior in the organization.

In the face of this situation the formal organization at times is supplemented by an *informal organization* of precedence, experience, and mutual friendship. A person may delay an action by going by the book, or he may speed one by going out of channels. In order to change a light bulb, it may be necessary

---

[4] To the extent that an innovation is something the supervisor would *not* have done, the burden of proof is on the creative person. To the extent that an innovation must move up many levels of supervisors, any one of whom may veto it, innovation is either discouraged or introduced through informal rather than formal channels. This may lead the very large corporation to become obsolete, since smaller companies may more readily adopt new ideas about people and products.

officially to put in a work order and wait for the housekeeping or engineering department to do the job. This may easily mean a wait of three days until the maintenance men meet prior commitments, and the person making the request may literally work in the dark. The alternative is cutting across channels and having the maintenance man do a favor before the paper that justifies the time and inventory is approved up and down the line. A network of informal reciprocal obligations and associations develops alongside the formal channels.

The informal network is always vulnerable to the official channels and a person caught off base may be reprimanded. This is necessary, since the authority system might well be undermined if the informal channel diluted the assignment of authority and left a person responsible for actions of which he was ignorant. But the informal organization may, if not veto, at least sabotage actions and people in the formal channels. One technique is to be overscrupulous and flood an official with all the memos and requests officially required. He is bogged down, then, in extraneous information.

Another function of the informal organization is protection. Not only may employees cover for each other, they may set rules that discourage eager beavers or rate busters. The informal network also carries rumors. Because an official communication going through channels may be delayed for days or even weeks as it moves up and down the proper channels, friends may tell each other likely changes in rules or personnel. The informal channels also permit trial balloons: neither a superior nor an employee need lose face if an idea is presented informally. A typical maneuver in the university is for a professor to let his close friends know "in deepest confidence" that another school is about to make him an offer. He is likely to obtain feedback helpful in determining how far he can bargain before becoming the guest of honor at a farewell party.

Different from and not to be confused with the informal organization is what has come to be called the *human relations movement*. Following the results of the Hawthorne experiments (Roethlisberger and Dickson, 1939) which found that workers improved their output regardless of the physical changes in their work setting, as long as *changes were made and management was explicitly interested in them*, a great amount of effort was expended on workers' attitudes. This led to an interest in nonfinancial motives and workers' personalities. The present authors follow Moore (1962), who believes that this more personal view was welcome to management because it served to reduce costs in terms of wages, and Brayfield and Crockett (1959), who wrote after a painstaking review: "We have arrived at two conclusions: first, that satisfaction with one's position in a network of relationships need not imply strong motivation to an outstanding performance within that system, and, second, that productivity may be only peripherally related to many of the goals toward which the industrial worker is striving [p. 421]." Put differently, a kiss on the hand is nice, but diamonds are a girl's best friend.

A third important feature of the organizational landscape is the distinction between professionals and nonprofessionals. In most industrial settings the professionals feed their expertise to the manager and are called *staff*. The people who work in ways that lead directly to the product are called *line* personnel. In hospitals and schools this situation is reversed, with physicians and teachers applying their professional expertise to the avowed purpose of the organization, the patients and students, while supported by nonprofessionals. A nonprofessional is at a disadvantage in evaluating the capability and production of the professional. He must take the word of professionals as to the competence of the physicians, teachers, and scientists working for him.

The professional who has kept up with his field can increase his professional status. He is *cosmopolitan* in terms of his reference group when his visibility is not limited to the place of his work. The administrator increases his value as he gains knowledge of his organization, but he loses through disuse and lack of study the professional skills he may once have had (in a university). The administrator is *local*, since his value is visible at his place of employment and is within rather than outside the organization. Because their future is not necessarily tied to it and their bargaining power with the organization resides in opinion outside it, cosmopolitans are less loyal to the organization than locals.

Reinforced Behavior in an Organization

First and foremost, a person is paid to do his job. The more explicit the task, as on the assembly line, the more clearly the work is related to compensation. When one moves up the hierarchy, the association of productivity to compensation becomes less clear. Assignment of duties and supervisory checks do lead to work being accomplished. The best prediction of what a person will be doing during the working day is the task specified in his position (job) description. Despite all individual differences in personal and professional styles, the best guess is that students and teachers will meet at the times and places assigned, that mailmen will make their appointed rounds, and that secretaries will type the memos produced by administrators.

As one moves from a situation in which there is a clear specification of desirable behavior, however, advancement in grade or increased salary for merit poses problems of measurement. A chronic difficulty is the specification of what is a good administrator or a good teacher. The latter position illustrates an additional problem: there may be many tasks and potential criteria for evaluation. A typical psychology professor may teach large undergraduate lecture sections and smaller graduate classes, give seminars, and supervise research or clinical practice. Competence in one area is not highly correlated, if at all, with competence at other forms of teaching.

The university teacher may also serve on committees of faculty or students, perform housekeeping chores on grants and budgets, advise or counsel students, or do that sort of teaching of fellow teachers known as consulting. He may be an editor of a professional journal; work for local, state, or federal agencies such as hospitals; and serve on boards of his professional associations. Some of these jobs provide an honorarium; most do not. Finally, a university teacher is supposed to be an expert, to be abreast of his field and ahead of his textbooks: he is supposed to create information as well as communicate it to students. The question becomes not only how the data for these divergent behaviors will be collected, but also how they will be weighed.

The answer for the professional such as the university professor is that most annual increases in compensation are a result of "outside offers." That is, another university bids for his services and the teacher moves to that one or remains at his present university if it matches the new offer. This leads professors to select certain behaviors—those that are cosmopolitan and visible beyond the confines of one institution, notably publication and involvement in the national professional organizations—as more likely to lead to reinforcement and advancement than the local activities of teaching or counseling students.

For nonprofessionals within a service organization, the situation is both similar and different. The person is evaluated for grade enhancement on the basis of his performance in his current job. The problem is how to do an outstanding job, and by this is meant one that will be recognized as such by people responsible for promotion. Just as the university teacher is biased toward scholarly production, so other biases may be introduced into other positions. For example Baker (1968) has noted that in advertising,

> most commercials are not written primarily to reach the general audience but *to impress other ad men.* Many Mad Avenuers, I believe, don't consciously realize this fact themselves. Ad men producing commercials look first for the gimmicks, camera tricks, "new" twists that will bring a reaction of "Oh, how clever!" from their peers and bosses. TV commercial writers and artists want to impress their personal originality on others in the creative departments, the agency, other agencies, on the client, other advertisers, the . . . field in general.

That is, the ostensible mission involving the consumer is *displaced* for the more immediately reinforced behavior of a supervisor or customer. The same point has been made by Henry (1964) in a study of nurses:

> "When you go off duty, they don't know whether you have spent time with the patients, but they do know whether you have written in the chart." This raises the important ancillary problem of the *hidden deficit,* which may be stated as follows: when a subordinate worker has a choice of tasks of unequal visibility, he will tend to perform the task of greater visibility and neglect the task of lower visibility—visibility referring, of course, not to what the worker sees, but rather to what his supervisor can see [p. 32].

One thing that can be seen is the *size* of a *budget* and the *number of people supervised*. Many position descriptions are graded on the basis of administrative responsibility, and this in turn means that the person whose department spends the most, whether wisely or otherwisely, will be in line for a raise. W. E. Moore (1962, pp. 119–120) is explicit on this matter. The budget may be a symbol of the person's importance, and in each step up the line, inflated budgets (leading at times to the invention of new missions to justify increases) are submitted as "first offers." Since most organizations have a "use it or lose it" policy, money left over toward the end of the year will be used to purchase furniture and new machines or to hire consultants, so that no evidence will exist that the original budget estimate was excessive and possibly incompetent.

To summarize and bring this section to a close: a large percentage of the work force (W. E. Moore, 1962, p. viii) labors in organizational settings. The basic aspect of organization is an ordering of work so that the outcome of the effort of many people will be predictable. The need for authority, specialization, rules, and impersonal application of rules develops when large groups of people are interdependent in attaining a common goal. The pressure to follow the rules and adapt to the organization overrides many personal preferences and the need to protect and enhance one's job leads additionally to types of behavior not originally envisioned. Finally, adjustment to the work situation (Presthus, 1962; Thompson, 1961; Whyte, 1956) may lead to the development of types of behavior patterns as well as specific task behaviors. But again the *setting* and the *behavior reinforced* in that setting (Lichtman and Hunt, 1971), not some organizational structure or personality, should be used to describe, evaluate, and hopefully modify people toward greater effectiveness and satisfaction.

LAST WORD

From the kinship and taboo systems of preliterate people to the interaction in contemporary formal organizations such as universities, the possible reinforceable behaviors a person may make are as limited by a socioeconomic environment as they are by the physical environment described in Chapter 13. In explanations of differences in overt behavior, these factors must be taken into account.

A relatively small and therefore more comprehensible example of the interaction of educational, economic, and technological variables is the current crisis in archeology (Coggins, 1972; Davis, 1972), which may serve as a summary of the complexities involved. To increase archeological knowledge, it is necessary to take into account the contextual earth, the remains of houses, and even the trash in which objects are found. As one result of increased public knowledge and sophistication, the number of amateurs who dig for artifacts and looters who sell to the art antiquities market has increased. Both groups seek objects rather than knowledge and disturb the sites, so that they yield little if any historical information.

While the mass media may spread interest in and appreciation of archeology, other technological advances may lead to the use of power saws to shave off parts of buildings so that they may be more readily transported. Ease of transportation makes sites that were previously difficult to reach, and thus protected, a goal for the amateur with increased leisure. Finally, the use of bulldozers to level earth for dams and roads may first destroy sites and then later put the remains under water or concrete. Here progress destroys the past; and it is possible that the professional by creating the understanding and taste of the general population may have hastened the demise of his source of knowledge and expertise.

We have used the large industrial and educational institution as an example in this chapter to show how economic, political, technological, and organizational considerations influence the behaviors and reinforcers available to the individual. Settings both create and limit the individual's opportunities to make acts and give meaning to the acts he makes.

16

Persuasion and Propaganda: Communication and Coercion

One of the most difficult things for an individual to accept is that he has been had. We all want to feel that we are free people, masters of our own destiny, captains of our own ship. Yet the thrust of the preceding fifteen chapters is that a multitude of influences—from our genes to our peers to our social class—affect, guide, and to a large extent control our behavior. Still we are not helpless puppets, and there are many ways in which we can control our environment (for example, see Chapter 12). In this chapter, however, we explore one influence process which arouses resentment and concern, that of being controlled for the *explicit benefit of someone else*.

In order to understand and appreciate the kinds of influences that are labeled as *propaganda* and *coercion*, we must present some concepts to provide a framework for pressures which attempt to have us do what we might not have done if we had an informed choice in the matter. We act and the physical and social environment reacts to us. As the environment changes and we find ourselves in an altered situation, we react to it. Our actions and the environment in which they are made may be thought of in terms of *bits of information.* Even at the sensory level we are continually rearranging and interpreting. We look at the solid rectangular door and "know" it is there, but as a retinal stimulus it appears actually upside down. The door changes shape as we or it moves and yet it appears to us as solid and stable despite the varying inputs.

Our ultimate molecular "reality" may be viewed as a matter of electrochemical interchanges functioning on a yes-no, on-off basis in a manner similar to a computer. This information is decoded by learned linguistic and cultural programs. We learn to scan information, to depend on prior experience to provide contextual clues, and to ignore or adapt information which is confirmatory and does not contradict too greatly our quality control standards. We may reprogram and learn new patterns as a result of changes throughout life such as those that come as we move from childhood through adolescence to maturity and senility and as political, economic, and technological systems change the *context* of reinforcement (see Chapter 15).

One of the ways of describing man's uniqueness among animals is that tools enable him to extend and alter his capacities for coping in a matter of years, whereas natural selection would require many generations to make the necessary evolutionary adjustments. The most familiar of these changes are physical tools that extend spatial range such as the airplane and the radio or ones that alter personal climate such as home heating and air conditioning. But the really major alterations are *intellectual*, as in the organization of the efforts of numerous people and the patterning of events into religious, political, social, and scientific concepts.

Just as a constant interchange occurs between a person and his physical environment, a constant interchange also occurs between a person and his intellectual environment. In this process of interchange of information, we cannot help but influence others and be influenced by them. In many regards this interchange is similar to the work of historians (see Chapter 7).

INFORMATION INPUTS, ORGANIZATIONS, AND OUTPUTS: SOME DEFINITIONS

We are interested in conditions that lead to differences in behavior and the behaviors of people such as psychologists who formulate that behavior. We emphasize the use of an overt behavior that may be differentiated from other actions as the measure of the effect of inputs or different stimulus conditions. It should be kept in mind that a person's output may serve as a condition for subsequent behavior and that to *continue* in a course of action is as much differential behavior as to increase, decrease, or otherwise alter a course of action. Francis Bacon (1963, p. 65) knew this, as much as current university presidents, when he wrote, "a forward retention of customs is as turbulent a thing as an innovation."

Output, or overt behavior, then, is an observable, differentiable act. *Input* refers to environmental conditions that may be manipulated. Various words used to designate input in this chapter are *communication, advertising propaganda,* and *coercion*—all of which refer to the general category of *the transmission of information.* We will be particularly interested in dealing with impact upon groups of people, but we should note that (*a*) all groups are composed of individuals; (*b*) the definition of a group, audience, or population is not an easy task; and (*c*) the principles applying to individuals should also serve, at least at the start, for individuals in group situations.

This does not mean that distinctions cannot be made between individual and mass communications. Boorstin (1970), for example, has distinguished between advertising and salesmanship. The communication of a salesman is directed at an individual, while an advertisement aims to bring individual members of a population into a community of consumers. The distinction may break down, as when a husband and wife shop together. The most central difference seems to be the direction of the communication.

An example that appeals to the present authors is the distinction they make as professors between lecturing and teaching. *Lecturing* is designated as talking to so large a group that the presentation is likely to be formal and starts (and usually ends) with the professor. There is very little opportunity to tailor the lecture to the student, and certainly not to all the students present. Teaching is possible with a small group of students who are comfortable with each other; in this situation the teacher can respond to where each student is intellectually (also note comments on the open classroom in Chapter 14). The ultimate of lecturing is the taped or televised presentation in which there are no cues such as questions, blank faces, or shifting bodies to provide the speaker with information (feedback) about how he is coming across. But the distinction between lecturing and teaching also becomes tenuous: there are times in a seminar when one of the participants lectures and there are blessed moments in large lectures when a dialogue develops among some of the audience and the speaker.

Television taping and book writing are not completely devoid of feedback. Student enrollment for a television course provides some guides as to its reception; the number of students entering similar courses subsequent to the televised one provides another measure. Scores on examinations both in the TV course and in subsequent classes and students' statements about the course (ratings, responses to questions) may also be used. For a textbook, a measure dear to the hearts of publishers is called *sales* and is similar to class enrollment. There is feedback, but it is delayed in time and is relatively impersonal.

As we move on the continuum from personal to mass communication, we know less about the audience; operationally, feedback of responses by the audience are less prompt, less clear, and less personal. The television lecturer or the author, however, must continue his job of communicating, just as candidates for election and producers of consumer products must continue their tasks. This leads to the construction of the audience as an *abstraction* or *image*.

We have applied the word *image* to the audience, but refined categories for investigative purposes have used words such as *opinion, attitude, belief, feeling,* and *value*. With college lectures, we may add *completion of prerequisites* and *training in studying and evaluating new information*. How information will be processed between input and output we have called *organization*.

Attitude as an Organizing Concept

The person emitting behaviors such as speech does so to have an effect on a recipient, listener, or message decoder. Both what he hopes to accomplish and the increased likelihood of attaining his goal are served by knowledge of the decoder or audience. A lecturer looking at his class can make some predictions about how his messages will be received; the question is how to increase and organize his information about the audience to heighten the impact of the messages sent. The first question is whether there are commonalities that will help us predict audiences' responses to different messages; such prediction may be called *improved control*.

The reader will note that we keep returning to a basic premise: the desirability of increasing one's effectiveness with other people. In the realm of mass audience and general messages, the target variables of the intellectual organization of the receivers have been called attitudes and opinions—or in earlier times opinions, sentiments, and predilections. We have pointed out (Chapter 4) that attitudes are strikingly analogous to personality traits. Hilgard (1962) has defined attitude as, "An orientation toward or away from some object, concept, or situation; a readiness to respond in a predetermined manner to the object, concept, or situation [p. 614]" and a trait as, "A persisting characteristic or dimension of personality according to which individuals can be rated or measured [p. 635]." This requires a definition of personality, which Hilgard (1962) has given as, "The individual characteristics and ways of behaving which, in their organization or patterning, account for an individual's unique adjustment to his total environment [p. 627]." A trait, then, is a characteristic used to account for individual behavior, and an attitude is a readiness to respond in a particular manner. Both traits and attitudes are inferred from behavior, whether directly in terms of situations or indirectly in terms of self-report tests.

Psychologists have devoted considerable effort to the area of attitudes. Allport has observed (1935) that "attitude is probably the most distinctive and indispensable concept in contemporary American social psychology. No other term appears more frequently in experimental and theoretical literature." This frequently cited as being descriptive of the interest and belief in this concept. McGuire (1969) has noted that "the last five social psychology textbooks which have appeared devoted an average of 25 percent of the space to attitude work, far more than any of the other topics, such as group processes and socialization [p. 138]."

General Comments

We are interested in having an impact on an audience. The audience's prior experiences (for example, learning a common language) and current concerns influence the material communicated. We presume that knowing the audience's position and feelings will help us in making an effective appeal. However, we can measure the effectiveness of the appeal only by action, and that is exactly what has not been clearly measured by psychologists or when measured has been found to be disappointing. To quote McGuire (1969):

> It would appear that [observing how the individual actually behaves in a situation] is the most directly measurable of the three [potential criteria of], and hence the most useful as the criterion component of attitude. However, closer examination shows that it tends to be measured, as frequently as do the cognitive and affective components, by a paper-and-pencil inventory which indicates how the person says he would behave in the presence of the object, rather than by observation of how he actually behaves. Attitude research has long indicated . . . that the person's verbal report of his attitude has a rather low correlation with his actual behavior toward the object of the attitude [p. 156].

This is illustrated by a report of LaPiere (1934), who traveled 10,000 miles across the United States with a young Chinese couple in the 1930s and was served at 184 eating and 66 different sleeping establishments. The group was turned away only once, and it was not clear if this was due to racial prejudice. When LaPiere sent questionnaires to all these places, one item was about serving Chinese persons. Questionnaires were returned by 128 of the establishments, and 90 percent of the places that had served the Chinese said they would not serve Chinese, and only one establishment said it definitely would. De Fleur and Westie (1958) found that one-third of their college students "behaved in a manner quite inconsistent with that which might be expected from their verbal attitudes [p. 673]."

Whether one is observing a parent telling his offspring to do what he says and not what he does, a campus freedom fighter denying the right to speak to someone with whom he disagrees, or a young lady displaying a worldly sophistication that is as great as her skirt is short, one finds that what a person says and what he does are frequently correlated at discouragingly low levels. A persons' expression of an attitude or opinion is itself an act and subject to all the environmental influences on overt action described previously.

An interesting debate is whether a change in attitude will be followed by a change in behavior or whether changed behavior is likely to lead to changed expressed attitudes. Data for the latter is far stronger, particularly from the *cognitive dissonance* (Festinger, 1957, p. 30) and *commitment* literature (Kiesler, 1971). In fact, Kiesler's working definition of commitment is "pledging or binding of the individual to behavioral acts [p. 30]"; his intuitive and quite operational comment is that "Explicit behavior, like an irrevocable decision, provides the pillar around which the cognitive apparatus must be draped. Through behavior, one is committed [p. 17]." Overt behavior is not irrevocable, but it certainly has an impact; and within the laboratory situation, behavior indicates a greater direction and stability than attitudes. Overt action makes the person more open to some aspects of his environment and more closed to others. To quote Kiesler (1971) again, "If you want someone not only to behave in a particular way but also to believe accordingly, then induce the behavior under conditions of very little external pressure. Give the person the feeling that he was free to do otherwise if he wished [pp. 164–165]." If the person can designate an external pressure, whether accurate or not, he may disavow the behavior as his own.

Commitment may be viewed phenomenologically as self-attribution, a self-labeling in the manner noted above. We agree with Kiesler (1971) that "if we fail, if the other refuses to act as we intended, we are not left with a null effect but rather the opposite effect. The subject we tried to commit may now be less resistant to counter-propaganda than before, more open to opposing views [p. 65]." Going beyond Kiesler to setting events, the person *learns not only acts but also relations to sources of influence.*

Having the person do favors (Freedman and Fraser, 1966), answer a biased questionnaire (Dillehay and Jernigan, 1970), or sign a petition (Kiesler, 1971) are acts that may precede expressed attitude change. It should also be remembered that refusing to give help or to sign a petition is also a social act and the justification for a refusal may be just as committing, but in an opposite direction, as compliance with the request.

Finally, attitudes may be a crucial part of a social role, and similar attitudes an aspect of attractiveness (Byrne, 1968). The person who was once a student but is now a teacher is likely to learn a new set of attitudes either through peer reinforcement or harsh experience. The converse may also be demonstrated: role playing may alter expressed attitudes (Greenwald, 1970; Janis and Mann, 1965). In short, *overt action usually precedes attitude change* rather than the reverse.

That attitude and behavior are not clearly related has not discouraged the existence of a major attitude change and opinion measurement industry in the United States. Hennessy (1970, pp. 134–135) has cited studies that "facts" given in public opinion surveys may deviate from objective truth. In one study, nearly two-fifths of the sample misrepresented their educational level; in another 10 percent falsely claimed that they had valid drivers' licenses. The subjects seemed to want to be helpful and to look good.

McGuire (1969) has put the matter as follows:

> A tremendous amount of applied research has been carried out to test the effectiveness of the mass media by those who work in the marketing, advertising, and political-behavior areas. . . . The outcome has been quite embarrassing for proponents of the mass media, since there is little evidence of attitude change, much less change in gross behavior such as buying or voting . . . Indeed, some of the results make it appear that mass media campaigns may even have the reverse of the intended persuasive impact; for example, Belson (1956) found that television programs designed to enhance the viewers' confidence in their ability to speak French had the reverse effect, and political behaviorists (for example, Berelson, Lazarsfeld, and McPhee, 1954) have found that those who expose themselves most to the presidential campaigns on the mass media seem to be the least affected by the campaign [p. 227].

Opinion

Hennessy (1970) has written, "There are almost as many definitions of public opinion as there are writers on public opinion [p. 21]." It seems from the various definitions that (a) there must be an issue on which there is significant disagreement, (b) the issue must be of widespread (but certainly not universal) concern, and (c) some expression or decision must be made by people in public. This last requirement refers to the goal of public opinion study, but also seems a useful way to help categorize the various terms. By this criterion *values* may be considered long-term enduring preferences or orientations, matters of principle that may be at a metacommunication level, that is, that deal with general relationships. Attitudes deal with general preferences and orientations in regard to designatable objects or people. *Opinions* are even more specific as to objects, situations, and people and more overt, factual, and short-term. This categorization is unfortunately unidimensional; for example, *internal* or *covert* or *unexpressed* opinions merge into attitudes.

A number of authors have distinguished between opinion as—dealing with potential facts that may be checked with expert or technical opinion—and attitude—feeling for which there is no ostensible right or wrong other than possible consequences. In this view the dimension moves from fact (opinion) to feeling (attitude). Hilgard (1962) arrived at this by defining opinion as "a judgment or belief involving an expectation or prediction about behavior or events [p. 626]." This definition means that an opinion can more easily be empirically verified, which in turn means that it is more specifiable. The same definition may be found in English and English (1958) who have defined an opinion as, "a belief that one holds to be without emotional commitment or desire, and to be open to reevaluation since the evidence is not affirmed to be convincing [p. 358]." That is, an opinion is a view *weakly* but *rationally* held. Public "opinion" about political events and leaders either belies this definition or in actuality deals with attitudes.

Public opinion aims to find out the status of *information* and *verifiable expectation* in a relevant population. The words *facts* and *information* may be used to designate specific bits of data available or not to members of the population, but the very nature of the historical process (as outlined in Chapter 7) is such that the type and amount of information available to an individual is highly preselected and biased. For example, less than half the American population seems to be very interested in presidential elections (Hennessy, 1970, p. 37). And the amount of information in any complex society or field of social endeavor such as a science is so great that even if a person devoted all his time to information gathering and organization, he probably could not be completely informed. Even in the field of science, the information sources are selected, the data are organized, and different views on topics become legitimate subjects for dispute. It is a fortunate event, but not necessarily a certain one, when such disputes lead to collection of relevant data.

People reason from facts which are incompletely or unevenly available and subject to manipulation by methods such as mass communication. At present the effectiveness of mass advertising seems not to have been proven; and this raises problems of how opinions and attitudes may be formed and changed.

With all these problems, why do we devote time and space to attitudes and opinions as a prelude to mass communications? There are a number of cogent reasons. Primarily, public opinion is part of our scene as psychologists. As noted in the quotations above and the material in Chapter 4, great amounts of professional energy are devoted to the topic. Further, there are parallels between the fields of social psychology and personality (as in Chapter 3); and attitude measurement and personality measurement share strong commonalities in theory, methodology (a verbal or questionnaire report), and generalizability.

Attitudes seem to have become an interest in themselves on both an academic and an applied level. By "academic" we are referring to the professional studies and theories on such topics as contrast, assimilation, balance, and cognitive dissonance. By "applied" we are referring to the efforts made to change attitudes about race or drug use with little investigation or followup.

Finally, attitudes represent an area that deals with the problem of the things people may *say to themselves*. We see such acts as (*a*) *parts of chains* in which an individual's responses are discriminative stimuli for his further acts; (*b*) *anticipatory goal responses*, which provide practice or predictions of how a person *might* act; and (*c*) related to both of the above, possession of knowledge of expected *role expressive behavior*. The relevance of attitudes and opinions for behavior influence has achieved such popular belief status that we could not cover this field of influence without commenting on this aspect of mass communication.

MASS COMMUNICATION

In this section we use *mass communication* as a generic term and *mass media* and *propaganda* as subtypes of such communication. Our comparison of lecturing to a class versus teaching foreshadowed this definition (following Wright, 1959) of mass communication. The communication is directed to a relatively *large, heterogeneous,* and *anonymous* audience. Mass communications have many functions: they may be a tool in daily living, as are newspaper ads of sales and listings of television programs; they may publicize norm violations that many people were privately aware of but thought unique and thus may mobilize people to action; they may lull people into a false sense of security or provide interpretations of events that might otherwise be confusing or upsetting; and they may transmit information from how to dress to how to regard fundamental values.

Our greatest interest is in how people's acts are altered, *if indeed they are*, by radio, television, movies, newspapers, books, lectures, magazines, and other forms of mass communication. While the audience may be anonymous to the sender of a mass communication, its members are neither anonymous nor homogeneous. Differences in age, sex, race, education, and the like influence what members of the audience will attend to and how they will be affected. More importantly, a person may be a member of several audiences, and each audience may be a social situation with its own meaning. A mass communication may be received in a social context that alters the response to the communication. For example, being in a well-lit room with one's parents may make a television mystery less frightening to a child (for examples see Himmelweit, Oppenheim, and Vince, 1966).

Audience and influence come together in the notion that the effect of information through the mass media is, at least, a two-step affair. This key concept was introduced by Robert K. Merton (1957a), who identified people to whom others turned for advice. His data analysis did not satisfy him until he realized that his subjects were using information in two different ways. This led him to identify two patterns of interest and influence. One group of people, called *locals*, are interested in their own community and the people in it. The locals' influence rests on a network of personal relationships and understanding service. The local is more likely to read the hometown newspaper and to belong to groups such as Kiwanis and Rotary. In contrast, the *cosmopolitans* are those whose interests are not centered on their place of residence. The cosmopolitan is more likely to belong to professional organizations, to be interested in national and international news, and to read news magazines and large city papers. Where the local may be influential by *who he is*, the cosmopolitan is influential by *what he knows*.

Both types of influentials have information available to them which they share with others. While their sources of information differ, they use media to gain a commodity, information, that they can exchange for continued prestige. An example would be a professor who reads journals to help prepare for a lecture.

The impact of the influential, whether cosmopolitan or local, is through the information he collects and uses to interpret events for those whom he influences. Mass media probably serve to provide topics of conversation or to confirm ideas, but face-to-face (personal, nonmass) contact seems to be of greater importance in the formulation of ideas.

In keeping with the thrust of the present volume, we quote Merton (1957a):

> Although one often speaks of "men of influence," it is clear that this phrase is an elliptical way of saying, "men who exert influence upon a certain number of other people in certain situations." . . . Influence is not an abstract attribute of a person, it is a process implicating two or more people. Accordingly, in an analysis of these patterns, we must look not *only* at the man who is influential, but also at the people who are influenced by him. Otherwise put, we have much to learn by exploring the question, who is influential for whom? [p. 410].

One variable is whether the person has knowledge that has been useful in the past or that is documented by his possession of an official degree. The person may be influential in one or in many areas, with locals probably having influence in a wider range of areas than cosmopolitans, who usually have specialized knowledge. Merton (1957a) also noted that high social status was not a major determinant of influence: a person was most likely to be affected by an influential of his own social level. In a more common example, adolescents are influenced by their age-peers rather than by their fathers regardless of how well-known the latter may be. And the influence of peers is most pronounced where the fathers' knowledge is presumptively least or is out of touch with the times. It helps (but is not absolutely essential) for a person who wants to be an opinion leader or an influential to know whereof he speaks. As documented by Katz and Lazarsfeld (1955), different types of people were leaders in fashions (younger women) than in shopping and other homemaking skills (older women).

What conditions make a personal contact more effective than a mass media communication? The personal contact is in a social context: it is more difficult to avoid, and its purpose of influencing may be disguised to both the listener and communicator. The message may be tailored to the listener with feedback, that is, with reward and punishment. These last two—tailored pace and feedback to the influencers—are what distinguish teaching from lecturing, as we described earlier. Finally, a personal acquaintance may be a more valued authority than a stranger; familiarity need not necessarily breed contempt.[1]

---

[1] The Soviet Communist concept of *agitator* is essentially that of a person who spreads the concepts of the party in small meetings. He is a link between mass media and the individual (see, for example, Barghoorn, 1966).

Mass Media

Mass media is usually defined more narrowly and specifically than mass communication. Weiss's use (1969) of the term is most typical: "Mass media may be said to include the print media of newspapers, magazines, and books; the broadcast media of radio and television; and the movies [p. 79]." Weiss goes further in evaluating the impact of these media on behavior:

> Part of the meaning of modern society, and one of its essential characteristics, is the ubiquitous presence of mass media. To people born into the urban centers of the world, the rich diversity of formal media is a natural element of the environment. Like current modes of transportation, kinds of occupations, and styles of dwelling, the mass media compose one of the characterizing features of the modern scene. Obviously, they contribute to the carrying out of daily routines, to relaxation and respite, to an informed understanding of the world, to action, to personal education and intellectual stimulation. However, their larger significance for societies and nations extends beyond their contributions to individual lives; for modern society not only uses mass media, but requires and is fostered by them. . . .
> In this perspective no large society can meet current requirements of viability and growth without efficient, rapid, varied, and repeatable means of communicating to multitudes of people. The political significance of the media is evident in the tight control exercised by dictatorships over all means of communication. Seizure of the media is one of the first acts of modern revolutionaries. . . . To the extent that a relatively homogeneous symbolic environment is provided by the media, either through governmental direction or through common actions of private controllers, uniformity of political and social behavior is fostered. Since the contents of the media not only refer to topical events but may also reflect societal values, norms of behavior, and traditional perspectives for interpreting the environment, the media may be said to contribute to the transmission of culture to the native-born and to the acculturation of immigrants and long-term residents [p. 77].

In short, mass media provide a common language to society and models for a multitude of social roles.

A considerable amount of field research, primarily of survey or content analysis, has been done on mass media, in addition to the more laboratory-oriented communication research. The mass media research touches upon many dimensions of influence such as the nature of the audience; the length of time of effects; the specific nature of the effects; how influences are mediated; the relationships between media and attitude changes; and the kinds of relationships between media and "personality."

For our purposes we focus on two aspects of the mass media research: the characteristics of opinion leaders and the influence of television viewing on children.

Lazarsfeld, Berelson, and Gaudet's study (1944) of the 1940 presidential campaign introduced the concept of "opinion leader." These authors concluded that the effects of the mass media are not transmitted directly to the general public. Rather, the information and attitudes of the media are first conveyed to a small, attentive, and concerned segment of the public. This smaller group then communicates to the more general public, most frequently by personal, face-to-face communication. Thus, in this two-part communication process people are more directly influenced by other individuals than by the mass media. "Knowledge of an individual's interpersonal environment is basic to all understanding of his exposure and reactions to the mass media [Katz and Lazarsfeld, 1955, p. 133]."

Opinion leaders have also been found to be more likely to read magazines and books, to be in contact with opinion leaders or "experts," and to be found at all social levels (except in public affairs, where they tend to be of high social status). Their leadership is generally limited to a particular area of decision making (Katz and Lazarsfeld, 1955). But as Weiss (1969) has noted:

> The voluminous literature on general studies of leadership . . . makes it clear that, except for a few characteristics, such as small-group leaders being somewhat more intelligent or more self-confident than nonleaders, the search for generalized traits of leadership without regard for the social situation in which leadership is expressed has been fruitless. This approach has been supplanted by an orientation that emphasizes analysis of situational and social determinants, acts of leadership, and the social definition of roles as a means of illuminating the behavioral meaning and requirements of leadership. [Weiss, p. 145].

A recent illustration of this new, behavioral approach is work by Wright and Worthy (1971) in which effectiveness on a similar previous task increased the likelihood of the person assuming a spokesman role; that is, the study found that leadership or influence is tied to task and situation rather than to some personality trait.

Violence and the Media

One of the major questions of our time is the impact of violence on television on the behavior of its viewers, particularly children. In this section we do not attempt to present and evaluate the voluminous research in the field of aggression, imitation, and modeling, which was touched on in previous chapters.

Rather, we are interested in the psychology of the investigation of this phenomenon. Throughout the 1960s there was increasing public concern that violence on television, particularly in cartoons, was having an adverse effect on children. Earlier, in the 1950s, several books and papers by the psychiatrist Frederick Wertham (1954) had presented clinical anecdotes to show the effects of violence in comic books on children. Through the efforts of Wertham and others including parents' groups, publishers voluntarily diminished their portrayal of violence in comic books.

In the late 1960s, the U.S. Surgeon General created a panel of leading investigators to produce research on the relationship between television and violence. A 300-page summary report was formally issued in January 1972. The findings of the commission were summarized as follows:

> First, violence depicted on television can immediately or shortly thereafter induce mimicking or copying by children. Second, under certain circumstances television violence can instigate an increase in aggressive acts. The accumulated evidence, however, does not warrant the conclusion that televised violence has a uniformly adverse effect nor the conclusion that it has an adverse effect on the majority of children. It cannot even be said that the majority of the children in the various studies we have reviewed showed an increase in aggressive behavior in response to the violent fare to which they were exposed. The evidence does indicate that televised violence may lead to increased aggressive behavior in certain subgroups of children who might constitute a small portion or a substantial proportion of the total population of young television viewers. We cannot estimate the size of the fraction, however, since the available evidence does not come from cross-section samples of the entire American population of children.
>
> The research studies we have reviewed . . . tell us something about the characteristics of those children who are most likely to display an increase in aggressive behavior after exposure to televised violence. There is evidence that among young children (ages four to six) those most responsive to television violence are those who are highly aggressive to start with—who are prone to engage in spontaneous aggressive actions against their playmates and, in the case of boys, who display pleasure in viewing violence being inflicted upon others [Cisin, et al., 1972, p. 123].

Thus, it would appear from this summary that television violence has an impact primarily on children who are already "prone" to aggressive behavior. Some investigators (for example, Liebert and Neale, 1972) have argued that the evidence was equivocal as the summary indicated, but strongly suggested that TV violence does have marked effects upon the behavior of children.

Immediately after the issuance of the summary report, a political dispute broke out about whether the report was whitewashing television. Critics of the report pointed out that among the twelve scientists and prominent persons selected by the government to make the report there was a vice president of the National Broadcasting Company and the research director of the Columbia Broadcasting System. Further, when the Surgeon General established the Committee on Television and Social Behavior, his office submitted a list of potential candidates for the committee to the television industry to allow it to raise objections to any investigator whose scientific impartiality it doubted. The individuals the television industry objected to were *not* selected for the final committee. As Boffey and

Walsh (1970) have stated, "The broadcasting industry was allowed to veto the appointment of potentially hostile critics, and at the same time, the industry was given prominent representation on the panel [p. 949]." Among the candidates rejected by the television industry were two of the major investigators of aggression in children, Bandura and Berkowitz, both of whom had previously published research indicating that aggressive behavior in children is related to viewing aggressive behavior on film.

The relationship between the mass media and aggressive behavior is still far from clear. The social impact of this question goes well beyond a simple experimental problem. As we have seen, it involves the direction and social ethics of a major American industry, the relationship between government and mass media, and the relationship between the ethical values of the investigator and how his research is utilized by society (see Sjoberg, 1967). While this brings us to the next topic, propaganda, it also illustrates how the very research information that is generated and disseminated is a result of the larger social and economic contexts of a given time and place.

Propaganda

One of the difficulties in defining *propaganda* is the line drawn between education (the influences which have influenced me) and propaganda (the influences which have influenced you). For example, as Barghoorn (1966) has noted "By way of contrast with western usage, Soviet writers, nurtured in a tradition of what one might call political messianism, have tended to use the term 'propaganda' in a highly positive sense, as more or less equivalent to education [p. 364]." The same tendency may be observed in Westerners. For example, the historian Carr (1961) has written:

> Educators at all levels are nowadays more and more consciously concerned to make their contribution to the shaping of society in a particular mould, and to inculcate in the rising generation the attitudes, loyalties, and opinions appropriate to that type of society; educational policy is an integral part of any rationally planned social policy. The primary function of reason, as applied to man in society, is no longer merely to investigate, but to transform; and this heightened consciousness of the power of man to improve the management of his social, economic, and political affairs by the application of rational processes seems to me one of the major aspects of the 20th Century revolution [p. 190].

Mass media lend themselves to educational and propaganda goals. To again quote Carr (1961):

> Education, which is a necessary and powerful instrument in promoting the expansion of individual capacities and opportunities, and therefore of increasing

individualization, is also a powerful instrument in the hands of interested groups for promoting social uniformity. Pleas frequently heard for more responsible broadcasting and television, or for a more responsible press, are directed in the first instance against certain negative phenomena which it is easy to condemn. But they quickly become pleas to use these powerful instruments of mass persuasion in order to inculcate desirable tastes and desirable opinions—the standard of desirability being found in the accepted tastes and opinions of the society. Such campaigns, in the hands of those who promote them, are conscious and rational processes designed to shape society, by shaping its individual members, in a desired direction. . . . Professional advertisers and campaign managers are not primarily concerned with existing facts. They are interested in what the consumer or elector now believes or wants only insofar as this enters into the end-product, i.e., what the consumer or elector can by skillful handling be induced to believe or want [pp. 192–193].

An example of educational values in operation and empirical data relevant to total institutions has come from a study of the effects of television in Great Britain (Himmelweit, et al., 1966).

When programmes such as *Science Review*; *Animal, Vegetable, or Mineral?*; *Meet the Commonwealth*; *From Tropical Forests*; *Have You a Camera?* come on the screen, children with access to one channel only must either stop watching or view programmes which they do not expect to be very interesting. Under these circumstances, quite a number of children chose to see such programmes and in fact enjoyed them. Children with access to one channel only *get the chance to discover* such programmes, but those with two channels hardly ever.

The more the child can follow his favourite choices by switching from channel to channel, the less likely he is to come in contact with programmes which, from an educational viewpoint, would *prove more worthwhile and which would enable him to experience new things and so broaden his taste* [p. 421; italics added].

The above comments tend to emphasize: (*a*) the tenuous line between education and propaganda; (*b*) the role of values in preselection of material in the media; (*c*) the role of alternative views, offerings, or activities as a reduction in the force of a mass communication, with the implication that (*d*) for the "good of the audience" alternatives should be reduced.

Definitions of Propaganda

Choukas (1965) has defined propaganda as "the controlled dissemination of deliberately distorted notions in an effort to induce action favorable to predetermined ends of special interest groups [p. 37]." It is worth noting that propaganda is defined as deliberate distortion to separate it from random, everyday error. This may also help distinguish propaganda from education: presumably the educator does not deliberately disseminate error or distortions. At its best education helps free the person for independent judgment, while propaganda channels his ideas and actions. Propaganda is an instrument of policy—hence the concept of controlled rather than free pursuit of knowledge. Propaganda is characterized as being bad, misleading, distorted, and inaccurate; its sources and aims may well be concealed. The propagandist may use the values and symbols of the group he hopes to weaken: he may couch his arguments in favor of free enterprise when his aim is to change such an economic system. Finally, propaganda works most effectively when it is combined with censorship, so that alternative arguments are suppressed and only information favorable to the propagandist is permitted.

In short, propaganda is not informative but *manipulative*. Its ultimate value is a change in action: to engage in an activity that the propagandist finds favorable or at least not to resist such an action as strongly as one would if one had an impartial knowledge of facts. We may note here that this analysis draws on concepts such as impartial array of facts that our knowledge of historiography, as detailed in Chapter 7, might well dispute as nonexistent. Finally, propaganda is persuasive rather than coercive. We may say that propaganda falls in the category of influence that uses neither force nor legitimate (honest) persuasion. Propaganda serves a special interest rather than an abstract notion of truth (that is, an impartial array of evidence). A propagandist is an advocate rather than a reporter, although he may pose as the latter.

The fostering of action by propaganda may be preparational or operational. There is a dimension of how soon the impact should be manifested. Choukas (1965, p. 239) has argued that if the time is immediate, suggestion and opinion may be fostered with an aim to action; in the near future, feelings may be the target; and the target may be symbolic in the remote future. In this last case the method may be more thoughtful than emotional and the material more informational in nature.

As with history, the object of propaganda is the generation of a scheme of the world and events that will serve to make sense of the past and help center attention on data helpful for the future. A propagandist may provide images and theories or he may stage events that facilitate such images. He may try to get the person to engage in mild acts consistent with the new role such as writing letters or making up arguments on both sides of the issue.

Use of Propaganda

Lerner (1959) has stated, "In the arena of world politics . . . policy uses four instruments to achieve its goals: propaganda, diplomacy, economics, war. These dominate, respectively, in strategies of persuasion, negotiation, bargaining, and coercion. Their respective vehicles are symbols, contracts, commodities, and violence [p. 481]." Lerner continues, as do the majority of writers in this field, in a manner that indicates *effective propaganda must first be effective communication.* The audience's attention must be obtained and its credence gained; the modification sought must be plausible to the audience and possible in the environment.

There are two views of propaganda. The first is that it is enormously effective and the individual easily manipulated; the second is that it is barely effective. While the former notion is more popular, the latter notion is probably more accurate, *especially when alternative information is available.* That is, 1984 may occur when control of communication is relatively complete, when institutions are total, and group loyalties and opportunities to verify alternative ideas are severely reduced. An example of the former view follows:

> In general, continuous propagandistic manipulation tends to transform the individual into an automaton, a puppet, the direction and intensity of whose actions are chiefly determined by an agitated impulse or instinct rather than by calm, sober thought. This result is inevitable. Under the constant bombardment of propagandistic ideas, an individual is sooner or later detached from the real, since any rational footing he might have had in reality is gradually destroyed. One by one, the links that might have held him to the world of reality are broken off; and with the propagandist always at hand to supply him with answers, his natural curiosity is satisfied; all initiative vanishes, and his mental horizon becomes fixed and stable. His whole personality becomes frozen and static [Choukas, 1965, p. 257].

The opposite side of the coin may be gleaned by examples from Shils and Janowitz (1954) on the effects of Allied propaganda on the German army:

> The fundamentally indifferent reaction to Allied propaganda was most interestingly shown in an intensive study of 150 Prisoners of War [Ps/W] captured in October 1944 of whom 65 per cent had seen our leaflets and for the most part professed that they read their contents. This was a group which had fought very obstinately, and the number of active deserters, if any, was extremely small. . . .
>
> In Normandy, where the relatively small front was blanketed with printed material, up to 90 per cent of the Ps/W reported that they had read Allied leaflets, yet this period was characterized by very high German morale and stiff resistance. . . .
>
> Despite the vast amount of space devoted to ideological attacks on German leaders, only about five per cent of the Ps/W mentioned this topic. . . .
>
> . . . the themes which were most successful, at least in attracting attention and remaining fixed in the memory, were those promising good treatment as prisoners of war. In other words, propaganda referring to immediate concrete situ-

ations and problems seems to have been most effective in some respects [pp. 511–514].[2]

In 1948 Lasswell (1960) made a classic and often repeated statement:

> A convenient way to describe an act of communication is to answer the following questions:
> Who
> Says what
> In which channel
> To whom
> With what effects? [p. 117].

Lasswell's statement not only provides an outline of variables for experimentation but is also remarkably similar to Paul's statement (1969a) about the evaluation of behavior modification research: "What treatment, by whom, is most effective for this individual with that specific problem, under which set of circumstances, and how does it come about? [p. 44]." Paul (private communication) did not have Lasswell in mind when he wrote the statement, nor has Paul been influenced by "propaganda" literature. Rather, both investigators independently arrived at a similar outline not only of communication but of all behavior influence experiments. This is as it should be, since both communication and therapy are forms of behavior influence. We might note that good therapy is effective therapy. The same is true for communication; when a spouse says, "We don't communicate," what is usually meant is that a lot of messages are sent that do not have the effect on the receiver desired by the sender. In short, poor communication is communication that does not change behavior.

Schramm (1954) has made a remark that puts the importance of mass communication in some perspective: "Lest all this talk of mass communication throw perspective awry, we should mention here that the average person in the United States seems to devote *only* a little over four hours a day, about one-fourth of his waking hours, to mass communications [p. 34, italics added]." *Only* indeed! Another way of considering the pervasiveness of the mass media is to think of the money spent on newspapers, movies, television, books, plays, and the like.

A repeated finding (for example, Schramm, 1954, p. 83) is that the person who uses one medium above average tends to be above average in his use of all media. Or more accurately, there is a positive correlation between the use of different media.

Finally, mass media are possible only where mass-produced symbols are

---

[2] Martin (1971) has done a recent study on international propaganda that is consistent with these findings.

possible and meaningful, that is, in a society with the time to indulge in mass media and the wealth to support it. People must be able to buy TV sets, or the society must have the specialization that permits the gathering of large groups of people, as is possible through the growth of cities.

The famous devices of propaganda given by Lee and Lee (1939; reprinted in Schramm, 1960, pp. 417–418) are *name calling*, or giving a bad label; *glittering generality*, in which the object is associated with a virtue; *transfer*, which carries over the authority of something respected; *testimonial*, in which the idea is presented as the product of some respected or hated authority; *plain folks*, which implies that the idea is true because it is common sense or of the common people (like us); *card stacking*, which involves selection of facts and illogical statements; and *bandwagon*, which argues that everybody (at least all of us) is doing it. Such procedures are common to discourse; while such devices may be used erroneously or more accurately, inconclusively, they are classified as propaganda when they are employed deliberately to deceive.

We have noted that mass media and propaganda are not as frighteningly effective as some fear, especially when there is not a monopoly or a single source of information, when the direction is not one that the receiver has already selected (for example, if a person is going to buy a tube of toothpaste, then a commercial may influence his choice of the brand), and if an interpersonal link (two-stage flow of influence, personal influence) is not available.

But mass media do have an impact or at least a sociological function. Lazarsfeld and Merton (1960) have noted that mass media may confer and validate status on public issues, persons, or social organizations. The attention of the mass media not only enhances but may also legitimize individuals, issues, and groups. A syllogism seems to exist: if you are important, the mass media will present you; and because the mass media present you, you must be important. A subclass is that if you are not attended to, you are not very important. A classic example is that peoples' opinions that crime had increased were associated with newspaper coverage of crimes rather than with the actual rate of commission of crimes. Another example of this validating effect is interest in the quality of black life in America: a decade ago, the black was the invisible man and while data were readily available, they were not disseminated.

A correlated mass media effect pointed out by Lazarsfeld and Merton (1960) is that the availability of information may lull the receiver. He is aware and informed, but should not let being informed take the place of action. This concept may be rephrased by saying that because his "attitudes" have changed due to the information, the receiver may think he has accomplished something; but attitudes without action are insights without behavior change, so that the person may feel virtuous when he is not.

Mass media may also be used to enforce social norms. When a matter becomes public, officials may have to take action in order to do their duty, even though they would prefer not to act. An example is the effect of being publicly known as a psychotic or marijuana smoker (H. Becker, 1963; Scheff, 1966; Ullmann and Krasner, 1969). A behavior that was previously rationalized, tolerated, or ignored, must now be acted upon (Edgerton, 1969).

COERCIVE INFLUENCES

"To coerce" is "to force, to act, or to think in a given manner; to compel by pressure or threat; to dominate, restrain or control forcibly [Morris, 1969, p. 258]." In practice, however, the line between influence and coercion is a subtle one. In this section we discuss two concepts which can be seen as coercive influences: brainwashing and sensory deprivation. We classify these behaviors as coercive because most of the individuals exposed to these techniques in nonlaboratory situations have been involuntary subjects.

Brainwashing

Like so many other concepts, brainwashing has many meanings attached to it and it has come to signify something quite evil. The use of the term may have cost George Romney, former governor of Michigan, his chance at the 1968 Republican presidential nomination, because he admitted he had been "brainwashed" on Vietnam.

The term was first used by a reporter (Hunter, 1951) in referring to the early reports of the procedures used by the Chinese Communists on prisoners of war during the Korean conflict. The term appears to have two related origins. It is a literal translation into English of the Chinese phrase more generally translated as "thought reform" (Lifton, 1956). The other origin derives from a phrase in Orwell's *1984* in which the protagonist of the novel is so thoroughly influenced by the procedures applied by a totalitarian society to wipe out his past that it is as if his brain had been washed and cleansed of all impurities of thought (that is, ideas undesirable to the political authorities).

Prior to the end of the Korean conflict, there were indications that the American prisoners were behaving in ways considered unusual for Americans. Charges of prisoners' collaborating with the enemy and Air Force officers' confessions of their involvement in germ warfare greatly concerned American officials. As a result, returning American prisoners were intensively studied by government psychiatric teams (Kinkead, 1959; Lifton, 1954, 1956, 1957; Segal, 1954; Strassman, Thaler, and Schein, 1956), who were to determine whether the prisoners' behavior had been influenced and if so by what techniques.

The initial behavior of the returned prisoners was characterized by apathy, detachment, lack of spontaneity, confusion, and suspiciousness. This "zombie-like" reaction was similar to the reactions of individuals who have been through a major catastrophe such as a fire or earthquake. These reactions decreased after a brief period, but the returned men had feelings of alienation, confusion, and apprehensiveness for a considerable period of time. It was first believed that the Chinese had used some secret techniques or drugs to bring about apparently dramatic changes in behavior. The reports of the various investigations, however, indicated that the procedures involved using many of the techniques of behavior influence in a clearly coercive manner.

Farber, Harlow, and West (1957) hypothesized that the basic ingredients of the thought reform process were debility, dependency, and dread (DDD). When an individual is weak, frightened, and realizes that he is dependent upon his captors for his very life, he is likely to be susceptible to influence. The Chinese captors made maximum use of the prisoners' expectancy of torture and possibly death. They tried to decrease the prisoners' ability to predict behavior. Instead of the expected torture, prisoners were greeted with cigarettes and friendly smiles. Just as the prisoners came to expect friendliness, the captors became harsh and demanding. Such alternations of positive and negative behavior were seemingly unrelated to anything the prisoners did and hence were unpredictable. Under such conditions, the individual became more susceptible to influence and responsive to whatever reinforcement he received.

The concept of "milieu control" introduced by Lifton (1956) is a useful one that links brainwashing with total-control institutions such as mental hospitals (Goffman, 1961) and also with the concept of sensory deprivation. By *milieu control* is meant the process by which an influencer can control all the environmental stimuli to which the influencee is exposed. For example, a prisoner's access to the "reality" of the outside world lies in the letters he receives, the radio, magazines, newspapers, visitors, and guards. If the captors control all the information in these channels, then the prisoner has no way of obtaining information counter to his captors' views. As an example, the prisoners were allowed to receive only letters that expressed their loved ones' dissatisfaction or desertion (the infamous Dear John letters: "farewell, I have a new boyfriend") or unpaid bills. Letters of affection and warmth from wife or girl friend were less likely to reach the prisoner.

Another technique used by the captors was similar to techniques in conventional group therapy, particularly in encounter groups. Self-examination and confession in a group setting were strongly reinforced by peer and captor approval. The coercive element entered when a group activity such as eating or ending the group session was made contingent upon every participant's emitting some sort of self-expression and self-condemnation. The individual only had to say a little initially but as time progressed more and more self-criticism was expected of him.

The effectiveness of these procedures has never been fully clarified. That an usually high number of American GIs collaborated with their captors seems clear. However, one of the goals of the captors seems to have been to influence the prisoners to be generally sympathetic to their point of view. The achievement of this goal is far more difficult to measure.

Sensory Deprivation

American Air Force officers who were physically isolated during the Korean conflict frequently acceded to the demand of their captors and signed false confessions that they had been involved in germ warfare. Early reports of the purported effects of isolation spurred the first of a series of laboratory studies at McGill University by Hebb and his associates (1958). These first studies analyzed the effects of the deprivation of perceptual stimuli on behavior. Hebb and other early investigators such as Bexton, Heron, and Scott (1954); Heron, Doane, and Scott (1956); Azima and Cramer-Azima (1957); Lilly (1956); and Solomon et al. (1961) found that isolation resulted in hallucinations, disturbed self-perception, impaired intellectual functioning, changed electroencephalogram (EEG) records, and visual disturbances. Hebb reported that these effects ceased a few days after the end of the isolation. However, when he told subjects "ridiculous" things during their isolation, he found that "propaganda effects" were longer lasting.

Later investigators of sensory deprivation tended to replicate many of the effects identified in the early isolation studies. Subjects in these later studies were put in isolation rooms, in which as much external stimulation as possible was removed. Subjects wore translucent goggles or were immersed in a tank of water or placed in a tanktype respirator. Orne and Scheibe (1964; described in Chapter 8 of this text) were skeptical of the interpretations, which ignored the demand characteristics implicit in such experimental procedures of isolating individuals.

The material on brainwashing and sensory deprivation belongs within the more general context of a psychology of behavior influence, particularly since these topics involve variables such as expectancy, reinforcement, and stimulus control.

LAST WORD

Just as a person is influenced by his physical environment (Chapter 13) and his political, economic, and organizational environment (Chapter 15), he is influenced by his *informational* environment. A person organizes information in much the same way as a historian; he actively selects what is significant and alters it on the basis of the events to which he attends. While research indicating the realistic impact of attitude-changing measures such as the mass media has been disappointing, we expect that important formulations will be developed. One repeated theme in this volume has been the importance of ideas. The process by which ideas are spread and translated into action by the general population requires investigation. Such work may contribute to improved effectiveness or help to protect the individual from undue or unfair influence.

In this chapter on a major aspect of behavior influence—the mass communications of a society—we have dealt with a number of concepts. As in every other influence process, we are dealing with key ideas (in this instance attitudes and opinions); the study of those concepts by professional investigators; the consequences of such concepts; and the similarity of investigated methods and findings to those for other influence processes. Mass communications deals with influence in situations involving more than one individual. Having considered this topic, we can now move on to the more general situations involving influence in the mass and the various theories dealing with crowds and mass movements.

CHAPTER 17

Collective Behavior

An important source of influence on individual behavior as setting event, instrumental act, and source of reinforcement is participation with other people in a larger aggregate frequently labeled "collective behavior." Blumer (1964) has included in this category "collective excitement, social unrest, crowd behavior, riots, manias, crazes, fads, mass alarms, mass hysteria, public revolts, protest movements, and revolutionary movements."

Milgram and Toch (1969) have used collective behavior to refer to "group behavior which originates spontaneously, is relatively unorganized, fairly unpredictable and planless in its course of development, and which depends upon interstimulation among participants [p. 507]." They have distinguished this category from very small groups of individuals such as two men fighting; from large aggregates of people together in one location but not interacting or engaging in joint activity; and from collective behavior involved in social institutions and ceremonies of established groups such as the Methodist Church, Harvard University, and the Republican Party.

The boundaries between these categories are not sharp and groups can evolve from one category to another. But most authors (see Ullmann, 1969c) contrast, as does Smelser (1963, p. 66), collective and conventional behavior. Smelser (1963), for example, has written: "Collective behavior, then, is the action of the impatient [p. 66]."

Although the users of propaganda or persuasion seek to influence *many people*, the basic focus of the previous chapter was on the *individual*. An emphasis on the individual characterizes this chapter as well. An organization, a social movement, or a culture exists only as it is manifested by the actions and interrelations of people. People erect buildings, factories, and hospitals which become the locale for the subsequent "organization" which develops in such institutions. People raise and allocate funds, drive rivets, and devise business forms for other people to fill out. Organizations, social movements, cultures, and the like are abstractions, a shorthand way of designating ideas which are dependent on an observer for recognition. As with other labels, the visible criteria for inclusion in the particular category may change over time and surplus and sometimes unusual meanings become associated with it. Participation in group action is a behavior in and of itself. We can and should therefore specify the *conditions* that *lead to group activities*.

The basic question in evaluating the influence of social movements on individual behavior is whether such group or collective behavior is different from individual behavior. There is considerable debate on this matter. Our view is that the behavior of individuals in groups (*a*) is still the behavior of individuals and hence (*b*) should be capable of description, analysis, and manipulation by the same principles applied to individual behavior. What is different is the increased importance of other people—the audience or the group members—as sources of discriminative (setting or controlling) stimuli, models, and reinforcing stimuli.

What is fascinating, stimulating, and potentially misleading in the literature on collective behavior is the degree to which the *forms* of collective behavior are similar, even though their content may be diametrically different. The techniques, appeals, and logic of the anti-Semite of the late 1930s resemble in a startling manner those of the extreme student activist of the late 1960s.

It is tempting to argue that a special group process affects and alters people regardless of the group's content and rationale; such an approach would further contend that this group process transcends other principles or conditions for action. If we described and explained behavior as merely "the result of the group process," however, we would be making the same error involved in using a label as an explanation for individual behavior. This chapter seeks to go beyond labeling to ask, *what is group process?*

Another objective, especially in our analysis of the human potential or encounter group movement, is to illustrate a central thesis of this volume: the impact of a theory of personality on human behavior. The effect is reciprocal: the theory alters behavior, and as a result of specific behaviors, further experience is directed to a sample of acts likely to verify the theory and away from experiences likely to disconfirm it.

THE CROWD

Interest in collective behavior and the crowd has been an integral part of social psychology since the texts by Ross (1908) and McDougall (1908; see Chapter 2 of this book). The concept of the crowd as a type of collective behavior relates to how the behavior of an individual is affected by his being part of an aggregate of other individuals: "*Crowd* is a generic term referring to highly diverse conditions of human assemblage: audience, mob, rally, panic all fall within the definition of crowds. Common to these terms is the idea of human beings in sufficiently close proximity that the fact of aggregation comes to influence behavior [Milgram and Toch, 1969, p. 509]."

There are many nouns in the English language to describe various kinds of crowd behaviors including mobs, riots, panic, rallies, demonstrations, audiences, picketing, marches, lynchings, sports spectators, sit-ins, and boycotts. In terms of influences one question is that of *leadership* and *intent of leadership*. The role of the "outside agitator" is often attributed to riotous crowds. This phrase implies that "leaders" have manipulated the crowd for their own benefit and against the best interests of the other individuals. How one conceptualizes the role of leadership in crowds depends upon one's formulation of crowd behavior.

Gustave Le Bon (1896) introduced a conception of large aggregates of people, a theory of crowds, which had two aspects. First, he argued that specific crowd action was a manifestation of the social and cultural processes of a given period.

Second, Le Bon postulated that a radical transformation occurs in a person when he enters a crowd; characteristics emerge which result in the development of a "collective mind." As Le Bon (1896) put it: "whoever be the individuals that compose it, however like or unlike be their mode of life, their occupations, their character, or their intelligence, the fact that they have been transformed into a crowd puts them in possession of a sort of collective mind which makes them feel, think and act in a manner quite different from that in which each individual of them would feel, think, and act were he in a state of isolation [p. 27]."

To explain the development of the crowd's collective mind, Le Bon postulated the mechanisms or conditions of anonymity, suggestion, and contagion. *Anonymity* implied that the individual loses his sense of responsibility as he merges with the crowd. As discussed in Chapter 9, on hypnosis, *suggestion* is a more observational than explanatory concept. The concept of *contagion* is interesting because of its medical connotations. Le Bon was a physician and used the contagion metaphor because he believed that what occurred in a crowd was analogous to the transmission of a disease from one person to another. The notion of contagion, with its medical and germ connotations, is a good illustration of how a metaphor can become an explanation.

Le Bon's ideas on the crowd had an impact on Freud, who incorporated and extended them into a psychoanalytic view of crowd behavior. Freud accepted the concept of a group mind and attributed to the crowd many of the same processes and mechanisms that he used to explain the individual and family relationships. In a crowd the individual renounces his own superego and relegates it to the crowd leader. Freud resorted to an analogue of hypnosis, with the relationship of the leader to the crowd being made similar to the hypnotist's relationship with his supposedly helpless subject who had regressed to a state of childhood dependence.

Many variations and criticisms of Freud's theories of crowds have evolved. Of chief interest is the Dollard, Doob, Miller, Mowrer, and Sears (1939) hypothesis that aggressive behavior follows a frustrating experience. One object of the theory was to explain destructive crowd behavior and to predict the targets of crowd aggression. For example, the theory might predict a significant negative relationship between frequency of Negro lynchings in the South and the value of the annual cotton crop. This theory linked crowd behavior and current social events.

Subsequent theories, particularly by sociologists, moved the conceptions of the crowd further away from the "collective mind" to that of the crowd as a *social phenomenon* in a specific time and place. Turner (1964) has offered a theory of crowds with a focal concept of "emergent norms" derived from experimental work with small groups by people such as Asch (1956), Lewin (1947), and Sherif (1936). These investigators indicated that groups of people interacting among themselves soon develop common standards, or norms, of acceptable behavior. "Norm theory states, then, that a person acts in a crowd as he does because he perceives it appropriate or required, and not because he is mechanically infected by group emotion or because he has a blind propensity to imitate [Milgram and Toch, 1969, p. 553]."

Social Movement

The most challenging and complete taxonomy of collective behavior is that of Smelser (1963). First, Smelser limited the scope of his inquiry: "Collective behavior, as we shall study it, is not institutionalized behavior. According to the degree to which it becomes institutionalized, it loses its distinctive character. [And] we define collective behavior as *mobilization on the basis of a belief which redefines social action* [Smelser, 1963, p. 8]." Later he noted that "our formal characterization of collective behavior is this: *an uninstitutionalized mobilization for action in order to modify one or more kinds of strain on the basis of a generalized reconstitution of a component of action* [p. 8]." Central to Smelser's theory are what he terms as the

> basic components of social action. These components are: (*a*) values, or general sources of legitimacy; (*b*) norms, or regulatory standards for interaction; (*c*) mobilization of individual motivation for organized action in roles and collectivities; (*d*) situational facilities or information, skills, tools, and obstacles in pursuit of concrete goals . . . (*a*) . . . the value-oriented movement is collective action mobilized in the name of a generalized belief envisioning a reconstitution of values; (*b*) the norm-oriented movement is action mobilized in the name of a generalized belief envisioning a reconstitution of norms; (*c*) the hostile outburst is action mobilized on the basis of a generalized belief assigning responsibility for an undesirable state of affairs to some agent; (*d*) the craze and the panic are forms of behavior based on a generalized redefinition of situational facilities [p. 9].

Smelser also postulates six systematic determinants for each incident of collective behavior: *structural conduciveness*—the general social conditions that exist in a given time and place and are conducive to the likelihood of a collective event occurring, such as a United States seething with civil rights unrest and earlier riots in New York and Rochester contributing to the riots in Watts in the summer of 1965; *structural strain*—a concept analogous to the physical strain on the fault lines of an earthquake zone; *the growth of a belief*—an estimate of the causes of the strain in a situation and suggestions about what can be done to alleviate the strain or at least prevent it from becoming worse; *precipitating factors*—the specific events that trigger the crowd action such as the shooting of a black or the placing of a campus off limits; *mobilization for action*—the behavior of certain individuals called leaders, who bring together and focus the activities of others; *social control*—the ways in which the agencies of control in the broader social system such as police, faculty, or ministry discourage or encourage the collective behavior. Social controls may prevent the emission of acts or punish them after the fact. Any particular incident of crowd behavior can be analyzed in terms of these six determinants and the four components of social action—values, norms, concrete social roles, and situational facilities.

Smelser (1963) has also noted:

> It is the combination of conduciveness and strain, not the separate existence of either, that radically reduces the range of possibilities other than panic. Before collective action can be taken to reconstitute the situation brought on by structural strain, this situation must be made meaningful to the potential actors. This meaning is supplied in a generalized belief which identifies the source of strain, attributes certain characteristics to this source, and specifies certain responses to the strain as possible or appropriate [p. 16].

Collective action may also be viewed as a form of behavior modification: "Every form of collective behavior attempts to 'solve' certain problems [Smelser, 1963, p. 66]." Smelser endeavors to predict or at least to order the forms of collective action by hypothesizing that as simple or direct solutions to problems fail, more general (or basic) aspects of the social system become the objects of change. Thus, the effect of a value-oriented movement would be a change in the fundamental *values* of the social organization.

In the next chapter we discuss collective activities in which individuals have attempted to organize large-scale living patterns of a community. At this point we explore *one specific social movement*, that of "human potential," and in so doing we touch upon the kinds of variables that are an integral part of investigating the social phenomenon of collective behavior.

We have selected this particular movement for a variety of reasons, including currency, relevancy, and field setting, and—we must add—our own interests as clinical psychologists.

THE HUMAN POTENTIAL MOVEMENT

Forerunners

Because human activity is ongoing, the starting point of any movement is arbitrary. The human potential movement may be traced to many different sources, including the early church during the decline of Rome, the English empiricists (in terms of the perfectibility of man) and Rousseau and other romantics (in terms of the value of naturalness).

The major forerunner of contemporary human potential concepts was Freud. His theory of personality remains central, implicitly and explicitly, to the formulations of the vast majority of persons engaged in sensitivity training and encounter groups. Further, Freud devised some of the procedures used as part of the movement such as free association and, early in his career, catharsis.

The early circle of students, colleagues, and friends who met at Freud's home would analyze each other's slips of the tongue, providing the sort of interpretive feedback to each other that is not uncommon in contemporary groups. These associates and students, when extending or revising Freud's work, introduced techniques and ideas that continue to have impact. For example, many of the concepts about the existence of *positive* aspects of the unconscious may be traced to Jung's formulation (1953) of the development of symptoms as due to the person not fully utilizing his capacities of thinking, feeling, sensation, and intuition. Jung and his followers were particularly interested in pictorial representation of concepts and in Eastern philosophies. Adler did much of his clinical work before audiences and made use of group participation and influence.

Ferenczi acted the role of loving parent at certain points in therapy and actively encouraged the acting out of regressive behaviors. Wilhelm Reich's theories of sexual energy and his emphasis on bodily health may be found in the current encounter scene. The psychosomatic theories—which link bodily manifestations to psychological deprivations—are heavily indebted to Abraham (1949), Dunbar (1954), and particularly Franz Alexander (1934).

The most important of Freud's students in terms of impact on current human potential work is Otto Rank (1929), who had three areas of influence. In making the child's separation from his mother at birth and his efforts at return central to his theory of neurosis, he moved in a manner congruent to the themes—ultimate failure in death—of contemporary existential analysis. Second, he had a major influence on the work of Jessie Taft, who in turn had a great impact on Carl R. Rogers. After Freud, Rogers' theoretical ideas (1959) are most prevalent in the human potential movement. Finally, Rank's theory led to a number of specific therapeutic procedures: "It gave him the idea that an analysis should consist in one gigantic 'living out' experience, and before long this assumed the form of rebirth [Jones, 1953, p. 408]."

The Viennese psychiatrist Victor Frankl (1962), influenced by his own experiences in a concentration camp and by the slaughter of millions in World War II, tried to *find meaning to life*, a problem also approached by the philosopher Jean Paul Sartre (1947). Other major existential authors are Binswanger (1958) and May (1953). These men spread the influence and theories of the existential philosophers, particularly Heidegger and Kierkegaard. Dictatorship, inflation, depression, war, and genocide had focused attention on both the vulnerability of man and the weakness of the financial, political, and social institutions on which he had built his life. The questions of how to be, how to survive, and how to make some sense of surviving needed answering.

In a broader context the Industrial Revolution had led to a marked change in family structure and eventually to changes in most social structures in Western society. In an agrarian society the family was separated geographically from others and lived and worked close together. With a shift to a manufacturing economy, work was not only segmented into assembly-line specialization, but the location of employment was moved out of the home. The family was no longer a vital economic unit. Sources of education and recreation were found, especially by the adolescent and young adult, outside the home. Whenever there is rapid change, respect for the knowledge of the elders is likely to decrease. In addition, as the number of people increases, formal ways of acting which emphasize civility rather than feeling develop.

Many actions intended to alter one's environment became more distant, impersonal, and abstract. This was so whether one worked for economic and social change through political action, a union, or any other organization. At the same time, much work became dull and trivial (as on the assembly line) or so abstract that only fellow specialists could understand it.

As the environment became less directly controllable and more abstract and distant in terms of action, the methods of organizing and evaluating which had worked in the past also deteriorated. The spread of communications, the devastation of warfare, the realization of social injustices such as poverty, led to a questioning of established beliefs and a feeling that these beliefs had little to do with one's own behavior. In the area of sexual behavior, for example, improved communication—both in terms of personal travel and knowledge from radio, television, and the written word—led to a questioning of accepted morality.

An increasing percentage of the population received a more formal education, first as a result of the World War II "GI Bill" and later as an expectation developed for at least some college education for nearly everyone. While more were being educated, the interval between the student's learning and the student's use of what he had learned increased. At worst the material taught was irrelevant—consistent with an ideal society that no longer existed if it ever had, rather than with the actualities the student could clearly observe outside the classroom. The major formal and informal agencies of teaching the culture— the family, the church, the school, the neighborhood, and the job—all decreased in effectiveness.

A major source of strain in our post–World War II society has been affluence. (In Chapter 15 we touched on the influences of economic variables on individual behavior.) In the presence of a surplus of the stimulus (satiation), a reinforcer loses its effectiveness. Parents who had experienced the depression of the 1930s and the anguish of World War II provided their children with as many of the good things of life as they could. In fact, the goal in life for many families was to provide for the children. Things once considered as marvelous gifts and even miracles now became expected as normal and a person's right. However, the segment of the American population reared in this condition of affluence was and remains a minority. Blacks, Mexican-Americans, Indians, the children of un-skilled laboring and farm parents, and the like have not shared directly or pro-portionately in the prosperity. However, it is the affluent minority that generally supplies the images of America in movies, television, theater, novels, and com-mercials.

Many definitions have been advanced for the word *alienation*. We offer the concept that one person is alienated from another when one person's behavior fails to have a meaningful impact on another; that is, when one person does not have a way of reinforcing another, of providing differential and meaningful con-sequences that influence another person's behavior. There are two sources for such loss of impact on another person. One is *extinction* and may be observed in the minority member who says the rules and concepts of the white middle class are irrelevant, essentially meaning that he has not been rewarded suffi-ciently for learning them. The other is *satiation* and may be observed in the white middle-class college student, who essentially has the material benefits for which such an education previously opened the way.

Where people are forced to focus on survival via attaining food, clothing, and shelter, the successful attainment of these necessities gives meaning to life. In a period of abundance people seek meaning elsewhere. In this light, it is not surprising that authors who dealt with the topic of meaning (Bugental, 1966; Maslow, 1968; May, 1953) had a major impact not only on students but on professional peers who also faced the problems of existence in their own lives. These authors brought together material and asserted the presence of motives, structures, propensities, and directions. The word *assertion* is used advisedly. These authors found both the traditional Freudian formulation and the experimental behavioral approaches wanting. The Freudians were rejected for biological reductionism and for dealing only with pathology; the experimentalists for their objectivity, which supposedly ignored the individual's subjective feelings and inner life. Almost by definition, within this approach system, experimental data based on systematic observation constituted a superficial and invalid statistical comparison. The very notion of experimental design was considered dehumanizing.

The existential psychologists practice what they preach. They have the honesty and consistency to be what they are. However, communication with them by people not committed to their view is difficult and they eschew the common psychological notion of validation of their efforts: a person feels something or he doesn't—resorting to the typical scientific validation procedures would be selling out. Yacorzynski (1963) has provided an example of this view: "a rigid definition recognized and accepted by everyone cannot be stated because such understanding will stem largely from the reader's own feeling in terms of the introjections already present and his ability to project these to the thesis which has been advanced [p. 103]."

Work with Groups

Therapeutic work with groups of individuals has been another major source for the development of the human potential movement. In exploring the origins of the movement, Ruitenbeek (1970, pp. 11–16, 42–45), took particular note of Dr. Joseph Pratt's group work with tuberculosis patients in Boston in the early 1900s; the group approaches within the psychoanalytic context by Lazell, Marsh, and Burrow during the 1920s; and Dr. Jacob Moreno, who "spoke then of encounter in much the same way as it is experienced in groups throughout the world today [and who published] an invitation to an encounter [Schloss, Siroka, and Siroka, 1971, p. 3]" in 1914.

Religious revival rituals preceded these efforts and yet are strikingly similar in many features to current procedures. Many religious services appeal to the senses, and much in Mowrer (1964) echoes Frances Trollope's observations of Cincinnati in 1832: "When the room is full, the company, of whom a vast majority are always women, are invited, entreated, and coaxed to confess before their brothers and sisters all their thoughts, faults, and follies. These confessions are strange scenes; the more they confess, the more invariably are they encouraged and caressed [as quoted by Ruitenbeek, 1970, p. 45]."

In *Wayward Youth*, August Aichhorn (1935) described work in which young males were allowed an almost leaderless group situation so that they would devise their own structure for survival. Psychoanalytically influenced teachers transferred the ideas of therapy to the educational field, the most famous application of which was Summerhill (Neill, 1960), although Bertrand Russell himself had earlier developed a school in which many of the same freedoms and personal responsibilities were granted. Maxwell Jones in his *Therapeutic Community* (1953) and *Beyond the Therapeutic Community* (1968) has described procedures for adult treatment that are also generalizations from the psychoanalytic therapy hour and found in the human potential movement.

Work with groups of patients rather than individuals received major impetus as a result of the shortage of trained therapists during and immediately after World War II. Aside from meeting a manpower need, group work was found to have advantages in and of itself. In a group the individual obtains feedback from the peers with whom he will interact in the future. This is far more useful that interacting only with a professional, the therapist, in his accepting, nonjudgmental, and socially unusual role. Various forms of group therapy developed, usually along the lines of major schools of psychotherapy such as psychoanalytic (Powdermaker and Frank, 1953; Slavson, 1950) or Rogerian (Hobbs, 1955).

Groups Outside the Psychoanalytic Tradition

There has always been a strong tradition in America of self-help through group activity. It is difficult to designate a starting place because one example leads back to another. In the United States, a long series of utopian and sectarian small groups have striven to maintain a community of interest both to improve their own lives and to provide a model for others. Certainly the spirit of Emerson, Thoreau, and the New England transcendentalists is not foreign to the human potential movement. We refer again to these groups in Chapter 18, on planned societies.

The combination of self-revelation and/or belief in a higher power may be found in Alcoholics Anonymous, Synanon, and other groups of nonprofessionals who have provided some of the techniques of the human potential movement. These groups were preceded by the movement called Moral Rearmament, Buchmanism, or the Oxford group. Buchman was a Pennsylvania Lutheran minister who in 1908 had a revelation that he had been selfish, dishonest, and petty. He confessed his faults to his former adversaries. The goals of his movement were absolute purity, honesty, unselfishness, and love. The last three—albeit not the first in the more general usage of the term—are synonomous with the current goals of the human potential movement. The sharing and self-revelation procedures of the Buchmanites are still attractive to many groups.

The openness, reciprocal confession and criticism, and focus on group rather than individual orientations may also be found in some forms of coercive social control (see Chapter 16). The goals of brainwashing are diametrically opposite to those of the human potential movement, but both have techniques in common. The marathon technique has been used with increasing frequency in both coercive and human potential movements to reduce resistance. Other procedures which are common to total institutions (Goffman, 1961), to brainwashing, and to the human potential movement involve giving up ties and identifications with established roles. The person uses only his first name or takes a new name. The location of the marathon or training sessions may purposely be a retreat from the person's hometown or place of work. Contacts with the outside world such as listening to news broadcasts are frowned upon. One symbolic ultimate is for the person to shed his clothes, that is, in a nude marathon. Clothes help distinguish people and provide identity—in a more dynamic jargon they are defenses, and in a behavioral jargon they are discriminative stimuli. If the purpose is to "be oneself" or to change, such identity deprivation is a useful procedure of persuasion.[1]

The Contributions of Industrial and Social Psychology

A distinction has developed in the human potential movement between a relatively more expressive trend symbolized by Esalen on the West Coast and a relatively more formal, task- and institution-oriented group on the East Coast represented by the National Training Laboratory (NTL). Both groups change over time and share members. We are dealing with a continuous range of behavior rather than with polar opposites. NTL is considerably older than Esalen and has in its background the contribution of social scientists in the fields of industrial and social psychology.

Industrial psychology originally centered on the arrangement of the work situation and personnel selection (Maier, 1952). From these tasks to the study of morale was a small and logical step, and it was hastened by the findings called the "Hawthorne effect" mentioned previously (Chapter 15) in which it had been found that regardless of the specific level of illumination, mere change and the implied interest of management led to the workers' increased production. This placebo effect in an industrial setting—the specific level of illumination was not associated with productivity—indicated the importance of interpersonal

[1] It is unfortunate that Dale Carnegie (1936) is so often ridiculed and so seldomly read. In helping people to participate and express themselves effectively, Carnegie arrived by trial and error at many exercises, such as hitting inanimate objects, that are frequently used in contemporary human potential groups.

variables. An emphasis on personal needs developed, which involved the training of foremen and other supervisory personnel in techniques for dealing with employees that were centered on workers' feelings rather than on the specifics of the task.

Kurt Lewin had worked with small groups on problems of types of group leadership and the changing of limited target behaviors. In 1946 and 1947, he and his coworkers came to the conclusion—in a manner similar to Carl R. Rogers in 1950—that telling people what or how to do something was less effective than letting them discover it themselves (Rogers, 1967; Schloss, Siroka, and Siroka, 1971). This led to a leaderless, usually agendaless, group situation in which the "dynamics" of how the group formed itself was the subject of later discussion. This emphasis on investigation of the *process* rather than the result or outcome, that is, provision of feedback to the members of how they had affected each other, is a major feature of the contemporary growth or human potential movement.

Other Background Influences

Two of the other major contributors to the techniques used in the human potential movement were the psychiatrist Jacob L. Moreno (1934) and the psychologist Fritz Perls (1969). Moreno was the major developer of the technique of psychodrama and for many years held meetings that were open to the public. His procedure emphasized the importance of spontaneity in solving many vexing interpersonal problems. Perls, Ralph Hefferline, and Paul Goodman, published in 1951 *Gestalt Therapy*, which had great subsequent impact. The object was for the person to regain direct contact with his environment and many still popular exercises were outlined. Basing his ideas on a very different model of man, Andrew Salter suggested and outlined a number of techniques for increasing "excitation" in his *Conditioned Reflex Therapy* (1949). Some of the procedures of the two volumes are strikingly similar.

Space does not permit us to do justice to all the people who contributed to the human potential movement. We may, however, point to some of those who contributed to its jargon, spirit, and intellectual context. Marshall McLuhan's concept (1964) that the medium is the message, that *how* something is said rather than *what* is said is of intense importance to the current culture, and fits well with the practice of the human potential movement. A common term, usually used derogatorily when attributed to someone else's behavior, is "game." Eric Berne's *Games People Play* (1964) has been read, enjoyed, and discussed by many of the leaders and participants of the movement.

Another source of movement jargon has been the popular use of adolescent, drug, and black expressions. In part this may be because in purpose and spirit the human potential movement borders on and at times overlaps with the counter-culture (see Roszak, 1969). The human potential movement and the various protest movements of the late 1960s (the black, antiwar, woman, homosexual, draft resisters, drug, hardhat, youth) all developed out of the uneasiness generated in all levels of American society by the turmoil of the period. Increasingly, all parts of society were trying in different ways to understand themselves, their society, and to seek direction. The protest movements do not place much premium upon the value of delaying gratification that is an outstanding feature of the Protestant ethic of the older generation and to which the human potential movement is a reaction. It has a sense of urgency that life is for *now*. One final observation is that the human potential movement is to the present time what mesmerism and romanticism were to the early nineteenth century (see Chapters 2 and 9).

HUMAN POTENTIAL BEHAVIORS

What do people in human potential situations *do*? What are the operants? And —more germane to purposes of behavior influence—to what extent is the emission of these behaviors under discriminative control, that is, highly associated with if not unique to the situations labeled as *human potential, sensitivity training,* or *encounter groups*?

We begin by placing the situation in a context in which a major proponent of the approach, the psychologist William Schutz, has put it. In his book describing the movement, Schutz used the title *Here Comes Everybody* (1971) to convey the spirit and philosophy of life he sees as integral to the movement:

> "Here comes everybody" is borrowed from Joyce's character H.C.E. in *Finnegan's Wake*. When people are regarded superficially their differences are accentuated —black and white, male and female, aggressive and passive, intellectual and emotional, happy and sad, radical and reactionary. But as we understand each other, differences fade and the oneness of man emerges—the same needs, the same fears, the same struggles, the same desires. Here comes everybody.
>
> The body-mind concept—the unity of all levels of man—and the encounter group offer ways of penetrating deeply, of contacting people at their core, of getting to the parts of everyone that are alike. These methods help people get past the different ways that each copes with his life, to look around and find that everyone is trying to cope with the same problem, just using different methods. Here comes everybody [p. xii].

Within this context we can look for the specification of what is actually done in the group. Mann (1970) has made the point that encounter groups really have no set limits as to potential behaviors which may occur.

> In an encounter group we can find the energies within us and around us, experiencing them and begin to learn to control them, rather than denying or repressing them. From this point of view any technique is appropriate if it

enables us to contact either the defense limiting our energy in a particular area, or helps us to contact the energy itself so that we can experience it and learn to live with it, like an unruly animal whose existence we have denied, but who appears, nevertheless, when we finally accept the possibility of its existence [p. xiii].

The encounter situation does include behaviors *not usual* for the relatively *highly educated*, usually *white* and *professional* or *middle-class people* who currently form the majority of the encounter group population. In fact, one of the attractions of the encounter is that behavior not permissible in everyday typical situations is accepted and even encouraged.

The group situation has two emphases: (*a*) total candor in expression and (*b*) experience that is bodily or sensation oriented. The unifying theme is "feeling" rather than "ideation." Some observations by Howard (1970) are focused on the specific kinds of acceptable and desirable group behavior:

[Quoting Charles Seashore of NTL] "You have to learn oblique intervention, too, and develop a repertoire of fantasies, analogies and games to provide people with ways to experience directly things that aren't intellectual [p. 41]." [Quoting Schutz:] "The further you go toward violence, sexuality, and loneliness . . . the better trainer you are, almost linearly [p. 42]." . . . Schutz asked men in one of his groups to urinate in front of each other [p. 43]. At these workshops . . . everyone is obliged to confess publicly to his mate three secrets which might seriously jeopardize the relationship [pp. 65–66].

These quotations also illustrate the encounter emphasis on *regression* and *catharsis*. Howard (1970) has also described activity happening—but typical of other kinds of human potential groups—at a nude marathon conducted by Paul Bindrim:

"Tell her!" urged Bindrim.
"You goddam bitch!" said Lloyd. "You're punishing me for no reason! I'd like to tear your hair out by the roots!"
Bindrim leapt across the room and grabbed from a box a Sears, Roebuck catalogue, which he thrust at Lloyd.
"Here's her hair," he said. "Go ahead! Tear it out!"
Lloyd did so, ravaging the catalogue into a mass of ragged confetti. But he still looked frustrated.
"Your face looks as if you'd like to bite somebody," Bindrim said. "Would you?"
"Yes," said Lloyd. "My father." This time Bindrim gave him a raw potato. Lloyd gagged as he bit into it, but seemed to feel better. To every workshop Bindrim brings a kit of such supplies: potatoes to bite, catalogues and phone books to rip, magazines to roll up and use as clubs, pieces of snappable wood to fracture, pillows to punch and nippled plastic baby bottles to bite or sometimes to fill with warm milk.

"Different people," he said, "express anger differently. There are whippers, biters, slappers, stranglers, and throwers. The idea is to regress, if possible, to the trauma that caused the distortion [pp. 94–95]."

Another observation made by Howard (1970) at an NTL-sponsored "Advanced Personal Growth Laboratory" follows:

Instead of [passing the butter] he rose from his chair, walked all the way down and around the long table to bring it to her personally. He smeared some of it, very gradually, all over her face. Amazed but then enchanted, she smeared some back at him. For a full fifteen minutes they stood there, amiably massaging butter into each other's faces [p. 124].

Finally, we quote a segment of an outline of procedures by Ellis (1969):

The leader says: "With what members of this group would you like to have a love experience? Ask this person if he or she will cooperate with you in having this kind of experience. If she or he consents, engage in it as much as you can do, right now. If both of you feel that you would like to have or to continue this love experience outside the room, you may leave the group for a maximum of five minutes and have it in one of the other rooms of this building. Be sure, however, to return after five minutes are up!" The leader then sees that (a) individuals having love experiences in the room are asked about what they felt during the experience; (b) individuals who do not choose to have love experiences with anyone are asked why they did not choose to do so; (c) individuals who choose to go out of the room for five minutes to have their love experiences are asked, when they return to the room, to describe in detail exactly what they did and what they felt while doing it. In one way or another, all the members of the group are induced either to have love experiences with at least one other member or to report why they do not desire to have them [p. 115].

It should be noted that Ellis follows these procedures in the context of his theory of rational-emotive therapy (Ellis, 1969, pp. 123–127). While not denigrating the value of experience or the reduction of defenses, Ellis also encourages cognitive and intellectual processes.

The general point of this section is that adults engage in activities in the encounter, or human potential setting, that are not usual among strangers in the strata of society of the participants in general or typical for the particular participants. The group sanctions, calls for, legitimizes, and offers models for these unusual behaviors.[2]

---

[2] T. X. Barber, in a colloquium, August 31, 1972, at the University of Hawaii, made the point that effects usually considered "hypnotic" may be obtained without trance or mention of hypnosis if introduced as ways of enhancing a person's range of experience or personal growth. This line of investigation, which is at its beginning at the time of this writing, promises further integration of different areas of behavior influence.

HUMAN POTENTIAL IDEOLOGY

One of the major theses of this book is that *theories and beliefs about personality affect overt behavior*. We may say that a personality theory is a link in a chain or sequence of behavior: it is a human response that influences other human responses. The theory one holds may call attention to certain behaviors and thus decrease others; a particular theory may also rationalize or legitimize one segment of behavior and lead to avoidance or condemnation of another.

In this section, we use the word *ideology* in the strict, dictionary sense: "1. the body of doctrine, myth, symbol, etc., of a social movement, institution, class, or large group. 2. such a body of doctrine, myth, etc., with reference to some political and cultural plan . . . along with the devices for putting it into operation [Stein, 1967, p. 707]."

What sort of background of ideas, doctrine, myths, or ideology makes the behavior observed in an encounter or human potential group acceptable, "good," and even necessary? In line with Smelser's theory (1963) of collective behavior, we may note that all social organizations involve values, doctrines, symbols, myths, procedures, and implicit and explicit formulations of behavior. Some "strain" (in Smelser's language) or failure of reinforcement (in our words) must develop in the social structure, so that a person is prepared to try some new behavior. This preparation may be through a failure to be taught the dominant ideology of the time or may be related to a period of extinction which might be called "disaffection" or "disillusionment" (Toch, 1965; Ullmann, 1969c). A person's overt behavior may change in an apparently sudden and dramatic fashion (which Toch calls "conversion"), or it may be shaped in a series of steps such as in a career (H. Becker, 1963). There are two complementary processes: the loosening of ties to one ideology and the gradual adoption of an alternative.

Supply of the ideology for this process occurs in a roughly stepwise progression. The first step is for someone (including the person himself) to point out that something is wrong; the second step is to pinpoint what is wrong and to offer a solution; the third step is to sell the doctrine and procedure, that is, to place the alternative in operation; the fourth and final step occurs when the new alternative has attracted a considerable body of followers and achieved such a degree of acceptance that implementation occurs and with it associations, institutions, and bureaucracies.

The adoption process for the individual may also be presented in a schematic, stepwise fashion. First, an alternative must exist and the individual must learn of it. The second stage is that of interest and curiosity, in which the person will gather information. Gathering information may be a crucial step, for in doing so the person is likely to place himself physically as well as mentally closer to people practicing the alternative and hence further away from the current practices. The third stage is that of weighing pros and cons, a "mental trial and error," possibly involving vicarious reinforcement as the individual anticipates what consequences he may expect from the alternative. The fourth stage is that in which the person tries out the alternative behavior. This may involve a considerable departure from conventional norms. Sociologists such as H. Becker (1963), Lemert (1967), and Scheff (1966) have labeled the rule breaking that currently falls in the province of forensic and psychiatric practice as primary deviance. The fifth and final stage is the evaluation of the consequences or impact of the fourth stage. These sociologists believe that if the person is labeled by institutionalized social agencies, the label and processes of social control (hospitalization for the labeled schizophrenic; prison for the labeled criminal) may have a greater effect than the person's actual behavior in the fourth stage. The label may lead to a more permanent change in social categorization and consequent behavior. This result is called secondary deviance. Ullmann and Krasner (1969) have pointed out that the individual himself may be the labeler. Even though no external social agent labels him publicly, the person may describe himself as an adulterer, sinner, or psychotic. In the same fashion, but in a favorable sense, the person may evaluate the effects of his new experiences as beneficial and reach a stage of self-acceptance.

A social movement starts with a felt need by people to make efforts to bring about a change in their environment. The change in experience—something added or avoided—need only be so labeled. It need not be something that all observers agree is desirable. The strain is defined operationally by the behavior of people.

Some of the social and historical events leading to the dissolution of the traditional pattern of interpersonal ties have been noted earlier in this chapter. A complex society creates many diverse social forms. Considerable "individuality" is lost in order that people may act "correctly" with others whom they meet even briefly. Many people feel that there is an everincreasing gap between their behavior and genuine feeling for other people. Midtwentieth-century Americans face seemingly compulsive consumption, passive spectator roles, and meaningless delay of gratification (Davis, 1970).

Roszak (1969) has placed the blame on technocracy, "that social form in which an industrial society reaches the peak of its organizational integration. It is the ideal men usually have in mind when they speak of modernizing, updating, rationalizing, planning [p. 5]." Social life reaches such a level of complexity that the typical citizen must defer to experts on matters that concern him vitally. An example is the modern corporation in which ownership is so diffuse among stockholders that the expert-managers possess position, information, and power with at most fractional legal ownership. The shareholder and the voter have a similar relationship to the presidents of General Motors and the United States; their impact on large, important organizations is small and very delayed.

Charles Reich (1970) has listed such modern problems as disorder, hypocrisy, and war; poverty and distorted priorities; decline of democracy and powerlessness; artificiality of work and culture; absence of community; and loss of self. Reich's concept of "consciousness" is very similar to definitions of personality. As he has put it, "Included within the idea of consciousness is a person's background, education, politics, insight, values, emotions, and philosophy, but consciousness is more than these or even the sum of them. It is the whole man; his 'head'; his way of life [p. 15]."

Consciousness III fits the ideal of the human potential movement, as the following quotations from Reich (1970) reveal:

> The foundation of Consciousness III is liberation. It comes into being the moment the individual frees himself from automatic acceptance of the imperatives of society and the false consciousness which society imposes . . . III declares that the individual self is the only true reality [pp. 241–242].

> One device is particularly important: an individual cannot hope to achieve an independent consciousness unless he cultivates, by whatever means are available, including clothes, speech mannerisms, illegal activities, and so forth, the feeling of being an *outsider*. Only the person who feels himself to be an outsider is genuinely free of the lures and temptations of the Corporate State. Only he can work in a bank or go to a cocktail party in "safety" because he will not be taken in [p. 276].

> Consciousness III is deeply suspicious of logic, rationality, analysis, and of principles [p. 278].

> The young people of Consciousness III see effortlessly what is phony or dishonest in politics, or what is ugly and meretricious in architecture and city planning, whereas an older person has to go through years of education to make himself equally aware." [p. 283].[3]

The type of strain that leads to Consciousness III can be linked with the Freudian concept of id impulses being held in check first by the ego and later the superego. But in the Freudian tradition the "real" desires, impulses, or instincts are socially unacceptable, and symptoms and adult personality are sublimations of the "genuine" underlying needs. Most intellectuals believe in these Freudian concepts, and as a result view the socialized and even ritualized behavior they feel forced to perform as not really genuine or representative of their real "me."

This uneasiness and discontent is both recognized and encouraged by leaders of the human potential movement, since it is in effect identical with their diagnosis of what is troubling our society.

---

[3] Consciousness III, however, does not seem to be very robust: "a truly sensitive person just could not stand to ride to New York on the Penn Central Railroad [Reich, 1970, p. 280]."

A sample of this view is provided by Mann (1970):

> From the individual's point of view, he may become socialized at the expense of his native responses. He becomes that which is *rewarded* and loses contact with that which he *is*. To perform effectively, he must, in a sense, avoid contact with his sensations, aspirations, and feelings. They might lead him to deviate from his established patterns [p. viii].

A second example is from Burton (1969):

> Social training is therefore a process of becoming a person with suitably refined sensibilities. . . . Parents limit sensitivity, awareness, and bodily feeling, and they very carefully circumscribe the child's experiences. This is not so much a lack of basic trust as a covert conspiracy to reduce ecstasy to their own level of experience. . . . They want fruitful, happy children, but strictly within the mold of their own super-ego. Thus it is that the person grows up feeling that he has dislocated parts of himself somewhere [p. 19].

As noted in Chapter 3, the central concept of Freud's theory is libido (energy). The human potential movement deals with energy. To continue the last quotation from Burton (1969), "Whatever is missing in the personality drains energy until it is found and reconciled with the totality of self [p. 19]."

And in similar fashion Mann (1970) has written:

> People who deal with the nature of human potential consider energy as a key concept in their explanations of their work and their goals. . . . Every defense, every emotional tension, every situation we avoid, drains us of energy. Further, resistance itself requires energy. Our personality is in part an energy-binding system that limits our access to our own resources [p. viii].

If the person were complete or "whole," the energy spent on correcting his deficit—whether of omission or commission—would be unnecessary and he would be able to live his life better. The solution offered by the human potential movement is to engage in some activity that will (*a*) do away with the defense, (*b*) satisfy what has not been satisfied, (*c*) provide an insight that people are not as the individual construes them because of his defenses, or (*d*) all of these at the same time. The ideas and jargon are strikingly Freudian, but the contemporary analyst would brand them as oversimplified and dated by at least half a century. The general goal is to free energy now being used to hold back the unacceptable or undeveloped. The concept of a "block," especially of energy, returns us to the psychoanalytic, thermodynamic analogy and to the assumption of an innate concept of healthy or normal man altered by external pressures.

The problem becomes one of attaining the general goal. The rubric would be to put the person "in touch" with his feelings. This process may occur by inducing the feeling through various forms of active role playing of the emotion or situations that invoke it. Schutz (1967) has written, "Often the feelings take over, the pent-up fury comes through, and the patient pounds until he's exhausted. This opens up important childhood material for analytic use . . . [p. 35]."

A second, related concept is regression. The person is encouraged to act in a unself-critical and nonintellectual manner. For example, Burton (1969) has written that "Encounter is experientially introjective rather than interpretative and it places little premium on intelligence with its function of rapidly manipulating symbols and placing and displacing them [p. 14]."

Stoller (1969, esp. pp. 88–91) has given a good summary of general ground rules. The first one is, "Accuracy of response—being 'right' is downgraded over honesty and spontaneity." The second rule is, "Being reacted to rather than understood is a consistent group goal. Understanding implies explanation and speculation, operations which impede the encounter." The third rule is, "Concentration is upon what is present within the group, the here-and-now rather than out-of-group data. . . . What counts is not the content of what is being said but its effect upon others." The next three rules deal with feedback, the expression of the effect of others on the individual. The seventh and last rule is, "Finally the group must learn when words are superfluous, when contact and communication must be attempted on an entirely different level. Resorting to nonverbal techniques permits the group members to explore new ground, to risk what they ordinarily avoid. It also enables them to stop what they customarily do and allow other response patterns to emerge."

A number of consequences follow from these rules. The first is the marked parallel between the stance of being *truthful* and the *correct* or *rational* of the human potential encounter. Schutz (1967) has put it this way: "The underlying philosophy behind the human-potential thrust is that of openness and honesty. A man must be willing to let himself be known to himself and others. He must express and explore his feelings and open up areas long dormant and possibly painful . . . [p. 16]."

Such honesty makes two presumptions. The first is that radical, unselected honesty is necessarily good. But knowing when to say something and when to be quiet may not only be a matter of courtesy and tact in general life but also one of the major accomplishments of the therapist. Timing influences whether a verbal message is effective rather than destructive. The second presumption is that what is said without consideration, with honesty and candor, is valuable and accurate. This presumption involves a model of man in general and of psychoanalysis in particular: that which is socially unusual and unacceptable expresses the "real" person. There have indeed been reports of "groupheads," people who feel alive and real only in encounter group situations (Howard, 1970, p. 33; Kuehn and Crinella, 1969, p. 841).

Rather than reducing "defenses," the social situation is used as a pressure to emit unusual, alternative, or novel behavior. Attitude change may indeed follow emission of novel behavior (Festinger, 1964). Modeling, role playing, shaping, and relabeling may be observed in the techniques of the human potential movement. Further, the emission of the new behavior may lead to the person relabeling himself or his acts. Touching, talking, and many of the other acts occurring in encounter groups are novel, pleasant, and fun. They may be relabeled as for the person's psychic good.[4]

Leadership

A social movement has different stages, and different types of leadership are effective at each stage. The stage of formal acceptance of the program of the human potential movement has led to institutionalization of both leaders and organization. Centers are rapidly growing in all parts of the country, accompanied by an outpouring of books, lectures, schools, and magazine articles. Esalen and NTL are examples of a movement attaining an organizational and bureaucratic stage.

As Howard (1970) has expressed it:

> Kahn [an encounter leader] and hundreds of men and women like him are today's circuit riders. In the spiritual life of this century, they occupy a niche similar to that of itinerant preachers in the last. They travel by jet instead of horseback . . . but their message is not much different. The kingdom of heaven, they say in their various jargons, is within: within you and within me and within us all. They are . . . received in some quarters with the degree of adulation usually reserved for Mary Poppins, Johnny Appleseed and the Easter Bunny [p. 40].

Evaluation

Formal investigation with evaluation of behavior, the use of groups to control for the effect of expectation of help (Goldstein, 1962), placebo effects, observer bias, and all the variables of treatment situations are not within the mainstream of the human potential movement. Such traditional scientific procedures are intellectual and focus on the externally, reliably observed as opposed to the phenomenological and personalistic. While it would be unfair to place a value on the human potential movement, we may discuss its worth within a scientific framework. Evaluative, followup studies of the human potential movement, and

---

[4] We note *Conduct Your Own Awareness Sessions* by Hills and Stone (1970) for two reasons. The first is its emphasis on the activity itself; the implicit promise is that if one but follows the actions, one will be better. The second is its rationale that these are "games people *should* play." A person may have his cake and eat it, too.

especially its more recent techniques have been at best discouraging (for example, Burton, 1969, p. 23). Burton (1969) has stated that "Each leader builds a personal following by collecting testimonials and quickly forgets his obligation to science. While industry has set some standards for its human relations consultants, the broader exponents of encounter have not and do not promise to do so [p. 24]."

Training laboratory groups preceded the human potential groups and were used in industrial settings for many years. In a major review of the use of such "T-groups" for managerial training and development, Campbell and Dunnette (1968) arrived at a summary evaluation: "Examination of the research literature leads to the conclusion that while T-group training seems to produce observable changes in behavior, the utility of these changes for the performance of individuals in their organizational roles remains to be demonstrated [p. 73]." Similar disappointing effects have been reported for group psychotherapy in clinical settings (Pattison, 1967; Powdermaker and Frank, 1953; Rickard, 1962), although it should be noted that these studies were of traditional psychiatric methods and populations.

Generalization from Group to Nongroup

Howard (1970), after considerable encounter group experience, noted that back home, "I felt lonelier than ever [p. 239]."

The problem is stated by Gottschalk and Pattison (1969):

> The T-group may provide a forum for more honest confrontation of self and others. It may also be a "hit-and-run" game. For example, one may talk quite freely to a stranger on an airplane but be totally incapable of confiding in one's real life relations. Thus the T-group may foster a sense of pseudo-authenticity and pseudo-reality—that this is really living while the rest of life is phony. The reality of the situation may be that the T-group participant can afford to act in ways that ignore reality because he does not have to live with the consequences of his behavior. Some people return to national sensitivity groups year after year because, they feel, "here I can really be myself." They are in fact unable to be themselves. Or they may be inappropriately capable of sharing intimate details of their psychological experience in a group of people without being able to do so when they should with a single individual.
>
> The T-group may foster a sense of new-found patterns of relationship that may be inappropriate to a participant's real life circumstances.[5] For example, T-group participants may return to their organization with "new ways of being"— only to find that the new self is not accepted by the old work group. The result may be ostracism or more likely a quick extinguishment [sic] of the new T-group

[5] We take the position that all behavior is real. The problem might be better put as: How frequent will the behavior be? And in what situations is it appropriate?

self through involvement in everyday life and work that provides negative rein-forcement [sic] of the new learning. For example, if a patient talked to all his friends as he talks to his therapist, he would soon run out of friends [p. 834].

This quotation touches on many points covered earlier. It is included here because of its distinction between behavior in the training or encounter situation and behavior in other situations that are more frequent in the person's life and that have more pervasive and enduring consequences. *Desirable behavior in one situation is not necessarily desirable in another.* The problem is to provide a benefit from the training situation that will carry over to the nontraining situation.

At this point the theory of personality enters. If a unitary "personality" which must be changed in order to achieve behavior change (and if the be-havior following insight is "right" for other situations) is postulated, then the sensitivity training situation should lead to widespread improvement. But if behavior is situation specific and there is no "personality" other than what people conceptualize, the results of sensitivity training may be diverse and not neces-sarily related to situations outside the group.

To illustrate this point and elaborate on it as do Gottschalk and Pattison in the above quotation, we may note informal reports from school and industrial settings. "In one large city school system an encounter group recently included teachers, most of whom were white, and students, most of whom were black, from the same school. The result was the opposite of what was sought—increased physical and verbal hostility of students to teachers in the school [Birnbaum, 1969, p. 96]." A similar effect in an industrial setting has been noted by Calame [1969]: the training group may lead to behavior that *decreases* the person's effectiveness. Sensitivity to another person's feelings and the modification of one's own behavior that is aversive to some others may decrease an executive's ability to act decisively and enforce his wishes. While positive feelings towards a superior may engender greater effectiveness, this hypothesis need not always be true. Vacillation of decision making—a prime example being the time and effort expended in many leaderless group discussion situations on procedural matters—may foster failures of goal attainment in military, industrial, and educational settings and resultant unpleasant feelings.

A distinction may be made between an emphasis on process and one on outcome. A process is usually evaluated by its effects, that is, its outcome. Con-versely, once an outcome criterion has been established, one looks for processes that will increase or decrease the result in the desired manner. Process may refer to methods, outcome to result. While it should be clear that the two cannot or at least should not be completely separated, specific studies and techniques tend to emphasize one or the other. The ultimate is such an emphasis on the process, or delivery system, that the medium becomes the message and not enough attention is paid to what is delivered.

This overemphasis on process may occur in sensitivity training groups, as it may in other forms of psychotherapy. It has been humorously described by Howard (1970), who recounted her visit to a restaurant on a night out from an NTL advanced personal growth laboratory: "The restaurant we would go to was just a few miles away, but the psychological distance was immense. No nuance of the journey was too trivial, in plan or execution, for us to pounce on and magnify. Every time we passed the salt back and forth, we would analyze what the gesture meant [pp. 118–119]." The behavior generated in one situation—in this case human potential movement groups—may not have useful or effective outcomes in another setting such as the army, business, or school. This does not mean that the values current in these latter situations are not in need of change.

Earlier we indicated that Smelser's notion of value (1963) applied to social institutions is the usual starting place in the development of social movements. We end this discussion with several quotations illustrating the emphasis given by the leaders of the human potential movement to changing social values.

Howard (1970) has quoted Maslow as stating, "[Individual therapy is] not the right answer if you think, as I shamelessly do, in terms of changing the whole world. We need more shortcuts. We have to teach everyone to be a therapist [pp. 36–37]." Howard has quoted Elizabeth Bugenthal as stating, "Right now, encounter groups are a kind of vestibule experience. What they do so far is help people get their feet in the door and give them a taste of how things *can* be [p. 139]."

Burton (1969) has offered this all-encompassing summary: "I am in all seriousness when I say that [the encounter movement] may soon represent the Judeo-Christian emphasis on individualization applied to vast numbers of people who can no longer be formally Christian but who want to be fully human [p. x]." And Reich (1970) has a nearly mystical belief that Consciousness III will save society and make the corporate state obsolete. These ideas may be compared with those of politically oriented mesmerists presented in Chapter 9.

LAST WORD

People respond to other people and serve either directly or indirectly as major sources of discriminative and reinforcing stimuli. This chapter has focused more directly on the question, Does the presence of other people alter one's behavior? While the group, crowd, or collective had been formulated through hypnotic, medical, and psychoanalytic analogues, the present authors center on general social influence principles to deal with group behavior. While behavior in groups does not call for new concepts, the group does provide new models, new sources of reinforcement, and new definitions of what is permissible or desirable. Group activity provides both a *setting event* and a *process for potentially rein-forcing activity.*

The current human potential movement has been used to illustrate the many historical roots of a social movement, the development of ideology, and the spread of a movement offering a new solution after social conditions have led to the inadequacy of established institutions. The movement's ideology and the overt activities of the members offer opportunity and inducements to *novel behavior*, that is, behavior that previously was emitted rarely if at all in other situations. We have touched briefly on the effects of new enactments on the person himself and on his fellow group members. But of prime importance to a theory of behavior influence is that the different behavior observed is not symptomatic of a deeper "realer" person that "must come out" so that available energy may be "liberated." Rather, the person was always capable of the acts, and in the setting of the encounter group the acts become appropriate and are modeled, primed, and reinforced. Observations may be formulated in terms of personality traits, as human potential proponents do, or in terms of a functional analysis of the behavior in the situation as presented in this chapter.

People become interested in, join, participate in, and relate to themselves through group activity. In an increasingly complex, impersonal society, group activity—from trade unions to various liberation fronts—may be an increasingly major method of altering the social and political climate as well as gaining interpersonal contact. Collective behavior is both a setting for behavior and a source of reinforcement for behavior. Collective behavior is an influence, and an understanding of it may aid in describing and predicting human activity in a way that the concept of a reified "personality" does not.

PART 4
Psychological, Ethical,
and Social Implications

CHAPTER 18

Planned Societies: People Controlling Their Own Destinies

Thus far we have focused on the ways in which individual behavior is influenced by environmental, social, cultural, economic, and historical forces. We have also stressed that human behavior is not a one-way street; the individual is not a helpless puppet pulled by environmental strings to act beyond his control. Man has always responded to and "improved" his physical and social environment. People plan a town, a commune, a hospital, an army camp, a monastery, a prison, a school, a labor union, a church, or a home. The resulting locale, institution, or social movement in turn influences behavior by its architecture and social structure, and its rules and role expectancies. The individual influences the institution and is influenced by it.

Recognizing that social structure always influences behavior, people endeavor to improve society. The wide range of behaviors intended to *change* society include making laws, voting, petitioning, revolting, and trying to plan for and/or carry out "better" societies.

Many human behaviors are oriented toward changing some aspects of society. More often than not, the individual plans to change society, so that the behavior of others will be influenced in a positive direction (operationally defined as "act in a way that pleases me"). Laws are considered necessary to control *others*. It is difficult for people to realize that they themselves are *the others* to others.

In this chapter we examine the attempts of people to establish social arrangements that are *alternatives* to or improvements on their current living situations. In reviewing communities and utopias we are not dealing with a phenomenon that differs from ordinary living. Just as there is no dichotomy between normal and abnormal, between personality and behavior, between hypnosis and behavior influence, there is no dichotomy between utopian life and other forms of social living. The *concept* of utopia has had a long history with changing meanings and consequences. And many communities have labeled themselves as communes or utopias. But their development is no different from that of any other group of people who try to give order to their lives and to control their destinies by the educations they receive, the jobs they work in, the homes they buy, or the people they marry.

UTOPIA

The American Heritage Dictionary (Morris, 1969) defines *utopia* as, "Any condition, place, or situation of social or political perfection. . . . Any idealistic goal or concept for social and political reform. . . . [Utopia] An imaginary island that served as a subject and title of a book by Sir Thomas More in 1516 and that was described as a seat of perfection in moral, social, and political life. [From Greek—no place.] [utopian] Excellent or ideal but existing only in visionary or impractical thought or theory [p. 1411]."

Thus, the term has two general meanings; (*a*) a *perfect society*, (*b*) *social reform*. These two usages have caused some confusion because of their incompatibility—reform implies something achievable, while perfection implies an absolute that cannot be attained. This distinction must be kept in mind throughout this chapter. We prefer to use utopia to signify its second meaning—social reform or innovation—because of its more positive, attainable implications and continuity with "normal" living (Krasner, 1971b).

The concept of utopia is an old one; Plato's *Republic* is an example. However, *utopia* did not become a household word until 1516, with the publication of More's book. *Utopia* is a recounting of the adventures of a fictitious Portuguese sailor, Raphael Hythlodaye, who made three voyages to America with the explorer Amerigo Vespucci and traveled through wild and unexplored places. The greatest wonder Hythlodaye described to More was the island of Utopia—this was the ideal commonwealth, in which all men are equal, prosperous, educated, and wise.

More's *Utopia* had a major impact on the behavior of subsequent generations. But, like many other seminal works, its intent and implications depend upon the concerns of the interpreter. As Negley and Patrick (1952) put it:

> Published in Latin in 1516, often reprinted, translated into English . . . in 1551, retranslated into English . . . in 1684, put into almost all European languages, and, in the twentieth century, into several Asiatic ones, the Utopia of Sir Thomas More is obviously universal in its appeal and ubiquitous in its influence. But great caution is necessary in interpreting it, for it is acclaimed by Protestant and Catholic, by Christian and Communist, by Progressivists and Reactionaries, indeed, by men of all schools of thought, though for widely different reasons. That More himself was recognized as a Saint by the Roman Catholic Church, and, in the same decade, that his Utopia was adopted as a textbook in Soviet Russia, indicates the need for caution in assessing both the man and the book [pp. 258–259].

As we have seen earlier in evaluating Machiavelli's impact, each age, each country, each social critic may use More's *Utopia*, the book and the concept, for his own purposes and within his own conceptual view of man. The possible interpretations of *Utopia*, the book, have been summarized by Ames (1949):

> The description of Utopia by itself may be considered one or more of a great many different things: 1. A fantastic escape from unpleasant reality. 2. A blueprint for a better society which More thought men might soon establish. 3. A better society which might exist in some far-off time. 4. A better society which More desired but did not believe possible. 5. A reconstruction of medieval social virtues. 6. A revival of primitive Christian communism. 7. A speculative portrait of rumored American societies like that of the Incas. 8. A strictly rational philosophic construction, minus Christianity, for the purposes of moral instruction. 9. A pleasant fable written by a humanist for the amusement of himself and his scholarly friends. 10. A fruit of classical studies, following Plato's Republic. 11. An early plan for British imperialism. 12. A Christian humanist account of a scholar's paradise, where philosophers are kings and the church is purified. 13. A society constructed as the direct opposite to England for the purpose of disguising social criticism. 14. A description of a desirable and possible organization of city republics [as quoted by Negley and Patrick, 1952, p. 264].

Ames' own preference was for the view common to his critical generation that More's book is really social satire and criticism. He concluded that the Utopian society was intended as a "protective disguise for the satire and dangerously progressive projects of a humanistic reformer and middle-class citizen [p. 263]."

These details of Utopia once more make the point that ideas, especially those that deal with people in general and personality in particular, are *human creations* that serve human purposes in a time and place.

Categorization and Background

Utopian ideas and practices have had two major sources: first, the body of general and science fiction labeled as *literary utopias*; second, the utopian communities of the eighteenth to twentieth centuries.

Manuel's classification of utopias (1967b), past and present, postulates three stages or epochs in Western utopias. "The first group might be called utopias of calm felicity, running roughly from More to the age of the French Revolution; the second comprises the dynamic socialist and other historically determinist utopias, which span the greater part of the 19th century; and the last are the psychological and philosophical utopias of the 20th century, for which I borrow from Professor Abraham H. Maslow the term 'eupsychia' [p. 71]."

There has always been a relationship between theoretical views about the nature of man and the belief in the possibility of utopian planning. The eighteenth and nineteenth centuries represented the height of optimism about man's nature and his inherent goodness. However, the theories of Darwin and Freud changed this optimism.

> In the latter part of the 19th century, two scientific hypotheses about the nature of man appeared to raise almost insurmountable barriers to the prolongation of the utopian dream: the discoveries of Darwin and Freud. Both were shattering to those men of the nineteenth century who had had visions of a peaceful, orderly, progressive world from which antagonism and aggression were virtually banished and where men's creativity would flower forever. . . . In many ways Freud's was the most trenchant and devastating attack on utopian illusions—what he called the lullabies of heaven—that had ever been delivered (Manuel, 1967b, pp. 86–87).

But despite the intellectual attacks on the optimistic underpinnings implicit in a notion of man as a changeable creature, the belief in the possibility of human betterment survived. Indeed, social planning, political efforts, laws, social ferment, and planned societies are currently gaining and merging both in conception and in behavior. In his "psychological history" of utopias Manuel (1967b) has described the close relationship between social and political processes and utopian planning:

> But despite their [e.g. Freud, Orwell] flood of bitter mockery the utopian energy of man was not irretrievably dissipated. The creature, it seems, could not stop dreaming even as he stood beneath the gallows of the atomic launching pads. Certain of the hopes of the old-fashioned . . . Saint-Simonian utopias had in

the meantime become partial political realities, through social legislation, in restricted areas of the world; or they had at least been incorporated as programmatic statements of intent by major institutions. The social encyclicals of Pope John XXIII, the speeches of Khrushchev at Soviet Party Congresses, and the preambles to Democratic Party platforms are a fairly wide-ranging sample of the penetration of early 19th century utopian motifs into the contemporary political arena [p. 87].

Who are the utopians? We define them here as individuals who use the behavior influence process to bring about change in the behavior of at least some fellow members of their society. Innovations have a high degree of social value. That is, the influencers have made a decision, implicitly or explicitly, that certain behaviors are better than others (for example, cooperation is better than competition). The focus of a utopia indicates the major concerns, both desired and undesired, of the particular society. Given this definition, far more individuals can be labeled utopian than would be under the narrower definition of the creator or planner of a "perfect" society. "The list of social critics and utopians whose visions have sometimes captured the dreams (but little else) of large numbers of people is long and varied. . . . Aldous Huxley and Charlie Chaplin, B. F. Skinner and Karl Marx, Edward Bellamy and C. Wright Mills, Germaine Greer and Ralph Nader (*Science News*, Feb. 12, 1972, p. 100)." This merging of the social critic and the utopian represents the context of current usage of the utopian concept.

However, utopia is also frequently used as a term of denigration:

Scorn is still the standard attitude toward utopia. The good liberal continues to echo the spirit that Macaulay once expressed when he said that he would much rather have "an acre in Middlesex than a principality in Utopia." The good Marxian continues to accept Engels' verdict that utopian socialism is "unscientific" and a shameful heresy. And even a dissenting Marxist like Milovan Djilas equates utopia with dogmatism and tyranny and opts instead for an "unperfect" society [Plath, 1971, p. ix].

The alternative position—which equates utopian and planned daily living— is summarized by Nisbet's observation (1962) that "Utopianism, after all, is social planning, and planning is indispensable in the kind of world that technology, democracy, and high population bring [p. xvii]."

ARCHITECTURE AND UTOPIA

The planned use of space is a major feature of every human community. The deliberately planned utopia or commune is usually spatially separated from other social units (although as may be seen in the human potential "utopia," this is not an absolute necessity); and Sommer (1969) has stated, "The American utopia rests on spatial segregation [p. 145]." This segregation implies that the planners of new societies should be able to make their decisions about the use of space independent of the existing usage. Commune members are usually reacting against the conventional use of space, since it is related to behaviors which they work to change. Sommer (1969) has pointed out the close relationship between the profession of architecture and utopian communities:

> The concept of Utopia as well as the word itself is surprisingly frequent in architectural books and articles. It seems to fill much the same role for architects as does health for medical practitioners and efficiency for engineers. As laymen continue to strive toward a Utopia through laws intended to produce harmonious and frictionless social intercourse, designers use environmental programming to develop physical forms that will increase the sum-total of human happiness [p. 148]."

The issue of privacy provides a major framework for relating space to behavior. The commune's objectives range from complete privacy to a merging of individual identity within the group. These objectives are manifested by the availability of private rooms and tents, as against a large undifferentiated unistructure.

Another factor related to the use of space is the size of the community. In his review of American communes, Roberts (1971) has concluded that "modern communal societies all maintain that the scale of society as currently organized is too large. Unlike Marxist utopians who conceive of an entire world community, communalists tend toward the anarchistic idea that man can relate in a meaningful way with a limited number of like-minded individuals [p. 12]." But what is the optimal size for a community? Some have argued that the ideal situation is one in which every member knows the first name of every other member.

Most communes have failed and will continue to fail because they have not dealt realistically with the relationship between space utilization and behavioral objectives. The members must agree on the goals of the commune before its space is designed. A survey of the commune literature indicates that, with some exceptions, very little advance consideration is given to the problem of what behavior the group really wants of its participants. There is also inadequate knowledge of how space affects behavior. The objective may be agreed on, but unless it is clear *how* the space can be utilized to bring about the objective many mistakes will occur. This is illustrated by a report (J. Rosenthal, 1971) on the new town of Columbia, Maryland. The town planners wished to provide teen-agers with facilities for recreation and other positive social behaviors, but the design and location of the center allocated for the purpose proved to be inadequate and fostered interracial friction between teenagers. In effect, poor architectural planning may defeat the best of intentions.

UTOPIAS AS SOCIAL MOVEMENTS

Although planning for new communities has taken place throughout American history ("in order to establish a more perfect union"), new communities such as communes have been particularly active in certain times—usually periods of social stress and upheaval or what Smelser (1963) would call a "strain."

> Every social movement must appeal to a segment or segments of society which are potentially amenable to the movement's ideology. The potential constituency of the modern communal-utopian movement is the young, disaffected, post-high-school, college and post-college individual. In contrast to working-class youths, many middle-class college students speak of their resentment of the "plastic" or "inauthentic" nature of bourgeois occupations, politics, religion, and respectability" [Roberts, 1971, pp. 15–16].

We now describe three kinds of communities: emotive groups, Walden Two, and Oneida. In different ways, each has been influenced by and has had influence upon American society.

The Emotive Group as Utopia

Utopian planning is not separate from day-to-day decision-making social influence but merges with other activities which call for a change in the existing value structure. Such human behaviors may include changing a school curriculum, setting up a new commune, or participating in a weeklong marathon encounter group.

From its origins in novels and in reality, the utopian community has had two functions: to achieve specific goals for its members and to influence the behavior of individuals in the outside society by serving as a *model* for them. Jacobs (1971) has referred to the emotive (encounter) groups as a "laboratory for solution for social problems, many have found a new locus for utopian hopes counter to prevailing conditions in mass society [pp. 235–236]." Although human potential groups are "part-time" rather than full-time living situations, their *value* orientation is so predominant that they supply the individual with patterns of behavior and a belief system as a full-time community would.

Utopia repeatedly merges with personality theory, be it that of Freud, Skinner, or neo-Rogerians (see Chapter 3). Maslow's theory has been crucial to the utopian-human potential social movement (see Chapter 17).

Even psychoanalysis can be viewed as a utopian social movement. As Jacobs (1971) has noted:

> The work impetus . . . was transmutted by the psychoanalytic utopians into psycho-analytic child-rearing designed to mold nobler humans. . . . Those who had been or might have been socialists or other reformers in the early decades of the 20th century were, in the 40's and 50's, analysts and analysands and the popularizers of the new panacea for individuals and society. Their popularizations filtered psychoanalytic utopian thinking through the mass media [p. 241].

As we have indicated previously, the human encounter movement developed out of the strains of the American life in the 1960s. As Jacobs (1971) has put it:

> Since the early 1900s human engineering through group techniques had been labeled 100 per cent American by its acceptance at the heart of America's social system—her economic enterprises. These techniques had become increasingly sophisticated. . . . The retreat movement in the churches, for example, bor-rowed personnel and techniques from group therapy and human relations insti-tutes and grew rapidly . . . varied kinds of control and emotive groups sprang up to handle myriad difficulties, almost to the point that one existed for every type of personal or social problem from interpersonal constraints to racial discord. Therapeutic and encounter entrepreneurs—professional and amateur—prospered, and some became "wholesalers" of groups [p. 242].

These groups were culminations of views of man that emphasized the im-portance of values and of the roles of "others": "Individuals, unequal to or cowed by the task of defining truth in a relativistic, secular world, sought a socially derived ethic. . . . Seeking value definition and self-validation, the heirs of Mead's generalized other—Riesman's 'other-directed men'—groped for identity with a group. Under contemporary mass conditions, they were ripe for involvement in that special variety of utopian community; the control and emotive group [Jacobs, 1971, p. 242]."

The founders of utopias emphasize behaviors that are the converse of those expected in the larger society. As Jacobs (1971) has observed, "Our society, dominated by routinized, restrained daily activities and suppressed emotionalism, has produced utopias steeped in spontaneity as its escape or reaction. In an increasingly cold, uncaring, bureaucratic society, the control and emotive groups offer opportunity, protection, and approval for catharsis [p. 247]." In fact, a major attraction of the human potential utopia is that it calls for behaviors not encouraged or permitted in the community.

Perhaps the major social institution which the utopian groups react against is the family. The human potential groups "are actually antifamilistic, as were most past utopian groups. They become more important to the individual than his family. They resocialize him away from its norms and values, weaning him from dependence on family [Jacobs, 1971, p. 249]."

Related to the antitraditional family attitudes are the community's attitudes about the importance and function of sexual relationships. "Since sex harbors perhaps the most powerful potential for particularized and privileged relations between individuals, it needs to be stringently controlled if the utopian community is to be successful. This seems to account, by the way, for the strong anti-familistic bias of many literary utopias from Plato to Campanella [Coser, 1967, p. 209]."

It is not surprising, then, that notions of sexual promiscuity have become associated with some of the human potential groups. The popular belief is typified by the behavior of the leading characters of the movie "Bob & Carol & Ted & Alice," in which the two couples in the title approach swinging as a result of the first couple's sensitivity group experience in California. Utopian communities consider exclusive dyadic relationships as dangerous to the group since such a relationship represents withdrawal into a private noncommunal world. As Coser (1967) has stated:

> Once this is understood an important sociological truth comes into view: *Celibacy and promiscuity, though opposed sexual practices, fulfill identical sociological functions.* From a structural point of view they are but variants on the same theme —the prevention of particularistic, dyadic attachments. Whether members refrain from all sexual relations, as among the Shakers, or whether there is complex marriage as in Oneida, where man and woman within the community may and do freely cohabit for short periods of time, turns out upon inspection to be sociologically unimportant. The true enemy of community are those "exclusive and idolatrous attachments" between two persons of opposite sex against which not only Noyes but also the Shakers and many others never ceased to warn [p. 209].

Finally, the human potential utopias desire to change the society *out there.* To the extent that they are successful, they destroy the purpose, need, or rationale for a separate grouping: "Members see themselves as elite pioneers showing the way to reform society and compensate for rigidities and impersonalities in its large structures. This is consistent with the history of utopia [Jacobs, 1971, p. 250]."

Maslow's utopian thinking was influenced by the anthropological studies of Margaret Mead and Ruth Benedict (see Chapter 3). These studies suggested that, contrary to Freud's theory, aggressiveness could be culturally determined and hence was not a universal characteristic of man. From this conclusion Maslow conceived of the desirable society as one in which individuals would spontaneously manifest altruistic behavior. In the good society all individuals would achieve self-actualization and have no need to express aggression or hostility.

The following description by Manuel (1967b) of the relationship between Maslow's personality and utopian theories was written prior to his death when Maslow's influence on the human potential movement was increasing.

> Along with the neo-Freudians, Maslow rejects such absolute concepts as the death instinct. He believes that through the discovery of the pure sources of one's own

nature there can be a free outpouring of creativity, even the birth of a new way of cognition uncorrupted by the inherited categories of Aristotelian thinking. His seems to be a utopia of the will, emancipated and untrammeled, that somehow achieves direct realization of the traditional love of the great universal religious illuminations of the sixth century before Christ. . . . Maslow is a psychological utopian not in the sense that he is blind to the economic and social miseries that inspired most past utopias, but that with a utopian's license he moves on to another plane, where, beyond basic needs, he posits requirements for a psychic utopia that are more or less autonomous of any existing political order; the fulfillment of "idiosyncratic potentials, of expression of the self, and of the tendency of the person to grow in his own style and at his own pace."

Of late, one can detect in Maslow's writings a movement away from the definition of self-actualization in romantic terms as the expansive realization of *all* potentialities, and the acceptance of a hierarchy of values in which a kind of religious experience again becomes the highest good to which others must be made subordinate. In this he seems to join those philosophers of history who foresee a new spiritualization of mankind and an end to the sensate culture of our times [pp. 93–94].

Walden Two

Skinner's utopian novel *Walden Two*—published in 1948 and reprinted several times, most recently in 1972—is a major landmark in the psychology of behavior influence because of its link with other aspects of the field. The book itself belongs in the long history of fictional planned (or feared) societies dating from Plato's *Republic* through Thomas More's *Utopia* and Edward Bellamy's *Looking Backward* to Aldous Huxley's *Brave New World*. *Walden Two* also provides a link with experimental psychology and behavior modification because it represents an extension to social life of basic experimental studies. The society described in *Walden Two* anticipated subsequent behavior modification procedures such as token economy in various institutional living situations. In so doing, it accentuated the importance of economic influences (for example, supply and demand) on individual behavior.

We now cite a passage from *Walden Two*, which describes the utopia's use of economic relationships to affect very specific job behaviors. Frazier, the planner of the society, is explaining the concept of labor credits to the visitor-narrator:

"Labor-credits are a sort of money. But they're not coins or bills—just entries in a ledger. All goods and services are free, as you saw in the dining room this evening. Each of us pays for what he uses with twelve hundred labor-credits each year—say, four credits for each workday. We change the value according to the needs of the community. At two hours of work per credit—an eight-hour day—we could operate at a handsome profit. We're satisfied to keep just a shade beyond breaking even. The profit system is bad even when the worker gets the profits, because the strain of overwork isn't relieved by even a large reward. All we ask is to make expenses, with a slight margin of safety; we adjust the value of the labor-credit accordingly. At present, it's about one hour of work per credit."

"Your members work only four hours a day?" I said. There was an overtone of outraged virtue in my voice, as if I had asked if they were all adulterous.

"On the average," Frazier replied casually. . . . "A credit system also makes it possible to evaluate a job in terms of the willingness of the members to undertake it. After all, a man isn't doing more or less than his share because of the time he puts in; it's what he's doing that counts. So we simply assign different credit values to different kinds of work, and adjust them from time to time on the basis of demand. Bellamy suggested the principle in *Looking Backward.*"

"An unpleasant job like cleaning sewers has a high value, I suppose," I said.

"Exactly. Somewhere around one and a half credits per hour. The sewer man works a little over two hours a day. Pleasanter jobs have lower values—say point seven or point eight. That means five hours a day or even more. Working in the flower gardens has a very low value—point one. No one makes a living at it, but many people like to spend a little time that way, and we give them credit. In the long run, when the values have been adjusted, all kinds of work are equally desirable. If they weren't, there would be a demand for the more desirable, and the credit value would be changed. Once in awhile, we manipulate a preference, if some job seems to be avoided without a cause."

"I suppose you put phonographs in your dormitories which repeat, 'I like to work in sewers. Sewers are lots of fun,' " said Castle.

"No. Walden Two isn't that kind of brave new world," said Frazier. "We don't *propagandize.* That's a basic principle. I don't deny that it would be possible. We could make the heaviest work appear most honorable and desirable. Something of the sort has always been done by well-organized governments—to facilitate the recruiting of armies, for example. But not here. You may say that we propagandize *all* labor, if you like, but I see no objection to that. If we can make work pleasanter by proper training, why shouldn't we?" [Skinner, 1948, pp. 51–53].

Walden Two has also had impact upon society in a broader sense because the novel has served as the basis for a number of communes or planned societies. In these instances, individuals were influenced by the kind of society described in the book and determined to use it as a model for their own "real" community. All these attempts are based in part on decisions by individuals as to what, for them, are the "good things" in life and how they are going to go about seeking them. Skinner (1969) has stated:

The important thing about the good things in life is what people are doing when they get them. "Goods" are reinforcers, and a way of life is a set of contingencies of reinforcement. In utopian literature, the arrangements of contingencies have seldom been explicit. . . . If we ask someone to describe the kind of world in which he would like to live, he will probably begin to list the reinforcers he would want to find in it. . . . A utopian community is a pilot experiment, like the pilot plant in industry or the pilot experiment in science, where principles are tested on a small scale to avoid the risks and inconvenience of size [pp. 37–38].

During the 1960s there was an upsurge in interest and attempts to set up a Walden Two–type of community in real life. The best known is the Twin Oaks Community, which started on a 134-acre farm near Louise, Virginia, in 1967. Mertens (1971) has culled the following statement from newsletters which describe the intentions, values, and plans for the community.

> Twin Oaks is an intentional community based on the book *Walden Two*. Its purpose is to set up and maintain a society aimed at and operated for the benefit of its citizens, to create a culture which produces happy and useful people, a people who cooperate with one another for the general good and who deal with problems in a peaceful and rational way. We avoid institutions which promote competition, exploitation or aggression. We reject the assumption that anyone who knows how to make other people serve his ends has a right to do so, and the notion that "success" consists of being envied by one's neighbors. We hold that superior intelligence or talent do not entitle a person to a larger share of the world's goods than other people, but simply oblige him to employ his talents for the good of society. We believe, not that everyone is equal (obviously not the case) but that everyone is entitled to be treated equally not only before the law, as the U. S. Constitution tried to guarantee, but also in income and leisure and opportunities for education. Twin Oaks has and is a radical life style, and we want to provide a genuine alternative to the competitive, consumer-oriented life offered by society [p. 6].

This gives us a clear picture of the value orientation of this society. We may also note the implicit desire, as in all social movement utopias, to bring about change in the outside world by providing a desirable model that will demonstrate how change can be brought about and maintained.[1] At the time of this writing, the Twin Oaks group is still in existence—small, poor, struggling, with turnover—but still functioning and in contact with the world through its newsletter, "Leaves of Twin Oaks."

THE ONEIDA COMMUNITY

In this section we outline the growth, development, and decline of a midnineteenth-century utopia. Oneida Community puts in sharp focus most of the topics of a psychology of behavior influence: social movement; the impact of an influ-

---

[1] American mental hospitals were originally designed (in the early nineteenth century) not only to help individuals with problems but to reform society.

> The asylum would also exemplify for the public the correct principles of organization. The new world of the insane would correct within its restricted domain the faults of the community and through the power of example spark a general reform movement. The broad program . . . resembled in spirit and outlook the communitarian movements of the period, such as Brook Farm and New Harmony. . . . Medical superintendents . . . were almost as eager as Owenites to evolve and validate general principles of social organization from their particular experiments [Rothman, 1971, p. 133].

encer; utopian plans; self-control; encounter groups; the social role of women; the impact of belief or ideology on behavior; education; and the need to approach an influence process such as a utopia in the social context of its time.

The Oneida Community, like many other American utopias, developed during the Jacksonian era. Holloway (1966a) has given a broad view of the commune scene in the 1800s:

> Over a hundred communities, with a total membership of more than one hundred thousand men, women, and children, were tried out in the course of the century. Some features of these experiments, whether they were sectarian or not, were more revolutionary than those of the much larger democratic and working-class movements in Europe, from which they differed fundamentally in that they attempted to dissociate themselves completely from established society. Instead of trying to change society from within, by parliamentary reform or by violent revolution, they tried to set up models of ideal commonwealths, thus providing examples which (in some cases) they hoped the world would follow. The ideals they sought, and often succeeded in achieving, included equality of sex, nationality, and colour; the abolition of private property; the abolition of property in people, either by slavery or through the institutions of monogamy and the family; the practice of non-resistance; and the establishment of a reputation for fair-dealing, scrupulous craftsmanship, and respect for their neighbours. . . . The history of these experiments is one of few successes, many failures, and constantly renewed endeavour. Only three of four communities have lasted longer than a hundred years. Many vanished within a few months of their foundation. But all have contributed something of value, not only to the fund of experience upon which succeeding experiments of the same kind have relied, but also to the history of American society. . . . Slightly mad, indeed, some of them were. From the emaciated Kelpius, who searched the heavens night after night for a portent of the Millennium, to Fourier, who thought that the sea would turn into lemonade; from the two Shaker girls who were ordered to whip one another for watching the "amour of two flies in the window," to Bronson Alcott, who refused to "enslave" animals by using them on his farm—from first to last, as was inevitable in a movement that tested the validity of almost every belief and almost every convention, there was a large number of cranks and a high proportion of fanatics. Emerson was certainly thinking of some of them when he wrote to Carlyle in 1840: "We are all a little wild here with numberless projects of social reform. Not a reading man but has a draft of a new community in his waistcoat pocket. . . . One man renounces the use of animal food; and another of coin; and another of domestic hired service; and another of the State . . . [pp. 18–20]."

Within this context of strain, discontent, hope, and ferment were established the communities of the Shakers, Rappites, Zoarites, Brook Farm, Hopedale, Amana, Oneida, and many others. These ventures had one thing in common: individuals were attempting to plan and to control their own environments.

The founder of Oneida was John Humphrey Noyes, born in 1811 of a well-to-do family (his father a congressman) and trained for the ministry at Yale Divinity School. Carden (1969) has described Noyes' ideas as follows:

He taught that one should follow only the inspired spirit of the Bible, not the letter of its law. To him, there were no absolute standards of morality. What is right for one time is wrong for another: it is a higher form of ethics to be responsible to oneself than to an external set of rules. In less specifically religious terms, although not without religious justification, he insisted that life is supposed to be happy. Men, and women too, should cultivate and desire the joys of all experience—including the joys of sexual intercourse. With regard to matters ranging from religion to sex, this nineteenth century prophet rejected the conventions of his day and often anticipated more than a century of change [pp. 1–2].

Noyes was described by George Bernard Shaw in *The Revolutionist's Handbook* as, "one of those chance attempts at the Superman which occur from time to time in spite of the interference of Man's blundering institutions (as quoted by Holloway, 1966b, p. vi)." ". . . as far as morals are concerned, particularly sexual morals, he was one of the most extreme revolutionaries that Western Civilization has produced (Holloway, 1966b, p. vii)."

Noyes' variation of the Calvinist doctrine of his time was *perfectionism*, the belief that man can achieve perfection on earth. Once man was convinced of his inner perfection, his outward behavior would be automatically above reproach. Noyes' views on religion were to have the greatest impact on the future community. As Carden (1969) has noted, "He came to look upon monogamous marriage as a tyrannical institution that did not exist in heaven and eventually would be abolished on earth [p. 8]."

After being thrown out of the church for his deviation from doctrine, he spent the next twelve years studying and teaching the principles of salvation from sin. A small group of believers gradually gathered around him, including his mother, two sisters, a brother, and their spouses. Noyes and his relatives were joined by other families and individuals from various parts of the United States. They built a chapel and devoted much of their time to study and to printing religious tracts.

Noyes felt that man was at the point where "ideal marriage" on earth could be started, but only in a society isolated from the secular world. "Noyes also believed that the need for a community was justified in other ways. He realized that 'the external character of the mass of mankind is, and must be to a great extent, molded by the society in which they live.' . . . Here was utopia—where earthly perfection would reach its highest form and Perfectionist ideals would be put into practice [Carden, 1969, p. 17]."

About a dozen adults and their children set up home at the site of an old sawmill on Oneida Creek and invited Noyes to join them. He did with about thirty other adults and fourteen children. The perfectionists incorporated themselves in 1847 as the Oneida Association which was to last for over thirty years with the same structure.

All descriptions of the community indicate that those joining had been solid citizens while in conventional society. They were described in 1853 as "sober, substantial men and women, of good previous character, and position in society [Carden, 1969, p. 26]." This is a particularly important point, because the group practiced what was then considered bizarre and highly unusual sexual behavior.

Nor were the members of the Oneida Association wanderers from group to group in a constant searching for "truth." These people knew the kind of environment they wanted. In fact, one of the points that differentiated the original founders from the next generation (their own progeny) was that the parents retained their original enthusiasm for the community, while the children eventually rebelled against it. Noyes believed that the kind of planned mating which he had in mind, which we would call *eugenics*, required "sound stock" to begin with.

From among the enthusiastic perfectionists, Noyes carefully selected those who were not only committed to his teachings *but who were also good craftsmen and farmers*. Thus, these skilled persons could provide for the material necessities of the community in its mill, smithy, shoe shop, and farm. These people also brought their life savings, and Carden has reported that "By 1857 the members had invested almost $108,000 in the community and its branches. Without this large capital investment, Oneida would almost certainly have perished [p. 39]." These economic considerations were major factors in the longevity of the community. These were individuals who had been successful in economic life before the formation of the community and who continued to be so. Eventually the Oneida Community stabilized at about 250 individuals.

Two major principles dominated community life: the belief in *individual perfection* and the belief in *doing what is good for the community*. Noyes emphasized the importance of the individual displaying behavior that was consistent with and a reflection of moral and spiritual character. The individual was expected to develop his intellectual capacity and to realize fully all his "potentialities." Self-realization was a goal of life in much the same way as it is in the current human potential movement.

The members of the community put heavy emphasis on arranging their environment so as to stimulate thought, inquiry, and the education of themselves and their children. They had an extensive library with heavy emphasis on the works of the heretics of the day such as T. H. Huxley and Darwin. They valued art, amusement, orchestras, dances, plays, chess, card games, and frequent picnics. They believed that "every man, woman, and child should be surrounded with circumstances favoring the best development of heart, mind, and body and that no one should be excluded on account of age, sex, or race, from engaging in any occupation for which he or she is adapted by nature or culture [Holloway, 1966a, p. 191]."

The most unusual feature of the Oneida Community was its practice of Noyes' concepts of "complex marriage" and "male continence." Both follow from Noyes' religious views of perfectionism. The system of *complex marriage* was deduced from Noyes' view that it was unhealthy for two people to be exclusively attached to each other. But everyone was not available to everyone else as a sexual partner. The system at Oneida was carefully controlled and regulated by the principle of *ascending fellowship.* Noyes believed that some perfectionists were more perfect than others and that the members could be ranked on a scale of perfectness. Older persons were considered to be higher on the scale, so that younger people were supposed to gain wisdom by having sexual relationships with an older person. Thus, sexual relationships generally occurred between young men and older women (often post-menopausal), and young women and older men. This arrangement also helped avoid unwanted conceptions. Frequent changes of partners were required to avoid any hint of exclusiveness in love. Nevertheless, some partners, young women in particular, seemed to be more in demand than others.

Male continence, as Noyes thought of it, involved a considerable amount of self-control. Noyes (1872) described the procedure as follows:

> Now we insist that this whole process, up to the very moment of emission, is *voluntary,* entirely under the control of the moral faculty, and *can be stopped at any point.* In other words, the *presence* and the *motions* can be continued or stopped at will, and it is only the final *crisis* of emission that is automatic or uncontrollable. . . . If you say that this is impossible, I answer that I *know* it is possible—nay, that it is easy. . . .
>
> Brutes, animal or human, tolerate none. Shall their ideas of self-denial prevail? Nay, it is the glory of man to control himself and the Kingdom of Heaven summons him to self-control in All Things [as quoted by Carden, 1969, p. 50].

The Oneida Community took an egalitarian stand on men and women's roles. For example, the community felt that women should enjoy sex as much as men. Noyes' views about sex as an act of love in its most natural form were not unlike those expressed in some modern hippie communes. Ironically, one of Noyes' major problems was to prevent the development of love affairs between couples. "Exclusive love" between a male and a female represented a threat to complex marriage. The mechanism of control was public confession and peer censure.

The system of male continence worked well as a birth control procedure, and the community under Noyes established a strict eugenics program in which a committee approved attempts at procreation by carefully selected couples. Noyes coined the word *stirpiculture* for this procedure of controlling the roots or stock of the new generation. Carden (1969) has described the result of these eugenic efforts:

> During the decade 1869–79, fifty-eight live children were born at Oneida, to a total of forty-four women. Although all are usually classed as stirpiculture children, thirteen were the result of accidental conceptions. . . . The distribution

of fathers was less even. John Humphrey Noyes believed sincerely in the superiority of his family line. He sired ten of the stirpicults—five boys, four girls, and one stillborn child [p. 63].

Education at Oneida

Enormous concern and effort went into children's education at Oneida. About 135 children—either born into the community or brought there by their parents—were involved. The children lived in a home away from their parents and received an education similar to that of wealthy children in the larger society.

Noyes and elders of the community had specific goals in the education of their children. Noyes continually lectured the children on "the importance of pleasing God by being good."

> Indeed the adults were particularly concerned about the children's spiritual state: they must be unselfish, they must respond to a quarrelsome friend by "turning the other cheek," they must report any backslider, and they must avoid the selfishness of "excessive partiality" or else be separated from their friends. In the 1850's and 1860's a child was reproved severely for even the smallest deviation from these standards. In the 1870's, when the stirpiculture children were being raised, discipline was still strict but not so harsh [Carden, 1969, p. 64].

This educational experiment was both enormously successful and unsuccessful. Carden (1969) has reported as follows:

> It is impossible to assess the results of the stirpiculture experiment. Many of the children were rated as superior and above average by the schoolmaster who taught in the Mansion House school after the breakup. Many went on to college. Some were successful in business, in scholarship, and in the arts. They were healthy, and they lived a long time. But these evidences of mental and physical superiority may be attributed solely to environmental factors. The stirpicults were brought up in a healthy country environment with plenty of fresh air, good food, and attention, and Oneida was isolated from chronic diseases that might have affected children in more crowded areas [p. 65].

On the other hand the failure in educating the young in the Oneida spirit was a major factor in the eventual breakup of the community. Carden (1969) has offered the following analysis of this failure.

> The community was threatened, too, by its inability to imbue its young with the spirit of the founders. Since Oneida children, unlike their parents, were members of the Community by virtue of family ties rather than by choice, their appreciation of Community ideals had to be developed. . . .
> Exposure to the system did not necessarily result in total acceptance of it,

however, although there is no evidence that the failure of the religious aspects of Perfectionism to inspire the young was the result of any deliberate rejection on their parts. Rather, unlike their parents, they were not a psychologically select group predisposed to accept the religion; and like their parents, they existed in an atmosphere in which a concern for the Community as a social entity was supplanting the reverence for its original reason for being. It is understandable, then, that the young did not greet Perfectionism with the convert's fervor.

Ironically, it was probably not the community's inconsistent attitude toward its own religious principles but its consistently strong emphasis on education which allowed children to follow a somewhat different course from that taken by their parents. All children were encouraged to read widely. To the detriment of their devotion to community ideas, they grew up with an appreciation of literary scholarship, with scientific training, and with at least a vicarious taste of the attractions of the outside world. . . . The adults, recognizing that the community's future professional needs must be met by those being educated at the time, abrogated that part of the ideal of self-perfection urging maximum realization of one's innate potential and advocated instead that young people be educated to fill the special needs of Oneida. In so doing, they introduced an element of disharmony that had not been in the early community: once, that which had been in the interest of the individual was simultaneously in the interest of Oneida; now, the individual's interests were to be sacrificed so that the goals of the community might be achieved. Despite the limitations imposed in the name of the good of the system, however, Oneida's youth faced adulthood with educational backgrounds that were very different from and much broader than those of their parents.

Although it might seem that disillusionment with the community would have stimulated the young people to make their way elsewhere, the fact is that they seceded from the Community no more frequently than did their elders. Oneida still had much to offer the younger generation although less than even it could have recognized. Whether broadened educational experience or the decline of religion at Oneida or Community membership by inheritance rather than choice was the principal cause of the failure of the young to embrace Oneida with the zeal that their parents had, the effect was that the Community was to experience the greatest threat to its existence without the benefit of a "spirit of unity" [pp. 93–96].

The young had not experienced the strains which had led their parents to establish the community. This is similar to the current young generation's inability to understand its parents' experience of economic depression and/or ideological and military struggle with fascism.

Self-Criticism as Control

A major technique of control at Oneida was self-criticism, a procedure described in Chapter 16 under brainwashing. Noyes was the only individual above criticism. Everyone else was exposed to continual self-examination and criticism by his peers.

Having undergone criticism, a member often sealed the evaluation by publicly confessing his failings and resolving to follow his fellow Perfectionists' recommendations for improvement. . . . If anyone reacted to criticism with sullen silence or with angry defense, he was reproved again. Stripped of all social support, he found no reassurance until he submitted completely to the Community's judgment. Submission brought Community approval and personal catharsis. Members found confession a "great source of relief," a "spiritual bath" that "cleansed" them of "self loathing." In search of further gratification they sometimes entered into a "course of historical self-criticism" that brought forth "numerous confessions of wrongs in the past," once secret, "perhaps half-forgotten—but necessarily darkening and poisonous to present experience [Carden, 1969, pp. 74–76].[2]

LAST WORD

The Oneida Community illustrates how an alternative life style involving some very specific and unusual human behaviors can develop and flourish at least for a time. This is not a startling statement, since changes in life style behaviors continually occur in any society. The Oneida experience is of note because it has been so well documented and illustrates many features of the successful commune. Oneida had strong leadership, a clear ideology, and specific influencing procedures such as the development of social control, confession groups, prescriptions for sexual behavior, positive reinforcement in labor relations, continual revision and evolution of belief systems, and continuous interaction with the outside world.

Oneida illustrates that unusual behaviors may be considered normal if so labeled. Complex marriage, male continence, economic communism, and even their garb differentiated the Oneidans from their fellow Americans. Yet none of these behaviors were considered "abnormal" or "sick" within the community or outside—as long as they were practiced within the community. Oneida also demonstrated the close relationship between people's conception of man's nature and the type of societies that they build for themselves. Utopian literature and communities such as Oneida extend the range of possible human experience.

In similar fashion, Maslow was and Skinner is a psychological theorist and utopian. Their theories as to what "human nature" is lead to different deductions and activities, but the activities of people in a growth group and a token economy commune are influenced by both the initiating theories and the resulting group expectations and goals. Toffler (1970) has concluded:

> In short, we can use utopianism as a tool rather than an escape, if we base our experiments on the technology and society of tomorrow rather than that of the

---

[2] This description may be contrasted with that of Frank (1961, chs. 5, 7).

past. And once done, why not the most rigorous, scientific analysis of the results? The findings could be priceless were they to save us from mistakes or lead us toward more workable organizational forms for industry, education, family life or politics [pp. 414].

Whether or not one agrees with Toffler, he illustrates one of the major themes of this chapter: while being influenced by them, people may deliberately devise their social as well as physical environments. A second point Toffler highlights is that scientific methods may be used to make decisions about future direction. The choice of directions, or values, is the topic to which we turn in the concluding chapter.

CHAPTER **19**

Ethical Implications: Behavior Influence and the "Good" Life

Throughout this book we have noted that ethical issues cannot be divorced from the behavior influence process. However, for convenience of exposition we have delayed focusing on the implications of alternative concepts of personality. We now discuss how goals of what is "good" may be selected; the values of science; ethical problems in research on humans; limitations on the control of behavior; and a concept of freedom.

We have been presenting evidence about the changeability of human behavior as a function of the environment. Implicit in such material are the ethics and values of the influencer who systematically alters the environment. It should be recalled from Chapter 12, on self-control, that people can alter their own environments. All individuals are influencers, and hence the question becomes influencers for what?

SELECTING AND EVALUATING "GOOD"

We have been using the terms "ethics" and "values" and now must define them. "Ethics" may be defined as "The study of the nature of morals and of the specific moral choices to be made by the individual in his relation with others . . . the rules or standards governing the conduct of the members of the profession"; (Morris, 1969, p. 450). Among the definitions of "value" is the following; "A principle, standard, or quality considered worthwhile or desirable [Morris, 1969, p. 1415]."

All of these definitions add up to an individual's deciding what conduct he considers *good* or *desirable*. After this decision the value problem becomes more complex and asks *good for whom* and *under what circumstances*. In our own lexicon, we have translated the concept of good as "having positive consequences."

The core of our argument is that *personality is human behavior* and *every act implies a value decision*. Following a behavioral model, values are not constant across situations (the same person may differ when he is acting as a taxpayer, churchgoer, teacher, or parent). Moreover, even in the same situation, professionals may differ in what behavior they wish to encourage. Classroom teachers and mental health workers have traditionally argued about the degree of conformity desirable in the classroom, and both may differ with what students find most agreeable. This difference is but a small example of the general point of this volume, that *personality theories have an impact on which behaviors are reinforced*.

Explicit in our view of personality is the assumption that the individual influences his environment—especially the part composed of other people—by his own considerations of what constitutes good behavior. What might be desirable behaviors to design into an ongoing society? Behaviors that can be labeled as altruism ("concern for the welfare of others as opposed to egoism; selflessness," Morris, 1969; p. 39) provide an example (Macaulay and Berkowitz, 1970). Other and similar positive behaviors are generosity and cooperation (Azrin and Lindsley, 1956). The teaching of academic skills is an example of increasing prosocial behaviors through behavior influence procedures (O'Leary and O'Leary, 1972). In the classic science-fiction fantasy *Last and First Men*, Stapledon (1931) conceived of the development of a "new man" (after many catastrophes had decimated the current species).

> In the earlier species . . . altruism occurred only in exceptional persons. In the new species, however, all normal men and women experienced altruism as a passion.

Assertiveness had also greatly changed. Formerly very much of a man's energy had been devoted to the assertion of himself as a private individual over or against other individuals; and very much of his generosity had been at bottom selfish. But in the Second Men, this competitive self-assertion, . . . was greatly tempered [pp. 101–102].

Bertrand Russell put the same idea succinctly: "It is obvious that a world in which the aims of different individuals or groups are compossible is likely to be happier than one in which they are conflicting. It follows that it should be part of a wise social system to encourage compossible purposes, and discourage conflicting ones, by means of education and social systems designed to this end (Russell, 1962, pp. xiv–xv)."

In Stapledon's novel it takes man approximately 200,000 years to arrive at a state of positive behavior toward others. Behaviorists such as John B. Watson or Skinner could conceive of arriving at this point in man's behavior in one generation *under the appropriate circumstances.*

Personality and Values

The more we know about antecedent, current, and consequent conditions, the less likely we are to use the concept of personality. The more we understand or manipulate a situation, the less we gain by referring to an act as an indication or result of a reified "personality." The usage of the concept of personality may itself be an obstacle to posing the most fruitful research questions or dealing with the environment in an effective manner. And, as we have continually emphasized, such usage is itself a learned behavior. We learn what is *denoted* by a concept from the study of the *conditions* under which people *devise, elaborate,* and *use* that concept.

We have tried to demonstrate that the concept of "personality" as a descriptive or explanatory term for observed data is superfluous. This in turn has implications for a variety of behaviors which have been dependent on models of personality and implicit assumptions about people. Explanations and predictions of others' behavior which depend on their "personality" would probably be more effective—or at least closer to reality as it is investigated scientifically—if they took greater account of the social conditions which affect behavior.

If there is no "personality," then where is the person? Where is the "I" or the "me" all of us know and love? If behavior is so dependent on situations, the I or me seems flotsam on a sea controlled by others or, even worse, by caprice and "luck." Concepts of responsibility, identity, and the like appear challenged. The situation is conceptually not dissimilar to the epigrammatic summary of progress in the history of psychology: first psychology lost its soul, then its mind, and recently (with the attack on psychoanalysis) its consciousness.

There is little left to man but human behavior. The situation reduces to the same apparent simplification as in any other scientific pursuit; only material phenomena—that is, heredity and environment—can be investigated empirically. The mode of investigation is a crucial aspect of the meaning of a proposition. If we limit ourselves to data based on the observations of our senses, we are limited in discourse to the domain of *material* events.[1]

Although the "continuity" of the self is more apparent than real—the result rather than the determinant of experience—this does not mean that the individual is irresponsible. He has learned contingencies which may be physical, such as laws of gravity, or social, such as the criminal code. In either case the person is not "irresponsible," if this word means that behavior does not have consequences. Quite the contrary; not only does behavior have consequences but the verbalization of likely consequences which is the result of the person's prior experience may be a major influence on whether or not an act is emitted.

Under this behavioral view the person becomes the *source* of the emission of behavior rather than the locus of a "personality." The lament for this untouchable "core" comes most loudly from therapists who talk of "self-actualization" as an end in itself (without specification) or who claim that treatment should never involve response contingent reinforcement, or what they call "coercion" and behaviorists call "assumption of responsibility."

If the situation accounts for much of the variance in behavior and the core personality accounts for little, then the next conceptual step is to investigate what kind of situational conditions should be fostered. Again, this step follows from a view that human beings are not passive, robotlike recipients of influence but are responsible for the consequences of their choices.

Selection of Goals: Values

Any answer to the question of what environmental conditions we should foster presumes that we know what we wish, what behavior we consider to be "good." The solution of this problem may have even greater social implication than the abandonment of the concept of a reified personality. As social scientists we have no unique conceptualization of what is "good," save the *description* and *understanding* of things as they are. *The value of truth or accurate observation is accepted because it makes science possible.* From this value we can deduce and weigh the worth of procedures and results as data. But it should be explicit that the "fundamental value" of science—honesty of observation—is itself an example of how purpose and value are interdependent.

---

[1] A reaction against such a model of man treated as natural phenomenon and measured as any other object or event may be found in existential psychology, especially May (1961).

We have pursued our discussions on the assumption that honesty, truth, and knowledge are worthy goals. This assumption leads to a paradox that must now be made explicit: the valuing of accurate observation of reality is as much a myth as is the concept of personality. The concept of accuracy is a standard devised by humans which influences our behavior. Accuracy serves as a goal (to know what is) and as a source of evaluation, but it does not exist as an independent entity.

The crucial point is that we must start with a value, and the "proof" of a value is not in the realm of our method. There is no fundamental or self-evident proof that either science or truth is valuable. Indeed, much in the current application of science might lead one to wish that science as we know it had never existed.

There is no way in the realm of logic or social science to define "good" absolutely. Our concepts of good are tied to specific instances and are not abstractions. In this regard our concepts of good are social acts and our designation of something as good is a form of approval similar to the emission of other verbal reinforcing stimuli. This line of reasoning leads to a situation involving a choice. We can decide that we have an insoluable problem and let the matter rest. Or we can *select a value* and acknowledge that our selection cannot be defended on purely rational or scientific grounds. The second approach is the one we prefer. At a later time we can determine by scientific investigation of the *consequences* of our choice how the selection of this particular value affected the goals or reasons for its selection. The question may be stated: Did the decision to consider "truth" as a fundamental value (independent variable) lead to an increase in happiness, health, cultural productivity, or wealth (dependent variable)? The circularity involved is manifest in the formulation of the problem: *we evaluate the value of a value by another value.*

We therefore advocate an overt, active selection and experimental investigation of values. This approach is in contrast to a passive acceptance of values as givens. Whether values are conceived of as set by society, deity, or parents is beside the point. The choice is between an active or a passive approach. If we cannot function at a personal and policy level without myths, we can at least select or devise myths and test them in terms of helping us attain ends that we consider desirable.

Our personal preference is for myths that diverge as little from observed reality as possible and that provide as great a range of meaningful choices to people as possible. Giving up the possibility of an absolute good does not lead to a concept of people as powerless or irresponsible; quite the contrary, it leads to the *freedom and responsibility to select starting points.* Fromm (1941) has termed this distinction as between "freedom from" and "freedom to." *If we cannot escape myths, we can choose them. Because we cannot find absolute starting points, we must select them.*

Obligations to the Influencee

We now focus on the learner, student, or recipient—the object of the socialization process. First, in the very nature of what has gone before, he is not inert or passive. An argument advanced by theorists such as Skinner (1953) is that influence processes are ubiquitous and are better placed in the hands of scholars and scientists than in the hands of politicians and advertisers. While agreeing personally with this view (we identify ourselves naturally enough with the good guys—the scholars and scientists), we must note its presumption that scholars are more proper wielders of influence than politicians or advertisers.

Earlier in this volume (Chapter 6) we described the begging of bears in the zoo: if they do not respond to the food, the humans visiting the zoo stop throwing it. To this extent the bears control the humans; if the bears "want" food thrown at them, that is, find it reinforcing, they must respond. Reinforcing contingencies are not a one-way street. The responses shape the reinforcer. This has been illustrated in the description of the token economy programs (Chapters 11 and 14) and other procedures which involve helping people learn how to interact with each other. This also has been illustrated by the famous cartoon of the rat in the Skinner box turning to his companion and saying, "Boy, have I got this guy trained. Every time *I* press this bar, *he* gives me food."

Contemporary ethical theorists often stop their investigations at the point at which observation of what people *do* is used to define "good." Empirical definitions are the domain of the field of psychology. If "good" or another label of approval is what moves people, it is a matter for observation. As one author (Stevenson, 1944) has noted:

> The "descriptive meaning" of a sign is its dispositions to affect cognition, provided that the disposition is caused by an elaborate process of conditioning that has attended the signs used in communication, and provided that the disposition is rendered fixed, at least to a considerable degree, by linguistic rules [p. 70].

> The emotive meaning of a word is the power that the word acquires, on account of its history in emotional situations, to evoke or directly express attitudes, as distinct from describing or designating them [p. 33].

The descriptive and emotive meanings of words are essentially acquired reinforcing stimuli. This is not surprising in the light of the prior discussions of language (see Chapters 8 and 12). The point is that *the psychological study of good (in the philosophical usage of the word) is the study of reinforcing stimuli.* The use of *good* as an admonition (that is, people should act in a certain manner) is the act of reinforcing someone else (that is, I want him to act in this manner; I will reinforce him for acting in this manner because it is reinforcing to me).

The use of *good* as an exhortation is a statement of contingencies (that is, if you act in this manner, it will in some way be reinforcing to you).

The similarity between the concepts of good and of reinforcement must be emphasized. Neither can be defined in vacuo. Rather, both may be studied so that it becomes possible to say what is good or what is reinforcing *for a particular person.*[2] Carrying the similarities between good and reinforcement further, we may note that both alter behavior. We may say the good is what man strives for; we may say quite operationally that the increase of positive reinforcement and the escape or avoidance of displeasure are the consequences that alter the rates of emission of various behaviors.

Reinforcers are defined by their effect on behavior, not on some other abstract evaluative basis. If good is equated with reinforcing stimuli, it ceases to be a unique, definable concept except as it operationally overlaps with the reinforcing stimulus.

Collection of Data on Hard Choices

The necessarily personal and arbitrary bases of values should lead to a constant recognition and reiteration of the embeddedness of the operational definition of *good* in time and culture. *This awareness of the cultural influence on the operational definition of good should prepare us for both the pluralism of good and the development of operations to evaluate the effects of how good is defined.*

We cannot help but influence others. We reconfirm or deny previous experiences; we become part of the other person's history of reinforcement and part of his knowledge of people. The question is not whether we should influence, but how and what we should influence.

Let us give an example. Research workers who were investigating academic and learning problems in a ghetto school observed that many of their pupils came to school without breakfast. A token economy was organized in which food reinforcers (juice, candy, and other edibles) were used as backup reinforcers for academic accomplishment. However, the situation presented a dilemma: the children were hungry, the researchers had food. Should the investigators not have given the food to the children regardless of their efforts or accomplishment?

Whether or not they gave food contingently on academic accomplishment, the workers would have been teaching the pupils something about people and the world in which they live. If food were given contingently, academic accomplishment might be accelerated. Further, it could be argued that when food is

---

[2] Vives, a Spanish philosopher and educator of the early Renaissance, introduced the notion against the beliefs of his day, that what the soul *is* is of little import, but *how it functions* is crucial.

given contingent upon academic accomplishment, the pupil would also learn that his accomplishments have meaning, that his behavior has differential consequences upon his environment. In simplest terms he would learn that work pays off. The converse must also be true for this type of teaching: those who do not work, do not get paid. While a well-designed program gradually shapes the child's behavior and ensures that the task is always within his ability to accomplish, there may be times, particularly in the beginning, when the child may test the program and not receive food.

The alternative, the giving of food noncontingently, would also teach the children about themselves and the world. No matter what they accomplished, they would receive the food; this response would imply that accomplishment is not a crucial behavior. Again, the issue is not whether the eventual gain from increased academic competence justifies the occasional withholding of a food reinforcer; the key point is that whether the food is given contingently or not something is communicated and taught to the child about the world he lives in and the impact, including lack of any, of his own behavior. No matter what we do, we influence others by our behavior.

We may put the matter in another way. If we give food noncontingently, we are implicitly saying that *being* is enough. Given our respect for human beings, this is a good thing to say; but we may also ask whether in the long run this is the most helpful thing to say to students. If we give the food contingently, we are faced with another question: *Who* is to select the academic content that is to be mastered before the child obtains food?

The investigator must sample the domains of his own values, those of his institution, and those of his society, as well as the benefits to the people who are influenced. We must be prepared to study not only the process of reinforcement but the effects of reinforcement on people, including the person giving the reinforcement as well as the person being reinforced. Relatively little data are available on the effects of being an influencer (for example, Milgram, 1963 provided some, although his interest was "compliance"). We need to obtain data, and as an offshoot of these data, we may find that two values previously considered different are similar in actual operation, and, conversely, that values presumed to be consonant are in reality not so.

THE VALUES OF SCIENCE

In the previous section we explored the consequences of looking at some accepted goals of science as value decisions in a given time, place, and culture. The concept of science can be examined in much the same way. The definition of *science* as a *process*—"The observation, identification, description, experimental investigation and theoretical explanation of natural phenomena [Morris, 1969,

p. 1162]"—offers a rationale for the view that science should not be dealt with as a separate entity with an existence of its own.

In effect ours is a view of "science" rather than "Science." A *current social role* in our society is that of a scientist, or investigator of natural phenomena, who follows a *current methodology* and *value system* in his work. The methodology, the belief system, and values of the scientist are continually changing. We emphasize what should be an obvious point because of the current myth among many scientists and nonscientists that there exists in our society an entity called Science, which by its very nature calls for and justifies certain human behaviors.

Some of the issues are illustrated by the controversy sparked by the publication of a paper by Jensen (1969). In a 1971 symposium discussing the ethical issues of behavioral research, the major topic of discussion was the implications of investigating the relationship between heredity and intellectual abilities. Jensen had reviewed the studies on the relative intelligence of white and black children and had focused on the implications of genetic racial differences in intellectual ability for compensatory education programs. The publication of his article led to a furor in the press and among the public, educators, and scientific groups. Our interest here is not in the scientific merit of Jensen's arguments or those of his critics. Rather, the *ethical* and *value problems* which this controversy raised illustrate many of the value issues in a psychology of behavior influence.

Scriven (1970) has reviewed the critical reactions to Jensen's original article and argued that most of them were emotional considerations of the substantive and methodological issues of the paper and ignored the major ethical issue of whether a researcher *should* publish results that could be used to further unjust causes and whether value judgments are legitimate in science. Scriven's major concern was that universities were failing in their obligation to teach "the skills, the data or the attitudes necessary for handling and acting on controversial moral, political, and scientific issues. In the Jensen case, we are reaping on the first fruits of that neglect. Worse will surely come."

Each of the participants in the above-mentioned symposium on ethics utilized the Jensen controversy to present his own point of view on ethical implications. Jensen's own views came closest to those of scientists belonging to a separate entity, Science, membership in which demands certain prerequisites such as the divorce of value consequences from truth-seeking behavior. Jensen (1972) has expressed this view as follows:

> Moral decisions apply to the uses of knowledge and must be dealt with at that point. My own value system—and it *is* a value judgment, the basic postulate of my own philosophy—holds that knowledge and understanding are preferable to dogma and ignorance.

In a free society, one which allows freedom of speech and of the press, both to express and to criticize diverse views, the social responsibility of the scientist, it seems to me, is clear. It is simply to do his research as competently and carefully as he can, and to report his methods, results, and conclusions as fully and as accurately as possible.

The scientist, in speaking as a scientist about his research, should not make it subordinate to his nonscientifically arrived-at personal, social, religious, or political ideologies [p. 2].

In effect this position holds that values should enter only into the *usage* of the scientific discovery but should not be related to the discovery itself. Horn (1972) has taken issue with Jensen's position by pointing out that it

implies that acts which serve the advancement of science necessarily are morally right. When stated thus bluntly, the argument is rather analogous to an argument that what is good for General Motors is good for America. This argument cannot stand, it seems to me, for the simple reason that it is not generally true. Much as I am strongly committed to a belief that science represents a major hope for life on this planet, I find it difficult to accept a belief that what is good for science necessarily is good for America, or for all mankind, or for all living matter. Surely it is not right for a scientist to take a calculated, high-probability risk of destroying man, purely in the name of science—i.e., in the belief that the results of this act might advance scientific knowledge [p. 5].

Thus, while Horn accepts science as a separate entity, he has argued that it does not have an overriding justification by its mere existence.[3]

In this same symposium on ethical values, Bressler (1972) saw a close connection between scientific findings and their consequences:

There exists actual or potential logical or psychological connections between scientific findings at various levels of certainty and specificity which may be incompatible either with the personal values of the investigator, with his perception of desirable social policy or with the consensus of the academic or scientific community. Moreover, such findings carry with them some probability of influencing social behavior. . . .

. . . The normal way to deal with this issue among those who argue that scientific findings have an autonomy of their own and may be advanced without much concern for the uses to which they are put, is put in the context of whether the ultimate loyalty of the scientist is to the scientific ethic itself. Science itself is, after all, an ethical system. It assumes, as an example, a preference for truth. It

---

[3] "What such textbook methodology usually ignores is that the scientific ethic (values and norms) is only one in a system of many conflicting, competing ethics making up the social fabric. It tends, instead, to assume there is a hierarchy of ethics with the scientific ethic at the pinnacle. But in actual practice, especially in field research . . . ethical issues are much more problematic (Vaughan, 1967, p. 71)."

assumes that we will share findings. . . . For we, as scientists, shielded behind the badge of innocence, have no special expertise in indicating what values men should pursue [pp. 1–3].

Here is a position closer to our view that value consequences are tied in with every aspect of scientific work and cannot be divorced from the work itself. Our view is that it is incumbent upon the investigator to spell out to the fullest extent that he can the possible consequences of his discovery and his own value orientation, which is a factor both in his selection of the area for investigation and his mode of investigation.

The explicit statement of values is the best safeguard we can presently devise against the person who poses as a scientist devoted to truth who manipulates and edits his results so that they confirm a particular social viewpoint. That is, the person who lies, regardless of the nobility of the cause, is not following the scientific ethic; at best he may be labeled advocate rather than reporter. At worst, he is a propagandist as described in Chapter 16.

Science in Time and Place

Another aspect of the controversy over the Jensen paper illustrated that science is a human behavior of a time and place. Jensen was criticized for raising questions about what is presently a generally accepted truth, namely, that genetically determined racial differences in intelligence have not been demonstrated. To question this opinion was in itself an act with important social consequences.

Haller (1971) has put this issue into historical perspective in his review of the beliefs and research of the scientists of the latter half of the nineteenth century. The issues then were pretty much the same as now: namely, whether there were differences in the inherited potentialities for intellectual functioning between racial groups. The scientists of that day concluded from the best data of their times that such differences did indeed exist. Every scientist believed that Americans of African descent were inferior to Americans of Caucasian descent. Haller reported that there were *no* dissenters from this position among the scientists during that era. Also, the social and political policy of that day (institutionalized discrimination against blacks) both reflected and influenced these scientific views.

Limits in Therapy

A model behavior influence situation in which ethical standards may be developed is *treatment*, which aims explicitly to foster a relatively permanent and significant change in the person treated. In this text and elsewhere (Ullmann and

Krasner, 1969) we have repeatedly argued that abnormal behavior may be defined as behavior that someone, including the person himself, considers change-worthy by society's sanctioned professionals. No behavior is abnormal in and of itself; a social reaction is an integral part of the definition of abnormality.

Given this view and a model of treatment as an educational rather than medical enterprise, the questions arise as to what behaviors may be changed and what, if any, limits should be placed on the manipulations used by the change agent. Ullmann (1969c) has argued that since "mental illness" does not represent a special class of behavior, the limits set by social and legal concepts should be followed. Ullmann has argued that particularly in his treatment of non-hospitalized adults the therapist as influencer is in the same role as the leader of a social movement. The limits on such an influencer also apply to the therapist, both as to what is permissible and what is not. The influencer himself may not break the laws of the society that sanctions his behavior. He is constrained not only in his goals but also in his methods by the society which he implicitly represents and in which both he and his client must live. This does not require dogmatic conformity of the therapist, but it does mean he must respect the procedures of change and the rules of the group.

FREEDOM

We conclude this book with a suggestion about the goal of a psychology of behavior influence. We would opt for the goal of *freedom* for the individual. But the concept of freedom has certainly been used in many diverse and frequently antithetical ways. As a result, what is freedom is (like "justice") one of the most debatable issues of all time, and freedom (like motherhood in the old days) is something everyone is for, because the consequences of being "against freedom" are usually disastrous.

Again we make an effort to pin a concept down in behavioral terms: "freedom" is "The condition of being free of restraints. . . . Liberty of the person from slavery, oppression, or incarceration. . . . Exemption from unpleasant or onerous conditions . . . the capacity to exercise choice; free will: '*the only freedom which deserves the name is that of pursuing our own good in our own way*' (John Stuart Mill) [Morris, 1969, p. 524]." The two key elements here are (*a*) *lack of coercion* and (*b*) *ability to choose*.

If we have made anything clear in this book, it is that a human being living in any society is never free of influence. Skinner (1971) has expressed a view of freedom as involving avoidance of aversive stimuli.

> Man's struggle for freedom is not due to a will to be free, but to certain behavioral processes characteristic of the human organism, the chief effect of which is the avoidance of or escape from so-called "aversive" features of the environment.

Physical and biological technologies have been mainly concerned with natural aversive stimuli; the struggle for freedom is concerned with stimuli intentionally arranged by other people. The literature of freedom has identified the other people and has proposed ways of escaping from them or weakening or destroying their power. It has been successful in reducing the aversive stimuli used in intentional control, but it has made the mistake of defining freedom in terms of states of mind or feelings, and it has therefore not been able to deal effectively with techniques of control which do not breed escape or revolt but nevertheless have aversive consequences. It has been forced to brand all control as wrong and to misrepresent many of the advantages to be gained from a social environment. It is unprepared for the next step, which is not to free men from control but to analyze and change the kinds of control to which they are exposed [pp. 42–43].

Using token economy as an illustration Krasner (1968) has argued that planning and individual choice are not antithetical.

Token economy programs are far from deterministic or mechanistic. Systematization does not mean mechanization. In fact the major element in these programs is flexibility. Unless the program continually changes by incorporating new behaviors, changing values, and bringing in new "good things," it becomes as static as any traditional program. When a token program begins it is impossible to predict contingencies that may be available within a year. This is perhaps the most valid criticism against Utopias which try to offer solutions on an eternal basis. Even *Walden Two* represents a fixed society in which all human problems have been worked out. Change itself must be programmed into the design. The goal of the program is for an individual to be enabled to make choices in his life. If he has more than one behavior in his repertoire, an individual is obviously freer than if he has no alternatives [p. 170].

Patients, children, or any other human beings should be reinforced for revising their economy, for making new environments for themselves, and for controlling their own behavior in every sense. There is every reason to make independence, creativity, and decision making valued or reinforced behaviors.

Having choice or alternatives available as a major aspect of freedom does not mean that free will—in the sense of an autonomous inner person free of outside influence—is a viable concept. It means that we are comfortable with a *metaphor* of man—that of freedom—which relies upon the availability of acceptable alternative learned behaviors as its major element.

A saving grace of viewing man's behavior in the context of behavior influence is that influence or control is *never absolute*. At best the converging of influences on man make one behavior or another *more likely to occur*. There is a paradox when we say that despite the multitude of influences upon him, man is able to select which one of a number of alternative behaviors is most likely to lead to positive consequences for himself. Man is influenced; man influences his environment. Can we have our proverbial cake and eat it too? The *belief* that man does have choice is necessary to increase the likelihood of man's being able to choose. If we believe this as parents, teachers, and therapists, we will design programs to make such behaviors possible on the part of our students.[4]

The Scope of Ethical Involvement

In this final section we can only hint at the many other ethical problems that are integral to a psychology of behavior influence. For example, a current area of concern is the ethical implications of research with human beings: How does one investigate the influence process when an explanation in advance to the subject of what one expects to happen will certainly affect the results? But to deceive the subject about the real purpose of the study may be to denigrate him and to raise the question of whether the research study is unethical in its relationship to its subjects.

Ethical concerns about research extend into the entire social, medical, biological field (Freund, 1969). Should the individual not be told of the possible effects of the drug or any other procedure he might be expected to undergo? What is meant by "full disclosure" or "informed consent" when one is setting up a study? Who is to have access to such life-saving devices as the kidney dialysis machine, which is in short supply, and who is to make the decision? This instance clearly raises the question of *who has the right to live*. Similarly, how are decisions to be made about the continuation of life for a defective baby or a terminally ill individual? The era of genetic engineering into which society is now entering will raise very clear value questions as to, among other things, which physical and perhaps emotional characteristics are most desirable.[5]

There is an area in which the influencer has literally "no place to hide" from his social responsibilities and from dealing with the myths and metaphors of his own discipline (Bartz, 1970; Krasner, 1962a, 1965b, 1966, 1969; Krause, 1970; Walker, 1969). But creating alternative myths and metaphors is only a partial fulfillment of social responsibility. The influencer must also take an active role in guiding the social usage of his research findings. One illustration of scientists undertaking such a deliberately influencing role is in the field of population control (for example, Ehrlich, 1968).

[4] A recent experiment by Davidson and Steiner (1971) has indicated that the perception of freedom may itself depend upon reinforcement schedules. This study illustrates one way in which research on freedom may be conducted within a behavioral model.

[5] Nothing here denies the major role of genes in determining the *limits* of human behavior. But the *impact* of genetic endowment is achieved through the behavior influence paradigm we have been presenting. Genetic impact (who will mate and have offspring) is mediated and influenced by many diverse social behaviors such as marriage; love; abortion; sperm banks; divorce; sexual practices; current social labels; poverty; welfare; nutrition; homosexuality; genetic intervention and repair as determined by "scientific findings"; racism; religious beliefs, and so on.

We have, in the earlier chapter on the impact of the physical environment on behavior, discussed the relationship between space and populations. One of the great issues of our time involves the question of population limitation and its various manifestations such as abortions, contraceptives, government incentive programs, and economic aid to underdeveloped countries. Callahan (1972) has presented the ethical problem this way:

> Throughout its history, the human species has been preoccupied with the conquest of nature and the control of death. Human beings have struggled to survive, as individuals, families, tribes, communities, and nations. Procreation has been an essential part of survival. . . . There remained a presumptive right of individual procreation, a right thought to sustain the high value ascribed to the outcome: more human beings. That the premise may now have to be changed, the value shifted, can only seem confounding . . . excessive population growth . . . poses critical dangers to the future of the species, the ecosystem, individual liberty and welfare, and the structure of social life. These hazards are serious enough to warrant a reexamination and, ultimately, a revision of the traditional value of unrestricted procreation and increase in population. The main question is the way in which the revision is to proceed. If the old premise—the unlimited right of and need for procreation—is to be rejected or amended, what alternative premises are available? By what morally legitimate social and political processes, and in light of what values, are the possible alternatives to be evaluated and action taken? These are ethical questions bearing on what is to be taken to constitute the good life, the range and source of human rights and obligation, the requirements of human justice and welfare. If the ethical problems of population limitation could be reduced to one overriding issue, matters would be simplified. They cannot [p. 487].

This view of the ethical issues involved in human behavior can and must be extended to many of the major issues of our time such as environmental and social control.

LAST LAST WORD

The unique dominance of the human species may be traced to three of its creations: language, technology, and social organization. Humans can mitigate, control, and increasingly create their own environments. But with each new freedom, new problems arise.

At this writing few people would argue with the need for some restrictions on the actions of people in terms of antitrust, antipollution, and antidiscrimination laws. Every freedom seems to require a limitation. Control of human behavior does not seem to be so much the issue, for we are accustomed to such control in political, economic, and criminal areas. What seems to be new is the degree of control of human behavior in areas thought of as personal, private, or mental rather than physical. The erroneousness of a physical-mental dichotomy has long been recognized; what is newer and reflected in the present work is the degree to which environmental manipulations have been found to account for behavior, so that the internal autonomous personality ceases to be either scientifically or socially useful.

If we believe that a technology of behavior influence is developing, we are faced with a choice. We may stamp it out and make it a punishable offense to pursue this line of investigation. We may decide not to do anything and to leave the application of such psychological findings to whoever wishes to use them for whatever ends he desires. Or we may try to face the hard problems of *what* procedures may be used by *whom* to attain *what* permissible ends. We may pursue this undertaking not in an attempt to discover something already given, but to help create something new.

Our hope is that this third alternative will be taken. The best way to increase freedom is not merely to say people *may* choose but to work so that people *can* choose. Just as humans have gone far in changing their physical environments, we hope the next decade will see humans controlling and changing their psychological environments. The how is being developed rapidly in schools, clinics, families, and formal organizations. An attempt is being made to reduce the gap between decision makers and the populations they affect, especially in the areas of education and consumer affairs and to a lesser extent in political and industrial settings. Communication among students, parents, and teachers, for example, not only increases the efficiency of the teacher but becomes increasingly the best way to help the teacher decide what ends will best serve all concerned. We need to foster greater communication and awareness between influencers (all of us) and influencees (all of us). We consider this a desirable outcome and hope this book is a step in that direction.

REFERENCES

Abraham, K. *Selected papers on psychoanalysis.* London: Hogarth Press, 1949.

Adelson, J. Personality. In P. H. Mussen (Ed.), *Annual review of psychology,* Vol. 20. Palo Alto, Calif.: Annual Reviews, 1969. Pp. 217–252.

Aderman, D., & Berkowitz, L. Observational set, empathy, and helping. *Journal of Personality and Social Psychology,* 1970, **14,** 141–148.

Adler, A. *Practice and theory of individual psychology.* New York: Harcourt Brace Jovanovich, 1927.

Adler, A. *Social interest: A challenge to mankind.* New York: Putnam, 1939.

Adler, N. The antinomian personality: the hippie character type. *Psychiatry,* 1968, **31,** 325–338.

Adorno, T. W., Frenkel-Brunswick, E., Levinson, D. J., & Sanford, R. N. *The authoritarian personality.* New York: Harper & Row, 1950.

Agnew, S. T. Agnew discusses child development. *Congressional Record,* Nov. 18, 1971, **117,** No. 177.

Aichorn, A. *Wayward youth.* New York: Viking, 1935.

Aiello, J. R., & Jones, S. E. Field study of the proxemic behavior of young school children in three subcultural groups. *Journal of Personality and Social Psychology,* 1971, **19,** 351–356.

Albert, S., & Dabbs, J. M. Physical distance and persuasion. *Journal of Personality and Social Psychology,* 1970, **15,** 265–270.

Alexander, F. The influence of psychologic factors upon gastrointestinal disturbances: general principles, objectives and preliminary results. *Psychoanalytic Quarterly,* 1934, **3,** 501–539.

Alison, D. *Searchlight: An exposé of New York City schools.* New York: Teachers Center Press, 1951.

Allport, F. H. *Social psychology.* Boston: Houghton Mifflin, 1924.

Allport, G. W. Attitudes. In C. Murchison (Ed.), *Handbook of social psychology.* Worcester, Mass.: Clark University Press, 1935. Pp. 798–884.

Allport, G. W. *Personality: A psychological interpretation.* New York: Holt, Rinehart and Winston, 1937.

Allport, G. W. What units shall we employ? In G. Lindzey (Ed.), *Assessment of human motives.* New York: Holt, Rinehart and Winston, 1959. Pp. 239–258.

Allport, G. W. *Pattern and growth in personality.* New York: Holt, Rinehart and Winston, 1961.

Allport, G. W. The general and unique in psychological science. *Journal of Personality,* 1962, **30,** 405–422.

Allport, G. W. The historical background of modern social psychology. In G. Lindzey & E. Aronson (Eds.), *The handbook of social psychology,* Vol. 1 (2nd ed.). Reading, Mass.: Addison-Wesley, 1968. Pp. 1–80.

Ames, R. *Citizen Thomas More and his Utopia.* Princeton, N.J.: Princeton University Press, 1949.

Anderson, D. C. Skinner: "It is science or nothing." *Wall Street Journal,* Oct. 6, 1971.

Anderson, D. F., & Rosenthal, R. Some effects of interpersonal expectancy and social interaction on institutionalized retarded children. *Proceedings of the 76th Annual Convention of the American Psychological Association,* 1968, 479–480.

Anspach, K. *The way of fashion.* Ames, Iowa: Iowa State University Press, 1967.

Appley, M. H. Derived motives. In P. H. Mussen & M. R. Rosenzweig (Eds.), *Annual review of psychology.* Vol. 21. Palo Alto, Calif.: Annual Reviews, 1970. Pp. 485–511.

Argyle, M., & Dean, J. Eye-contact, distance, and affiliation. *Sociometry,* 1965, **28,** 289–304.

Asch, S. E. Studies in the principles of judgments and attitudes: II. Determination of judgments by group and ego standards. *Journal of Social Psychology,* 1940, **12,** 433–465.

Asch, S. E. Forming impressions of personality. *Journal of Abnormal and Social Psychology,* 1946, **41,** 258–290.

Asch, S. E. *Social psychology.* Englewood Cliffs, N.J.: Prentice-Hall, 1952.

Asch, S. E. Studies of independence and conformity. A minority of one against a unanimous majority. *Psychological Monographs,* 1956, **70** (9).

Asch, S. E., Block, H., & Hertzman, M. Studies in the principles of judgments and attitudes: I. Two basic principles of judgment. *Journal of Psychology,* 1938, **5,** 219–251.

Ascough, J. C., & Sipprelle, C. N. Operant verbal conditioning of autonomic response. *Behaviour Research and Therapy,* 1968, **6,** 363–370.

Atkinson, R. C. Computerized instruction and the learning process. *American Psychologist,* 1968, **23,** 225–239.

Atthowe, J. M., Jr., & Krasner, L. A preliminary report on the application of contingent reinforcement procedures (token economy on a "chronic" psychiatric ward). *Journal of Abnormal Psychology*, 1968, **73**, 37–43.

Ayllon, T., & Azrin, N. H. The measurement and reinforcement of behavior of psychotics. *Journal of the Experimental Analysis of Behavior*, 1965, **8**, 357–383.

Ayllon, T., & Azrin, N. H. *The token economy: A motivational system for therapy and rehabilitation.* New York: Appleton-Century-Crofts, 1968.

Ayllon, T., & Michael, J. The psychiatric nurse as a behavioral engineer. *Journal of the Experimental Analysis of Behavior*, 1959, **2**, 323–334.

Azima, H., & Cramer-Azima, F. J. Studies on perceptual isolation. *Diseases of the Nervous System Monograph Supplements*, 1957, **18** (8).

Azrin, N. H., & Holz, W. C. Punishment. In W. K. Honig (Ed.), *Operant behavior: Areas of research and application.* New York: Appleton-Century-Crofts: 1966. Pp. 380–447.

Azrin, N. H., & Lindsley, O. R. The reinforcement of cooperation between children. *Journal of Abnormal and Social Psychology*, 1956, **52**, 100–102.

Bachrach, A. J., Erwin, W. J., & Mohr, J. P. The control of eating behavior in an anorexic by operant conditioning techniques. In L. P. Ullmann & L. Krasner (Eds.), *Case studies in behavior modification.* New York: Holt, Rinehart and Winston, 1965. Pp. 153–163.

Bachrach, A. J., & Pattischall, E. G. An experiment in universal and personal validation. *Psychiatry*, 1960, **23**, 267–270.

Back, K. W. *Beyond words.* New York: Basic Books, 1972.

Bacon, F. The complete essays of . . . New York: Pocket Books (Washington Square ed.), 1963.

Baer, D. M., Peterson, R., & Sherman, J. A. The development of imitation by reinforcing behavioral similarity to a model. *Journal of the Experimental Analysis of Behavior*, 1967, **10**, 405–416.

Baer, D. M., & Sherman, J. A. Reinforcement control of generalized imitation in young children. *Journal of Experimental Child Psychology*, 1964, **1**, 37–48.

Baer, D. M., Wolf, M. M., & Risley, T. Some current dimensions of applied behavior analysis. *Journal of Applied Behavior Analysis*, 1968, **1**, 91–97.

Baird, R. R., & Lee, H. L. Modification of conceptual style preference by differential reinforcement. *Child Development*, 1969, **40**, 903–910.

Baker, S. S. *The permissible lie: The inside truth about advertising.* Cleveland: World, 1968.

Baldwin, J. M. *Mental development in the child and the race: Methods and processes.* New York: Macmillan, 1895.

Bandura, A. Psychotherapy as a learning process. *Psychological Bulletin*, 1961, **58**, 143–159.

Bandura, A. Social learning through imitation. In M. R. Jones (Ed.), *Nebraska symposium on motivation.* Lincoln, Nebr., University of Nebraska Press, 1962. Pp. 211–269.

Bandura, A. Behavior modifications through modeling procedures. In L. Krasner & L. P. Ullmann (Eds.), *Research in behavior modification.* New York: Holt, Rinehart and Winston, 1965. Pp. 310–340. (a)

Bandura, A. Influence of models' reinforcement contingencies on the acquisition of imitative responses. *Journal of Personality and Social Psychology*, 1965, **1**, 589–595. (b)

Bandura, A. A social learning interpretation of psychological dysfunctions. In P. London & D. Rosenhan (Eds.), *Foundations of abnormal psychology.* New York: Holt, Rinehart and Winston, 1968. Pp. 293–344.

Bandura, A. *Principles of behavior modification.* New York: Holt, Rinehart and Winston, 1969.

Bandura, A., Blanchard, E. B., & Ritter, B. Relative efficacy of desensitization and modeling approaches for inducing behavioral, affective, and attitudinal changes. *Journal of Personality and Social Psychology*, 1969, **13**, 173–199.

Bandura, A., Grusec, J. E., & Menlove, F. L. Vicarious extinction of avoidance behavior. *Journal of Personality and Social Psychology*, 1967, **5**, 16–23.

Bandura, A., & Kupers, C. J. Transmission of patterns of self-reinforcement through modeling. *Journal of Abnormal and Social Psychology*, 1964, **69**, 1–9.

Bandura, A., Lipsher, D. H., & Miller, P. E. Psychotherapists' approach avoidance reactions to patients' expressions of hostility. *Journal of Consulting Psychology*, 1960, **24**, 1–8.

Bandura, A., & McDonald, F. J. The influence of social reinforcement and the behavior of models in shaping children's moral judgments. *Journal of Abnormal and Social Psychology*, 1963, **67**, 274–281.

Bandura, A., & Menlove, F. L. Factors determining vicarious extinction of avoidance behavior through symbolic modeling. *Journal of Personality and Social Psychology*, 1968, **8**, 99–108.

Bandura, A., & Rosenthal, T. L. Vicarious classical conditioning as a function of arousal level. *Journal of Personality and Social Psychology*, 1966, **3**, 54–62.

Bandura, A., Ross, D., & Ross, S. Vicarious reinforcement and imitative learning. *Journal of Abnormal and Social Psychology*, 1963, **67**, 601–607.

Bandura, A., & Walters, R. H. *Adolescent aggression.* New York: Ronald Press, 1959.

Bandura, A., & Whalen, C. K. The influence of antecedent reinforcement and divergent modeling cues on patterns of self-reward. *Journal of Personality and Social Psychology*, 1966, **3**, 373–382.

Barber, B., and Hirsch, W. *The sociology of science.* New York: Fress Press, 1962.

Barber, T. X. Physiological effects of "hypnosis." *Psychological Bulletin*, 1961, **58**, 390–419.

Barber, T. X. "Hypnotic" phenomena: A critique of experimental methods. In J. E. Gordon (Ed.), *Handbook of clinical and experimental hypnosis.* New York: Macmillan, 1967. Pp. 444–480.

Barber, T. X. *Hypnosis: A scientific approach.* New York: Van Nostrand, 1969.

Barber, T. X. *Suggested ("hypnotic") behavior: The trance paradigm versus an alternative paradigm.* Harding, Mass.: Medfield Foundation, 1970.

Barber, T. X., Dalal, A. S., & Calverley, D. S. The subjective reports of hypnotic subjects. *American Journal of Clinical Hypnosis*, 1968, **11**, 74–88.

Barghoorn, I. Soviet doctrine on the role of propaganda. In B. Berelson and M. Janowitz (Eds.) *Reader in public opinion and communication* (2nd ed.). New York: Free Press, 1966, pp. 360–378.

Barker, R. *Ecological psychology.* Stanford, Calif.: Stanford University Press, 1968.

Barker, R., Dembo, T., and Lewin, K. *Frustration and regression: an experiment with young children.* Iowa City: University of Iowa Press, 1941.

Bartlett, C. J., & Green, C. G. Clinical prediction: Does one sometimes know too much? *Journal of Counseling Psychology*, 1966, **13**, 267–270.

Bartz, W. R. While psychologists doze on. *American Psychologist*, 1970, **25**, 500–503.

Barzun, J. *The American university.* New York: Harper & Row, 1968.

Batchelor, I. R. C. *Henderson and Gillespie's textbook of psychiatry.* London: Oxford University Press, 1969.

Bateson, G. A. Some systematic approaches to the study of culture and personality. *Character and Personality*, 1942, **11**, 76–84.

Bateson, G. A., Jackson, D. D., Haley, J., & Weakland, J. Toward a theory of schizophrenia. *Behavioral Science*, 1956, **1**, 251–264.

Baughman, E. E. *Personality: the psychological study of the individual.* Englewood Cliffs, N.J.: Prentice-Hall, 1972.

Becker, C. L. *Everyman his own historian.* New York: Crofts, 1935.

Becker, H. S. *Outsiders: Studies in the sociology of deviance.* New York: Free Press, 1963.

Beecher, H. K. The powerful placebo. *Journal of American Medical Association*, 1955, **159**, 1602–1606.

Beecher, H. K. *Measurement of subjective responses: Quantitative effects of drugs.* New York: Oxford University Press, 1959.

Beecher, H. K. Increased stress and effectiveness of placebos and "active" drugs. *Science*, 1960, **132**, 91–92.

Beez, W. V. Influence of biased psychological reports on teacher behavior and pupil performance. *Proceedings of the 76th Annual Convention of the American Psychological Association*, 1968, 605–606.

Belson, W. A. Learning and attitude change resulting from viewing a television series, Bon Voyage. *British Journal of Educational Psychology*, 1956, **26**, 31–38.

Bem, D. J. Self-perception: An alternative in interpretation of cognitive dissonance phenomena. *Psychological Review*, 1967, **74**, 183–200.

Benedict, R. *Patterns of culture.* Boston: Houghton Mifflin, 1934.

Benedict, R. *The chrysanthemum and the sword.* Boston: Houghton Mifflin, 1946.

Bentham, J. *An introduction to the principles of morals and legislation.* Oxford: Clarendon, 1789.

Bentler, P. M., O'Hara, J. W., & Krasner, L. Hypnosis and placebo. *Psychological Reports*, 1963, **12**, 153–154.

Berelson, B., Lazarsfeld, P. L., & McPhee, W. N. *Voting.* Chicago, Ill.: University of Chicago Press, 1954.

Berger, S. M. Conditioning through vicarious instigation. *Psychological Review*, 1962, **69**, 450–466.

Berger, S. M., & Lambert, W. W. Stimulus-response theory in contemporary social psychology. In G. Lindzey and E. Aronson (Eds.), *The handbook of social psychology*, Vol. 1 (2nd ed.). Reading, Mass.: Addison-Wesley, 1968. Pp. 81–178.

Berkowitz, L., & Knurek, D. A. Label-mediated hostility generalization. *Journal of Personality and Social Psychology*, 1969, **13**, 200–206.

Berlin, I. The question of Machiavelli. *New York Review of Books*, 1971, **17** (7), 20–32.

Berlyne, D. E. Behavior theory as personality theory. In E. F. Borgatta & W. W. Lambert (Eds.), *Handbook of personality theory and research.* Chicago: Rand McNally, 1968. Pp. 629–690.

Bernard, L. L. *Instinct: A study in social psychology.* New York: Holt, Rinehart and Winston, 1924.

Berne, E. *Games people play.* New York: Grove Press, 1964.

Bernstein, D. A. Problems in behavioral fear assessment in psychotherapy outcome research. Paper presented to Western Psychological Association, Los Angeles, 1970.

Bernstein, D. A. Behavioral fear assessment: Anxiety or artifact? In H. Adams & I. P. Unikel (Eds.), *Issues and trends in behavior therapy.* Springfield, Ill.: Charles C Thomas, 1973.

Betz, B., & Whitehorn, J. C. The relationship of the therapist to the outcome of therapy in schizophrenia. *Psychiatric Research Reports*, 1956, **5**, 89–105.

Bexton, W. H., Heron, W., & Scott, T. H. Effects of decreased variation in the sensory environment. *Canadian Journal of Psychology*, 1954, **8**, 70–77.

Biddle, B. J., & Thomas, E. J. (Eds.). *Role theory.* New York: Wiley, 1966.

Bijou, S. W., & Baer, D. M. *Child development, Vol. 1: A systematic and empirical theory.* New York: Appleton-Century-Crofts, 1961.

Billingsley, A., & Giovannoni, J. M. *Children of the storm.* New York: Harcourt Brace Jovanovich, 1972.

Binet, A., & Simon, T. *A method of measuring the development of the intelligence of young children.* Chicago: Chicago Medical Book, 1913.

Binswanger, L. Existential analysis and psychotherapy. *Psychoanalysis and Psychoanalytic Review,* 1958, **45,** 79–83.

Birnbaum, M. Sense about sensitivity training. *Saturday Review,* November 15, 1969, 82–98.

Birnbrauer, J. S., Wolf, M. M., Kidder, J. D., & Tague, C. E. Classroom behavior of retarded pupils with token reinforcement. *Journal of Experimental Child Psychology,* 1965, **2,** 219–235.

Bischof, L. J. *Interpreting personality theories* (2nd ed.). New York: Harper, 1970.

Blake, R. R., Rhead, C. C., & Mouton, J. S. Personality. In P. R. Farnsworth (Ed.), *Annual Review of Psychology,* Vol. 10. Palo Alto, Calif.: Annual Reviews, 1959. Pp. 203–232.

Blake, R. R., Wedge, R. B., & Mouton, J. Housing architecture and social interaction. *Sociometry,* 1956, **19,** 133–139.

Blau, P. M. *Bureaucracy in modern society.* New York: Random House, 1956.

Blau, P. M., & Scott, W. R. *Formal organizations.* San Francisco: Chandler, 1962.

Block, J. *The challenge of response sets.* New York: Appleton-Century-Crofts, 1965.

Bloom, S. W. *The doctor and his patient.* New York: Russell Sage, 1963.

Blumer, H. Collective behavior. In J. Gould and W. L. Kolb (Eds.), *Dictionary of the social sciences.* New York: Free Press, 1964. Pp. 100–101.

Boas, F. *Race, language, and culture.* New York: Macmillan, 1940.

Boffey, P. M., & Walsh, J. Study of TV violence: Seven top researchers blackballed from panel. *Science,* 1970, **168,** 949.

Boorstin, D. J. *The decline of radicalism: Reflections on America today.* New York: Random House, 1970.

Borgatta, E. F. Introduction. In E. F. Borgatta (Ed.), *Social psychology: Readings and perspective.* Chicago: Rand McNally, 1969. Pp. 1–42.

Boring, E. *History of experimental psychology,* (2nd ed.) New York: Appleton-Century-Crofts, 1950.

Bowerman, C. E., & Kinch, J. W. Change in family and peer orientation of children between the 4th and 10th grades. *Social Forces,* 1959, **37,** 206–211.

Brady, J. P. Brevital-relaxation treatment of frigidity. *Behaviour Research and Therapy,* 1966, **4,** 71–77.

Braginsky, B. M., & Braginsky, D. D. Schizophrenic patients in the psychiatric interview: An experimental study of their effectiveness at manipulation. *Journal of Consulting Psychology,* 1967, **31,** 543–547.

Braginsky, B. M., Braginsky, D. D., & Ring, K. *Methods of madness: The mental hospital as a last resort.* New York: Holt, Rinehart and Winston, 1969.

Braginsky, B. M., Grosse, M., & Ring, K. Controlling outcomes through impression management: An experimental study of the manipulative tactics of mental patients. *Journal of Consulting Psychology,* 1966, **30,** 295–300.

Brandt, L. W. American psychology. *American Psychologist,* 1970, **75,** 1091–1093.

Brayfield, A. H., & Crockett, W. H. Employee attitudes and employee performance. *Psychological Bulletin,* 1959, **52,** 396–424.

Bressler, M. Comments on ethical issues and behavioral science research. *Catalog of Selected Documents in Psychology,* 1972, **2,** 1–11.

Brim, O. G., Jr. Personality development as role-learning. In I. Iscoe & H. W. Stevenson (Eds.), *Personality development in children.* Austin, Texas: University of Texas Press, 1960. Pp. 127–159.

Brodbeck, M. The influence of propaganda without social support. In D. Willner (Ed.), *Decisions, values and groups.* New York: Pergamon, 1960. Pp, 241–245.

Bronfenbrenner, U. *Two worlds of childhood: U.S. and U.S.S.R.* New York: Russell Sage, 1970.

Brown, R. W. A determinant of the relationship between rigidity and authoritarianism. *Journal of Abnormal and Social Psychology,* 1953, **48,** 469–476.

Bruch, H. Obesity and orality. *Contemporary Psychoanalysis,* 1969, **5,** 129–144.

Bruehl, D., & Solar, D. Systematic variation in the clarity of demand characteristics in an experiment employing a confederate. *Psychological Reports,* 1970, **27,** 55–60.

Bruner, J. S., & Postman, L. Perception, cognition, and behavior. *Journal of Personality,* 1949, **18,** 14–31.

Bryan, J. H., & London, P. Altruistic behavior by children. *Psychological Bulletin,* 1970, **73,** 200–211.

Bryan, J. H., & Test, M. A. Models and helping: Naturalistic studies in aiding behavior. *Journal of Personality and Social Psychology,* 1967, **6,** 400–407.

Bryan, J. H., & Walbek, N. H. Preaching and practicing generosity: Children's actions and reactions. *Child Development,* 1970, **41,** 329–353.

Buckner, H. T. The transvestic career path. *Psychiatry,* 1970, **33,** 381–389.

Bugental, J. F. T. *The search for authenticity: An existential-analytic approach to psychotherapy.* New York: Holt, Rinehart and Winston, 1966.

Burchard, J. D. Systematic socialization: A programmed environment for the habilitation of antisocial retardates. *Psychological Record,* 1967, **17,** 461–476.

Burchard, J. D. A methodology for conducting an experimental analysis of cheating behavior. *Journal of Experimental Child Psychology,* 1970, **10,** 146–158.

Burchard, J. D., & Tyler, V. The modification of delinquent behavior through operant conditioning. *Behaviour Research and Therapy,* 1965, **2,** 245–250.

Burnham, J. C. Historical background for the study of personality. In E. F. Borgatta & W. W. Lambert (Eds.), *Handbook of personality theory and research.* Chicago: Rand McNally, 1968. Pp. 3–81.

Burnham, J. R., & Hartsough, D. M. Effects of experimenters' expectancies on children's ability to learn to swim. Paper presented at Midwestern Psychological Association, Chicago, Ill. May 1968.

Burris, D. S. (Ed.) *The right to treatment.* New York: Springer, 1970.

Burton, A. (Ed.) *Encounter: The theory and practice of encounter groups.* San Francisco, Calif.: Jossey-Bass, 1969.

Burton, R. *The anatomy of melancholy* (F. Dell, & P. Jordan-Smith, Eds.). New York: Tudor, 1927.

Bushell, D., Jr., Wrobel, P. A., & Michaelis, M. L. Applying "group" contingencies to the classroom study behavior of preschool children. *Journal of Applied Behavior Analysis,* 1968, **1,** 55–61.

Byrne, D. The repression sensitization scale: Rationale, reliability and validity. *Journal of Personality,* 1961, **29,** 334–349.

Byrne, D. Repression-sensitization as a dimension of personality. In B. A. Maher (Ed.), *Progress in experimental personality research,* Vol. 1. New York: Academic Press, 1964.

Byrne, D. *An introduction to personality.* Englewood Cliffs, N.J.: Prentice-Hall, 1966.

Byrne, D. Attitudes and attraction. In L. Berkowitz (Ed.), *Advances in experimental psychology.* New York: Academic Press, 1968.

Calame, B. E. The truth hurts. *Wall Street Journal*, July 14, 1969 (Vol. 49, No. 191), 1, 23.

Calhoun, J. B. Population density and social pathology. *Scientific American*, 1962, **206**, 139–146.

Callahan, D. Ethics and population limitation. *Science*, 1972, **175**, 487–494.

Campbell, P., & Dunnette, D. Effectiveness of T-Group experiences in managerial training and development. *Psychological Bulletin*, 1968, **70**, 73–104.

Campbell, P. T., & Stanley, J. C. *Experimental and quasi-experimental designs for research.* Chicago: Rand McNally, 1966.

Caplan, R. B. *Psychiatry and the community in nineteenth century America.* New York: Basic Books, 1969.

Carden, M. L. *Oneida: Utopian community to modern corporation.* Baltimore: Johns Hopkins, 1969.

Carlson, E. T., & Simpson, M. M. Perkinism vs. Mesmerism. *Journal of the History of the Behavioral Sciences*, 1970, **6**, 16–24.

Carnegie, D. *How to win friends and influence people.* New York: Simon and Schuster, 1936.

Carr, E. H. *What is history?* New York: Random House, 1961.

Carson, R. C. *Interaction concepts of personality.* Chicago: Aldine, 1969.

Cartwright, D. Social psychology and group processes. In P. R. Farnsworth (Ed.), *Annual review of psychology*, Vol. 8. Palo Alto, Calif.: Annual Reviews, 1957. Pp. 211–236.

Cattell, R. B. *The sixteen personality factor questionnaire: Handbook and tabular supplement.* Champaign, Ill.: Institute for Personality and Ability Testing, 1950. (a)

Cattell, R. B. *Personality: A systematic theoretical and factual study.* New York: McGraw-Hill, 1950. (b)

Cattell, R. B. *Personality and motivation: Structure and measurement.* Yonkers-on-Hudson, N.Y.: World Book, 1957.

Cautela, J. R. Treatment of compulsive behavior by covert sensitization. *Psychological Record*, 1966, **16**, 33–41.

Cautela, J. R. Covert sensitization. *Psychological Reports*, 1967, **20**, 459–468.

Centers, R. *The psychology of social class.* Princeton, N.J.: Princeton University Press, 1949.

Chaplin, J. P. *Dictionary of psychology.* New York: Dell, 1968.

Chapman, L. S., & Chapman, J. P. The genesis of popular but erroneous psychodiagnostic observations. *Journal of Abnormal Psychology*, 1967, **72**, 193–204.

Chapman, L. J., & Chapman, J. P. Illusory correlation as an obstacle to the use of valid psychodiagnostic signs. *Journal of Abnormal Psychology*, 1969, **74**, 670–675.

Chapman, L. J., Chapman, J. P., & Brelje, T. Influence of the experimenter on pupillary dilation to sexually provocative pictures. *Journal of Abnormal Psychology*, 1969, **74**, 396–400.

Chartier, G. M. A-B therapist variable: Real or imagined? *Psychological Bulletin*, 1971. **75**, 22–33.

Chaves, J. F. Hypnosis reconceptualized: An overview of Barber's theoretical and empirical work. *Psychological Reports*, 1968, **22**, 587–608.

Choukas, M. *Propaganda comes of age.* Washington, D.C.: Public Affairs Press, 1965.

Christie, R., & Geis, F. L. Some consequences of taking Machiavelli seriously. In E. F. Borgatta & W. W. Lambert (Eds.), *Handbook of personality theory and research.* Chicago: Rand McNally, 1968. Pp. 959–973.

Christie, R., & Geis, F. L. *Studies in Machiavellianism.* New York: Academic Press, 1970.

Christie, R., & Lindauer, F. Personality structure. In P. R. Farnsworth (Ed.), *Annual review of psychology*, Vol. 14. Palo Alto, Calif.: Annual Reviews, 1963. Pp. 201–230.

Cisin, I. H., et al. *Television and growing up: The impact of televised violence*. Washington, D.C.: U. S. Government Printing Office, 1972.

Clarizio, H. Stability of deviant behavior through time. *Mental Hygiene*, 1968, **52**, 288–293.

Clark, E. T. *The small sects in America*. New York: Abington Press, 1949.

Clark, K. B. The pathos of power: A psychological perspective. *American Psychologist*, 1971, **26**, 1047–1057.

Clark, M., Lachowicz, J., & Wolf, M. A pilot basic education program for school dropouts incorporating a token reinforcement system. *Behaviour Research and Therapy*, 1968, **6**, 183–188.

Clements, C. B., & McKee, J. M. Programmed instruction for institutionalized offenders: Contingency management and performance contracts. *Psychological Reports*, 1968, **22**, 957–964.

Coe, W. C., & Sarbin, T. R. An experimental demonstration of hypnosis as role enactment. *Journal of Abnormal Psychology*, 1966, **71**, 400–406.

Coe, W. C., & Sarbin, T. R. An alternative interpretation to the multiple composition of hypnotic scales: A single role-relevant skill. *Journal of Personality and Social Psychology*, 1971, **18**, 1–8.

Coggins, C. Archeology and the art market. *Science*, 1972, **175**, 263–266.

Cohen, H. L. Educational therapy: The design of learning environments. In J. M. Shlien (Ed.), *Research in psychotherapy*, Vol. 3. Washington, D.C.: American Psychological Association, 1968. Pp. 21–53.

Cohen, H. L., Filipczak, J. A., Bis, J. S., & Cohen, J. M. *Contingencies applicable to special education of delinquents*. Silver Spring, Md.: Institute of Behavioral Research, 1966.

Collins, J. K. Muscular endurance-normal and hypnotic states: A suggested catalepsy. Honors thesis, Department of Psychology, University of Sydney, 1961.

Condry, J. C., & Siman, M. L. An experimental study of adult versus peer orientation. Unpublished manuscript, Department of Child Development, Cornell University, 1968. Cited in U. Bronfenbrenner, *Two worlds of childhood*. New York: Simon & Schuster, 1972.

Cooley, C. H. *Human nature and the social order*. New York: Scribner, 1902.

Corey, S. M. The nature of instruction. *Programmed instruction*. Sixty-sixth yearbook, Part II, National Society for the Study of Education. Chicago: University of Chicago Press, 1967. Pp. 5–27.

Coser, L. A. Greedy organizations. *European Journal of Sociology*, 1967, 8, 196–215.

Cottrell, L. S., Jr. The adjustment of the individual to his age and sex roles. *American Sociological Review*, 1942, **7**, 618–625.

Couch, A., & Keniston, K. Agreeing response set and social desirability. *Journal of Abnormal and Social Psychology*, 1961, **62**, 175–179.

Craig, K. D. Physiological arousal as a function of imagined, vicarious, and direct stress experiences. *Journal of Abnormal Psychology*, 1968, **73**, 513–520.

Craig, K. D., & Lowery, H. J. Heart-rate components of conditioned vicarious autonomic responses. *Journal of Personality and Social Psychology*, 1969, **11**, 381–387.

Craig, K. D., & Weinstein, M. S. Conditioning vicarious affective arousal. *Psychological Reports*, 1965, **17**, 955–963.

Craig, K. D., & Wood, K. Physiological differentiation of direct and vicarious affective arousal. *Canadian Journal of Behavior Science*, 1969, **1**, 98–105.

Craik, K. H. Environmental psychology. In R. Brown et al. (Eds.), *New directions in psychology*, Vol. 4. New York: Holt, Rinehart and Winston, 1970. Pp. 1–121.

Crichton, M. A scientist can always say "no" to secrecy. *The New York Times*, October 29, 1971, 41.

Crocker, T. D., & Rogers, A. J. *Environmental economics.* Hinsdale, Ill.: Dryden Press, 1971.

Cronbach, L. J. Educational psychology. In C. P. Stone and D. W. Taylor (Eds.), *Annual review of psychology*, Vol. 1. Palo Alto, Calif.: Annual Reviews, 1950. Pp. 235–254.

Cronbach, L. *Essentials of psychological testing* (3rd ed.). New York: Harper & Row, 1969.

Crossman, R. (Ed.). *The God that failed.* New York: Harper & Row, 1950.

Crowne, D. P., & Marlowe, D. A new scale of social desirability independent of psychopathology. *Journal of Consulting Psychology*, 1960, **24**, 349–354.

Crutchfield, R. S. Conformity and character. *American Psychologist*, 1955, **10**, 191–198.

Dahlstrom, W. G. Personality. In P. H. Mussen (Ed.), *Annual review of psychology*, Vol. 21. Palo Alto, Calif.: Annual Reviews, 1970. Pp. 1–48.

Dahlstrom, W. G., & Welsh, G. S. *An MMPI handbook: A guide to use in clinical practice and research.* Minneapolis: University of Minnesota Press, 1960.

Daniels, G. H. *Science in American society: A social history.* New York: Knopf, 1971.

Darnton, R. *Mesmerism and the end of the enlightenment in France.* Cambridge, Mass.: Harvard University Press, 1968.

Davenport, B. F. The semantic validity of TAT interpretations. *Journal of Consulting Psychology*, 1952, **16**, 171–175.

Davidson, A. R., & Steiner, I. D. Reinforcement schedules and attributed freedom. *Journal of Personality and Social Psychology*, 1971, **19**, 357–366.

Davis, F. Focus on the flower children. Why all of us may be hippies someday. In J. D. Douglas (Ed.), *Observations of deviance.* New York: Random House, 1970. Pp. 327–340.

Davis, H. A. The crisis in American archeology. *Science*, 1972, **175**, 267–272.

Davison, G. C. Elimination of a sadistic fantasy by a client: A controlled countercondi-tioning technique. *Journal of Abnormal Psychology*, 1968, **73**, 84–90.

Davy, J. Exploding the science myth. In review of J. D. Watson, *The double helix. The Observer*, May 19, 1968.

DeCecco, J. P. *The psychology of learning and instruction: Educational psychology.* Englewood Cliffs, N.J.: Prentice-Hall, 1968.

DeCecco, J. P. The social psychology of learning and change, civic man, and demo-cratic polity. In M. E. Meyer and F. H. Hite (Eds.), *The application of learning principles to classroom instruction.* Bellingham, Wash.: Western Washington State College, 1971. Pp. 63–82.

De Fleur, M. L., & Westie, F. R. Verbal attitudes and overt acts: An experiment on the salience of attitudes. *American Sociological Review*, 1958, **23**, 673.

Delgado, J. M. R. *Physical control of the mind.* New York: Harper & Row, 1969.

De Ropp, R. S. (Ed.). *Drugs and the mind.* New York: Grove Press, 1961.

DeVos, G. A., & Hippler, A. E. Cultural psychology: Comparative studies of human behavior. In G. Lindzey and E. Aronson (Eds.), *The handbook of social psychology.* Vol. 4 (2nd ed.) Reading, Mass.: Addison-Wesley, 1969. Pp. 323–417.

Dewey, J. The need for social psychology. *Psychological Review*, 1917, **24**, 266–277.

Dillehay, R. C., & Jernigan, L. R. The biased questionnaire as an instrument of opinion change. *Journal of Personality and Social Psychology*, 1970, **15**, 144–150.

Dimont, M. I. *The indestructible Jews.* New York: World, 1971.

Dohrenwend, B. S., Feldstein, S., & Plosky, J. Factors interacting with birth order in self-selection among volunteer subjects. *Journal of Social Psychology*, 1967, **72**, 125–128.

Doland, D. J., & Adelberg, K. The learning of sharing behavior. *Child Development*, 1967, **38**, 695–700.

Dollard, J., Doob, L. W., Miller, N. E., Mowrer, O. H., & Sears, R. R. *Frustration and aggression.* New Haven, Conn.: Yale University Press, 1939.

Dollard, J., & Miller, N. E. *Personality and psychotherapy: An analysis in terms of learning, thinking, and culture.* New York: McGraw-Hill, 1950.

Doubrovsky, C. P. *Report on sex bias in the public schools.* New York: National Organization for Women, 1971.

Draper, J. W. *History of the American civil war.* New York: Harper & Row, 1867–1870, 3 Vols.

Drucker, P. F. *The concept of the corporation.* New York: Mentor, 1964.

Dubos, R. *Man adapting.* New Haven, Conn.: Yale University Press, 1965.

Duke, J. D. Intercorrelational status of suggestibility tests and hypnotizability. *Psychological Record*, 1964, **14**, 71–80.

Duke, J. D. Failure of inner/other directedness to correlate with waking indices of hypnotizability. *Psychological Reports*, 1968, **23**, 270.

Dunbar, F. *Emotions and bodily change.* New York: Columbia University Press, 1954.

Dunham, H. W., & Weinberg, S. K. *The culture of the state mental hospital.* Detroit: Wayne State University Press, 1960.

Dunlap, K. *Habits: Their making and unmaking.* New York: Liveright, 1932.

Durkheim, E. *The rules of sociological method.* Chicago: University of Chicago Press, 1938.

Durkheim, E. *Suicide: A study in sociology.* New York: Free Press, 1951.

Edgerton, R. B. On the "recognition" of mental illness. In S. C. Plog & R. B. Edgerton (Eds.), *Changing perspectives in mental illness.* New York: Holt, Rinehart and Winston, 1969. Pp. 49–72.

Edwards, A. J., & Scannell, D. P. *Educational psychology: The teaching-learning process.* Scranton, Pa.: International Textbook Co., 1968.

Edwards, A. L. *The social desirability variable in personality assessment and research.* New York: Dryden Press, 1957.

Edwards, A. L. *Manual for the Edwards personal preference schedule.* New York: Psychological Corporation, 1959.

Efran, J. S. Looking for approval: Effects on visual behavior of approbation from persons differing in importance. *Journal of Personality and Social Psychology*, 1968, **10**, 21–25.

Efron, P. *Gesture and environment.* New York: King's Crown Press, 1941.

Ehrlich, P. *The population bomb.* New York: Ballantine Books, 1968.

Elliott, R., & Vasta, R. The modeling of sharing: Effects associated with vicarious reinforcement, symbolization, age, and generalization. *Journal of Experimental Child Psychology*, 1970, **10**, 8–15.

Ellis, A. *Reason and emotion in psychotherapy.* New York: Lyle Stuart, 1962.

Ellis, A. A weekend of rational encounter. In A. Burton (Ed.), *Encounter: The theory and practice of encounter groups.* San Francisco: Jossey-Bass, 1969.

Ellsworth, P. C., & Carlsmith, J. M. Effects of eye contact and verbal content on affective response to a dyadic interaction. *Journal of Personality and Social Psychology*, 1968, **10**, 15–20.

Endler, N. S., Hunt, J. McV., & Rosenstein, A. J. An S-R inventory of anxiousness. *Psychological Monograph*, 1962, **76** (17, Whole No. 536).

English, H. B., & English, A. C. *A comprehensive dictionary of psychological and psychoanalytical terms.* New York: McKay, 1958.

Eriksen, C. W. Personality. In P. R. Farnsworth (Ed.), *Annual review of psychology*, Vol. 8. Palo Alto, Calif.: Annual Reviews, 1957. Pp. 185–210.

Erikson, E. H. *Young man Luther*. New York: Norton, 1958.

Erikson, E. H. *Childhood and society*. (2nd ed.) New York: Norton, 1963.

Erikson, E. H. *Gandhi's truth on the origins of militant nonviolence*. New York: Norton, 1969.

Esser, A. H., Chamberlain, A. S., Chapple, E. D., & Kline, N. S. Territoriality of patients on a research ward. In J. Wortis (Ed.), *Recent advances in biological psychiatry*, 1965, **7**, 36–44.

Exline, R. V. Exploration in the process of person perception: Visual interaction in relation to competition, sex, and need for affiliation. *Journal of Personality*, 1963, **31**, 1–20.

Exline, R. V., Gray, D., & Schuette, D. Visual behavior in a dyad as affected by interview content and sex of respondent. *Journal of Personality and Social Psychology*, 1965, **1**, 201–209.

Eysenck, H. J. *Dimensions of personality*. London: Routledge and Kegan Paul, 1947.

Eysenck, H. J. The effects of psychotherapy. *Journal of Consulting Psychology*, 1952, **16**, 319–324. (a)

Eysenck, H. J. *The scientific study of personality*. London: Routledge and Kegan Paul, 1952. (b)

Eysenck, H. J. Personality. In C. P. Stone (Ed.), *Annual review of psychology*, Vol. 3. Palo Alto, Calif.: Annual Reviews, 1952. Pp. 151–174. (c)

Eysenck, H. J. *The dynamics of anxiety and hysteria*. London: Routledge and Kegan Paul, 1957.

Eysenck, H. J. Learning theory and behaviour therapy. *Journal of Mental Science*, 1959, **105**, 61–75.

Eysenck, H. J. (Ed.). *Behaviour therapy and the neuroses*. London, England: Pergamon, 1960. (a)

Eysenck, H. J. *The structure of human personality*. London: Methuen, 1960. (b)

Eysenck, H. J., & Prell, D. B. The inheritance of neuroticism: An experimental study. *Journal of Mental Science*, 1951, **97**, 441–465.

Farber, I. E. Anxiety as a drive state. In M. R. Jones (Ed.), *Nebraska symposium on motivation, 1954*. Lincoln, Neb.: University of Nebraska Press, 1954. Pp. 1–46.

Farber, I. E., Harlow, H. F., & West, L. J. Brainwashing, conditioning, and DDD (debility, dependency, and dread). *Sociometry*, 1957, **20**, 271–285.

Featherstone, J. *Schools where children learn*. New York: Liveright, 1971.

Fenichel, O. *The psychoanalytic theory of neurosis*. New York: Norton, 1945.

Ferenczi, S. *Final contributions to the theory and technique of psychoanalysis*. New York: Basic Books, 1955.

Ferster, C. B., & DeMyer, M. K. The development of performances in autistic children in an automatically controlled environment. *Journal of Chronic Diseases*, 1961, **23**, 312–345.

Ferster, C. B., Nurnberger, J., & Levitt, E. B. The control of eating. *Journal of Mathetics*, 1962, **1**, 87–109.

Ferster, C. B., & Skinner, B. F. *Schedules of reinforcement*. New York: Appleton-Century-Crofts, 1957.

Festinger, L. Architecture and group membership. *Journal of Social Issues*, 1951, **7**, 152–163.

Festinger, L. Social psychology and group processes. In C. P. Stone (Ed.), *Annual review of psychology*, Vol. 6. Palo Alto, California: Annual Reviews, 1955. Pp. 187–216.

Festinger, L. *A theory of cognitive dissonance*. Stanford, Calif.: Stanford University Press, 1957.

Festinger, L. Behavioral support for opinion change. *Public Opinion Quarterly*, 1964, **28**, 404–417.

Festinger, L., Schachter, S., & Back, K. *Social pressures in informal groups.* New York: Harper & Row, 1950.

Fiedler, F. E. The contingency model: A theory of leadership effectiveness. In H. Proshansky and B. Seidenberg (Eds.), *Basic studies in social psychology.* New York: Holt, Rinehart and Winston, 1965. Pp. 538–551.

Fineman, K. R. An operant conditioning program in a juvenile detention facility. *Psychological Reports*, 1968, **22**, 1119–1120.

Fishbein, M. (Ed.). *Readings in attitude theory and measurement.* New York: Wiley, 1967.

Flanders, J. P., A review of research on imitative behavior. *Psychological Bulletin*, 1968, **69**, 316–337.

Flanders, J. P., & Thistlethwaite, D. L. Effects of informative and justificatory variable upon imitation. *Journal of Experimental Social Psychology*, 1970, **6**, 316–328.

Forer, B. R. The fallacy of personal validation: A classroom demonstration of gullibility. *Journal of Abnormal and Social Psychology*, 1949, **44**, 118–123.

Frank, J. D. *Persuasion and healing.* Baltimore: Johns Hopkins Press, 1961.

Frank, J. D. Galloping technology, a new social disease. *Journal of Social Issues*, 1966, **22**, 1–14.

Frankel, A. S., & Barrett, J. Variations in personal space as a function of authoritarianism, self-esteem, and racial characteristics of a stimulus situation. *Journal of Consulting and Clinical Psychology*, 1971, **37**, 95–98.

Frankl, V. E. *Man's search for meaning: An introduction to logo-therapy.* Boston: Beacon Press, 1962.

Franks, C. M. (Ed.). *Conditioning techniques in clinical practice and research.* New York: Springer, 1964.

Freedman, J. L., & Fraser, S. C. Compliance without pressure: The foot-in-the-door technique. *Journal of Personality and Social Psychology*, 1966, **4**, 195–202.

Freud, S. *New introductory lectures in psychoanalysis* (1932). New York: Norton, 1933.

Freud, S. *The standard edition of the complete psychological works.* J. Strachey (Ed.). London: Hogarth Press, 1953.

Freud, S. *Leonardo da Vinci: A study in psychosexuality* (1910). In *Standard edition*, Vol. 11. London: Hogarth Press, 1957.

Freud, S. *The interpretation of dreams* (1900). In *Standard edition*, Vols. 4 and 5. London: Hogarth Press, 1962.

Freud, S. *Moses and monotheism* (1939). In *Standard edition*, Vol. 23. London: Hogarth Press, 1964.

Freud, S., & Bullitt, W. C. *Thomas Woodrow Wilson, twenty-eighth president of the United States: A psychological study.* Boston: Houghton Mifflin, 1967.

Freund, K. Some problems of the treatment of homosexuality. In H. J. Eysenck (Ed.), *Behaviour therapy and the neurosis.* New York: Pergamon Press, 1960. Pp. 312–326.

Freund, P. A. (Ed.). *Experimentation with human subjects.* New York: Braziller, 1969.

Fried, M. Grieving for a lost home. In L. J. Duhl (Ed.), *The urban condition.* New York: Basic Books, 1963.

Fried, M., & Gleicher, P. Some sources of residential satisfaction in an urban slum. In H. M. Proshansky, W. H. Ittelson, & L. G. Rivlin (Eds.), *Environmental psychology: man and his physical setting.* New York: Holt, Rinehart and Winston, 1970. Pp. 333–346.

Friedan, B. *The feminine mystique.* New York: Norton, 1963.

Friedrichs, R. W. *A sociology of sociology.* New York: Free Press, 1970.

Fromm, E. *Escape from freedom.* New York: Holt, Rinehart and Winston, 1941.

Fromm, E. *Man for himself.* New York: Holt, Rinehart and Winston, 1947.

Fromm, E. *The sane society.* New York: Holt, Rinehart and Winston, 1955.

Fromm, E. *The revolution of hope.* New York: Harper & Row, 1968.

Fuller, P. R. Operant conditioning of a vegetative human organism. *American Journal of Psychology,* 1949, **62,** 587–590.

Gage, N. L. Paradigms for research on teaching. In N. L. Gage (Ed.), *Handbook of research on teaching.* Chicago: Rand McNally, 1963.

Gage, N. L., & Unruh, W. R. Theoretical formulations for research on teaching. In R. C. Anderson, G. W. Faust, M. C. Roderick, D. J. Cunningham, & T. Andre (Eds.), *Current research on instruction.* Englewood Cliffs, N. J.: Prentice-Hall, 1969.

Gagné, R. M. *The conditions of learning.* New York: Holt, Rinehart and Winston, 1970.

Galbraith, J. K. *American capitalism.* Boston: Houghton Mifflin, 1956.

Galbraith, J. K. *The new industrial state.* Boston: Houghton Mifflin, 1967.

Galle, O. R., Gove, W. R., & McPherson, J. M. Population density and pathology: What are the relations for man? *Science,* 1972, **176,** 23–30.

Gandolfo, R. L. Role of expectancy, amnesia, and hypnotic induction in the performance of posthypnotic behavior. *Journal of Abnormal Psychology,* 1971, **77,** 324–328.

Gans, H. *The urban villagers.* Cambridge, Mass.: Harvard University Press, 1960.

Geer, J. H., & Turteltaub, A. Fear reduction following observations of a model. *Journal of Personality and Social Psychology,* 1967, **6,** 327–331.

Gelfand, S., Ullmann, L. P., & Krasner, L. The placebo response: An experimental approach. *Journal of Nervous and Mental Disease,* 1963, **136,** 379–387.

Gergen, K. J. *The psychology of behavior exchange.* Reading, Mass.: Addison-Wesley, 1969.

Gericke, O. L. Practical use of operant conditioning procedures in a mental hospital. *Psychiatric Studies and Projects,* 1965, 3–10.

Gibson, W. B. (Ed.). *The fine art of swindling.* New York: Grosset & Dunlap, 1966.

Gilbert, G. M. *Personality dynamics: A biosocial approach.* New York: Harper & Row, 1970.

Gilman, R. The femlib case against Sigmund Freud. *New York Times Magazine,* January 31, 1971, 10–47.

Girardeau, F. L., & Spradlin, J. E. Token rewards on a cottage program. *Mental Retardation,* 1964, **2,** 345–351.

Glaser, R. Toward a behavioral science base for instructional design. In R. Glaser (Ed.), *Teaching machine and programed learning* II *Data and directions.* Washington, D.C. National Education Association, Department of Audiovisual Instruction, 1965. Pp. 771–809.

Glass, B. *Science and ethical values.* Chapel Hill, N.C.: University of North Carolina Press, 1965.

Glenn, M. Introduction. In J. Agel (Ed.), *The radical therapist.* New York: Ballantine, 1971. Pp. ix–xiv.

Gleser, G. C., & Ihilevich, D. An objective instrument for measuring defense mechanisms. *Journal of Consulting and Clinical Psychology,* 1969, **33,** 51–60.

Goffman, E. *Asylums.* New York: Doubleday, 1961.

Goffman, E. *Stigma.* Englewood Cliffs, N.J.: Prentice-Hall, 1963. (a)

Goffman, E. *Behavior in public places.* New York: Free Press, 1963. (b)

Goffman, E. *Interaction ritual.* New York: Doubleday, 1967.

Goffman, E. *Relations in public: Microstudies of the public order.* New York: Basic Books, 1971.

Goldberg, L. R. Simple models or simple processes? Some research on clinical judgments. *American Psychologist*, 1968, **23**, 483–496. (a)

Goldberg, L. R. Seer over sigh: The first good example? *Journal of Experimental Research in Personality*, 1968, **3**, 168–171. (b)

Goldberg, L. R., & Slovic, P. The importance of test item content: An analysis of a corollary of the deviation hypothesis. *Journal of Counseling Psychology*, 1967, **14**, 462–472.

Golden, M. Some effects of combining psychological tests on clinical inferences. *Journal of Consulting Psychology*, 1964, **28**, 440–446.

Goldiamond, I. Self-control procedures in personal behavior problems. *Psychological Reports*, 1965, **17**, 851–868.

Goldman, R., Jaffa, M., & Schachter, S. Yom Kippur, Air France, dormitory food, and the eating behavior of obese and normal persons. *Journal of Personality and Social Psychology*, 1968, **10**, 117–123.

Goldstein, A. P. *Therapist-patient expectancies in psychotherapy*. New York: Pergamon, 1962.

Goldstein, A. P. *Psychotherapeutic attraction*. New York: Pergamon, 1971.

Goldstein, A. P., Heller, K., & Sechrest, L. B. *Psychotherapy and the psychology of behavior change*. New York: Wiley, 1966.

Goodman, P. *Growing up absurd: Problems of youth in the organized system*. New York: Random House, 1960.

Gordon, J. E. (Ed.). *Handbook of clinical and experimental hypnosis*. New York: Macmillan, 1967.

Gorer, G. Themes in Japanese culture. *Transactions of the New York Academy of Science* (Series II), 1943, 106–124.

Gottschalk, L. A., & Pattison, E. M. Psychiatric perspectives on T-groups and the laboratory movement: An overview. *American Journal of Psychiatry*, 1969, **126**, 823–839.

Graziano, A. M. An historical note: J. Stanley Gray's, "Behavior modification," 1932. *Journal of the History of the Behavioral Sciences*, 1970, **6**, 156–158.

Greenspoon, J. The reinforcing effect of two spoken sounds on the frequency of two responses. *American Journal of Psychology*, 1955, **68**, 409–416.

Greenwald, A. G. When does role playing produce attitude change? *Journal of Personality and Social Psychology*, 1970, **16**, 214–219.

Griffitt, W. Environmental effects on interpersonal affective behavior: Ambient effective temperature and attraction. *Journal of Personality and Social Psychology*, 1970, **15**, 240–244.

Griffitt, W., & Veitch, R. Hot and crowded: Influences of population density and temperature on interpersonal affective behavior. *Journal of Personality and Social Psychology*, 1971, **17**, 92–98.

Groen, G. J., & Atkinson, R. C. Models for optimizing the learning process. *Psychological Bulletin*, 1966, **66**, 309–320.

Gross, H. S., Herbert, M. R., Knratterub, G. L., & Donner, L. The effect of race and sex on the variation of diagnosis and disposition in a psychiatric emergency room. *Journal of Nervous and Mental Disease*, 1969, **148**, 638–642.

Grossberg, J. M. Behavior therapy: A review. *Psychological Bulletin*, 1964, **62**, 73–88.

Grusec, J. E., & Skubiski, S. L. Model nurturance, demand characteristics of the modeling experiment and altruism. *Journal of Personality and Social Psychology*, 1970, **14**, 352–359.

Guilford, J. P. *Personality*. New York: McGraw-Hill, 1959.

Guthrie, E. R. *The psychology of learning*. New York: Harper & Row, 1935.

Guthrie, E. R. *The psychology of human conflict*. New York: Harper & Row, 1938.

Gutman, R. Site planning and social behavior. In H. M. Proshansky, W. H. Ittelson, & L. G. Rivlin (Eds.), *Environmental psychology: Man and his physical setting.* New York: Holt, Rinehart and Winston, 1970. Pp. 509–517.

Haas, H., Fink, H. & Hartfelder, G. The placebo problem. *Psychopharmacology Service Center Bulletin,* 1963, **2**, 1–65.

Haase, R. F., & Di Mattia, D. J. Proxemic behavior: Counselor, administrator, and client preference for seating arrangement in dyadic interaction. *Journal of Counseling Psychology,* 1970, **17**, 319–325.

Hagen, R. L. Group therapy versus bibliotherapy in weight reduction. *Dissertation Abstracts International,* 1970, **31**, 2985–2986B.

Hale, N. G., Jr. *Freud and the Americans: The beginnings of psychoanalysis in the United States, 1876–1917.* New York: Oxford University Press, 1971.

Haley, J. The art of psychoanalysis. *ETC.,* 1958, **15**, 190–200.

Haley, J. *Strategies of psychotherapy.* New York: Grune & Stratton, 1963.

Haley, J. *The power tactics of Jesus Christ and other essays.* New York: Grossman, 1969.

Hall, C. S. and Lindzey, G. *Theories of personality,* (2nd ed.). New York: Wiley, 1970.

Hall, E. T. *The hidden dimension.* New York: Doubleday, 1966.

Hall, E. T. *The silent langauge.* New York: Fawcett World Library, 1969.

Haller, J. S., Jr. *Outcasts from evolution: Scientific attitudes of racial inferiority, 1859–1900.* Urbana, Ill.: University of Illinois Press, 1971.

Haring, N. G., & Hauck, M. A. Improved learning conditions in the establishment of reading skills with disturbed readers. *Exceptional Children,* 1969, **35**, 341–351.

Harlow, H. F. The formation of learning sets. *Psychological Review,* 1949, **56**, 51–65.

Harlow, H. F., & Harlow, M. K. Learning to love. *American Scientist,* 1966, **54**, 244–272.

Harlow, H. F., & Suomi, S. J. Nature of love simplified. *American Psychologist,* 1970, **25**, 161–168.

Harmatz, M. G., & Lapuc, P. Behavior modification of overeating in a psychiatric population. *Journal of Consulting and Clinical Psychology,* 1968, **32**, 583–587.

Harris, M. B. Self-directed program for weight control: A pilot study. *Journal of Abnormal and Social Psychology,* 1969, **74**, 263–270.

Harris, M. B. Reciprocity and generosity: Some determinants of sharing in children. *Child Development,* 1970, **41**, 313–328.

Hartshorne, H., & May, M. A. *Studies in deceit.* New York: Macmillan, 1928.

Hartung, J. R. A review of procedures to increase verbal imitation skills and functional speech in autistic children. *Journal of Speech and Hearing Disorders,* 1970, **35**, 203–217.

Hartup, W. W., & Coates, B. Imitation of a peer as a function of reinforcement from the peer group and rewardingness of the model. *Child Development,* 1967, **38**, 1003–1016.

Hashim, S. A., & Van Itallie, T. B. Studies in normal and obese subjects with a monitored food dispensing device. *Annals of the New York Academy of Sciences,* 1965, **131**, 654–661.

Hastorf, A. H. The reinforcement of individual actions in a group situation. In L. Krasner & L. P. Ullmann (Eds.), *Research in behavior modification.* New York: Holt, Rinehart and Winston, 1965. Pp. 271–284.

Hauser, A. *The social history of art.* 4 vols. New York: Vintage, 1958.

Hebb, D. O. *The organization of behavior.* New York: Wiley, 1949.

Hebb, D. O. The role of neurological ideas in psychology. *Journal of Personality,* 1951, **20**, 39–55.

Hebb, D. O. The motivating effects of exteroceptive stimulation. *American Psychologist,* 1958, **13**, 109–113.

Hefferline, R. F. Learning theory and clinical psychology: An eventual symbiosis? In A. J. Bachrach (Ed.), *Experimental foundations of clinical psychology*. New York: Basic Books, 1962.

Hefferline, R. F., Keenan, B., & Harford, R. A. Escape and avoidance conditioning in human subjects without their observation of the response. *Science*, 1959, **130**, 1335–1339.

Heine, P. J. *Personality in social theory*. Chicago: Aldine, 1971.

Henderson, J. D. The use of dual reinforcement in an intensive treatment system. In R. D. Rubin and C. M. Franks (Eds.), *Advance in behavior therapy, 1968*. New York: Academic Press, 1969. Pp. 201–210.

Hennessy, B. C. *Public opinion* (2nd ed.). Belmont, Calif.: Wadsworth, 1970.

Henry, J. Space and power on a psychiatric unit. In A. F. Wessen (Ed.), *The psychiatric hospital as a social system*. Springfield, Ill.: Charles C Thomas, 1964, 20–34.

Herguth, R. J. *Herguth's people*. Chicago: *Chicago Daily News*, July 8, 1970.

Heron, W., Doane, B. K., & Scott, T. H. Visual disturbances after prolonged perceptual isolation. *Canadian Journal of Psychology*, 1956, **10**, 13–18.

Hersen, M., & Greaves, S. T. Rorschach productivity as related to verbal reinforcement. *Journal of Personality Assessment*, 1971, **35**, 436–441.

Hess, E. H. Imprinting. *Science*, 1959, **130**, 133–141.

Hewett, F. M. *The emotionally disturbed child in the classroom*. Boston: Allyn and Bacon, 1968.

Hewett, F. M., Taylor, A., & Artuso, A. A. The Santa Monica project: Evaluation of an engineered classroom design with emotionally disturbed children. *Exceptional Children*, 1969, **35**, 523–529.

Heyns, R. W. Social psychology and group processes. In P. R. Farnsworth (Ed.), *Annual review of psychology*, Vol. 9. Palo Alto, Calif.: Annual Reviews, 1958. Pp. 419–452.

Hilgard, E. R. *Introduction to psychology* (3rd ed). New York: Harcourt Brace Jovanovich, 1962.

Hilgard, E. R. Individual differences in hypnotizability. In J. E. Gordon (Ed.), *Handbook of clinical and experimental hypnosis*. New York: Macmillan, 1967. Pp. 391–443.

Hilgard, E. R. Hypnotic phenomena: The struggle for scientific acceptance. *American Scientist*, 1971, **59**, 567–577.

Hills, C. and Stone, R. B. *Conduct your awareness sessions*. New York: New American Library, 1970.

Himmelweit, H., Oppenheim, A. N., & Vince, P. Television and the child. In B. Berelson and M. Janowitz (Eds.), *Reader in public opinion and communication*. (2nd ed.) New York: Free Press, 1966. Pp. 418–445.

Hingtgen, J. N., Coulter, S. K., & Churchill, D. W. Intensive reinforcement of imitative behavior in mute autistic children. *Archives of General Psychiatry*, 1967, **17**, 36–43.

Hobbs, N. Client-centered therapy. In *Six approaches to psychotherapy*. New York: Dryden Press, 1955. Pp. 11–60.

Hoffman, P. J. The paramorphic representation of clinical judgment. *Psychological Bulletin*, 1960, **57**, 116–131.

Hollingshead, A. B. *Elmtown's youth*. New York: Wiley, 1949.

Holloway, M. *Heavens on earth*. (2nd ed.) New York: Dover, 1966. (a)

Holloway, M. Introduction to J. H. Noyes, *History of American socialisms*. New York: Dover, 1966. (b)

Holt, E. B. *The Freudian wish and its place in ethics*. New York: Holt, Rinehart and Winston, 1915.

Holt, J. *How children fail*. New York: Pitman, 1964.

Holt, J. *How children learn.* New York: Pitman, 1967.

Holt, J. *The underachieving school.* New York: Pitman, 1969.

Holt, R. R. Individuality and generalization in the psychology of personality. *Journal of Personality,* 1962, **30,** 377–404.

Holtzman, W. H. Personality structure. In P. R. Farnsworth (Ed.), *Annual review of psychology,* Vol. 16. Palo Alto, Calif.: Annual Reviews, 1965. Pp. 119–156.

Homans, G. C. *Social behavior: its elementary forms.* New York: Harcourt Brace Jovanovich, 1961.

Homme, L. E. Control of coverants, the operants of the mind. *Psychological Record,* 1965, **15,** 501–511.

Homme, L. E., De Baca, P. C., Cottingham, L., & Homme, A. What behavioral engineering is. *Psychological Record,* 1968, **18,** 425–434.

Honigfeld, G. Non-specific factors in treatment I: Review of placebo reactions and placebo reactors. *Diseases of the Nervous System,* 1964, **25,** 145–156. (a)

Honigfeld, G. Non-specific factors in treatment II: Review of social-psychological factors. *Diseases of the Nervous System,* 1964, **25,** 224–239. (b)

Horn, J. Some ethical issues in reporting behavioral science research: A point of view. Comments in Symposium on Ethical Issues of Behavior Science Research. Annual Meeting, Western Psychological Association, San Francisco, April 1971. Abstracts in *Catalog of Selected Documents in Psychology,* 1972, **2,** 1–17.

Howard, J. *Please touch: A guided tour of the human potential movement.* New York: McGraw-Hill, 1970.

Howard, K. L., & Orlinsky, D. E. Psychotherapeutic process. In P. H. Mussen & M. R. Rosenzweig (Eds.), *Annual review of psychology.* Vol. 23. Palo Alto, Calif.: Annual Reviews, 1972. Pp. 615–668.

Hughes, H. S. Emotional disturbance and American social change. *American Journal of Psychiatry,* 1969, **126,** 21–28.

Hull, C. L. *Principles of behavior.* New York: Appleton-Century-Crofts, 1943.

Hull, C. L. *Essentials of behavior.* New Haven, Conn: Yale University Press, 1951.

Hunt, J. McV. *Intelligence and experience.* New York: Ronald Press, 1961.

Hunt, J. McV. Traditional personality theory in the light of recent evidence. *American Scientist,* 1965, **53,** 80–96.

Hunt, M. *The affair: A portrait of extra-marital love in contemporary America.* New York: World, 1969.

Hunter, E. *Brainwashing in Red China.* New York: Vanguard, 1951.

Hurlock, E. B. An evaluation of certain incentives used in school work. *Journal of Educational Psychology,* 1925, **16,** 145–159.

Hutcheson, F. An inquiry concerning beauty, order, etc. In P. McReynolds (Ed.), *Four early works on motivation.* Gainesville, Fla.: Scholars' Fascimiles & Reprints, 1969. P. 93.

Ihilevich, D., & Gleser, G. C. Relationship of defense mechanisms to field dependence-independence. *Journal of Abnormal Psychology,* 1971, **77,** 296–302.

Illich, I. *Deschooling society.* New York: Harper & Row, 1971.

Inkeles, A., & Levinson, D. J. National character: The study of model personality and sociocultural systems. In G. Lindzey & E. Aronson (Eds.), *The handbook of social psychology.* Vol. 4 (2nd ed.). Reading, Mass.: Addison-Wesley, 1969. Pp. 418–506.

Ittelson, W. H., Proshansky, H. M., & Rivlin, L. G. The environmental psychology of the psychiatric ward. In H. M. Proshansky, W. H. Ittelson, & L. G. Rivlin (Eds.), *Environmental psychology: Man and his physical setting.* New York: Holt, Rinehart and Winston, 1970. Pp. 419–439.

Jackson, C. W., Jr., & Kelly, E. L. Influence of suggestion and subjects' prior knowledge in research on sensory deprivation. *Science,* 1962, **135,** 211–212.

Jackson, D. N., & Messick, S. Content and style in personality assessment. *Psychological Bulletin*, 1958, **55**, 243–252.

Jackson, P. W. *The way teaching is: Report of the seminar on teaching.* Association for supervision and curriculum development and the center for the study of instruction. Washington, D. C.: National Education Association, 1966. Pp. 7–27.

Jacobs, R. H. Emotive and control groups as mutated new American utopian communities. *Journal of Applied Behavioral Science*, 1971, **7**, 234–251.

Jacobson, E. *Progressive relaxation.* Chicago: University of Chicago Press, 1938.

Jakubowski, P. A. Expectancy and the effects of consistent and inconsistent contingent social reinforcement. *Dissertation Abstracts*, 1968, **29**, 771.

James, W. *Principles of psychology.* New York: Holt, Rinehart and Winston, 1890.

Janis, I. L., & Mann, L. Effectiveness of emotional role-playing in modifying smoking habits and attitudes. *Journal of Experimental Research in Personality*, 1965, **1**, 85–90.

Janson, H. W. *History of art.* Englewood Cliffs, N. J.: Prentice-Hall, 1962.

Jay, A. *Management and Machiavelli.* New York: Holt, Rinehart and Winston, 1968.

Jensen, A. R. Personality. In P. R. Farnsworth (Ed.), *Annual review of psychology,* Vol. 9. Palo Alto, Calif.: Annual Reviews, 1958. Pp. 295–322.

Jensen, A. R. How much can we boost IQ and scholastic achievement? *Harvard Educational Review*, 1969, **39**, 1–123.

Jensen, A. R. Genetic research on human mental abilities: Ethical issues. *Catalog of Selected Documents in Psychology*, 1972, **2**, 1–10.

Jones, E. *The life and work of Sigmund Freud.* Vol. 1. New York: Basic Books, 1953.

Jones, E. *The life and work of Sigmund Freud.* Vol 2. New York: Basic Books, 1955.

Jones, M. *The therapeutic community.* New York: Basic Books, 1953.

Jones, M. *Beyond the therapeutic community.* New Haven, Conn.: Yale University Press, 1968.

Jourard, S. M. *Disclosing man to himself.* Princeton, N.J.: Van Nostrand, 1968.

Jourard, S. M., & Friedman, R. Experimenter-subject "distance" and self-disclosure. *Journal of Personality and Social Psychology*, 1970, **15**, 278–282.

Jowett, B. *The dialogues of Plato.* New York: Macmillan, 1892; Random House, 1937.

Jung, C. G. *Psychological types.* New York: Harcourt Brace Jovanovich, 1933.

Jung, C. G. *Collected works.* H. Read, M. Fordham, & G. Adler (Eds.). Princeton, N.J.: Princeton University Press, 1953.

Jung, C. G. Concerning the archetypes, with special reference to the anima concept. In *Collected works*, 1954, Vol. 9, Part I. Princeton, N.J.: Princeton University Press, 1959.

Jung, C. G. *Memories, dreams, reflections.* New York: Random House, 1961.

Juster, F. T. Microdata, economic research, and the production of economic knowledge. *The American Economic Review*, 1970, **60**, 138–148.

Kadushin, C. *Why people go to psychiatrists.* New York: Atherton, 1969.

Kagel, J. H., & Winkler, R. C. Behavioral economics: Areas of cooperative research between economics and applied behavioral analysis. *Journal of Applied Behavior Analysis*, 1972, **5**, 335–342.

Kalish, H. I. Behavior therapy. In B. B. Wolman (Ed.), *Handbook of clinical psychology.* New York: McGraw-Hill, 1965.

Kamiya, J. Conscious control of brain waves. *Psychology Today*, 1968, **1**, 57–60.

Kanfer, F. H. Issues and ethics in behavior manipulation. *Psychological Reports*, 1965, **16**, 187–196. (a)

Kanfer, F. H. Vicarious human reinforcement: A glimpse into the black box. In L. Krasner & L. P. Ullmann (Eds.), *Research in behavior modification.* New York: Holt, Rinehart and Winston, 1965. (b)

Kanfer, F. H. Verbal conditioning: A review of its current status. In T. R. Dixon and

D. L. Horton (Eds.), *Verbal behavior and general behavior theory*. Englewood Cliffs, N.J.: Prentice-Hall, 1968.

Kanfer, F. H. The maintenance of behavior of self-generated stimuli and reinforcement. In A. Jacobs & B. Sachs (Eds.), *The psychology of private events*. New York: Academic Press, 1971. Pp. 39–57.

Kanfer, F. H., & Duerfeldt, P. H. Effects of pretraining on self-evaluation and self-reinforcement. *Journal of Personality and Social Psychology*, 1967, **1**, 164–168.

Kanfer, F. H., & Karoly, P. Self-control: A behavioristic excursion into the lion's den. *Behavior Therapy*, 1972, **3**, 398–416.

Kanfer, F. H., & Marston, A. R. Conditioning of self-reinforcing responses: An analogue to self-confidence training. *Psychological Reports*, 1963, **13**, 63–70. (a)

Kanfer, F. H., & Marston, A. R. Determinants of self-reinforcement in human learning. *Journal of Experimental Psychology*, 1963, **66**, 245–254. (b)

Kanfer, F. H., & Phillips, J. S. A survey of current behavior therapies and a proposal for classification. In C. M. Franks (Ed.), *Behavior therapy: Appraisal and status*. New York: McGraw-Hill, 1969. Pp. 445–475.

Kanfer, F. H., & Phillips, J. S. *Learning foundations of behavior therapy*. New York: Wiley, 1970.

Kanter, R. M. *Commitment and community: Communes and utopias in sociological perspective*. Cambridge, Mass.: Harvard University Press, 1972.

Kantor, J. R. *Principles of psychology*. New York: Knopf, 1924–1926. 2 vols.

Kardiner, A. *The psychological frontiers of society*. New York: Columbia University Press, 1945.

Kardiner, A., & Preble, E. *They studied man*. New York: World, 1961.

Kateb, A. *Utopia and its enemies*. New York: Schocken, 1963.

Katona, G. *Psychological analysis of economic behavior*. New York: McGraw-Hill, 1951.

Katz, D. Social psychology and group processes. In C. P. Stone (ed.), *Annual review of psychology*, Vol. 2. Palo Alto, Calif.: Annual Reviews, 1951. Pp. 137–172.

Katz, E., & Lazarsfeld, P. F. *Personal influence*. New York: Free Press, 1955.

Kaufmann, C. B. *Man incorporate*. New York: Doubleday, 1967.

Kazdin, A. E., & Bootzin, R. R. The token economy: An evaluative review. *Journal of Applied Behavior Analysis*, 1972, **5**, 343.

Kelley, H. H. The warm-cold variable in first impressions of persons. *Journal of Personality*, 1950, **18**, 431–439.

Kelly, E. L., & Fiske, D. W. *The prediction of performance in clinical psychology*. Ann Arbor, Mich.: University of Michigan Press, 1951.

Kelly, G. A. *The psychology of personal constructs*. New York: Norton, 1955. 2 vols.

Kemp, D. E. The AB Scale and attitudes toward patients: Studies of a disappearing phenomenon. *Psychotherapy: Theory, Research & Practice*, 1969, **6**, 223–228.

Kemp, D. E. Routinizing art: Implications of research with the A-B Scale for the practice of psychotherapy. *The Journal of the American College Health Association*, 1970, **18**, 238–240.

Kessel, F. S. The philosophy of science as proclaimed and science as practiced: "Identity" or "dualism?" *American Psychologist*, 1969, **24**, 999–1005.

Kessel, P., & McBrearty, J. F. Values and psychotherapy: A review of the literature. *Perceptual and Motor Skills*, 1967, **25**, 669–690.

Kiesler, C. A. *The psychology of commitment: Experiments linking behavior to belief*. New York: Academic Press, 1971.

Kim, Y. H. The blind as a minority group. Paper presented to the American Sociological Association, Denver, Colorado, 1971.

Kimmel, H. D. Instrumental conditioning of autonomically mediated behavior. *Psychological Bulletin*, 1967, **67**, 337–345.

King, C. W. *Social movements in the United States.* New York: Random House, 1956.

Kinkead, E. *In every war but one.* New York: Norton, 1959.

Kinsey, A. C., Pomeroy, W. B., & Martin, C. E. *Sexual behavior in the human male.* Philadelphia: Saunders, 1948.

Kinsey, A. C., Pomeroy, W. B., Martin, C. E., & Gebhard, P. H. *Sexual behavior in the human female.* Philadelphia: Saunders, 1953.

Kintz, B. L., Delprato, D. J., Mettee, D. R., Persons, C. E., & Schappe, R. H. The experimenter effect. *Psychological Bulletin,* 1968, **69,** 316–337.

Kinzel, A. F. Body-buffer zone in violent prisoners. *American Journal of Psychiatry,* 1970, **127,** 59–64.

Kleck, R., Buck, P. L., Goller, W. L., London, R. S., Pfeiffer, J. R., & Vukcevic, D. P. Effect of stigmatizing conditions on the use of personal space. *Psychological Reports,* 1968, **23,** 111–118.

Klein, G. S., & Schlesinger, H. J. Where is the perceiver in perceptual theory? *Journal of Personality,* 1951, **20,** 2–23.

Klineberg, O. Recent studies of national character. In S. Sargent & M. W. Smith (Eds.), *Culture and personality.* New York: Viking Fund, 1949, 135–136.

Klinger, B. L. Effect of peer model responsiveness and length of induction procedure on hypnotic responsiveness. *Journal of Abnormal Psychology,* 1970, **75,** 15–18.

Kluckhohn C., & Murray, H. A. (Eds.) *Personality in nature, society, and culture.* New York: Knopf, 1948.

Kogan, K. L., & Wimberger, H. C. Behavior transactions between disturbed children and their mothers. *Psychological Reports,* 1971, **28,** 395–404.

Kohlberg, L. Moral development and identification. In H. W. Stevenson (Ed.), *Child psychology.* Yearbook of the National Society for the Study of Education, Part I. Chicago: University of Chicago Press, 1963, 277–332.

Kolaja, J. *Social system and time and space.* Pittsburgh: Duquesne University Press, 1969.

Kolb, L. C. *Noyes' modern clinical psychiatry.* (7th ed.) Philadelphia: Saunders, 1968.

Komarovsky, M., & Sargent, S. S. Research into subcultural influences. In S. Sargent & M. W. Smith (Eds.), *Culture and personality.* New York: Viking Fund, 1949. Pp. 143–158.

Kostlan, A. A method of the empirical study of psychodiagnosis. *Journal of Consulting Psychology,* 1954, **18,** 83–88.

Kozol, J. *Death at an early age.* Boston: Houghton Mifflin, 1967.

Kraft, T., & Al-Issa, I. Behavior therapy and the treatment of frigidity. *American Journal of Psychotherapy,* 1967, **21,** 116–120.

Krasner, L. The use of generalized reinforcers in psychotherapy research. *Psychological Reports,* 1955, **1,** 19–25.

Krasner, L. Studies of the conditioning of verbal behavior. *Psychological Bulletin,* 1958, **55,** 148–170.

Krasner, L. Behavior control and social responsibility. *American Psychologist,* 1962, **17,** 199–204. (a)

Krasner, L. The therapist as a social reinforcement machine. In H. H. Strupp & L. Luborsky (Eds.), *Research in psychotherapy,* Vol. 2. Washington, D.C.: American Psychological Association, 1962. (b)

Krasner, L. Verbal conditioning and psychotherapy. In L. Krasner & L. P. Ullmann (Eds.), *Research in behavior modification.* New York: Holt, Rinehart and Winston, 1965. Pp. 211–228. (a)

Krasner, L. The behavioral scientist and social responsibility: No place to hide. *Journal of Social Issues,* 1965, **21,** 9–30. (b)

Krasner, L. Behavior modification research and the role of the therapist. In L. A.

Gottschalk & A. H. Auerbach (Eds.), *Methods of research in psychotherapy.* New York: Appleton-Century-Crofts, 1966.

Krasner, L. Assessment of token economy programmes in psychiatric hospitals. In R. Porter (Ed.), *Learning theory and psychotherapy.* London: Churchill, 1968.

Krasner, L. Behavior modification: Values and training. In C. M. Franks (Ed.), *Behavior Therapy: Appraisal and status.* New York: McGraw-Hill, 1969.

Krasner, L. Behavior therapy. In P. H. Mussen (Ed.), *Annual review of psychology,* Vol. 22. Palo Alto, Calif.: Annual Reviews, 1971. Pp. 483–532. (a)

Krasner, L. The token economy and utopian planning. Paper presented at Annual Meeting of Western Psychological Assoc., San Francisco, Calif., April, 1971. (b)

Krasner, L. Token economies. In W. C. Becker (Ed.), *Uses of reinforcement principles in education.* Champaign, Ill.: Research Press, 1973.

Krasner, L., & Atthowe, J. M. The token economy as a rehabilitative procedure in a mental hospital setting. In H. C. Rickard (Ed.), *Behavioral intervention in human problems.* New York: Pergamon Press, 1971. Pp. 311–334.

Krasner, L., Knowles, J. B., & Ullmann, L. P. Effect of verbal conditioning of attitudes on subsequent motor performance. *Journal of Personality and Social Psychology,* 1965, **1,** 407–412.

Krasner, L., & Krasner, M. Token economies and other planned environments. In C. E. Thoresen (Ed.), *Behavior modification in education.* National Society for the Study of Education, 72nd Yearbook. Chicago: University of Chicago Press, 1973.

Krasner, L., & Ullmann, L. P. Variables affecting report of awareness in verbal conditioning. *Journal of Psychology,* 1963, **56,** 193–202.

Krasner, L. and Ullmann, L. P. (Eds.) *Research in behavior modification.* New York: Holt, Rinehart and Winston, 1965.

Krasner, L., Ullmann, L. P., & Fisher, D. Changes in performance as related to verbal conditioning of attitudes toward the examiner. *Perceptual and Motor Skills,* 1964, **19,** 811–816.

Krause, M. S. Use of social situations for research purposes. *American Psychologist,* 1970, **25,** 748–753.

Krebs, D. L. Altruism: An examination of the concepts and a review of the literature. *Psychological Bulletin,* 1970, **73,** 258–302.

Krech, D., & Crutchfield, R. *Theory and problems of social psychology.* New York: McGraw-Hill, 1948.

Kretschmer, E. *Physique and character.* Berlin: Springer-Verlag, 1951.

Kryter, K. D. *The effects of noise on man.* New York: Academic Press, 1970.

Kuehn, J. L., & Crinella, F. M. Sensitivity training: Interpersonal "overkill" and other problems. *American Journal of Psychiatry,* 1969, **126,** 840–845.

Kuhn, T. S. *The structure of scientific revolutions.* (2nd ed.) Chicago: University of Chicago Press, 1970.

Kuypers, D. S., Becker, W. C., & O'Leary, K. D. How to make a token system fail. *Exceptional Children,* 1969, **35,** 101–109.

LaBarre, W. Some observations on character structure in the Orient: The Japanese. *Psychiatry,* 1945, **8,** 319–342.

LaBarre, W. *The human criminal.* Chicago: University of Chicago Press, 1954.

Lambert, W. W. Social psychology in relation to general psychology and other behavioral sciences. In S. Koch (Ed.), *Psychology: A study of a science,* Vol. 6. New York: McGraw-Hill, 1963. Pp. 173–243.

Lang, P. J. Experimental studies of desensitization psychotherapy. In J. Wolpe, A. Salter, & L. J. Reyna (Eds.), *The conditioning therapies.* New York: Holt, Rinehart and Winston, 1965, 38–53.

Lang, P. J. Stimulus control, response control, and the desensitization of fear. In D. J.

Levis (Ed.), *Learning approaches to therapeutic behavior change.* Chicago, Ill.: Aldine Publishing Co., 1970. Pp. 148–173.

Lang, P. J., & Melamed, B. G. Avoidance conditioning therapy of an infant with chronic ruminative vomiting. *Journal of Abnormal Psychology*, 1969, **74**, 1–8.

Lanyon, R. I., & Goodstein, L. D. *Personality assessment.* New York: Wiley, 1971.

LaPiere, R. T. Attitudes vs. actions. *Social Forces*, 1934, **13**, 230–237.

Lapointe, F. H. Origin and evolution of the term "psychology." *American Psychologist*, 1970, **25**, 640–646.

Lasswell, H. D. The structure and function of communication on society. In D. M. Schramm (Ed.), *Mass communications.* Urbana, Ill.: University of Illinois Press, 1960. Pp. 117–130.

Latane, B., & Schachter, S. Adrenalin and avoidance learning. *Journal of Comparative and Physiological Psychology*, 1962, **55**, 369–372.

Lazarsfeld, P. F., Berelson, B., & Gaudet, H. *The people's choice: How the voter makes up his mind in a presidential campaign.* New York: Duel, Sloan, and Pearce, 1944.

Lazarsfeld, P. F., & Merton, R. K. Mass communication, popular taste, and organized social action. In W. Schramm (Ed.), *Mass communications.* Urbana, Ill.: University of Illinois Press, 1960. Pp. 492–512.

Lazarus, A. A. New methods in psychotherapy: A case study. *South African Medical Journal*, 1958, **32**, 660–663.

Lazarus, A. A. The treatment of chronic frigidity by systematic desensitization. *Journal of Nervous and Mental Disease*, 1963, **136**, 272–278.

Lazarus, A. A. *Behavior therapy and beyond.* New York: McGraw-Hill, 1971.

Lazarus, A. A., & Abramovitz, A. The use of "emotive imagery" in the treatment of children's phobias. *Journal of Mental Science*, 1962, **108**, 191–195.

Le Bon, G. *The crowd: History of the popular mind.* London: E. Benn, 1896 (New York: Viking Press, 1960).

Lefcourt, H. M., Rotenberg, F., Buckspan, R., & Steffy, R. A. Visual interaction and performance of process and reactive schizophrenics as a function of examiner's sex. *Journal of Personality*, 1967, **35**, 535–546.

Lefkowitz, M., Blake, R. R., & Mouton, J. S. Status factors in pedestrian violation of traffic signals. *Journal of Abnormal and Social Psychology*, 1955, **51**, 704–706.

Lemert, E. M. *Social pathology.* New York: McGraw-Hill, 1951.

Lemert, E. M. Paranoia and the dynamics of exclusion. *Sociometry*, 1962, **25**, 2–25.

Lemert, E. M. *Human deviance, social problems, and social control.* Englewood Cliffs, N.J.: Prentice-Hall, 1967.

Leontief, W. Theoretical assumptions and non-observed fact. *American Economic Review*, 1971, **61**, 1–7.

Lerner, D. Effective propaganda: Conditions and evaluations. In W. Schramm (Ed.), *The process and effects of mass communication.* (1st ed.) Urbana, Ill.: University of Illinois Press, 1959.

Levitz, L. S. The experimental induction of compulsive gambling behaviors. *Dissertation Abstracts International*, 1971, **32**, 1216–1217.

Levitz, L. S., & Ullmann, L. P. Manipulation of indications of disturbed thinking in normal subjects. *Journal of Consulting and Clinical Psychology*, 1969, **33**, 633–641.

Levy, L. H. Anxiety behavior and behavior scientists' behavior. *American Psychologist*, 1961, **16**, 66–68.

Levy, M. R., & Kahn, M. W. Interpreter bias on the Rorschach Test as a function of patients' socio-economic status. *Journal of Projective Techniques and Personality Assessment*, 1970, **34**, 106–112.

Lewin, K. *Principles of topological psychology.* New York: McGraw-Hill, 1936.

Lewin, K. Group decision and social change. In T. M. Newcomb & E. L. Hartley (Eds.),

Readings in social psychology. New York: Holt, Rinehart and Winston, 1947. Pp. 330–344.

Lewin, K., Lippitt, R., & White, R. Patterns of aggressive behavior in experimentally created 'social climates.' *Journal of Social Psychology*, 1939, **10**, 271–299.

Lichtman, C. M., & Hunt, R. G. Personality and organization theory: A review of some conceptual literature. *Psychological Bulletin*, 1971, **76**, 271–294.

Liebert, R. M., & Fernandez, L. E. Vicarious reward and task complexity as determinants of imitative learning. *Psychological Reports*, 1969, **25**, 531–534.

Liebert, R. M., & Fernandez, L. E. Effects of vicarious consequences on imitative performances. *Child Development*, 1970, **41**, 847–852.

Liebert, R., & Neale, J. M. TV violence and child aggression. *Psychology Today*, 1972, **5**, 38–40.

Liebert, R. M., & Spiegler, M. D. *Personality: An introduction to theory and research.* Homewood, Ill.: Dorsey Press, 1970.

Liebert, R. M., & Swenson, S. A. Association and abstraction as mechanisms of imitative learning. *Developmental Psychology*, 1971, **4**, 289–294.

Lifton, R. J. Home by ship: Reaction patterns of American prisoners of war repatriated from North Korea. *American Journal of Psychiatry*, 1954, **110**, 732–739.

Lifton, R. J. "Thought reform" of western civilians in Chinese communist prisons. *Psychiatry*, 1956, **19**, 173–195.

Lifton, R. J. Thought reform of Chinese intellectuals: A psychiatric evaluation. *Journal of Social Issues*, 1957, **13**(3), 5–20.

Lifton, R. J. *Thought reform and the psychology of totalism: A study of "brainwashing" in China.* New York: Norton, 1961.

Lifton, R. J. *History and human survival.* New York: Random House, 1970.

Lilly, J. C. Mental effects of education of ordinary levels of physical stimuli on intact, healthy persons. *Psychiatric Research Reports*, 1956, **5**, 1–9.

Lindsley, O. R. Operant conditioning methods applied to research in chronic schizophrenia. *Psychiatric Research Reports*, 1956, **5**, 118–153.

Lindsley, O. R. Characteristics of the behavior of chronic psychotics as revealed by free-operant conditioning methods. *Diseases of the Nervous System*, Monograph supplement, 1960, **21**, 66–78.

Lindsley, O. R., Skinner, B. F., & Solomon, H. C. *Studies in behavior therapy, Status Report I.* Waltham, Mass.: Metropolitan State Hospital, 1953.

Linton, R. *The cultural background of personality.* New York: Appleton-Century-Crofts, 1945.

Little, K. B. Personal space. *Journal of Experimental Social Psychology*, 1965, **1**, 237–247.

Lloyd, K. E., & Garlington, W. K. Weekly variations in performance on a token economy psychiatric ward. *Behaviour Research and Therapy*, 1968, **6**, 407–410.

Loeb, M. B. Role-definition in the social world of a psychiatric hospital. In M. Greenblatt, D. J. Levinson, and R. H. Williams (Eds.), *The patient and the mental hospital.* New York: Free Press, 1957.

London, P. *The modes and morals of psychotherapy.* New York: Holt, Rinehart and Winston, 1964.

Lovaas, O. I. Effect of exposure to symbolic aggression on aggressive behavior. *Child Development*, 1961, **32**, 37–44.

Lovaas, O. I. Some studies on the treatment of childhood schizophrenia. In J. M. Shlien (Ed.), *Research in psychotherapy.* Washington, D.C.: American Psychological Association, 1968. Pp. 103–121.

Lovaas, O. I., Berberich, J. P., Perloff, B. F., & Schaeffer, B. Acquisition of imitative speech by schizophrenic children. *Science*, 1966, **151**, 705–707.

Lovaas, O. I., Freitag, G., Gold, V. J., & Kassorla, I. C. Experimental studies in childhood schizophrenia: Analysis of self-destructive behavior. *Journal of Experimental Child Psychology*, 1965, **2**, 67–84.

Lovaas, O. I., Freitas, L., Nelson, K., and Whalen, C. The establishment of imitation and its use for the development of complex behavior in schizophrenic children. *Behaviour Research and Therapy*, 1967, **5**, 171–181.

Lovaas, O. I., Schaeffer, B., & Simmons, J. Q. Building social behavior in autistic children by use of electric shock. *Journal of Experimental Research in Personality*, 1965, **1**, 99–109.

Luft, J. Implicit hypotheses and clinical predictions. *Journal of Abnormal and Social Psychology*, 1950, **45**, 756–760.

Luft, J. Differences in prediction based on hearing versus reading verbatim clinical interviews. *Journal of Consulting Psychology*, 1951, **15**, 115–119.

Lundin, R. W. *Personality: A behavioral analysis.* London: Macmillan, 1969.

Luria, A. R. *The role of speech in the regulation of normal and abnormal behavior.* Oxford: Pergamon, 1961.

Luria, S. E. Reply to E. Chargaff. *Science*, 1968, **160**, 603–604.

Lynd, R. S., & Lynd, H. M. *Middletown: A study in contemporary culture.* New York: Harcourt Brace Jovanovich, 1929.

Macaulay, J. R., & Berkowitz, L. (Eds.) *Altruism and helping behavior.* New York: Academic Press, 1970.

MacKinnon, D. W. Personality. In C. P. Stone (Ed.), *Annual review of psychology*, Vol. 2. Palo Alto, Calif.: Annual Reviews, 1951. Pp. 113–136.

Maddi, S. R. *Personality theories: A comparative analysis.* Homewood, Ill.: Dorsey Press, 1968.

Madsen, C. H., Jr., & Ullmann, L. P. Innovations in the desensitization of frigidity. *Behaviour Research and Therapy*, 1967, **5**, 67–68.

Maier, N. R. F. *Principles of human relations' application to management.* New York: Wiley, 1952.

Makarenko, A. S. *Road to life.* London: Stanley Nott, 1936.

Mann, J. *Encounter: A weekend with intimate strangers.* New York: Grossman, 1970.

Mann, J. H. The relationship between cognitive, behavioral, and affective aspects of racial prejudice. *Journal of Social Psychology*, 1959, **49**, 223–228.

Mann, L., & Hagevik, G. The new environmentalism: Behaviorism and design. *Journal of the American Institute of Planners*, 1971, **37**, 344–347.

Manning, E. J. Personal validation: Replication of Forer's study. *Psychological Reports*, 1968, **23**, 181–182.

Manuel, F. E. Introduction. In F. E. Manuel (Ed.), *Utopias and utopian thought.* Boston: Beacon Press, 1967. Pp. vii–xxiv. (a)

Manuel, F. E. Toward a psychological history of utopias. In F. E. Manuel (Ed.), *Utopias and utopian thought.* Boston: Beacon Press, 1967. Pp. 69–101. (b)

Maris, R. W. *Social forces in urban suicide.* Homewood, Ill.: Dorsey Press, 1969.

Marks, J., Sonada, B., & Schalock, R. Reinforcement versus relationship therapy for schizophrenics. *Journal of Abnormal Psychology*, 1968, **73**, 397–402.

Marquis, J. N. Orgasmic reorientation: Changing sexual object choice through controlling masturbation fantasies. Paper presented at California State Psychological Association Annual Meeting, 1970.

Martin, L. J. Effectiveness of international propaganda. *The Annals of the American Academy of Political and Social Science*, 1971, **398**, 61–70.

Martin, M., Burkholder, R., Rosenthal, T. L., Tharp, R. L., & Thorne, G. L. Programming behavior change and reintegration into school milieu of extreme adolescent deviates. *Behaviour Research and Therapy*, 1968, **6**, 371–383.

Masling, J. The influence of situational and interpersonal variables in projective testing. *Psychological Bulletin*, 1960, **57**, 65–85.

Maslow, A. H. Our maligned animal nature. *Journal of Psychology*, 1949, **28**, 273–278.

Maslow, A. H. *Motivation and personality*. New York: Harper & Row, 1954.

Maslow, A. H. *Toward a psychology of being*. (2nd ed.) Princeton, N.J.: Van Nostrand, 1968.

Maslow, A. H. *The farther reaches of human nature*. New York: Viking, 1971.

Masters, W. H., & Johnson, V. E. *Human sexual response*. Boston: Little, Brown, 1966.

Masters, W. H., & Johnson, V. E. *Human sexual inadequacy*. Boston: Little, Brown, 1970.

Matarazzo, J. D. The interview. In B. B. Wolman (Ed.), *Handbook of clinical psychology*. New York: McGraw-Hill, 1965, 403–450.

May, R. *Man's search for himself*. New York: Norton, 1953.

May, R. The origins and significance of the existential movement in psychology. In R. May (Ed.), *Existence*. New York: Basic Books, 1958. Pp. 3–36.

May, R. (Ed.) *Existential psychology*. New York: Random House, 1961.

Mayer, J. *Overweight*. Englewood Cliffs, N.J.: Prentice-Hall, 1968.

Mayer, M. The full and sometimes very surprising story of Ocean Hill, the Teachers' Union and the Teacher Strikes of 1968. *New York Times Magazine*, Feb. 2, 1969, 18–40.

McClelland, D. C. *Personality*. New York: Dryden Press, 1951.

McClelland, D. C. *The achieving society*. Princeton, N.J.: Van Nostrand, 1961.

McCelland, D. C., Atkinson, J. W., Clark, R. A., & Lowell, E. L. *The achievement motive*. New York: Appleton-Century-Crofts, 1953.

McDougall, W. *Introduction to psychology*. London: Methuen, 1908.

McDougall, W. *The energies of men: A study of the fundamentals of dynamic psychology*. London: Methuen, 1932.

McGinnies, E. *Social behavior: A functional analysis*. Boston: Houghton Mifflin, 1970.

McGuigan, F. J. The experimenter: A neglected stimulus object. *Psychological Bulletin*, 1963, **60**, 421–428.

McGuire, W. J. The nature of attitudes and attitude change. In G. Lindzey and E. Aronson (Eds.), *The handbook of social psychology* (2nd ed.), Vol. 3. Reading, Mass.: Addison-Wesley, 1969. Pp. 136–314.

McHugh, P. *Defining the situation*. Indianapolis: Bobbs-Merrill, 1968.

McKeachie, W. Lipstick as a determiner of first impressions of personality. *Journal of Social Psychology*, 1952, **36**, 241–244.

McKelway, S. C. Old 880. In W. B. Gibson (Ed.), *The fine art of swindling*. New York: Grosset & Dunlap, 1966. Pp. 110–111.

McLaughlin, B. *Learning and social behavior*. New York: Free Press, 1971.

McLuhan, H. M. *Understanding media: The extensions of man*. New York: McGraw-Hill, 1964.

McMains, M. J., & Liebert, R. M. Influence of discrepancies between successively modeled self-reward criteria on the adoption of a self-imposed standard. *Journal of Personality and Social Psychology*, 1968, **8**, 166–171.

McNair, D. M., Lorr, M., & Callahan, D. M. Patient and therapist influences on quitting psychotherapy. *Journal of Consulting Psychology*, 1963, **27**, 10–17.

McReynolds, P. A restricted conceptualization of human anxiety and motivation. *Psychological Reports Monograph*, 1956, Supp. 6, 293–312.

McReynolds, P. Anxiety as related to incongruencies between values and feelings. *Psychological Record*, 1958, **8**, 57–66.

McReynolds, P. Anxiety, perception, and schizophrenia. In D. Jackson (Ed.), *The etiology of schizophrenia*. New York: Basic Books, 1960. Pp. 248–292.

McReynolds, P. (Ed.) *Four early works on motivation.* Gainsville, Fla.: Scholars Facsimiles and Reprints, 1969.

Mead, G. H. *Mind, self, and society: From the standpoint of a social behaviorist.* Chicago: University of Chicago Press, 1934.

Mead, M. *Sex and temperament in three primitive societies.* New York: Morrow, 1935.

Mead, M. *And keep your powder dry: An anthropologist looks at America.* New York: W. Morrow, 1942.

Meehl, P. E. *Clinical versus statistical prediction.* Minneapolis: University of Minnesota Press, 1954.

Meehl, P. E. Seer over sign: The first good example. *Journal of Experimental Research in Personality*, 1965, **1**, 27–32.

Meeker, W. B., & Barber, T. X. Toward an explanation of stage hypnosis. *Journal of Abnormal Psychology*, 1971, **77**, 61–70.

Mehrabian, A. Inference of attitudes from the posture, orientation, and distance of a communicator. *Journal of Consulting and Clinical Psychology*, 1968, **32**, 296–308. (a)

Mehrabian, A. Relationship of attitude to seated posture, orientation and distance. *Journal of Personality and Social Psychology*, 1968, **10**, 26–30. (b)

Mehrabian, A. *An analysis of personality theories.* Englewood Cliffs, N.J.: Prentice-Hall, 1968. (c)

Mehrabian, A. Significance of posture and position in the communication of attitude and status relationships. *Psychological Bulletin*, 1969, **71**, 359–372.

Mehrabian, A. *Tactics of social influence.* Englewood Cliffs, N.J.: Prentice-Hall, 1970.

Mehrabian, A. *Silent messages.* Belmont, Calif.: Wadsworth, 1971.

Mehrabian, A., & Diamond, S. G. Effects of furniture arrangement, props and personality on social interaction. *Journal of Personality and Social Psychology*, 1971, **20**, 18–30.

Mehrabian, A., & Ferris, S. R. Inference of attitudes from nonverbal communication in two channels. *Journal of Consulting Psychology*, 1967, **31**, 248–252.

Meichenbaum, D. H. Effects of social reinforcement on the level of abstraction in schizophrenics. *Journal of Abnormal and Social Psychology*, 1966, **71**, 354–362.

Meichenbaum, D. H., Bowers, K. S., & Ross, R. R. Modification of classroom behavior of institutionalized female adolescent offenders. *Behaviour Research and Therapy*, 1968, **6**, 343–353.

Meichenbaum, D. H., Bowers, K. S., & Ross, R. R. A behavioral analysis of teacher expectancy effect. *Journal of Personality and Social Psychology*, 1969, **13**, 306–316.

Meichenbaum, D., & Goodman, J. The developmental control of operant motor responding by verbal operants. *Journal of Experimental Child Psychology*, 1969, **7**, 553–565. (a)

Meichenbaum, D., & Goodman, J. Reflection-impulsivity and verbal control of motor behavior. *Child Development*, 1969, **40**, 785–797. (b)

Meichenbaum, D., & Goodman, J. Training impulsive children to talk to themselves: A means of developing self-control. *Journal of Abnormal Psychology*, 1971, **77**, 115–126.

Meichenbaum, D. H., & Smart, I. Use of direct expectancy to modify academic performance and attitudes of college students. *Journal of Counseling Psychology*, 1971, **18**, 531–535.

Meisels, M., & Guardo, C. J. Development of personal space schemata. *Child Development*, 1969, **40**, 1167–1178.

Melton, A. W. Learning. In C. P. Stone (Ed.), *Annual review of psychology*, Vol. 1. Stanford, Calif.: Annual Review, 1950.

Menen, A. *The space within the heart.* New York: McGraw-Hill, 1970.

Menninger, K. The anatomy and physiology of the personality. *Bulletin Menninger Clinic*, 1950, **14**, 75–80.

Mertens, G. C. Towards (or the flank attacks towards) the expanded behavioral laboratory: The experimental community. Paper presented at Annual Meeting of Western Psychological Association, San Francisco, California, April 1971.

Merton, R. K. The self-fulfilling prophecy. *Antioch Review*, 1948, **8**, 193–210.

Merton, R. K. Patterns of influence: Local and cosmopolitan influentials. In R. K. Merton (Ed.), *Social theory and social structure*, revised edition. New York: Free Press, 1957. Pp. 387–420. (a)

Merton, R. K. Priorities in scientific discovery: A chapter in the sociology of science. *American Sociological Review*, 1957, **22**, 635–659. (b)

Messick, S., & Jackson, D. N. Acquiescence and the factorial interpretation of the MMPI. *Psychological Bulletin*, 1961, **58**, 299–304.

Mesthene, E. G. *Technological change: Its impact on man and society*. New York: Mentor, 1970.

Metz, J. R. Conditioning generalized imitation in autistic children. *Journal of Experimental Child Psychology*, 1965, **2**, 389–399.

Metzger, W. P. Generalizations about national character: An analytical essay. In L. Gottschalk (Ed.), *Generalization in the writing of history*. Chicago: University of Chicago Press, 1963.

Michelson, W. *Man and his urban environment*. Reading, Mass.: Addison-Wesley, 1970.

Milgram, S. Behavioral study of obedience. *Journal of Abnormal and Social Psychology*, 1963, **67**, 371–378.

Milgram, S. Some conditions of obedience and disobedience to authority. *Human Relations*, 1965, **18**, 57–76.

Milgram, S., & Toch, H. Collective behavior: Crowds and social movements. In G. Lindzey & E. Aronson (Eds.), *The handbook of social psychology*, Vol. 2. Reading, Mass.: Addison-Wesley, 1969. Pp. 507–610.

Miller, G. A., Galanter, E., & Pribram, K. H. *Plans and the structure of behavior*. New York: Holt, Rinehart and Winston, 1960.

Miller, L. K. Freedom money: A token economy approach to organizing self-help activities among low-income families. O.E.O. Grant CG 8719 A/O: Annual Report #1, 1969.

Miller, N. E. Learning of visceral and glandular responses. *Science*, 1969, **163**, 434–445.

Miller, N. E., & DiCara, L. Instrumental learning of heart-rate changes in curarized rats: Shaping and specificity to discriminative stimulus. *Journal of Comparative and Physiological Psychology*, 1967, **63**, 12–19.

Miller, R. J., Lundy, R. M., & Galbraith, G. G. Effects of hypnotically induced hallucination of a color filter. *Journal of Abnormal Psychology*, 1970, **76**, 316–319.

Millett, K. *Sexual politics*. Garden City, N.Y.: Doubleday, 1970.

Millon, T. (Ed.) *Approaches to personality*. New York: Pitman, 1968.

Mischel, W. Theory and research on the antecedents of self-imposed delay of reward. In B. A. Maher (Ed.), *Progress of experimental personality research*, III. New York: Academic Press, 1966. Pp. 85–132.

Mischel, W. *Personality and assessment*. New York: Wiley, 1968.

Mischel, W. *Introduction to personality*. New York: Holt, Rinehart and Winston, 1971.

Mischel, W., & Grusec, J. Waiting for rewards and punishments: Effects of time and probability on choice. *Journal of Personality and Social Psychology*, 1967, **5**, 24–31.

Mischel, W., & Masters, J. C. Effects of probability of reward attainment on responses to frustration. *Journal of Personality and Social Psychology*, 1966, **3**, 390–396.

Mischel, W., & Staub, E. The effects of expectancy on waiting and working for larger rewards. *Journal of Personality and Social Psychology*, 1965, **2**, 625–633.

Mithaug, D. E., & Burgess, R. L. The effects of differential reinforcement contingencies in the development of social cooperation. *Journal of Experimental Child Psychology,* 1968, **6,** 402–426.

Modigliani, A. Embarrassment, face work, and eye contact: Testing a theory of embarrassment. *Journal of Personality and Social Psychology,* 1971, **17,** 15–24.

Money, J. *Sex errors of the body: Dilemmas, education, counseling.* Baltimore: Johns Hopkins Press, 1968.

Montessori, M. *The Montessori method.* New York: Schocken Books, 1964.

Moore, H. T. The comparative influence of majority and expert opinion. *American Journal of Psychology,* 1921, **32,** 16–20.

Moore, W. E. *The conduct of the corporation.* New York: Random House, Vintage Edition, 1962.

Moore, W. E. *The professions: Roles and rules.* New York: Russell Sage, 1970.

Moreno, J. L. *Who shall survive? A new approach to the problems of human interrelations.* Washington, D.C.: Nervous and Mental Disease Publishing Co., 1934. (Rev. ed. Beacon House, 1953).

Morris, D. Must we have zoos? *Life,* Nov. 8, 1968, **65,** 75–80.

Morris, W. (Ed.) *The American heritage dictionary.* New York: American Heritage Publishing Co., 1969.

Mowrer, O. H. A stimulus-response analysis of anxiety and its role as a reinforcing agent. *Psychological Review,* 1939, **46,** 553–566.

Mower, O. H. What is normal behavior? In L. A. Pennington & I. A. Berg (Eds.), *An introduction to clinical psychology.* New York: Ronald Press, 1948. Pp. 17–46.

Mowrer, O. H. *Learning theory and personality dynamics.* New York: Ronald Press, 1950.

Mowrer, O. H. *Learning theory and the symbolic process.* New York: Wiley, 1960.

Mowrer, O. H. *The new group therapy.* Princeton, N.J.: Van Nostrand, 1964.

Mullahy, P. (Ed.) *The contributions of Harry Stack Sullivan.* New York: Hermitage House, 1952.

Muller, H. J. *The children of Frankenstein: A primer on modern technology and human values.* Bloomington, Ind.: Indiana University Press, 1970.

Murchison, C. A. *History of psychology in autobiography.* Worcester, Mass. Clark University Press, 1930.

Murphy, G. *Personality.* New York: Harper & Row, 1947.

Murphy, G., Murphy, L. B., & Newcomb, T. M. *Experimental social psychology.* New York: Harper & Row, 1937.

Murray, H. A. *Explorations in personality.* New York: Oxford University Press, 1938.

Murray, J. P., Rubinstein, E. A., & Comstock, S. A. (Eds.) *Television and social behavior.* Vol. 2. *Television and social learning.* Rockville, Md.: National Institute of Mental Health, 1972.

Nash, M. M., & Zimring, F. M. Prediction of reaction to placebo. *Journal of Abnormal Psychology,* 1969, **74,** 568–573.

Negley, G., & Patrick, J. M. *The quest for utopia.* New York: Doubleday (Henry Schuman, Inc., 1952), 1962.

Neill, A. S. *Summerhill: A radical approach to child rearing.* New York: Hart Publishing Co., 1960.

Newcomb, T. M. *Social psychology.* New York: Dryden Press, 1950.

Nikelly, A. G. Ethical issues in research on student protest. *American Psychologist,* 1971, **26,** 475–478.

Nisbet, R. A. *Community and power.* New York: Oxford University Press, 1962.

Nisbet, R. A. *Emile Durkheim.* Englewood Cliffs, N.J.: Prentice-Hall, 1965.

Nisbet, R. A. *The social bond: An introduction to the study of society.* New York: Knopf, 1970.

Nisbett, R. E. Determinants of food intake in obesity. *Science*, 1968, **159**, 1254–1255. (a)

Nisbett, R. E. Taste, deprivation, and weight determinants of eating behavior. *Journal of Personality and Social Psychology*, 1968, **10**, 104–116. (b)

Nisbett, R. E., & Kanouse, D. E. Obesity, food deprivation, and supermarket shopping behavior. *Journal of Personality and Social Psychology*, 1969, **12**, 389–394.

Noyes, J. H. *Male continence*. Oneida, N.Y.: Office of the Oneida Circular, 1872.

Ober, D. C. The modification of smoking behavior. Unpublished doctoral dissertation, University of Illinois, 1967.

O'Leary, K. D. The effects of self-instruction on immoral behavior *Journal of Experimental Child Psychology*, 1968, **6**, 297–301.

O'Leary, K. D., & Becker, W. C. Behavior modification of an adjustment class: A token reinforcement program. *Exceptional Children*, 1967, **33**, 637–642.

O'Leary, K. D., Becker, W. C., Evans, M. B., & Saudargas, R. A. A token reinforcement program in a public school: A replication and systematic analysis. *Journal of Applied Behavior Analysis*, 1969, **2**, 3–13.

O'Leary, K. D., & Drabman, R. Token reinforcement program in the classroom: A review. *Psychological Bulletin*, 1971, **5**, 379–398.

O'Leary, K. D., & O'Leary, S. G. (Eds.) *Classroom management*. New York: Pergamon, 1972.

Orlansky, H. Infant care and personality. *Psychological Bulletin*, 1949, **46**, 1–48.

Orne, M. T. The nature of hypnosis: Artifact and essence. *Journal of Abnormal and Social Psychology*, 1959, **58**, 277–299.

Orne, M. T. On the social psychology of the psychological experiment: With particular reference to demand characteristics and their implication. *American Psychologist*, 1962, **17**, 776–783.

Orne, M. T., & Evans, F. J. Social control in the psychological experiment: Antisocial behavior and hypnosis. *Journal of Personality and Social Psychology*, 1965, **1**, 189–200.

Orne, M. T., & Scheibe, K. E. The contribution of nondeprivation factors in the production of sensory deprivation effects: The psychology of the panic button. *Journal of Abnormal and Social Psychology*, 1964, **68**, 3–12.

Orne, M. T., Sheehan, P. W., & Evans, F. J. Occurrence of posthypnotic behavior outside the experimental setting. *Journal of Personality and Social Psychology*, 1968, **9**, 189–196.

Orwell, G. *1984*. New York: Harcourt Brace Jovanovich, 1949.

Osgood, C. E., & Suci, G. J. Factor analysis of meaning. *Journal of Experimental Psychology*, 1955, **50**, 325–338.

Osgood, C. E., Suci, G. J., & Tannenbaum, P. H. *The measurement of meaning*. Urbana, Ill.: University of Illinois Press, 1957.

Oskamp, S. The relationship of clinical experience and training methods in several criteria of clinical prediction. *Psychological Monographs*, 1962, **76** (28, Whole No. 547).

Oskamp, S. Overconfidence in case study judgments. *Journal of Consulting Psychology*, 1965, **29**, 261–265.

Parrish, M., Lundy, R. M., & Leibowitz, H. W. Hypnotic age-regression and magnitude of the Ponzo and Poggendorff illusions. *Science*, 1968, **159**, 1375–1376.

Parsons, T. The principal structures of community. In C. Friedrich (Ed.), *Community* (Nomas II). New York: Liberal Arts Press, 1959.

Pascal, G. R. *Behavioral change in the clinic: A systematic approach*. New York: Grune & Stratton, 1959.

Pastore, N. *The nature-nurture controversy.* New York: King's Crown Press, 1949.

Patterson, G. R. An application of conditioning techniques to the control of a hyperactive child. In L. P. Ullmann and L. Krasner (Eds.), *Case studies in behavior modification.* New York: Holt, Rinehart and Winston, 1965. Pp. 370–375.

Patterson, G. R. Behavioral techniques based upon social learning: An additional base for developing behavior modification technologies. In C. M. Franks (Ed.), *Behavior therapy: Appraisal and status.* New York: McGraw-Hill, 1969. Pp. 341–374.

Patterson, G. R., & Reid, J. B. Reciprocity and coercion: Two facets of social systems. In C. Neuringer and J. L. Michael (Eds.), *Behavior modification in clinical psychology.* New York: Appleton-Century-Crofts, 1970. Pp. 133–137.

Patterson, G. R., Shaw, D. A., & Ebner, M. J. Teachers, peers, and parents as agents of change in the classroom. In F. A. M. Benson (Ed.), *Modifying deviant social behaviors in various classroom settings.* Monograph No. 1, Department of Special Education, University of Oregon, 1969.

Pattison, E. M. Evaluation studies of group psychotherapy. *International Journal of Psychiatry,* 1967, **4,** 333–343.

Paul, G. L. *Insight vs. desensitization in psychotherapy.* Stanford, Calif.: Stanford University Press, 1966.

Paul, G. L. Insight versus desensitization in psychotherapy two years after termination. *Journal of Consulting Psychology,* 1967, **31,** 333–348.

Paul, G. L. Two-year follow-up of systematic desensitization in therapy groups. *Journal of Abnormal Psychology,* 1968, **73,** 119–130.

Paul, G. L. Behavior modification research: Design and tactics. In C. M. Franks (Ed.), *Behavior therapy: Appraisal and status.* New York: McGraw-Hill, 1969. Pp. 23–62. (a)

Paul, G. L. Outcome of systematic desensitization. I: Background, procedures and uncontrolled reports of individual treatment. In C. M. Franks (Ed.), *Behavior therapy: Appraisal and status.* New York: McGraw-Hill, 1969. Pp. 63–104. (b)

Paul, G. L. Outcome of systematic desensitization. II: Controlled investigations of individual treatment, technique variations, and current status. In C. M. Franks (Ed.), *Behavior therapy: Appraisal and status.* New York: McGraw-Hill, 1969. Pp. 105–159. (c)

Paul, G. L. Inhibition of physiological response to stressful imagery by relaxation training and hypnotically suggested relaxation. *Behaviour Research and Therapy,* 1969, **7,** 249–256. (d)

Pavlov, I. P. *Conditioned reflexes: An investigation of the physiological activities of the cerebral cortex.* London: Oxford University Press, 1927.

Pellegrini, R. J. Some effects of seating position on social perception. *Psychological Reports,* 1971, **28,** 887–893.

Perls, F. *Ego, hunger and aggression.* New York: Vintage Books, 1969.

Perls, F., Hefferline, R. F., & Goodman, P. *Gestalt therapy.* New York: Julian Press, 1951.

Pervin, L. A. *Personality: Theory, assessment, and research.* New York: Wiley, 1970.

Peterson, R. F. Some experiments on the organization of a class of imitative behaviors. *Journal of Applied Behavior Analysis,* 1968, **1,** 225–235.

Peterson, R. F., & Whitehurst, G. J. A variable influencing the performance of generalized imitative behaviors. *Journal of Applied Behavior Analysis,* 1971, **4,** 1–9.

Petras, J. W. Changes of emphasis in the sociology of W. I. Thomas. *Journal of the History of Behavioral Science,* 1970, **6,** 70–79.

Phillips, E. L. *Psychotherapy: A modern theory and practice.* Englewood Cliffs, N.J.: Prentice-Hall, 1956.

Piaget, J. *Judgment and reasoning in the child*. New York: Harcourt Brace Jovanovich, 1928.

Piaget, J. *The child's conception of the world*. New York: Harcourt Brace Jovanovich, 1929.

Piaget, J. *Construction of reality in the child*. New York: Basic Books, 1954.

Piaget, J. *Logic and psychology*. New York: Basic Books, 1957.

Plath, D. W. (Ed.) *Aware of Utopia*. Urbana, Ill.: University of Illinois Press, 1971.

Plato, The Republic. In B. Jowett, *The dialogues of Plato*. New York: Random House, 1937. Pp. 591–879.

Plowden, L. (Ch.) *Children and their primary schools*. A report of the Central Advisory Council for Education (England), Vol. 1. New York: British Information Service, 1967.

Polya, G. *How to solve it*. Garden City, N.Y.: Doubleday, 1957.

Powdermaker, F. B., & Frank, J. B. *Group psychotherapy: Studies in methodology of research and therapy*. Cambridge, Mass.: Harvard University Press, 1953.

Premack, D. Toward empirical behavior laws. I: Positive reinforcement. *Psychological Review*, 1959, **66**, 219–233.

Presthus, R. *The organizational society*. New York: Knopf, 1962.

Priest, R. F., & Sawyer, J. Proximity and peership: Bases of balance in interpersonal attraction. *American Journal of Sociology*, 1967, **72**, 633–649.

Proshansky, H. W., Ittelson, W. H., & Rivlin, L. G. (Eds.), *Environmental psychology*. New York: Holt, Rinehart and Winston, 1970.

Rachman, S. Introduction to behaviour therapy. *Behaviour Research and Therapy*, 1963, **1**, 3–15.

Rachman, S. Studies in desensitization. II. Flooding. *Behaviour Research and Therapy*, 1966, **4**, 1–6.

Rachman, S., & Teasdale, J. *Aversion therapy and behaviour disorders: An analysis*. London: Routledge and Kegan Paul, 1969.

Rank, O. *The trauma of birth*. London: Routledge and Kegan Paul, 1929.

Razin, A. M. A-B variable in psychotherapy: A critical review. *Psychological Bulletin*, 1971, **75**, 1–21.

Razran, G. H. S. Conditioning away social bias by the luncheon technique. *Psychological Bulletin*, 1938, **35**, 693.

Razran, G. H. S. A quantitative study of meaning by a conditioned salivary technique (semantic conditioning). *Science*, 1939, **90**, 89–90.

Razran, G. H. S. Conditioned response changes in rating and appraising sociopolitical slogans. *Psychological Bulletin*, 1940, **37**, 481.

Redd, W. H., & Birnbrauer, J. S. Adults as discriminative stimuli for different reinforcement contingencies with retarded children. *Journal of Experimental Child Psychology*, 1969, **7**, 440–447.

Rehm, L. P., & Marston, A. R. Reduction of social anxiety through modification of self-reinforcement: An instigation therapy technique. *Journal of Consulting and Clinical Psychology*, 1968, **32**, 565–574.

Reich, C. A. *The greening of America*. New York: Random House, 1970.

Reisman, J. M. *The development of clinical psychology*. New York: Appleton-Century-Crofts, 1966.

Rhyne, L. D., & Ullmann, L. P. Graffiti: A nonreactive measure? *Psychological Record*, 1972, **22**, 255–258.

Rickard, H. C. Selected group psychotherapy evaluation studies. *Journal of General Psychology*, 1962, **67**, 35–50.

Rickard, H. C., Dignam, P. J., & Horner, R. F. Verbal manipulation in a psychotherapeutic relationship. *Journal of Clinical Psychology*, 1960, **16**, 364–367.

Riegel, K. F. Influence of economic and political ideologies on the development of developmental psychology. *Psychological Bulletin*, 1972, **78**, 129–141.

Riesman, D. Some questions about the study of American character in the twentieth century. *The Annals of the American Academy of Political and Social Science*, 1967, **370**, 36–47.

Riesman, D., Glazer, N., & Denney, R. *The lonely crowd: A study of a changing American character.* New Haven, Conn.: Yale University Press, 1950.

Risley, T. R. The effects and side-effects of punishing the autistic behaviors of a deviant child. *Journal of Applied Behavior Analysis*, 1968, **1**, 21–34.

Roberts, R. E. *The new communes: Coming together in America.* Englewood Cliffs, N.J.: Prentice-Hall, 1971.

Roe, A. A psychological study of environment, psychologists and anthropologists, and a comparison with biological and physical scientists. Washington: American Psychological Association, 1953. (a)

Roe, A. *The making of a scientist.* New York: Dodd, Mead, 1953. (b)

Roe, A. Individual motivation and personal factors in career choice. In F. N. Arnhoff, E. A. Rubinstein, & J. C. Speisman (Eds.), *Manpower for mental health.* Chicago, Ill.: Aldine, 1969. Pp. 131–148.

Roethlisberger, F. J. & Dickson, W. J. *Management and the worker.* Cambridge, Mass.: Harvard University Press, 1939.

Rogers, C. R. *Client-centered therapy: Its current practice, implications and theory.* Boston: Houghton Mifflin, 1951.

Rogers, C. R. A theory of therapy, personality, and interpersonal relationships as developed in the client-centered framework. In S. Koch (Ed.), *Psychology: A study of a science*, Vol. II: *General systematic formulations, learning, and special processes.* New York: McGraw-Hill 1959.

Rogers, C. R. *On becoming a person: A therapist's view of psychotherapy.* Boston: Houghton Mifflin, 1961.

Rogers, C. R. Process of the basic encounter group. In J. F. T. Bugental (Ed.), *Challenges of humanistic psychology.* New York: McGraw-Hill, 1967. Pp. 261–276.

Rogers, C. R., & Skinner, B. F. Some issues concerning the control of human behavior: A symposium. *Science*, 1956, **124**, 1057–1066.

Rogers, D. *110 Livingston Street: Politics and bureaucracy in the New York City schools.* New York: Random House, 1968.

Rogow, A. A. *The psychiatrists.* New York: Dell, 1970.

Rorer, L. G. The great response-style myth. *Psychological Bulletin*, 1965, **63**, 129–156.

Rosekrans, M. A. Imitation in children as a function of perceived similarity to a social model and vicarious reinforcement. *Journal of Personality and Social Psychology*, 1967, **7**, 307–315.

Rosenberg, B. G., & Sutton-Smith, B. *Sex and identity.* New York: Holt, Rinehart and Winston, 1972.

Rosenhan, D. On the social psychology of hypnosis research. In J. E. Gordon (Ed.), *Handbook of clinical and experimental hypnosis.* New York: Macmillan, 1967. Pp. 481–510.

Rosenhan, D., & White, G. M. Observation and rehearsal as determinants of prosocial behavior. *Journal of Personality and Social Psychology*, 1967, **5**, 424–431.

Rosenthal, J. A tale of one city. *New York Times Magazine*, Dec. 24, 1971, 16–26.

Rosenthal, R. *Experimenter effects in behavioral research.* New York: Appleton-Century-Crofts, 1966.

Rosenthal, R. Covert communication in the psychological experiment. *Psychological Bulletin*, 1967, **5**, 356–367.

Rosenthal, R., & Fode, K. L. Psychology of the scientist. V: Three experiments in experimenter bias. *Psychological Reports*, 1963, **12**, 491–511.

Rosenthal, R., & Jacobson, L. Teachers' expectancies: Determinants of pupils' I.Q. gains. *Psychological Reports*, 1966, **19**, 115–118.

Rosenthal, R., & Jacobson, L. *Pygmalion in the classroom.* New York: Holt, Rinehart and Winston, 1968.

Rosenthal, T. L., Moore, W. B., Dorfman, H., & Nelson, B. Vicarious acquisition of a simple concept with experimenter as model. *Behaviour Research and Therapy*, 1971, **9**, 219–227.

Rosenthal, T. L., & White, G. M. On the importance of hair in students' clinical inference. *Journal of Clinical Psychology*, 1972, **28**, 43–46.

Rosenthal, T. L., Zimmerman, B. J., & Durning, K. Observationally induced changes in children's interrogative classes. *Journal of Personality and Social Psychology*, 1970, **16**, 681–688.

Ross, E. A. *Social psychology.* New York: Macmillan, 1908.

Roszak, T. *The making of a counter culture.* New York: Doubleday, 1969.

Rothman, D. J. *The discovery of the asylum.* Boston: Little, Brown, 1971.

Rotter, J. B. *Social learning and clinical psychology.* Englewood Cliffs, N.J.: Prentice-Hall, 1954.

Rubin, Z. Measurement of romantic love. *Journal of Personality and Social Psychology*, 1970, **16**, 265–273.

Rubovits, P. C., & Maehr, M. L. Pygmalion analyzed: Toward an explanation of the Rosenthal-Jacobson findings. *Journal of Personality and Social Psychology*, 1971, **19**, 197–203.

Rudolph, F. *The American college and university, a history.* New York: Knopf, 1962.

Ruitenbeek, H. M. *The new group therapies.* New York: Avon, 1970.

Russell, B. *Human society in ethics and politics.* New York: Mentor, 1962.

Russell, B. *The autobiography of Betrand Russell, 1872–1914.* Vol. I. New York: Bantam, 1968.

Rychlak, J. E. *A philosophy of science for personality.* Boston: Houghton Mifflin, 1968.

Saenger, G., & Gilbert, E. Consumer reactions to the integration of Negro sales personnel. *International Journal of Opinion and Attitude Research*, 1950, **4**, 57–76.

Salter, A. *Conditioned reflex therapy.* New York: Farrar, Straus, 1949, and Capricorn, 1961.

Salzinger, K. Experimental manipulation of verbal behavior: A review. *Journal of Genetic Psychology*, 1959, **61**, 65–94.

Salzinger, K., & Pisoni, S. Reinforcement of affect responses of schizophrenics during the clinical interview. *Journal of Abnormal and Social Psychology*, 1958, **57**, 84–90.

Salzinger, K., & Pisoni, S. Some parameters of the conditioning of verbal affect responses in schizophrenic subjects. *Journal of Abnormal and Social Psychology*, 1961, **63**, 511–516.

Sapir, E. *Selected writings in language, culture, and personality.* Berkeley, Calif.: University of California Press, 1948.

Sarason, I. G., Verbal learning, modeling, and juvenile delinquency. *American Psychologist*, 1968, **23**, 254–266.

Sarason, I. G. *Personality: An objective approach.* (2nd ed.) New York: Wiley, 1972 (1st Ed., 1966).

Sarason, I. G., & Harmatz, M. G. Test anxiety and experimental conditions. *Journal of Personal and Social Psychology*, 1965, **1**, 499–505.

Sarason, I. G., & Smith, R. E. Personality. In P. H. Mussen (Ed.), *Annual review of psychology.* Palo Alto, Calif.: Annual Reviews, 1971. Pp. 393–446.

Sarbin, T. R. A contribution to the study of actuarial and individual methods of prediction. *American Journal of Sociology*, 1942, **48**, 593–602.

Sarbin, T. R. Contributions to role-taking theory. I: Hypnotic behavior. *Psychological Review*, 1950, **57**, 255–270.

Sarbin, T. R. Role theory. In G. Lindzey (Ed.), *Handbook of social psychology*. Cambridge, Mass.: Addison-Wesley, 1954. Pp. 223–259.

Sarbin, T. R. Anxiety: Reification of a metaphor. *Archives of General Psychiatry*, 1964, **10**, 630–633. (a)

Sarbin, T. R. Role theoretical interpretation of psychological change. In P. Worchel & D. Byrne (Eds.), *Personality change*. New York: Wiley, 1964. Pp. 176–219. (b)

Sarbin, T. R. Hypnosis as a behavior modification technique. In L. Krasner & L. P. Ullmann (Eds.), *Research in behavior modification*. New York: Holt, Rinehart and Winston, 1965. Pp. 343–357.

Sarbin, T. R. Ontology recapitulates philology: The mythic nature of anxiety. *American Psychologist*, 1968, **23**, 411–418.

Sarbin, T. R., & Allen, V. L. Role theory. In G. Lindzey & E. Aronson (Eds.), *The handbook of social psychology*, Vol. 1. Reading, Mass.: Addison-Wesley, 1968. Pp. 488–567.

Sarbin, T. R., & Andersen, M. L. Role-theoretical analysis of hypnotic behavior. In J. E. Gordon (Ed.), *Handbook of clinical and experimental hypnosis*. New York: Macmillan, 1967.

Sarbin, T. R., & Coe, W. C. *Hypnosis: A social psychological analysis of influence communication*. New York: Holt, Rinehart and Winston, 1972.

Sarbin, T. R., & Juhasz, J. B. The historical background of the concept of hallucination. *Journal of the History of The Behavioral Sciences*, 1967, **4**, 339–358.

Sarbin, T. R., & Juhasz, J. B. Toward a theory of imagination. *Journal of Personality*, 1970, **38**, 52–76.

Sargent, S. S. *Social psychology*. New York: Ronald Press, 1950.

Sargent, S. S., & Smith, M. W. (Eds.) *Culture and personality*. New York: Wenner-Gren (for Viking Fund), 1949.

Sartre, J. P. *Existentialism*. New York: Philosophical Library, 1947.

Sattler, J. M. Racial "experimenter effects" in experimentation, testing, interviewing and psychotherapy. *Psychological Bulletin*, 1970, **73**, 137–160.

Scarf, M. Normality is a square circle or a four-sided triangle. *The New York Times Magazine*, October 3, 1971, 16–17, 40–50.

Schachter, S. Obesity and eating. *Science*, 1968, **161**, 751–756.

Schachter, S., Goldman, R., & Gordon, A. Effects of fear, food deprivation, and obesity on eating. *Journal of Personality and Social Psychology*, 1968, **10**, 91–97.

Schachter, S., & Gross, L. P. Manipulated time and eating behavior. *Journal of Personality and Social Psychology*, 1968, **10**, 98–106.

Schachter, S., & Singer, J. E. Cognitive, social and physiological determinants of emotional state. *Psychological Review*, 1962, **69**, 279–399.

Schaefer, H. H., & Martin, P. L. Behavioral therapy for "apathy" of hospitalized schizophrenics. *Psychological Report*, 1966, **19**, 1147–1158.

Schaefer, H. H., & Martin, P. L. *Behavioral therapy*. New York: McGraw-Hill, 1969.

Scheff, T. J. *Being mentally ill*. Chicago: Aldine, 1966.

Scheff, T. J., & Sundstrom, E. The stability of deviant behavior over time: A reassessment. *Journal of Health and Social Behavior*, 1970, **11**, 37–43.

Schein, E. H. The effect of reward on adult imitative behavior. *Journal of Abnormal and Social Psychology*, 1954, **49**, 389–395.

Schein, E. H., Schneier, I., & Barker, C. H. *Coercive persuasion*. New York: Norton, 1961.

Scheler, M. F. *The nature of sympathy*. New Haven, Conn.: Yale University Press, 1954.

Schloss, G. A., Siroka, R. W., & Siroka, E. K. Some contemporary origins of the personal growth group. In R. W. Siroka, E. K. Siroka, & G. A. Schloss (Eds.), *Sensitivity training and group encounter*. New York: Grosset & Dunlap, 1971. Pp. 3–10.

Schofield, W. *Psychotherapy: The purchase of friendship*. Englewood Cliffs, N.J.: Prentice-Hall, 1964.

Schramm, W. Mass communications and their audiences in other countries. In W. Schramm (Ed.), *The processes and effects of mass communication*. Urbana, Ill.: University of Illinois Press, 1954. Pp. 74–83.

Schramm, W. (Ed.). *The impact of educational television*. Urbana, Ill.: University of Illinois Press, 1960.

Schur, E. M. *Crimes without victims: Deviant behavior and public policy: Abortion, homosexuality, drug addiction*. Englewood Cliffs, N.J.: Prentice-Hall, 1965.

Schutz, W. *Joy*. New York: Grove Press, 1967.

Schutz, W. C. *Here comes everybody*. New York: Harper & Row, 1971.

Schwartz, D. C. On the ecology of political violence: "The long hot summer" as an hypothesis. *American Behavioral Scientist*, 1968, **11**, 24–28.

Schwitzgebel, R. *Street-corner research: An experimental approach to the juvenile delinquent*. Cambridge, Mass.: Harvard University Press, 1964.

Scott, R. A. The factory as a social service organization: Goal displacement in workshops for the blind. *Social Problems*, 1967, **15**, 160–175.

Scott, R. A. *The making of blind men*. New York: Russell Sage, 1969.

Scott, W. A. Social psychological correlates of mental illness and mental health. *Psychological Bulletin*, 1958, **55**, 65–87.

Scriven, M. The values of the academy. *Review of Educational Research*, 1970, **40**, 541–550.

Sears, R. R. Experimental analysis of psychoanalytic phenomena. In J. McV. Hunt (Ed.), *Personality and the behavior disorders*, Vol. 1. New York: Ronald Press, 1944. Pp. 306–332.

Sears, R. R. Personality. In C. P. Stone (Ed.), *Annual review of psychology*, Vol. 1. Palo Alto, California: Annual Reviews, 1950. Pp. 105–118.

Sechrest, L., Gallimore, R., & Hersch, P. D. Feedback and accuracy of clinical predictions. *Journal of Consulting Psychology*, 1967, **31**, 1–11.

Secord, P. F. Stereotyping and favorableness in the perception of Negro faces. *Journal of Abnormal Social Psychology*, 1959, **59**, 309–315.

Secord, P. F., & Backman, C. W. *Social psychology*. New York: McGraw-Hill, 1964.

Segal, H. Initial psychiatric findings of recently repatriated prisoners of war. *American Journal of Psychiatry*, 1954, **111**, 358–363.

Seitz, F. C. Five psychological measures of neurotic depression. A correlational study. *Journal of Clinical Psychology*, 1970, **26**, 504–505.

Seligman, M. E. P., Maier, S. F., & Geer, J. H. Aleviation of learned helplessness in the dog. *Journal of Abnormal Psychology*, 1968, **73**, 256–262.

Sennett, R. Review of *Beyond freedom and dignity* by B. F. Skinner. *New York Times Book Review*, Oct. 24, 1971, 12–15.

Seward, J. P. Learning theory and identifications: II. The role of punishment. *Journal of Genetic Psychology*, 1954, **84**, 201–210.

Sewell, W. H. Infant training and the personality of the child. In A. M. Rose (Ed.), *Mental health and mental disorder*. New York: Norton, 1955. Pp. 325–340.

Shapiro, A. K. The placebo effect in the history of medical treatment: Implications for psychiatry. *American Journal of Psychiatry*, 1959, **116**, 298–304.

Shapiro, A. K. A contribution to a history of the placebo effect. *Behavioral Science*, 1960, **5**, 109–135.

Shaw, M. J. Some postulates concerning psychotherapy. *Journal of Consulting Psychology*, 1948, **12**, 426–431.

Shearn, D. Operant conditioning of heart rate. *Science*, 1962, **137**, 530–537.

Sheldon, W. H. *Varieties of delinquent youth: an introduction to constitutional psychiatry*. New York: Harper & Row, 1949.

Sherif, M. A study of some social factors in perception. *Archives of Psychology*, 1935, **27**, 187.

Sherif, M. *The psychology of social norms*. New York: Harper & Row, 1936.

Sherif, M. *An outline of social psychology*. New York: Harper & Row, 1948.

Shibutani, T. *Society and personality*. Englewood Cliffs, N.J.: Prentice-Hall, 1961.

Shils, E. A., & Janowitz, M. Cohesion and disintegration in the Wehrmacht in World War II. In D. Katz, D. Cartwright, S. Eldersveld, & A. McC. Lee (Eds.), *Public opinion and propaganda*. New York: Holt, Rinehart and Winston, 1954. Pp. 553–582.

Shneidman, E. S., & Farberow, N. L. (Eds.) *Clues to suicide*. New York: McGraw-Hill, 1957.

Silberman, C. E. *Crisis in the classroom: The remaking of American education*. New York: Random House, 1970.

Silverman, H. F. Characteristics of some recent studies of instructional methods. In J. E. Coulson (Ed.), *Programmed learning and computer-based instruction*. New York: Wiley, 1962. Pp. 13–24.

Simon, H. A., & Stedry, A. C. Psychology and economics. In G. Lindzey & E. Aronson (Eds.), *The handbook of social psychology*, Vol. 5. Reading, Mass.: Addison-Wesley, 1969. Pp. 269–314.

Sines, L. K. The relative contribution of four kinds of data to accuracy in personality assessment. *Journal of Consulting Psychology*, 1959, **23**, 483–492.

Singer, E. *Key concepts in psychotherapy* (2nd ed.) New York: Basic Books, 1970.

Sjoberg, G. (Ed.) *Ethics, politics, and social research*. Cambridge, Mass.: Schenkman, 1967.

Skinner, B. F. *The behavior of organisms*. New York: Appleton-Century-Crofts, 1938.

Skinner, B. F. *Walden two*. New York: Macmillan, 1948.

Skinner, B. F. Are theories of learning necessary? *Psychological Review*, 1950, **57**, 193–216.

Skinner, B. F. *Science and human behavior*. New York: Macmillan, 1953.

Skinner, B. F. A case history in scientific method. *American Psychologist*, 1956, **11**, 221–233.

Skinner, B. F. *Verbal behavior*. New York: Appleton-Century-Crofts, 1957.

Skinner, B. F. The design of cultures. *Daedalus*, 1961, **90**, 534–546.

Skinner, B. F. Operant behavior. *American Psychologist*, 1963, **18**, 503–515.

Skinner, B. F. *The technology of teaching*. New York: Appleton-Century-Crofts, 1968.

Skinner, B. F. *Contingencies of reinforcement*. New York: Appleton-Century-Crofts, 1969.

Skinner, B. F. Creating the creative artist. In Anonymous (Ed.), *On the future of art*. New York: Viking, 1970. Pp. 61–75.

Skinner, B. F. *Beyond freedom and dignity*. New York: Knopf, 1971.

Skolnick, P., Moss, R., Salzgeber, R., & Shaw, J. I. The effects of population size and density on human behavior. Unpublished manuscript. San Fernando Valley State College, 1971.

Slavson, S. R. *An introduction to group therapy*. New York: Commonwealth, 1943.

Slavson, S. R. *Analytic group psychotherapy*. New York: Columbia, 1950.

Sletten, I. W., Hughes, D. D., Lamont, J., & Ognjanov, V. Work performance in 76 psychiatric patients: Tokens versus money. *Diseases of the Nervous System*, 1968, **29**, 261–264.

Slocum, W. L. *Occupational careers.* Chicago: Aldine, 1966.

Smelser, N. J. *Theory of collective behavior.* New York: Free Press, 1963.

Smelser, N. J., & Smelser, W. T. (Eds.) *Personality and social systems.* New York: Wiley, 1963.

Smith, A. *The theory of moral sentiments.* London: A. M. Miller, 1759.

Smith, P. *The historian and history.* New York: Random House, 1964.

Snygg, P., & Combs, A. W. *Individual behavior.* New York: Harper & Row, 1949.

Solomon, P., et al. (Eds.) *Sensory deprivation.* Cambridge, Mass.: Harvard University Press, 1961.

Solomon, R. L. Punishment. *American Psychologist,* 1964, **19,** 239–253.

Solomon, R. L., & Brush, E. S. Experimentally derived conceptions of anxiety and aversion. In M. R. Jones (Ed.), *Nebraska Symposium on Motivation,* Vol. 4. Lincoln, Nebr.: University of Nebraska Press, 1956. Pp. 212–305.

Sommer, R. *Personal space.* Englewood Cliffs, N.J.: Prentice-Hall, 1969.

Sommer, R., & Becker, F. D. Room density and user satisfaction. *Environment and behavior,* 1971, **3,** 412–417.

Spence, K. W. *Behavior theory and learning: Selected papers.* Englewood Cliffs, N.J.: Prentice-Hall, 1960.

Spencer, H. *First principles.* New York: Appleton-Century-Crofts, 1899.

Spitzer, S. P. (Ed.) *The sociology of personality.* New York: Van Nostrand, 1969.

Staats, A. W. (Ed.) *Human learning.* New York: Holt, Rinehart and Winston, 1964.

Staats, A. W. *Learning, language and cognition.* New York: Holt, Rinehart and Winston, 1968.

Staats, A. W. Social behaviorism, human motivation, and the conditioning therapies. In B. Maher (Ed.), *Progress in experimental personality research,* Vol. 5. New York: Academic Press, 1970. Pp. 111–168.

Staats, A. W., & Staats, C. K. Attitudes established by classical conditioning. *Journal of Abnormal and Social Psychology,* 1958, **57,** 37–40.

Staats, A. W., & Staats, C. K. *Complex human behavior: A systematic extension of learning principles.* New York: Holt, Rinehart and Winston, 1963.

Staats, A. W., Staats, C. K., Schutz, R. E., & Wolf, M. M. The conditioning of textual responses using "extrinsic" reinforcers. *Journal of the Experimental Analysis of Behavior,* 1962, **5,** 33–40.

Staats, C. K., & Staats, A. W. Meaning established by classical conditioning. *Journal of Experimental Psychology,* 1957, **54,** 74–80.

Stampfl, T. G., & Levis, D. J. Essentials of implosive therapy: A learning-theory-based psychodynamic behavioral therapy. *Journal of Abnormal Psychology,* 1967, **72,** 496–503.

Stanton, A. H., & Schwartz, M. S. *The mental hospital.* New York: Basic Books, 1954.

Stapledon, O. *Last and first men.* New York: Dover, 1968 (original edition, 1931).

Staples, E. A., & Wilensky, H. A controlled Rorschach investigation of hypnotic age regression. *Journal of Projective Techniques and Personality Assessment,* 1968, **32,** 246–252.

Starr, R. J., & Katkin, E. S. The clinician as an aberrant actuary: Illusory correlation and the incomplete sentence blank. *Journal of Abnormal Psychology,* 1969, **74,** 670–675.

St. Augustine. *The confessions.* New York: Pocket Books, 1952.

Steffy, R. A., Hart, J., Craw, M., Torney, D., & Marlett, N. Operant behavior modification techniques applied to a ward of severely regressed patients. *Canadian Psychiatric Association Journal,* 1969, **14,** 59–67.

Stein, J. (Ed.) *The Random House dictionary of the English language.* New York: Random House, 1967.

Steinem, G. Why we need a woman president in 1976. *Look*, Jan. 13, 1970, **34**, 58.

Stern, W. *General psychology from the personalistic standpoint*. New York: Macmillan, 1938.

Stevenson, C. L. *Ethics and language*. New Haven, Conn.: Yale University Press, 1944.

Stoller, F. H. A stage for trust. In A. Burton (Ed.), *Encounter: The theory and practice of encounter groups*. San Francisco: Jossey-Bass, 1969. Pp. 81–96.

Stolurow, L. M. Model the master teacher or master the teaching model. In J. D. Krumboltz (Ed.), *Learning and the educational process*. Chicago: Rand McNally, 1965. Pp. 223–247.

Strassman, H. D., Thaler, M. B., & Schein, F. H. A prisoner of war syndrome: Apathy as a reaction to severe stress. *American Journal of Psychiatry*, 1956, **112**, 998–1003.

Stuart, R. B. Behavior control of overeating. *Behaviour Research and Therapy*, 1967, **5**, 351–363.

Stuart, R. B. Situational versus self-control. In R. D. Rubin, H. Fensterheim, J. D. Henderson, & L. P. Ullmann (Eds.), *Advances in behavior therapy III*. New York: Academic Press, 1972. Pp. 129–146.

Stunkard, A. J. Eating patterns and obesity. *Psychiatric Quarterly*, 1959, **33**, 284–295.

Suinn, R. M., Jorgensen, G. T., Stewart, S. T., & McGuirk, F. D. Fears as attitudes: experimental reduction of fear through reinforcement. *Journal of Abnormal Psychology*, 1971, **78**, 272–279.

Sullivan, H. S. *The interpersonal theory of psychiatry*. New York: Norton, 1953.

Sullivan, H. S. *The psychiatric interview*. New York: Norton, 1954.

Sullivan, H. S. *Clinical studies in psychiatry*. New York: Norton, 1956.

Sullivan, H. S. *Schizophrenia as a human process*. New York: Norton, 1962.

Sullivan, H. S. *The fusion of psychiatry and social science*. New York: Norton, 1964.

Sutcliffe, J. P. "Credulous" and "skeptical" views of hypnotic phenomena: A review of certain evidence and methodology. *International Journal of Clinical and Experimental Hypnosis*, 1960, **8**, 73–101.

Sutcliffe, J. P. "Credulous" and "skeptical" views of hypnosis: Experiments on esthesia, hallucinations, and delusion. *Journal of Abnormal and Social Psychology*, 1961, **62**, 189–200.

Szasz, T. S. *The myth of mental illness: Foundations of a theory of personal conduct*. New York: Hoeber-Harper, 1961.

Szasz, T. S. *Law, liberty, and psychiatry: An inquiry into the social uses of mental health practices*. New York: Macmillan, 1963.

Szasz, T. S. The moral dilemma of psychiatry: Autonomy or heteronomy? *American Journal of Psychiatry*, 1964, **121**, 521–523.

Szasz, T. S. *Psychiatric justice*. New York: Macmillan, 1965. (a)

Szasz, T. S. *The ethics of psychoanalysis: The theory and method of autonomous psychotherapy*. New York: Basic Books, 1965. (b)

Szasz, T. S. *The manufacture of madness*. New York: Delta, 1970.

Tate, B. G., & Baroff, G. S. Aversive control of self-injurious behaviour in a psychotic boy. *Behaviour Research and Therapy*, 1966, **4**, 281–287.

Taylor, J. A. A personality scale of manifest anxiety. *Journal of Abnormal and Social Psychology*, 1953, **48**, 285–290.

Taylor, J. A., & Spence, K. W. Conditioning level in the behavior disorders. *Journal of Abnormal and Social Psychology*, 1954, **49**, 497–502.

Taylor, J. G. *The behavioral basis of perception*. New Haven, Conn.: Yale University Press, 1962.

Temerlin, M. K. Suggestion effects in psychiatric diagnosis. *Journal of Nervous and Mental Disease*, 1968, **147**, 349–353.

Terman, L. M. *The measurement of intelligence*. Boston: Houghton Mifflin, 1916.

Tharp, R. G., & Wetzel, F. J. *Behavior modification in the natural environment.* New York: Academic Press, 1969.

Thibaut, J. W., & Kelley, H. H. *The social psychology of groups.* New York: Wiley, 1959.

Thomas, D. R., Becker, W. C., & Armstrong, M. Production and elimination of disruptive classroom behavior by systematically varying teacher's behavior. *Journal of Applied Behavior Analysis*, 1968, **1**, 35–45.

Thomas, K. (Ed.) *Attitudes and behaviour.* Harmondsworth, Middlesex: Penguin, 1971.

Thomas, W. I. *Social behavior and personality.* New York: Social Science Research Council, 1951.

Thomas, W. I.; & Znaniecki, F. *The Polish peasant in Europe and America.* 5 vols. Boston: Badger, 1918–1920.

Thompson, V. A. *Modern organization.* New York: Knopf, 1961.

Thorndike, E. L. Animal intelligence: An experimental study of the associative processes in animals. *Psychological Monographs*, 1898, **8**, 1–109.

Thorndike, E. L. *Animal intelligence: Experimental studies.* New York: Macmillan, 1911.

Thorndike, E. L. *The psychology of learning.* New York: Teachers College Press, 1913.

Toch, H. *The social psychology of social movements.* Indianapolis: Bobbs-Merrill, 1965.

Toffler, A. *Future shock.* New York: Random House, 1970.

Tornatzky, L. G., Fairweather, G. W., & O'Kelly, L. I. Psychology in action. *American Psychologist*, 1970, **25**, 884–888.

Troffer, S. A., & Tart, C. T. Experimenter bias in hypnotist performance. *Science*, 1964, **145**, 1330–1331.

Turner, R. H. Collective behavior. In R. E. L. Faris (Ed.), *Handbook of modern sociology.* Chicago: Rand McNally, 1964. Pp. 382–425.

Tyler, V. O., Jr., & Brown, G. D. Token reinforcement of academic performance with institutionalized delinquent boys. *Journal of Educational Psychology*, 1968, **59**, 164–168.

Ullmann, L. P. *Institution and outcome: A comparative study of psychiatric hospitals.* New York: Pergamon, 1967.

Ullmann, L. P. From therapy to reality. *The Counseling Psychologist*, 1969, **1**, 68–72. (a)

Ullmann, L. P. Making use of modeling in the therapeutic interview. In R. D. Rubin & C. M. Franks (Eds.), *Advances in behavior therapy, 1968.* New York: Academic Press, 1969. 175–182. (b)

Ullmann, L. P. Behavior therapy as social movement. In C. M. Franks (Ed.), *Behavior therapy: Appraisal and status.* New York: McGraw-Hill, 1969. Pp. 495–523. (c)

Ullmann, L. P. Beyond the reinforcement machine. In S. H. Osipow & W. B. Walsh (Eds.), *Behavior change in counseling: Readings and cases.* New York: Appleton-Century-Crofts, 1970. Pp. 35–44. (a)

Ullmann, L. P. On cognitions and behavior therapy. *Behavior Therapy*, 1970, 201–204. (b)

Ullmann, L. P. From childhood to adolescence: The current status of behavior therapy. *Career Directions*, 1971, **2**, 27–41.

Ullmann, L. P. Who are we? In R. D. Rubin, H. Fensterheim, J. D. Henderson, and L. P. Ullmann (Eds.), *Advances in behavior therapy.* New York: Academic Press, 1972. Pp. 213–223.

Ullmann, L. P., Bowen, M. E., Greenberg, D. J., Macpherson, E. C., Marcum, H. B., Marx, R. D., & May, J. S. The effect on rapport of experimenters' approach and avoidance responses to positive and negative self-references. *Behaviour Research and Therapy*, 1968, **6**, 355–362.

Ullmann, L. P., Forsman, R. G., Kenny, J. W., McInnis, T. L., Jr., Unikel, I. P., & Zeisset, T. R. Selective reinforcement of schizophrenics' interview responses. *Behaviour Research and Therapy*, 1965, **2**, 205–212.

Ullmann, L. P., & Krasner, L. (Eds.) *Case studies in behavior modification*. New York: Holt, Rinehart and Winston, 1965.

Ullmann, L. P., & Krasner, L. *A psychological approach to abnormal behavior*. Englewood Cliffs, N.J.: Prentice-Hall, 1969.

Ullmann, L. P., Krasner, L., & Collins, B. J. Modification of behavior through verbal conditioning: Effects in group therapy. *Journal of Abnormal and Social Psychology*, 1961, **62**, 128–132.

Ullmann, L. P., Krasner, L., & Edinger, R. L. Verbal conditioning of common associations in long-term schizophrenic patients. *Behaviour Research and Therapy*, 1964, **2**, 15–18.

Ullmann, L. P., Krasner, L., & Gelfand, D. Changed content within a reinforced response class. *Psychological Reports*, 1963, **12**, 819–829.

Ullmann, L. P., & Sikora, J. P. An extension of Coleman, Katz, and Menzel's *Medical Innovation*, using behavior therapists. Paper presented at Western Psychological Association, Los Angeles, April, 1970.

Ullmann, L. P., Weiss, R. L., & Krasner, L. The effect of verbal conditioning of emotional words on recognition of threatening stimuli. *Journal of Clinical Psychology*, 1963, **19**, 182–183.

Underwood, B. J. *Psychological research*. New York: Appleton-Century-Crofts, 1957.

Vaughan, T. R. Governmental intervention in social research. Political and ethical dimensions in the Wichita Jury Recordings. In G. Sjoberg (Ed.), *Ethics, politics, and social research*. Cambridge, Mass.: Schenkman, 1967.

Vollmer, H. M., & Mills, D. L. (Eds.) *Professionalization*. Englewood Cliffs, N.J.: Prentice-Hall, 1966.

Volpe, A., & Kastenbaum, R. Beer and TLC. *American Journal of Nursing*, 1967, **67**, 100–103.

von Neumann, J., & Morganstern, O. *Theory of games and economic behavior*. Princeton, N.J.: Princeton University Press, 1944.

Wahler, R. G. Oppositional children: A quest for parental reinforcement control. *Journal of Applied Behavior Analysis*, 1969, **2**, 159–170.

Wahler, R. G., Winkel, G. H., Peterson, R. F., & Morrison, D. C. Mothers as behaviour therapists for their own children. *Behaviour Research and Therapy*, 1965, **3**, 113–124.

Walker, E. L. Experimental psychology and social responsibility. *American Psychologist*, 1969, **23**, 862–868.

Walker, H. M., Mattson, R. H., & Buckley, N. K. Special class placements as a treatment alternative for deviant behavior in children. In Monograph 1. Department of Special Education. University of Oregon, Eugene, Oregon, 1969.

Walmsley, D. M. *Anton Mesmer*. London: Robert Hale, 1967.

Walters, R. H., & Parke, R. D. Influence of response consequences to a social model on resistance to deviation. *Journal of Experimental Child Psychology*, 1964, **1**, 269–280.

Warner, W. L., & Lunt, P. S. *The social life of a modern community*. New Haven, Conn.: Yale University Press, 1941.

Watley, D. J. Counselor confidence in accuracy of predictions. *Journal of Counseling Psychology*, 1966, **13**, 62–67.

Watson, J. B. Psychology as a behaviorist views it. *Psychological Review*, 1913, **20**, 158–177.

Watson, J. B. *Psychology from the standpoint of a behaviorist*. Philadelphia: Lippincott, 1919.

Watson, J. B., & Rayner, R. Conditioned emotional reactions. *Journal of Experimental Psychology*, 1920, **3**, 1–14.

Waxler, C. Z., & Yarrow, M. R. Factors influencing imitative learning in preschool children. *Journal of Experimental Child Psychology*, 1970, **9**, 115–130.

Webb, E. J., Campbell, D. T., Schwartz, R. D., & Sechrest, L. *Unobtrusive measures: Nonreactive research in the social sciences.* Chicago: Rand McNally, 1966.

Weber, L. *The English Infant School and informal education.* Englewood Cliffs, N.J.: Prentice-Hall, 1971.

Weber, M. *The Protestant ethic and the spirit of capitalism.* New York: Scribners, 1930.

Weiner, H. Some effects of response cost upon human operant behavior. *Journal of Experimental Analysis of Behavior*, 1962, **5**, 201–208.

Weiner, H. Human behavioral persistence. *Psychological Record*, 1970, **20**, 445–456.

Weiss, R. L., Krasner, L., & Ullmann, L. P. Responsivity of psychiatric patients to verbal conditioning: "Success" and "failure" conditions and pattern of reinforced trials. *Psychological Reports*, 1963, **12**, 423–426.

Weiss, W. Effects of the mass media of communication. In G. Lindzey & E. Aronson (Eds.), *The handbook of social psychology* (2nd ed.), Vol. 5. Reading, Mass.: Addison-Wesley, 1969.

Weitzenhoffer, A. M. *Hypnotism, an objective study in suggestibility.* New York: Wiley, 1953.

Weitzenhoffer, A. M., & Hilgard, E. R. *Stanford hypnotic susceptibility scale.* Palo Alto, Calif.: Consulting Psychologists Press, 1959.

Wellford, C. Factors associated with adoption of the inmate code: A study of normative socialization. *Journal of Criminal Law, Criminology and Political Science*, 1967, **58**, 197–203.

Wells, B. W. P. The psycho-social influence of building environment: Sociometric findings in large and small office spaces. *Building Science*, 1965, **1**, 153–165.

Welsh, G. S. Factor dimensions A and R. In G. S. Welsh & W. G. Dahlstrom (Eds.), *Basic readings on the MMPI in psychology and medicine.* Minneapolis: University of Minnesota Press, 1956. Pp. 264–281.

Wertham, F. *Seduction of the innocent.* New York: Holt, Rinehart and Winston, 1954.

Whalen, C. K., & Henker, B. A. Creating therapeutic pyramids using mentally retarded patients. *American Journal of Mental Deficiency*, 1969, **74**, 331–337.

Whalen, C. K., & Henker, B. A. Pyramid therapy in a hospital for the retarded: Methods, program evaluation and long-term effects. *American Journal of Mental Deficiency*, 1971, **75**, 414–434.

Whitehorn, J. C., & Betz, B. J. A study of psychotherapeutic relationships between physicians and schizophrenic patients. *American Journal of Psychiatry*, 1954, **111**, 321–331.

Whitehorn, J. C., & Betz, B. J. Further studies of the doctor as a crucial variable in the outcome of treatment with schizophrenic patients. *American Journal of Psychiatry*, 1960, **117**, 215–223.

Whiting, J. W. N., & Child, J. L. *Child training and personality.* New Haven, Conn.: Yale University Press, 1953.

Whorf, B. L. *Language, thought and reality.* New York: Wiley, 1965.

Whyte, L. L. *The unconscious before Freud.* New York: Basic Books, 1960.

Whyte, W. H., Jr. *The organization man.* New York: Simon and Schuster, 1956.

Wiggins, J. S. Convergence among stylistic response measures from objective personality tests. *Educational and Psychological Measurement*, 1964, **24**, 551–562.

Wiggins, J. S. Personality structure. In P. R. Farnsworth (Ed.), *Annual review of psychology*, Vol. 19. Palo Alto, Calif.: Annual Reviews, 1968. Pp. 293–350.

Wiggins, J. S., Renner, K. E., Clore, G. L., & Rose, R. J. *The psychology of personality*. Reading, Mass.: Addison-Wesley, 1971.

Williams, R. I., & Blanton, R. L. Verbal conditioning in a psychotherapeutic situation. *Behaviour Research and Therapy*, 1968, **6**, 97–103.

Winder, C. L., Ahmed, F. Z., Bandura, A., & Rau, L. C. Dependency of patients, psychotherapists' responses, and aspects of psychotherapy. *Journal of Consulting Psychology*, 1962, **26**, 129–134.

Winett, R. A., Richards, C. S., Krasner, L., & Krasner, M. Child monitored token reading program. *Psychology in the Schools*, 1971, 8, 259–262.

Winett, R. A., & Winkler, R. C. Current behavior modification in the classroom: Be still, be quiet, be docile. *Journal of Applied Behavior Analysis*, 1972, **5**.

Winkler, R. C. Ward management of chronic psychiatric patients by a token reinforcement system. *Journal of Applied Behavior Analysis*, 1970, 3, 47–55.

Winkler, R. C. The relevance of economic theory and technology to token reinforcement systems. *Behaviour Research and Therapy*, 1971, **9**, 81–88.

Winkler, R. C., & Krasner, L. The contribution of economics to token economies. Paper presented to the Eastern Psychological Association, New York, April 15, 1971.

Witkin, H. A., Lewis, H. B., Hertzman, M., Machover, K., Meissner, P. B., & Wapner, S. *Perception and personality*. New York: Harper & Row, 1954.

Wittrock, M. C. The learning by discovery hypothesis. In L. S. Shulman & E. R. Keislar (Eds.), *Learning by discovery: A critical appraisal*. Chicago: Rand McNally, 1966.

Wohlwill, J. F. The emerging discipline of environmental psychology. *American Psychologist*, 1970, **25**, 303–311.

Wohlwill, J. F., & Carson D. M. (Eds.) *Environment and the social sciences*. Washington, D.C.: American Psychological Association, 1972.

Wolf, M. M., Giles, D. K., & Hall, V. R. Experiments with token reinforcement in a remedial classroom. *Behaviour Research and Therapy*, 1968, **6**, 51–64.

Wolfle, H. M. A fundamental principle of personality measurement. *Psychological Review*, 1949, **56**, 273–276.

Wollersheim, J. P. Effectiveness of group therapy based upon learning principles in the treatment of overweight women. *Journal of Abnormal Psychology*, 1970, **76**, 462–474. (Doctoral dissertation, University of Illinois, 1968.)

Wolpe, J. Reciprocal inhibition as the main basis of psychotherapeutic effects. *Archives of Neurology and Psychiatry*, 1954, **72**, 205–226.

Wolpe, J. *Psychotherapy by reciprocal inhibition*. Stanford, Calif.: Stanford University Press, 1958.

Wolpe, J. Psychotherapy by reciprocal inhibition. *Conditioned Reflex*, 1968, 3, 234–240.

Wolpe, J. *The practice of behavior therapy*. New York: Pergamon, 1969.

Woodworth, R. S. *Contemporary schools of psychology*. New York: Ronald Press, 1931.

Wright, C. R. *Mass communication*. New York: Random House, 1959.

Wright, J. M., & Worthy, M. Volunteering as group spokesman as a function of task effectiveness, leader success, and task similarity. *Psychological Reports*, 1971, **28**, 911–917.

Yacorzynski, G. K. *Frontiers of psychology*. New York: Philosophical Library, 1963.

Yates, A. J. *Behavior therapy*. New York: Wiley, 1970.

Zanna, M. P., Kiesler, C. A., & Pilkonis, P. A. Positive and negative attitudinal affect established by classical conditioning. *Journal of Personality and Social Psychology*, 1970, 14, 321–328.

Zeidel, S. F., & Mehrabian, A. The ability to communicate and infer positive and negative attitudes facially and vocally. *Journal of Experimental Research in Personality*, 1969, 3, 233–241.

Zigler, E., & Phillips, L. Psychiatric diagnosis and symptomatology. *Journal of Abnormal and Social Psychology*, 1961, **63,** 69–75.

Zilboorg, G. *A history of medical psychology.* New York: Norton, 1967.

Zimmerman, E. H., Zimmerman, J., & Russel, C. D. Differential effects of token reinforcement on instruction-following behavior in retarded students instructed as a group. *Journal of Applied Behavior Analysis,* 1969, **2,** 101–112.

Ziv, A. Children's behavior problems as viewed by teachers, psychologists, and children. *Child Development,* 1970, **41,** 871–879.

Zweig, S. *Mental healers: Franz Anton Mesmer, Mary Baker Eddy, Sigmund Freud.* New York: Frederick Ungar, 1932.

Name Index

Subject Index

AB variable in psychotherapy, 176–177
Accuracy, effectiveness and, 17–19; guidelines for, 19; methodology and, 17–19
Achievement, need for, 65
Acquiescence, 101, 102
Advertising, impact on behavoir, 424–435
Affiliation, 34
Age, behavior and, 340–341
Alcoholics Anonymous, 448
Alienation, 446
Altruism, 34, 35
Anal stage of development, 50
Analogues, limitations of, 226–230
Analysts, factor, 74
Annual Review of Psychology, 83 n.
Anxiety, historical development of, 184; measures of, 18; research concerning, 94–100
Applicability, accuracy and, 19
Archetypes, 53
Architecture, utopia and, 471–472
Arousal theories, 61
Attitudes, 16, 32–33, 73; as an organizing concept, 419–420
"Attribution theory," 279
"Aunt Fanny effect," 130
Authoritarian personality, 85
Autokinetic effect, 41 •
Autonomic functions, control of, 299
Autonomy, functional, 74
Aversion techniques, 293–297
Avoidance behavior, 162

"Barnum effect," 130
Baserates, 129–130
Behavior, 15–17; avoidance, 162; concepts of, 31–39; changeworthy, development of, 256, 261–269; maintenance of, 269–270; changing of, 277–302; cognitions as, 300–301; collective, 439–463; con-

forming, studies in, 215–217; consistency of, over time, 165–166; cultural influences on, 391–415; economic influences on, 391–415; environments and, 329–359; formal education and, 360–390; heredity and, 87–88; maintenance of, over time, 164–165; midtwentieth century approach to, 83–90; new, 159–161, maintenance of, 275–276; operant, 58–59; political influences on, 391–415; research concerning, 82–109; seemingly self-defeating, 161–164; social influences on, 21–22, 86–87, 391–415; superstitious, 265; theories of, 47–81
Behavior influence, 21; as alternative approach to personality, 139–167; complexity of, 143–145; experimental laboratory and, 202–230; "good life" and, 487–502; hypnosis as example of, 231–250; interactive nature of, 141–143; measurement, 110–138; psychology of, 13–23, development of, 24–109; research on, 169–326
Behavior sampling, personality measurement as, 115–118
Behavior therapy. *See* Therapy
Behaviorism, 56–61; radical, 58–60; social, 63
Behaviorists, social, 61
Bias, experimenter, 91
Blindness, 334–340
Books, impact on behavior, 424–435
Brainwashing, 435–437
Buchmanism, 448

Canalization, 65–66
Chaining, 160
Change, openness to, 20
Classical conditioning, 154
Classroom, as planned en-

vironment, 377–389; open, 387–389; token economy in the, 286–287, 377–387
Closeness, intrusion and, 353–354; likability and, 352–353
Coercion, 435–437
Cognitions, as behavior, 300–301
Collective behavior, 439–463
Collective representation, 62
Collective unconscious, 53
Communication, behavior and, 416–438; mass, 424–435
Conditioned response, 154
Conditioned stimulus, 154
Conditioning, classical, 154; operant, 56, 156–158; verbal, 224–226; Pavlovian, 154; respondent, 153–156, meaning and, 223–224; semantic, 155
Conflict, 154
Conformity, 140
Consciousness of kind, 34
Consciousness III, 454, 462
Consistency of measurement, 124–125
Constitutional typologists, 74–77
Constructs, 70
Contagion, 39, 442
Control, 304–305; self-, 303–326; stimulus, 304
Coping, 90
Covert sensitization, 296
Creative self, 54
Creativity, 18
Crowd, 39–40, 441–442
Crowding, 354–356
Cues, 17, 66; response-produced, 152–153
Cultural differences, 344–345
Cultural influences on behavior, 391–415

Defense Mechanism Inventory, 89 n.
Demand characteristics, 91, 203–205
Deprivation, sensory, 437
Desensitization, 288–293; studies of, evaluation of, 288–289

555